WRITING AND FIGHTING THE CIVIL WAR

SOLDIER CORRESPONDENCE TO THE NEW YORK SUNDAY MERCURY

Foreword by

EDWIN C. BEARSS

Edited by

WILLIAM B. STYPLE

With chapter introductions by

BRIAN C. POHANKA

EDWIN C. BEARSS

Dr. JAMES M. McPHERSON

Dr. RICHARD J. SOMMERS

WILLIAM B. STYPLE

Epilogue by

ROBERT LEE HODGE

Belle Grove Publishing Company
P.O. Box 483
Kearny, N. J. 07032

Printed in the United States of America

ISBN 1-883926-13-0

Library of Congress Control Number: 00-131730

All photographs in this book are from the collection of the
U. S. Army Military History Institute at Carlisle Barracks.

Contents

Foreword

by

Edwin C. Bearss

It was with more than passing interest that I received a late summer 1999 telephone call from William B. Styple of Kearny, New Jersey. I had not previously spoken with Bill, but knew of his work and reputation. I knew of his long association with the Civil War community as an author/editor with such titles as *The Andersonville Diary & Memoirs of Charles Hopkins*; *Our Noble Blood*, the translated Civil War letters of Philippe Régis de Trobriand; *The Little Bugler*, a true story of a twelve-year-old boy in the Civil War; and finally a particular favorite of mine *What Death More Glorious*, a biography of Brig. Gen. Strong Vincent. Styple, a scholar and living history enthusiast, has expanded his horizons teamed with Brian Pohanka to co-author, direct, and produce the *Echoes of the Blue & Gray* video series. Styple told me of his continuing research and the significance of the New York *Sunday Mercury* to his work in the Civil War and as historian for the Town of Kearny.

The *Sunday Mercury* devoted much space to the publication of correspondence received from Union soldiers and sailors, principally the former. These letters, written from the field or on shipboard, he said, provided excellent first person overviews on camp-life, marches, battles, leaders, why they fought, etc. His goal was to review the newspaper columns and select at least one letter from each issue to tell the story of the war as seen by the correspondents of the *Sunday Mercury*. The resulting book would be organized by chapters, each devoted to a year of the conflict.

Styple asked if I would be interested in reviewing the 1862 chapter and writing an introduction. "Yes," I replied.

Late in October, I received a typescript of the subject chapter and spent the next two months with Union soldiers and sailors, and their thoughts, hopes and fears. As I did, initial curiosity changed to enthusiasm, echoing Styple's view of the letters and how their publication would benefit scholars, living historian groups, and those of the reading public savoring the lifestyles of the Union rank and file and the jacktars of the t'ween decks.

Unlike too many letters found in the *National Tribune*, a popular source for many present-day historians with their old soldiers' reminiscences and sea tales, the *Sunday Mercury*'s correspondents wrote of contemporary events, scenes, and personalities. They did not write from hindsight, nor are they as prone to exaggerate their personal roles. The practice of the old soldier over-emphasizing his actions and placing himself on center stage has resulted in wags referring to Henry Kyd Douglas' *I Rode With Stonewall* as "Stonewall Rode With Me."

Military censorship of Civil War soldiers' and sailors' letters was not the rule, and many of their letters were routinely published in newspapers. The only government oversight, except in a few unusual circumstances, was moral suasion on the part of authorities. Generals, such as Robert E. Lee and U. S. Grant, made it a practice to read enemy newspapers. It has been said that General Lee, because of the skill of the Confederate spy network in the Maryland counties fronting Chesapeake Bay and the Potomac River, would within 24 hours be reading a New York City newspaper. If true, insofar as it applies to the *Sunday Mercury*, the information reaching Lee from this source would be a spymaster's dream.

Edwin C. Bearss
Historian Emeritus
National Park Service

Preface

"Our army of military correspondents are writing and fighting at the same time, and are, therefore, competent to describe the actions in which they bear their parts."—Sunday Mercury, April 26, 1863.

I first encountered the soldier correspondence to the New York *Sunday Mercury* in 1996 while researching my book, *The Little Bugler: The True Story of a Twelve-Year-Old Boy in the Civil War*. My subject had enlisted in Manhattan in 1861 and served for three years in the 40th New York Infantry, prompting me to search period newspapers for articles or letters pertaining to that regiment. During the Civil War, letter writing provided the crucial link between the soldier and home, and newspapers commonly published soldier correspondence. This material is a preferable source for historians: unlike post-war recollections, which can become clouded by the passage of decades, a letter written from the battlefield describes the event as it unfolds. On a tip from my friend and fellow historian, Brian Pohanka, I examined the *Sunday Mercury*, where he had found several letters written by soldiers in the 5th New York Infantry.

I began at the New-York Historical Society, where I found original bound copies of the *Sunday Mercury* for the years 1862 and 1863. Immediately, I saw that this paper published more military correspondence than most, with some issues containing nearly twenty letters apiece. I quickly became thoroughly entranced by the revealing content of everyday soldier life and the vivid descriptions of battle. Here was a collection of first-person wartime accounts that told the story of the Civil War in a way that no historian could. Perhaps the most thrilling aspect of reading through the letters was the fact that these soldiers were unaware of their fate, and sometimes their naïveté was painfully evident. I was hooked. I knew then that this material, if brought to light, would provide new insight into the life of the Union soldier and serve as a fresh source for all students of the Civil War.

I decided to undertake the mission of finding and copying each letter from every issue of the *Sunday Mercury* published during the war—approximately 225 weeks of correspondence—not knowing whether this task was realistic or even possible. I also thought it necessary to collect the historically significant editorials to better understand the opinions and political stance of the publishers.

Next I visited the New York Public Library to examine their extensive microfilm collection of 19th Century newspapers. Although the visit was fruitful, I was frustrated to find their *Sunday Mercury* collection incomplete and, even worse, that little care and attention was paid by the technicians during the microfilming process. Many pages of the newspaper were carelessly flattened, which caused creasing and rendered several historically important letters illegible. Despite these difficulties, I was able to collect most of the letters from 1861 and 1865. My search came to a successful conclusion at the Center for Research Libraries in Chicago, where the remaining issues (with the exception of three weeks) of the year of 1864 were located.

After amassing and reading more than 3,000 letters and editorials, I selected 500 that would best tell the story of the Civil War as it was seen through the eyes of the common soldier. Letter selection was based on importance, content, descriptive quality, and the ability to guide the reader through the conflict. The letters appear in the order in which they were published in the *Sunday Mercury* rather than as chronologically written (owing to distance and the slowness of the mails, some letters took longer than others to get to New York City). I have included biographical notes on the identified *Sunday Mercury* correspondents; the information is taken from service and pension records located in the National Archives. Unfortunately, I have not included battle maps for it would take an atlas to depict every location, campaign or battle mentioned in this book. For editing purposes, the publication date of each issue is underlined; brackets identify persons or regiments, locations and dates; parentheses are original to the letter writer, and braces reveal the comments of the editors of the *Sunday Mercury*. Misspellings, whether by the soldier or the paper's typesetter, have been left uncorrected and without a *sic*. Some letters contain racial epithets and other disturbing terminology; however, in order to preserve the integrity of the *Sunday Mercury* correspondence, I have refrained from removing any offensive material. To better understand the course of military events, a brief historical overview is provided for each year of the war. With a debt of gratitude I acknowledge the distinguished historians who provided these valuable introductions: Mr. Brian C. Pohanka of Alexandria, Va., Mr. Edwin C. Bearss of Arlington, Va., Dr. James M. McPherson of Princeton, N. J., and Dr. Richard J. Sommers of Carlisle, Pa.

It is with great pleasure that I would like to mention all those who have assisted me in the preparation of this volume. Looking back, this project has been one of the most fulfilling and enjoyable experiences in my life. My sincere thanks to Sonia Krutzke, Roger Hunt, Daralee and Colleen Ota, Jim Nevins, Victoria and Marta Lopes, Buddy Kruk, Jack Fitzpatrick, Bill Dekker, Peter Doroshenko, Tom Brown, Garry Wetstein, John Valori, Lance Ingmire, and Doug Reed. Additional thanks to Mike Winey and Randy Hackenburg at the Military History Institute at Carlisle Barracks, Mariam Touba of the New-York Historical Society, Thomas Burke at the New York Public Library, and Daniel Lorello at the New York State Archives. I would also like to thank Historian and Preservationist Robert Lee Hodge who has supplied a fitting epilogue for this book. Finally, love to my family for putting up with me for all this time.

If a dedication is appropriate, it is to the memory of the editors of the *Sunday Mercury* and their heroic correspondents—some are known; most are unknown. Not a moment passed while working on this book that I did not feel their presence. Without them, this book would not exist.

William B. Styple
Kearny, New Jersey

Frequently used abbreviations:

A.A.A.G.	Acting Assistant Adjutant General
F.F.V.	First Families of Virginia
F.Z.	Fire Zouave
N.G.S.N.Y.	National Guard State of New York
N.Y.S.M.	New York State Militia
N.Y.S.N.G.	New York State National Guard
N.Y.S.T.	New York State Troops
N.Y.S.V.	New York State Volunteers
N.Y.V.V.	New York Veteran Volunteers
Zou-zou	Zouave

Introduction

"What we want is news, news from the army—from the battle front!"
Editor William Cauldwell of the *Sunday Mercury.*

"WAR!, WAR!!, WAR!!!," thundered the April 21, 1861 headline of the New York *Sunday Mercury.* The editors were outraged that the pusillanimous new Confederacy of Cotton States had fired upon the flag of the United States at Fort Sumter in Charleston Harbor. As war fever swept New York, the city's militia units assembled to respond to the urgent need of protecting the threatened capital of Washington, D. C.

A special notice appeared in the April 28 edition of the *Sunday Mercury*: the editors asked the departing volunteers to write and "inform us of any events of interest." As an incentive to the prospective correspondents, a free copy of the newspaper would be sent to any contributing soldier; to safeguard against receiving any bogus news, no anonymous letters would be accepted. At the editors' insistence, a correspondent had to include his name, rank, company, and regiment, although a *Nom de plume* might be utilized for publication. Any letter received by the *Sunday Mercury* without the required identification would be promptly placed in the waste-paper basket.

This simple request for news generated the largest and most impressively detailed collection of journalistic correspondence ever written during the Civil War. Hundreds of soldiers wrote thousands of letters to the New York *Sunday Mercury*, creating a unique history of the great American conflict. These soldier correspondents were truly writing and fighting the Civil War.

William Cauldwell was born on Bayard Street in New York City on October 12, 1824, the son of Scottish immigrants Andrew and Margaret Cauldwell. When William was eleven years old, he was sent to an uncle in Louisiana and enrolled in Jefferson College, near Plaquemine on the Mississippi River. Returning to New York City in 1839, young Cauldwell first obtained a position in a dry-goods business at the salary of $50 a year, but found the job not to his liking. He then drifted into the employ of Samuel Adams, the owner of a printshop and showed an aptitude for typesetting. Cauldwell worked for Adams nearly three years, until Adams was murdered. (The homicide was one of the most sensational to have ever occurred in old New York. Adams had done work for John C. Colt, brother of Samuel Colt—inventor of the Colt revolver, and was owed a considerable sum. One day Adams called upon Colt, who was engaged in nailing a lid on a packing-crate. The two men quarreled, and in a fit of rage Colt struck Adams with a hammer and killed him. Colt then put the body in a box, nailed it up, and sent it to a ship bound for a Southern port. He subsequently confessed, and committed suicide on the day appointed for his execution).

A few weeks after the death of Adams, William Cauldwell procured a position on the *Sunday Atlas*, and quickly rose to become foreman of the office. He remained with the *Atlas* from early 1841 to the autumn of 1849, during which time he managed to save about $600 from his earnings. In 1850, with the assistance of his uncle in Louisiana, Cauldwell purchased a share in the New York *Sunday Mercury* for $1,200. The enterprising new editor promptly enlarged the paper and expanded its coverage of literature, city news, and sports.

Soon afterward, Sylvester Southworth and Horace P. Whitney joined the firm as additional editors, and the *Sunday Mercury* began to flourish. In those days most daily newspapers did not publish a Sunday edition in deference to strict Sabbatarians, and as a result a few independent weeklies were able to find an audience. Of these, the *Sunday Mercury* became the most widely read weekly newspaper in the United States. Unlike the weekly "illustrated pictorials" such as *Harper's Weekly* and *Frank Leslie's Illustrated Newspaper*, the *Sunday Mercury* contained no artist pictures or cartoons, and only rarely included a simple woodcut illustration.

Appealing to the American fondness for literature, the serialization of novels, poetry, and humor became the foundation of the paper's success. America's classic humorists "Orpheus C. Kerr" (Robert H. Newell), "Artemus Ward" (Charles Farrar Browne), "Doesticks" (Mort. G. Thompson), "Disbanded Volunteer" (Joseph Barber), and Mark Twain (Samuel L. Clemens), and a host of other brilliant writers all rose to literary fame in the pages of the *Sunday Mercury*.

Besides devoting much of its space to literary works, the *Sunday Mercury* also covered domestic and international news, local politics (it was a Democratic paper in a Democratic town), police news, and information relevant to the many volunteer fire companies in the city. A sports section was featured, and Cauldwell's love of the game of baseball was evident (one historian of the sport credits Cauldwell with being the first newspaperman to write about baseball). But Cauldwell soon found the work of editing the newspaper, along with attending and writing about baseball matches, too exhausting, so he hired a young man named Henry Chadwick to cover the sport. Chadwick became a devotee of the game and wrote about it extensively. At the time of his death in 1908, he was considered *the* authority on baseball, and was later elected to the Hall of Fame as one of the great contributors to the game.

Vital to the many militia organizations in New York City—collectively known as the First Division—the paper regularly featured a column entitled "Military Matters," wherein all military maneuvers and concerns were reported and discussed at length. More importantly, regimental and company commanders were able to notify their members of upcoming drills and gatherings through the column, making the *Sunday Mercury* a must-read for any member of these organizations.

In early 1861, the circulation of the *Sunday Mercury* stood at 145,000, and editors Cauldwell, Southworth and Whitney were satisfied that their fortunes were made. Shortly following the attack on Fort Sumter, however, catastrophe overtook the paper in the stoppage of communication between the North and the South. A majority of the paper's readers were in the South and Southwest, and this misfortune of war cut off 90,000 subscribers in only a few hours. "It was indeed disheartening," recalled a contemporary journalist, "but the trio did not sit down and mourn."

William Cauldwell had another idea.

"What we want is news, news from the army—from the battle front!" a galvanized Cauldwell announced to his partners.

But war correspondents did not come cheap, and with limited resources it seemed impossible for the paper to provide interesting news coverage from the war zone. For the *Sunday Mercury* to survive, Cauldwell needed to broaden the definition of a war correspondent. Several friends and employees of the paper were militia volunteers heading south to Washington, and they offered to send dispatches from the front. Cauldwell liked the idea: soldiers as journalists. The paper could obtain news by finding a correspondent from each regiment passing through New York City on its way to the scene of strife. Instructions were simple: get as much accurate information as you can by personal observation—do not speculate—and forward it with haste. The result was the column entitled "Our War Correspondence," where a single letter from a regiment could provide important information for hundreds or perhaps thousands of worried friends and family.

"Every publication day, crowds anxious to get the paper, blocked up the corner of Fulton and Nassau streets where the office was then located," recalled a correspondent, "and the paper found its way down South in the thousands, and was eagerly read around the camp-fires."

While the original intention of the column was to provide news and information from the front, it was the national prestige of the *Sunday Mercury* that transformed the column into a platform for a soldier to voice his opinion about the war and his government. The result was that the *Sunday Mercury* became the public oracle of the Union soldier and sailor. In a war where "freedom" was the battle cry, the letters to the *Sunday Mercury* came to represent the cherished freedom of expression.

Writing and fighting came with a price. Casualties ran high among the soldier correspondents, and no fewer than eight of them were killed, wounded, or captured during the first year of war. Just how many correspondents became casualties cannot be known with certainty; but in most cases, the editors would notify their readers upon the death of a correspondent. For the writer whose fate in battle was unknown, the editors would appeal for another letter to arrest their fears while the readers were left to wonder.

With all of the military details and movements being carefully described and published, it is no wonder that difficulties regarding military censorship arose. In late 1861, several correspondents were arrested for letter-writing, and for awhile the future of the column was uncertain. Guidelines for correspondence were codified and, fortunately, the letters continued, but on more than one occasion, the mails were halted for fear of providing information to the enemy. In another matter, regarding breach of discipline, at least one soldier was court-martialed and found guilty for criticizing a superior in a letter to the *Sunday Mercury*.

In their final letters before discharge, many of the veteran correspondents profusely thanked the *Sunday Mercury* for faithfully advocating the rights of the soldier:

"We shall not forget, that we, as well as every regiment in the service, are under many obligations to your valuable journal for not only furnishing us with the latest intelligence, but in carefully guarding the soldiers' interests while we have been performing our duty at the front."

Said another:

"In behalf of the regiment, allow me, Mr. Mercury, to offer you our sincere thanks for the generous manner in which you have advocated the rights of the soldier. Wishing the Mercury every success...."

Success lasted another thirty years for the *Sunday Mercury*. Southworth retired before the close of the war, and by 1876 Whitney's health broke down and he retired. The paper was now left to the sole management of William Cauldwell. In the early 1890s the rise of yellow journalism and fierce competition for readership among the daily papers in New York City brought financial woes. Cauldwell struggled to keep his paper afloat, but the final curtain came in 1895 after a failed attempt to transform the *Sunday Mercury* into a daily, the *Morning Telegraph*. After fifty years of life, the newspaper that was known during the Civil War as "the soldier's friend" ceased publication.

William Cauldwell died in 1907. In his obituary, the New York *Tribune* paid homage by calling him "the Father of Sunday Journalism." Unfortunately, overshadowed by a host of famed newspapermen, Cauldwell has been ignored by historians and students of journalism. He and the favorite newspaper of the Union soldier—the *Sunday Mercury*—have been all but forgotten. This book is recognition long overdue.

W. B. S.
January 31, 2000

Sources:
Jarrold, Ernest. *Hon. William Cauldwell*, The Journalist. New York, 1890.
Spink, Alfred H. *The National Game*. New York, 1910.
Dictionary of American Biography, 1984.
The National Cyclopedia of American Biography, 1890.
New York, *Tribune*, Dec. 3, 1907.

Chapter I

<u>1861</u>

by

Brian C. Pohanka

Vested with the responsibility of providing "reliable information," and granted a forum in which to do so, the soldier correspondents of the New York *Sunday Mercury* marched off to war fired with a patriotic enthusiasm that was fueled by zealous naïveté. Fate had chosen them to settle the National crisis, a sacred obligation owed to their country, their homes, their families. The rhythmic tramp of the volunteer legions, the rolling drums and piercing fifes, the flapping banners and cheering crowds made every man feel he was a hero, and service seem a glorious adventure. Fledgling warriors, borne to their destiny on a surging tide of martial ardor, those "Boys of '61" could scarcely have imagined the trials and suffering that lay ahead.

This remarkable compendium of letters to the *Sunday Mercury* provides a rare opportunity to gauge the wartime experiences of a diverse group of individuals representative of those Walt Whitman called "the actual soldier...the unnamed, unknown rank and file." Through their words, faithfully and regularly conveyed via Cauldwell's weekly to comrades and homefront alike, we can trace the inevitable transformation from eager "fresh fish" to weary, battle-hardened veteran. Though their devotion to country was at times tinged with cynicism and a propensity to critique the actions of military and political authority, the honesty of their letters, like their immediacy, serves as a genuine barometer for the cumulative morale of the Federal armies.

The vast majority of volunteers who paraded through Manhattan en route to the front had never fired a shot in anger and could only imagine what battle was like. They had not, in the parlance of the time, "seen the elephant." That many would pass through that fiery crucible by year's end, coupled with the novelty of military life in all its aspects, make these 1861 letters all the more fascinating and poignant.

Many of the early war Union troops were members of state militia units, while others sought to emulate the fame of European regiments. Their great variety of uniform reflected those origins and pretensions, and it was a colorful army indeed that began to gather in the environs of the Federal capital at Washington, D. C. Some, like the 7th and 8th New York, were clad in gray attire, the traditional garb of the state militia, while others sported the immensely popular French styles of the Zouave (5th and 9th New York) and Chasseur (14th Brooklyn). The 39th New York, or "Garibaldi Guard," wore a uniform modeled on that of the Italian *Bersaglieri*, while the 79th New York "Cameron Highlanders" were garbed in part in glengarry caps and tartan trews. It was not uncommon for each company of a particular regiment to wear its own distinctive outfit, Company K of the Irish-American 69th New York—Meagher's Zouaves—being but one of many examples. Quite a few of the *Sunday Mercury*'s correspondents in those first months of the conflict were members of these colorfully-clad volunteer commands.

No Federal regiment marched to war with such high expectations of military glory as the 11th New York Infantry, popularly know as The Fire Zouaves. The unit's rank and file was largely comprised of members of Manhattan's Volunteer Fire Department—men famed for their physical prowess, reckless courage and swaggering bravado. Their charismatic commander, 24 year old Colonel Elmer E. Ellsworth, was martial enthusiasm personified. Known far and wide as the founder of the "Zouave Craze" that swept America on the eve of the conflict, his very name was an inspiration to the zealous volunteers who rallied to the cause of the Union. And, at a time when most Americans believed the sectional conflict would be settled in a matter of months, Ellsworth's Fire Zouaves seemed certain to immortalize themselves with valorous deeds on the field of battle. Their high-spirited exploits and zeal for "immediate action," as one Fireman put it, were prominently featured in the pages of the *Sunday Mercury*, though events would prove that they would have spent their time more profitably on the drill field, than in fighting fires and engaging in patriotic braggadocio.

Colonel Ellsworth's death at the hands of Alexandria innkeeper James W. Jackson during the Federal occupation of the town on May 24 made the young officer an early martyr for the North. But the sobering reality of what one soldier decried as Ellsworth's "brutal murder" became much more evident to the *Sunday Mercury*'s readership when blood was spilled on the field of battle. "It was a horrible time," a 5th New York sergeant wrote of the June 10 clash at Big Bethel on the Virginia Peninsula; "on we pushed, the balls crashing all over us." The fight was in fact little more than a large scale skirmish, but at the time it was big news, and a portent of things to come.

These preliminary encounters paled by comparison with the battle of Bull Run on July 21, 1861. Urged on by Northern war fever and the desire for a decisive engagement, the reluctant General Irvin McDowell's Federal army suffered a resounding defeat, the effects of which would resonate for months to come. The soldier correspondents of the *Sunday Mercury* ascribed the debacle to a number of factors: the Rebel "masked batteries," the enemy's "treachery" in allegedly flying US Colors, and on McDowell committing his units piecemeal, "regiment by regiment." One New Yorker even blamed the sightseers who had come out from Washington, claiming "the civilians started the panic." Few volunteers were willing to admit that their own military inexperience and innocence of war caused even the most vainglorious units—like the vaunted Fire Zouaves—to become disordered and demoralized. But no survivor could even begin to construe the battle as glorious. "It was," wrote a 2nd New Yorker, "a wholesale slaughter."

Not surprisingly, grumbling and complaints multiplied in the weeks following the disaster. Along with accusations of Southern atrocities—bayonetting and throat-cutting of wounded, and the like—were hints of treasonous proclivities on the part of some senior Federal officers. Problems of administration and supply came to the fore, as disgruntled volunteers excoriated the issuance of "shoddy" clothing, "ragpickings…fit only for manure." Some units had not been paid since entering service. Other regiments clamored to be allowed to return to New York to "reorganize," and many of the Fire Zouaves did just that. The 79th New York Highlanders were in a state of mutiny. It was all a far cry from the exuberance and soul-stirring panoply of April and May.

It was against this backdrop of faltering morale and organizational disarray that 34 year old General George Brinton McClellan made his grand entrance on the stage of History. The very image of confidence, dash and military zeal, the "Young Napoleon" began to bring order out of chaos in the Federal forces at Washington. The editors of the *Sunday Mercury* echoed the sentiments of the uniformed correspondents, praising McClellan for his enforcement of military discipline at the same time as the General ensured that his troops were "comfortably fed and clothed, and properly provided for." By "encouraging officers and men to feel confidence in one another," McClellan won the trust and devotion of his soldiers, and forged a unique and powerful bond—one that would continue to incite frequent and often impassioned comment in the pages of the *Sunday Mercury*.

Through the months that followed the volunteers learned and mastered the intricate choreography of battalion drill, came to accept the arbitrary enforcement of military authority, and inexorably made the transformation from civilian to soldier. With the exception of General Ambrose Burnside's expedition to the North Carolina coast, and the calamitous Federal defeat at Ball's Bluff on the Potomac, the autumn and winter of 1861 passed without a significant confrontation between the Eastern armies. But there now were few illusions in the blueclad ranks that victory could be attained at small cost. A soldier of the 40th New York made that clear when he cautioned the *Sunday Mercury*'s readers, "believe not that peace can soon be established without blood."

Brian C. Pohanka
Alexandria, Va.

One week after the surrender of Fort Sumter, the following editorial appeared in the April 21, 1861 edition of the Sunday Mercury:

THE WAR

The greatest and most important war ever waged on this continent has now begun, and will be prosecuted with a vigor, an enthusiasm, and an intensity never equaled since the days of the Crusades.

The whole North, is aroused and united. Party lines are swept away, and partisan feelings have vanished. Those who boldly expressed Southern sympathy and opposition to our own Government, one week ago, have been convinced of the treasonable designs of the mutineers of the South, and now rally, as one man, to the support of the American flag—the banner of the Free North.

And it was time that the twenty millions of the freemen of the North should be united, and aroused to the danger that threatens Country, Constitution, and Liberty. The artillery that rained *hot shot* and shell upon Fort Sumter has not only united the North in one irrepressible outburst of indignation, but it has also fired anew the revolutionary madness of the South. We have no longer a puny confederacy of seven Gulf States to contend against. Virginia, which contains the ashes of the immortal Washington within her once loyal precincts, has turned traitor to the Union. Kentucky, too has been dragooned into the vile conspiracy, and arms her citizens to resist the Federal authority. Tennessee proffers her troops to the usurpers of the National Government. North Carolina seizes the forts within her boarders. Missouri has refused to defend the integrity of the nation. And though Maryland may appear to stand firm, her strength is neutralized by traitors.

Thus the civil war inaugurated by the attack on Fort Sumter, swells into tremendous proportions. Rebel States, with a population of ten or twelve millions, and covering a territory almost twice as large as the free States east of the Rocky Mountains, are in arms against the Government, and at this moment threaten to seize upon the National Capitol at Washington.

But the more imposing the force of treason—the greater the danger—the higher will rise the patriotism and courage of the North to resist, to conquer and to punish that treason.

The President has already called for seventy-five thousand men. He must call out three hundred thousand, and prepare a reserve of a million. It is no war of idle blockade and protracted sieges. We have to defend Washington. We have twelve States, at least, to conquer and subdue.

It is not enough to blockade a few ports, or retake a few fortresses. Our Government must either conquer treason in the whole South, and subdue it utterly, or it must itself be overthrown. The time is past for any terms of peace. When the shout of war goes up from thirty millions of people, the voice of peace is like a whisper in a hurricane!

Not only is this one of the greatest wars in human history, but it will be for the weaker side to be overwhelmed as by an avalanche, one of the most terrible. We do not impeach the courage of the would-be usurpers. They have brave and skillful officers. We acknowledge all this; but they have terrible odds against them.

First. The prestige of a regular Government, acknowledged and honored by the whole world, with a flag that has been like a bow of promise to the nations.

Secondly. An overwhelming disparity of numbers. The North is more than two to one against them. They can be crushed out of existence by the mere force of numbers.

Thirdly. The North has the sinews of war. A hundred millions of dollars gorge our bank-vaults, and our Government can borrow all that is required in Europe. Though the rebellious States might, through the maddening influences of their selfish leaders, raise a million of men, they cannot command the means to clothe, feed, or move them.

Finally. There hangs over the South the black and horrible thunder-cloud of Slavery. Four millions of slaves, once aroused to rebellion, would be enough, alone, not only to conquer the South, but to make it such a scene of horror as the sun has never gazed upon.

And whether the Northern armies, which are about to be precipitated upon the usurpers—which will soon be upon the banks of the Potomac, and sweeping down the Mississippi—proclaim *freedom* to the slave, or not, the effect will be the same. Four millions of slaves will rise upon their masters from the Potomac to the Rio Grande. A few strokes of the spade will flood the whole Valley of the Lower Mississippi. The first bugle note of freedom from the North, will open the sluices of a far more terrible inundation.

Treason is bringing upon itself a fearful retribution!

April 28, 1861
MILITARY MATTERS

WAR CORRESPONDENCE.—Several members attached to the different companies and regiments have kindly proffered to write to us frequently, wherever they may stationed, and inform us of any events of interest transpiring among them. It is necessary to obtain reliable information, so as not create any false impression or circulate bad news among the thousands of relatives and friends of the citizen soldiers of the First Division, and of the different Volunteer Regiments who read the SUNDAY MERCURY at home.

We therefore hope that all who may be writing to us will send their names along, to guard against bogus news. In these days of rebellion, when traitors are apt to cut telegraph wires, and in some cases obtain possession of the lines, much caution must be used in publishing hurried statements.

One copy of the SUNDAY MERCURY will be mailed, *free of expense*, to each company from this city, during the war, for the use of the men, if the Captain or Orderly Sergeant sends us the direction.

We shall also take much pleasure in transmitting any military books, or equipments, which may be ordered through this establishment.

FIRE AND MILITARY ITEMS

THE FIRE ZOUAVES.—This regiment is now equipped, and ready for service. It is just ten days since Col. [Elmer E.] Ellsworth first reached town from Washington, and communicated to us his project. On Thursday week [April 18], he called the prominent members of the Department to meet him at the Astor House. They approved of the plan; and on Friday, Saturday, and Sunday the companies were enrolled. He drilled the battalion on Monday. On Tuesday they were mustered into service. On Wednesday and Thursday, equipped and quartered. On Friday morning ready to march! They had to wait for supplies, however; but they depart to-day, carrying with them the blessings and God-speeds of a million true lovers of the Union, who dwell around and upon this patriotic island home.

As it is decreed that we cannot go with this regiment—in whose ranks may be found some of our best friends—we implore Head-quarters to place them in the position they ask for. That is—*the nearest to the enemies of their country*, and face to foe with the bragging, yellow-faced Southern traitors, if they *dare* to face honest men! We fear not for the result.

May 5, 1861
SEVENTY-FIRST REGIMENT, N.Y.S.M.
NAVY YARD, WASHINGTON, April 26, 1861.
To the Editors of the Sunday Mercury:

At last we are here. We have had a rough old time of it getting to Washington. Being all for glory, we are in high spirits. We left in the R.R. Cuyler, as you know, about 4 P.M., and got along very well until night, when there was a lively time among the boys in finding room enough to lie down—every available spot being occupied—the deck, hold, and cabin, being full; for you must recollect, that we had one thousand one hundred and forty in the regiment, not including the ship's crew.

The rations were dealt out in the most horrible manner; and they consisted, the first day, of a small piece of roast beef, and a piece of bread; the second day, first rations, a cup of *swill*—an excuse for coffee—two sea biscuits, and a chunk of salt beef boiled, and so salty that it could not be eaten; and, second, half-boiled rice, similar chunk, swill again repeated. On Monday [April 22], all but one hundred of the boys were sea sick.

There were seven vessels in our fleet, headed by the Harriet Lane. On Tuesday night we anchored off the Severn River, on account of some rockets being sent up, as we supposed, from the Maryland shore, but which afterward proved to be from the frigate Constitution, anchored a short distance from Annapolis. They thought we were the enemy, and going to attack them; we thought the same of them. All hands were immediately ordered up on deck, and furnished with ten cartridges each, and kept up until ten o'clock, at which time we were ordered to bed. The next morning we sailed for Annapolis, and landed. We were quartered at the Naval Academy Grounds.

We had a visit from Gov. [William] Sprague, who commands the Rhode Island Regiment. He is a very young man, and wears spectacles. You would take him to be about twenty-eight years old.

Thursday, we started from Annapolis for Annapolis Junction, about thirty miles, with loaded muskets. We marched our company behind baggage-carts, it being the rear company; toiled slowly along until nine o'clock; rested for two hours; had our rations, consisting of two sea biscuits; marched on again until sunset; rations and rest again; rest, two hours, rations, one sea biscuit.

The colonel purchased seven horses and carts to carry the officers' luggage, and our "rations," paying for each $300 a piece, and the horses were almost worthless—the men pushing them along half the time. The next morning, about half-past four, we arrived at the Junction, having marched thirty miles in twenty-four hours, with nothing for the inner-man but three biscuits; the sun broiling hot, through the day, and carrying our heavy knapsack and gun.

About half-past five o'clock our company started to guard the track from the Junction to Washington. We met a carriage containing two men, and on asking them a question, they gave us a wrong answer. Then one of the boys asked them how much they would charge to take us to Washington, and one of them said $5, but that he would take us to Baltimore for nothing, and continued: "We will see you in Washington in about a week, and you won't be quite so jolly, you d—d Northern abolitionists."

In an instant every musket was cocked and pointed at them, when the captain jumped in front of the two men and said:

"For God's sake, boys, don't shoot them!"

They both turned deadly pale, and left in as quick a time as could be.

We guarded the track until dark, when the train went down to fetch up the regiment. They took us up to relieve another guard of the Pennsylvania (Sixth) regiment, leaving us no guard for half an hour, at the end of which time we found a large iron rail across the track. We kept a sharp lookout, and pretty soon a man came upon the track, and attempted to lay another obstruction upon it. One of the guard fired at him, but missed him, at the same time giving him chase; but he escaped.

We arrived in Washington on Saturday, at 6:30, A.M., and marched to the Inauguration Ball Building; but in the afternoon came to the Navy Yard, where we have a good, permanent place, having sole command of it while here. It is on the banks of the Potomac, and is really a beautiful place.

The New York regiments seem to be the favorites, generally.

We arrived without a sick or disabled man in the whole regiment.

The President passed through our quarters yesterday, and took up a gourd—which we stole in Maryland—to take a drink from a pail of water. Standing just a few feet away from him, I said:

"Mr. Lincoln, that is a secession dipper."

"Gourds are a great institution, nevertheless," he replied.

R. P. VAN Z. [Ruthven P. Van Zandt]

May 12, 1861
OUR WAR CORRESPONDECE.

On our sixth and seventh pages will be found several letters of interest from special correspondents of the SUNDAY MERCURY, now at the seat of War. Others, of a later date, also appear in our pages.

We urge upon every company and regiment the necessity of keeping their friends posted through our columns. There is not a soldier or fireman here who does not read the SUNDAY MERCURY, and it is the "Pet of the Ladies."

Demands for five thousand copies to supply the City of Washington and vicinity, have been sent to us. We shall try and make arrangements whereby every soldier in the service may be enabled to get the paper.

We enjoin all who can to write at least once every week, not later than Thursday. We will attend to any of their little private wants or wishes.

EIGHTH REGIMENT N.Y.S.T.

ANNAPOLIS, MD., May 2, 1861.

To the Editors of the Sunday Mercury:

I hasten to give you a few matters which may be of some interest. The regiment (Eighth, N.Y.S.T.) left New York on Tuesday evening, April 23rd, by steamer Alabama, at 11½ o'clock, with about 1,000 men, to go to—I don't know where. On Wednesday, the men paid their respects to old Neptune almost to a man. Nothing of particular interest occurred until Thursday morning, when we went on deck and found ourselves in company with the steamers James Adger and Marion. The former had the United States brig Perry in tow, and the Sixty-ninth Regiment, numbering some 1,200 men on board. The Marion had the Thirteenth Regiment on board; they number about 600 men. The decks and rigging of the different vessels were covered with human beings; the bands were all playing our national airs and "Dixie," and cheer after cheer were given by the men, making it one of the grandest occasions I have ever witnessed. While going up the river, a British brig was hailed by the Perry, and called upon to show her colors, which, at first, they refused to do; but a gun across her bows raised the colors, amid the cheers of the men on the three vessels. The three vessels kept together all day, and arrived here at 7 o'clock in the evening. The steamer Montgomery, which had Capt. [Joshua M.] Varian's Battery, arrived during the night; and on Friday (26th), about noon, we were landed.

The Twelfth Regiment, of New York, left on Friday for Washington. We arrived in time to see them off.

The Sixty-ninth left for the purpose of guarding the railroad between this place and Washington—a distance of forty miles. Both regiments looked well, and were in excellent spirits.

The grounds occupied by us belong to the U. S. Government, and have been used as a Naval School, which has been broken up and ordered to Newport. The dwellings occupied by the professors have been given up to the military for barracks, which makes us very comfortable, although a little crowded. Our food is very fair, considering the circumstances; but I assure you there is very little fault found. Two of our companies have been sent some eight miles up the bay on special duty; also two squads of Captain Varian's Battery.

There are about 4,500 men at this place at the present time, and two steamers are now in the bay with more (probably Ellsworth's Zouaves and the Fifth Regiment, from New York).

I will try to give you some more information in a day or two, but we have been so busy that we hardly know what is going on here.

Yours, etc.,   S. M. B—, Eighth Regiment.

FIRE ZOUAVES (Eleventh New York Infantry)

WASHINGTON, D.C, Wednesday, 9, A.M.

To the Editors of the Sunday Mercury:

Hurrah for the Zouaves! A working fire, under *Chief Engineer Ellsworth*!

I have just returned from a working fire in Pennsylvania avenue, next door but one from Willard's Hotel. At 4 o'clock this morning, we were started from sleep by the ringing of the city bells; and, on turning out found that a large five-story building in the locality above-mentioned was in a blaze. We had to roll the engines and hose carriages, get them to work, man the brakes and take charge of the pipes. Our gallant little colonel got a trumpet, and officiated as Chief, assisted by [William] Hackett, [John] Wildey, [John B.] Leverich, [John] Downey, and other assistants. The splendid hotel was in imminent danger, owing to the miserable machines here, and an insufficient supply of water. We got street-pipes on, and also got on the roof of the building next to Willard's—a mighty hot spot, too—and after about two-and-a-half hours of hard work, got the fire confined to the building in which it originated. The truckmen threw down the cornice and chimneys, and when all danger was past, our new Chief formed us in line, when we were addressed by the well known Col. [Joseph K.] Mansfield, of the U. S. Army, and Mr. Willard, proprietor of the hotel—the latter of whom invited us to partake of the best his house afforded. Forming by companies, we proceeded to the special dining-room, where we had the best meal since leaving New York. After complimenting us for our bravery, Mr. Willard stated, that he owed the preservation of his hotel to the Firemen Zouaves, and would long bear us in remembrance. With a hearty cheer and a Zu zu shout, we marched off to quarters, Chief Ellsworth in command, with his trumpet under his arm. Major [Robert] Anderson was also at one of the hotel-windows. We cheered him heartily; and he returned the compliment by repeatedly saluting us.

A very cool piece of impudence was enacted on this occasion. As our Chief was marching along with the men, one of the Washington firemen, who arrived on the ground when we had the fire down, walked up to him and demanded the trumpet. The "boss" looked at him steadily for a moment, and replied: "I am going to send this trumpet to New York. If you have more men here than I have, you can take it—not without!" All along the route home we were cheered heartily. Some of our detractors here have found out that we are fit for any kind of duty, and ask nothing but a "clear field and no favors."

Pony [Noah] Farnham, our Lieutenant-Colonel, was out on the camp ground, some two miles from the Capitol, with forty men, pitching tents; and last night we were ordered to have breakfast, and be on the parade ground, fully equipped for the route, at 7 o'clock. This fire has interfered with our plans, but we shall certainly be off within a few hours. Farnham and his squad, of course, missed the fire, so we have a "peg" the best of them.

Our movements since our arriving here, you are, of course, acquainted with. On Monday, we were under arms for ten hours, and were mustered into service *for the war*; the regiment thus being the first to take the general oath. Some scamps, who crept into our ranks before leaving New York, have committed outrages here; but they have been taken, and will be sent home in irons. Five of the vagabonds will be turned over to the civil authorities.

It seems strange to see the red-shirts from New York occupying the desks and splendid rooms of the Senators. I am now writing to you on the desk of the "Little Giant," Senator [Stephen] Douglas. Some of the Massachusetts men are roaming around in front of me, looking for Senator [Charles] Sumner's desk. The boys address each other by the names on their desks thus: "Senator Bright, lend me your envelope." "Senator Powell, oblige me with a penful of ink." "Senator King, your knife, if you please." "Senator Doolittle, give me half that cracker," etc. Rather a *big thing*, this, for the fellows, and the "*Pet Lambs.*"

All the men are anxious to meet the Southern pirates in a fair fight; and you may rely on it, that every crack of their rifles will bring a man down.

The MERCURY is in great demand here. It is meat and drink to the boys. A couple of thousand more than the usual quantity taken here would hardly begin to meet the demand. Please send me a couple of copies regularly. Let the friends of our members in New York know, that they ought to direct their letters to the care of Col. Ellsworth; and in the multitude of correspondence the letters are delayed somewhat.

Everything is going on smoothly, and we will be at home in our tents very shortly. Those tents are of the Sibley pattern—the first ever given to a regiment by the United States Government. They are, as you know, in the shape of *marques*, and will accommodate sixteen men each. All of the camp equipage goes with them. Another big thing for the "Pet Lambs." We were told by the colonel that our new parade and inspection uniform will be here in a day or two. The sooner the better, for our present rig looks pretty shabby, in consequence of having to rough it out on the dirty decks of the Baltic during the passage.

Major [John A.] Cregier is always on the alert, and attends strictly to his responsible duties. This, of course, every one knew he would do; but he does even more. He is here, there, and everywhere, looking after the comfort of the men, and has already gained the good wishes of every one in the regiment. He is "every inch a soldier."

Rumors are flying thick, relative to an attack on the city this week. Let it come. The Fire Department banner will head the van, and we will bring back with us some of the pirate's colors besides.

Yours, etc.,   J. A. S.

P.S.—In consequence of the fire, our departure for camp is postponed until to-morrow morning in order to let the boys have a chance to dry their clothes. How do you suppose they are drying them? By the fire! Not a bit of it. They are kicking foot ball; playing base ball; jumping over piles of flour barrels; taking standing jumps, etc. A few are washing their duds in the shape of handkerchiefs, stockings, and the like. Some have learned more of housekeeping in a few days than they ever knew before. I will write next from the camp.

J. A. S.

John A. Smith, age 29, was five feet eight inches tall with light hair and blue eyes. Before the war he worked as a printer and fire reporter for the Sunday Mercury. *He resigned from the 11th New York on Oct. 11, 1861. On Jan. 28, 1862 he enlisted as a private the 47th New York Infantry and was later commissioned Lieutenant on Dec. 22, 1863. Smith was killed in action at Chester Station, Va., on May 7, 1864.*

ELLSWORTH'S ZOUAVES (11th New York Infantry).

WASHINGTON, D.C. May 8th, 1861.

To the Editors of the Sunday Mercury:

This is the first opportunity I have had of communicating with you since I left New York. We are quartered in the Senate Chamber of the United States—the last place which should be occupied by American troops fighting Americans. The boys are in excellent health, never better in the world; and are all anxious and eager for a fight. You mark my word, no regiment ever left New York at any time that will do the execution in battle that the Zouaves will do. We had six bad-minded men in the regiment and they came very near disgracing us all. It appears that three of the men applied to Captain [Michael A.] Tagen for administration to his company, but he would not receive them unless they were members of the Fire Department. Somehow or other, they obtained possession of badges, and—unfortunately for ourselves—the real characters of the men were not known till it was too late. When discovered they were drummed out of the regiment, and will be sent to New York to-morrow in irons.

We got into camp some day this week, and I will send you the full particulars of our movements in a weekly letter hereafter.

I have twenty-eight members and ex-members of Hose Co. No. 41, and I must say they are doing very well.

Send me some of your Sunday paper regularly. The boys can't do without it. If you forget it, and I am shot; I will haunt you.

COMPANY C., Ellsworth's Fire Zouaves.

TWELFTH REGIMENT N.Y.S.M.

WASHINGTON, May 1st, 1861.

To the Editors of the Sunday Mercury:

There are, it is estimated, over twenty thousand troops in the capital this moment. It is nothing but the roll of the drum, the sound of the bugle, and drill, drill, and tramp, tramp of soldiers all day long. The officers and men are unceasing in their endeavors to acquire the necessary proficiency in the manual of arms, to fit them for the strife. We were pleased to hear that some of our members, who were compelled to remain behind, have raised a fund to assist the families of those who rallied to the call of their country; it is a praiseworthy deed; they will reap their reward.

Companies H, F, and A are quartered in a church, corner of Fifth street and Louisiana avenue; and yesterday, about 3, P.M., as we were sitting in our quarters, some of the men employed mending their clothes, others variously employed, there arose one of the most terrific yells at the door I ever heard, and for a moment I could not imagine where I was; but I soon learned the cause, for in a few moments I saw, from the pulpit, where I was standing, the tall form of President Lincoln, and at his side, that favorite son of New York, Gov. [William H.] Seward, making their way through the dense mass, up to the pulpit. After silence was obtained, the Governor said he had brought the President to see the New York boys, and the Twelfth Regiment in particular, for he thought they could shout as loud and fight as well as any others in the country.

These remarks were received with a perfect yell. Silence again being restored, the President thanked them for the alacrity they had shown in responding to the call of the Government, to defend the glorious Stars and Stripes; he said, that millions yet unborn would thank them for their ready response and privations, which they had and may still have to endure in the cause of their country. They then retired, shaking hands with all who were within their reach.   D. G. McK., Twelfth Regiment.

May 19, 1861
FIRE ZOUAVES
CAMP LINCOLN (opposite Alexandria), May 13, 1861.
To the Editors of the Sunday Mercury:

I have just received a copy of the MERCURY, and sat down to read it, whilst eating my bread, rice, and coffee. I was very much pleased with the account you gave of the Union Rangers [25th N.Y. Infantry]; and I hope the old fogies at Albany will not keep [James] Kerrigan and his men dangling at their heels, as they have some of the other regiments. Give us the Rangers as side partners, and if we don't make things howl, then I am no judge of what New York boys are made of.

I see by the *Herald* that there are 7,000 troops in Alexandria. All bosh! At the present moment there are not 700, much less 7,000. Our boys are opposite the city every hour of the day, and can see the movements of the people there almost with the naked eye. The feeling amongst the people all around this portion of the country is for the preservation of the Union, under any and all circumstances. This you can depend upon as being entirely true.

The men are in as fine condition as it is possible to bring them to. They are ready and anxious to obey their officers; so much so, indeed, that half the time they do not wait to receive their orders before they are off to execute them. Col. Ellsworth is a very strict disciplinarian, and is thought very much of by the regiment. Pony Farnham is every inch a soldier, and after the boys earn his worth and military abilities, will not stop at liking him—they will love him.

If the boys in New York were to see us here, it would make many of them laugh. Just imagine to yourself a thousand men playing leap frog; dancing, groups of singers, card-players, smoking, cooking, washing, growling, talking fire; and just as I am writing, I hear one exclaim to a red-headed mischief-maker: "Say, McIntyre, do you recollect the night 57 passed — truck?"

The regiment is turned out every morning at five o'clock to wash and prepare breakfast, and are allowed from that time till nine to amuse themselves in any way they choose, when they are called to the parade-ground. They are kept on the parade-ground from 9 to 12 o'clock, when they are dismissed for two hours to prepare dinner. On assembling, at 2 o'clock, they are drilled until 6, when they are formed in line of battle, Wallace's Band playing some favorite airs. After parade, the men are dismissed for the day. Every man in the regiment is compelled to be in his tent and lights out at twenty minutes after nine, always excepting the guard.

Dan Collins, of 5 Engine enlivens the boys every night with his corps of musicians; and it is really gratifying to see how much interest the boys manifest whilst listening to the music. I remain,
                         Yours etc.,   M. C. Company G.

May 26, 1861
FIRE ZOUAVES
CAMP ELLSWORTH, May 18, 1861.
To the Editors of the Sunday Mercury:

Here we still remain, directly opposite our enemies and the enemies of our country, leading and holding the "even tenor of our way." Why don't the knights of the red-tape councils (for, you know, red tape is predominant) order us into immediate action? Here we remain, in dull inactivity, rusting for want of excitement. The "boys" would rather attack a second Sebastopol than have days and weeks pass away with "nothing to do." If an order was promulgated to the effect that we were to have a daring brush or engagement with the rebels, it would be hailed as a god-send.

Directly across the river is the rebel rendezvous—Alexandria. Is it not tantalizing to see the secession flag flying there, and we unable, though anxious, to pull it down? Between you and me, and the guardhouse, there was a plot that some fifty of us would secretly cross the river to-night, and bear it away in triumph; but the colonel, by some means unknown to us, discovered the plot, and positively refused to countenance it, therefore, we must let the matter drop for the present.

I wish to contradict at least one of the many reports concerning us which is at present causing considerable uneasiness to our many friends in New York. I understand that it was published in one of the dailies that we were almost starved. I declare, fearlessly and unhesitatingly, that this rumor is a foul slander, and is utterly devoid of truth. Please tell our friends that our fare is excellent—far better, perhaps, than any other volunteer regiment here. There is always some grumblers, who, were they fed on roast turkey and plum-pudding every day, would still grumble. It is the earnest wish of the majority of the regiment (and they are good and brave men), that all such men as I have mentioned will be rooted out from among us. To tell the truth, even though we are not quite fed on "the fat of the land and fish of the sea," still we have excellent rations. Should I ever get home, I am afraid you will scarcely recognize me; for, at the present time, I am as stout as "a feather-bed tied around the middle"; and if I continue to increase in the same proportions, I will have to resign myself to the tender mercies of Barnum.

After leaving Washington, we, for the first time since we left for New York, pitched our tents on an open plain, some three miles from Washington. Here we remained for one week, and I never, up to that time, was aware there was such a material and marked difference between the soft side of a pine plank and the soft, comfortable beds of yore. Sleeping under the canvas, with no other protection from the damp ground save our blankets, came rather hard to us at first; but we are now the more reconciled. The day we left the Capital, after arriving at our new encampment, as we were compelled to dig trenches in the midst of a driving storm of wind and rain, I was only too happy to "turn-in," and throw myself into the arms of Morpheus. It was the sweetest sleep I ever had.

Yesterday, we again removed our tents some two miles further down. We are now encamped on the banks of the Potomac, one of the finest spots that could be chosen, and which the eyes would never tire of gazing on. Here we enjoy superior facilities for fishing and bathing.

The weather here is delightful. We have had several visitors from New York to see us, during the week.

We drill five or six hours daily. It would make you laugh to see such heavy men as Dan Collins, the vocalist, puff and perspire turning somersaults in the Zouave drill.

We fairly idolize the Colonel. He is working like a "honey-bee," endeavoring to make us comfortable and contented. Wherever he leads, we will follow.

Yours, etc., R. W.

THE MURDER OF COLONEL ELLSWORTH

We hope, and do not doubt, that every fireman, every patriot, and every American citizen will recollect, and hold in eternal remembrance, the assassination of the young, the gallant, and glorious Colonel Ellsworth whose fate, at Alexandria, on Friday last [May 24], sealed the last red seal which consecrates the book of martyrs to the cause of human liberty. He died at the hands of an assassin—not at the hands of a foeman who met him in the field of war; for, had he died on the field of battle, we might have ascribed his sacrifice to the chances incident to a glorious, or even inglorious, fight. Young, honorably ambitious, patriotic, and zealous in the cause of his country, he entered the lists of the nation to win a glorious name or a soldier's grave. He fell too early and young, but his death shall not go unavenged. The whole North and North-west will rally to punish the cowards and braggart, who to propagate and advance the cause of human slavery.

The murder of Ellsworth will carry fire, faggot, and flame to every region where his assassination shall be applauded by rebels, knaves, and thieves!

Ellsworth! Brave, determined and gallant! He led to the field of war our Fire Zouaves, and will they not, and all their sympathizers, rally to avenge the death of their chosen leader and chieftain.

Colonel Ellsworth, though not a resident of the city of New York, and, in some sort, a stranger to our firemen, yet commanded their respect, confidence, and lasting love. They will not permit his assassination to go unpunished, and woe to be those who hereafter fall into the hands of his enemies. His death has awakened a feeling, excited loud notes from the tocsin of war, and called into action, which cannot be subdued or silenced until every road of land between the Potomac and the Rio Grande is conquered!

June 2, 1861
SEVENTY-FIRST REGIMENT N.Y.S.M.
WASHINGTON NAVY YARD, May 23, 1861.
To the Editors of the Sunday Mercury:

I notice, in your last issue, a letter from a member of the Seventh Regiment N.Y.S.M., which contains a statement in regard to this regiment, so utterly untrue and without foundation, that we all feel it a duty we owe to ourselves to have it corrected. It is to the effect, that "the Seventy-first Regiment were induced to take the oath of allegiance for three months by the promise of General [Winfield] Scott that they should return to New York in thirty days." The statement is so manifestly absurd, that had it not appeared in your widely-read and reliable sheet, no one would have considered it worthy of notice; and even now, I shall only pronounce it *unqualifiedly false*. There exists among many members of the Seventh, the delusion that the Seventy-first are "down on them," and it causes some of the "weaker brethren" of that gallant corps to make spiteful remarks about us, to the great shame and annoyance of the better-informed members of the Seventh.

The Seventy-first took the "three months' oath" *cheerfully*, and expect to *serve it out* to the best of their ability, at such places, and in such manner, as their superior officers may direct.

We are very comfortably quartered at the Navy Yard; all the boys are in good health, and, with the exception of the sorrow caused by the death of our late gallant commander, in the best of spirits; in fact, the jolliest set of boys in the service. Lieutenant-Colonel [H. P.] Martin, who is now in command of the "Seventy-onesters," is too well known in New York for me to attempt any description of him. Suffice it to say, that he is the most thorough soldier and perfect gentleman in the First Division, and possesses the confidence and esteem of every officer and man in the regiment. We have just received the new uniforms and equipments, sent by our friends in New York, with which we are exceedingly pleased, and grateful accordingly. You would be astonished to see how well the boys look in their new uniforms, which I will endeavor to describe, for the benefit of such of your readers as are not "posted" about us. It consists of a bluish gray kind of woolen jacket, or coat, with side-pockets (*à la* Fulton-market butcher), gray satinet pants; canal-boat brogans; coarse black, United States body-belt, and bayonet-sheath attached, and one black cross-belt, with spread eagle medallion on the breast; our regular, fatigue-cap with white Havelocks; and last, but not least, a generous-sized canteen, covered with gray flannel, with striped web-strap. Taken altogether, it is a cool, comfortable, serviceable uniform—in fact, "just the thing" for "Johnny to go for a sojer" in.

We have about two hundred and fifty men on guard all the time in the Yard, on the bridge, and on the guard-boats. A party of twenty men from Company E, under command of Lieut. T. B. Prendergast, and about forty United States sailors and gunners, under Capt. [Henry] Morris, U. S. Navy, are now on the Mount Vernon, ready for a start, and will probably go down the river to-day, to look after the Virginia shore-batteries, and the new pirate-steamer, Lady Davis. There will probably be music aboard before they come back. I find I have written quite a lengthy document, probably quite too long for your patience and column, but I trust your good-nature to publish it.

Very truly yours,   SEVENTY-ONESTER.

SEVENTY-FIRST REGIMENT

WASHINGTON, D.C., May 30th, 1861.

To the Editors of the Sunday Mercury:

I have a few leisure moments at present in which to give you a few incidents. We left the Navy Yard at 2 o'clock on Tuesday morning to proceed to Alexandria, as we had orders that our presence was wanted there, in case there was an attack made on that city by the rebels. We were conveyed thither in the steamer Philadelphia, and arrived at the wharf in one hour from the time of starting. We were landed in less than half an hour, and formed in line of march—whither, we knew not. We proceeded to the Marshall House, where we took quarters for the night—the house where Ellsworth was killed. Some of the men went to sleep as soon as they could, while others went on a voyage of discovery. Some got a piece of the oilcloth from the hall where the tragedy occurred; others got a piece of the door where the slugs entered that killed the colonel; while others were in the pantries, seeing if there was anything good to eat. One of the men got the coat that [James] Jackson wore when he went out with the company he belonged to; others got secession caps; and, others, things too numerous to mention. One young man had a very interesting letter, written by Jackson's daughter to some friend of hers. All of which were kept as mementos of the place. Lieutenant [James R.] Klots, of Co. B, found a small secession flag stowed away in one corner of a desk, which he took possession of. The whole house has been sacked by visitors. About 1½, I retired to the room allotted and four others, feeling quite tired. We thought we would turn in. We had a splendid bed (the dirty floor) to lie on, and slept soundly until the drum beat for us to get ready to start on another tramp.

I was very much pleased with the majority of the people I met there, all appearing to be Union men now. Alexandria is a very pretty place. There are a great many pretty women there, more so than there are in Washington.

About 8 o'clock the Michigan Regiment came along to take our place, and we were called upon to fall in (which we did very reluctantly, as we wanted a chance to further visit the place) and prepare to leave.

About 4 o'clock P.M., we left on board the steamer Baltimore for our old quarters (the Navy Yard) at Washington, which we reached in safety. I regret to state, that our worthy friend, Frederick May (commonly called "Yaller"), was left behind, as he was on guard; so, so pass away the time, he formed a company of his own, and called them the "Left Guard." All you have got to say to him is: "Yaller, was you down to Alexandria?" his answer will be: "Left!"

Yours etc.,   A MEMBER OF CO. C.

June 9, 1861
LETTER FROM A VIRGINIAN
To the Editors of the Sunday Mercury:

I frequently see statements in the different journals of this city, touching the sudden and unexpected revolution in the sentiments of the people of Virginia. Different journals assign different reasons for that change.

We all know that Virginia was sound on the Union question at the election for delegates to the State Convention, by a majority of 60,000 in favor of the Union. But why this sudden change? Ask your secession politicians; ask your secession journals; ask those who, for the last seven months, have been belching for their treasonable sentiments from the city and State of New York. From them you will get an answer.

When the loyal citizens of Virginia were struggling for their rights with the horde of armed traitors at home, the treasonable sentiments of your politicians, and journals, were scattered broadcast throughout the State, to convince the people of Virginia that a majority of the citizens of New York were with them, and ready to aid them with men and money if required. The minority in Virginia have set the sacred rights of the ballot-box and the sovereign will of the people, at defiance, and are now forcing their secession doctrines down the throats of the people with armed traitors from the Gulf States.

When that glorious banner left Norfolk, and that piratical flag was raised in its stead, it caused the tears to flow from many an eye, with a prayer that the Stars and Stripes would yet wave in triumph over their heads, in defiance of all traitors, whether at home or abroad.

The Union men of Eastern Va. are forced to take up arms against the Government; but will they fight? Not against their country's flag. The traitors know it; and, therefore, fear them. They will not risk a battle with equal numbers if they can avoid it, for they cannot depend upon the Union men in their ranks, and they know it. Let General [Benjamin F.] Butler plant the Stars and Stripes in the vicinity of Norfolk, and issue a proclamation, offering protection to all loyal citizens and their families, and he will find true and loyal men flocking around his standard, who will help to defend it to the last extremity. All they ask is to get out of the clutches of the secessionists and rally under the true flag. I see the traitors, while professing to ignore the Constitution and laws of the United States, claim the benefit of the Fugitive Slave Law: they are willing and anxious to receive the benefit of that law, while they ignore and repudiate all others. Gen. Butler has decided that matter in the proper way; and if they want to receive the benefit of any portion of the law, let them take an oath to support and obey all laws of the United States, or receive the benefit of none.

For the last thirty years, the institution of slavery has threatened the destruction of this Government, and the time has arrived when it is necessary to choose between free and slave labor, for this Government cannot longer endure half slave and half free. Any other than a permanent settlement would be useless; experience has taught us the folly of compromise, and it would be madness to trust them. Self-preservation is the first law of Nature, and it is evident to every man of ordinary intelligence, that slavery is the cause of this rebellion, and there never can be a final settlement while the cause exists. I have always, heretofore, been opposed to interfering with slavery in the States where it exists; but I now find that slavery or this Government must perish in this struggle—one or the other must fall; and I do not think there can be a final settlement of this question while the foot of the slave presses American soil.

The secessionists of the South claim that slavery exists by virtue of the Constitution of the United States. Fatal delusion! The Constitution of the United States is the supreme law of the land; and if slavery exists in any State or Territory, by virtue of that instrument, it must exist in all the States and Territories of the United States, and any action taken by the people of a State to abolish slavery is unconstitutional, and therefor null and void. They also claim, a man's first allegiance is due his State. If such is the case, what position does a man occupy who leaves one State with intention of becoming a citizen of another State? It requires a residence of two years in Virginia; and, during his probation, I ask, where is his allegiance due? Again, when a citizen of the United States, sojourning in a foreign country, is oppressed, does a State Government or the United States Government protect him? That, in my opinion, is enough to convince any man where he owes his allegiance.

You will see statements in the secession papers of slaves who are loyal to their masters, and volunteer to fight for them. They volunteer like the horse, and have about as much say in the matter as that animal has, and instead of fighting for their masters, the slave population of the South keep the whites in a constant state of fear, for there is nothing, to them, so fearful to contemplate as a servile insurrection, and there has never been a time, in the history of this country, when the dangers of one was so imminent as there is at the present time.

The programme of the secession leaders at the South is not generally understood. They know, while they are in the Union, they cannot re-open the African slave-trade; and for that reason they want to destroy the Government. They intend to supply all demands for slave labor with slaves, and force the laboring whites into a standing army to protect their property; but the eyes of the non-slaveholders of the South are opening;

light begins to dawn on them; and they are now getting a glimpse of the true state of affairs, and it will not be long before they will rise in their might and crush the authors of all their sufferings. There is a majority in the South to-day in favor of the Union, who are forced at the point of the bayonet to smother their feelings, and will hail the return of the Stars and Stripes with joy, and will thank God they are once more restored to all the rights and privileges of citizens of the United States.

OLD VIRGINIA.

EIGHTH REGIMENT N.Y.S.M.

ARLINGTON HEIGHTS, VIRGINIA, June 4th, 1861.

To the Editors of the Sunday Mercury:

In my last I promised to give you further account of our travels. Immediately upon our arrival at Washington, we took up our line of march across the city to our camp grounds on the heights overlooking Washington. It was a long march, and most every other person we saw was a soldier. Washington presented a truly warlike appearance; all the large buildings being crammed with soldiers. Soldiers on the corners, soldiers in board shanties, soldiers in tents—soldiers everywhere. Our regiment was much admired; the appearance of the men being very fine, their step solid, and their sunburnt faces giving them the appearance of veterans. The spot we encamped on was called Kalorama. It is a very beautiful spot, surrounded with fine shade trees, the rear protected by a steep declivity, along the base of which flows a stream called Rock Creek, with a bridge crossing it leading to Georgetown, which is close on the other side. The creek is a perfect godsend to the boys, who enjoy its cool waters exceedingly. While here we were mustered into the United States service for three months, from April 25th to July 25th. It was a very solemn and impressive ceremony.

We received marching orders on Saturday, May 25th, and on Sunday morning, about 8 o'clock, we started for Arlington Heights, Virginia. It was a long and fatiguing march, and we suffered considerably from the heat of the sun, particularly in crossing the Long Bridge, which is about a mile and a quarter long, and where we were exposed to Sol's full rays, with not a breath of air stirring.

On the Virginia end of the bridge we passed the Seventh, some of whom were busy digging trenches. They were anything but enthusiastic in their reception of us, allowing us to pass their lines in almost perfect silence, much to the surprise of our boys, who expected a better reception from their brother graybacks and neighbors from the Empire City. One thing is certain, the Seventh, or, in fact, any other regiment, could not have passed our quarters in such a quiet manner. Shortly after passing the Seventh Regiment, we came to a canal bridge, on which was suspended an effigy of Jeff Davis, with a very good pair of boots on—better, in fact, than the original should be allowed to wear. We were halted on the other side, in a shady wood, for half an hour; and then, much refreshed, proceeded on our way. We soon passed the Twenty-eighth New York Regiment; and, after another long stretch, and a short rest, we discovered that we had gone about a mile out of our way. We turned, and soon gained our camp ground, which is on the estate of the late George Washington Parke Custis, and lately the residence of General [Robert E.] Lee, of the Confederate army, about one hundred of whose slaves yet remain about the estate.

This is a lovely spot, well shaded by large trees, under which our tents are pitched. There is a splendid view of Washington and the surrounding country from the family mansion, which is situated on the brow of the hill, facing the Potomac. *Harper's Weekly*, of June 8th gives a very good sketch of the country.

The boys are in good spirits and in good health. We had a large drove of cattle sent to us a few days ago, and our butcher troop immediately started a slaughter-house in the woods. We have had fresh meat ever since, which had the effect of making a good many of the men sick in the consequence. To-day, orders have been issued that no more fresh meat shall be given to the men for three days.

We have had beautiful weather. The days are very warm and the nights very cold. We sleep on the bare ground, which, in consequence of the shade, is very damp, and we get up in the morning well soaked; but we don't mind it now, we are getting used to all that kind of thing.

Our muskets were inspected by a United States officer yesterday, and all our ammunition taken from us, which was replaced by better, the officer saying it was fortunate we had not been attacked, as our ammunition was good for nothing; and such was actually the case, for the regiment had target practice on Saturday, the targets placed 120 yards out in the water. In nine cases out of ten, the balls struck the water twenty yards short of the target. No matter what the elevation—from 100, 200, 300 yards—it was all the same. No more at present.

NEMO, H Company, Eighth Regiment.

June 16, 1861
FIRE ZOUAVES
CAMP ELLSWORTH, ALEXANDRIA, Va., June 6, 1861
To the Editors of the Sunday Mercury:

A rainy, dismal morning is not the best time in the world to attempt to give a description of one's mode and manner of living; but as I must write, in order that your patrons may read, I shall have to go on in the best way possible. It was only the night before last that we moved our camp to a spot about two hundred yards from its former site, in order to make way for the ditch and embankment of the new earth-fort that we are building; and since then, we have had an incessant fall of rain; rain that comes searching into all accessible quarters—down your neck, through the openings of your leggings and into the shoes, along the side of your face, until you begin to think that a channel has been made which connects under the chin and down the breast. And yet in this merciless, pelting storm our lads have had to stand double guard, without overcoats, and otherwise but poorly clad; and they have done it without a murmur? No matter how the wind might blow, or the rain beat, there stood the sentry, all his faculties alive, ready to hail the approach of friend and foe.

Last Sunday we buried our comrade of Co. G—young [Henry C.] Cornell. It was a beautiful, calm morning—the country families around us looking quiet and peaceful, and holy—when the mournful *cortège* came slowly past, and then through they came. The drum and fife led off with the funeral march, after which followed the adjutant, preceding a corporal and eight men of the deceased's company. Next came the coffin, covered with the "Flag of our Union," borne by six of the Co, with crossed muskets, then his friends and more immediate companions of Capt. [Michael A.] Tagen's command. The members of the regiment, line and staff-officers, brought up the rear. Arrived at the grave, which was under a tree on the brow of a hill, suitable funeral ceremonies were performed by the chaplain, the earth was thrown in, three volleys fired, and we walked away—many, perhaps, thinking how soon such might be their burial.

In the afternoon of Sunday the regiment was formed in a square, when the "Articles of War" were read. That section which prescribes kind treatment to all prisoners of war, particularly attracted the attention of Co. G, and from their significant looks and actions, I could not help imagining that the number of prisoners they will bring in will be very small. The Virginia cavalry—those "chivalrous" gentlemen who boast of the purity of their blood—will have a chance to show their courage when they come near Tagen and his troop, while the memory of Cornell is still fresh in their minds.

J. A. S.

Private Henry C. Cornell, age 21, was killed while on picket near the Fairfax Road, on May 30, 1861.

June 23, 1861
SIXTY-NINTH REGIMENT
FORT CORCORAN, ARLINGTON HEIGHTS, Va., June 13, 1861
To the Editors of the Sunday Mercury:

We are just now busy mounting sixteen heavy guns in our works, which are almost finished, and, when done, we shall be able to hold our position against all the efforts of Jeff Davis and as many traitors as he may choose to send; that is, if commanded by our own officers, in whom we have the highest confidence—in their ability as well as their great personal courage. We have had pretty hard work since our encampment here, but everything has been done cheerfully and without a murmur. It would astonish any person to see the immense works that we have thrown up in such a short space of time, and in one of the most exposed places here, right on top of an eminence with not a shrub or tree to protect us from the rays of a scorching sun, and not even a breath of air. In the tents it is almost suffocating, but we heed it not. Our country calls for it—many thousands of our brave countrymen in all parts of the world are anxiously watching the movements of our gallant fellows. They shall not be disappointed; we are determined to a man the traitors shall pass over our dead bodies before we shall suffer defeat at their hands. We are in the best possible health and spirits; hardly any sickness among us, and what there is, is not from the nature of the climate here. Indeed, when other regiments are suffering from change of food and climate, it takes no effect on us. On the contrary, we grow stronger and healthier everyday, which I attribute all together to the great care taken of us by our gallant colonel and officers. Col. [Michael] Corcoran spends all his time with us, principally in the trenches; and his presence seems to make the work lighter—even the burning noon-day sun seems to lose its great power when he rides past us—his rich voice ever and anon is heard: "Well done, boys." When that comes, I tell you the dirt flies.

I cannot see how it is some men hold such influence over others. Yet, so it is. Col. Corcoran is one of them. A rigid disciplinarian, yet a generous commander, one that would punish his most intimate friend when an aggressor against military laws. Yet he would give his last cent to comfort the greatest stranger in the regiment when in need.

Ever ready when he meets you, no matter what your position maybe be, with a kind word. He is one of those men, only sometimes met with, who take your eye immediately, and for whose sake you would go through fire to please. In such men I would never had my confidence shaken. Few commanders ever gained such an enviable position as Col. Corcoran has gained here among all classes of people. With such a commander and such officers as we have, "We will and must conquer."

Our Commissariat is of the best description, thanks to our gentlemanly Commissary, R.C. Downing, Esq. We get all that men can eat of good, wholesome, well-cooked food, and also kill our own cattle (we buy them though). In fact, we had everything an Irishman needs to make him happy, not the least of which is some good "old rye," which some generous soul (knowing the natural propensities of Irishmen) sent, where by we might quench our thirst while digging "sacred soil." Just fancy how we are fed; men that hardly weigh 150 pounds leaving NY, now bring down the beam at 180, with all our heavy work. It shows conclusively the spirit of the men in such a cause, and the uniform system of discipline adopted, and faithfully carried out in the regiment. Last Tuesday night four companies of our regiment advanced toward Fairfax, but with no other success then capturing a few prisoners. Our company had since returned, after gaining their point. The others, I have not heard from as yet. The rebels seem to give the Sixty-ninth a "wide berth." And I assure you it will be a very wise thing for them if they continue to do so. We have an old score to wipe out when we get an opportunity. We shall give them "Ellsworth," we have not yet forgotten his brutal murder, nor are we likely to for some time to come.

NEMO.

FIFTH REGIMENT (DURYEE'S ZOUAVES)

{The following extract is from the pen of Dan. Hart, Orderly Sergeant Co. F, of Duryee's Zouaves (or Advance Guard) formerly clerk to the Central Park Commissioners. It tells the whole story of the battle of Big Bethel in a nutshell, and shows that a necessity exists for better arms.}

When the company came in from evening parade on Sunday [June 9], I noticed the captain examining the muskets, etc., and immediately "smelt a mice." Later in the evening, he ordered me confidentially to see that the men were supplied with ammunition and rations for a day, which I did; and after tattoo, was ordered to rouse them silently at 11 o'clock, and, as orderly, was informed that we were bound on business. Of course there was little sleep in my tent. We put our house in order, wrote a little note to the folks, in case we should be unfortunate, and inclosed them where they would be found. At 11 o'clock we were mustered, and, to our surprise, found the whole regiment under arms, not a light being visible, or a word spoken above a whisper. We marched out to the road from camp, and, joining with the artillery, proceeded to Hampton, where we crossed the creek in large boats, and resumed our march. It was a curious occasion; the darkness and silence, and the steady, firm step of such a body of men, trained like a machine—nobody knowing where or what we were ordered to, but all feeling that something was impending, and that probably the time of some of us was come. So we continued until after daylight, where we heard the quick discharge of arms at our front—a few cries, and then all was still. A moment afterward, the skirmishers took to the rear several prisoners, and we learned that we had driven in the enemy's pickets.

In this condition, and without any time for rest, we were ordered to form line, and make ready for a charge on the enemy. The artillery advanced, and galloped up a road directly in our front. In a moment or two we heard a heavy report, followed by a volley from the concealed foe, and the way the shivers of grape and cannon-balls came whistling around us, and tearing up the ground, was neither interesting nor pleasant. Thereafter, as we saw the flash, we each dropped to mother earth in quick time. We were ordered to a wood by the roadside, under cover of which we hoped to proceed; but the enemy soon had our range, and the boys began to fall around me. It was a horrible time, and one to appeal the stoutest heart. However, on we pushed, the balls crashing all over us, and through the trees, as if through a wheat-field. A man who was crouching beside a tree by me, was killed instantly by a cannon-ball, and numbers were hurt close by. All we could do was to crouch on the ground and remain quiet. Some of our men went to the enemy's flank and endeavored to harass them, but only partially succeeded, as our miserable muskets will not carry; they are almost worthless.

DANIEL H. HART.

SEVENTY-FIRST REGIMENT

WASHINGTON NAVY YARD, June 15, 1861

To the Editors of the Sunday Mercury:

There was an election in Maryland yesterday, and some of our boys that were on the bridge, learning that secessionists had things all their own way, the boys "sailed in," and you talk about voting—they voted once for their right hand, and once for their left, and then declared themselves so that Jeff Davis' crew left the polls in disgust.

In speaking of elections, this is the way that the secessionists carried Virginia: The troops quartered there were ordered to march, and in marching, they voted in every place where they saw a ballot-box—some of them voting as often as ten times! The secession Captain that our regiment took prisoner, told us he voted forty-three times! This beats New York all hollow. His name is Wm. Hadden. He got drunk, and began to talk about Jeff Davis, and pulled out his pistol, when one of the "old boys" grabbed him. You know the grabber, I guess, he was fireman of 44 Engine once—Jube Harrison. He (the Captain) says he has got one hundred and twenty-five in his company, in Virginia, three miles this side of Acquia Creek; but we intend to tame him before we let him go.

There is a rumor here that a secession flag is flying on the Maryland side, about seventeen miles from here, and ten of us have sent in our names as willing to volunteer to go for it. We expect to be gone five days. If I should be lucky enough to get it, I will send it on to you. I will have my share of it, anyhow, as those things are always divided.

With respects,   W. H. R.

SEVENTY-NINTH REGIMENT

GEORGETOWN HEIGHTS, D.C., June 17, 1861

To the Editors of the Sunday Mercury:

A great deal of boasting has been done by officers and men in the rebel army, that one of them is equal to five of the Northern troop. In regard to our regiment (the Seventy-ninth) we are satisfied to engage them, giving them two to one, as soon as it will suit their convenience to stop for fear of being hurt in running away; and we are not alone in that respect, for I have visited all the New York militia regiments, who are all willing to give them the same terms, and, I am proud to say, they would be more liberal with them, by giving them, greater odds, for the sake of having a brush with them.

Of all the regiments our here, of whom New York ought to be proud, in my opinion, and I express it fearlessly, the Sixty-ninth, N.Y.S.M., are entitled to the first position to receive the thanks of the citizens of New York and the United States.

They have erected and completed as perfect a fortification as was ever finished by Todelben for the Russian Government during the Crimean war. Their strength in their present position is equal to ten regiments unprotected, and they are just the boys who will have a hand in where there is any fighting to be done.

I must say that their officers are not excelled by any in the other regiments for perfection in drill and soldierly deportment.

I think the Eighth and Seventy-first will go home when their three months are up, which I am very sorry for, as they are very fine regiments, and are well acquainted with their duty.

The Second N.Y.S.M. Regiment have a very fine camp, and their ranks are filling up fast. For cleanliness, their camp is a perfect model, and their men are a stout, hardy class of worthy mechanics, many of whom I have worked with, as well as several of their officers. They will give a good account of themselves.

It is very hard to get New York papers. When we first came, we could get as many in the camp every afternoon, at five o'clock, as we wished, for five cents each; but the carrier has either stopped or been stopped. If we had one of the enterprising Fulton-street newsboys out here, it would pay him well, as this is the only place I have ever been where no spirit of enterprise is displayed.

Yours, sincerely,   ONE OF THE SEVENTY-NINTH, N.Y.S.M.

June 30, 1861

EIGHTH REGIMENT

ARLINGTON HEIGHTS, VA., June 21, 1861

To the Editors of the Sunday Mercury:

On Thursday, June 13th, President Lincoln reviewed the New Jersey Brigade and the Eighth Regiment. Our marching orders were received late, and we were forced to proceed to the parade-ground close to the Long Bridge at quick time. We reached there, after our sweating march of three miles, a little before his Excellency, and we were assigned the right. After the review, we returned to our camp by moonlight, and reached the Heights at 9 o'clock.

On Friday, the corps surveyed the roads (of which there are many) between the camp and the Fairfax Court-House Road, and the Turnpike to Manassas Junction. We were not disturbed or did we meet with any scouts of the enemy, to the extreme disappointment of our boys.

Saturday, President Lincoln, Secretary of State Seward, Secretary of War [Simon] Cameron, and staff, visited our camp. The Troop fired a salute, and every man not on special duty turned out. The regiment was drawn up in line of battle and his Excellency was received with all the honors due to his high position. The escort consisted of about 250 U. S. dragoons. The President and suite visited everything of interest about the camp, and returned to Washington at 7 o'clock.

On Monday, June 17, several scouting parties left our camp, among them twenty-five engineers; though our particular duty was surveying, and making ourselves conversant with the different roads, and the advantages which they offered, we still considered ourselves acting in a capacity which required us to proceed with extreme caution. We carried our arms, and threw out pickets in advance, and the main body or reserves performed the surveying duties. We advanced nearly eight miles from our camp, and gained a great deal of valuable information. We feel perfectly at home here, and know every road, nook, and corner for miles around. Several prisoners were taken by the different scouting parties from the regiments belonging to the division under command of Gen. [Irvin] McDowell.

From present appearances it cannot be long before the two armies meet; for both are advancing, and the maneuvers become every day more and more interesting.

The several companies in the regiment are making great proficiency in drilling. Company A (Capt. [James O.] Johnston) are entitled to great praise. They are conversant with every duty of the infantry soldier; and at this writing, Lieut. [Anthony S.] Woods is drilling the company in street-firing, which they execute admirably.

Twenty men of the Eighth Regiment succeeded in carrying safely from Washington to this place Professor [Thaddeus] Lowe's balloon, and have proceeded with it to Ball's Cross Roads. It is used for taking observations, and must prove decidedly advantageous to our forces. From the elevated position which he attains, he can view the country for miles around, and by counting the tents of the enemy, we are also enabled to get a very fair estimate of their number. The professor made several ascensions on Monday last.

Yesterday, [Mathew] Brady, the photographer, visited our camp, and took several fine pictures—the Staff, Engineer Corps, Warrant Staff, and a group of Captain Johnston's company. We will send copies to our friends next week.

A great deal of complaint is made by the members of the regiment about not receiving the SUNDAY MERCURY. I have not had one in three weeks, and sometimes have to wait until Wednesday or Thursday before my turn comes to read the one or two which do manage to get into the camp. The New York Sunday papers are a source of pleasure which we New Yorkers cannot possibly get along without, and to us military men the SUNDAY MERCURY is indispensable. I trust our friends will take the pains to send them along in future.

Adieu for the present.　　　　　　　Yours, etc.,　　　　　　　T. R. T.

P.S.—The regiment has, within the last few days, been supplied with light-blue pants, of the same material as the overcoats; also, with steel-gray and purple mixed jacket, loosely made, and extending about four inches below the waist. The dress looks well, and are just the articles to fight in; add but the gaiters, and we have a very neat Zouave uniform.

July 7, 1861
SIXTY-NINTH REGIMENT
FORT CORCORAN, ARLINGTON HEIGHTS, VA., July 2, 1861.
To the Editors of the Sunday Mercury:

I have now been two days amongst the officers and men of the Sixty-ninth Regiment, and will therefore give you all the information sustained from both the rank and file, commencing with Company A, Captain [James] Haggerty, or, as it is more familiarly called, the "bullies," from the fact that when danger is nigh there is to be found "Old Ironsides" company. They number one hundred and twenty men, real fine fellows, and full of fun and frolic.

Captain James Kelly's command is in an excellent state of discipline. Captain K is the senior line officer, and therefore takes the right in line. His officers—the first and two junior lieutenants—are clever tacticians, and deserve credit for their constant labor in behalf of the company. Captain Kelly is well known to the officers of the Moonlight Brigade as the holy "Friar Tuck."

Company C—or "O'Mahony Guard"—is commanded by the energetic little Captain [James] Cavanagh, and are considered by all to be the best drilled in the manual of arms and column marching.

Next follows the Faugh-a-Ballaghs, Co. E, Captain P. Kelly, or, as he is sometimes called, Bishop O'Toole. Company E is well known to the public, from the fact that Lieut. [John] Bagley, with ten men of a picket-guard, made a descent upon Falls Church, nine miles from here, and there capturing a captain, first-lieutenant, and five men of the secession army, four flags, muskets, and numerous letters of a treasonable nature.

Company B, acting captain Lieutenant [John J.] Gorson, is a fine command of intelligent men. They number one hundred and twenty-five, rank and file, and occasionally act in concert with the Faugh-a-Ballaghs in scouting the country hereabouts. His lieutenants are [Thomas] Leddy and [William] Fogarty; good fellows.

Company D, is commanded by Capt. Tom Clark, who, you remember, served in the Sixth Regiment a number of years; has good men, and very excellent officers, Company K, or the Zouaves, Capt. Thomas F. Meagher, is the junior company of the regiment. They are all young men, none exceeding 28 years of age. They are improving wonderfully in the use of the musket, and will, no doubt, teach some of the older hands. Prince Rory O'Moore is the Grand-Master and President of the Moonlight Brigade (Capt. Meagher).

Capt. Melver has a very good company, known in the fort, as the "sports." They were formerly commanded by Capt. [Robert] Nugent, who is now here on business.

Company F, Capt. [John] Breslin, has 130 men, and is officered by Lieuts. [Patrick] Duffy and Hicks. Capt. Breslin is known, by the Fraternity of the M. B., as the "White Horse of the Peppers."

Company G, commanded by Lieut. [William] Butler, who has his assistants Lieuts. [Bernard] McDermott and Murphy, are considered by the other officers to be the best on guard-mounting and sentry duty. Number of men, 120.

The Engineer Corps is composed of select men, taken from the line companies, and numbers 50. Capt. [James] Quinlan (a Don Juan) is commandant. He is ably assisted by Lieuts. Louis D. Momergue and P. McQuade.

Now, a word for the members of the staff, and I have done. Quartermaster [Joseph] Tully is well known in the legal-reading New York to be a perfect gentleman and soldier.

Paymaster [Matthew] Kehoe is a real jolly, good head officer we all know. "Mat" puns on the officers. The officers — him.

Dr. [J. Pascal] Smith (or "Damn it."), Dr. Nolan (or "Gad-fly"), Dr. Barron (or "Seidleis Powder") are able men in their profession, and are great favorites with the officers and men of the Sixty-ninth Regiment.

The mysterious order of the Moonlight Brigade—the names of a few of its members you have above is offered as follows: President—Prince Rory O'Moore (Capt. T. F. Meagher); Secretary—Jefferson Brick (Lieut. John Bagley); Chaplain—Bishop O'Toole (Capt. P. Kelly). Meeting every night, in a grove on the banks of the Potomac.

VISITOR.

July 14, 1861
NINTH REGIMENT N.Y.S.V.
CAMP BUTLER, NEWPORT NEWS, July 5th, 1861.
To the Editors of the Sunday Mercury:

I thought I would give you an idea of what fatigue-duty (most appropriately named) consists of. When on that kind of duty you are generally armed with an axe or a shovel, instead of a musket and bayonet, and have to fell trees, cut and split wood for the cook-house, or get out posts and cut brush to make a building with for some purpose or another; and after having got ready a sufficient quantity, you load yourself with enough to break the back of a jackass and start for camp—a corporal or sergeant standing by to see that no man shrinks, but takes his full load; or you are set to digging a well, or carrying buckets full of sand and small pebbles to put round it; cleaning up the quarters, working in the trenches, or carrying the quartermaster's stores from the wharf to his quarters—nearly half a mile. These, and twenty other equally pleasant modes of killing time, all come under the denomination of fatigue duty. However, we all know that it has to be done, and generally fall to cheerfully.

We had a full-dress parade on last Sunday, and afterward divine service. The regiment was marched by what we call a flank-movement, and formed in a kind of solid square in a beautiful orchard surrounding the house of one of the very few of the natives of this part who have not cleared out, and he is believed to be a rank secessionist at heart, although he has got a protection from head-quarters. We then stacked arms, unslung our knapsacks, and sat on them, or reclined on the ground, with them for pillows, in the shade of the apple and peach trees, and were ready for the service—the chaplain and officers being provided with chairs in a nice, cool porch, or verandah, which run round the house. The sermon was preached by the Rev. Mr. Conner, our chaplain, and was a good one. We had prayers and singing, all in the regiment who choose joining in the singing. On the whole, it was one of the most striking and impressive scenes I ever remember to have witnessed, the men lying so perfectly at their ease; and, although it was an intensely hot day, there was a cool breeze which, in the shade, made it delightful. Listening to the words of the preacher with rapt attention, their minds apparently intent on anything but the stern realities of a soldier's life. I shut my eyes once or twice and almost imagined I was in some country meeting-house, far away from all war-like scenes; but when I opened them, the first thing to catch the eye was the stacks of bright, glistening bayonets, somewhat resembling a corn-field, with a stack of bayonets everywhere where a hill or corn should be. The men, to a casual looker-on, would, I have no doubt, appear to be a promiscuous crowd without order or regularity in their placement; but, after all was over, the two words—"Attention, battalion!"—from the colonel, produced, instantaneously, strait-serried ranks, every man in his exact place, and ready, if necessary, for immediate service, either offensive or defensive. The next orders were: "sling knapsacks—take arms"; and so we marched off to our quarters, every man, I believe, feeling refreshed and better for spending an hour or two in that manner. During the service, an occasional grin was elicited from our men by the grim look of the old secessionist—who, with his daughter, was leaning out of a window, listening—when our chaplain touched on political matters, and compared the loyal people of the United States with the Israelites, as the chosen people of God, and the secession rebels with the Amalekites, and others, whom they were ordered to make war upon.

Yours truly,   G. E.

July 21, 1861

OUR WAR CORRESPONDENCE

In consequence of all our correspondents being now occupied with handling swords and muskets, in place of the pen, we cannot expect many letters just now. As soon as they come to a stand (perhaps at Richmond), we shall have reliable details from them.

TENTH REGIMENT NEW YORK STATE VOLUNTEERS

FORTRESS MONROE.

Your much-prized paper was received on Tuesday. We look for the arrival of the SUNDAY MERCURY more than any other paper—that being the only paper in which we can see any correspondence from our friends and relatives in the New York regiments.

Things in general are very dull around here at present, and the boys of our regiment—and, in fact, of all the other regiments in this part of Virginia—are growing extremely impatient at the (to them) inexcusable delay in making some forward movement; besides our present life in the fortress is rather dull and unsavory, compared with our former adventurous, rough camp-life, of which we have had a full taste since we arrived here from New York. Our last encampment was not a miracle of cleanliness, owing to the sloping of the grounds around us; and in case of a storm during the night, it was not a very extraordinary matter to awaken the next morning and find ourselves and our knapsacks, blankets, etc., floating in a foot of mud and water.

It would interest some of our New York friends to see how anxiously the letters are looked for in the morning. The mails are generally assorted at about 8 o'clock; but an hour before that time crowds begin to gather around the small apartment in one of the case-mates, which is used as the post-office; and if the folks at home could see the varied looks of joy, hope, disappointment, and despair which are depicted upon the faces of the expectant and patient ones who await news from home, they would not be chary or dilatory in sending letters to the far-off, wandering volunteer.

At the express office the same scene is enacted over again. The large piles of boxes and packages are anxiously examined and closely scanned; and when a box is discovered by its owner, it is instantly captured and carried off, amid the envious looks of his companions. And then the different varieties of boxes, and the inscriptions thereon, would be a source of amusement to a stranger. Here is a box supposed to contain cakes, sugar, tea, etc.; and a bottle or two of wine. On the side however, is the inscription, "25 bars soap," or "24 pairs boys' pegged boots," or some other equally uneatable article.

It is getting toward "tattoo," and soon the whole fortress and its occupants will be enwrap in slumber, so I think I'll close.

Yours, truly,   C. W. C.

FIRST WISCONSIN REGIMENT

MARTINSBURG, July 8th, 1861

To the Editors of the Sunday Mercury:

I suppose, ere this, you have read in the New York papers of the engagement of the Wisconsin First, to which I belong, with the rebels at Falling Water, Va. Having a good opportunity this morning, I will write a few lines and give you an account of our movements. I wrote last at Hagerstown, Md. Since then we have been on the continual march. We moved from Hagerstown to Williamsport, remaining there a day or two, then we went back to Hagerstown at noon, 27th of June. We struck our tents and moved on to Downsville, a distance of six miles, when our company was sent out on the heights along the Potomac as pickets. We remained there two days, when we again were ordered back to Williamsport where we remained two days.

On the morning of the 2nd of July, at 3 o'clock, we again struck our tents, and as the advance guard of Gen. [Robert] Patterson's army forded the Potomac. Our company was then sent out as skirmishers. This was the hardest work we have had to perform, as we had our knapsacks on, and had to go through wheat fields, woods, and ravine, and hills 80 feet high, and wooded for some 4½ miles. We came out near Falling Water, on the cross-road, where we waited for the main body of our regiment. After a rest of half an hour, we again took up our march. Co. B, of our regiment relieving us as skirmishers, we were sent on as advance guard. We had proceeded but a short distance, when we were informed that the enemy was but a short distance ahead, concealed. A few minutes after, we heard heavy firing, and knew that our Co. B was attacked. We were then ordered forward, "double-quick," to support them. We moved at once, and passed through field after field, over fences, when we received a heavy fire, which we returned, and deployed as skirmishers, in Zouave style, loading and firing at will. After our third volley, we had a battery stationed in the rear of us, throwing shells at the enemy. Ours and Co. B, were the only two companies of our regiment engaged in the action. We had scattered the rebels, and were advancing upon them, when two Pennsylvania regiments came up, forming in line of battle on our right and left. When the rebels began to retreat, the regiment on our right got a sight on them, and gave them one volley. It was a warm reception we got, the balls rattling around us like rain. They were under cover, while we were in an open field; and it is a wonder to me that more of us were not killed. Only one member of our company—my messmate, G. Drake—was killed. A number of the other company were wounded. We drove the rebels some 2½ miles, when we encamped. At daylight next morning we struck tents, and moved for Martinsburg. Our entrance into the town was received by the citizens with delight and enthusiasm. In half an hour after, tents were pitched. We were visited by large numbers of citizens, ladies and gentlemen, and the town seemed to be waked up to new life. Our flag now waves over the principal buildings in town.

The rebels just before their flight from this place, destroyed all the engines belonging to the Baltimore & Ohio Railroad, some 60 in number, also the bridge belonging to the same. The rebels are encamped some five miles from us on Bunker Hill. They number some 12,000. I expect we shall advance upon them in a day or two. On the Fourth of July, our brigade, consisting of our regiment and the Pennsylvania Eleventh, went back to Williamsport to guard the baggage-wagons and battery. We returned on the 5th, and have been expecting an attack ever since. At midnight of the 5th, we were called up by an alarm—but it was a false one. Day before yesterday we heard the rebels were advancing upon us. We were immediately turned out. Our regiment was kept in reserve. All the other regiments, with the battery and cavalry, advanced about a mile and formed in line of battle—the battery and cavalry commanding the roads. For two hours we stood upon our guns, waiting for them had they made their appearance, for we have 25,000 troops within a half mile.

It is a pretty sight to see 25,000 men all under arms; besides, it is very exciting. At 2 o'clock last night we heard firing among our pickets, and supposed the enemy was advancing upon us, as the firing grew closer and closer. The drums were beat, bugles sounded, and we were again in line for their reception; but it proved to be the firing of pickets upon a patrol of cavalry of the enemy. Our guns were all loaded, our cartridge-boxes well filled, and we felt quite like "pitching in." We did. We lay upon our arms every night, and in five minutes from the first tap of the drum, or sound of the bugle, we were in line and ready.

When I see so much waste of property, and so many defenceless women and children retreating from their homes, it makes my blood boil with indignation at the conduct of these rebels, and I long to be in action. I have seen, within the past few weeks, many things which would cause the blood of any loyal citizen of the United States to boil, and to make them willing to lay down their lives for their country.

I may perhaps, in our next fight, fall; if so, I have the consolation of knowing that I die in a glorious cause. I hope, however, that I shall be spared to send a few messages of death into the hearts of those who have made all this trouble. Our regiment has but five weeks longer to serve out its first enlistment, and whether we will re-enlist is not yet decided upon.

We have had very hard times the few past weeks, and the money which we received for our first month's service is now gone; so we will not be able to procure for ourselves vegetables, and such other articles of comfort as we have been wont to enjoy when at "our homes, far away," and with which camp life is rendered more agreeable. We have only four small tents for sixty men, and we have to sleep upon the bare ground. For the past five nights I have slept in the open air, with no covering at all; still we are all in good health, and as rugged as bears. I feel better than I have for a long time past.

The scenery along the Potomac is beautiful, and I have enjoyed many a pleasant hour in beholding it. Along the Alleghanies the scenery is most beautiful and captivating; and among those beauties is to be seen, in all its splendor, the rising and setting of the sun.

We have just received an order to have three days' rations cooked, so I suppose we shall leave to-morrow. There are more regiments coming to-day. The New Hampshire has just passed here, and the Second Wisconsin, with others, will be here to-day; and before you receive this, we shall, in all probability, have another battle. There has just passed, also, a New York regiment, and one from Massachusetts, and in the New Hampshire wagons were some ten young ladies brought out as nurses.

I understand that we are to be sent out as pickets this afternoon. So good-bye for a while—perhaps forever.

Truly, yours,   J. B., First Wisconsin Regiment.

July 28, 1861
FIRE ZOUAVES

WASHINGTON, Thursday, July 25.

To the Editors of the Sunday Mercury:

My communications with you have been interrupted for some time by events connected with the movements of our regiment, advancing from time to time, rendering the means of communication with Washington more difficult and uncertain. But to resume from my last letter, written at Shuter's Hill, I have to say that the regiment broke camp, and move down the road some four miles, to a spot nearly opposite Cloud's Mills, where we found ourselves supported on one side by the Scott Life Guard (Thirty-eighth Regiment), First Michigan, two Maine, and one Vermont regiments. We here remain for some days, until orders were received for the column to advance in light marching order. The men were given three days' provisions in their haversacks, consisting solely of six pilot biscuits, a piece of salt pork, one small cup of ground coffee, and a cup of sugar.

Leaving our encampment at about 10 o'clock in the morning [July 16], we took the road for Fairfax Station. The rest of the troops marched toward Fairfax Court House, while our brigade, consisting of the Michigan First, Scott Life Guard, and our own regiment, took a circuitous route through the woods to outflank the enemy at Fairfax Station. Company B, Captain Edward Burns, was sent forward as skirmishers, and entered Fairfax Station about an hour in advance of the main body. As they came within sight of the railroad station, they found the enemy retreating down the railroad-track, and, taking a side-path, captured eleven in the woods, and in their camp, behind a masked battery, also took the flag of the Teusas Rifles, presented to them by the lady's of Teusas, Alabama. This flag was taken possession of by Colonel [Orlando B.] Willcox. It was a handsome blue-silk standard, with eight stars on a blue field, and a representation of a bale of cotton, wrought in white silk. It was afterward delivered up to Brigadier-General McDowell, who complimented the company on their bravery, and trusted the regiment would continue to do its duty as well in the future as in the past.

The next morning Capt. Andrew Purtell, of Co. K, assisted by John Wildey, of Co. I, and your correspondent, raised the American flag on the camp-ground of the rebels, amid the stirring music of the drum and fife and the enthusiastic cheers of the men. This flag which was thus raised was presented to Company K by Messrs. Whitton, Forsyth and other friends from the neighborhood of Washington Market, in New York City. After taking up the line of march, at 3 o'clock that afternoon, we proceeded along the road past Fairfax Court House onto Centreville, when we were apprised of a battle going on by the report of artillery, which could be distinctly heard. Orders were immediately given to proceed as rapidly as possible, and at the same time we heard the most extravagant rumors that the New York Second and Twelfth Volunteers, and the Sixty-ninth, had engaged some batteries near Bull's Run, and were badly cut up, so as to need immediate assistance. The men made the most super-human exertions until we arrived at the foot of the hill near Centreville, when we were told that our services were not required, as they had beaten the enemy, and taken possession of a battery, at a place near Bull's Run. We then again took up the line of march, with only a rest of a half and hour. We passed there the main body of our army, and lay for the night in full view of the village of Centreville. Here, by orders of Colonel Willcox, foraging parties were sent out, and some forty or fifty head of cattle brought in, shot, and dressed for the use of the men, and distributed to them. Our brigade—under Colonel Willcox—was thus the only one, nearly, that was supplied with fresh food that night and the ensuing morning. Resting that day, and up to Saturday evening, we were ordered again to fall in line for a forward movement. Company rolls were called, and the men responded with alacrity, after which, we were told to lie down by our guns until 2 o'clock in the morning of Sunday. At that hour we were called up, and were fairly on the march a little after 4 o'clock.

Again striking a circuitous path through the woods, so as to flank the enemy's batteries, accompanied by Gen. McDowell (the Scott Life Guard and the Michigan Regiment still with us), we marched steadily on until between 12 and 1 o'clock in the day. During the last four miles on the march we were in sight of the battle-field, from whence we could see clouds of smoke arising, and distinctly hear the report of the guns. Coming nearly within a mile of the actual battle-field, our men halted, threw off their overcoats, and haversacks, and, with only their canteens and equipments, marched immediately on the field. Arriving at the foot of the hill, our two associate regiments were detached from us, while we marched over the brow of the hill, through a heavy wheat-field. Our red shirts had no sooner glanced in the sunlight then the enemy, noticing our approach, began to throw their six-pound shot at us. Falling back to the foot of the hill, Companies A and H of the regiment were ordered to be held back as reserve, while the remainder pressed eagerly onto the fight. These two companies in less than five minutes, were ordered forward and join the regiment in the battle. Our first point of attack was the nearest position held by the rebels. Some three regiments of riflemen were drawn up in front of a fence, with a masked battery on their left, at the edge of a wood which run down to our right, filled with their sharp-shooters and cavalry. From two to three hundred yards distant from the enemy's line was another fence, up to which our regiment charged and delivered their fire. From here we could plainly see the rebel soldiers with the Confederate flag in the centre. While the men were loading, a charge was made on our rear, from the wood, by the now celebrated Black Horse Cavalry. Col. [Samuel P.] Heintzelman, of the Regular service was at this time with us; and he, like ourselves mistook this cavalry for troops of our own. Waving a small American flag at each end of their line, they advanced to within almost pistol shot, when our men discovered their mistake, and, flanking round, poured a volley into them, and then made a charge. It was one indiscriminate fight, hand to hand, and men fell on all sides, the enemy in front firing at us. Bowie-knives and pistols were used with deadly effect, until in this way the cavalry were driven back, their horses scampering riderless and wildly over the hills. At this point Col. Farnham was shot from his horse, wounded on the left side of the head, but was picked up and again placed on his charger, and led us to the charge against the battery. Major Loeser's horse was also shot from under him; but being again mounted, he rode around our line as coolly as ever, urging the men to the charge. Being again driven back, we retired some distance down the hill, attempting to carry our wounded off with us, when the colonel rode around to the rear and again brought the men to the charge. It was all in vain, however; for our comrades were fast falling by the fire from the woods, while the enemy were too strongly intrenched for us to attempt to get nearer then the fence of which I first spoke. At this point the Michigan First were brought up and driven back. Then the Rhode Island men charged with Gov. Sprague riding at their head; and, fighting all that the men could do, were still repulsed. While we were thus carrying our wounded slowly with us, we observed the Sixty-ninth Regiment coming along in full line of battle. They asked what the matter was, and being told that we had been driven back, answered that they would take satisfaction for us. Marching up to the particular point from where we had been driven, they delivered in their fire, loaded and fired again, and staid until actually driven back without the least chance of forcing the enemy from his position. It was at this time that their flag was taken (the green banner of their nationality) and carried though the woods.

Capt. Wildey, of Co. I, rallying a few men, charged through the wood after those who had the flag in their possession, and with his own pistol shooting the two rebels who had it, rescued and brought in back in triumph. In this way, with the flag of the Sixty-ninth at the head of our regiment we marched on towards Centreville. We had gone but a short distance, when from the clouds of dust on the roads to the right and left, and, on our rear, we could notice that the enemy were in full pursuit. Before proceeding a half mile, we were warned of their being within range by cannon-ball plowing the ground at our sides. We then took to the woods the colonel still riding at our head, bareheaded, and bleeding and after a march of about a mile, were charged upon by their infantry. Turning and delivering a volley which drove them back, we again marched on, and in a short time, gained the wide open road which brought us to Centreville, and from thence about two miles further down where those who were most fatigued made a halt for the night under charge of Capts. Wildey and Purtell, Lieut. [Jacob] Willsey, Capts. Bill Burns, [John B.] Leverich, and a few other officers.

At about 10 o'clock that evening we were roused by the wagoneers, who told us that they had orders to retreat, as the enemy were endeavoring to cut us off at Fairfax Court House. There was no recourse but to again take the road; and, weary, footsore, and travel-worn, those that were left in our party reached Alexandria next morning.

There were many incidents connecting with the battle which it might be interesting to your readers, did time permit or space suffice. The first one carried from the field was Lieut. [Daniel] Divver, of Company G. Shortly afterward, we saw a sergeant, whom we supposed to be Dan Collins, so well known and celebrated as a singer in New York, carried off. Then small troops of men were scattered over the field, four or five in each, endeavoring to bear off some wounded comrade. Some were shot through the head, and lived perhaps five minutes; but most of the wounded were shot about the stomach and thigh—the majority of missiles being rifle-balls. On the road down, Capt. Leverich told me that he had left three of his sergeants on the field. [Edward] Lyons, [Patrick] Connolly, of Engine 51, were left behind, also [John D.] Babcock, of Engine 38, and many others whose names it would be impossible to give in this brief space. It will perhaps be three or four days yet before the actual loss in killed and wounded can be ascertained; but it has been very heavy— perhaps too heavy for our friends in New York to believe. Still, many are reported as missing who will yet turn up. Quite a number are undoubtedly in the woods between Fairfax and Centreville, and may yet come home safe.

It will take at least a month for our regiment to be fully recruited and ready to enter the field again. The general feeling among the men is, that of wanting satisfaction for the loss they have already suffered. So far as the officers of our regiment are concerned, one and all fought as bravely and manfully as the men could do. The colonel himself, bleeding, and faint, and weary, stood by us, and led us on in this disastrous route; and even took the precaution to have the guns that were thrown away by men in the fight placed under the wheels of the wagons so as to be broken and rendered useless, if picked up by the enemy.

Where the fault rests, it's impossible for me to say. General McDowell, who was near our regiment, seemed to act cool and collected; and I cannot believe that the mistake was his. The one great mistake, in bringing the men up, regiment by regiment, to charge on the batteries, where a full brigade was required.

If our friends in New York will only send on money, if they can, it will be the means of keeping many here, who, otherwise, will be likely to go away, and endeavor to reach home.

Many acts of kindness were exhibited toward our men by citizens in Washington, and also by our friends in New York, who came on, prominent among whom I noticed Hon. John Haskin, Alderman Brady, James Cameron of Hose Comp. 28, and many others, who did not spare their money in providing food and quarters for those who are here suffering. The stories told of the barbarity of the rebels toward our troops are in many cases, perhaps, exaggerated; but that cruelty was practiced toward them, there can be no doubt. Our hospital, with the yellow flag, and the letter H in its centre, flying from the roof of the building was fired on with shells and cannonry, and set on fire. Many poor fellows very likely lost their lives in it. Capt. [John] Downey, it is reported, was butchered by them; but for the truth of this I cannot vouch, although many men assert it as an actual fact within their own knowledge. Certainly we were led to believe, before going into battle, and even on the retreat, that we need expect no mercy, and those who sank from exhaustion, intending to deliver themselves up, lay down with but little hope of ever regaining their regiment or meeting their friends. We ascertain from a sergeant of the Alabama Rifles whom we captured that their orders were to spare no man wearing a red shirt, but whether this inhuman mandate was fully carried into execution or not, it is impossible to say. Possibly those who may come in within the next day or two, will be able to state the truth on this point. I have thus briefly given such particulars as can be hurriedly noted down; and in my subsequent letters, will endeavor to give full information relative to all those who have been reported as missing, who are not with the regiment.

J. A. S.

P.S.—I shall furnish you with an official list of our killed and wounded as soon as our loss can be definitely ascertained. At present, all is rumor; and I would not harrow the feelings of any family by forwarding an unreliable statement.

SEVENTY-FIRST REGIMENT N.Y.S.M.

WASHINGTON NAVY YARD, July 23, 1861.

To the Editors of the Sunday Mercury:

Since my last from here, we have had a terrific battle, which, you will learn by the telegraphic accounts, resulted in our being repulsed, although the loss on our side is small in comparison with that of the enemy. The battle commenced at 9 A.M., on Sunday, the 21st inst., the first engaged being the Seventy-first and the Rhode Island First and Second Regiments. We opened a heavy fire of musketry upon the Alabamians, and slaughtered them badly. We could see them fall one after another very fast. They returned our fire with great activity and killed many of us, and wounded some thirty of our boys; and, the killed is supposed to be about ten, although we were at first reported badly cut up. We stood our ground well, and were the last to leave the field. Our colors were completely riddled, and a shell passed through the centre of the flag, just above the color-bearer's head. We had almost succeeded in taking the battery on our left, when, by a ruse, the rebels stopped our firing by raising the Stars and Stripes. We thought they were our friends, and stopped firing, whereby a great advantage was gained by them. We were marched some twenty miles, and then entered the fight much worn out; but, nevertheless, we sustained the previous good reputation of the gallant Seventy-first, of Gotham. One of our Company H was struck by a cannon-ball in the face, which carried away his upper jaw and part of the nose—a horrid sight indeed. Another was struck by a ball in the thigh; he fell near me, and exclaimed: "My God, I'm shot!" One other was wounded in the left hand; and our gallant Lieut. [Andrew] Embler was also wounded in the fleshy part of the leg, but it will not prove serious, we all hope. He is a brave man and gentleman. Col. Martin lost his horse, and had to foot it during the engagement. He walked up and down, cheering the boys and encouraging us on to victory. We finally all retreated in order, and reached Washington on Monday. Capt. [Augustus Van Horne] Ellis was wounded slightly. Only four of our boys are missing. The rebels were seen cutting the throats of our wounded and bayoneting them to death. Oh, what a terrible sight! I hope never to see it again. The groans and cries of the wounded were too horrible to be depicted, amid the roaring cannon and the bursting of shell over and around us. Our total loss is about thirty in all. But few balls fell among us, as they were fired too high as a general thing. We expect to be home on Friday. The boys are under orders to leave for home to-morrow (Thursday), and all is bustle and confusion. I can write no more at present; but hoping you will set matters all right with relatives and friends of the regiment, believe me, yours, as ever, in the Union cause.

J. H. G.

Co. H, Seventy-first Regiment N.Y.S.M.

LETTER FROM HARRY LAZARUS

{We are permitted to copy the following private letter from Harry Lazarus, well-known as a prize-fighter and champion of the light weight of America, who, as a member of Company G Fire Zouaves, bore himself gallantly in the contest at Bull's Run:}

FORT RUNYON, VIRGINIA

July 22, 1861.

As you will see by the heading of this letter, I am at Fort Runyon, the quarters of the Twenty-first, of Buffalo. I arrived here this morning, and will remain for a short time, to get a little rest. I suppose you are already acquainted with the particulars of the great fight which took place on Sunday. We were at first victorious, and had driven the enemy three miles before us, when they received a very strong re-enforcement of fresh troops, and our wearied and worn out troops were in turn forced to retreat. Some of our regiments were badly cut up. Our regiment suffered as severely as any. At the present writing we can find only thirty men out of the one hundred and nine who were in our company when we went into battle. I was accidentally caught between two pieces of cannon and somewhat hurt, although not seriously.

I would like to give you a full description of the battle, but time and space will not permit. It is impossible, as yet, to tell who is killed and wounded—our troops are so scattered.

I find that fighting is rather warm work, especially when you hear the bullets whistling around you like hail-stones. I had the stock of my musket shot off in my hand; my cartridge-box was fairly riddled with bullets; although, strange to say, I escaped without a wound.

I send inclosed a handkerchief, which I "captured" on our road from Fairfax Court-House. We saw a company of ladies in a house waving their handkerchiefs to the secessionists. We surrounded the house, and got some prisoners among the crinoline. I took the handkerchief from a lady who was said to be a daughter of General Lee. I send it to you; not for its intrinsic worth, but as a slight memento of the incidents of battle.

Yours, etc.,   HARRY LAZARUS.

SECOND REGIMENT

{Extract from a private letter}

VIRGINIA, July 22, 1861.

Dear—: —I write to inform you that I am alive, unhurt and well. We have just got out of a severe battle, in which many of our brave boys were slaughtered; but I have not time now to give you many particulars. We were marched up a road made expressly for us by the rebels. They opened their battery at the head of this road, and drove us back to the woods. We rallied, and, by the mismanagement of our incompetent general—[Robert] Schenck—we were brought back on the same masked battery. We could not see any obstruction, or an enemy to fire at. The ground seemed to vomit out grape and canister in torrents. It is the general opinion among the men, that we were betrayed by our commanding general of division. Indeed, Col. [George W. B.] Tompkins was under that impression, although he did not express it; for, when he received orders to attack the hole where these infernal machines were, he told the general he would not, and commanded his men to obey no orders that they did not receive from him—he would lead them to victory, and not to needless slaughter. When the order to lie down was given, a battery opened on the edge of a wood, tearing everything before it. Had our colonel followed the order of the general, we should have been all cut to pieces. The Eighth suffered severely, as also did the gallant Sixty-ninth, and brave boys of the Zouave regiment. They deserve immortal honor for their many gallant deeds.

This was no battle—it was a wholesale slaughter. The very ground opened, and blew us to atoms. Col. Tompkins deserves great praise. He saved two-thirds of our regiment by flanking us into the woods. The enemy seemed to understand our move; for, in less time than I can write, the Black Horse Cavalry dashed out on us; but O God! what a bloody reception they got from us. Nearly, if not quite, one hundred of them were left dead upon the field of their exploit.

I was attacked on the way from Vienna by a few straggling dragoons. We had provisions for our men, and I was in command. We made two horses by the operation, and I lost the little pistol which you presented to me. I missed it when two miles from the place where we were attacked; but I went back with ten men and a dark lantern and recovered it. This was very risky; but it was your gift.

We cut the Eighth Regiment of Georgia all to smash. We have several prisoners. We were badly beaten, but not defeated or discouraged in the least. We will give it to them again. We are ordered to Washington, for the reason that this temporary success may encourage the enemy to attack the city. Our battle-flag is pretty well used up. I will send it home as a memento of what we have gone through. An infernal scoundrel on horseback tried to capture it from our sergeant; but he fell to the earth like lead. The pole and spear is broken, and the flag is all in ribbons.

As I said before, it is the opinion of the men that some of our generals were in league with the secessionists; if they were not, they are inexcusable on the ground of utter incompetency for their positions. Give us better officers in command, and we will face the devil and all his hosts in secessiondom.

Yours, etc., *****.

August 4, 1861
MILITARY MATTERS
NEGRO SOLDIERS FOR THE REBELS—The Legislature of Tennessee has passed an act "for the relief of volunteers," which authorizes the governor to impress into the army all the free negroes of that state between the ages of fifteen and fifty years, being sound in mind and body. These "volunteers" are to perform such menial services in the camp as may be required, and to receive therefor regular rations, with eight dollars per month as wages. Why don't our Government, if we *have* a Government, at once put an end to negro property in rebellious States? Why is President Lincoln so subservient and timid toward the slaveholding enemies of the Union?

PRESIDENT LINCOLN'S REBEL BROTHERS-IN-LAW.—At Big Shanty; a few miles from Atlanta, there was, last week, a rebel camp of 5,000 men—among them a brother of Mrs. Abe Lincoln, named [David] Todd, who held a captaincy. He had charge of thirty-five Union prisoners, taken near Fort Monroe; and, when our informant left, was wrangling with some ruffians who wished to enter the cars and insult the captives. Dr. [George] Todd, another brother of Mrs. Lincoln, was a private in an Alabama regiment. He had been arrested in Texas, for speaking disrespectfully of Jeff Davis; but was afterwards released, and enlisted. Is this why the President deals so tenderly with armed traitors? Must family ties continue to stand between the people and rigid justice, and shall Mr. Lincoln be always permitted to discharge prisoners guilty of high treason, with an "oath of allegiance" and a God speed back to the Confederate Army? Forbid it, spirit of Washington!

SEVENTY-NINTH REGIMENT
NEW YORK, August 3, 1861.
To the Editors of the Sunday Mercury:
You have, no doubt, given me up as one of those numbered with the dead or missing in the late advance, and engagements, and retreat, all of which I have been in, and, no doubt, think I tried to do my duty; however, I will let others judge of that, and endeavor to give you as good a sketch as I can from memory, as I lost my bag and books (but not my implements of war, which many did), and, of course, I will make some mistakes, which I think my friends of the Seventy-ninth will excuse, when they know that it is a severely-wounded soldier that writes it.

Since I wrote you last, we have been advancing from place to place in Virginia, and as nothing of importance happened until we reached Centreville, except that the road was barricaded in several places with trees, which was soon cleared by our pioneers, and the sight of several camps deserted, in some which the fires were still burning—all of which, to us, was the cause of much prospecting on what a set of cowards we had to encounter, but which was set at rest by our arriving, on Thursday, July 18th, at about two miles west of Centreville, where, at midday, we were run (not marched) in at double-quick time, which was the order, for the last three miles; and when we drew up in line of battle, we were more ready to fall down than fight, although the spirit was there; but we had no fighting to do, as the enemy's cannonading soon ceased. The troops that were engaged in close quarters with the enemy were ordered to retreat, and our brigade (*i.e.*, [Col. William T.] Sherman's) to cover the rear, which we did, having in the Seventy-ninth only one man wounded, in the Sixty-ninth, three men wounded, Wisconsin Second, 1 killed; at the battery, two of the gunners were killed. The New York Second Volunteers suffered most; but the whole of it only amounted to a good skirmish.

We retired on Centreville about 4, P.M., as near as I can guess, having no time-piece; then we were marched through the village, taking a road leading westward for about a mile, and there encamped in an open field, until Sunday morning at 2 A.M., at which time we started for the big Bull Run, which we understood very little about, and of which our higher officers, be they generals or gomerals, seemed to know far less. We marched about five miles. When passing through and to the outer or westerly side of a large wood, we got the first sight of the enemy on the rising ground beyond the river. We halted there for about an hour, Col. Sherman, at the same time, trying to discover their batteries by firing shot and shell, which all fell short. We then got the order to march, which we did, crossing Bull Run in double-quick time, and up the hill through a very thick pine wood of small trees, the Sixty-ninth on the right, the Wisconsin Second next, the Rochester Thirteenth next, and the Seventy-ninth (our own) next; another brigade followed, whose I know not. Suffice it to say, on emerging from the wood, the Sixty-ninth attacked the right flank of the enemy (then engaged with our troops, who attacked them from the north), and before the whole brigade got out of the wood and formed, had them completely routed and flying in all directions; but it proved to be only a feint, so as to get us to following them to hotter quarters. The line of battle then was formed on the hill from which the enemy was driven (and where we ought to have intrenched ourselves until we found out their strength), and from which I must say that the grandest scene of my life appeared to me, although awful in the extreme. For a time all was as still as death in the ranks.

Our artillery opened upon them with fury, doing great execution—the shot and shell falling in their midst; their batteries at the same time playing upon us, but generally falling short—their whole army being now (as it appeared to us) only a few scattered regiments in full retreat; when our generals or gomerals, like the fish with the fly, snapped the bait, and gave the order to advance, which was duly obeyed. An attack on their batteries was ordered, the Fire Zouaves taking the lead, covered by a troop of United States cavalry, who, when the first volley was fired upon the Zouaves, wheeled and galloped off, striking terror to the hearts of many brave men. The Zouaves poured volley after volley among the enemy, but having as yet no support, withdrew, although quickly, yet in good order, and formed on the brow of the adjacent hill, and nearer the enemy than the cavalry even dared to go. The panic, at the same time, took hold on another New York regiment, then lying in the road over which the horse and Zouaves past, who fled in consternation out of the strongest position on that field, and not even waiting to get a chance to fire off their guns at the enemy, who took the precaution not to follow at this time. Our position was then changed from the back of a hill about two hundred yards from the same road, but to the left and rear of where that last regiment run from, our right resting near that ill-fated hospital, which was said to be burned on account of no flag being flown on it, and where we could not see what happened at the next attack on the batteries; but it soon came to our turn—the whole Sherman Brigade being marched in along with the Zouaves on the right; and as it would be hard to say to what I saw happen ourselves. Our portion was to attack the right of the enemy, which we did. When at twenty paces from their batteries, they having taken correct aim, the enemy poured into us the most deadly volley that has ever been showered on an army since killing with powder was invented, and in which volley many of our best and bravest fell. Col. [James] Cameron had but uttered the words, "Give it to them, my brave Scotch laddies!" which I distinctly heard, when the word rang along the line, "The colonel's dead!"

Captain [David] Brown fell at the same time. All of which happened quicker than time it takes me to tell it. But suffice it to say, that the Seventy-ninth never faltered; but gave and took as coolly as ever did the regiment from which they take their name. Twice did they rally on the field, and drove back three times the fresh regiments of the enemy, at the same time they received the musketry of the masked batteries from right and left by oblique firing (the deadliest of all firing); nor did they leave the ground until several minutes after the retreat was sounded—the Sixty-ninth and the Zouaves acting in the same cool and decisive manner. During the last charge I was taken from the field, having given way from loss of blood from a wound I received in the beginning of the action; and feeling a little refreshed, after getting a drink of water at a small brook in the valley below (and at which place I saw resting themselves several prominent members of the Seventy-ninth, a number of whom are now in New York; showing holes made in their clothes by themselves, telling of the narrow escape they had, and how many they killed; but whom, I am led to believe, were never in the engagement, and when told to go back refused to go—they may rest assured that they will be exposed as soon as the regiment returns). I proceeded toward the second hospital (the first being crowded). The second was also crowded; but I got a place under a tree, and got the wound dressed and the bleeding stopped; but the doctor could not take the time to extract the ball. I ate a cracker, drank some water, and, after resting a little, joined in the general stampede which followed, coming back by the northern road toward Centreville, and which proved, afterward, to be the safest, as on the other, or direct, road the rear was attacked by cavalry, and several taken prisoners, amongst them Captain W. Manson, First Company—which place we passed about one hour after, and arrived in Centreville, about eight or nine o'clock, where I entered the hospital for the night, sending the man who conveyed me—by resting my weight on his arm—on after the regiment, as I felt perfectly secure, there being two regiments covering our retreat half a mile below Centreville. I there got the ball dug out, and lay down and slept sound until morning.

At daylight rose; looked for the two regiments that covered us the night before; they were gone; had left at 2 A.M. on Monday; was told that the rebel cavalry had visited us at 3 A.M., and had gone to Fairfax, which I reached about 1 P.M., seeing nothing to disturb me, the road being literally covered with wagons, provisions, and the implements of war, such as swords, muskets, cartridge-boxes, knives, etc. Passed a captain and lieutenant of another regiment; asked them where was their company or regiment; said they did not know, which I believed, as they looked like men who knew nothing. Traveled until within three miles of Arlington, when an Eighth-Regiment ambulance wagon picked me up, and took me into the hospital of the Brooklyn Twenty-eighth Regiment, where I found several of our wounded, and where I, as well as all the others, received the kindest treatment and care from Dr. P. B. Rice and assistant, as well as from the Hospital Steward, Geo. G. Holman, whose attentions for two days and nights were unceasing. The services of such men are invaluable to a regiment; and, I must say, are rarely to be found.

On Wednesday, we moved into Washington, into several houses in Massachusetts avenue, Sixth street. Our tents were brought over on Friday and Saturday, and we moved into camp on Saturday, on which day I left for New York. Arrived in Philadelphia at 9 P.M.; put up at the Continental Hotel, J. E. Stevens & Co. proprietors; went to the office for my bill at 4 P.M. on Sunday; found some friend had paid it; but on asking Dr. Gross, who visited me twice while there, for my bill, it was only five dollars—paid it. He is a strong Union man, lives corner of Eleventh and Walnut streets, and has a son in the army. Left with the 5½ train for New York; arrived home—where I now am—at 11 P.M., and where I expect to be confined for a month to come. I now find, on arriving in New York, that a statement is going the rounds that we, while in Columbia College, destroyed furniture, pictures, etc.—in fact, everything that appeared not in accordance with our views of religion. I pronounce the whole an unmitigated falsehood, and I refer the authors of the same to the president of said college, who, when we left there, stated to the officers of this regiment that he was sorry that we were going to leave, as we had conducted ourselves with more propriety than even the Sixty-ninth had done. I may also state, that in our regiment there was, and is, many good Catholics, whom, I am certain, would have let the writer of this know had anything of the kind occurred.

And now as to a Colonel of our regiment. I find that Secretary Cameron has appointed Governor [Isaac I.] Stevens, who, on Tuesday last, was presented to the regiment—they being drawn up in line—and who, when he gave the first command, was answered with silence—not a man took notice of him. The fact is, they want a colonel of their own choice, and will have him.

And I would caution all interested in this regiment to beware of impostors here in New York, as plenty are going around representing that they belong to the regiment, and were at the battle, and work on the finer feelings of the afflicted for their own nefarious purposes. One has already been arrested by the activity of Captain Wm. Bruce, 280 Eighth avenue, and is now receiving his deserts. Captain Bruce is always ready and willing to do anything for the regiment, and is one of those men in whom both officers and privates of the regiment has entire confidence.

Excuse the length of this letter, and believe me to be your sincere friend.

ONE OF THE SEVENTY-NINTH REGIMENT, N.Y.S.M.

{This correspondent received a musket-ball through the collar bone, and was extracted at the bottom of the shoulder blade. We shall be happy to give his name and address to any one desirous of seeing the gentleman.—ED.}

SEVENTY-FIRST N.Y.S.M.

NEW YORK, August 3, 1861.

To the Editors of the Sunday Mercury:

Permit me to contradict, through the medium of your extensively circulated journal, the assertion made by the Washington correspondence of the *Daily Times*, that Col. Martin, of the Seventy-first Regiment, did not fully attend to his duties on the field of battle at Bull Run, on Sunday, the 21st ult. Until he lost his horse, he never left the immediate presence of his regiment; and even after; when his duties were performed on foot, he encouraged and ordered his regiment wherever their duty called them. Few regiments maintained their position so well as ours—although others have been more highly praised. We were in the hottest of the fight, and among the first in the field, and certainly the last to leave it, and know not of the full retreat until we reached the road, having left the field in regular military order. The First and Second Rhode Island regiments fought by our side, and did bravely, having lost many killed and wounded. Among the latter was Lieutenant [Henry A.] Prescott. I saw him struck with a ball on the upper part of his head. He probably died in ten minutes from the time the ball struck him. [John J.] Morrissey, of our company, I learn has had his leg taken off—he, too, having been struck by a ball from a rifled cannon. [John G.] Cobb, poor fellow, has lost his upper jaw, and a portion of his nose. Others in the regiment that were wounded are doing well. It was an awful sight to see the dead and dying, and to hear the wounded cry for water and assistance—enough to chill the heart's-blood. One poor fellow, of an Alabama regiment, crawled to our lines wounded in the left thigh. He asked me for water. I gave him a drink from my canteen, rebel though he was.

I asked him how many were in his regiment; he said some nine hundred. I told him all we asked was, a fair shot at them. He said he was compelled to take up arms against us, but I thought of the same old story; so I let that pass, for what it was worth. He was uniformed in a pair of blue overalls, no coat, a straw hat, and had a double-barreled shot gun. A poor specimen of a soldier, I thought, although he was some thirty-five years of age. He said we would have hard fighting at those batteries; and so it proved. In my opinion, the torch to those woods would have smoked them out, and given us a fair chance to try Northern steel and Southern chivalry; but the cowards fought in woods and behind entrenchments. Some one or two regiments came forward, and were soon cut to pieces by us. There was no general order given to retreat; and the supposition is, that the civilians, in a great measure, started the panic. It is certain, that it was no place for them, unless they did some fighting and not take the lead in running.

Our position was very much exposed; and for an hour and a half we were ordered to lie down, and load and fire! pretty close work, I assure you—with bullets whistling around you in endless number and variety, together with the dull roar of a cannon ball, and the shrill whistle of a shell, bursting within a few feet of where you were. I will now close; but before doing so, I would state that any and all statements made by papers, in detriment to the Seventy-first, are wholly false and unwarranted; and, as far as I am aware of, we each and all did our duty as upholders of the Stars and Stripes; and many of us are willing to return again, to teach a rebel foe a loyal lesson.

J. H. G., Seventy-first Regiment, N.Y.S.M.

SEVENTY-FIRST REGIMENT N.Y.S.M.

NEW YORK, August 2nd, 1861

To the Editors of the Sunday Mercury:

I wish to draw your attention to an act of gallantry performed by a member of the Seventy-first Regiment, named John Fitz Maurice, in the awful retreat from the battle of Manassas. A short time after crossing the bridge where the enemy opened on us from his concealed batteries, and at a moment when every one was looking out for himself, he saw one of our brave "fire boys" trudging moodily along with a broken arm and a horrible scar on the cheek. He went up to him, cheered him by his words, and promised to stay by him. Just then one of our cowardly teamsters came tearing along at full gallop, riding over everything in his rapid flight. The gallant Seventy-firster jumped into the centre of the road and stopped him; he requested a ride for his poor wounded friend, and offered a five-dollar gold-piece to the cowardly wretch; but he would not listen to anything but the promptings of his own cowardly soul; when, before his horse had time to move a step, he struck him a stunning blow with the butt of his musket, which knocked the wretch senseless to the ground. The poor Zouave shed tears like a girl, and, with a grip of the hands, the two friends parted—the one on the back of the teamster's horse; the other, to rejoin his regiment.

ONE WHO WAS THERE.

August 11, 1861

THIRD CONNECTICUT INFANTRY

WASHINGTON, D.C., July 30, 1861.

On Sunday morning at two o'clock, the long roll (the battle signal) beat, and up we started, with gun and blanket, and three days' provisions, and fell into line. We were then about four miles from the battle-ground. We took up the march ahead, as were in the advance; and after going, under a most beautifully-bright moon, for about three miles half the time up hill, stony, rough, and at double-quick, we were halted, and let the "Grand Army" file past us. It was such a splendid sight!—artillery parks, a few cavalry, and then regiment after regiment of infantry, until some thirty thousand had passed, when we again fall in.

About ten o'clock the cannonading commenced, and we could see regiment after regiment fall back, but, at the same time, we steadily advanced and drove back the enemy; and about half-past eleven we were called upon to advance, still under a load of blankets and provisions. We were the reserve of our brigade and know it meant something. They took us a mile at least, through fields, over fences, through the broiling sun, heavily loaded, at the double-quick. Our men now and then fell down exhausted. If there were any cowards, they had a good excuse. Suddenly we faced the enemy—then, laid aside only our blankets, formed in line of battle, and then the Second Maine (with whose officers I was well acquainted) and Third Connecticut went in together. The First and Second formed further off to our right. We advanced, again up hill, firing at the retreating army. Some of our regiment dropped back; not many—two or three of our company. Presently we were staggered just on the brow of the hill, by a thundering discharge of musketry from two houses. We rushed on, up the lane, my company directly in front of it, but all circling around it. The enemy left it and fell back. We gained the houses and were rushing in, when we saw the American flag hoisted by what we supposed the enemy. The cry ran along: "Cease firing; you're killing our men!" There was a slack on our part; we hoisted our American flag and Connecticut Third Regiment colors on the house; and, "honor to whom honor is due," Major Warner and Capt. Jack Nelson did it (so let it be recorded), when instantly there was the most terrific fire of grape, canister, shell, and rifled cannon, from what we afterward found to be a masked battery of sixteen guns (ten in front and six on the flank.) We charged at the point of the bayonet; a shell burst within six feet of me; cannon-balls, musketry, fire, flame, smoke, and noise; something struck me on the side; I fell heels over head forward, and lay bewildered for a minute, then up again. There lay some ten or twelve men all cut up to pieces, John H. Sellick shot through both legs; Thomas Winton, through one leg; the others (not of my company) mangled here and there. Another rifled shot came through the house, tearing everything, and it passed within four feet of where I stood in the opening, cutting down eight or ten men. Another shell struck the roof of the house, tearing it all to pieces; and then the order was given to fall back. We did so, under the brow of the hill, under a terrific discharge of shot, which cut us fearfully, so that when I mustered my company in again, thirty were missing. As I left the field, I picked up a very pretty sword, which I gave to one of my men to carry, but which he finally threw away. We brought off Sellick and Winton, badly shot. Just as we were lying down flat to avoid the shot, which were flying around (and I lay flat on my face, panting like a dog—no water, and wet through with perspiration), I saw an officer gallop across the field, I started up (at first supposing, from the gray uniform, that it was one of my Maine friends). He said: "Where's the rest of 'em?" Says I: "What regiment do you belong to?" Said he: "Oh, yours. Hallo! where did you get that sword?" Says I: "Why that's mine." That made me smell a mice; and, at the same time, I saw S. C. with a palmetto tree on his buttons. I seized him by the collar and jerked him off his horse, and said: "You're my prisoner!" and brought him, horse and all, in. He was the aid de camp of Gen. [Joseph E.] Johnston, coming to give us orders, supposing, from the position which we held, that we were rebels. I delivered him up to head-quarters. His sword I still carry. Presently up dashed another horseman from our rear, who also mistook us for a Georgia regiment. We took him prisoner. We saw then that we (the Third Connecticut Regiment alone) were surrounded and unsupported. We fell back, as we all supposed, to recruit our energies, and go in again; but suddenly a panic seemed to take hold of the troops (not ours); they scattered, and started in all directions. The fight became general; the enemy followed up; our reserves were not there to cover our retreat; every opening or road we crossed we were fired at with shell and grape, and men fell back exhausted, and were cut off by cavalry. I came along and found poor Winton abandoned; he called on me to save him. Curtis and I took him in our arms and bore him along; we each handed our sword to one of our men to carry; we have not seen them since, and never will. The men ran away and abandoned us, and lost our swords; but we got Winton along on to a horse, and he is safe. Poor Sellick! I have not seen since; we carried him under a tree and left him. We got, of course, behind, and separated. I got separated from Curtis, and lost in the woods.

I found two of my men, and some eight or ten of other regiments. We went along together; and just as we emerged into a road, alongside of a stream (Bull Run), some twenty feet wide, and about three feet deep, down dashed a large body of rebel cavalry. Of course, there was nothing to be done but to leap into the stream, which we did, from the bank, some eight or ten feet high. They fired a few shots as they went by, and one of our party fell dead in the water. Poor fellow! I thought for a few moments, "Have we been spared thus far to fall in such a miserable hole as this?" I went up to my waist, and waded through, dragging my canteen as I went along to get a little water in it, as I was almost gone with exhaustion. We got on to the opposite bank, and along about five hundred yards, and there we found Lieutenant Gray (honor to him for it) had made a stand, with what he could find of my company and some others. We stood the charge of cavalry, and drove them back; they charged again with three cannon. Gray led the boys, and took one of the cannon and brought it into camp, and the cavalry fled, with considerable loss of life. We finally came along, leaving the baggage-wagons, etc., and got into our field at Centreville, where we lay down to rest without anything to eat; nothing under us, nothing over us, having lost all our blankets. We lay down at about 8 P.M. At 10 P.M. we were ordered up, fell in, and were marched to Falls Church, twenty miles, the way we took—*via* Vienna—without a halt of one hour, all told, during the entire route, and most of it double-quick.

Twenty-eight hours steady fighting; double-quick marching; nothing to eat; mud to drink—for I was glad to get a little moisture from where the horses drank—and the men tramped through, and we arrived at Falls Church at about 6 A.M., put up our tents, which we had left there, in a heavy rain, and I lay down to sleep.

In two hours we were ordered to strike our tents and be ready to march. We did so. The cars to take our baggage to Alexandria got off the track, and we waited, in a pelting rain, until dark. We then marched, leaving a guard to look after the baggage, etc., and went along about three miles, through mud up to our knees—without exaggeration—when we turned into the Ohio camp, which they had abandoned. I lay down wet through, as I went into a stream up to my knees to wash off the mud, this being the eighth night I had lain on the ground in the open air without taking off my clothes or boots.

About 6 A.M. the colonel called the captains, and said it would be necessary to send back to Falls Church to bring in our baggage; the guard left there had been frightened away by the enemy, and all would be lost. I jumped out and told him I would go back; Gray also. We got thirty-five privates (volunteers), all told, out of the Third Regiment. And we went back, through mud and mire, got to the camp, loaded up our (Third) baggage, then the Second Maine's, and then the First and Second Connecticut's, and brought back everything off all right. Of these forty-five men, twenty were from my own company; twelve from Capt. Brook's; two from Capt. Moore's; one from Capt. Cook's. So let it be recorded.

Our few Union friends treated us very kindly; but, at the same time, packed up and abandoned everything they couldn't carry. It was melancholy.

When we came into Washington, yesterday, amid here and there a cheer—though I held my head up, and my company came along proudly in good order, for they did their duty—I felt sad at the result.

Well, we got back to our regiment safely; immediately took up the line of march (though we had been six miles without a halt) and again at double-quick. I kept my company in order and steadily in rank.

We got to Arlington, through mud, soaked through, and again had to lie out on the wet ground with no covering, or walk all night; and the dew which came down was like a rain.

Yesterday, about five P.M., we again started, and marching (still double-quick) about eight miles, arrived at Washington, where we turned in, weary and hungry, into tents vacated by the New York Twenty-sixth. At about 11 P.M., our colonel ([John L.] Chatfield) took the responsibility of giving each company crackers and cheese and a gallon of whisky—the first that had been dealt out to us since we left Hartford—and if ever men needed it, it was after that battle. We stayed here last night, and now to-day we are pitching our own tents close by, and are moving in; but how long to stay, or what to do, we cannot tell.

I do not ask to take more credit to my company than they deserve; but they certainly had the thickest of that fight, as they went up a lane where they were most exposed. But I do say that the Third, together with the Second Maine, stood the brunt.

Speidel performed feats of valor; he was attacked by three horsemen, and had his sword knocked out of his hand, but he jumped from his horse. At the same time a foot soldier shot one of the horsemen. Speidel seized the dead horseman's sword, killed the second man, and the third ran away.

Our friend Singer (and a better soldier never lived) is gone. He was wounded, and put into a wagon; but they fired into the wagon and killed him.

Our surgeon and the Second Maine surgeon were taken prisoners while attending the wounded.

FREDERICK FRYE, Captain, Third Connecticut Regiment.

August 18, 1861
MILITARY MATTERS

MUTINY AND DISSATIFICATION AMONG OUR TROOPS.—We are pleased to see the stringent measures adopted by Gen. [George B.] McClellan, to put a stop to some of the unnecessary grumbling and downright mutinous conduct of some of the troops in and about Washington. This commandant is doing all he can to have his officers and men comfortably fed and clothed, and properly provided for. He does not allow the humblest private to be neglected or ill-treated, and tells them all there is a mode by which they can obtain every redress for grievances. But he permits no insubordination or mutiny. This is right. Let him go on with the good work. If we are to have an army, let us have disciplined soldiers in it; or else let the Army be disbanded, and end the War by a surrender of all law and authority. There has been too much laxity of discipline. When once order is enforced and exists, all trouble will be at an end.

Gen. McClellan's prompt measures for the enforcement of discipline and the suppression of mutinies awaken applause everywhere. He seems disposed to place the Army upon a secure footing, and is encouraging officers and men to feel confidence in one another, so that when they shall again go to the field, they may be relied upon, and will stand together. Unless there is discipline—unless every man in the field is taught to know the power there is in aggregated numbers, and the necessity of a bold front in the face of any odds—there is no use in attempting to obtain victories; for if soldiers are permitted to believe they are beaten when they retreat from a sudden repulse, they will soon consider it an impossibility to rally. If every individual on a field is determined to die rather then yield, and swears he cannot and will not be taken prisoner, the result is, an army irresistible, by force of mind, which is superior at times to physical matter. His energy becomes a weapon more formidable than bayonet or bullet; his coolness and unconquerable valor dismay and confuse any enemy, and is sure to overpower him when finished with momentary triumph or desperation.

FIRST NEW YORK INFANTRY

CAMP BUTLER, NEWPORT NEWS, VA., August 13th, 1861.

To the Editors of the Sunday Mercury:

Your welcome paper was received here to-day. Since my last, nothing has occurred here to fill a very interesting letter. On Friday night we were aroused from our slumbers by the firing of muskets by our outer picket-guard. We were on the alert in a moment, ready for an attack, feeling sure this time that we should have a fight. But alas! we were doomed to be again disappointed. The picket had been alarmed by the approach of some cows, which here run wild in the woods and which the guards supposed to be the enemy. We therefore went back again to our tents, feeling that we had been again fooled—though, we are used to that.

Col. [Rush C.] Hawkins' Zouaves are having quite an interesting time this week, being in a state of insubordination verging on mutiny, in consequence of the expiration of their three months enlistment, and the delay in receiving their pay. They refused to do any duty except guard, and elected three men from each company to act as delegates to represent them. They have continued in this state until yesterday, when General Butler visited this place. The troops were called out to receive him, and after review he promised the Zouaves that they should be paid within forty-eight hours, which may satisfy them when they—see it. He also called out the delegates, and sent them to Fortress Monroe. The Zouaves are a hardy lot, and well drilled, their regiment making a fine appearance on parade or drill.

Our regiment has been for the past two weeks without a field officer to command, as Colonel [William H.] Allen still remains at Fortress Monroe, awaiting the settlement of his case, and Lieut.-Col. [Garrett] Dyckman has been to New York on furlough. He took home with him his son and only child to die. He was the pet of the regiment, who all unite in sympathy for the bereaved parents. Although but a dozen summers had passed over his head, he had won the love of all who knew him.

Our men are all sobered down from the excitement attendant upon receiving their pay. King Alcohol has been banished from the post; every barrel, keg, or bottle of liquor, ale, or beer belonging to sutlers, men, or even the officers, has been broken up, and contents spilled upon the ground. All boxes or packages of any kind received here are opened by the Provost Marshal before being delivered to their owners, everything of a spirituous nature being confiscated and destroyed, so that we are all perforce temperance men, and a bottle of whisky would be a prize indeed. Our kind friends in New York will therefor take due notice, and govern themselves accordingly. Send no liquor to us, as there is no way in which we can receive it.

I remain yours, etc.   SIGOURNEY.

A BASE BALL BATTALION.—We are informed by a correspondent that several gentlemen well known in base ball circles, have a project under consideration for the formation of a battalion or regiment, exclusively of base ball players; and it is seriously contemplated to recommend a call for a special meeting of the National Association of Base Ball Players, for the purpose of bringing the matter more immediately before the representations of all the clubs. There are now eighty clubs belonging to the Association; and there are upwards of a hundred others located throughout the State, which it is thought would gladly join in such a movement. An average of five men from each club would form a regiment; and better material for soldiers than could there be gathered together cannot be found.

Of course, the whole idea is as yet mere suggestion. From the fact that a large number of ball players have already been carried off to the war in different regiments, we do not know that the project under consideration is practicable. We have no doubt, however, that hundreds would flock to the standard of such an organization, if it were put in proper hands. In order to test the matter, we are willing to receive answers and suggestions from officers of different clubs, for the purpose of ascertaining the practicability of the project prior to any decided movement being made. Let us hear what would be the chances for a Base Ball Battalion.

August 25, 1861
FOURTEENTH REGIMENT, N.Y.S.M.
ARLINGTON HEIGHTS, VA., Aug. 21, 1861.
To the Editors of the Sunday Mercury:

You, perhaps, have expected me to drop you a line or two long ere this; but the fact is, I have been so busy attending to the duties devolving on me, that I have not been able to let you know how I was getting along. You know that the Fourteenth had a taste of Bull Run, I suppose—as you also know that the "seceshers" tasted the metal of Brooklyn in that fight. I happened *not* to be there, on account of being ordered to remain behind to protect our camp. You may judge those that were left behind felt had when listening to the distant thundering cannon, and feeling, as I did, that at each boom many a brave spirit was passing away. Some half a dozen or more left our camp contrary to orders and got on teams that were going toward Fairfax, Centreville, or Manassas. I felt almost disposed to do the same, but for the necessity of my being present as charge d'affaires at our camp (Porter).

It was a lamentable sight, the return of our troops. The day was a very gloomy one in almost every respect, for it was raining very fast a great part of that morning after the fight, and to see men, wounded and fatigued as they were, ambulances, wagons, and teams filled, was indeed a sight. Everywhere along the road were scattered arms and ammunition; and though it was raining very fast, our fatigued troops could be seen in gulleys, under trees, in barns, or wherever a spot could be found where they would not be sure to be trampled upon. As I met the men from the many different regiments, they would inform me that the Red Legs were all cut to pieces. It looked much like truth when I met our men—but occasionally and few in number. We have not, however, lost as many as we at first thought; and some of those that were seen killed, in I don't know how many different ways, have at last turned up as being prisoners at Richmond, four of whom belong to my company (I), viz: Felix Cuscadden, Simon H. Richardson, and Lewis Francis, privates, and our first lieutenant, Clayton Scholl. Gen. [Fitz John] Porter seems to think our boys did well; and from what conversation the Prince Napoleon had with Gen. McDowell, it seems to be verified; for it is reported here that Napoleon informed McDowell that the Red Legs did more harm and were the greatest source of trouble to the secessionists (and this information was given by [Gen. P. G. T.] Beauregard to Napoleon) than all the rest, and that they lost 900 killed and wounded from one regiment, by the Red Legs. My cousin returned from the fight to the encampment; and though he was shot through the calf of his left leg, he made out to bring back his musket and accoutrements, and walked a distance of over 40 miles—clean through from the battle-field to Arlington Heights. It was indeed a curious spectacle to witness; some with bullet-holes through their caps, some through their clothing, in many different places—even to the splitting of the stocks of muskets, holes through cartridge-boxes, and belts actually cut away from the person—and in most of these cases the men unharmed. My cousin had three bullet-holes through the right leg of his pants, without grazing the skin even.

One man I noticed with about seven different shotmarks, with but three to touch the flesh, and they but scratches, all bullet impressions. There is no doubt but bad management caused that defeat to terminate as it did. There are a great many things transpiring which seem very unlike what ought to be "military." It was not a whipping our men got, but it was a panic they were seized with. The teamsters and the regular troops are looked upon as the great cause of that trouble. Great credit appears to be due—from the many versions I have listened to of the battle—to the Rhode Islanders (Sprague's Battery and Regiment particularly), the Fourteenth of Brooklyn, Ellsworth's Zouaves, the Sixty-ninth, with its glorious Zouaves, the Wisconsinites, the Minnesotians, Michaganders, the New York Second, Eighth, and Seventy-first, Garabaldians, and New York Blenker's Rifles, also.

The next time we try the boasted chivalry, who are well versed in treachery, as they have shown themselves by raising the United States flag to draw our troops in their midst unguarded, I think it will be necessary to try a few of the heavy artillery and mortars. It is folly to send such brave men as our forces were composed of to rush into masked batteries and traps.

But there are still screws loose somewhere else. I cannot be led to believe but that, in Washington, in the departments, there are traitors conniving at our destruction, and men who will give all the information necessary to Jeff Davis on the eve of our next battle, as it was done for Bull Run.

There appears to be some efforts made to resist the enemy, should they attack us about here, which I think is not probable. There appears to be places between here and Baltimore, as far as I understand the geography of this section of country, more easy of passage, and, when once across the border, great destruction of both life and property seems inevitable.

I have now more confidence since McClellan has taken the command, and hope that he is doing the same as he is doing about here on all the ridge of hills between here and the Relay House. It is probable we will hear of an attack on Fortress Monroe or Newport News ere long, and if that point is gained, it is considerable toward a defeat of our forces.

Last night and yesterday was my turn as sergeant of the guard at this point. About 11½ o'clock, Colonel Kerrigan, accompanied by a lieutenant and about four files of men, brought six strapping negroes, who were captured, armed to the teeth, in a piece of woods just above here. The colonel was in good spirits, as well as accompanied by a flask of the genuine, of which the officer of the guard and myself became once or twice inspired, if not spirited; and after about three hours' conversation we parted, assenting to his request that we should call at his camp and drink a bottle of wine with him at an early period.

There is a general feeling of a desire to return home by our boys, so as to rid themselves of some of the officers they have over them. The officers, of course, are opposed. The general seems to think that the Fourteenth Regiment is composed of lawyers; that they are not fit to be either tree cutters or trench diggers; but that they would make good lawyers or musicians—they have such a faculty of arguing points and whistling Yankee Doodle.

Yours, truly,   J. J.

Company I, Fourteenth Regiment, N. Y. S. M.

John Jenkins, age 27, was born in England; he stood five feet seven inches tall, with grey eyes and brown hair. On June 1, 1861, Jenkins enlisted for three years in Co. I, 14th Brooklyn State Militia. He was soon promoted to third Sergeant but later was reduced in ranks to private after being absent without leave (returned voluntarily). On May 8, 1864, Jenkins was shot through the left shoulder during the battle of Laurel Hill, Va. He was a frequent correspondent to the Sunday Mercury, *contributing dozens of letters throughout the war. John Jenkins died in 1905.*

MOZART REGIMENT, (Fortieth New York Infantry).

FLAG HILL, near ALEXANDRIA, Thursday, Aug. 22, 1861.

To the Editors of the Sunday Mercury:

"Rain, rain, go away, and come again another day."

My thoughts fly back to childhood's peaceful days, and I repeat, insensibly and earnestly, the above poetical petition. All of us would be willing to make most any sacrifice to the clerk of the weather, if he would "shut pan" on his water-works, and give us at least one day to dry ourselves. Talk about Jersey! Why, its mud is no more to be compared with the "sacred soil," than the rocky hills of Massachusetts does to the golden plains of California—(isn't this a beautiful metaphor?) The people about here say that the said weather will continue until the "moon goes out!" I pray that her royal highness may soon have occasion to "go out."

Considerable excitement has existed for the last day or two, in consequence of the unusual number of rumors flying about, relating to the enemy. First it will be: "They are ten miles off!" and then will be: "We will undoubtedly be attacked to-night!" So it goes; first one thing, then another. I hardly think that, should the "seceshers" really attack us, we would believe it was them until some satisfactory evidence should prove them so to be.

Our brigade, consisting at present of the Third and Fourth Maine, and New York Thirty-eighth and Fortieth (Mozart) regiments, were reviewed by General McClellan this afternoon. We were marched to an open field about a mile distant, and there formed in line of battle, and the usual exercises were enacted. After review, General McClellan had a conversation with our colonel, in which he (the general) stated that he was most agreeably disappointed in the Mozart Regiment. He said that he had heard of it very often, but really did not presume that it made so fine an appearance. He congratulated Col. [Edward J.] Riley, and seemed well pleased with us. This must be a very flattering as well as hopeful acknowledgement to our colonel and his officers. To the men I know it is.

I am really glad to perceive that an action is taking place to suppress all rebellious journals in the city and elsewhere. We all hail the intelligence with delight, and hope that soon these traitorous sheets will be extinguished. I have no doubt that these vile publications have aided materially the cause of rebellion, by preventing many from enlisting. I am of the opinion, however, that no true *Union* man can be persuaded by their lying editorials. Let me say to one and all who stand doubting, *believe not that peace can soon be established without blood. It is a base fabrication, gotten up by a certain few, who are traitors at heart,* and whose only prayer is, that the subjugation of the Southern States may never be accomplished. Come on! Your country calls, and needs your help. Under the star-spangled banner, we *must* be successful at last.

All are well, and in good fighting trim. Perhaps before my next epistle, we will have a chance of displaying our skill and bravery. No news of importance has your correspondent gathered, and he sits woefully, gazing alternately from mud to sky, wondering, in the meantime, why the chaste moon doesn't "go out."

Yours,   FORRENS.

The 40ᵗʰ New York Infantry was also known as the "Mozart Regiment"—named after the Mozart Hall faction of the Democratic Party in New York City.

September 1, 1861

BRAVERY OF A FIRE ZOUAVE—A private letter from a young soldier in Co. F, Eleventh Massachusetts Regiment, who was in the Stone Bridge battle relates the following instance of the bravery of one of the New York Fire Zouaves:

"I must tell you of the noble bravery of one of Ellworth's Zouaves. He had been shot in the wrist, and the ball had severed an artery. It was after we had made the second charge upon the battery, and I had lost my gun, which had been knocked from my hands by a cannon ball, and I was now in the rear of the company, when I saw the Zouave creeping toward me. 'Boy,' said he, 'for God's sake hold me up a minute, I am gone under; but let me fire once more on them!' I held him up, and, facing him round toward the enemy, steadied his arm while he fired six shots from his revolver at them. I then helped him down the hill toward the hospital, a short distance, when he asked me to examine his side, as he felt a pain there. I opened his clothes, and found that a ball had passed through his body. I carried him a little further, when suddenly our whole body, artillery, infantry, and all, were rushing upon us in full retreat and crying out: 'All save themselves who can.' 'Go,' said the Zouave, 'go, my boy; you are not hurt, and I am a dead man; they cannot hurt me any more. Go, for God's sake, go!' And I had to leave him."

September 8, 1861
A NEW DIET FOR THE ARMY—HOW TO OBTAIN SUPERHUMAN POWER. The Erythroxylon Coca has attracted the attention of Mr. J. F. Maisch, who contributes an article in regard to it to the August number of the *Medical and Surgical Reporter*, in which he recommends the surgeons of our army and navy to test its power of preserving human life.

This plant is indigenous to the mountainous regions of Bolivia and Peru, and is cultivated in districts elevated from 2,000 to 5,000 feet above the sea. It is valued chiefly for its narcotic properties, which it possesses in a greater degree than any other vegetable production, not excepting opium and tobacco.

The Peruvians gather the leaves, and after drying them in the sun, chew them in connection with the lime, or the alkaline ashes of some plants, which they affirm renders the flavor of the plant sensible to the taste.

Prescott, in his *Peru*, says the Coca is of so invigorating a nature, "that the Peruvian, with a small supply of it in his pouch, and a handful of roasted maize, performs his wearisome journeys, day after day, without fatigue."

Dr. Thompson says the Indians, under its influence, work twenty and thirty hours without sleep. They travel on foot, seventy leagues in three days, using very little food, but chewing constantly on the Coca, which they carry in a pouch thrown over the shoulder, together with a bottle of quick-lime.

The Coca has no injurious effect on health or life, save when used in excess, and then, like all other excesses, it sooner or later causes death.

If these statements are true, and they seem to be well authenticated, the recommendation of the *Reporter* would appear to be worthy of attention. Such an increase in vigor and the power of enduring and resisting fatigue would amply repay almost any cost.

Armed with so powerful an invigorator, fifty thousand troops might march successfully against five times their number. The strength of armies could not then consist in their numbers, and the battalions that chewed Coca would be assured of the help of Providence.

SINGULAR MEETING OF BROTHERS AFTER A BATTLE—BOTH OF THEM WOUNDED.—A correspondent of the Richmond *Dispatch*, writing from "Camp near Manassas, July 27," relates the following affecting incident of the meeting, after the separation of seven years, between two brothers, one a member of the New Orleans Washington Artillery, the other belonging to the First Minnesota Infantry. He says: "We went into a stable in Centreville where thirteen wounded Yankees were, and upon entering, found a Washington Artillery man seated by the side of a wounded soldier, evidently ministering to him with great care and tenderness. He remarked that it was very hard to fight as he had fought, and turn and find his own brother fighting against him, at the same time pointing to the wounded soldier from whose side he had just risen. I asked if it were possible that was his brother. 'Yes, sir, he is my brother Henry. The same mother bore us—the same mother nursed us. We meet the first time for seven years. I belong to the Washington Artillery, from New Orleans—he to the First Minnesota Infantry. By the merest chance I learned he was here wounded, and sought him out to nurse and attend him.' Thus they met—one from the far North, the other from the extreme South—on a bloody field in Virginia, in a miserable stable, far away from their mother, home and friends, both wounded—the infantry man by a musket ball in the right shoulder, the artilleryman by the wheel of a caisson over his left hand. Their names are Frederick Hubbard, Washington (Louisiana) Artillery, and Henry Hubbard, First Minnesota Infantry."

Frederick Hubbard, age 22, was discharged from the Confederate Army on October 30, 1861 as a result of his disabled arm. Brother Henry, age 19, was sent to Richmond as a prisoner and was later exchanged on October 6, 1861. According to his pension file, it is claimed that Henry died from the effects of his Bull Run wound on March 6, 1879.

MOZART REGIMENT
Thursday, August 29th, 1861

What might have been the precise position of those old heroes who forsook the half-buried plow and the rugged acre for the trusty rifle and the tented field—what might have been their reflections when for the first time they "wrapped their martial cloaks about them," and laid them down, beneath the canvas white, to balmy sleep—I am unable to conjecture. Still, a philosophy of my own teaches me that men and manners vary only a little in a generation or two. Accepting this to be true, I allege that, could some of their old epistles be brought to light—that is, epistles dated from this section of the country—that they would exactly correspond with mine so far as barometrical observations are concerned. I assert that men and manners alter little. The weather changes less. I guess those same old heroes would have laughed if they could have peered into the future, and read the appellation which history and events were to attach to the "moistened" soil of Virginia. The idea of its being designated by the term "sacred" would, methinks, have been received with loud demonstrations of mirth—especially on such a day as this. Although the moon isn't visible at present, still it is evident that she hasn't "gone out" yet. But I will make no further remarks on the weather, lest my mind should become clouded too, and my epistle prove as unacceptable as the said weather.

Still, withal, we are in a high state of excitement, and live in constant expectations of being summoned to the field. For three of four days past we have dispatched pickets; and as they return, they all report having seen the enemy, and he hard at work, upon the hills near Ball's Cross Roads. Even at this moment, the booming of cannon comes over the hills, and the sound, though muffled, stirs within our breasts a desire for action. It may come soon; and all of us are prepared for it. We desire to settle the question as soon as possible. We came here for the sole purpose of crushing out this infamous rebellion; and the sooner it is done, the better for us and our own cherished country.

Lest our friends should presume that our thoughts are upon war, and war only, I give below the result of a well contested ball-match, which came off some week or so ago. Among the number I have no doubt some of our Brooklyn friends will recognize old players, who more than once have gained the applause of enthusiastic hundreds. The following is the score:

FIRST.	O.	R.	SECOND.	O.	R.
Bennet (P.)..................2		4	Brown (U.)..................2		4
Lowery (C.)..................2		4	Garrleen (1st b.).............2		4
Wood (1st b.)................3		4	Ward (P.)......................2		4
Forrens (2d b.)..............2		3	Shute (c.f.)...................3		3
Short (3d b.)................4		3	Leahy (3d b.)................4		3
Airy (c.f.)....................x		3	Godfrey (r.f.)................4		2
Raynor (r.f.)................4		2	Harnion (s.s.)................3		2
Decker (s.s.)................3		2	Millen (2d b.)...............4		1
Munson (l.f.)...............4		3	Triqudet (l.f.)...............3		3

INNINGS...........................1	2	3	4	5	6	7	8	9
First.................................2	3	3	0	2	1	4	6	7-28
Second.............................2	5	0	3	3	4	2	0	7-26

As you perceive, the game was a close one, and ended as creditable to the one as to the other. Among the "Firsts" there were some good players. Corporal Bennet made some splendid batting, and proved himself a good pitcher also; he was a member of the Atlantic (of Jamaica). Lowery done well, and there is none who can excel him in catching; he formerly belonged to the Mattano (of Brooklyn). Wood and Short were both excellent players, and are old hands at it. On the other side we noticed Corporal Brown especially. His batting was excellent, and generally gained for him a home run. Ward and Garrison played well also. Ward pitched with admirable swiftness, and gave that peculiar "twist" which won for Creighton so much praise. Altogether it passed off well, and was applauded by all who witnessed it.

Another match may come off soon, when the whole eighteen will be joined. The ball, however, will be made by "Minié"—a little harder, I believe, than those usually used. I sincerely trust that we may be as successful in the new game as in the old.

Well, I know not whether I have penned an interesting letter or not, but still I trust that the reader will imagine the author to be knee-deep in the mud, and almost wet to the skin; then consider, whether this is not as much as could be expected, when every thing so teems with inspiration.

All are well, and in good spirits.

Yours,   FORRENS, Co. I, Mozart Regiment.

September 15, 1861

OUR FIRE ZOUAVES IN RICHMOND.—{The following letter, written by Lieut. A. M. Underhill, of Company G, First Fire Zouaves, and foreman of Mechanics' Hose Co. No. 2, of Brooklyn, will be read with interest}

RICHMOND, VA., Aug. 16, 1861.

DEAR BROTHER:—Your letter of the 3rd came to hand on the 13th, by way of Louisville and Nashville. As I had written before, I have waited a few days, and have nothing new to write about. Please send a copy of that portion of my last letter relating to my capture to the colonel of my regiment, and state also that Captain Downey and forty-three non-commissioned officers and privates are prisoners with me. I was very glad to know that you learned of my situation so soon as you did. It had worried me considerably, as I know it did you all until you heard from me.

We hear all kinds of rumors here—some of them very extravagant; among others, that our regiment is disbanded, and that in the battle they broke, and ran at the first fire. To my own certain knowledge, they were broken and formed again three separate times, and held the hill and the battery (Sherman's, as the folks here call it, but in reality Captain Ricketts') longer than any other regiment that attempted it. Five different regiments in succession were ordered to hold that hill, and every one of them was in turn driven back. This I know, for I never left the field during the entire fight. Sometimes we were driven clean over the fence, but never beyond it. Three times the battery was taken away from us; the second time we retook the guns and attempted to run them off by hand (the horses being all killed), but were compelled to leave them. Shortly after that, I met Col. Farnham, who ordered me to retire from the field, which I did with him, endeavoring to rally the men. When we had succeeded in getting about two hundred of them together in another field, the order to retreat was given. Then it was that I gave way entirely, from mortification and the revulsion from such intense excitement. I had also sprained my ankle in endeavoring to draw off the cannon, so that, what with pain and want of food and rest, I proceeded but a short distance, and fainted. When I became sensible again, all was still; so I crept into the woods, and lay down to sleep. I awoke about three o'clock in the morning, and made my way slowly back to Centreville, at which place I arrived about seven o'clock. I found a number of wounded men there, with no one to attend them. I gave them all the assistance that I could in bandages, food, and drink, until late in the day, when I was made prisoner, and sent to Manassas.

Our regiment—had they been the veterans that you read about in the life of Napoleon—might have held that hill, but it would have been held in a short time only by their dead bodies; such, at least, is my opinion, which may not be worth much to other people, or those who have been in battles before. At any rate, I don't think I shall alter it until experience teaches me that I am or was wrong. I have not received any pay from the Government. Can you send me some money? I will need very little here—enough to buy a cot to sleep on, a blanket, and some under-clothes, will last me through the winter very comfortably. My bed at present is a soft plank, which I am satisfied with when it is necessary; but if it can be bettered at small expense, I decidedly prefer that it should be. Such delicacies as milk, eggs, butter, etc., can be dispensed with; but when to be had by paying for them, I decidedly prefer to have them. Give my love to all, and let me know the news from Jay street, who is elected foreman in my place, and how they are getting along.

FOURTEENTH BROOKLYN

ARLINGTON HEIGHTS, VA., September 10, 1861.

To the Editors of the Sunday Mercury:

As I have a few moments' leisure, and supposing that you would like to hear from our camp—and though I have not anything very special to write about—it, nevertheless, is a pleasure to me to write of some of those matters apparently of minor importance. It would seem strange, no doubt, to some people at home, that we here have not plenty of news to communicate at all times, however, such being far from the case, we have to get along as well as circumstances will admit. I happened to see a copy of the SUNDAY MERCURY, the other day, and found an article from a sergeant of Co. I. That article was read all through camp—many of our boys being regular subscribers to your Sunday publication—and so there was more truth than policy in that article, you may judge it was read with pleasure.

The regiment now has plenty to do—having every other day one-half nearly on picket duty. You can imagine that the boys don't have to wait long for their turn at work, *i.e.*, digging or throwing up breastworks, and leveling trees—guard and picket duty . We have been in readiness for a march—having constantly on hand two days extra rations for nearly a week, and supposed, from surrounding reports, that we should have a right smart engagement with "secesh" before this—but I reckon they are not quite ready for us yet. It is possible that when we dash at them again, "secesh" will be "*done gone* a right smart heap," from which even South Carolina will learn to know "heow to guess the rail Deown Easters' mode of *toting* them on the other side of Jordon."

The last time I was on picket—and, in fact, each time we are out—there were plenty of seceshers to be seen on the hills, at work. We are very often within speaking range of them in the day-time, and at night can hear them conversing. They often use—or, at least, try—their treachery on us; but we make out to *guess* their *reckoning* too well for us to receive much injury from their crack shots at night. We make out to be better posted than to allow them to be posted about our posts at night, within range of them. Several Union pickets, however, have been reckless enough to secede from duty, and while out scouting, have been so unfortunate, as, in some instances, to receive shots from the prowling seceshers hidden in bushes, or in the woods.

There has been great preparations made within the past two weeks toward a movement somewhere about here. The tramp, tramp, tramp of infantry, the rattling and rumbling of cavalry and artillery, breaking the stillness of night, as they have passed night after night over the Long Bridge, from Washington to this side of the Potomac—everything being kept so secret, and the restrictions that have been placed over all the troops so different to what it was before Bull Run, certainly means something else than a Bull Run, or anything like trifling or joking, this time, at any rate.

The news of the capture of Forts Clark and Hatteras, with the prisoners and arms, and added to it, also, the confirmation of the death of Jeff Davis, has tended to a degree to inspire some of those who felt a desire to get rid of soldiering, to enter into the martial spirit with vigor again.

The Fourteenth Regiment now have but about five hundred men, rank and file. Two officers have gone on a recruiting expedition to Brooklyn. It may be a very good idea in the present state of affairs in the regiment, but it is possible the good idea will not be seen. There are many little affections existing that cannot be cured until a better confidence is engendered by the men, in professions and representations made to them by their commanders. I think, however, that the Fourteenth of Brooklyn fare as well in some things as can be expected. We do not get all that Uncle Sam allows his children, through the selfishness of somebody who has his misplaced confidence; but we get along better than some regiments about here do. The two last companies out here I and K—are still without their overcoats, and those who do not make out to borrow from the other portion of the regiment suffer much from the heavy dews and cold, chilly night-winds of this clime. Brooklyn has shown herself ever ready to furnish all that her sons of the Fourteenth have required, but, of course, she cannot attend to the negligences of others. Our boys make out to keep up their spirits finely. The old members call the new companies artillery and cavalry I and K respectively. It is, Fall in for your horses, Company I, and fall in for your howitzers Company K, saddles, spurs, and what not from reveille till tattoo. If a piece happens to be discharged, the general cry is, either put him in the guard-house, or else send him home. Dreadful punishment, for it is just what most of the members have been in hopeful anticipation of doing soon—the going-home part, particularly.

We are in daily expectation of receiving a two-months' pay, when there will be some smiling, in more ways than one, with many.

                                                                                          J. J.

September 22, 1861

HAWKINS' NINTH REGIMENT N.Y.S.V.

ON BOARD STEAM TRANSPORT S. R. SPAULDING

CAPE HATTERAS, September 12, 1861.

To the Editors of the Sunday Mercury:

I write you, having an opportunity to send this by the transport which leaves for Fortress Monroe to-day.

We struck tents at Newport News, Va., at 4 o'clock, P.M., of the 10th inst., but did not get aboard of the steamer until 10 P.M., when we left under cover of the night. We arrived here yesterday, 12 P.M., after a pleasant voyage. The steamer was somewhat crowded, and of course we hadn't everything we wanted. We slept on deck, down in the hold, and in fact in every place we could find. We disembarked at 1 P.M., Wednesday, and remained on shore until 6 P.M., when we were ordered aboard again for the night. The same inconvenience we had to experience again. All the companies, with the exception of our own, are ashore. We are detained aboard for something; I don't know what. To tell the truth, this is the most dreary place I have ever seen. The soil is all sandy, like Coney Island exactly. Our colonel [Rush Hawkins] is in possession of Fort Clark, which is at the upper end of the island. Fort Hatteras, in possession of Col. [Max] Weber, is nearest the landing, and is, I think, the best fort. I stood upon the ramparts yesterday, and viewed the country all around. It is a very curious sight. Shot and shell were strewed all around. I have got plenty of shell and shot, and will endeavor to send you some. Fort Hatteras is not a regularly-built fort, like any that are in the Harbor of New York; it is built of sand and sod, and has no barracks.

Our boys have all sorts of trophies taken here. Some had watches, and others had knives and pistols; and when we arrived, we were received by some of our boys who were dressed up in all sorts of clothes, taken from the "seceshers"—green, blue, gray, and every color imaginable. It was rather an amusing sight, and one I won't soon forget. Yesterday we met two schooners (prizes) on their way to Philadelphia. It appears they came in here supposing it to be still in possession of the secessionists. Lieut. Crosby met them, and they asked to be towed in by the Fanny, and the captain of the "secesher" said he was glad to get clear of the "d—d Yankee," meaning the frigate Cumberland, who tried to deceive them by letting them run the blockade. Lieut. Crosby afterward said he was a United States officer, and claimed him as his prisoner. The captain then was so surprised that he went aboard and got drunk, and remained so all day. The colonel had a beautiful stand of colors captured, and he hoisted them on the fort. We have captured five vessels since our boys have been here, and we expect a number to arrive from the West Indies daily. The prizes we took yesterday had on board coffee and ammunition.

Our boys lived high at first. They captured all their provisions. The people, they say, come from miles around into camp, and sell articles, such as fish, etc. They are all loyal. To my utter surprise, we have not seen a contraband since we arrived. There are none around. All the people are white. There is a small church a little way up the main land, where an old minister preaches, and who seems to be their leader. He comes into camp under a flag of truce, and gets all the inhabitants to swear allegiance to the Union. About five hundred have already done so. They say there is no rebels nearer than sixty miles. This I guess is so, because we have no picket-guard posted, only an interior guard. We are on the Cape, and nothing can be seen to the North but a wide expanse of water; and it reminds me of the island that Robinson Crusoe lived on; at the back you can see a few houses. Our men seem to have everything they want; figs are in abundance; a little back in the country, fishing is of the first class, but the water is awful. We have no well save those that are dug in the sand, and the water is almost unfit to drink. When a storm is brewing, they say, it carries everything before it, washing clear over the sand. You may not hear from me for one or two weeks. I understand we are to have communications with the fortress twice a week, and then of course I will write you often.   R. H. J.

September 29, 1861
FOURTEENTH REGIMENT, N.Y.S.M.
ARLINGTON HEIGHTS, VA., Sept. 24.
To the Editors of the Sunday Mercury:

Having a few moments to spare, I take the opportunity to write a few lines to you before a grand battle takes place, or we, perchance, leave this camp at head-quarters. Five companies lately returned from picket-guard duty, and the company I belong to was stationed so that we had very good opportunities of seeing the rebels often. At night, our posts were changed; and it so happened that some of us got a pretty close view of the rebel scouts—one of which came within fifteen feet of the tree behind which I stood watching him; but as soon as he saw our men, he retreated behind the barn-sheds, into the woods, and vanished. I felt a strong inclination to fire—which could not have been resisted, had the individual approached closer—for I already felt it unsafe to allow such proceedings from strangers to go on unheeded—but our orders were strict, and to the effect that we must not fire unless advanced upon, after a challenge.

We imagined we saw any quantity of scouts, but I feel liberal enough, after what I felt positive of having witnessed, to let some of them go for mere freaks of imagination, caused by the presence of a cow or two, a horse, and a young colt, which were innocently going their rounds in quest of fodder around about the out-houses of the farm-house at which I, with six men, were posted. If said animals only know what excitement they were making during that dark and quiet night, and the dangers they were laying themselves liable to of being shot, through such influences, they would certainly be more careful, and perhaps get the countersign—or, at least, be more considerate of their safety than the old sow, who, on one occasion, being challenged, and told to halt, heeded not the request, but walked along, apparently well assured of being quite safe; and to the inquiry, "Who comes there?" only answered with a gruff grunt and a whiff. As our gallant guardsmen, the challenger, felt satisfied that Mrs. Pork was not one of the enemy, and attributing that peculiar kind of an answer to the ignorance of said sow, thought, no doubt, that where ignorance is bliss, 'twas folly to be wise.

During the night, it being but partial moonlight most of the time, in a field we imagined we saw the seceshers forming. The clouds passing gave an apparent movement to objects in the distance, which we supposed must be seceshers. It turned out, on a close examination, to be a lot of bean poles, with the vines around them. So you see what night does, and the excited imagination—so apt to picture forms to our view.

The regiment has just been paid off—in part gold, and the other Treasury Notes. The Fourteenth, of Brooklyn, are once more happy—now they have the means at hand for necessities, and payment of little debts incurred. The majority are acting on a wise principle, by sending all they can spare to their friends and relatives; and Mrs. Inskip, wife of our chaplain, has—true to her womanly character—taken the part of an angel, by offering to convey, for the benefit of the members of the regiment, all moneys that can be spared for future purposes, and for friends and relatives, and deliver to all personally—for which I am sure she now receives the thanks and love of all.

Through the diligent energy of ladies who are here on a visit—Mrs. Inskip at the head—and the prompt acquiescence of our General ([Erasmus D.] Keyes), Colonel [Edward B.] Fowler, Major [Robert B.] Jordan, and the chaplain, we have had a large tent erected, and seats laid fit to accommodate a large number of men. It is proposed that the tent shall be called "Fowler's Chapel," in honor of our lieutenant-colonel, now in command in the regiment—Colonel [Alfred M.] Wood being a prisoner at Richmond. The evenings are selected for divine service, lectures, and union conferences. It pleases me much to see such a disposition manifested as I witnessed at the inauguration of the "Big Tent," it being crowded. It is very pleasant to listen to the singing, and particularly so to have the opportunity of hearing a grand and patriotic speech from Mr. [Joseph S.] Inskip, as we often do. I looked for a copy of your paper, but I don't see it yet. It may be that something occurs through the Post-office Department. Hoping you are as well as this leaves me. I am,

Yours, truly,   J. J.

SPECIAL CORRESPONDENCE TO THE SUNDAY MERCURY.

WASHINGTON, D.C., Sept. 24, 1861.

To the Editors of the Sunday Mercury:

I am again, as you perceive, in the vicinity of the seat of war; and, although not engaged directly in a military capacity, my business frequently draws me to the other side of the Potomac.

On my first visit—since our regiment left Arlington Heights, July 24—I assure you, I was greatly surprised at the many changes made all over that portion of the country, for miles; trees have been felled, and innumerable batteries and fortifications erected; new roads built; and, in fact, had I been conveyed there blindfolded, I would have failed to recognize (after having been brought to light) anything except Lee's House.

On Saturday I went to Bailey's Cross Roads, and was there all day Sunday. Munson's Hill is about 1¼ miles from the Cross Roads, and the men's uniforms can be minutely described with the aid of a glass. They (the rebels) have a barricade of felled trees across the road, on the other side of which those who are off duty frequently assemble. Their pickets extend about half a mile from the hill, and ours about the same distance from Bailey's Roads. This brings both bodies a quarter of a mile from each other. At half-past eleven A. M., Sunday, their pickets commenced firing on ours, and succeeded in wounding two of our men. The captain of the Michigan regiment (who, by the way, is a trump) then went forth with a white pocket-handkerchief, and succeeded in reaching their barricade without being fired on; and was met by the officer, of whom he inquired the cause of their firing, and stated that he understood that an agreement had been entered into, between General [James] Longstreet (rebel) and General [William] Franklin (Union), that no firing should be continued on pickets, unless in case of an advance, to which the rebel officer replied: "That he knew of no such an agreement; and that he would take care of his pickets, and we could look to our own."

The captain then returned by the main road, where we all stood, anxiously watching his maneuvers; and after a little consultation with several officers, concluded to pay them off in their own coin; he doubled his pickets, and sent none except those armed with Enfield Rifles; in less than ten minutes, several shots were fired by their pickets, and a body of about twenty men advanced down the road to the barricade, and our pickets replied promptly, and with good effect. I saw two drop, and were carried to the fort; and half a dozen well-directed shots sent the party in the main road, apparently, reluctantly back to their supposed stronghold. I think, from what I can see now in the army of the Potomac, that Jeff Davis & Co. will truly have a hard road to travel. It seems to me to be almost an utter impossibility for an army to approach within three miles of the Potomac in the direction of Arlington or Alexandria. On all sides, no matter which way you turn, field-pieces are before you, and there is no end to forts, breastworks, gabions, facines, stockades, etc., etc.

In visiting the different regiments of my acquaintance, and also those on whom I have called on business matters, I have had several opportunities (and you can bet I availed myself of the chance to take a crack at them) to witness several engagements between pickets. Secesh are tall game, and the excitement beats duck-shooting at least so one of Kerrigan's boys state.

I have just returned from Alexandria, and visited again the Marshall House, where poor Ellsworth was murdered. It is now a complete ruin, not one solitary pane of glass remains in the building; from the cupola of the house, however, still defiantly flies the Stars and Stripes.

The evenings are now becoming very cold—equal to our Northern evenings in the month of November—and I think the rebel volunteers will not only suffer from the place likely becoming too hot, but also from it being already decidedly too cold. As long as they shake, who cares what the agency is that brings around the effect? And now, having been on horseback for the last ten hours, allow me to bid you adieu, and retire to rest. My regards to all the boys of the old Eighth Regiment.

Yours, etc.,   T. R. T.

MILITARY MATTERS

THE ARMY SUTLER AND HIS PROFITS.—The sutler's tent is the same in all camps we ever visited. Be it understood, for the benefit of those who are uninformed, that the sutler is the merchant of the regiment. He sells lemonade, tobacco (in papers and plugs), cigars (of cabbage, oak leaves, or tobacco), red herrings, crackers, and molasses-cake. He would sell whiskey if he dared. His tent is always lumbered up with barrels and boxes, and at the customers' end of it a board across two pork-barrels does duty for a counter. Here the men come in crowds every hour in the day, to get some little delicacy (after salt fat pork and no vegetables, with the sun at ninety-eight degrees, even molasses-cake is a delicacy) to eat, or for a glass of cool lemonade to drink and make much of.

As the regiments are mostly supplied with water from muddy springs of their own digging (to prevent poisoning by our amiable Virginia neighbors); and as the sutler generally has the only ice in camp, a glass of even the sutler's lemonade is a grateful beverage under the torrid circumstances.

The currency used by the sutler is paste-board tickets, representing respectively the value of five cents, ten cents, or twenty-five cents, payable in goods at the sutler's store. When a soldier desires to enter into commercial negotiations with the sutler, and has no money wherewith to achieve that mercantile desideratum, he naturally concludes to anticipate some portion of his pay. He, therefore, obtains from his captain a printed order on the paymaster for one dollar or more, as the case may be, which is signed by himself, of course, as drawer of the order, and is then countersigned by the captain, as a guaranty that the sum of money called for in the order is actually due the man. This document is now negotiable, and the sutler will take it and give for it its "face," not in money, but in tickets, which are simply due-bills on himself, which he binds himself to redeem in store goods.

All the goods are sold at his own prices; and as the tickets must eventually all find their way to his establishment, it follows that the office of regimental sutler usually pays better than that of major-general. When pay-day comes round, the men, having spent all their tickets, have, as a general rule, little interest in the paymaster. The sutler presents all the orders for pay which are in his possession, and from the paymaster receives the gold. This whole system is very objectionable and the French plan of paying the soldiers every ten days would be an infinite improvement. As it is, the men do the work and dare the danger, while the sutler pockets the lion's (or rather the sutler's) share of the pay.

All sutler's stores or tents are alike—are always thronged, and always make money. There is usually a rear entrance for the officers, who are thus admitted behind the counter; and occasionally a sportive major takes a fancy to ride a frolicsome horse in at the back door, and a smashing sensation is the result.

Though the sutlers are prohibited from selling spirits to the men, which rule they obey in most regiments, still, as a general thing, an officer need not languish for his liquor. A colonel can have his cocktail, a major can procure his mint-julep, a captain his "cold without," a lieutenant his "lemonade with," and even a sergeant can procure his favorite "smash."

But the whole sutler arrangement is bad, though it is so intimately connected with the system of army payments that a reform touching only the sutler's department would be but half skin-deep.

WHAT IS SHODDY?—There has been a great deal of talk about the clothing furnished to our soldiers being made of "shoddy." The tailors of New York are said to have used this article, in some cases, in making uniforms, though they stoutly deny it; but that it has been used for that purpose in Pennsylvania there is no doubt whatever. And what is "shoddy"? the reader will naturally inquire. Well, it is one of the mysteries of the cheap clothing and big profits of the slop-shops. Among the Jews the "shoddy" trade is quite extensive, originating, we believe, in John Bull's dominions, but now extensively carried on in this country.

The invention of machinery to prepare old woolen rags, and mould them into "shoddy," has resulted in making valuable the cast-off clothes of even our beggars. This stuff, which was formerly rejected by paper-makers as worthless, or fit only for manure, has now become suddenly in demand at from seven to ten dollars per ton. The black-cloth "shoddy" is the most valuable, and is used in the manufacture of clothing, such as was furnished to a portion of our volunteers, about which so much has been said.

Old woolen rags are now collected by the rag-men, and are sorted into whites, carpets, shawls, stuffs, shirtings, linseys, and black cloth. When thus assorted and baled, they are sold to the "shoddy" manufacturer, who takes all the woolens, carefully re-assembles them, and passes them through the rag-machine, which is a cylinder, set with teeth; this, revolving at a great speed, tears or pulls the rags to wool. When thoroughly pulled apart, and reduced to soft wool, it is saturated with oil or milk, and has the appearance of balls about the size of a pea. The common "shoddy" requires scouring in heaters, filled with chemical matter. When thus completed, it is mixed with new wool, in as large proportions as possible, to escape detection. The Simon-Fare "shoddy" is made of soft woolens; but the hard or black cloths, when prepared in the same way, will produce what is called "mungo"—an article used extensively in superfine cloths, which is usually finished in a way that will deceive the best judges. Many persons, no doubt, have been surprised at the accumulations between the cloth and lining of the garments, which is, in reality, the sequel for the sudden falling to pieces of their garments. The recent disgraceful developments is "shoddy" cloth, made into soldiers' uniforms, we presume, will injure the "shoddy" trade a good deal.

FOURTEENTH REGIMENT, N.Y.S.M.
THROGMORTON'S HILL, VA., October 3rd, 1861.
To the Editors of the Sunday Mercury:

In haste I take the opportunity of dropping a line or so. Since my last to you the regiment had the pleasure of greeting the return of their brave Lieutenant [Rollin A.] Goodenough, who, when taken by secesh at Bull Run, happened to be aiding the wounded and acting in the capacity of a surgeon at the hospital, and came to us on parole of honor.

Last Saturday afternoon [Sept. 28], an order came to the old camp for marching directly after our return from parade and inspection by Gen. McDowell and staff. Our time was so brief that we had not sufficient to pack all our knapsacks in, but slinging our blankets over our shoulders, and with accoutrements, etc., we marched forth. As soon as we arrived at the crossroads we made a halt, and got our position, and then proceeded. The night was very dark, and as regiment after regiment, cavalry and artillery, were passing to and fro, or rattling over the rough roads—with the views of signal lights and fires—it really was a soul-stirring theme to contemplate. Several halts had to be made in consequence of having to cut away trees and logs that were thrown across the roads by the retreating enemy. We arrived on this hill at about half-past nine o'clock, and our pieces being stacked, prepared for bivouacking. We soon had our camp-fires burning in honor of our new position.

Early on the following morning (Sunday) our boys were to be seen, with their red caps, on each surrounding hill. After I had swallowed my piece of bread and cup of tea—an article that I happened to stow away—I also took a stroll, and visited the different places where secesh were but a few days since quartered with their cavalry and infantry. One house I went to the top of was sacked completely, and showed considerable artistic skill in the way of writing. A large hole in the wall had written above it: "This is the hole that gave the secesh fun!"; and, underneath: "This is the hole that made the Yankees run." The First Maryland Volunteers were well represented in writing, and South Carolina and Virginia.

Our flag can be seen waving in many different places, and over many rude looking forts, vacated by secesh.

The boys have had considerable fun over practicing the loadings and firings with two or three imitations of war implements, in the way of stove-pipe mounted on wheel-barrow, and a pump log on a wagon. In fact, stove-pipes were rather universal in the neighborhood for such purposes.

On Monday, we had most of our regiment on duty, digging for a new fort, and yesterday every man—non-coms, included—was engaged in the work of clearing the woods of some heavy timber, and the way the giants of the forest fell before the axes of the Brooklyn Fourteenth was truly a caution—every moment told of the death-groan of many a brave old oak as the earth shook with the fall of their tremendous forms.

Since our arrival here we have witnessed the burning of many a beautiful house with furniture included. I am proud at the thought none of it was the doings of any of this regiment. I don't mean to praise our men over others in that respect by that, for I believe most of the fires were caused by secesh stragglers, whom, I believe, are yet prowling about.

In conclusion, I will state that your paper now comes regularly.

Yours,   J. J.

NINTH REGIMENT (CITY GUARD), N.Y.S.M.
CAMP SMITH, DARNESTOWN, MD., October 5, 1861.
To the Editors of the Sunday Mercury:

Pray accept my apologies for my not writing to you ere this; but the fact is, that we have very little time to ourselves; and when we do have a spare moment, we hardly feel like employing it in writing. Since my last, our colonel has been made a brigadier-general *pro. tem.*, and the boys do not mourn their loss to any great degree, and more especially the drum corps. On our march to this place, some five weeks ago, some of the drummers being in advance of the regiment, stopped at a house to get something to eat. The good lady of the house (and whose name is Dawson) complied with their request, and got them up a good dinner, and just as they were sitting down, the colonel came in, and seeing the drummers, he ordered them to join the regiment, and, of course, they had to submit to his orders. After they had gone, the colonel very considerately sat down and ate their dinner which by right belonged to the drummers. And once in a while you will hear the boys saying: "Who ate the drummers' dinner?" And the echo will answer "Colonel." But now he has gone, and may peace go with him. The lieutenant-colonel is now in command, and a better man I don't think could be found, as also with our major.

Now for a few words for our sutler. He is to outsiders a very pleasant-spoken man, but he has what the boys say, "gone back on us." His charges are outrageous, and what is still worse, he will not allow any outside peddler to come anyways near the camp; so we are thus compelled to patronize him, and he has got us at his mercy. We are unable to buy any luxuries from the farmers, as he buys up everything to supply the officers' table. It would do you good to hear the boys grumble when pay-day comes. As soon as they receive their hard-earned money from Uncle Sam, the sutler stands by the desk, and nine out of ten of the boys turn most of their money over to him to settle their accounts, and then commence the grumbling; but there is no use of saying a word, as he will only tell that he don't care for your custom. But, at the same time, he knows that he has got things that most of the boys need, and so they are compelled to patronize him. By recent orders from Head-quarters, we have to sling our knapsacks at battalion drill, and I can tell you it hurts the boys' feelings very much; but "orders are orders," and they must be obeyed.

As to our food, we cannot complain, as we have plenty. But we complain very much at the way the "Clerk of the Weather" has used us lately, and we don't like to see rain, as our tents do not stand water very good, and there is no sleep for us when it rains.

We have been looking for a chance to have a pop at the enemy, but as yet it has not been granted. And when we do, we will meet them with a will.

Yours, etc.,   A MEMBER.

October 20, 1861
SEVENTY-NINTH REGIMENT, N.Y.S.M.
CAMP BIG CHESTNUT, VIRGINIA, October 15, 1861
To the Editors of the Sunday Mercury:

I have no doubt but you are surprised at not hearing from me lately, but a small explanation will, no doubt, satisfy you that I ought to be excused. In returning from home, after recovering from my wounds, I found myself rather unpleasantly situated with regard to the company to which I belong. That is now happily arranged to the satisfaction of all concerned, and I am doing my duty—at least, with satisfaction to myself.

Now about how we are getting along. Well, we have been into four successful skirmishes lately, and helped to build two first-rate fortifications and several bridges. (But you must excuse the further knowledge of them, as it might give aid and comfort to the enemy.) All has been done under the able direction of General I. I. Stevens. Our late colonel, but who has, with the consent of the proper authority, retained us in his brigade, as well as with the unanimous consent of the regiment, who have the utmost confidence in his abilities as a commander. Our pickets are now within two thousand yards of the enemy's, and we have several exchanges almost every day. Yesterday, the Forty-ninth Regiment, N.Y.V., were on picket, and sent out a skirmishing party, by orders of General Stevens who also sent three of the Seventy-ninth to act as guides. Your friend happened to be one of those selected, and by their—the Forty-ninth's—own knowledge of the ground, and that of Colonel [Edward] Cross, who commanded the expedition, and ours combined, we arrived within three hundred yards of their pickets before the perceived us, when they opened fire upon us. They advanced their reserve to strengthen their pickets, and our officers advanced ours to strengthen our skirmishers, and a steady fire was kept up for about an hour. Only one of our men—of the Forty-ninth—was wounded. How many of the enemy, we know not, but we saw several of them fall, when the shades of evening notified us that it was time for us to return, we having obtained the necessary information, namely, the true position of the enemy. And one thing I must say of the Forty-ninth Regiment and their officers, that they engaged the enemy, and stood the fire, as well as any veterans. I was very much surprised when told that this was the first time they had been under fire, and they knowing that five times their number was in front of them. They returned in as good order as from parade. Nor did we return far until we found that the Seventy-ninth were out to a man to our assistance, should it have been required, when we—the guides— joined our own regiment—the Seventy-ninth—and we all returned to camp together, which was only about two miles distant from where we encountered their pickets.

In the Seventy-ninth, there has been many changes since Bull Run, especially among the officers. There are three captains and three lieutenants prisoners, one captain was killed; one took French leave, one resigned; and one has not yet so far recovered from his wounds as to take command; two are on furlough, and only one of the original captains who left New York with the regiment is with it in camp at present. There has been two elections for captains held—one in the Fourth Company (of which David Brown was captain, and was killed at Bull Run while leading on his company). First Lieutenant John Moore (who was severely wounded at the same time) has been elected captain, to fill that vacancy, he having returned to duty, and First Lieutenant Robert McNie has been elected Captain of the Sixth Company in place of Captain [James] Christie, who has retired from the service. Orderly Sergeant A. Graham has been elected Second Lieutenant of the Eighth Company, and Orderly Sergeant Keith Gilmore Second Lieutenant of the Seventh Company. Several other officers are filled *pro. tem*, until the prisoners, or wounded, or furloughed return. Yet, with all the difficulties, no regiment in the service has better line officers, nor is there one that his done more service for the country, nor is there one that there is less said about in the service than the Seventy-ninth.

As to our field officers, we have neither yet elected colonel, lieutenant-colonel, nor major, all of which offices are now vacant. The first is vacant on account of Colonel I. I. Stevens being appointed a brigadier-general; the second on account of Lieutenant-Colonel [Samuel] Elliot having resigned, and the third on account of Major [David] McLelland having resigned. It is supposed that at last will be filled from the present line officers of the regiment. Several have been spoken of for colonel, but most prominent amongst the number is Captain [George L.] Willard, United States Army, and Brigade-Major Robert Taylor, of the Fourth Brigade, N.Y.S.M. Both are excellent officers, and the only difficulty is to ascertain whether either one will accept, which, I believe, will be settled in a few days.

I will now give you an account of the duty of last week. We had eight hours rest in our bed in camp. We got wet through all our clothing three times, with the privilege of letting them dry on our backs. One of the rain and hail storms lasted for eight hours. I picked up one piece of hail as large as a hen's egg. It being the largest hail ever seen by the natives in this part. The balance of the time we were skirmishing or on picket duty, or taking a nap on the roadside or field when relieved from duty. And for all its being the hardest week we have had in the service, every one seemed satisfied, and made no complaint.

Our camp is now advanced, and we are again snug in our tents except when an alarm happens, or our turn of picket duty, every fifth day. The strictest discipline is enforced with all now, and has made us what we think ourselves at the present time—good—soldiers.

I must now say a little about our arms. We have six different kinds of muskets in our regiment; the most of them are the common Harper's Ferry or Springfield smooth bore, the balance are a few Enfield rifled-muskets, the best arm in the service, some Springfield and Harper's Ferry rifles, and Minié rifles—the three last described were picked up by the men at Bull Run. Now, I must tell our friends, and those having control of arms of our State, that this regiment has agreed upon one thing; that is, that they are entitled to Enfield rifled muskets, and ought to have them, as we know that we have earned them. Just fancy a regiment, on skirmishing duty, meeting face-to-face with the enemy; at five hundred yards they open fire on us, their balls wounding our men, and going as far beyond us. We return the fire with the common musket; our shot fall short, or take no effect; they roar out and laugh at us, their outer pickets, and skirmishers, and reserves are armed with the Harper's Ferry and Springfield rifle, which are equal to the Enfield, only a little heavier.

Now, this has actually happened under my own observation, and in which I have been a party, who, at least, tried to do my duty under the said circumstances. Several of our friends promised and tried in vain to obtain the Enfield musket for us; and now the only chance we think that is left is, to appeal to our friends in the Old Country, whom we at least know have some regard for their children.

Why not give those common muskets to companies forming, until they are fit to take the front in the field? Or are we denied them because we claim this as our adopted country? We should like to have these questions answered, as our minds are made up to have them in some way or other.

We have just (at 6 A.M., Oct. 16) returned from hunting up the cause of another false alarm—the long-roll beat at 1 A.M.—cause was, putting green soldiers on picket.

Oct. 16th, 3 P.M.—We have just now received the serious intelligence that our general, I. I. Stevens, is ordered to another command by the War Department—to what place or for what cause we know not; but we think it is on some secret engineering expedition. He has just received a dispatch, and packed up his things, and taken a farewell with us in less time than it took to feed his horse, and I can assure you it brought the big tears to the eye of many a brave man. He was much affected himself at the same time. The Board of Officers met immediately after, and passed resolutions commendatory of his conduct, knowledge, and bravery while in command of the Seventy-ninth Regiment, a copy of which I will forward you as soon as I can procure it.

I understand that all officers and non-commissioned officers and privates now on furlough or detailed on recruiting service are to be ordered to report themselves for duty at the camp immediately—their places to be filled by wounded members who are now able to perform that duty. I think that is a very good move, and will be very satisfactory to the regiment.

Hoping that you will excuse the length of this letter, also the imperfections in it, I remain,

　　　　Yours, respectfully,　　　　　　　　　　ONE OF THE SEVENTY-NINTH REGIMENT, N.Y.S.M.

October 27, 1861
FIFTY-FIFTH REGIMENT N.Y.S.M., LAFAYETTE GUARD
CAMP GAINES, NEAR TENALLYTOWN, D.C., October 19, 1861.

For the first two days after I had dispatched to you my letter, dated the 29th of Sept., we were kept ready to march at a moment's notice; but the order for our departure, though ardently expected, did, not arrive, and we heard on Thursday. The 1st of October, that the enemy, after having made a general advance upon our lines, had again retreated, when things throughout the camp once more resumed their former monotonous course, varied only by several inspections, that took place within a week after.

We were inspected on Saturday, the 5th inst., by Col. [Randolph B.] Marcy of Gen. McClellan's staff, accompanied by the Count de Paris and the Duke de Chartres, and not by the Prince de Joinville, as your correspondent from the Anderson Zouaves [62nd N.Y. Infantry] erroneously states.   They expressed themselves highly satisfied with our drill, deportment, and equipments; and we had the gratification of seeing, a few days after, nailed up at Headquarters, an extract from a Washington paper (the *Republican* I believe) speaking of this review, as near as I can remember, in the following terms: "On Saturday, Col. Marcy, of Gen. McClellan's staff, went to inspect the regiments, forming the brigade of Gen. [John J.] Peck. He found them all very efficient, especially one regiment composed mainly of Frenchmen, and commanded by Colonel [P. Régis] de Trobriand and other French officers, most of whom have seen active service in Algiers, the Crimea, or Italy.   This regiment was found to be in so high a state of efficiency, that they could compete even with our regulars."

You can easily imagine that this praise, bestowed upon our regiment, made us feel very proud of it, and created a general satisfaction throughout the camp.

Camp Gaines derives its name from Fort Gaines, erected here lately. We are in possession of it, and squads of men are detailed daily to work at mounting the guns. The view from here over the surrounding country is very beautiful. Our camp is kept very neat and clean, and affords in itself a very picturesque view.

On Saturday (the 13th) evening we got orders to prepare to march. Were drummed out at 9 P.M.; stood ready in ten minutes, but were ordered back again to our tents. In half an hour were drummed out once more. This time the order to march had arrived. Such a cheering I never heard in my life. We all expected sure to go to Virginia this time, but we were doomed to disappointment again, as the sequel will show.

We marched over a road leading through the woods down toward the river. The night was clear and beautiful, and the moon shone so brightly down upon us through the foliage of the trees bordering the road on both sides, that I would have considered the expedition quite romantic, if the constantly increasing weight of my knapsack on my shoulder had not driven all romantic ideas out of my head. We halted at a place near the Chain Bridge, and encamped there for the night.

It grew very cold toward morning, and the camp-fires we had lit did not make up for the tents we had left behind us. Next morning got orders to march back again to our camp. As we had found out that we were not going to Virginia yet anyhow, we were very glad to get back to our camps and its tents once more.

Friday, the 18th, the Paymaster, for whom we had waited so long already, arrived at last, to pay us that one month due us from the State. From that time up to this moment I have seen nothing but smiling faces; and the farmers around here, and others who trade with the soldiers, are reaping a rich harvest.

The health of our regiment has, so far, been very good, and I trust will remain so, unless the men should now eat too much of the good things suddenly within their reach, which I hope they will have sense enough not to do.

For the papers you sent me, accept my thanks; and now, as my letter is very long already, and I do not know anything more to write, I will close, remaining,

     Yours, respectfully,   H. D., YORKVILLE.

November 3, 1861
UNITED STATES CHASSEURS (65th New York Infantry)
CAMP EVERGREEN, D.C., Oct. 28th, 1861.
To the Editors of the Sunday Mercury:

As we have the honor of belonging to the great metropolis of the Empire State, it has somewhat surprised me that our relatives and friends at home have not been kept better informed of our movements through the columns of your valuable paper, especially as our career has been so very favorable. Since we left our homes and kindred to do battle for the Union, our motto has been that of our native State: "Excelsior," and we have gone forward into the heart of secessiondom, and gained an enviable place in the hearts of such military chieftains as have at different times had the control of our movements. The gallantry displayed by the Chasseurs when they were stationed at the advanced post, commanded by the late Colonel [Edward D.] Baker, and their steadiness under fire during the engagement at Lewinsville, so elicited the gallant Baker's feelings of admiration that at the time he met his glorious death, he was about to request of General McClellan the return of our regiment to his Brigade.

We are at present encamped in a delightful meadow, encompassed by groves of majestic cedars. Nature and Art seem to have combined their efforts to make our camp at once attractive and fitted for its purpose; it has an excellent parade-ground. Springs of water, bordered by extensive woods, and with an active medical staff, to enforce the sanitary regulations, we are as comfortable as soldiers can expect.

Our commandant, Colonel [John] Cochrane, has fully realized the high expectations we had formed of him; his universal kindness and affectionate interest in the welfare of his men has so endeared him to us, that, should he be promoted to a higher grade, as has been rumored, it would be hard to fill the vacancy in our hearts, where he is so firmly established.

Not wishing to trespass too much on your valuable space, I will conclude, promising to keep such of your readers as are interested in the movements of the New York Chasseurs well posted.

Yours, truly,   UNDERTAKER.

November 10, 1861
FIRST U.S. CHASSEURS
CAMP COCHRANE, D.C., Nov. 4, 1861.

Since my last the name of our camp has been changed from Evergreen to that of Cochrane, in honor of our gallant colonel, who at present is in your city on special business. It is rumored in the regiment that when he returns he will bring with him as fine a band as can be procured. This will be an improvement on our drum corps; for although the fife and drum are considered the only true martial music, I have noticed that regiments accompanied by the music of a full brass-band go through their evolutions with more spirit and vigor than those who follow the monotonous six-eight time of a drum corps. The old adage, music hath charms to soothe the savage beast is beautifully illustrated in the following incident. One of our men who for some offence, had been confined in the guard-house and whose demeanor in consequence was sulky and defiant in the extreme, sat listening to the air of "Home, Sweet Home," eloquently discoursed by a fine band belonging to Birney's Zouaves [23rd Pennsylvania Infantry], attached to our brigade. His morbid feelings were banished by the melting strain, and he told me, as a tear stole down his cheek that in future no derelictions of duty on his part should prevent him giving a good account of himself to his loved ones at home. All men have music in their souls developed to a greater or less extent, and music has all the potency of a magician's wand to keep the finer sensibilities of the human race constantly exercised.

It is now an interesting period with us; the advent of pay-day is close at hand, and the men are disposing of their allowance in prospective. The unmarried ones laying plans for procuring Stone's Patent Bedstead, etc., in case we have to go into winter-quarters; those who have families, are estimating how much of their two months' pay they can remit home; and it is worthy the pencil of a painter to delineate the different expressions of pleasure lighting up the faces of the men as they come from the paymaster's office; some of the boys with a loud boisterous laugh, indicative of reckless expenditure at the sutler's, and unlimited outlays at the huckster's stand; peddlers contriving to hang around all camps in the vicinity of pay day. Then again, the warm sunbeams of satisfaction illuminating the countenance of some married man who is anticipating the pleasure of receiving an acknowledgment from his family of the receipt of his remittances. The sutler's assets are all squared up; and the boys, with the independence that ready money gives, vow never to run in debt again, and keep their resolution as long as their money lasts. We have hopes, now that Gen. McClellan holds the reins of military government in his hands, he will soon order an onward movement; for we understood one of the great objections to entering into any decisive engagements in the heart of the enemy's country was, the climate being too excessively warm for our Northern constitutions. I can assure you we find that objection entirely removed when we turn out at reveille without gloves to go through the exercise of the manual. A heavy frost shivers every tree and shrub, and it requires considerable animal heat to counteract the frigidity of the atmosphere, and the zero-like qualities of the gun-locks. I will now bring this to a close by guaranteeing you something more interesting next week. Till then, I remain, yours,

UNDERTAKER.

November 17, 1861
FIFTY-FIFTH REGIMENT, LAFAYETTE GUARD
CAMP TENALLYTOWN, November 12, 1861.

Although we have made no move whatever since my last and are still in our old encampment, formerly called Camp Gaines and although I have no very important news to give yet I will venture upon sending these lines, as I think that the few items of note I have joined to a short description of the way we pass our time, may not be without interest to many of your readers.

You will, perhaps, remember that I complained in my first about the thinness and insufficiently of our blankets. We have since received good heavy U. S. blankets. This is a decided improvement, and one that was very much needed.

On the 31st of October, we were again mustered in for pay preparatory to our receiving the two months due on that day.

Next day, at 4½ A.M., the first death occurred in our camp. John Peiser, a member of Co. F (Zouaves), died in the camp hospital after five days sickness of inflammation of the bowels. Poor fellow! It is a hard, sad fate to die thus in a hospital, far, far away from friends and loved ones at home. I will add, for the consolation of his relatives, that, from what I know of the gentlemen attending in the hospital, I believe they are very humane and kind-hearted, and sure to do everything in their power for a suffering patient.

The flag was hoisted at half-mast, and the body, neatly dressed up, was laid out for the day, to give the men a chance to take a last look at their late comrade. He was afterward, in accordance with the desire of his relatives, sent on to New York to be buried there. Peace be to his ashes!

Thursday, the 7th inst., Mr. Farmer, of Ludlow street New York, came to visit the regiment. He brought with him several barrels containing crackers, sausages, needles, tobacco, pipes, books, etc., which he distributed among the men. It was a very kind and philanthropic idea, and worthy of a notice in your paper.

Friday, the 8th inst., Gen. McClellan reviewed us on Meridian Hill; three brigades, [Darius] Couch, [Lawrence] Graham, and Peck. We left camp at 9 A.M., fully equipped, with knapsacks, etc. The regiment appeared on this occasion, for the first time in our new red pants, distributed a few days previous, and looked very well indeed. We marched through Tenallytown and Georgetown to Meridian Hill, a distance of over six miles. The weather, in contrast with that we had had during the last week or so, was, for once, really beautiful and highly favorable. There was quite a number of spectators on the field, both ladies and gentlemen. Of Gen. McClellan, I got a very good view, as he rode along our lines, followed by his staff. He is a very fine-looking man; his features indicates a high intellect, energy, and determination. He looked very sharply at our men, as he rode down our ranks, and seemed well pleased with their looks.

The review lasted until about 3 o'clock, when, after having rested half an hour, we marched back to our camp, where we arrived at 5 o'clock P.M., rather worn and tired.

H. D., YORKVILLE.

November 24, 1861
HAWKINS' ZOUAVES
CAMP WOOL, HATTERAS INLET, N.C., October 18th, 1861.

Having a little leisure time of my own, I thought a few lines would not be unacceptable to the readers of the SUNDAY MERCURY, knowing, as I do, that your paper is a welcome visitor at all times in our midst. The weather at Hatteras Inlet is, as you must know, none of the best at this season of the year. Our regiment is doing well, and we pride ourselves on our being one of the best-drilled regiments in the service. As regards to the health of the Zouaves, I can't say that they are in as good health as they might be. We sent twenty-two men to Fortress Monroe by the last steamer. Four of them were members of our company (A); and if we are kept on this accursed place much longer, we can send a squad of sick every time the steamer leaves for Fortress Monroe. I suppose you have seen the Rev. Mr. Taylor, who was on a visit to New York, along with our regimental chaplain. He arrived here from your city yesterday (Sunday); and I think he must have had a good string of luck, as I noticed that his trunk was pretty heavy. The members of his little flock are sadly in need of all the charity that New York city can possibly bestow.

Gen. [Thomas] Williams is pretty rough on the Zoo-Zoos, as we have more drill-calls than any other regiment in the service. Capt. [Andrew S.] Graham is now in your city on a furlough. If he thinks he is forgotten by Co. A, he is very much mistaken. We miss him every day, and I can assure you that he has the best wishes of the members of Co. A. That he may soon get well is the prayer of each and every one of the Zoo-Zoos. We expect to receive orders to pack up and leave our present delightful camping-ground, for— where? that's what bothers the boys. I see that our mail closes in about ten minutes, and I must draw my letter to a close.

Yours, truly   S.

December 1, 1861
OUR WAR CORRESPONDENCE.—We are sorry to hear that several of our correspondents have been placed under temporary arrest, or forbidden to write us any more letters for public perusal. If the service of the country demands this silence on their part and our concurrence, we must, as good and loyal citizens, comply; and shall cheerfully do so. If, however, on the contrary, a ban is attempted to be placed over the free thoughts and feelings of our volunteer soldiers, and a free press is to be restricted as to what it shall or shall not publish, at the mere caprice of one or two conceited officers, we intend to keep on printing our correspondents' letters.

December 8, 1861
MILITARY MATTERS
A LEGION OF HONOR.—We sincerely hope that Congress will, during its present session, institute a decoration of merit for every brave and loyal soldier now in the great army of the United States, to be called a "Union Medal"—and to be won and worn by all who deserve it by acts of heroism and soldierly virtue. It is

well known that the Cross of the Legion of Honor was scarcely second to his power of promotion in the hands of the First Napoleon; and in some instances, the desire to possess it brought out the most daring individual bravery from those who did not desire and would not accept command. The Queen of England, following in the French line of reward, has done wonders in inspiring the rank and file of her soldiers who took part in the Crimean War, as well as by recognizing the services of those who stood firmly during the Sepoy rebellion, in the distribution among them of appropriate medals. The proudest satisfaction an English war-worn veteran can enjoy is, the exhibition of his Waterloo medal.

Let our War Department not overlook this powerful incentive to the soldiers now serving in the army, and Congress, by public proclamation, make it possible for the humblest private in the ranks to be decorated with an honorable certificate of his valor. It would compliment personal honor and be something tangible to hand down to posterity as a proof that the soldier took honorable part in the great conflict. Not even the chance of promotion, in our opinion, could do more to evolve the best spirit of an army; and certainly the country should not grudge the item of *cost* to those who are now paying for her what cost cannot repay. We are quite well aware that the objection may be raised, that we should be aping the governments of the Old World in any such personal decoration; but let it be remembered that we are now aping them (if such is to be the word) in the raising of mighty armies in which the spirit of our institutions has heretofore been repugnant, and that if we accept, from necessity, the great points of their action, we should scarcely hesitate at a minor detail which may materially add to the spirit and efficiency of those armies when in the field.

December 15, 1861
HAWKINS' ZOUAVES
HATTERAS INLET, N.C., Dec. 6, 1861.

As we have just been paid off, I of course feel just like writing a short letter, which, I suppose, will be all the better because of its shortness.

The weather is terribly cold, and the men are getting the full benefit of the cold northern, as they come across Pamlico Sound.

Death has again been in our midst, and taken from our ranks one of our best men—poor Cameron! the neat little corporal. How hard it is to die so far away from home, with none of the dear ones to cheer his last hours! Captain Graham will have something to do when he fills his place.

The Forty-eighth Pennsylvania are our neighbors, and, of course, are some better than our crummy Twentieth.

I see the sutler has arrived by this steamer, and, of course, he expects to pocket all the small change which the boys are likely to have in their pockets. I don't see it. "That's what's the matter!"

I hope you will keep on printing your war correspondence. I, for one, will write just what I think, and ask nobody as to what I shall write or how I shall write it.

I have just been down to the wharf, and bought a quart of good, fat oysters, at only twenty-five cents per quart. Pretty good, don't you think so?

It is growing late, and we are to have an inspection to-night; so I shall draw my letter to an end.

Company A is, as it always was, Excelsior!

       Yours, truly,   S.

December 22, 1861
FIRST FIRE ZOUAVES
CAMP BUTLER
NEWPORT NEWS, VIRGINIA, December 16, 1861

I intended to write you before now, but have been very busy since my arrival among the "Zoo-zoos." Our regiment, though not full, is improving very much in discipline. The colonel ([Charles McK.] Leoser)
is putting the men through thoroughly every day, and before long we expect to be filled up to the required number.

We have now got the arms taken from the Hatteras prisoners, and we will see what success they meet with when employed in a better cause. We expect to be provided with Minié or Enfield rifles in due course of time.

The boys have not yet forgotten Bull Run. It is still the great topic of conversation around the camp and guard fires; and it is laughable to hear the reminiscences of that fight.

This part of the country is like all the rest of Virginia, where troops are now or have been encamped. The entire region is deserted by all but a few poor white people and negroes. Every house is torn or burnt down, and groves and gardens laid waste. It is a desolate, melancholy sight.

The Congress and Cumberland are lying off here for protection to our camp, and to blockade the river. The gunboats take their position near the shore, to keep vessels from running up at night. They attempt it sometimes, but always get driven back.

Everything is dull here now except drilling. That is mighty lively. There goes the roll-call. So, good-bye!

OCCASIONAL.

December 29, 1861
FIRST REGIMENT U.S. CHASSEURS.
HEADQUARTERS CAMP COCHRAN, D.C., December 31, 1861

The transactions of the past week have been of a numerous and varied character. First in order comes the substitution of Sibley tents for the small infantry ones formerly in use by us. The Sibley tents are spacious enough to contain twenty individuals; are of a sugar-loaf form, and have a stove in the centre—this affords us a sure preventative against the inclemency of the weather, and increases the beauty of our camp as well as the comfort of the men. The next item of interest is the arrival of our band—nineteen pieces—under the direction of Professor Monohan of New York. The band is worthy of the regiment and their leader's well-earned fame; and last, though not least, is a base-ball match, played by the field and line officers of the regiment, on Christmas day, of which I will give you an account—the runs made, and playing throughout being first class, and hard to beat by professional clubs. The match was organized the day previous, in the following manner: Lieutenant James King having finished a winter tent, boarded on the sides, and furnished with doors and windows, after the most approved European models, in the exuberance of his spirits, concluded to have a house-warming to celebrate the completion of his winter tenement. There was a good time generally, and the house was christened by the mysterious cognomen of the "Big Spoon." The only conjecture I can make as to the hidden meaning of this euphonious title is, that the house is noted for its hospitality and generous host, who always is on hand to dispense the creature comforts of life with a lavish hand. After the baptism, a base ball match was agreed upon for the day following. Two nines were selected, and captains chosen. The respective nines were named the "Old Bachelors," and the "Old Maids." The appellation could not be more antagonistic. Now for the match. The day was fine and the ground in good condition. The Old Bachelors were under the command of Lieut. King, the Old Maids of Lieut. [Henry B.] Dyer. Marshaled in battle-array, the toss was won by Lieut. King. Below I give the score:

KINGS	O.	R.	DYERS.	O.	R.
Lt.Kellinger(P.)..............2		1	Dr. McDonald (C).........2		7
Lt. Miln (c.f.)…...…......5		3	Lt. Bernard (l. f.)...........8		1
Lt. Bogert (s.s.).............3		0	Lt. Ellis (3d b.).............3		0
Lt. King (1st b.).............4		5	Lt. Dyer (2d. b.)............3		0
Capt. Bernard (l.f.).........3		3	Lt. Selover(c.f.).............4		5
Lt. Truesdale (2d b)........2		4	Cpt. Higgenbotham(1st) ..0		2
Q. M. Ford (r.f.).............3		1	Capt. Heely (s.s.)...........1		5
Rev. Burghart (3d b.)........4		4	Comm. Terry (r.f.).........5		2
Lt. Col. Shaler (C)...........1		8	Capt. D. Miller (P.)........1		7

INNINGS.....................1	2	3	4	5	6	7	8	9
First..............................2	4	3	4	2	1	6	3	2—29
Second..............................6	2	4	3	4	2	3	2	3—29

The match was well-contested throughout, and some splendid playing was made by a few of the contestants. Col. Shaler's catching was as perfect as his drill, and his batting was superb; the large number of runs—eight, three being home-runs, evince this. Captain D. Miller's pitching was very good, and he made four home-runs in splendid style. Captain Higginbotham played with his accustomed spirit, and was not cautioned to see to it during the entire game. The exertions of Lieut. Truesdale to catch balls flying over his head were not generally rewarded with success. This was not for want of activity, but an unfortunate lack of stature.

Yours truly,   UNDERTAKER.

HAWKINS' ZOUAVES
HATTERAS INLET, N.C., December 22, 1861.

To-day has been a glorious day for us. Our colonel has got back, and our captain has also arrived. I tell you, Mr. Editor, it would have done your heart good, if you could have heard the rousing cheers that went up to the heavens for each; and let me tell you that they were from the heart.

The weather is very fine, and the Zoo-Zoos stand it like Trojans. We have any quantity of work. We drill once in the morning, and once in the afternoon.

I went to church last Sunday, and was very much surprised to see our adjutant also there, intoxicated. In order to have you fully understand the particulars of the whole matter, I will say, that most of our officers are gentlemen; but I am sorry to say that one or two of the young ones, having no person to teach them any better, have been led away. The very idea of going to church, and, while the minister is engaged in prayer, to pass the bottle and take a drink. Shame on such men!

Why were they ever put over men that are their betters. Such men are a disgrace to the service, and a double disgrace to the brave Ninth.

Yours truly,   A. V. S.

Chapter II

<u>1862</u>

by

Edwin C. Bearss

Most of the letters published in the *Sunday Mercury* and selected for appearance in Chapter Two are from soldier correspondents in New York units. They number 89, and include five letters or more from each of these infantry regiments: the 73rd New York (2nd Regiment Fire Zouaves), 12th New York, 36th New York, 40th New York (Mozart Regiment), 51st New York, and 69th New York, and lesser numbers from 20 regiments and one company of artillery. Most of these New York units served in the Army of the Potomac, while some of them saw earlier service with Maj. Gen. Ambrose E. Burnside's Coast Division on the North Carolina Sounds or in the lower Shenandoah Valley and then with Maj. Gen. John Pope's Army of Virginia. There are also letters from four non-New York regiments in the Army of the Potomac: the 8th New Jersey, 1st U.S. "Berdan's" Sharpshooters, the 5th New Hampshire, and the 71st Pennsylvania (the California 500). Other eastern associated correspondence are found under these headings, Special Correspondent (2), Military Matters (3), Editorials (8) Paroled Prisoners, Camp Parole, Maryland (2), Novitiate and Ebanezer hospitals (1) each.

The western armies get short shift, with only two Shiloh letters, one from a soldier in the 2nd Iowa and the other from a U. S. Regular. A similar number of letters from Uncle Sam's webfeet—one from the brownwater navy and the other by a bluewater sailor grace this chapter.

For added interest, Editor Styple includes "The Rallying Song of the Fifth Zouaves" and a poem "Who Wouldn't be a Fire Zouave?" by one of the regimental sergeants.

Collectively these letters provide an excellent overview of the life of the soldier as seen through the eyes principally of New Yorkers in the eastern Union armies. Most of the correspondents were either company grade officers or enlisted people enabling us to see the war through their eyes rather than those of more exalted rank. The *Sunday Mercury* editors and most of the Army of the Potomac correspondents are McClellan loyalists and support the war to preserve the Union. The same cannot be said for the Lincoln Administration and General Burnside following the Fredericksburg debacle.

Eighteen hundred and sixty-two was a crucial year for Union fortunes in the east, giving an added dimension to the letters in the *Sunday Mercury*. After much prodding from President Lincoln and the new Secretary of War Edwin M. Stanton, Maj. Gen. George B. McClellan, in what the press hailed "as the stride of a giant," began with the mid-March transfer by water of three corps of the Army of the Potomac from the Washington area to the lower Peninsula. It was then "on to Richmond" with an unforeseen four-week delay in front of the Yorktown-Warwick Line, followed by the May 5 battle of Williamsburg. McClellan then became the "Virginia creeper" as his corps slowly felt their way forward. McClellan's army, now reinforced and reorganized into five corps, was caught astride the Chickahominy on May 31 by the Confederates. The two-day fight known to the North as the battle of Fair Oaks and to the South as Seven Pines ensued. The Federals gave ground, then stiffened, and held. Confederate Gen. Joseph E. Johnston was wounded and after a brief interlude, Gen. Robert E. Lee assumed command of what is known to history as the Army of Northern Virginia.

By the fourth week of June, the Army of the Potomac, one corps still north of the Chickahominy, had closed to within six miles of Richmond. General Lee called Maj. Gen. T. J. "Stonewall" Jackson and his small army down from the Shenandoah Valley. Since late March, Jackson and his foot cavalry had more than held their own against superior numbers of Federals west of the Blue Ridge. Boldly seizing the initiative, the Confederates in the Seven Days Battles hammered the Army of the Potomac. McClellan lost his nerve and by the morning of July 2, the Federals had retired into a fortified camp at Harrison's Landing, on the James River, 26 miles from Richmond.

Early August found the armies again on the move as attention shifted to Piedmont Virginia. On August 9, Jackson's wing of Lee's army battled N. P. Banks' corps of Maj. Gen. John Pope's recently constituted Army of Virginia at Cedar Mountain. Jackson won but only because he had more men. The Lincoln administration withdrew the Army of the Potomac from its Harrison's Landing enclave, and Lee prepared to "suppress" Pope. The race was on, ending on the Plains of Manassas. In a three-day fight beginning at Brawner Farm on August 28, the Confederates defeated John Pope's army, although it had been reinforced by two of McClellan's corps and units of Burnside's command recalled from the North Carolina Sounds.

Lee crossed the Potomac carrying the war into Maryland. Pope was sacked and sent to Minnesota to cope with the Sioux uprising, and his Army of Virginia folded into the Army of the Potomac. President Lincoln, rejecting the advice of his cabinet, retained McClellan in command of the Army of the Potomac. "Little Mac" justified the President's confidence by restoring the army's morale and taking the field on September 8. The next 14 days were action filled. Saturday, the 13th, found the Federals in Frederick, Md., and McClellan in possession of a copy of Lee's Special Order 191 and Stonewall Jackson closing on Harpers Ferry; by nightfall Sunday, Union forces had forced the South Mountain gaps and Jackson had invested Harpers Ferry; Monday, Harpers Ferry surrendered and Lee took position behind the Antietam; Wednesday, the 17th, along the Antietam, the landscape turned red, as America experienced its bloodiest day; Thursday evening, Lee's Confederates abandon the field, re-cross the Potomac, and return to Maryland; Monday, the 22nd, President Lincoln, McClellan and his men having won a victory, issued his preliminary Emancipation Proclamation.

Lincoln's visit to the Army of the Potomac in late September and his efforts to get McClellan to promptly follow-up on his Antietam victory proved frustrating. The President was heard to say "this is not the Army of the Potomac, it is McClellan's bodyguard." It was late October before the army crossed the Potomac in force and advanced cautiously southward through the Loudoun Valley. The elections over, Lincoln sacked McClellan, replacing him with General Burnside. Arguably November 7 would be the darkest day in the history of the Army of the Potomac, because Burnside was star crossed and his assumption of command set in motion a series of miscues that inexorably led the gallant soldiers of his army to disaster in front of Fredericksburg's Marye's Heights defended by Lee's grim veterans on December 13, 1862.

This barebone outline adds some context to the war in Virginia and Maryland as experienced by most of the correspondents of the *Sunday Mercury*. Now quoting Paul Harvey: "It is time for the rest of the story."

> Edwin C. Bearss
> Historian Emeritus
> National Park Service

January 12, 1862
SIXTY-NINTH REGIMENT

CAMP CALIFORNIA, NEAR ALEXANDRIA, VA., Thursday, Jan. 9, 1862.

Having a leisure moment or two, I drop you a few lines about the Sixty-ninth Regiment, N.Y.S.V. (or First Regiment, Irish Brigade). On Friday last we started, at very short notice, from this camp to go on picket-duty close to Springfield. The weather was very cold, and snow fell pretty freely. We arrived on the ground about dusk, and relieved the Sixty-sixth, N.Y.S.V., much to their joy. Four companies immediately went on outside picket, about two miles further out, and near Springfield, and one did garrison duty—this having half the regiment on duty at once. Nothing of any consequence occurred until Sunday night, when, about 11 o'clock, some dozen shots were fired in quick succession by our pickets on the right, which alarmed the whole line. In a short time a few shots were fired by Co. I, about the centre of the line; and immediately after the firing was taken up by Co. G, on the left. This alarmed the whole camp, and the boys expected an attack, but in a short time all again was quiet. I suppose there was not a rebel within a mile of our lines; and, notwithstanding the assertion of a daily paper in New York, our pickets that night were not fired into by the enemy. On Saturday afternoon, three soldiers, found straggling in the neighborhood, were taken into custody, and our men were delighted at having, as they supposed, arrested three of Jeff Davis' rebels, but they turned out to belong to a Pennsylvania regiment, and had been out shooting. We arrived here on Tuesday. The weather continues very cool, and the men of this regiment feel it severely, especially at night, having only one blanket. Accounts reach New York invariably that the men are in excellent health, but I can tell you that half the men in the Sixty-ninth are suffering more or less from colds. If one takes a walk about at night, when all is quiet, the continual coughing is astonishing. And how can it be otherwise? One blanket in the midst of winter! And the shoes are as bad, even worse, than those given to the three months' volunteers. I have seen a young man's shoes all worn in the sole after ten day's wear in camp! Pay day, to the rejoicing of all, and especially the sutler, is drawing nigh. It is no wonder the sutler of this regiment should look for pay-day. His regular charges is five cents for a clay pipe, two cents for a sheet of note-paper and two cents for an envelope; other necessaries in proportion. His bill of extortion must be a nice one. I say, abolish sutlers at once, or have them to sell at reasonable prices.

I see the SUNDAY MERCURY is anxious for an onward movement; but be patient. A defeat again in the neighborhood of Centreville would be most disastrous to our arms, while a victory followed up would break the spine of this rebellion. Let McClellan alone awhile longer. A word more, and I will close for the present. The army is allowed 1¼ pounds of fresh or salt beef. When this regiment is served out with fresh beef, 15 per cent is cut off, which, I understand, is allowed for shrinkage. That is, when a company's allowance is 100 pounds of fresh beef, the commissary gives them only 85 pounds, asserting that it evaporates 15 pounds in its transit from Alexandria, three miles distant. Such, I think, is not square. I mention the circumstance that it may be noticed by the proper authorities. What does the SUNDAY MERCURY think of the matter?

Yours, etc.   NON-COM, SIXTY-NINTH REGIMENT.

January 19, 1862
RALLYING SONG OF THE FIFTH ZOUAVES

We're a band of Zouave brothers,
We came from New York State;
To the traitors of our country
We bear immortal hate.
The rebels call us devils
Because our dress is red,
But we'll learn them what they
Do not know, that is, "their dog is dead."

Chorus. Then join in the chorus, boys,
And raise your voices high;
With Warren for a leader, we
Will win the day or die.

On Federal Hill we have built a fort
Of earth-works, strong and sound;
And ten-inch columbiads we have
Mounted all around;
If Jeff should cast his eye this way,
He'd look at it with dread

And say, in Baltimore, at least,
"My dog is surely dead."

If we are called away from here
To join the army grand,
We will show the bloody traitors
How New York men can stand,
We will haul their dirty banner down,
And plant our own instead,
And make them cry out, as they run,
"O Lord! our dog is dead."

And when we arrive at Charleston,
There for a while we'll halt,
We will burn that rotten city down,
And pack it well with salt.
So in the ages yet to come,
You'll ofttimes hear it said:
"'Twas there the dog first found its life,
And there they left it dead."

MOZART REGIMENT, Fortieth New York Infantry
CAMP SACKETT, VA., January 19th, 1862

Can you, by any manner of means possible, prompt or advise us (when I say us, I mean the Mozart Regiment)—I reiterate, can you tell us in what way the entire regiment (not forgetting old Shoenberger and "Snapper" in the cook-house) may at once show you how grateful it is to you, for ever having taken it into your heads, and coming to the conclusion to print such a paper as the SUNDAY MERCURY? Why, my dear sir, it is a perfect fountain of joy to our men. When the news boys of Alexandria are heard running through the streets of our encampment, calling out, "Soldiers of the Potomac, the SUNDAY MERCURY!" the sound of his voice is the cue. Here I must interrogate. Now, do you for a moment imagine when I say "cue" that I mean billiard-cue? If you do, dispel the thought. It is more in the style of an actor's cue, or that of the stage-carpenter; for as I remarked in some distant corner of this note, at the exclamation "SUNDAY MERCURY!" by the dirty-faced little news-boys, a complete change of scene takes place; the canvas-grained doors, which, until then, had been closed, are on the instant thrown open, and you behold a simultaneous growth of heads, that sprout out by hundreds from their stately muslin houses. They then strike up the chorus, with varied airs, of "This way, boy!" "SUNDAY MERCURY!" "Here, boy, can't you see me?"

By-the-by, I must tell you of peculiarly spicy dialogue that took place between an Irishman and a Dutchman, of our company, at the time your last number appeared in our midst. The Irishman was posted as sentinel at the head of our street, and the Teutonic brave one occupied the tent on the corner, and quite near Mickey M—y's post. The news-boy was summoned by soldiers—each one pulling and handling the poor boy a thousand ways at once. At one time he would be "right in front;" then "change front to rear;" anon some voice would sing out: "Change first five cents—forward on last MERCURY!" Then a delicate hand, that had but lately closed upon a piece of "salt horse," might have been seen to seize the poor little dirty-faced representative of "Southern chivalry" and the "sacred soil of the Old Dominion" by the coat-collar, and exclaimed "About face!" and suiting the action to the word, he did about face, and he made the darndest face about doing it that I ever saw.

It was at this interesting climax of things that my Dutch friend (who wanted to purchase a MERCURY, to read it upside-down, or downside-up—it would have been all the same to him), being buried up to his eyes in a loaf of bread, exclaimed, in a clear, unmistakable voice:

"Poy—leetle poy mit dings!"

At this, the news-boy looked down the street and caught the Dutcher's eye—that is, all that appeared above the margin of the loaf of bread; and Dutcher, being sure that he stood a good chance of getting a MERCURY, nodded his head three or four times, and at each time sent his nose about half an inch deeper into the loaf. But, speaking about noses, I must say that it is colored.

But not to swerve too widely from my subject, Dutchy, observing that the boy turned away his head without taking the slightest notice of him, added another tremendous nod, and vociferated an exclamation that made Camp Sackett howl. At this juncture his cap fell off, and brought up in a mud-puddle. Well talk of Ned Forrest hurling Lucullius to the "Cream of Tarterers." If that loaf of bread and piece of horse wasn't hurled you may shoot me. The boy being too far away for the loaf to reach him, the Dutchman came to the conclusion that he would not cast his bread and meat "upon the open air." So with one impetus he let her went, and it kissed the cheek of Mickey, who had been laughing at the failure of the crout.

MICKEY.—"Well, bad luck to ye for a Dutchman. What d'ye mane by that?"

DUTCHY.—"Hoo."

MICKEY.—"You, you crout,ye!"

DUTCHY.—"You Irisher, you tid said tat I tid was crout, ain't it?"

MICKEY.—"Yes. Well, it's nice to hear the likes uv you callin' yerself one ov the great sogers uv the army uv the Pot-o-mac."

DUTCHY.—"Hoo have got no shoulders on to arms of mi back, tid it was I, too, *furgannstorshumpter* Irisher, ain't it?"

MICKEY.—"What!—ah, go intil yer tent, yer dhrunk. Bad luck to ye! Go on now. Rub yer nose wid a tallow candle, and sleep off the whisky."

DUTCHY. (pulling in his head).—"You too it, too lumper Irisher. Kanter in my nose."

After the tent-door closed , echoed answered from the inside in the following tongue:

"We expect to have a fight in ten days, provided the roads dry up."

When Mickey, turning on his heel to walk his beat, was heard to murmur in a confidential tone:

"That Dutch is a quare Ingin-rubber language."

This is the same Irishman that, while on guard last week, and at midnight, as the officer of the day, with his escort, was visiting the several posts, gave the following challenge:

"Who comes there?"

"Grand round."

"Who is Dan Brown?"

At which the sergeant answered:

"The grand round, sir!"

"O ho!" says Mickey. "Bad cess til ye. I thought it was the second relief!"

The grand round passed.

Our regiment has just returned from the duties of a three-days' picket, the time of which reached from the Potomac to the Fairfax Road. I think the best way for me to express my gratitude, and that of the entire regiment to you and your paper, for the many pleasures you have afforded us, to extend to you an invite to go on one of our scouts and picket-expeditions. You shall have all the luxuries the soil provides; and amongst them I will mention some of the loveliest mud ever stuck "to boot." Besides, it would, I am certain, be a source of pleasure to you, just once to march to the "Mozart time".

I think that there is something going to take place in a few days, as the army on this side of the river, that has been quietly slumbering for some time past, like a great serpent, and is slowly uncoiling his heavy body, and the surrounding country begins to shake. As I am writing, I can hear volley after volley, which are being ushered from the mouths of the pieces that adorn the parapets of the rebel batteries down the river at the blockade. But let the bull bellow while he can; he will soon be compelled to pull in his horns.

R. McW.

Robert McWade, age 27, was five feet four inches tall with black hair and hazel eyes. He enlisted in Company C, 40th New York Infantry on June 12, 1861, and was soon promoted to sergeant. "R. McW" was a frequent contributor to the Sunday Mercury. *On June 9, 1862, McWade was commissioned Second Lieutenant. In his pension file, McWade listed his post-war occupation as an Actor. He died in 1907.*

FIFTY-FIFTH REGIMENT, N.Y.S.M., Lafayette Guard

CAMP TENALLYTOWN, D.C.

January 13th, 1862.

It having been impossible for me to write these lines in time for yesterday's publication, I hope you will give them a place in your next issue. I shall try to be more prompt in my communications hereafter. The great event of the past week was the presentation to the regiment of a magnificent set of colors, made by the lady of Lieut. [W. A.] Wood, and some friends of the family. When we heard that we were to have a new set of flags, we were all very glad, as our old ones looked so small, and so insignificant in comparison to those of other regiments round here, that it had often annoyed us. Great preparations were made to get everything in good order for the presentation, which was to take place on the 8th inst. (Wednesday), at 3 P.M. There having been snow on the ground for several days previous, we went to work to clear a space of ground for the regiment to form on, and another space on our drill-ground on which the presentation was to be made. The dining-saloon of the officers was beautifully decorated with flags, evergreens, and arms of all kinds, the arrangements of which reflected great credit upon the designer. A collation was prepared, and a small but select number of guests invited. The first on the list were President Lincoln and lady. I needn't tell you that their presence rendered the ceremony much more impressive than it otherwise could have been, and that we expressed our gratitude for the honor done us by the first magistrate of the republic, by welcoming him very warmly. There were, besides, Gen. [James] Shields, Gen. [Erasmus D.] Keyes, and staff, and some members of Congress, with their families, etc. Gen. Peck was not present. He has been sick for some time past.

The Hon. Fred. A. Conkling made a very good speech—Mrs. de Trobriand standing on his right, holding the French (regimental) flag, and the colonel on his left, with the American colors. At the close of the speech, he handed the former flag also to the colonel, who, wrapping up both flags together, made a short but appropriate answer, which was received with great applause.

After we had duly presented arms, and received our flags, we marched in defile past the President and other guests, and were then marched back to camp, while the guests and officers repaired to the dining saloon, to partake of the refreshments which had been provided. When, after awhile, the President and Mrs. Lincoln came out to get into their carriage, they found the whole regiment assembled to give them a parting ovation. Three times three cheers and a tiger were given, and silence only restored when the President signified his intention to speak. He thanked us for the kind welcome; said that he had been much pleased with the regiment, that he felt confident that they would fight well, and do their share toward subduing the rebellion; and then sat down, amidst tremendous cheering, which was kept up until the carriage had arrived outside the camp. Cheers were then given for the colonel, Lieut. Wood, etc., and the memorable day ended very pleasantly.

On New Year's day we had quite exciting time here. In the order of the day was written that the men were to have complete liberty for once; the officer of the day was requested to waive all punishment, on account of its being New Year's day; and the prisoners in the fort—except those tried by court-martial—were set free. We had just begun to enjoy our liberty, when at 10 o'clock the order arrived to get the regiment ready for an immediate advance. At 11 o'clock we were called out. When we stood in line, with knapsacks, etc., ready to march, the colonel read to us an order from Gen. McClellan, wishing us a happy New Year, and saying that he decided upon sending us as a New Year's gift the order to prepare for an immediate advance. The colonel said that he expected momentarily the order for our departure; that he had full confidence in us; that he knew we would do our duty, and that he would only ask to keep in readiness to march at a moment's notice. He then made us stack arms, and sent us to our dinner. The order, as well as the speech of the colonel's were received with great enthusiasm, and there was no end to the cheering. This was the more praiseworthy, as most of the men had just finished fixing their winter-quarters, and had by dint of hard work, succeeded in rendering their tents warm and comfortable; and it was no small thing to be suddenly ordered to give up the result of so much hard labor, to lie down again on the cold ground somewhere, with hardly anything to protect them.

In the afternoon, we were reviewed by Secretary Seward, and we lay down in the evening with the belief that we would be called out during the night. But we were not called on since, and the only thing we have left in memory of that grand hoax are the one hundred cartridges each of us received at that time. The supposition is, that the order was sent to keep the men in their camp during New Year's day; and, if this was the intention, it was well carried out.

Yours, very respectfully,

H. D., YORKVILLE.

EIGHTH NEW JERSEY VOLUNTEERS

HOOKER'S DIVISION, LOWER POTOMAC,
January 19, 1862.

We wish in behalf of a large number of friends and old readers of your valuable paper, to make a plain statement in regard to the manner in which some volunteers are served down here in Maryland. Many of the boys are in the habit of occasionally receiving a box containing a few little articles of comfort, such as shirts, gloves, stockings, and also cake, preserves, etc., and once in a while a quart or two (seldom more) of the ardent. In respect to the latter article, the boys are ever generous, the whole number of his messmates, (usually sixteen), sharing his pleasure by drinking to the health of the generous donor. Now, there are a few officers in our regiment who have taken it upon themselves to order every box that arrives in camp to be opened, and if they contain a bottle, it is immediately taken out and smashed, and the contents forever lost to the owner. As this thing has just been commenced, under the supervision of Maj. Joseph Trawin and Capt John Tuite, and knowing you, friend MERCURY, to be the champion of the soldiers' rights, you will kindly oblige us by giving your opinion whether the officers have any authority for thus destroying our private property. You are, of course, aware that if a soldier should get drunk, or become in any way disorderly, he is punished for it; but should a thousand individuals be punished for the misdeeds of two or three? By giving your opinion in this matter, you will confer many obligations upon the following friends, and readers of the MERCURY: Sergt. Browe, Sergt. Schooner, Corp. A. Jeroleman, Wm. E. Jacobson, Sgt. E. H. Preen, Theodore Mackey, James Harley, William Oliver, M. Clauson.

{The officers are ordered, and possess the authority to destroy all liquor sent into camp—no matter to whom intended—as its abuse leads to trouble. To a sober, discreet, and well-behaved soldier, some little leniency should be shown. It is optional with the commandant, however, and he is answerable for the conduct of his men. Liquor is good, once in a while; but the continual use of it leads to continual trouble, endangering life and our great cause of the Union.—ED.}

SECOND REGIMENT, N.Y.S.M. (82nd New York Infantry).

CAMP GORMAN, MARYLAND, January 14, 1862.
To the Editors of the Sunday Mercury:

Knowing that you are for a forward movement of our grand army, I will tell you the minds and feelings of the men in the regiments up here (Poolesville, Md.,). I get the SUNDAY MERCURY every week. The minute I get it—if it was between tattoo and the taps—I must read it out to them; and they go in for what you want— a forward movement.

We are now building log-houses to keep the cold out, and those that have them built are too lazy to go and cut wood for the fire. This is all for the want of something to do. We are all eager for the fray. When we get paid, there will be plenty ready to desert—not alone from this regiment, but from all the regiments along here. The fact is, we are disgusted with this lazy life. We left our work to come out here and fight for our glorious Stars and Stripes; but when we get back, we won't know how to do the work—we will be too lazy. I am speaking the minds of the First Minnesota, Fifteenth Massachusetts, Seventh Michigan, the Tammany Regiment, as well as ourselves.

YOUNG SOLDIER.

{We suppose the above correspondent does not really mean "to desert"—as that is a crime despicable in the eyes of a soldier; but he is, like many others, anxious to give expression to his feelings, and show the necessity for a forward movement. Wait a little longer, Young Soldier.—ED.}

February 2, 1862
SECOND REGIMENT FIRE ZOUAVES
CAMP LAWRENCE, MARYLAND, January 29, 1862

The boys lead a very easy life just now, being left on their own resources as to enjoyment, the weather not permitting the usual drills to take place. We have had two weeks of stormy weather already, and we have a fair prospect of two more. The roads will be rendered so bad that we will find it very hard to have our food transported; but I think, if it comes to that, the boys will save the trouble of transportation, by going where the food is.

The health of the regiment continues as favorable as usual, there being but one case in the hospital, and he is fast recovering his former health. The morning sick-list has been reduced from fifteen to five or six per day. "Healthy boys, aren't we?"

A few days ago, the members of Company I, of this regiment, were the recipients of a splendid tri-colored silk flag, trimmed with yellow fringe, as a present from their Brooklyn friends. On the white stripes, the following inscription was beautifully embroidered: "Presented to Company I, Second Regiment, New York Fire Zouaves, by the Brooklyn (F. D.), Fire Department." In fact, it was a most magnificent gift, and is very much appreciated by the boys.

The hearts of the boys were made glad once more by receiving a (most welcome) visit from the paymaster. The laddies received him with cheers, notwithstanding he was rather late in "calling." He was expected about the 12th of this month, but did not arrive until the 22nd, setting up accounts on the 23rd. Everything passed along swimmingly (especially under foot), the boys receiving their money with smiles; in the meantime, cracking jokes with the sutler, who, you may bet high, was close at hand to receive his share of the spoils—and in some cases it was the lion's share.

We are having another addition added to our camp, in the shape of a bake-house, which would have been finished some time ago, if the weather had permitted. I cannot comprehend why it has been put off so long, as the boys have been eager for the building of it ever since arriving in this camp. The other regiments of this brigade had theirs built long since, and have been enjoying themselves on fresh bread, while we have been relishing hard crackers.

Company A seems to be the leading company in almost everything. They commenced to prepare their tents for the winter first; they also took the lead in laying their street crossways with poles. Company B followed suit, and I presume the rest of the companies will do the same, as it is quite an improvement to the street, not only in appearance, but in comfort also. The style of work is known by the name of Corduroy Pavement.

We had a flag-raising here the other day. Our old flag, which was nailed to the staff, having braved many a storm, but at last received serious injuries, after which it was deemed necessary to replace it by a new one, which was done in due form. Our new flag is a beautiful affair, and I hope before it is worn out by the contaminating breath of Maryland, it will have a chance of paying a visit to Virginia, South Carolina, or some other foreign port. As I have some pressing duties which demand my present attention, I will bid you good-bye until my next, remaining,

Yours truly,   MARION BOY.

FIRST REGIMENT U.S. SHARPSHOOTERS
COMPANY G
WASHINGTON, D.C., January 29, 1862.

I am only too well aware that the reading public of Gotham are under the impression that the much-abused and silently-suffering Sharpshooters are entirely "used up," and "gone in," etc.; but in the spirit of "hoping ever," I protest against the report, and beg leave to assure all that we calculate to be a "big thing" yet. The charitable and sympathizing correspondent of a N. Y. paper (some weeks since) would fain make it appear that death, disease, and even worse—demoralization—were rife in our secluded camp. To an extent, the former was the case (now the general health is better), and the subject is one of deepest sorrow to us, who have seen some of our dearest comrades fall beneath the tough of dread disease; but still, the figures he used were considerably beyond the actual number, and that the First Regiment, as he says, could never muster more than 180 men on battalion drill, for weeks at a time, was—to use a gentle term—a tremendous exaggeration. As for demoralization, if I understand what that means—what it is, I have seen no symptoms of it as yet.

Berdan's Sharpshooters are now, as they have been, comfortably quartered, well fed, and well treated, if we except the fact that they have been promised much that they have never had; but which fact is not, by any means, attributable to Col. [Hiram] Berdan. They have had the best of military instruction; and I think I am safe in saying that we are as well drilled as any other body of light infantry in the field. Such, in fact, was the expressed opinion of Gen. McDowell and Gen. Sprague, and numerous others high in office, who personally inspected us in the fall. Moreover, the regiment is not a motley, untried body of men, as many in the North have an idea; they are shots, and if not all "crack" shots, they are at least riflemen, and know how to handle and take care of a rifle, which is more than every man knows, I believe.

The regiment I believe, to be unsurpassed either in their *physique* or *morale*, and if given the opportunity, will never disgrace their flag upon the field. Aware as a general thing, as men are, that much is expected of them, they mean to realize the expectations of the public by making their balls count where they have a chance, and are determined to "go in and win," or never come out again.

That we should have been kept here so long when we were needed—McDowell wanted us—[Ambrose] Burnside wanted us—[James] Lane wanted us—waiting for arms that it appeared were never, never coming, seems, to say the least of it, queer; but whatever one may think on such points—in my humble position "mum's" the word. Now, though, it is considered settled—no more deceiving promises—no more weary months of aching suspense. We are to have the genuine Sharpe's rifle in fifteen days, and the second Colt's five-shooters to-morrow. Once armed, it looks probable to me that we will be moved to a forward position, and then to start on that long-expected, soon-coming word which shall send the army of the Potomac down upon the hordes of Secessia as the "wolf on the fold," or more as the hound on the wolf to alter Byron slightly for the occasion.

The position of our present encampment is rather remote, and in a manner, I imagine, unhealthy; but Col. Berdan declares we should live and die here before we should leave with any other than the legitimate and chosen arm—the Sharpe rifle.

We are rejoicing now in the enjoyment of very pleasant weather—that is, as far as the atmosphere is concerned—mud abounds in fearful quantity and quality, for there is just enough of the old-fashioned yellow clay in this soil to make a patent suction boot-jack of every square foot of the land in wet weather. A movement, of course, is out of the question, with the roads in their present condition, and there is every prospect of their remaining bad for a month to come, judging from the statements of the old residents here, who speak of February as a month of storms and disagreeable weather generally.

RAMMER

February 9, 1862
SECOND REGIMENT, N.Y.S.M.
HEAD-QUARTERS, POOLESVILLE, MD., February 3, 1862.

Seeing a letter in your valuable paper of the 26th ult. signed "A Young Soldier," I have concluded to correct some of his misstatements for your valuable paper. This young (lazy) soldier says that we are all as lazy as he—that we are too lazy to cut wood for our fires. Now, sir, this is all false. The men all went to work with a will and built their houses; and every day they go out and lay in enough wood for the day's use, and some of them get in enough for a week. He says, also, that he speaks the mind of the Tammany Regiment, and the Fifteenth Massachusetts, and the Seventh Michigan, and First Minnesota. Now, I have been to all their camps, and they speak entirely differently. It's a fact they all want a forward movement, but they want no such move as the last one at Ball's Bluff. And he says the men will all desert. There isn't a man in the regiment but loves the Colonel (Tompkins) too well to leave him or the regiment; but I know that, if our little colonel was to leave us, that there would be a great many leave and join other regiments. The colonel has been absent about a month, and we all wish he was back, for the regiment don't look anything without he is here to command it. And if we go to move across the river again, we will miss him more; for it was him that saved us at Edward's Ferry from the fate of our neighbors, the Tammany and Fifteenth Massachusetts Regiments, under the brave Baker. Tompkins was in command opposite the ferry, near Goose Creek, and he ordered over two howitzers of Ricketts' Battery, and placed them in a small piece of woods. In fact, he played their (the rebels) own game—he made a masked battery. The second evening we were over there, a large body of rebels came out of the woods with a yell, and were going to pour down on us, when, to their astonishment, the shells flew into them thick and fast, and they broke and ran into the woods like a lot of cowards, and they did not show themselves again until we returned to Maryland.

The above is only a very small sketch of our brave little colonel's sagacity in warfare.

It is snowing like—now, and don't look like stopping, yet the regiment is in good health at present.

HENRY ECKFORD B. B. C.

SIXTY-NINTH REGIMENT, N.Y.S.V.

CAMP CALIFORNIA, VIRGINIA,

Thursday, Jan. 30, 1862.

Since writing to you before, nothing worthy of special mention has occurred in this camp, or in those of the other regiments composing the Irish Brigade, but, as it has been a few weeks since you have heard from this quarter, I thought I would write anyhow. Yesterday week, and the evening before, my companions in arms may be seen here and there about the camp, counting and re-counting the money given them by the pay-master, and nothing but jolity and good-humor pervaded. Three companies were paid on Tuesday evening, the paymaster arriving late in the afternoon, accompanied by the sutler, who went to Alexandria especially to meet him. The remainder received their money next day. As each man came up to get his pay, the amount due the plump sutler was deducted. Whether such a proceeding was legal or not I don't know; but one thing I do know, that more than three-fourths of what money he received was for villainous liquor, dispensed to the men for $1.50 per pint bottle. This stuff is sold the rank and file; I must say not openly, but, nevertheless, they always manage to get a superabundance; and when one manages to get a bottle of it, he thinks himself quite smart to be able to procure it at any price therefore its cost is never taken half so much into consideration as the means of getting it. The officers go in as they please to a separate apartment, and drink as much as they please; and it is not a very common occurrence for your correspondent to see some of them from time to time in a state unfit for the position they hold—a condition totally demoralizing to military discipline. In saying this, I do not by any means intend to censure the commanding officer of this regiment, who is an attentive, able and hard-working colonel; but he cannot see everything, and if he knows anything of the kind it is promptly reprimanded. Rumor has it that the paymaster has received a few hundred dollars from the sutler for his kindness. The Sixty-ninth Regiment have done well by their folks at home—no less a sum than $14,500 having been transmitted, by the Reverend Father [Thomas] Willett, to the families of the men in New York, and no doubt $3,000 more has reached your city through other hands. This is gratifying, and illustrative of the fact, that the poor Irish never forget those they have left at home. No matter, Messrs. Editors, where Providence has driven him, an Irishman thinks of those near and dear to him; he yearns for his family—for the comfort of his wife and little ones. It is a trait in his nature he cannot expunge.

The regiments in this neighborhood have no good drilling ground, and our colonel feels this much, as he is determined that the men shall go into the field as well disciplined as possible, which will be very shortly. He said yesterday at drill that it may be in two weeks or sooner, and battalion drills, superintended by Colonel Nugent, are the order of the day. Forming square, and charge bayonets at double-quick, accompanied by a terrible yell from every man is especially looked after. So you may imagine the "brigade" is not going to retreat while a show of victory remains. "No retreat," Mr. Editor, is our motto; but it is easier to say so than to stand ground strewn with blood and death. I know so, for I have been there, and those who talk most about "No retreat," may be depended upon least. But the next time we will have no cause to retreat.

The brigadier-generalship of our brigade engages the attentions of every individual in the Sixty-ninth Regiment, and much concern is evinced as to who will be appointed to this important position.

Thomas Francis Meagher's name is conspicuous, and he is endeavoring to procure it. He deserves it in one sense of the word; but, Mr. Editor, the great and important question is, Is he capable? The general opinion of the regiment is, that he is not; and one cannot help coming to that conclusion from his own words, a few months back, in public print. If a man had not military knowledge sufficient to be a colonel in August last, how could he gain that necessary to be a brigadier-general now, without seeing a week's service since? It is the opinion here that battles enough have been lost by incapable generals, and it is high time none but qualified men are so appointed. If the administration would like to place a man in that important position, let General Shields be the person; or let Colonel Corcoran be exchanged, if possible; and he would swell the numbers of the Irish Brigade, if he had the command, in one week, more than any other person in the Union in months. The name of Col. Corcoran is justly imprinted on the heart of every Union-loving Irishman. He, Mr. Editor, would be the right man in the right place. With a wide extent of military knowledge, calm under the most trying circumstances, courageous as a lion, and sober, he could do more for the thinned numbers of the Irish Brigade than any man now living.

The weather, ever since this regiment came off picket duty, has been very disagreeable—mud up to the knee. To-day has set in finer, and we are expecting a spell of fine days. The guard suffer much, as we have nothing but one tent to accommodate sixty men. They have to stand in mud and water all the time; so that, instead of two hours on and four off, it is just equal to twenty-four hours for each guard. The sutler, by some authority, occupies the only wooden building inside our camp, part of which is occupied as a stable by the staff, which, in the opinion of your correspondent, would be better suited for a guard-house, and let Mr. Sutler erect one at his own expense. The men need shelter those cold winter nights. Our polite and gentlemanly Adjutant (Smith) expects an appointment on the brigade staff. His position cannot be easily filled as ably. He is deservedly esteemed by officers and men. Our drum corps is a dead-head on the government. To each company two drummer-boys were appointed at Fort Schuyler, and since that time, one boy only, (the smallest of the lot) has learned sufficient to beat calls, etc. The drum-major, nevertheless, takes them to practice once or twice a week, but no further progress is ever made. They are mostly sons of some persons connected with the regiment, and receive their pay, rations and clothing for nothing.

The Rev. Father Willett is untiring in his exertions in looking after the spiritual care of the men, and never lets an opportunity pass without giving his hearers a good and wholesome advice. He is much regarded by all.

A good many of our "non-coms," have lost their chevrons since pay-day; but things are all right again—drill, drill, drill being the order, except when the weather interferes, which has been almost continually since the first of this year.

Yours, etc.,   NON-COM., SIXTY-NINTH REGIMENT.

SIXTY-NINTH REGIMENT, N.Y.S.V.

CAMP CALIFORNIA, February 1, 1862

I avail myself of the present opportunity to send you a few lines, informing you of affairs in this quarter. For the last three weeks we have had nothing but rainy, dark, and dismal weather, without a single ray of sunshine to brighten our hopes of a fight or an onward movement; and if it were not for the presence of our very dear friend, Paymaster [William] Richardson, with his rolls and strong box, we would have all died of *ennui.* It is surprising to see with what alacrity the sutler avails himself of a seat at the pay-table to collect his exorbitant bills off the poor men who come here, leaving wives, families, homes, and friends, to maintain, at the expense of their lives, the honor of that country and flag that has so generously given them a shelter and a home. To give you an idea of his charges, I will just mention a few of them. For a pair of common pegged boots, $7.50, worth in Alexandria and New York about $2; for a common Dutchman's pie, 20c., worth 6c.; a plug of tobacco, 15c. to 20c., worth 1c. to 4c.; a glass of beer or cider, 10c., bad at that; a very common half-Spanish cigar, 6c. to 10c. With an order from your captain, you can very easily get a small bottle of villainous whiskey for $1.25 to $1.50. For a small-sized molasses-cake, in shape like a three-cent pound cake, but much inferior, both in size and quality, he very modestly asks you to give him 10c. You are probably aware that the Government does not make any allowances to the enlisted men of writing materials; so that we have to purchase the necessary paper on which so much of the heart's thoughts are transferred from this place to our wives and little ones at home. The selling of this article gives the sutler one chance to show how much interested he feels in affording every facility to us to communicate with absent friends; and he does it with a vengeance; for the smallest sheet of the worst writing paper he charges 2c.; envelopes the same.

I could go on enumerating item after item. In every case, the article sold is disposed of for at least four times the retail price in any city in the Union. Taking into consideration that almost every man in the regiment (exclusive of the officers) has purchased from him to the amount from $6 to $20, and that the regiment numbers over 750 men, and that the average amount paid by each man was $8 (a very low average), the proceeds would be about $6,000, without any rent to pay or any other expenses, and that his profits are at least two-thirds of this sum, $4,000, is not a bad two-months' work for the sutler of the Sixty-ninth Regiment.

There were one or two incidents that occurred at the pay-table that I might mention. It is usual for the sutler to hand to the captains of companies, before pay, a list of names of men in his company who are indebted to the sutler. The list has the man's name on the left, the amount due on the centre, and on the right is a blank where the man signs his name if he recognizes the debt as just. This list must be signed before he can get a cent of pay. A man belonging to Capt. [James P.] McMahon's company had refused to sign his name to the list, and the sutler reduced it, when the man immediately signed his name; but what was his surprise at the pay-table, when being paid off to find the amount of one dollar inserted between the original sum and his name; the man objected, but had to contend himself with it, the paymaster could not keep a whole regiment waiting to arrange a small matter of one dollar. To his credit be it said, his captain did all that could be done for him, but other recognized dues were put down in the same form, and so the matter was dropped. Our worthy quartermaster said a word on this occasion; but I suppose it was with that spirit of dog eat dog that made him tap the venerable and burly sutler on the shoulder, and informed him that he, the sutler, reminded him of Shylock, waiting for his pound of flesh. But you will say that the regulations make all provisions, etc., for the government of sutlers; that the sutler shall have the tariff of prices fixed by the Council of Administration posted or exposed in a conspicuous place in his store. This has not been done. Also that there shall be no difference in price in cash or credit sales. Our sutler at one time, issued tickets of the value of one dollar, and then bought them back at the rate of thirty-six cents, cash, on the dollar. This was done when he was prevented from selling liquor, as they did it to get some with the cash outside of the camp. I suppose what he had made in that way he only considered a fair equivalent for the prohibition of the sale of rum at his store.

It is much to be regretted that there are not more efforts made to put into operation the allotment system, as it would have a good effect on the men. They would allot to their friends at least nine or ten dollars a month, and then would have only three or four dollars to spend at the sutlers. Once a man makes an allotment of his pay, it is some time before it can be changed, and the sutlers can only sell to the men the amount remaining of the pay after deducting the sum allotted.

I will endeavor, in my next, to give an idea of the way that business is transacted in the Quartermaster's Department out here, and why so many persons try to get that position.

L'IRLANDIAN.

FIFTH NEW HAMPSHIRE VOLUNTEERS

HEAD-QUARTERS CAMP CALIFORNIA,

FAIRFAX CO., VA., February 1, 1862

Here I am once more, a humble servant of our public friend, Uncle Sam. You will see by the heading of this sheet where I am and who with. I have been out this time about three months, and enjoyed good health all the while. Our living is very good, and we have plenty of bodily exercise every day. The regiment is one of the best in the army for drill, size, and discipline. Our colonel [Edward Cross] is an old Mexican veteran and a good soldier. He is a perfect gentleman, and one of my best friends. We are situated about three miles below Alexandria, and near Fort Worth. We go on picket duty once in four weeks near Springfield Station, and some two miles beyond Edsell's Hill. For the past three weeks the weather has been very unsettled. It rains or snows nearly every day now, and the mud is knee-deep all over the country. The roads are almost impassable.

We use the Enfield rifle, and drill as light infantry. About seven-eighths of the regiment are shoemakers by trade, and a finer set of fellows one seldom sees together. A member of our company wrote a song about the regiment, which we sing, together with other songs, to pass away the dull hours. I enjoy myself generally very well, and like the life as well as I could wish. I should like it better if we could have a brush with the enemy. I must now close and prepare to go on dress parade.

Yours,   L. C. S.

THIRD LIGHT BATTERY, NEW YORK ARTILLERY VOLUNTEERS

CAMP GRIFFIN, VIRGINIA, February 4th, 1862.

As I have written to you before, and not seen my letter published, I would even try again, I thought, as I did not notice any correspondence from this division in your columns. As an old subscriber to the SUNDAY MERCURY, I have felt my heart beat lighter upon the reception of the mail, and beheld my SUNDAY MERCURY wrapt up. And when I have sat at night by the camp-fire, with two or three of our New York "fire laddies" around me, and read them the news of the week out of the papers, it has often recalled thoughts of home; and in some cases, when engaged in reading the items of the Fire Department, their eyes enlarge, their muscles relax, and they utter aloud their heartfelt wishes, that they may live to hear the old Hall bell ring out its lively peals once more, and have one more good square race with the "masheen."

You have, doubtless, heard before of our battery, which has, of late, received the name of the Third Light Battery, New York Artillery Volunteers, although we still, and ever will, bear the name we have so long borne honorably, of Mott's Battery. Our commander, Thaddeus P. Mott, of New York city, is an officer of great experience, having served with distinction in several campaigns, both in this and foreign countries. He has been in a few little scrapes since we have been in the service, and in every one he has shown himself to be a cool and energetic commander.

Our first-lieutenant is also a Yorker, named [William] Stewart, who is now on furlough, in consequence of ill-health, has nearly all the qualities of our captain, and is beloved by all the our men, as is our second, George F. Fitzgerald, of New York. We have also a first-lieutenant named [Charles] Kiscerow, a Danish officer of thirteen years' experience, who has but lately come amongst us, but who has by his fairness, and kindness, already won the hearts of the men.

We have at present four ten-pounder rifled guns, and two twelve-pounder Napoleon guns. Our full strength now is 119 men. We are under the command of Brigadier-Gen. Winfield S. Hancock, an officer of considerable experience in military matters. The Fifth Wisconsin, Forty-ninth Pennsylvania, Sixth Maine, and Forty-third New York, with Banks Battery and [Romeyn B.] Ayres Battery (regular) compose our brigade, and is considered to be one of the best disciplined in the service. The Fifth Wisconsin and Sixth Maine, under the tuition of their efficient colonels, [Amasa] Cobb and [Hiram] Burnham, have attained a perfection of drill which would be a credit to many of our crack militia regiments.

There is a rumor of our brigade going South in the new expedition under Gen. [Samuel] Heintzelman, which is soon to be fitted out; and the men are all living in hopes that it may prove true, for the steady routine of camp-life day after day has afflicted many of them with a lasting *ennui*.

The weather here has been very bad for some past. The mud has been at least a foot thick for the last two weeks, and it has dried up, thanks to a hard frost last night. It has been snowing hard all day to-day.

We were visited to-day by Messrs. Wm. E. Dodge, Jr., and Theodore Roosevelt, of New York, who are commissioned by the President to receive the allotment rolls of those members of the battery who desire to send money to their families at home. I send you a copy of the bill passed by Congress relative to that subject, which may be of use to you. It met with general favor throughout the company, and will doubtless be adopted by many of our members.

Fearing that I may occupy too much space. I will draw to a close with my best wishes for the success of your excellent journal, and that it may long continue to cheer the hearts of the "fire-laddies" at home and abroad, is the earnest wish of

Yours, very respectfully.   HARRY BLAKE

February 16, 1862
WHO WOULDN'T BE A FIRE ZOUAVE?
BY SERGEANT FRANCIS MORAN, COMPANY H, SECOND FIRE ZOUAVES
CAMP LAWRENCE, Feb. 6, 1862.

> Who wouldn't be a Fire Zouave,
> And form the army grand;
> With bayonets bright we'll win the fight.
> Or perish hand in hand.
>
> Our foes are strong, we know full well,
> And eager to destroy
> The sacred land that gave them birth,
> The source of freemen's joy.
>
> We long to hear McClellan's voice
> Command us in the fight,
> To sweep rebellion from our land,
> And vindicate our right.
>
> We'll foil the traitors' foul designs,
> And withered be the hand
> That e'er shall dare to draw a blade
> Against our native land!
>
> Then gather, Second Fire Zouaves,
> And rally round our flag;
> We ne'er shall see its stars replaced
> By any rebel rag.

According to his service record, Sergeant Frank C. Moran, age 20, five feet five inches tall, dark complexion with grey eyes, worked as a printer before the war. He received a wound in the left hand during the battle of Williamsburg on May 5, 1862, and was again wounded at Bristoe Station on August 27. Promoted to Second Lieutenant, Moran was commanding his company at Gettysburg on July 2, 1863 when he was wounded in the head and ankle by an exploding shell and was captured. Lieutenant Moran spent the next twenty months a prisoner of war and made five escape attempts, finally being exchanged on March 1, 1865.

In a letter written after the war, Moran states: "During my imprisonment I suffered all but Death and my health was lost. One of my Brothers died in Andersonville prison and the other died from the effect of his sufferings as a prisoner after his release at the end of war. I am the only male member of our family left." Frank Moran died in Baltimore, Md., on Dec. 10, 1892 of Pulmonary Tuberculosis.

THIRTY-EIGHTH REGIMENT, N.Y.S.V.

CAMP SCOTT, NEAR ALEXANDRIA, VA., Feb. 12.

I fear that it is almost impossible to write anything of interest, as the clerk of the weather has been absent so long that mud has almost gained the upper hand of everything.

Last week, while on picket duty near Accotink Village, we had a grand conflagration on our post. It happened thus: The house was dug out of a hay-stack, which was supported by rails. We had the fire inside of the house, in order to conceal it from outsiders; and the straw being scattered around the place, it was in danger of taking fire at any time. But luck was in our favor; and the shanty did not take fire in the night. But just at daybreak, when part of us were making our coffee and toasting our bread for breakfast, and the rest making a late visit to dreamland, the flames from the fire communicated with that part of the picket-house which was made of both rails and straw. What fun! Guns, overcoats, haversacks, and canteens flew out of the place into the snow beyond, in a manner that reminded me of a New York fire.

Our next move was to save the stack. This we had hard work to do, but after working strenuously for half an hour we succeeded in putting it all out. Our loss amounted only to a few dollars, in haversacks, gloves, etc., with all our rations for three days (and we had not yet been on picket twenty-four hours), our tobacco, and a couple of pipes—no insurance. The rest of the day was spent in building a new house, and begging from the other posts.

The third day on picket we met with another misfortune. We had had quite a snow-storm, and it now began to thaw. Our tent was situated in a sort of hollow, and as it begun the water began to run in, and we were soon overflowed, and spent the third night in six inches of water.

Our theatre is at last completed, and a few musical performances have been given by the Third and Fourth Maine Bands. I understand that it is to be opened on Saturday night with "Don Cæsar" and "O'Callaghan On His Last Legs."

My letter, I fear, is a rather prosy, but with a hope of pardon, I inscribe myself,

TENT TWO.

P.S.—Our theatre is to be opened to-night. They have slightly changed the order of proceedings. I send you a programme, which, if you choose, you can light your cigar with.

T. T.

February 23, 1862

SECOND FIRE ZOUAVES, (73rd New York Infantry).

CAMP LAWRENCE, MD., Feb. 19.

To the Editors of the Sunday Mercury:

I have a great complaint to make against the Adams Express Company from Washington to Staten Island. I am a private in the Second Fire Zouaves, and took a notion to send my wife a portrait of her better-half, and with the above-named I concluded to send her a five-dollar bill as a present to my little ones. I placed the bill at the back of the portrait, not thinking for a moment that any of the Express Company's employees would be so base as to abstract the trifle sent as a token of fatherly love to the little prattlers, who have been deprived of his company these last seven months. My wife answered my letter by return of mail, stating therein that she had received the portrait, but that the parcel had been opened by some miscreant and the money abstracted. She then made a complaint to the superintendent of the express office, who assured her the parcel went safe from the city of New York to Staten Island. Now, there must be some great neglect on the part of the managers having dishonest members in their employ. By stating these facts to you, and at the same time knowing you to be the soldier's friend, I thought you would give this publicity. By so doing, it will not only be doing me a great service, but the public at large. Believe me, sirs,

Yours, most respectfully,   J. H.

March 2, 1862

OUR MILITARY CORRESPONDENCE—No paper in the country has so large a list of valuable correspondence in the army as has the SUNDAY MERCURY. To its columns everybody now looks to learn everything of interest that transpires in the respective camps. In this week's issue we have letters from fifteen or twenty different regiments, all detailing items of general interest, and information particularly gratifying to the soldiers' friends at home. In this department the SUNDAY MERCURY is far in advance of all competition. So we go! Half the papers in the country now supply themselves with news and other matters from our vivacious and enterprising columns.

SIXTY-NINTH REGIMENT

CAMP CALIFORNIA, VA., Feb. 26.

The "monotony of camp-life," as a good many of your military correspondents are wont to say, has been seriously disturbed within the past ten or twelve days in the camp of the Sixty-ninth.

On Thursday last [Feb. 20] the regiment returned from their second picket tour, having relieved the Fifty-seventh N.Y.S.V., the Sunday previous. Nothing at all occurred while on the outpost worthy of occurrence. The men did their duty cheerfully and willingly, although the weather was of the most disagreeable kind. There was none of that temerity or unsteadiness so apparent on our first picket duty. We were replaced by the Sixty-third, and the Eighty-eighth took their place Monday last. On Friday we were ordered to be ready to turn out next morning at 4 A.M., in light marching order, with one days' provisions.

Accordingly, a little after daybreak the line was formed, and we were just under way in the direction of Edsall's Hill, accompanied by the Illinois Cavalry and the Fourth United States Battery (six pieces), the Eighty-eighth following after. With bounding hearts we marched on our way, not caring what number we came in contact with, but not an opposing foe made his appearance.

After marching within a few hundred yards of Edsall's Hill, we dropped into the woods on the right of the road, and there patiently waited while the cavalry and Captain [Felix] Duffy's company were scouring the country in every direction. They returned reporting no sign of the enemy. We returned to camp about eight o'clock P.M., up to our knees in mud. The roads in Virginia are, I believe, the worst in the world.

On Monday we were visited by a terrific gale, which leveled tents and scattered their contents in every direction. All the tents in the Sixty-third's camp, adjoining, were blown down, and the greater part of those in the Eighty-eighth. Mostly all our officers' tents, magazine, chapel, guard-tents, and worst of all, our hospital, in which were two or three critical cases, were leveled to the ground. The hurricane continued, with more or less force, until about 2, A.M., Tuesday. Yesterday we had a brigade-inspection.

As the SUNDAY MERCURY is independent enough to denounce all unfair or fraudulent practices, whether existing in army, navy, or civil life, I thought I would mention what must be a source of enormous expense to the Government if carried on in every regiment as in this. I mean the system of taking enlisted men from the ranks and using them as servants. Those men draw their clothing, rations, and pay, from their respective companies, and work for commissioned-officers—stable men and servants of all kinds being detailed from the ranks. Even one officer has a corporal as his valet. Of course they pocket the allowance for servant, and diminish the ranks. It is a practice that ought to be speedily put an end to.

Brig.-Gen. Meagher has taken up his residence among us. He looks hale and hearty. He accompanied us on our reconnoisance on Saturday. There is a marked improvement in the Sixty-third Regiment since Col. [John] Burke has had command. He is a good commander, and looks the very embodiment of courage and determination. The news of our recent victories in other places has had a most encouraging effect on our men, and we almost expect to participate in the celebration of our national anniversary in the city of New York. We all hope so.

More from your correspondent in due time.

Yours, etc.,   NON-COM, SIXTY-NINTH REGT.

March 9, 1862

FROM A GUNBOAT VOLUNTEER

CAIRO, Ill., Feb. 28.

I know that you are always willing to lay before the readers of your valuable paper the grievances of the soldier, or to expose the rascality of those who transact business for our glorious Union; and now I take this opportunity to show them how some of our officers act toward those who have always commanded the respect of their fellow-soldiers and those that had command of them.

On the 12th day of February there was an order read to us at dress parade, calling for volunteers to man the Western gunboat flotilla. There was a response by some fifteen men, and we were told to hold ourselves in readiness to start in an hour's notice. We did so; and on the 17th of February we left for Edwards' Ferry with the understanding that there would be a propeller in waiting to convey us to the Point of Rocks. There had been one, but it had started before we got there; so we had to walk twenty-one miles with knapsack on our backs, canteen and haversack, and three days' rations; not a small load for those that had been lying in winter quarters, with very little drill and very little walking, except on picket duty twice a month, being all the exercise we have had for these last three months. But to return to my story. We arrived at the Point of Rocks, at 5 o'clock, P.M., making seven hours' tramp. The train that was to convey us to Baltimore had run off the track, so we were in time, and we thought that we were lucky—but it was unlucky, as you will see.

We arrived in Baltimore about 12 o'clock, and were marched to the Union Defence Committee rooms and were told that we would have supper there; but were doomed to disappointment, as nothing presented itself to our view except the bare boards.

We had a guard placed over us like prisoners, to keep us together; but still the boys found a way to get out, and they got a little in for it, as two got stabbed by those loyal citizens of Baltimore (Gen. [Charles P.] Stone's pets), and are now in hospital there. But I will pass over the little ups and downs of the journey, except one more incident, which happened at Indianapolis, where we were received at the depot by a company of Home Guards, not with a friendly shake of the hand or a cheer, but by the point of the bayonet, like the enemy or a parcel of prisoners. Such was the reception we received there by the Home Guard. We, that volunteered our services to man the river gunboats, and we that have been in the service of the Government these last six, eight, and fourteen months—that was our welcome. Thank God! that is not the way we show our welcome in the Eastern or Northern States; if it was, few soldiers would we have. This treatment so exasperated the boys, that they tore up the seats, and broke the windows, and fired them at the soldiers, and told the captain of them that if he did not draw them off there would be a riot. So he did so, and all was quiet again; but none of the boys were allowed to leave the depot, and we soon bade farewell to that inhospitable city. The next town worthy of remark was Terre Haute, where we received coffee, fresh bread, and beef. We soon left there; and every town or village we came to after, we were received with cheers, and the people would do anything for us, until we reached Cairo City, on the 21st, and were placed on board the Maria Denning, receiving-boat; and of all the miserable, dirty, unventilated, and untenantable boats I ever was on, this was the worst. There were about 300 on board before we came, and we swelled that number to 450. Those that came in first occupied the covered deck, but we had to lie as best we could.

The boat is stowed with shell, provision, or in fact anything they can get on board of her. Sleeping is almost out of the question unless you sleep standing up, sitting on your knapsack, which is not very comfortable after a long and tedious journey of six days and five nights. We are kept aboard there under a strong guard, and not allowed to leave on any pretence, and half fed. Our rations consists of half a pint of coffee twice a day, and one gill of rum twice a day, raw salt pork (if you are expert at stealing), and crackers the same. Tough fodder I think for U.S. soldiers. Remember I do not blame Uncle Sam one mite, for he allows us more than we can eat. I have eaten his rations for these last eight months and know what I am entitled to; but the officers are making money off us, and no mistake. Now there is a boat alongside us called the Hazel Dell, with some one hundred secession prisoners on board, and they are treated far better than we are. We have now been aboard this receiving-boat six days, and I have not received one meal of cooked rations and no convenience for cooking, as there is neither pot, kettle, nor pan of any kind to be got aboard, so we have to eat it raw. Hard fare for one that has seen what Uncle Sam allows his soldiers and sailors! If we were the refuse of our companies, there would be some excuse for this kind of treatment. But we are not. The majority of us are picked men—are New York mechanics.

There are no officers here to appeal to, or if there are any, they keep themselves scarce as cheese. Knowing that you are always ready to help in exposing those that are guilty, and to do justice to the soldier, as I have seen by being a constant reader of your paper, I have taken the liberty to appeal to you, I remain yours with respect,   JUSTICE.

March 16, 1862
FIRST FIRE ZOUAVES
CAMP BUTLER, NEWPORT NEWS, VA., March 3.

On Saturday afternoon about ten o'clock, most of the boys were engaged in cleaning up for Sunday's inspection, when word was passed through the camp that the rebel battery Merrimac [C.S.S. Virginia] was coming up river, followed by two other rebel boats. She came up with other two firing, from all appearances, at her. She passed the frigate Congress, and fired a few shots at her, which the Congress returned, and kept on until she came to the frigate Cumberland, which vessel, on the battery approaching her, poured a broadside into her, when the battery fired into the Cumberland and then drew back, and rushing forward again, sunk a large augur she carried in her bow into the sick boy, making a large whole in her, so that she sunk in a half-hour. Two of our boys were on board of her when the battle was going on, and were to work on No. 1 guns. Their names are Charles McMannis and John Bracken, of Co. E. McMannis was wounded, but not severely, but Bracken escaped unhurt. To the officers and crew of the Cumberland too much praise cannot be showered on them, for they fought like tigers; and on being asked by the commander of the Merrimac whether they would surrender or not, they said they would sink first; and sink she did, with the American colors flying. At the time she sunk, the sailors jumped in the water to swim ashore. When in the water, the Merrimac opened on them with a shower of grape and cannister. Leaving the Cumberland, the Merrimac passed on to the Congress, and fired two broadsides into her, setting her on fire, and raking her fore and aft, when the officers run up a white flag. After the Congress surrendered, the battery threw shells over our camp. Our boys had plenty of work to do. Gen. Mansfield sent for us to work on some Parrot guns. We dragged the guns from the camp to the point and helped to work them, and some were firing with a part of the Indiana Twentieth, on the boarders, who tried to take the officers of the Congress prisoners, also to cover the retreat of the sailors.

In the evening, we were pretty well worn out. Sunday came, clear and bright, and had it not been for the Ericsson Battery (Monitor), I suppose we would have been shelled pretty well. The Monitor and the Merrimac both had steam up at the same time, when the Monitor went out and opened the ball, and they kept it up until one o'clock on Sunday afternoon, when the Merrimac was towed away. What harm was done to the Merrimac, I am unable to say, but there was no damage done to the Monitor.

On Sunday afternoon, scouts came in camp, and stated that a large land-force was advancing. The long roll was beat, and our little band was drawn up in a line, and had the order to rest. After waiting an hour or more, we were marched out about a mile and a half, and orders came to throw up breastworks, at which the boys went to work with a will. We were marched back into camp about eight o'clock in the evening. The work on the fortifications is still going on, and when it is done, I believe it will be called Fort Mansfield.

Everything is quiet to-day. Yesterday the Monitor passed the place, and anchored near the dock. Bands played the national airs, and crowds went down on the beach, and such cheering never was heard. The crew of the Monitor returned the cheers with a will. I suppose she will be stationed at this place.

There is nothing further of any importance that I know of transpiring. I will close by stating that the boys did all in their power to assist the poor sailors off the two ships, having had a great many in our camp during their stay.

Yours, with respect,   FRIENDSHIP

March 23, 1862

LINES

{For the Sunday Mercury.}

Written on the death of Corporal Edward Carroll, of Co.H, Eighth Regiment, Washington Grays, N.Y.S.M., killed at the Battle of Bull Run, Va., July 21, 1861.

By J.V.V.

We are waiting for thee, loved one,
  But O! we wait in vain,
Too well we know, alas! that thou
  Wilt ne'er return again.
Life's mission is accomplished;
  Ended all care and toil,
Far from us thou art sleeping
  Beneath a Southern soil.

But 'tis hard to think thou must die,
  With prospects here so bright,
That hopes that bid so fair as thine,
  Should know so sad a blight.
No friend was near in that dreaded hour,
  Not e'en thy gentle wife,
To wipe the death-damp from thy brow,
  As thou breathed away thy life.

But we've looked our last upon thee,
  Will see thee here no more,
Yet we trust that we again shall meet
  Upon a happier shore;
There the cry of war is never heard,
  No parting there is known:
Loved one, we hope to meet thee there,
  Around our father's throne.

SIXTY-NINTH REGIMENT, N.Y.S.V.

CAMP NEAR UNION MILLS, VA., March 17.

Early on Monday morning last, the Grand Army of the Potomac was in motion, and a few minutes before sunrise the Irish Brigade went on its way rejoicing in the expectation of wiping out the stain of the memorable 21st of July last. Though rumors were afloat on Sunday that the New Jersey Brigade occupied Fairfax, and that our arms generally met no opposition of consequence, still few believed that we could cross that memorable rivulet, Bull Run, with perfect impunity. Centreville and Manassas are in our hands, and at present everything looks gay. The "brigade" is encamped on the hill southeast of Union Mills, which we reached on Wednesday afternoon. We found that the rebels had retreated, and burned the railroad bridges as they went along. They were encamped here in strong force—perhaps to the number of 40,000 or 50,000— and with that number sneaked rather than give us battle, and a one-sided one at that, from having possession of the almost innumerable hills in this section of Virginia. I visited some of their encampments yesterday. They were comfortably housed in log huts, well put up, and from the appearance of things, the rebels must have beat a retreat. Flour in large quantities, rice, clothing of every description, cooking utensils, any quantity of axes, and innumerable little things necessary in camp-life, were left behind. Our boys availed themselves of the opportunity thus afforded, and for the last two days are taking whatever they can turn to account away. Cakes in abundance were immediately made and baked, rice cooked, and almost everybody partook of something secesh. In my travels, I found this sheet of paper tacked up in one of the log-houses in a conspicuous place. You can see what is on the first page. I send it as a curiosity. Also, another sheet, hung along side this, which I inclose. Each hut was built large enough to accommodate fifteen or twenty, and they seemed to have cooked for themselves. A good many deserters have come in. There are two in Company K, Sixty-third Regiment. They were found in the woods, before we reached this place, on Wednesday morning, and immediately joined the company of the men whom they first met. They say the rebels are disheartened, and will not show fight much nearer than Richmond. They are both Irishmen. Whether we will continue to march forward or not I cannot say, but we must follow by land or water. The men are in good spirits. Our troops are all around, and occupy the hills only just left by the enemy. We have had fine weather since we left Camp California, which is lucky, as we brought no tents with us. More at the next opportunity.

Your friend, NON-COM.

{The sheet of paper on which our correspondent writes bears evidence of the baseness of secesh literature. The reading is as follows: "Cood by, Yankees. I expect to meet you one of these days. Then look out for squals. W.W.".... "You cannot make us submit to Yankey hirelin's. Written by a Louisiana. J.F.H.".... "Beauregard Regiment—Punx, Secessionist." The writing is in three different hands.—EDS.}

NINETY-FIFTH REGIMENT

HEAD-QUARTERS, WASHINGTON, D.C., March 15.

I hope you will excuse me for intruding on your valuable time; but it is an affair of importance. I want to know whether a volunteer is to be treated as a dog or an American soldier. We arrived in Washington on Sunday last, pitched our tents on Monday, got three or four handfuls of straw to spread on the mud, as it rained all day; and after eating a piece of dry bread, I slept as only a fatigued soldier can sleep. After a day or two we got some coffee and fat pork, served to heighten our appetites. When we asked for more, we were told that some of us were deserving of nothing. Yesterday it rained incessantly, and not having flies to our tents, we were deluged with water. Went to bed supperless, and slept in the mud and water all night. We arose, wet, cold, and hungry; and after a delay of an hour we got breakfast. A thin slice of bread and a piece of pork, which a boy of three years old would refuse. One sergeant told us if we grumbled we would get nothing next time. I went to the colonel with my ration but could get no redress. He sent for our sergeant, who stated that some of the men threw their rations away, and, on that account he cut them short. I was dismissed with a caution not to grumble without cause next time. I want to know if a man who enlists to fight for his country, gives up his home and friends, all the ties that the heart clings to, to follow the banner of his native land and battle for its glory, is to be starved under the very dome of the capitol? Is he to lie kenneled like a hog on the bare wet ground, when five hemlock boards would floor a tent, and barrack-boards are only ten cents a-piece? Is the heart and sinew of the land—men buoyant with life and vigor—to have their constitutions broken and become wasted, emaciated wrecks, for the sake of a few paltry dollars? Why, it costs near as much to supply them with medicine and bury those who are cut off in their bloom, by cold, hunger, and improper exposure to the elements. Let them get them good clothing, shoes through which the water will not run as through a sponge, India-rubber sheets to protect them from the rain and damp ground, and food that will strengthen them. Let them have good officers, who will attend to their wants, and understand military tactics properly. Some of them pass a military examination by simply paying a hundred dollars, and it is these kind of men that are a curse to our volunteer army. They get leagued with the quartermasters, and then rob the poor soldier out of his food and wages.

PRIVATE, Company B, Ninety-fifth, N.Y.S.V.

March 30, 1862
NINETY-FIFTH REGIMENT, N.Y.S.V.
HEAD-QUARTERS, WASHINGTON, D.C., March 26.

In perusing the columns of your interesting paper, a few days since, I was somewhat surprised to find a correspondent from the Ninety-fifth complaining with such woe and bitterness. In reply to the writer of the article referred to, I must certainly say I differ from him materially. The life of a soldier differs from that of the private-citizen or the retired millionaire. We cannot expect to sit down to a meal composed of all the delicacies of the season, or to have a bill of fare thrust under our nose, affording us the privilege of selecting any article of food our dainty appetites many demand, or does the writer in question expect to be waited on in true *bon ton* style by some aristocratic tan-colored African. It is with regret that I have to say such articles as the one referred to injures not the regiment but the one guilty of asserting such slanderous reports.

As regards the food, the writer of this article is entirely wrong. The night we arrived at Washington we were taken into the large room near the depot, which, by-the-way, was well heated throughout, and there furnished with good hot coffee, wheat-bread, and good corned-beef. In the morning we partook of the same. We slept the first night in Washington on the floor, it is true; but we had our blankets, and this room, like the eating-room, was also well heated. True, it rained the day we went to camp; but I don't think the colonel or any officer could have prevented it; but we pitched our tents in true soldier style, and I believe every man rested good, enjoying a quiet sleep, and not in the mud, as the gentleman speaks about. He also says we are fed upon a thin slice of bread and small piece of pork—only enough to heighten our appetites. I don't know how thick the gentleman wants the bread; if his jaws are ponderous, and at the same time elastic, and having no fear of the lockjaw caused by being outstretched, then he might with safety take in one of our thin slices, which, I would inform the public, consists of whole loaf. As for the small piece of pork he speaks about, I must differ from him again. The men have all the pork they want, unless there may be some rare exceptions. For my part I would rather eat pork with some moderation, than run the risk of rushing the matter, thereby endangering the body with being covered with bristles. But to be plain about the whole affair, it is very seldom the men eat up their rations. They have more bread than they can eat, each man being furnished with a loaf per day, and it's no uncommon thing to find men selling bread for milk to the peddlers in camp, showing very plainly that in the place of being short, we have an overplus. We do not live entirely on bread and pork, as many would suppose from the purport of the article. Our food consists of bread, tea and coffee, salt pork, corned beef, fresh beef, rice and potatoes, and beans. I merely make mention of the articles to inform our friends and relatives at home, that the members of the Ninety-fifth are not treated like dogs, and its very seldom that we hear any one grumbling about the food. We have men in camp who always had plenty of the good things of this life while at home, men who were not obliged to leave the comforts of a home, or the ties that hold us by nature, but not a word or murmur escapes from their lips. I have but a small opinion of men who grumble at a full supply. The attack made upon the officers was very ungenerous, and far from what I consider right. I have the pleasure of an acquaintance with most of them, and I must say the officers attached to the Ninety-fifth are gentlemen, and deserve no such attack as was made upon them by the writer in question. I know no officers in the entire regiment but what would willingly deprive themselves of many wants rather than their respective commands should be neglected.

I am around about the camp every day, but I hear none of this terrible growling among the men. If the writer in question belongs to that class who are born to disappointment, then he may have been led to pen the article at the impulse of the moment. If this should be the case, the public would at once excuse him, and pronounce his letter "had a humbug." If the gentleman merely comes under the title "Private" when he don't rank there at present, it's rather unjust, or, if he is a good soldier, and feels himself so badly used, I hope he will come out again, and give us his name, or inform us in some way where he can be found, then, if his case is so bad as he pretends, we will cheerfully assist him in making everything right. Let me state, however, that if a soldier is misused, he has redress, and should not decline informing his comrades who he is or where he can be found. I have no hesitation in stating that I belong to Company A, Captain [Samuel L.]Harrison, for further particulars, inquire at head-quarters. It would be useless for me to publish an autobiography of the commissioned officers. Suffice it to say, they are all gentlemen, too well known to commend through the columns of a public journal, or be injured by such articles as the one in question. What I have asserted here I can back up; and if the gentleman is not satisfied with the military experience of our officers, why does he not come out with some new publication on military tactics, differing entirely from those now published, and show what he can do, wherein the officers of the Ninety-fifth are so deficient.

Yours, etc.,   UNION.

Company A, Ninety-fifth Regiment

FIRST REGIMENT N.Y.V.

NEWPORT NEWS, VA., March 26.

Troops are massing in vast columns at the fort, and Old Point Comfort is a scene of jostling bustle, the sea of soldiery surging out from the shore to Hampton itself, and extending half-way to Newport News.

The greatest anxiety reigns in the First. We will, indeed, be sadly disappointed if not included in the offensive movements obviously about being made. Long have we maintained the advanced post of the Army of the Union—the left flank of Camp Butler—the regiment of all the nearest to the capital of rebellion—and we will surrender our honorable, if perilous, position with the keenest regret, if compelled, which I trust will not be the case.

The Cumberland, sunken "fornent" the post of our regiment, it seems is parting with her dead. On Saturday, the body of a sailor came ashore at Signal Point. He was, of course, not recognized, but was carefully examined for identification. The initials, C.H.S., were graven with India-ink on his arm, and his clothing was marked 367, a number which shows him to have been a new man. Twenty dollars were found upon his person. He was young, and even so long after death, retained features which proved him to have been in life a fine-looking, prepossessing fellow. A wound on his brow bore evidence of the battle of the 8th.

We lost on the morning of the 20th, a sergeant, William H. Currie, Co. G, who died of an attack of typhoid, superinduced by exposure endured on a scout a month ago. Mr. Currie was born in Ohio, though long a citizen of New York, and was once well known at Cincinnati.

An old soldier, who has seen service in more than one army says, "Faith, I know the regiment will soon have the rout—cause why, it's clean crazy! It's stage struck!" If coming events throw their shadows before in this way, and sunny faces, joyous laughter, mad gambols, and quaint entertainments indicate the march, the bivouac, and the battle, they are certainly at hand. Every hour not employed on guard or drill is replete with sport, and almost every company has its theatre, whereat the night antecedent to "tattoo" is made amusing enough, with odd farces, songs, etc., mostly original.

The SUNDAY MERCURY affords its share of interest to this camp, and, I am glad to say, is the most popular weekly patronized by the soldiers.

No Merrimac yet. She is seen almost daily, with steam up, in the Elizabeth River, but does not venture forth.

Occasional desertions from the rebel lines occur—mostly from Louisiana and Mississippi regiments—generally of persons formerly from the North.

Fires seen still, almost continuously, on the other shore.

Rebel force at Warrick and Yorktown, variously estimated and undoubtedly immense.

Yours,   A.

THEATRE NEWS

MARY PROVOST'S THEATRE—J. WILKES BOOTH.—We are happy to be able to speak with some degree of commendation of the company gathered at this theatre. Such actresses as Mrs. Farron, Mrs. Chanfrau, and Mrs. Lottie Hough; and such generally capable actors as Messrs. Lewis Baker, George Ryer, and E. L. Tilton, are worthy of any dramatist. The minor performers, too, appear to understand their business, and appear less provincial than we expected to find them.

The "star" of the concern, Mr. J. Wilkes Booth, has had the good fortune to elicit from one of the more metaphysical daily critics a tribute of admiration for his "intellectual breadth." If this expression is used in contradistinction with "intellectual depth," we can detect some signs of its applicability to the actor in question. To speak in ordinary English, Mr. J. Wilkes Booth is an actor born to be a leader in the Edmund Kean school, but perverted by circumstances into a distant follower of Cooke. By his facile, nervous line-ments, soft, and almost womanish voice, and sensitive temperament, he is made to produce great effects, like Kean, by the magnetism of subtle gesture, and the electrical influence of strongly-defined expression of face. By availing himself of these natural powers, he would prove his possession of both intellectual breadth and depth. But he does nothing of the kind, if we may fairly judge him from his enacting of "Richard III," and "Charles de Moer," of late. With a countenance adapted to the utmost delicacy of expression in all its features, he expresses like an actor whose magnitude of eyes is the only sign of respectable intelligence about him; with the low, rich voice of an Orpheus, he aims to thunder like a Boanerges, or Lord North. It is but just to say, however, that inexorable circumstances have brought Mr. Booth to this perveration of normal-self; his experience as a "star" has been chiefly confined, hitherto, to localities where discrimination is not a part of criticism, and noise and buncombe are the *aut nullus* of the stage. In short, he has played to country audiences, in places where it is particularly true that,

"The drama's laws the drama's patrons give.
And those who live to please must please to live."

Now that he had gained a foothold on the stage that tries men's brains, let us hope that he will subside, by degrees, into his proper self, and become the fine intellectual artist he has evidently the gift to be.

After carefully considering the genius so fitfully exhibited by Mr. J. Wilkes Booth, in the few impersonations noted, we arrive at the conclusion that he may make, under intelligent tutelage, a better actor than his brother Edwin, and quite as good a one as his father ever was.

April 6, 1862
THIRTY-SECOND REGIMENT, N.Y.S.V.
CAMP NEWTON, ALEXANDRIA, VA., April 1.

This being "All Fool's day," I have concluded to let "all fools" play their pranks, and sit down to pen a peculiarly-interesting letter to the SUNDAY MERCURY. One is somewhat puzzled in consequence of the "suppression of the press in publishing army movements," how to commence, continue, or finish a letter for publication. Orpheus C. Kerr, in one of his recent side-splitting communications, has given us ample warnings as to the inevitable consequences attending the unlucky editor who publishes "a word too much."

Well, we are here, [William B.] Franklin's Division is here, McDowell's corps is here. Hientzelman has gone, Porter has gone, Keyes has gone, thousands more have gone. We are going when—ahem! Where, "Who am I?" as Jerry Bryant would say, were he living—and General McClellan's confidential adviser as your humble servant—"Honest Abe"—undoubtedly is. I have too much regard for the future welfare of the SUNDAY MERCURY to even say the destination appears to be down the river on vessels of all descriptions.

If you consider the above as committing you in any way, don't publish it. Let the reading world go hungry, or read [James G.] Bennett's editorials.

I refer to the *enormous* anticipations of those poor impoverished (?), half-loyal, half-secesh, on-the-fence F.F.V.s, who are still occupying this portion of the "sacred soil," in their expected recompense from Government. Our recent brilliant victories, combined with the flight of the rebels from Manassas, and other signs too plain to be mistaken, have set these poor persecuted individuals to "rec-on-in'" that Uncle Sam will gain the day "arter all;" and they are beginning to make our their estimates of the damage done them by our troops.

I have always been, and am still, in favor of Government making fair awards to all truly loyal people for their losses in this war. According to their estimates, a piece of half-brush, half-rail fence is worth more than the same space closely fenced with Enfield rifles. An acre or two (few of them more than that) of garden truck in seed trampled down by a troop of cavalry is worth more than the horse and trappings that did the damage.

Some of them, I find, have actually prevailed on commanding officers to pay them money for imaginary damage, hoodwinking said officers. Officer takes up his residence with said F.F.V.'s pretty wife, pretty daughter, or, perhaps, prepossessing contraband, and that's the secret.

I speak as one who knows what he's saying, having been encamped here nine months, and five of said nine months detailed as "safe guard" at the residences, gardens, etc., of these F.F.V.s. Moreover, being somewhat of an observer and listener of events transpiring in the immediate vicinity, I have arrived at the conclusion that some of these gents will either fleece Uncle Sam or get terribly disappointed.

Colonel (now general) [Thomas A.] Davis, on our return from Bull Run last July, said to all applicants for protection: "Gentlemen, hang the American flag from your house, tree, fence, or barn, and I guarantee each and every one of you complete protection." But two or three acted on his advice, and were protected, the rest thought "Beauregard might come along."

　　　　　　　　Yours, truly,　　　　　　　　　　　　　　　　CALIFORNIA.

One of the most popular features in the Sunday Mercury *was the weekly column of its Washington Correspondent Orpheus C. Kerr (Office Seeker), who was, in actuality, humorist Robert H. Newell whose political satire inspired and entertained a generation of Americans.*

April 13, 1862
MOZART REGIMENT, FORTIETH N.Y.S.V.
HAMPTON, NEAR FORTRESS MONROE, VA.

Here we are at last, safe and sound. Being busily engaged, this is the first chance I have had to write. On the 17th of March we left our camp near Alexandria, and marched to that city, and next morning we set sail down the river, the bands on the different boats playing their best airs as we steamed down past the city. The citizens crowded the wharves, and the ladies (bless them!) waved their handkerchiefs to us until we were out of sight. After the boat left the dock, I received a SUNDAY MERCURY from you. As soon as the boys found that there was a SUNDAY MERCURY on board, there was a general rush toward me for it, and I had it two days before I got a chance to read it, as I had to lend it—I may say—to all hands; and so it is, whenever I get a paper from you.

We passed the rebel batteries about three in the afternoon. As we came up, the boys gave nine cheers, and the bands again struck up their best, "So gayly O!" These batteries are on the right bank. After proceeding down a few miles further, we were joined by five of Uncle Sam's gunboats, who took the advance, and as night set in began shelling the woods in the Virginia side, to see that the coast was clear. As we got no response, we proceeded on our way. Nothing of interest occurred down the rest of the way. Suffice to say, we arrived at Fortress Monroe, where we saw the Monitor, and the other sights around the Fortress.

We did not land until next morning, as a heavy rain set in. We disembarked about ten o'clock, in a drenching rain, and marched about a mile and a half from the Fortress, where we encamped. When we arrived in the ground we were wet through, as well as hungry. We left our tents behind us, and we have to substitute our oil-blankets instead. Two men club together, joining their blankets, which form a kind of tent—open at both ends—and about two and a half feet high. In these we passed several wet nights. Last Saturday night especially, some of us were nearly floating about the field.

On Monday the 24th, we struck tents and crossed over to the burnt town of Hampton, where every house in the place is burned to the ground. We passed through it, and pitched our tents about a mile and a half south of it, where we now are.

I received a copy of the SUNDAY MERCURY from you on last Saturday afternoon; it was a week on the way, but it was welcome. We get plenty of drilling; we have a company or a battalion drill in the afternoon and a dress-parade after that again. Our rations are getting better and better; our supper last night consisted of two crackers (shingles) and a cup of miserable tea. Our rations of bread per day is nine crackers. We expect to march to-morrow, and I hope before you hear from me again, that the Mozart Boys will make their mark upon the enemy, as we now have the Austrian rifles in place of the old muskets.

I will write again as soon as possible, but as old Joe is calling the company to dinner, I must dry up.

Yours, truly,   HIGH PRIVATE, REAR GUARD.

NINTH REGIMENT, N.Y.S.V.—HAWKINS' ZOUAVES
ROANOKE ISLAND, N.C., March 28.

Being on guard to-day, and having nothing else to do but write, I thought I could not do any better than get a letter ready, in case there was a chance to send it on. I, being the next corporal on the list for duty to-day, I, of course, had to take my chances with some three or four others, and try for the picket, or Camp Foster, which is equally as good as the former. You must know that the main guard is not looked for with any great amount of pleasure; and when any of the non-coms. get on guard outside of the camp, they think, and justly, too, they have got a big thing. The place where I am now on guard is about eighty rods from our camp (Reno), and is the rendezvous for all the contrabands on the island. They are about 200 in number; and among them you can find the big, fat, greasy nigger, and the dainty "yaller" nigger. The whole camp belongs to them exclusively; and such times as they have every night after they are done work and had supper! They have "meetin'", as they call it; and such lungs as some of them got! You can hear them easy three miles; and if Dan Bryant could only drop in upon them when they are dancing, his fortune would be made sure. The regular old genuine fling! and such steps! And they are not to be laughed at either, by any means. They are as happy as fish in water, and seem to like the change of masters very much. The manner in which they worship God is also very queer. Just imagine forty or fifty darkeys sitting about the room, of both sexes, some as black as tar, and others the color of gold, and all going in on their own hook, some praying, and others singing, and now and then one of the "gemmen" gets excited, and jumps up and down, and makes Rome howl. Forrest ain't anything. They get $10 a month and a soldier's allowance of clothing. So you see that there is only $3 a month difference between the volunteer and the black man. The women also get $4 a month and rations, which is almost as good as some of the New York waiting-maids get. Sergeant [Walter] Thompson is the commander of the black forces now on the island; and he is as kind to them as though they were bone of his bone. Company G has been doing the nice thing by its late commander (now our major). Shortly after dress-parade the other day, the company marched in a body up to the major's quarters, where they halted, when the major was requested to step outside, as the boys wanted to see him, when a committee of three marched to the front, holding in their hands what I supposed to be a banjo-box, but what was in reality a box containing a splendid sword. The boys did it well, and took the gentleman all aback. On receiving the sword, the major returned thanks to the company in a happy manner; and at the same time he gave the Zou-zous an idea of what they might expect if they did not behave themselves. After which, the boys gave Major [Edward] Jardine three hearty cheers, and retired to their quarters to partake of some refreshments which were awaiting them. Well, the major means to make the regiment as good as the best; and he is well liked for it. Long may he live say the Zou-zous.

Lieutenant-Colonel [Edward A.] Kimball dropped in among us rather suddenly the other day; and for a while he thought he would get to his quarters without being seen by the boys, but some one more sharp than others caught sight of him, and gave a yell. The news spread like fire, and soon his whole *family* were about him. Cheer upon cheer went up for the old war-horse. He got clear of the boys after a while, and, I suppose, he thought himself safe; but he had hardly got into his quarters when the band made its appearance, which was a signal for the boys to close *en masse* around the major's quarters. After the band had played some of their best pieces, the old major made his appearance, when he received a perfect ovation. He made a short speech to his children, and retired to his quarters. The Zou-zous feel secure now that the old war-horse has returned.

The weather is warm by degrees, and we will soon have old Sol out in some of his warmest garments. The members of Company A are building a gymnasium, on which somebody is expected to break their heads. They have now in working order the parallel bars, swings, rings, single rope, and single bar; boxing-gloves are also to be had, whenever any one is inclined to spill a small amount of the ruby.

Colonel Hawkins is in command of the island; and the way the yokels stand around is a caution. They have got their match when they undertake to play D.B. on him; and what is more, they know that he has his eye upon them.

The mail arrived yesterday, and, I am sorry to say, it brought me no SUNDAY MERCURY, and I don't know what I will do with myself. If you ask anybody to lend you the SUNDAY MERCURY, you might as well take their dinner, for they would sooner give you the latter than the former.

I must close my letter, or I shall be in the dark, as I am now writing by candle-light (the candle I borrowed), and the candle at the present moment is only about an inch long. So "over the river" until the next mail.

Yours, truly,   ROANOKE.

April 20, 1862
MOZART REGIMENT
ON PICKET NEAR YORKTOWN, VA., April 15.

We left our camp, near Alexandria, on the 17th of March, and after parading through the principal streets we embarked on the transports, and the next morning we set sail down the river.

We arrived at Fortress Monroe on the evening of the 19th, after a pleasant excursion down the river, and the next morning we disembarked at the fortress through a heavy rain-storm. We marched about two miles from the landing place and pitched our blankets (we have no tents) for the night. We have to rough it now, for when we left Alexandria we left our good times behind. We left Old Point and crossed over to Hampton on the 24th, where we were treated to a battalion drill, or company drill, in the morning, and a brigade drill in the afternoon, and a dress parade after that. Roll call eight times a day and short allowance.

We left Hampton on the 4th of April, rested on the battle-field at Big Bethel, and arrived near our present location on the 5th, late in the evening. Several men belonging to other regiments were killed and wounded on the march (the rebel shell were flying around us like hail at one time), but not a Mozarter got touched. When we arrived at our quarters the shell and shot were flying over our heads, but our batteries were on hand, and soon silenced the enemy.

Next morning myself and several others took a walk out of camp and went down to see one of their forts; it was about ten hundred yards from where we stood. A crowd of us collected, when the rebels, thinking it a good opportunity, let drive a rifled shell at us. I rolled off the tree in double-quick time, and lay on the ground. The shell struck a fence and one of the rails struck a poor fellow (a member of the Fourth Maine Regiment) in the small of the back, breaking it; he died in a few hours. It was a lucky thing for some of us that the shell did not burst; if it did, you would not get this.

We left our camp in the fields and took to the woods, where we are at present, on the 9th inst., during a heavy rain-storm. Coming down we passed right in front of a large fort. We could see them running around inside the fort, but they did not fire at us. We lay in the woods all night, and the next morning we were sent off on picket. We had no supper the night before, and we had to go without any breakfast. Late at night we got some coffee and crackers, which did satisfy us somewhat. We were close enough to the enemy to hear them calling the roll in the morning. I will now pass over until to-day. We came here yesterday evening, and relieved the Thirty-seventh N.Y.V. We were ordered to "keep our eyes skinned," and to keep no fires burning. We had all to be awake. We were within three hundred yards of the rebel pickets. We could see their picket fires in front of us, and could see the enemy passing and repassing before the fires. This morning we discovered we were within three-eighths of a mile of one of their largest forts. They drew in their pickets at daybreak. We could see them with the naked eye going around in squads inside the fort. I procured a glass, and with its aid I had a good look at them. I saw them engaged in mounting a large gun, and a party of negroes working in another place. All hands seemed to be busy; some were cutting down trees; more were throwing up intrenchments. They have splendid winter-quarters. In one fort there are over two hundred houses made up of logs, and each capable to accommodate from eight to twelve men. They are built close to the breastworks; they will be a fine mark for our shells. We were left peaceably, not a shot exchanged while we were out. We are a lucky regiment. The enemy seem to know us, and respect us. We were relieved at dusk this evening by the Michigan Third, who (as soon as they took our places) fired off two guns. After supper we got some shoes, stockings, etc., which were much needed by us.

This morning (the 16th) the bombardment has begun. As I am writing the cannons are at it thick and fast. One of our boys went down to see the fun; he got up on a large tree, where he sat about five minutes, when a shell from the enemy struck the tree, bringing him and the tree down. The shell did not explode, and he brought it into camp, where it is now. He says we are giving them fits.

We will be out to-morrow to raise intrenchments; two regiments out of the brigade are at work to-day. We had an account of the capture of Island No. 10 and the battle of Pittsburg Landing. The boys are in great spirits, and they think this will be the last battle of the war. I hope so, at least. We will have a bloody fight; Yorktown is the Sebastopol of America.

Hoping when you next receive a letter from me that I can inform you of the capture of Yorktown, and to see you soon in Gotham, I remain

Yours, truly,   HIGH PRIVATE REAR RANK.

ON THE BATTLEFIELD, PITTSBURG LANDING
April 8.

I write this not knowing when or how I can send it. We had a famous battle yesterday, and entirely routed the enemy after a desperate fight, lasting from 7 A.M., until 6 P.M. The enemy numbered 100,000 and over; and our strength was 60,000. Our battalion [16th U. S. Infantry], and the other regulars (Fifteenth and Nineteenth), went into the action four times. In the first instance on the centre, where the enemy was pouring in fearful volleys by artillery and infantry. The centre was nearly broken, when we were ordered up, and in twenty minutes forced them to retire. We were then held in reserve; and went into action three times on the right and left flanks—the last time on the enemy's right, where the action lasted nearly an hour, when the order to cease firing was followed by that of "fix bayonets," and charge after the rebels, who were in full retreat. The cavalry then came up and continued the pursuit, and we bivouacked on the field of battle, and are this morning most uncomfortable, it having rained all night. We have no blankets, except the few we found in the rebel camp. We lost, killed, in our battalion, Capt. [William Henry] Acker, of Minnesota; Lieut. [Edward Lewis] Mitchell, of New York; wounded, Capt. [Patrick T.] Keys, of Pennsylvania; and four privates killed, and 56 wounded. The Fifteenth lost about the same number, but no officers killed—four were wounded, including Capt. [Henry] Keteltas, of New York. I will not attempt to give you any further particulars, or describe the horrors of a battle-field. I went out during the night with a lantern in search of provisions, etc., and the scene was awful. Our battalion fought splendidly, and are much praised, particularly as we saved the centre where several of the volunteer regiments broke and fled. I will write again as soon as possible. The way the bullets whistled around me was (as friend Bartlett says), "simply disgusting." The enemy was right upon us before I heard the order to fire, and I was then leading my men and giving orders; but to tell you I got to the rear and suddenly when the firing commenced, and immediately ordered the men to fall on their knees, and kept them in that position, with orders to fire only at the rebel flag; and, it is said, there is a pile of dead men there, and I am going to see them. We made a bayonet charge, but the Fifteenth was nearest, and took the battery. God grant I may be spared in our next engagement, which must take place soon, as we are to pursue them, or they may return with re-enforcements. Adieu.

April 10th, 1862.

I have another chance to send you a letter, and think best to do so, as the other may not have reached you. I wrote that we had a great battle, and that I came off unwounded. I searched in vain for some mark on my uniform, but discovered nothing but one hole through my canteen; so I may as well report myself wounded in the canteen. We have had all sorts of rumors about the position of the enemy, and their intention to return, but nothing has been heard from them yet. I don't believe we shall meet them again until we get to Corinth. A report got abroad that the Fifteenth and Sixteenth Iowa, who behaved shamefully. Our general [Alexander

McD. McCook] was over to see us yesterday, and he is as saucy as you please about his division, taking all the credit to himself of the victory. It was the largest battle ever fought on this Continent. We have ascertained from rebel officers (prisoners) that their strength was 110,000 men; ours engaged was 60,000. I believe this to be strictly true. General Sidney Johnston and [Governor] George Johnston, of Kentucky, were both killed, and their bodies lay near us, and were seen by all. Their uniforms were very rich. The battle extended over a front of six miles from right to left, and four miles to centre. I went to our extreme right today to see the wounded there, and the ground is covered with dead men of both sides, and what makes it more horrible is, that the dry leaves caught fire from the bombshells, and burned both dead and wounded. It will take several days yet to bury them all; horses and men lay piled together. I could collect plenty of trophies in the way of swords and small arms, but it would be of no use, as I cannot send them home or carry them with me. We could not send home the bodies of Captain Acker and Lieutenant Mitchell, as orders were against it, so we buried them near the Landing, where they can be easily found. We have done all we could for them, and preserved young Mitchell's watch, sword, and pistol. We must leave here soon, as it will be very unpleasant if it gets very warm; so far, it has been quite cool. Our wagons have not yet arrived, but it has ceased raining, and we have dried our clothes and feel quite comfortable.

It is wonderful how few of us were killed. At one place during the second action, where our battalion was engaged, there was a heavy growth of small trees and every one of them is either cut down with grape shot, or riddled with Minié balls. Hundreds of large trees in other places were cut down by shell and round balls of all kinds. Gen. [William T.] Sherman pursued the enemy on the evening after the battle, and discovered that they had burned their baggage trains, but left standing over 1,000 tents, which he brought back with him and presented a full set to our battalion.

Everybody expresses themselves quite satisfied with fighting, and none are anxious to have a duplicate of this last affair. Gen. [Ulysses S.] Grant told our major that the Fort Donelson fight was, as compared to this, as the morning dew to a heavy rain. It was most fortunate for him that Gen. [Don Carlos] Buell arrived, as he was thoroughly whipped on Sunday, and many regiments fled and took refuge under the cliff at the landing, and refused to return to duty. It is shameful how some of them acted; but most all fought splendidly, although one crack regiment (the Thirty-second of Indiana), broke through our line in retreat, during the fearful fire of the enemy. At one time we thought our little battalion would be annihilated, but he quickly rallied his men, and we did not partake of the fright. We know positively that in our third action, in which was engaged the Fifteenth, Sixteenth, and Nineteenth Regulars, and First Ohio and Third Kentucky, we were opposed by Gen. Beauregard in person, with 10,000 fresh troops. It was then that we gave them a continual fire, directed towards their flag, and the moment we ceased firing, and fixed bayonets and commenced the charge, they retreated, and as the growth of under-brush was so thick, we could not catch them, as they had gained the road. A report has just come in that the enemy are again advancing, and are within seven miles. I don't credit the report; however if they do come, I think they will be used up, as we are prepared and ready.

REGULAR.

SECOND IOWA INFANTRY
PITTSBURG LANDING, TENN., April 10.

Some days before this reaches you, you will have heard the particulars through the press of the greatest and bloodiest battle that has yet been fought on the Western Continent. This point is on the Tennessee River, nine miles from the Mississippi State line, and ten miles from the Alabama line. Beauregard, with a heavy force, advanced upon our outposts at daybreak, Sunday, the 6th last. Our troops gradually fell back, contesting the ground inch by inch. Our brigade consisting of the Second, Seventh, Twelfth, and Fourteenth Iowa, were ordered to the support of the centre, which was falling back. We were soon in the hottest part of the conflict, and three times the rebels were repulsed in their desperate charges on the Iowa Brigade. We held our position from 7 o'clock in the morning till 4 o'clock in the afternoon. At that time, it became apparent that we were outflanked by rebel re-enforcements. The order was given to retire. The Second and Seventh Iowa cut their way through, while a terrific cross-fire was poured into our flanks. The Twelfth and Fourteenth Iowa were surrounded before the order could reach them. They stood their ground manfully, but were compelled to surrender as prisoners of war after a spirited resistance. The Eighth Iowa were also taken prisoner, after doing some heavy old fighting.

Our regiment (Second Iowa) and the Seventh Regiment fell back about a mile, and rallied to the support of the heavy guns planted on a hill close by the river. The rebels advanced, ten regiments deep, confident of driving us into the river. They were allowed to advance within close range; then our heavy guns opened upon them, and our gunboats shelled them from the river. The slaughter was terrible, and they were forced to fall back.

During the night, we lay down by the batteries, amidst a drenching rain, the mortars and guns being worked at every half-hour, to give the rebels a lively remembrance, and keep them in a state of alarm. I never saw guns managed with such skill as ours were that afternoon and night. The noise was awful, sounded like continual peals of thunder and the crashing and smashing of the elements. The bombardment of Fort Donelson by the gunboats was no comparison to it.

At daybreak, Monday, having had re-enforcements from Gen. Buell's troops, our forces advanced upon the rebels, driving them back slowly. They fought with great determination, and acted like men determined to conquer or die. Toward the afternoon they were repulsed and driven back at every point. Our regiment was held as a support to the advancing columns during the morning; toward noon, our company were thrown out as skirmishers, and in the afternoon our regiment made one of the best bayonet charges of the day. The rebels don't seem to relish the point of the bayonet. Sunday, the battle was "nip and tuck," the fortunes of the day were wavering in the balance from side to side. Monday, we finally drove the rebels at every point, and the day was ours. It has been a dearly-bought victory, and I don't think that the battle is over yet. If we advance on Corinth, we are likely to have another terrible struggle. I suppose 30,000 men must have fallen in this combat, killed and wounded. On the rebel side, John C. Breckinridge is reported among the killed; also A. Sidney Johnston, and another brigadier-general killed. General [Braxton] Bragg is said to be wounded and a prisoner. Upon our side, General W.H.L. Wallace and General [Benjamin M.] Prentiss reported killed, and a host of officers, of all grades dead. I cannot obtain any reliable information about the result of the battle, the number killed, wounded, and prisoners, or the amount of artillery captured or taken. Everything is in confusion, so it will take a week to get at the truth.

I went through the engagement hardly getting a scratch. Several bomb shells exploded close to me, throwing dirt and mud over me, making me look as if I had been rolling in the gutters of New York on a rainy day. I felt thankful to think that I did not wear fine broadcloth that day, for they surely gave my ragged and dirty uniform a benefit. The battle was a sublime and yet an awful and terrible sight. The roar of musketry, the coarse thunder of the heavy artillery, belching out death and destruction; the explosion of shells, the groans and shrieks of the dying and wounded, the pools of blood, the dead and dying at every few steps, the shock and crash of small-arms, make up a scene of sublime horror that is indelibly stamped upon my memory. I had imagined such scenes in my earlier youth when reading tales of the Revolutionary struggle, Napoleon's battles, the war in the Crimea, but never dreamed that I should realize such scenes in my own experience. The fighting at Fort Donelson was completely cast in the shade by the cool courage and bull-dog obstinacy with which either side contested every inch of ground. The English press have spoken in rather a disparaging tone of the valor of the American nation. This action will show to the world that neither the North nor South can be excelled in courage or valor by any race upon the face of the globe. Although battling for the National Government, I could not but feel proud that the force engaged against us that displayed such desperate deeds of valor were of the same race, blood, and people. Of those opposed to us, I have no doubt the majority conscientiously believed that we were infringing upon the rights of the South. Holding those views, I do not wonder at their conduct on the field. We look at it from a different stand-point; but we cannot but regret that political differences should drive the South into rebellion against the best Government that, we think, has ever existed. I hope the time is not far distant when we will again be a united people. What a front we can then present to the world! Foreign powers will then be a little more cautious in their intervention, when they know what kind of material they have to contend against. A foreign war would re-unite the popular heart of the American people. The rebel prisoners with whom I have conversed speak as if they would like to return under the old flag, and live on terms of peace and harmony with the whole country. There has been much misrepresentation made to the people of the South by their leaders.

In the fight, our regiment had eighty-six killed and wounded, out of about four hundred men in the action. At Fort Donelson, our regiment had two hundred and nine killed and wounded. So, if we have another fight, the regiment will show rather a slim front.

April 11th.—This morning, we have reports that Beauregard is going to make another stand some eight miles from here. It is probable that Gen. Buell will wait a few days for re-enforcements before making another advance. We have reports again to-day, that Island No. 10 is captured, with some ten thousand prisoners. I hope it is correct; for our forces have been at it a long time.

What can Gen. McClellan be doing in Virginia? Thirty to fifty thousand of the rebels that fought here are said to be from Manassas! Many took an active part in the battle of Bull Run. It is probable that part of the "Army of the Potomac" will be sent to our assistance. Of the soldiers engaged in the contest, the average will be fully one hundred men killed and wounded in every regiment.

On the battle-field, some wounded rebels fell into our hands, to whom I gave some water from my canteen. They thanked me again and again, and said they had been led to expect different treatment. The celebrated Washington Artillery Battery, of New Orleans, fell into our hands. It is the same battery that did such awful execution on our troops at Bull Run.

        Yours truly,   H.

April 27, 1862
TWENTY-FIFTH REGIMENT, N.Y.S.V.

CAMP BEFORE YORKTOWN, VA., April 16.

An intense desire to know of the futurity and welfare of the SUNDAY MERCURY and its proprietors prompts me thus to encroach on your valuable time, hearing that no letters from soldiers in the Army of the Potomac are allowed to be published. In one of your recent issues I saw a letter from a member of Mott's Battery, dated from Hampton. I wish to know the particulars and limits as to writing. I have written from Alexandria, giving an account of our march to Fairfax and route to Alexandria. It was not published. I carefully avoided anything relating to the number of our forces. I would continue to write if it should be left to your discretion to insert it or not. I present, unless you wish it for personal perusal. My company being on skirmishing duty, we were the first to get a sight of this Sebastopol, and I shall, if you wish it, give you general views.

Guns are going off on the York River from the gun-boats continually; the Fifteenth New York [Engineers] Volunteers are making bastions and gabions; bridges are being built across the York River, and there is great excitement going ahead. Balloon ascensions have been made this last week continually, by Professor Wise [Thaddeus Lowe]. Our division being under the fire of the rebel batteries, we took position on the flank. There are great anecdotes told of our sharpshooters killing their gunners inside the batteries. Another battle like Corinth and good-bye to the fated hopes of Jeff. The breastworks for the siege guns are going up. Their centre fort is strong, and protected by a swampy ground in front. None of their heavy guns have opened yet. They sent up a balloon yesterday while we were on picket. It did not reach a great elevation, and came down suddenly. Last Saturday week was our day of coming up and engaging them until we found their positions and strength. I shall reserve an account of it, waiting your permission whether I shall write or not.

I feel rather lonesome; no paper to look at; it seems as if all my friends had forgot me. I await some news; I wish I could get your paper.

Yours, truly,   H. L.

{We understand the Government allows soldiers' letters to pass again. Don't predict or divulge movements to be made. Only give an account of what is past, or passing, and all will be right.—EDS.}

May 4, 1862
BERDAN'S SHARPSHOOTERS, (First U. S. Sharpshooters)

CAMP WINFIELD SCOTT, BEFORE YORKTOWN, April 27.

Last winter, in one of my notes to you, I predicted a good name for the Sharpshooters if ever they took the field, and already have they earned it, and earned it with an arm that, to say the least, suits us poorly. But for this one stumbling-block, our path hence onward were a smooth one. If we only had what for so long a period we have longed for—the Sharpe rifle—we could go forward with a heart in the cause , and ready for any post or duty. We have only the Colt rifle, and it is not the gun for sharpshooters. "Old California", of whom mention has already been made in your columns (we know him as Mr. [Truman] Head. of G. C., Michigan—a man of considerable property, somewhat aged, and of many years' experience in the Rocky Mountains), and of whom peculiar notice is taken on account of the execution he has done, carries one of Sharpe's rifles—not a telescopic one, as stated in the *Herald* of the 10th. Every time he fires it is bound to count; the fatality lies partly in the man, and partly in the splendid weapon that he has (bought with his own money), and a specimen of what we all should have.

In the affair of the Fifth, the work done with our Colt guns, though fully equal to our expectations—for we never expected much of them—proved them not to be such an arm as we should have. The principal part of the effective shooting on that day was done by the target-rifles of Cos. C and E. We are proud to have received the special commendation of the commander-in-chief, and feel the honor of the same; but among ourselves we are still dissatisfied, and cannot be otherwise while we lack what we always have looked for and have so often been promised, and are still promised. It may be we shall get them yet; I hope so.

More than a week has passed since we ran upon this hold of the enemy, and the great work of preparation goes on. I could tell you of thousands, and tens and twenties of thousands of infantry daily and nightly pouring in; of long trains of wagons, and acres of artillery; rows of shot and shell to be measured by the rod, and huge earthworks born in a single night. On the river, too, are dangerous-looking vessels—part and parcel of the "Anaconda"—and once in a while the white smoke puffs out from the side of one, and a hissing "reminder" rushes through the air to those who occupy the water-batteries at Gloucester and Yorktown. It is a deep and fearful study to see this machinery of war get ready for working. Science contributes its lion's share in the balloons, the electric wire, the nightly and daily signaling, the fearful complications of huge shells of unknown contents and curious construction, and a hundred different devices of destruction.

All the while we lie here patiently awaiting the word to go on, and more or less thoughtlessly employed, pass the time as the great work proceeds. Here, when or where the grand affair opens, we know not. We are but the humble tools of those who are to "boss the job". Of three things there is a certainty: the fight is coming soon—it will be a hard one—but Yorktown will fall.

Yours,   RAMMER.

May 11, 1862

To Richmond!

"Forward to Richmond"! are the talismanic words which now beckon our brave heroes to victory—and there should be no cloud-gathering in the shape of a halt. Let there be the same feeling of unanimity and good-will among all classes of our population that pervades throughout the several divisions of the great Union Army, and the Rebellion will go down crushed into oblivion. All eyes are now turned toward Richmond, to see if the three grand columns converging thither shall effectually free Virginia from the withering blight of insurrection which has well-nigh wasted her substance and expatriated her inhabitants. Next, every gaze is riveted upon Norfolk, and the rear attack of Burnside. Another glance reveals the operations of [David] Hunter between Savannah and Charleston. Here is our weakest point; and if we have 10,000 spare troops, thither should they hasten at once. So far as the extreme South and West is concerned, [Gen. Henry] Halleck and Butler are more than a match for Beauregard and [Mansfield] Lovell. The city of Mobile is at any moment within our reach. Between every point indicating the grand base of operations, parallel lines are being run by the continuous advance of the Federal army, which completely prevent any concerted plans of defence from being inaugurated by the enemy. He is virtually surrounded at all points, and "unconditional surrender" is the only hope to which he can turn.

We can but join our fellow-citizens and readers generally in mutual interchanges of congratulations at the brilliant achievements of our arms everywhere. Let the capture of Richmond be followed with rejoicings all through the land. Let us have a holiday—a triumphant merry-making to mark the successes of our arms at Yorktown, and New Orleans. Make the welkin ring with national salutes, and let the streets be gay with national emblems—make our houses bright with light, and our public places resound with music, in honor of the glorious conquests won by worthy sons of honored sires. We feel, we know, that the Republic is saved!

May 18, 1862

SIXTY-NINTH REGIMENT, N.Y.S.V.

YORKTOWN, VA., May 8.

Contrary to anticipations the army of the Potomac have entered Yorktown, as at Manassas, without fighting. Our army are following them up, and will, it is confidently expected, annihilate them before they leave this state. The Sixty-ninth Regiment reached Ship Point three weeks ago, from Alexandria, during which time the men have been variously engaged in making gabions, assisting in erecting a mortar battery, repairing roads, etc. About the time everything was ready to open fire on the traitors—works which required an enormous amount of labor—they found out they could not resist the pressure, and our troops entered into possession of the deserted forts on Sunday morning last. If they had made a stand here there must necessarily have been an awful loss of life, for the place is, in a great measure, naturally fortified; but of our success there could not be a doubt, for Gen. McClellan had made almost superhuman efforts for a glorious triumph. It is surprising how men will howl at such a man as Gen. McClellan. Let them come here and see what had to be accomplished before fear was struck into the hearts of the foe, and then forever "dry-up". This peninsula is a curious mixture of swamps and sandy earth, and the absence of any kind of stone is at once observable. The climate must be unhealthy in the summer months, as stagnant pools abound in every direction. The Sixty-ninth, nevertheless, has suffered little; Richard McGovern of Co. I, and Sergeant [John] Reed of Co. K, being our only loss, except one who was accidentally killed by the falling of a tree. There are a few men in the regiment who might be discharged, without disadvantage to the Government; but the "medical staff" say, curiously enough, they have not the power. It would seem worse than useless to have a poor fellow kept in the service who is of no earthly use as a soldier; still the doctors tell them they can do nothing for them, and they are compelled to remain to pine away and die, without any person interesting themselves in their behalf. The captains, who were glad to recruit them in New York, ask them to drink, etc., now don't care a cent what happens to them, whether they live or die.

It is amusing to see maps of Yorktown and its fortifications in some of the New York newspapers. The illustration in a daily paper of Tuesday last looked about as much like the Empire City and its defences as it resembled Yorktown. Those in the SUNDAY MERCURY, as a general thing, are correct. It was a source of gratification to the writer to receive, a few days after landing at Ship's Point, a copy of the SUNDAY MERCURY, the first since the 14th of March. It was extensively borrowed, and the boy's eyes brightened at the sight of their favorite paper.

The brigade will go on board ship here for West Point, some distance up the York River. The men are in excellent health and spirits. Peddlers and sutlers are making money fast around here, enormous prices being charged for everything. The poor soldier is robbed at every point. Contractors rob him out of clothing, money, and the patriotic sutler charges him fabulous prices for such things as tobacco, soft bread, pipes, pies, etc., etc. I dropped into a miller's house the other day, and found the old man selling his Confederate money to Union soldiers. Our men bought them as curiosities, $1 and $2 bills being freely given for 25 cents, the miller having no faith in the stability of Jeff Davis' Government. A member of the Second New York, a short time after landing at Ship Point, went to a house in the neighborhood to make some purchases, and, after having done so, tendered a five-dollar United States Treasury note in payment; but the woman would take no such money—nothing but rebel paper would satisfy her. Our friend bethought himself of a cut of a $20 Confederate bill in one of the New York illustrated papers, went to his knapsack, cut it out, brought it to the housewife, and received his full change in good money. Not a bad joke, that.

Your, etc.,   NON-COM.

MOZART REGIMENT
ON THE MARCH TO RICHMOND, VA., May 12.

I hope you will excuse me for my long silence, and I am sure you will when I tell you that we have been busily engaged during the last few weeks.

On the morning of Sunday, May 4, at three o'clock, we left our camp to go on picket in the trenches before Yorktown, after taking a round-about course, in order to escape observation by the enemy. We got to our posts at daybreak. The enemy kept up a sharp fire for about half an hour, when word came that they were evacuating Yorktown. We were ordered to leap over our trenches, and go over to the rebel works at double-quick, which we did, throwing away our overcoats and haversacks as we went. We soon came up to the enemy's trenches, and leaped over the parapet. Co. I was the first company to enter the works, followed by the regiment. We did not have our colors with us. The Second New York Fire Zouaves planted the first American flag on the enemy's intrenchments. Going over, we expected to have a large fight with their rear guard, but the birds had flown, leaving behind them all their camp equipage. A great many old United States muskets and some rifles were found in their works. I am sorry to tell you that we lost two of our best men, killed that morning by a torpedo, set in the ground, and seven wounded. The ground was full of torpedoes and percussion-shells, set in the ground, so arranged that when a man would step on one of them, it would explode and kill perhaps a dozen or more men, but we will have a reckoning with the rebels yet.

As soon as it was known that the enemy abandoned his works, our whole army was in motion. Our brigade ([David B.] Birney's) marched in the afternoon, and passed through the enemy's works. When night set in, we halted, and bivouacked on the roadside. We passed several deserted camps on the way. The enemy had some fine new tents and good log-houses, but they were in a filthy condition. It is no wonder the rebel soldiers die off so fast. The are too lazy to keep themselves or their quarters clean.

Next morning, we were on the march again. Rain set in during the night, and marching was unpleasant, on account of the liquid state of the mud. Before we started, we could hear the thunder of artillery. We soon became convinced that a fight was going on. When we got within four miles of Williamsburg, we could hear volley after volley of musketry, succeeded by artillery. We were ordered to throw off our knapsacks, and prepare for a fight.

We soon came up to the scene of action, and found our men in a woeful plight; they were fighting against an overwhelming enemy, who was in the act of turning one of our flanks as we came in.

The Thirty-eighth and Fortieth New York Regiments were ordered into the front as we went in. The band struck up "Yankee Doodle", and, with a wild cheer, we dashed upon the enemy, driving them back with terrible loss. The ground was covered with dead and wounded. As night set in, the firing ceased on both sides, and we lay down on the wet and bloody ground (without anything to eat or drink), ready to renew the fight in the morning; but the enemy withdrew during that night, and left us masters of the field, as well as the handsome little town of Williamsburg, which, of course, became Union after the rebels had left. Deserters come every day in crowds; they say the rebellion is played out, and not worth fighting for. We were engaged for three days after the battle in burying the dead. We got great praise for our gallantry from Gens. Heintzelman and [Philip] Kearny. We are to have the word "Williamsburg" on our banner in letters of gold. We are now on the march after the enemy. We are sixteen miles from Williamsburg; we have lost many men, but none of our courage; and if we meet the rebels in a fair fight, we will make them rue the day they met the Mozart Regiment in battle.

Hoping to write the next letter to you from Richmond, I remain yours, truly,

HIGH PRIVATE, REAR RANK.

SECOND FIRE ZOUAVES

NEAR WEST POINT, VA., May 13, 1862.

Our regiment was ordered on picket duty on the morning of Sunday, May 4, 4 A.M. Shortly after 6 A.M., a report reached us that Yorktown was evacuated (which we had already surmised), our colonel immediately sent our colors forward, and thus the colors of the Second New York Fire Zouaves, were the first to be planted on the rebel walls before Yorktown. At 10, A.M., we returned to our camp, and commenced preparations for the pursuit, which our brigade (the Excelsior), commenced at 1 P.M., during the afternoon we marched about 8 miles, and bivouacked in the woods. During the night it commenced raining, and at daylight the roads were almost impassable; every man felt cold, weary, and hungry. Still onward we pressed, anxious to meet the enemy, and drive him on!

At 6, A.M., Monday, May 5th, we were again on the trail, the rain still descending in torrents, our boys feeling more anxious for their rifles than for themselves. Between 9 and 10, A.M. (as near as I could judge), the action commenced, and from that time till about 3, P.M., General [Joseph] Hooker's Division—comprising the First and Eleventh Massachusetts, Twenty-sixth Pennsylvania, Second New Hampshire, Fifth, Sixth, Seventh, and Eighth New Jersey, and First, Third, Fourth, and Fifth Regiments Excelsior Brigade—contended against and held at bay 30,000 rebels.

The enemy's works extended from the York to the James River. An abattis was formed on their entire front, by the trees being felled in every possible direction, and behind this the enemy ensconced themselves. Rifle-pits were dug in every practicable position to rake our men. Nothing daunted, our men pressed on, and held their ground against overpowering numbers until 3 o'clock in the afternoon, when the Second Michigan, Thirty-seventh, Thirty-eighth, Fifty-fifth, and Sixty-second New York, and some others, arrived, and drove the enemy back. At 5, P.M., General [Winfield Scott] Hancock's Brigade came upon the enemy's left, and made his brilliant bayonet charge, losing but twenty killed and wounded.

Is it not enough to sicken a man to think that his honors are to be taken from him in this manner? Contrast Superb Hancock's loss with the loss of the Excelsior Brigade! The four regiments, in killed, wounded, and missing, have suffered a loss of 700—one-fourth of what went into action! General Hooker's Division, which I have named, including the Excelsior Brigade, has lost 1,570. Our four regiments have lost half of that number, and yet we get no credit. Who did the fighting? Who gets the praise? Comment is unnecessary. Let me not be accused of pilfering honor from other regiments. On the contrary, I wish it to be plainly understood that the fighting was all done before Hancock's Brigade came up, and by the regiments that I have named. There may be some regiments that I have not named, as in the excitement I could not see everything. No braver man can be found than Gen. Hooker. In the thickest of the fight, and where the bullets flew like hail, he was to be found urging his men on. I have just learned from authentic sources, that the rebel Capt. [John] Lea, who was taken prisoner, has asserted, on the honor of a gentleman, that there were no troops in the batteries that were charged on by Gen. Hancock's Brigade, as he was stationed there, and retired previous to the "celebrated charge". He acknowledges the bravery of Hooker's Division, and evinces regret that the honors they have won are not bestowed upon them.

The Second Fire Zouaves (Fourth Excelsior) have lost some of their best men. Our lieutenant-colonel, Lewis Benedict, Jr., wounded and taken prisoner; Captain John Feeney, I fear, mortally wounded; Lieutenant John J. Glass, killed; poor Glass, every man in the regiment loved him—kind and affectionate to everyone—I never heard him utter a harsh word to any; he was buried on the battle-field near the spot where he fell. Our entire casualties will amount to one hundred and twenty in killed, wounded, and missing. Our colonel [William R. Brewster] behaved nobly, over-exertion and exposure has been too much for him, and he is now very ill. Major John D. Moriarty is in command of the regiment, and is, as he always has been, a favorite with the boys.

The battle of Williamsburg is the first our regiment was engaged in, and while I have endeavored to speak for every regiment that went into the action before the enemy commenced his retreat, I leave our actions to others to relate, confident that we will command the admiration of the friends of the volunteer Fire Department, when the truth is known.

Yours,   EXCELSIOR.

May 25, 1862

FIRE DEPARTMENT NEWS

AN INCIDENT OF THE FIGHT AT WILLIAMSBURG.—During the desperate fight of the Second Fire Zouaves (and in fact the whole of the Excelsior Brigade) at Williamsburg, where they contended against a force three times numerically greater than there own, the heroic Glass (ex-foreman of Engine Co. No. 16) fell mortally wounded. Knowing that if the rebels came back upon the ground, according to their thievish and brutal instincts, they would strip the bodies of the Union soldiers of everything of valuable, he placed his badge under a log beside him. His supposition was correct; for, being re-enforced, a portion of the Division under Hooker fell back, and the sneaking villains began to search for plunder among our dead.

In a short time the brigade rallied, and drove the enemy in confusion before them. Poor Glass was discovered still living, but fast journeying to "that bourne whence no traveler returns." As his comrades bent over, and watched his eyes closing in death, he kept pointing to the log. None could understand him at first; but finally, on examining the spot they found the badge; and contented to know it was safe, he peacefully breathed his last.

NINETY-FIFTH REGIMENT, N.Y.S.V.

AQUIA CREEK, VA., May 21.

I stole away from my squad last Sunday, after working an hour, and went to take a stroll through the country. I find that the poorer class of people around here are as rank abolitionists as ever [Horace] Greeley or [William Cullen] Bryant were. They state that the niggers injure white labor. The large slaveholders all had slaves; and when they had more work than the slaves could do they hired the free niggers of the neighborhood in preference to whites—as they worked cheaper, and answered their purpose just as well. A poor white man could only get twenty-five cents per day and board. In fact, from the account that one man gave me, the poor whites are treated as bad as the negroes by the rich planters of the country.

The people, taking them altogether, as a class, are the most ignorant I have ever known. One of them—a man who is said to own a thousand acres of land—argued on me, the other day, that South Carolina was a part of Virginia State. The women, young and old, smoke or chew snuff. The most of them are dirty and slip-shod—although I have seen some exceptions, but, "like angel's visits, few and far between."

The rich people are morose and unsocial. They charge exorbitant prices for the butter, milk, and eggs that the soldiers buy from them. They would show their teeth if they dared; but that time has passed, and it is only in their dark and ominous glances that you can read the hatred they dare not express in words.

I met one man, whose name is Butler. He is a poor man, and, of course, is a Unionist. The accounts he gave me of the atrocities committed by the rebel soldiers are dreadful. How General [Theophilus H.] Holmes allowed such deeds to be committed are beyond my comprehension. He has told me that the North Carolina troops, who were stationed here last fall and winter, met a young married woman in the woods near Aquia Village and outraged her person. Her name was Gallatroin. She was found next morning dead where they had left her; and yet, the men who committed this barbarous deed were never punished for it.

The same fellows also went to a free negro's house and violated the persons of his wife and daughter, and shot him dead on the spot because he tried to prevent them.

Another man has told me that they could not enter a house without trying to violate the females, or else grossly insulting them, before they left.

They also burned or scuttled all the boats belonging to the poor fishermen, before they left, and were going to put the torch to the mill, and thus leave the people to starve, when the news arrived of our approach and prevented them from doing it.

The principal town in Stafford county is Stafford Courthouse. It is composed of a store, a court-house, and three or four private residences. There was a Dr. G. I. Conway who lived there. He was employed by the rebel authorities to hunt up the people of Union sentiments and report them. Two Northern men who had settled there and bought land from one of the planters were the first informed on. These men's names were Maury. A party of Arkansas soldiers went to their houses in the night-time, dragged them from their beds, and after treating them to a ride on a rail, gave them their choice to either join the Confederate Army or else be shot on the spot. Of course they joined. They were sent away to Louisiana, and the man that sold their land to them had the unparalleled impudence to try and sell it again.

There are a good many soldiers, who have deserted from the enemy, or else pretend they have deserted, living in their own homes. I, for my own part, consider them spies, and think that the officers ought to look sharper after them.

One of our captains was shot last week, and yet I saw him on Sunday sitting in the house of a man who was prevented from joining his regiment by the Rappahannock bridge being burned before he arrived there.

He is also employed to carry the cannon away from here. He has got a son in the rebel army, and is represented to me by the people around here as a professed Yankee-hater.

He has got two or three daughters, and that is the reason, perhaps, that the officers go there. But, in my opinion, they should hold no intercourse with the traitors, who have tried to destroy the Union, that they are paid for supporting.

I have heard a very laughable account about [Gen. Daniel] Sickles' Brigade. It seems that part of it went to Stafford Court House. They wanted tobacco from the store-keeper Morgan; he refused them. They took the tobacco by force, and fetched the old rascal out about half a mile from his house, and compelled him to run double-quick back again, at the point of the bayonet.

Troops are pouring in every day. A Maine Battery passed through here yesterday. The dock is loaded with ammunition and provisions. We are expecting to leave every day for Fredericksburg, but they still find something to detain us.

I send you a list of names polled in this county to know whether the action of the Convention that was held in this State 13th of Feb., 1861, should be submitted to the people for ratification or rejection. I have some more very curious papers that I will send you.

My letters, I know, are very faulty, but when a man has to work from sunrise to sunset, and then go to bed at 9 P.M., it will be seen that he has no time to spare, and anything he writes must be done in a hurry.

T. O. M.

June 1, 1862

AN ENGLISH CARTE DE VISITE—"Macmillan's Magazine" exults in a contributor who betrays his kindly feelings for America in the following gentlemanly and elegant portrait of our honest Chief Magistrate. Of Mr. Lincoln—"To say that he is ugly, is nothing; to add that his figure is grotesque, is to convey no adequate impression. Fancy a man six feet high, and thin out of proportion; with long bony arms and legs, which somehow seem to be always in the way; with great rugged furrowed hands, which grasp you like a vice when shaking yours; with a long scraggy neck, and a chest too narrow for the great arms at its side. Add to this figure a head cocoanut-shaped and somewhat too small for such a stature, covered with rough uncombed and uncombable hair, that stands out in every direction at once; a face furrowed, wrinkled, and indented as though it had been scarred by vitriol; a high narrow forehead, and, sunk deep beneath bushy eyebrows; too bright, somewhat dreamy eyes that seem to gaze through you without looking at you; a few irregular blotches of black, bristly hair in the place where beard and whiskers ought to grow; a close-set, thin-lipped, stern mouth, with two rows of large, white teeth, and a nose and ears which have been taken by mistake from a head of twice the size. Clothe this figure, then, in a long, tight, badly-fitting suit of black, creased, soiled, and puckered up at every salient point of the figure (and every point of this figure *is* salient); put on large, ill-fitting boots, gloves too long for the long, bony fingers, and a fluffy hat, covered to the top with dusty, puffy crape; and then add to all this an air of strength, physical as well as moral, and a strange look of dignity coupled with all this grotesqueness, and you will have the impression left upon me by Abraham Lincoln.

MILITARY MATTERS

OUR CORRESPONDENTS.—During the present war five of our special correspondents have been killed or severely wounded, and three more imprisoned. This shows that our letter-writers are not outsiders, and that when there is any fighting to be done they are where the balls fall thickest.

THIRTY-EIGHTH REGIMENT, N.Y.S.M.

EN ROUTE FOR RICHMOND, VA., May 28.

Now that our forces are so near Richmond, a few incidents of prison life in the tobacco manufactories might be interesting to the reader in search of truth. After the Battle of Bull Run, on the 21st of July, 1861, among those captured I was marched to Manassas Junction, where we remained in the drizzling rain, which fell all night. Owing to the extreme fatigue of body attending on the heat of the day, forced marching, and the battle-field, I slept peaceably and sound, and for a moment on awakening the next morning, it was almost impossible for me to decide where I was; but gradually a vivid sense of my position forced itself upon me, and I realized that I was a prisoner. All day on the 22nd, following the battle, we remained standing in the slowly-falling rain, wetting us to the skin. Around us stood guards, close together, and beyond them a gaping multitude of idle gazers, looking at the "Yankees"—evidently, from the way they eyed us, supposing us to be some curious animal, and remarking: "Why, they look just like our folks!" "Lord, they're white folks just like we are." And asking us: "What made you come down here for?" All day long we were kept in this position, nothing given to us to eat, and—must I say it?—water could not be obtained, unless, thanks to God for the falling rain of that day, when caught in an india-rubber blanket, poured into a tin-cup. And bitter, brackish, sickish to the taste as was this water, 'twas like nectar to the half-famished men who, many of them, had not tasted a drop of water since the previous bloody day. About 5 o'clock, P.M., however, some hard biscuit and rancid bacon were divided among us, and we were marched to the railroad depot, and placed in baggage and freight cars, *en route* for Richmond. Here Fortune was propitious, for the rain dripping from the tops of the cars presented a rich harvest of pure water to the thirsty men. It was a perfect godsend. It was hard in the extreme to see the avidity with which the poor fellows sought to catch the falling drops, as their thirst was doubly increased by the salt meat just served out.

About six o'clock the next afternoon, we arrived in Richmond, and, well guarded, were marched through the streets, hooted, hissed, and blackguarded in a manner I could hardly have believed would have occurred in a city belonging to a civilized nation. But seeing what I have of them has changed my mind considerably. About dark, we reached one of the vile tobacco factories destined to receive us, and from whose doors many of the brave boys who entered them were never more to pass, until in a pine coffin, conveyed in a rickety cart, they should fill a grave in some distant portion of the negro burying-ground of the capital city of Virginia. Is it too much to ask one passing thought to those who thus died and still fill the humble tenement? In the building with myself were five hundred and thirty-eight souls—two hundred on one floor, and three hundred and thirty-eight on the floor above, these floors being some one hundred by thirty feet. Here, for some three or four weeks—if I may be allowed the expression—we were left to rot; and ere that time, vermin had made their appearance, and, notwithstanding all endeavors to the contrary, "reigned supreme". It was a fine specimen of close packing, at night, when we turned in, and it would have been difficult to one not accustomed to moving among a crowd to have made their way through the room with stepping on some part of the human mass that strewed the floor. Even in the day it was difficult navigation.

Lieutenant [David] Todd, of Kentucky, C. S. A., notorious for his cruelty, was in charge of us. Much has been already said of his treatment of our suffering prisoners of war. An incident, however, which I do not think has been in print, occurring at this time, and in which he was chief actor, will better prove his cruel treatment than any other I could mention.

One morning, in passing through one of the crowded rooms, stopped by the crowd who obstructed his passage, he bade them give way; they not obeying his order as quickly as he wished, he drew his sword, and making a step toward one of the nearest of the crowd, who belonged to the First Minnesota Regiment, passed it through the lower portion of the leg, and in withdrawing it he literally cut the piece of flesh to the bone. Remarking coolly, as he passed on: "Take care of the man and clear the road." This act was on par with his other cruelties while in charge. By his orders our prisoners were fired on in the windows, and no less than five wounded and three killed. Another day we were refused water for more than six hours in the day, for the mere crime of spilling some on the floor; and frequently our meals were not served until late in the day. Some four weeks after our arrival, the wounded from Bull Run arrived in Richmond, and some placed in the general hospital, and the remainder—by far the largest portion—conveyed to our prison, Hanwood's Tobacco Factory, on Main, corner of Twenty-sixth street, it being the most convenient of access and best adapted to hospital purposes.

After remaining in the prison hospital till the middle of November, I was removed to quarters, as they called the prison; here I remained until my return home. During my short existence in the den I saw hard scenes, as well as amusing ones; spent sad hours, and a few happy ones. In the room, here you'd see a sick man lying on the hard floor groaning; there, another who had lost his reason—several cases of this kind occurred; again, a party of bluff players appear busily engaged transferring from one to another Confederate shinplasters. In one corner is the bone manufactory, where from beef bones, rings, brooches, breast-pins, hair-pins, shawl-pins, and other trinkets are constructed by the workmen, and many were done in a masterly manner, and the proceeds devoted to obtaining the meal not furnished by the Confederacy, viz., dinner. At dinner, we had, bread, five ounces; beef boiled, five ounces; soup, one pint. No wonder many went hungry, and couldn't help it. In the centre of the room the stove, prison made (it is quite singular how many things a man can make if he will only take a hold and try), with a variety of different concoctions—quite as difficult it is to discover what they are made of as it is to understand how the pans are constructed in which they are cooking. Here, again, we have a grand drill of cripples we have been discharged as cured from the hospital, some minus a leg, some an arm, and others with a leg some three or four inches short. And as they go marching around the room, merrily going through the military drill, it looks comical in the extreme. I must say, the ones who seemed to have suffered the most pain seemed to be the merriest party of the lot. Some singing, others promenading, fill up the heterogeneous mass of prisoners of war.

On the 1st of January, we received news of our approaching freedom; and on the 3rd were marched to the steamer Northampton, on which we received one good meal—coffee, fried bacon and pork, chickens and turkey stew, and boiled corned beef. I suppose that they were trying to erase the impression of our former feeds from our mind, thinking that if we went home with full stomachs it would pay for our fasting the whole time we had boarded at the expense of the Southern Confederacy. That afternoon the old flag floated before us once more, and when it came upon us it was too much for us to bear. Our hearts overflowed, and every eye filled with tears, that had been long locked up in the adamantine chambers of our hearts. The stirring moment was deepened by the band on board the steam transport George Washington, which received us from the Confederate steam transport, striking up the old loved tune, "Home Sweet Home". And as the gentle strains floated over the quiet waters of the James River, and the Stars and Stripes waved above us, it seemed the happiest moment of my life. At Baltimore we were received by the Union Relief Associations, who treated us in good style. Our boys gave us a splendid reception in the regiment, and our colonel, a furlough. Since its expiration, I have been with the regiment. While passing through Williamsburg, a few days after the late battle, I was informed by two of my prison comrades, who were standing guard over the Secesh, that a number of the Fifth Georgia Regiment, who stood guard over us in Richmond last summer, were inside, and that they had recognized some of them, and been remembered by them in return. At this moment, I heard some one calling from the window, and discovered a Secesh, who said:

"Say, wasn't you the man who used to carry the bottles over after medicine from the place whar de sick Yankees was in?"

"Just so," said I.

"I reckoned you was. I stood guard over dem dare. Doesn't you remember me?"

"No, sir," I answered.

I thought his face familiar, but could not place him. As he belongs to the Fifth Georgia, I suppose he told the truth. It would be difficult for a person to have seen me passing across the Main street of Richmond with my armful of bottles, and a guard with musket and bayonet marching stiffly behind me, to have forgotten so novel a picture. Several of our regiment, also prisoners of war, recognized some of the Secesh soldiers, and conversed with them of Richmond. Sergeant C. W. Fairfield, captured while on picket last August at Munson's Hill, Va., saw the same party who captured him immediately. Other recognizances have been also made on both sides.

I hope I shall soon be able to write to you from Richmond, and I hope I may chronicle the delivery of our gallant major, James Decatur Potter, who has been a prisoner since the 21st of July last.

I remain yours, respectfully,   E.H.K.

Edward H. Kellogg, age 23, of Company K, 38th New York Infantry was mustered out with the regiment on June 22, 1863. He later served in the 17th New York, and 39th New York Infantry. According to his pension file, Kellogg listed his occupation as a journalist. In 1875 he married Marie Curtin of Brooklyn and the couple had two children. Edward Kellogg died on February 21, 1898 of heart failure.

THIRTY-EIGHTH REGIMENT, N.Y.S.M.

EN ROUTE FOR RICHMOND, VA., May 22.

We are in pursuit of the chivalry and are soon to lay our clutches on them; that is if they stand at some place and give fight in earnest, not like they did at Williamsburg, where the darned mean skunks ran like so many sheep, leaving their dead and wounded behind them. We are but partly avenged on them for making us run at Bull Run. We will soon have full revenge, thanks to our Little Corporal.

I assisted in burying some of our dead, and I felt while laying some of my late comrades in the wet earth of Virginia, that I could whip about a whole regiment of rebel thieves myself. I noticed quite a number of Indians lying dead on the field.

Talk of mud in New York. Pshaw! you never saw any mud in New York in comparison with what we went through on our way to the battle. We went through mud up to our knees. It was near 4 o'clock before we got on the field. On nearing the field we were hailed with shouts and cheers by the regiments that had been engaged for some time. A band of music struck up "Yankee Doodle" and other patriotic airs. We little heeded much just at that time, splash up to our waists nearly in mud. All the same, boys, go in and give them fits. "There goes one of my shoes," cries Carney. He wanted a diving-bell to get it, he said, when he whipped a few Secesh. We then filed through a thick wood for near a half a mile, then came to a front face and marched to the edge of the wood, where we met the first fire of the enemy, and where we lost the first man. He cried out: "I am shot boys, but it is for the Union. Go in and give them fits." We went tumbling over felled trees to the open road, the balls coming thick and fast in the meantime. When we got on the road we met our general (Kearny). He was sitting composedly on his horse as if he was reviewing his troops. I shall never forget his cool, calm words to us. He said: "Boys, cross the fence, and charge on them; let them feel your bayonets." Over the fence we leaped, hardly stopping to discharge our rifles; our colonel leading and cheering us on, aided by the lieutenant-colonel. Two braver men I never saw. Our men were falling very fast. The Secesh began to waver and fall back. We put volley after volley into them as they retreated. It was by this time quite dark. We commenced to find our wounded and carry them to the surgeons. The most of them had to stay in the wet woods all night long, with their wounds unattended to. What officer is to blame, I cannot say. It was a great shame, whoever's fault it was. Very few of us got any sleep that night. The next morning we received orders to go to Williamsburg; we were encamped on the east side of the city. A detail was made from each company to go and assist to bury the dead, and the balance was put on guard.

In the city there is where you can see the Southern ladies promenade with a revolver and a dirk in their waist-belts. I had one say to me if a Yankee came into her house she would blow his brains out! I tried to talk Union to her, but she could not see it. We had to watch the niggers very close, to prevent them from setting the city on fire. They got awful independent, as an old gentleman remarked to me. "One would think," he said, "that they owned us, instead of us owning them."

I saw and conversed with a great many of the wounded and prisoners, most of them were conscript. They, as a general thing, said that they hoped we would be victorious. Some told me that half of the Southern army was getting greatly in favor of our cause, and a number of regiments would not fire at us when ordered. There are about ten surgeons belonging to the rebel army in Williamsburg, attending to their wounded. They have the liberty to go around the city as much as they please.

We go to-morrow to New Kent Court-House. I suppose we will have a skirmish or two on the way.

Our colonel (J.H.H. Ward) has been in his twelfth fight.

I have not seen the SUNDAY MERCURY for two weeks. It seems like meeting an old friend to get it. It is acknowledged by all to be the best paper for us to get. My paper is read by a great many. I think it would be quite a curiosity for you to see one of your papers after it has been read by us fellows.

Yours, truly,   BOWERY.

FIFTH REGIMENT, N.Y.S.V. (DURYEE'S ZOUAVES)

EN ROUTE TO RICHMOND, May 24.

Let me glorify our regiment and especially our company a little. We have had the post of honor—that is, of danger—on the right. While I was reading your paper, a shot or shell—yes, it was a shell, but from a rifled gun—flew directly over and not ten yards above our tent. Let me go back to our work at Battery No. 10—a battery directly in face of the enemy's works at Yorktown. It was a mere mound of earth in front of a trench. Two rows of gabions had to be placed behind this mound of earth, and then the earth thrown upon top (this was done under fire remember), and the magazines commenced. By Thursday—the first day on which I rejoined the company—one gun had been dragged up and placed into position; but the embrasures were fated never to be opened. Thursday, the body of the magazines was completed. About 500 rounds of ammunition—the solid shot weighing 32 pounds, the shells four or five pounds lighter, and the powder about five or six pounds to the round.

Five guns, each gun weighing 3,550 to 3,570 pounds, were mounted and dragged into position with their limbers and carriages, weighing about 2,000 pounds of themselves, by Companies E and B, of the Fifth New York Zouaves, reduced by various details to about one hundred men. Let me tell you, too, what this dragging of guns means. The horses drew the guns down a ravine to within about one hundred and fifty yards from the battery. From this ravine a road, rising thirty feet in the first thirty yards, leads to the trenches along which we had to drag, through deep sand; this weight of nearly three tons, and this five times. In addition to this, we dragged up some thirty timbers for heavy guns; each timber requiring from six to eight men to lift it on the limbers alone. This was one day's work, and was accomplished under a heavy fire, directed almost exclusively on our poor battery. Upwards of thirty shell exploded directly over the trench within an hour. Six shots, supposed to be solid, were driven, to my knowledge, through a bank of earth twelve feet thick in the rear of our battery. The work was herculean, and performed under unusual difficulties. Our battery was not finished, but might have been opened next day, but others were not ready. Next day we dragged up another gun, and performed various work around the battery, now mounting seven rifled guns. Only half the companies worked on this day, as we moved our camps two miles nearer the battery, into a ravine screened from the view of the enemy by a piece of woods, but within easy mortar range, and it was here I received your paper. Yesterday, (Saturday) I went to the battery about one o'clock, the splinter-proof blinds of the second magazine, were being put up. The wood having to be cut and carried from the same ravine where we had the guns.

Our battery was completed on the 3d inst. We had not enough to do on Sunday to keep ten men working an hour. The firing during Friday and Saturday had been warm, but somewhat distributed. The boys had for the most part got over dodging all but the shells that actually exploded among us. In fact, we feared far more a gun of our own which we named "Steamboat", from the peculiar sound of the shell. Instead of coming as a properly constructed rifle shell should, point foremost, it insisted on turning end for end, over and over, topsy-turvy, making a noise like a propeller. It then fell short generally in or near our trenches. At the word "there's the Steamboat!" every head sought the nearest splinter-proof on the right, instinctively. Saturday night, about five o'clock, the working parties left; the firing had almost ceased. I was left with five men of our company to guard the battery; a corporal came up with two men to join me, afterward. At six o'clock the firing was re-opened with a mortar shell, most exquisitely pitched into the trench about thirty yards to the left of our battery, where, during the day, there had been a crowd of men. Fortunately there were none there at that time or, it must have caused considerable damage. From this time till one o'clock, as I guess, the firing was almost continuous. Shell after shell was thrown toward our little camp; shot after shot was thrown at our battery and No. 1. How the boys slept in camp, I can not tell.

We watched the shells, which we could see from the minute they left the gun, and speculated upon their destination. A fire broke out toward the right of the enemy's line, it rose and fell, and rose and fell; a battery near it steadily throwing shell at our camps. About 1 o'clock, the firing on the enemy's side ceased entirely, and No. 1 battery on our side opened. I got relieved and went to sleep, but was wakened once by the Steamboat, and heard its fragments whirling around our heads, something like a volley of musketry.

Next morning, [May 4] the first word I heard was "Yorktown is evacuated". Nobody was to be seen in the rebel batteries. Two of our boys started over; stragglers from the pickets joined them. The Twenty-second Massachusetts was marched over. A cry of "down", and a shot comes whizzing from the right. "That's from Gloucester Point!" Two or three more shot are fired, as if in spite; but our boys are pretty well hardened. The working detail march into the trenches, and at the news spring upon the trenches. The American flag rises over the rebel batteries, and the whole line of more than four hundred yards of men break into one hearty spontaneous cheer, rising again and again. Battalion after battalion march over to prevent a return of the enemy.

Do you want to know how it feels to be under fire. Well, I will tell you. A rifle shell coming right at you (if it goes so far that the sound catches it, for at first it goes ahead of the sound) comes with a short rush of a most indescribable character, very provocative of intense fear. One instant it is by you, a sharp explosion, and you hear the fragments of the shot whirring away with a hum like twenty thousand bumble bees. I never got quite used to them.

The mortar shell is more insidious. You hear a slight report, and forget it; about a quarter of a minute after you hear a gentle whiss, whiss, like the soughing of the wind through the trees; a thud, an explosion, and the pieces go humming off like those from any other shell.

A solid shot whizzes by you more like a rifle shell, but not quite so loud, strikes two or three times, and is lost.

I have had some experience now, and must say there are much pleasanter things to hear. Last night, though, Corporal [George] Williams, senior corporal to me, sat up and watched them firing, never lowering his head beneath the parapet unless a shot came within a few yards. I must say I envied his coolness.

                                                                                ZOUAVE

SIXTY-SIXTH REGIMENT, N.Y.S.V.

BOTTOM'S BRIDGE, VA., May 26.

McClellan's army of the Peninsula (no longer of the Potomac), with a war appetite whetted to the keenest edge by the brilliant achievements of their arms at Williamsburg and West Point [Eltham's Landing], are eagerly pushing forward to Richmond, cherishing the hope, as they advance under their cautious and wary leader, that the rebels, realizing at last that it is no longer a chimera, but a fact, that the national forces are thundering at the gates of their capital, will see the propriety of making their long-boasted stand, and for once—just once—give the Yankees the satisfaction of an open battle.

The commander-in-chief yesterday advanced his head-quarters from White House, across the Chickahominy, two miles to the front of this the reserve of General [Edwin V.] Sumner's corps d'armée, and within eleven miles of Richmond. Up to 8 o'clock last night, 60,000 of our troops were thrown across the river, bridged by Cloud Murphy's pontoons.

General Sumner, following McClellan, moved his head-quarters from St. Peter's Church to this point yesterday morning. The divisions under his command broke camp as early as 5 o'clock in the morning but the long columns did not commence winding its sinuous course from the hill-sides until near 9 o'clock. By this time the sun was well up in the heavens, and shooting down his hot, scorching rays most unmercifully upon the heavily-knapsacked and accoutered soldiers. Many had failed to fill their canteens in the morning, expecting, as before, to find plenty of water along the way; but in this they found to their bitter experience that they were mistaken. The suffering, on this account, was great. Several fainted on the wayside; a number were sun-struck, and stragglers were more numerous than on any one day's march before. The experiences of yesterday will warn many a soldier that the hot, sultry season of the Southern country is already close upon them, and will, besides, be instrumental in teaching them the lesson, that to their corpulent haversacks must, of necessity, be added a well-filled canteen of water. The two go hand-in-hand with the soldier, and, next to his arms, are last to be parted with.

More or less has been written by the different army correspondents of the New York press concerning the peninsula, its swamps, its tillable soil, its inhabitants (what remains of them), its corduroy roads (built by the "Yankees"), its breakneck, bottomless mudholes, and various other things interesting to the reading public, treating them all as intelligently as the be-knighted, God-forsaken localities in which they were from time to time compelled to occupy would possibly permit. The lower peninsula—let me not speak of it! As a soldier, let me never see more of it. Our numerous buried dead from the swamp camps, and over hundreds of fevered, emaciated sick sent to Northern hospitals tell the story of regions between Shipping Point and Yorktown.

Leaving the interval between the latter place and West Point, which, by the way, is more prolific in spots of tillable, livable, hillable ground (the three terms go together, and are altogether proper, according to the peninsula dictionary), indulge me a word in speaking of the upper country of that region lying between West Point Landing and the Chickahominy. It is a region particularly interesting, from the fact that, ere the early history of Virginia had been given to the world by the author and the typo, here lived some of the wealthiest and most important F.F.V.s' Estates, the broad acres of which (told only by the thousand, "stocked" with hundreds of slaves, whose yearly increase filled the coffers of their conscientious and Christian masters) run parallel with the Paumunkey and Chickahominy Rivers. The splendid mansions, which, at intervals, attract the attention of the soldier as the abodes of these enormous landed proprietors and slave-breeders, are now all deserted. The different estates are only occupied by the human chattels who, through disability, could not, or, through disinclination, would not, leave with their masters for Richmond on the approach of the Federal army. The extended wheat and rye-fields, which a few days ago held out such promise to the Secession planters, were left to be overrun by Northern soldiers, to be occupied as camping grounds, or given over to the grazing of our horses.

In one of these mansions, a chaplain of one of the regiments of Gen. [Israel B.] Richardson's Division was called upon to perform the last sad rites over the body of the master of the house. He had been a captain in the rebel army for nearly nine months, up to April 27. He then sickened with a fever, of which he finally died. Before his death, he held a long interview with the chaplain, and among other sins of which he acknowledged himself guilty was the greatest one of his life—that of taking up arms against his government, and fighting against the old flag.

"I thought, at one time," said he, "that we could whip the Yankees, and succeed in successfully establishing a Southern Confederacy—a government in which no Northern State should participate or take part. I afterward saw my folly, and sorely repented me, both on my own account and that of Virginia, my native State, taking sides with this rebellion. Why, sir," said he, after a little pause, "the other day, when the advance of your army continued to pass my house hour after hour, your soldiers carrying knapsacks, the weight of which would kill half the Southern soldiers in a single month, I thought of the fallacy which so many of us Southerners held, that the Yankees could not live in our hot climate but a short time. And that was not all, sir; the men, as they filed past, seemingly never to stop, sang songs as they went along. My God, how have we Southern people been deluded! How can we hope to fight, much less to conquer, such men? It is impossible, sir, utterly impossible." Mr. Oliver Fraquer (that was his name), of the county of New Kent, Va., died with these sentiments on his lips, and asking, in the same connection, a prayer from the Union chaplain for his soul, and the return of his native Virginia to the old Government.

To-morrow morning, the gallant Sixty-sixth moves forward with the whole force of the Second Corps of McClellan. We count on being in Richmond inside of the next four days; and then, and not till then, you will hear from me again.

D. E. F.

June 8, 1862
FIRST LONG ISLAND REGIMENT (67th New York Infantry)
COLD HARBOR, VA., May 28.

The many duties incidental to the life of the soldier have hitherto prevented me from indulging in a description of the changing scenes through which we have been passing; but, presuming that the communications forwarded by our right *marker*, will have proved sufficient to inform our many friends of our varied locations, I shall confine myself, more particularly, to the events which are transpiring at the present time. We arrived at this camping-ground on the 25th inst., and have remained here since then, busily engaged in throwing up batteries and digging long rifle-pits, which are intended for use in case of an overpowering force obliging us to retreat. We are now within eight miles of the rebel capital, and expect soon to enter it in triumph. There are no thoughts of wavering, and our troops are eagerly looking forward to the time when they will be permitted to meet the foe on the field of strife. The rebel forces are but a short distance ahead, and frequently make reconnaissances in strong force. Our pickets are stationed within sight of theirs, and shots are sometimes exchanged, doing little or no damage on either side. The sanitary condition of our men is very favorable, and neither rains nor exposure of any kind are sufficient to dampen their ardor. On our arrival, we bivouacked near a pleasant forest, clothed in the vernal vestments of Spring; but, alas! for the beautiful prospect now; a large tract of forest trees has fallen beneath the axe, wielded by the sturdy hands of the soldier, and the green foliage is fast perishing under the influence of the scorching sun. As we advance, the country appears more and more beautiful; the fruit-trees have long since shed their blossoms, and the green fruit is now pendant on their branches. Sweet-smelling flowerets abound in the forests, and May-apples and strawberries are ripening rapidly. Limpid streams are abundant, and their musical murmurings fall pleasingly on the ear. Often am I tempted to take a solitary stroll beside them at the hour of eventide, for well do the hour and scenes accord with the spirit within. I cannot forbear reflecting on how soon, many—yes, very many of my fellow-soldiers will have ceased to inhale these pure airs of heaven, and to appreciate these scenes of nature, so romantic and picturesque. But, being unwilling to trifle with your time and space, I will close by promising to "call again" after the taking of Richmond, provided my life is spared to do so.

I am, with much respect, yours,　　　　　　　　　　　　A REDUCED CORPORAL.

June 15, 1862
TWENTY-FIFTH REGIMENT, N.Y.S.V.
GAINES' MILLS, VA., June 6.

As the rude hand of war has not silenced my lips up to this present moment, I wish to let you know some of the scenes that the Twenty-fifth has passed through. We got orders, on last Tuesday morning [May 27], to leave knapsacks behind, and without time to have breakfast, or coffee, to rally on our march, we knew not where. The rain came down in torrents all night, and at 4 o'clock we were pacing through the mud, knee-deep, arms at will. We immediately saw we were for a long march. The Sixth U.S. Cavalry took the lead, and we took the right of the division. We continued our march without incident for eight miles, and then got orders to halt. It is unnecessary stating about the country, as it was all through the woods, up hills, and down ravines. We halted about half an hour, and then started again, the cavalry keeping in advance of us. We knew then we were within seven miles of Hanover Court House. About two miles further on our cavalry made a dash, and diverging right and left, came on the enemy's cavalry pickets. We were on a narrow turnpike; we dashed down the rails, and our colonel ([Charles A.] Johnson), as cool as if on dress-parade, sung out, "Deploy skirmishers!" We advanced through wheat; the skirmishers not getting engaged, rallied, and advanced in front of us, coming up to the edge of the woods. We halted, and then the rattling commenced. Our lieutenant-colonel ([Henry F.] Savage) took the left, and deployed two companies, Captain [Michael] McMahon taking the lead. We on the right got into the woods; and then our adjutant came, without any cap on, singing out "Rally on the reserve!" We expected our skirmishers to be falling back; but no fall back; they blazed away desperately—the enemy trying to flank them. We supported them—our company and the rest of the regiment going to support the battery (Martin's)[Co. C, 1st Massachusetts] on the left. The enemy tried twice to get at us in the rear; but we, deploying suddenly, and keeping up the firing briskly, they fell back hastily. We, hearing a cheer on the left, knew our men had flanked them, and then we advanced on the right. Two of the rebels lay in the woods behind their knapsacks, not thinking, until two of my company chased them, and pursued them, firing at them, and bringing them both down. Upward of ten of the rebels had a fair shot at one of my company, named Charles McMaguire, but they only wounded him in the leg. The plundering of knapsacks now commenced. The enemy, being from North Carolina, was comfortably quartered, not expecting a visit from us. The rebels doing picket were the Eighteen North Carolina Regiment. The boys got revolvers and trophies, even letters; they were actually writing to their sweethearts and families. We lay down exhausted, drenched with rain, and hungry also. It was then we knew our loss. Captain McMahon fell dead, cheering on his men. If mortal man is regretted, it is him; his memory is wept over by all who knew him. He came out with the regiment, and sleeps the sleep of death. In a few moments, General [John H.] Martindale's son rode up and ordered our colonel to send the regiment to support the Second Maine regiment—the enemy trying the flanking movement on them also. General [Daniel] Butterfield's Brigade had passed us and were ahead, thinking the enemy was in front. Now was the critical moment of the day. The enemy advanced out of the woods, and thought to capture a battery in the open field. The Second Maine let them come, and then gave them a volley. They ran; but having good supports in the woods, they lay down and commenced bushwacking, as usual. We took position on the centre in an open ground. We contested the ground hotly, the Second Maine cheering us. Both regiments fought with desperation. The Second Maine fought bravely, and had a good position.

They saved us once from being totally destroyed and cut to pieces, the rebels getting us into a cross-fire. The colonel gave orders to fall back, but no run. He waved his sword while his horse fell dead, and he got wounded in the leg. He rallied us again, until receiving two balls in the leg. Such proof of bravery could not be equaled on any battle-field. Our adjutant got wounded, and fell also. They had seven regiments fighting. The Forty-fourth [New York Infantry] came up, and took an exposed position on our left, and fought bravely; they suffered heavily as well as our regiment. The battle grew fiercer; one of our guns was left totally useless, the men being shot down at their post. Things looked doubtful. We were used up badly. The Second Maine giving the rebels heavy volleys, contested the ground till the Eighty-third Pennsylvania and Ninth Massachusetts had at the time got on the rebels' rear, and charged them with the bayonet. For two hours, the Second Maine and the Forty-fourth also fought nine regiments of the rebels without giving in. Our artillery now advanced to the front, raking the woods with spherical-case, canister, and grapeshot. The rebels now gave way in disorder, and fled. Previous to this, I may mention about that section of [Charles] Griffin's battery [Co. D, 5th U.S.] of two guns. One of them being silent, the other was working by only two men. One would ram home, and the other fire the piece, for upward of twenty minutes. At last, in the act of charging the piece, one fell; the other man took the rammer and sponge, laid it down, and left the gun. Such instances of personal bravery never before exhibited on any battle-field.

As an instance of the boasted chivalry of the South, I may assert, with truth, we fought three regiments of the rebels without any supports, as we were engaged, and won our own fight in front, before any regiment was able to be up to our assistance. Our loss is heavy indeed—182 killed, wounded, and missing. It is thought our lieutenant-colonel (Henry Savage) will lose his arm. He and our colonel have gone to New York. What will be done with us we know not. No one to command us. There are left only one hundred and fifty men fit for duty. There is talk of attaching us to the Second Maine; but is our old number—Twenty-fifth of New York—that we have fought and bled for, to perish? We say, "No!" We await with patience the recovery of our colonel and officers. The officers killed were: Lieutenant [Charles] Halpin, Lieutenant [George E.] Fisk, and Captain McMahon. My mind is not collected to give you proper detail of all. Trusting that we have done our duty to our country, and wishing the SUNDAY MERCURY and its proprietors the success they are entitled to,

---

June 10.

On receiving orders, while at Hanover, that our work had been accomplished, we soon got under weigh for our old camp at Gaines Mills. We had been kept busy, all day, doing the last sad offices of burying our fallen comrades where they fell, and marking their names on pieces of rude boards. The fallen comrades of the Forty-fourth New York Volunteers lie alongside together. We left the battle-ground with heavy-hearts, although, while marching past the Ninth Massachusetts, they gave us a ringing cheer. The roads being dried up a good deal, we got along better than when going. When arriving in camp, all were weary and very much fatigued. It was an empty looking encampment, not one of the tents being occupied. Most of our wounded men have been sent to the White House, the rest, that is, those too heavily wounded, are left here; but in what condition. The arrangements are awful. The idea of a hard biscuit being offered to a wounded man with pallid cheek, looks rather wanting; but is it the fault or want of sympathy of the people of the North? I say no—they say so too. Might I ask what effect it has on us when some of our men steal into our camp for something to eat? It has its evils; but where is the fault? We have without a murmur stood the hardships and hunger, and privations on the march, stood the din and shock of battle without flinching; but when wounded, what is to cheer our drooping spirits? We augur better; but when hopes die, then the spirit of a soldier dies also. We have since done our duty, though no man slept two nights in the week, as we have been detailed as guards everywhere since our arrival in camp, and have done our fatigues also. Yesterday an order came for one hundred and seventy-five men for picket. They went on picket; and shortly after, an order came for one hundred men for fatigue. They could not be got. We had not forty men in camp. We think that we are entitled to a little rest somewhere until we can appear again as a regiment, or some duty assigned is that our members are capable of performing. We are not strangers to the activity and work that is progressing rapidly along the Chickahominy River. While on a picket, lately, we could see the rebel camps lie scattered before us; while, at the same time, a clustering group of the rebels lie picturesquely, squatted and smoking, gazing intently at us. It looks to me like the allies before Sabastopol, their pickets lining the Fechesnaya River, while the Russians are posted on the other bank of the river—no pickets firing, but each watching any encroachment from either side.

Professor Lowe's balloon seems soaring to the blue canopy above, and relieves your gaze of earth's scenes, transfixing your mind on the high state of science man has attained on earth, as well as floating through the airy space above us.

The whole of [Fitz John] Porter's division, formerly, but now commanded by General [George A.] McCall, was reviewed by General Prim, son, and staff. They seemed a little astonished at the numbers of the Twenty-fifth New York; but General Martindale explained the cause to the Spanish general. He seemed to take a close scrutiny of us. In general, the division looked well, and breaking up, all the bands struck up rather lively. It was a rather animated scene than usual, to see. Only the heavy booming of the cannon has stirred our nerves those last few weeks since. It is reported for a certainty that the rebels have been re-enforced here at Richmond. All last Saturday, the very earth shook with the heavy discharges of musketry and heavy cannon. From twelve o'clock until darkness set in, we thought the ball was up, and all was excitement and eagerness. All our division was ordered out; but the hour has not yet come. I may state that although our numbers seemed cut up greatly by our papers' account, the rebels got an awful salting when Gen. Heintzelman and Gen. Sumner supported Gen. [Silas] Casey and Gen. Couch. The rebels had seven divisions engaged, and lost over 8,000 in killed, wounded, and prisoners. It has been stated by Professor Lowe that the rebel retreat was an awful panic, throwing away muskets, overcoats, and every article that impeded their flight. It has been said by regiments in our brigade that we made tall traveling to Hanover Court House, they not having time to assist us in that battle; but we, I am aware, never made such tracks as those gentlemen on the right about march to Richmond. Those fair forms that in the morning graced every house-top in

Richmond, and held aloft many a snowy scarf that fluttered in the breeze, their prayers breathing softly after their chivalrous lads, must have a fatal effect, when seeing their warriors return in double-quick time, without, putting the Yankees into the river.

I must not forget to mention we owe a tribute of gratitude to several members of Duryee's Zouaves, for their brotherly love and soldierly conduct in decently interring two members of our regiment who they found in the woods, when we were engaged with the rebels, hanging suspended to two trees, with their throats cut. Will barbarity never end? Such was equaled only by the heathen Sepoys of India in their accursed career also. The bayonet is our answer. The same style of taking them prisoners as the Sixty-ninth and Eighty-eighth gave them last Sunday at Bottom's Bridge. No palliation for such murderers.

I have seen in your issue of June 1st a record of the death of Harry Clarke, of Hose Co. No. 15. He fell bravely, but not without avenging his death. He was wounded, and the rebels thought to take him prisoner; he resisted, as it is supposed, for he was found lifeless over the dead body of a rebel, having put his bowie knife through the rebel's throat.

Another fireman, Richard Edgeworth, of Engine Co. No. 9, has lost his right arm.

Our opinion is, that of all the troops when disciplined, none can equal the fireman for bravery.

The SUNDAY MERCURY is a rather rare prize among the camps, and sells at twenty-five cents a copy. I am favored by getting a copy now and then, but it soon is borrowed, and takes a circuit through many a camp; and for my civility in lending it I never see it again.

The morale of our army is good; no sickness in any of the camps to be seen.

Yours, respectfully,   OCCASIONALLY

The price of an eight page Sunday Mercury *in 1862 was four cents; by the end of the war it was eight cents.*

SIXTY-SIXTH REGIMENT, N.Y.S.V.

June 12.

You have already been informed of the position occupied by Sumner's corps, comprising the divisions of Richardson and [John] Sedgwick, up to Saturday, 2 o'clock, P.M. At that hour, we were at least six miles from the field of strife, on the opposite bank of the Chickahominy. The boom of cannon and the continuous rattle of musketry of the morning ought to have warned us that we were liable, at any moment, to be ordered forward; but instead of this, the men were drilled, first by the company and afterward by battalion, from 9 o'clock in the morning until nearly 1 o'clock, P.M. The result was, that, a little after 2 o'clock,, while many of us were still partaking of our soup and crackers, orders came for the several commands to fall in immediately, and be ready to march in ten minutes. Strange as it may sound, Gen. [William H.] French was at the head of his brigade, and leading it toward the Chickahominy Swamp, two full minutes inside of that time. No time was allowed for striking tents, packing knapsacks, or rolling blankets. Everything, save our arms, ammunition (sixty rounds), and rations (two days'), were left behind.

At 3 o'clock, our men were rapidly crossing the river in two columns. The swamp on either side of the river, for nearly a half mile, was flooded by two feet if water; while the river proper and the sluices adjoining proved so deep, that the shortest of us were compelled to carry our haversacks and cartridge-boxes on our heads. Gen. Richardson—or, as the boys will have it, "General Dick"—set the example to his men, by jumping from his horse, and wading through the turbid waters. Cheer after cheer greeted the general at this evidence of his willingness to lead where he asked his soldiers to follow. The Chickahominy once forded, the bluffs were immediately made, and obliquing to the right, the long column took the quick and double-quick step in the direction of "The Seven Pines."

An aid from Heintzelman reached Gen. Richardson within two miles of the battle-field. He was covered with mud, as his horse was with foam. Informing the general of the surprise and repulse of Casey, and the advance of Heintzelman to his relief, he wheeled his horse about and guided our division to the right of Heintzelman's line of battle, the place designated as that to which we could give him the greatest support. It was now past 6 o'clock; but the artillery was still belching forth its thundering tones, and the rattle of musketry was long and continuous. French's brigade, consisting of the Sixty-sixth, Fifty-seventh, and Fifty-second New York and Fifty-third Pennsylvania, held the advance. Quietly but quickly we moved down into the swamp, wading swollen streams, and contending with the yielding, muddy soil, until the large clearing of fallow-land (in which the Seventh Michigan Regiment, belonging to Sedgwick's division, had rescued the Fifty-sixth New York and Sixty-first Pennsylvania, and were even then pitted against a whole brigade of rebels, receiving and delivering a deadly fire) was reached. Filing to the left and rear of the Michigan boys just as night was closing in, the enemy discovered quickly our lines of battle, and commenced falling back to the woods. A volley of musketry, that was a volley, now poured in upon the retreating rebel column, and when the old general ordered a charge of bayonets to expedite their movements, the effect was magical; the whole column broke, run, skedaddled, crossed the railroad, and took to the woods. All night long our division stood to their arms in line of battle, on a swampy field, covered in many places by six and eight inches of water. Around us, on every side, lay the dead and wounded soldiers. They were mostly Mississippians and North Carolinians. A lieutenant of the Eleventh Mississippi lay just behind me, mortally wounded; his face livid, and turned skyward, with only the doleful frogs of the dismal swamp sounding mournfully his melancholy doom.

But the night at last wore away; the dawn appeared and with the setting in of the day also set in a renewal of the battle. The Sixty-sixth New York was ordered to move forward in line, right in front, within one hundred yards of the woods; the Fifty-seventh and Fifty-second New York debouched to the left, and took up their position under cover of the wood in that direction, while the Fifty-third Pennsylvania was thrown forward to our front, across the railroad, just outside of the wood. Throwing out skirmishers, it was shortly discovered that the enemy were moving forward their lines through the wood. On they came; the Fifty-third skirmishers were driven in, and the regiments taking advantage of the natural embankment of the railroad cut, hid themselves from view. A full rebel brigade moved majestically through the wood upon this one point, which they were not long in gaining. As they issued from the edge of the forest, seeing but one regiment in line to oppose them, they let fly a full volley of minié bullets, which we permitted to whiz harmlessly over our heads by a slight inclination forward. The front rank, and at a distance of thirty yards poured a deadly and destructive fire into the rebel ranks—all that were not killed or wounded; for such pedestrian time as was made through the thick underbrush swamp has not a precedent in the pages of history, or the annals of civilized warfare.

The battle of Fair Oaks had now fairly opened; the Sixty-sixth New York had received without flinching the first fire of the enemy. The Fifty-third Pennsylvania, following up the advantage gained over thrice their number by the stunning effect of their first volley, were in hot pursuit of the retreating rebels, raining their leaden bullets thick and fast into the enemy. The Fifty-seventh and Fifty-second, advancing well their line of battle into the swamp, had taken up a position from which a destructive fire was opened upon the rebel centre. The Sixty-sixth making a left half wheel, bore down in splendid order, and with unbroken front to the woods to support the Fifty-third Pennsylvania on the one hand, and the Fifty-second New York on the other. The Irish Brigade, or rather two regiments of it, the Sixty-ninth and Eighty-eighth, (the Sixty-third being on special duty), penetrated the swamp a half mile to the left, and with wild cheers and yells, took in hand the "clearing out" of any number of rebels might be brought to oppose them. For over three hours the battle raged fiercely, the rebels at each onset of our brave men, falling back in disorder. General Richardson's men, numbering less than nine thousand all told, following up their brilliant success of the early morning continued to press forward, combating and driving back, step by step, three, and sometimes four times their number of the enemy. The Irish Brigade, led on by Meagher, fought like tigers—now pouring in a deadly fire of buckshot and balls; now charging the enemy with cold steel, now clubbing their muskets and engaging the foe in a hand-to-hand encounter. The yells which from time to time rang through the woods along the Irish line of battle was enough to appall the stoutest rebel heart. A squad of North Carolinians, which we outflanked and took prisoners, averred that their general was reliably informed that the Irish Brigade numbered seventeen hundred strong, and that he had rather encounter so many demons. They proved "a terror to the enemy" indeed, mowing the rebels down at one time three or four deep.

The last offensive demonstration made by the rebels was to turn our right. The continued yells and cheers of Meagher's men, added to the frightfulness of their bayonet-charges, had the effect of so discouraging the flower of the rebel army (which attacked them, only to be repulsed each time with greater slaughter), that, as a last and desperate retort, the rebel general endeavored to gain their flank. The Sixty-sixth, as I said before, held the right of the line. The rebel column, strengthened by fresh troops, moved through the swampy wood, left in front, until nearly opposite our line, when, forming their line of battle, they came steadily, but quickly, forward. For a full hour previous, our regiment had not fired a shot, but lay prostrate upon the ground. Our general had so ordered it, to our wonderment and mystification, be it said. But the grand *finale* told the story, and revealed the strategic purpose of our brigade commander. Our silence would naturally lead the enemy to suppose that our right had changed its position and gone to the support of the regiments on our left; and with this view of the matter, they bore confidently down through the swamp in the direction of the railroad. Colonel [James C.] Pinckney commanded his gallant six hundred to "lie low", to wait until the enemy came close upon us, and then, at the word "fire!" pour in a full volley. We performed what we were bid, to the letter. The rebel column broke and ran, the numerous dead and wounded left behind telling how murderous had been our fire—how complete the rout of the enemy. Thus it was that, instead of succeeding in their maneuver to outflank our right, and obtain the rear of the Irish Brigade, our right turned the enemy's left in a manner so complete and powerful as virtually to bring the battle to a victorious close. To the Sixty-sixth is accorded this credit, both by our brigade and division commanders, of terminating with a successful issue the battle of Fair Oaks—one of the fiercest conflicts of the war, and the only principal engagement of the army in which infantry alone did the fighting.   R. E. F.

SIXTY-NINTH REGIMENT, N.Y.S.V.

CAMP ON THE RICHMOND AND YORK RIVER R.R.
SEVEN MILES FROM RICHMOND, June 3.

The Sixty-ninth Regiment, as you are aware of before now, was engaged in battle with the enemy on Sunday last. As the writer of this letter was not everywhere at the same time, a detailed account of the engagement cannot be expected; but such as is, every word can be relied on.

The rattle of cannon and musketry on Saturday forenoon made it evident a struggle was going on, and a little after 3 P.M., regiments were being rapidly moved to the scene of action, among them the Irish Brigade. We reached the ground about 9 P.M.,—ground hotly and manfully contested but a few hours previous by our troops, among which were the Second and Thirty-fourth N.Y.S.V., who fought like tigers. We rest Saturday night on a large open tract of land, from which the timber had been cleared years ago, the stumps being half decayed. During the night, doctors and their assistants were continually going to and fro, with lantern in hand, picking up the wounded. Their moans were heart-rendering. As the sun rose above the horizon on that beautiful Sabbath morning, a few scattering shots told us plainly that the ball was fairly opened. The scene of action was now on the railroad, distant from the open space in which we were in line, about four hundred yards, and screened from the observation by a thick wood. The Eighty-eighth and Sixty-ninth were in line on the edge of the road, fronting the railroad, waiting for the order to "go in", when the Fifty-third Pennsylvania Regiment came rushing from the railroad, unable or unwilling to hold their position. General Richardson, who was in the rear of the Sixty-ninth, immediately told them to form in line, and hold their position; or, said he, "I will get that battery up there (pointing his finger) to play on you." A few minutes after, an aide came for the Sixty-ninth to support the Fifth New Hampshire, who were nobly holding their ground, thirty or forty yards in advance of the railroad, against a whole brigade. "You cannot have the Sixty-ninth," said he, "I must reserve them for the charge. Take the Eighty-eighth." A short time only had elapsed, and on came the same aide, quicker than before, for the Sixty-ninth, saying the Fifth New Hampshire would be surrounded if not immediately re-enforced. True enough, when we reached the railroad left in front, we found that a rebel regiment had got around by the right of the Fifth New Hampshire, and had them nearly surrounded, when we opened fire. We came at an opportune moment, or they would be completely cut to pieces. Manfully did we do our duty. Not a rebel was in line, or to be found opposite our lines after the third round. They could not stand our fire. It was pronounced terrible by all parties. The Eighty-eighth, which was on our left, likewise drove the enemy before them like sheep. The Sixty-ninth and Eighty-eighth saved the day. The one turned the right, and the other the left flank of the enemy. During the engagement, the enemy tried to bring a battery to bear on the road on our right, which would sweep our lines, but quickly had to retire from the fire of one of our own pieces. We did not follow them, for reasons to me unknown, but, probably, in consequence of the thick woods, and not knowing their position or strength, it was prudent to do so.

The Eighty-eighth lost six killed and nineteen wounded; the Sixty-ninth, one killed and eleven wounded. The following is a correct list: Killed—Michael Herbert, of Company I. Wounded—Sergeant [William F.] Daly, Company G; Corporal [Arthur] Kelly, Company G; Private Maurice Quinlan, in the thigh, slightly; Corporal [John] Doran, Company H, in the leg; Jas. Heeney, Company C, flesh wound in thigh; Corporal Reilly, Company A, slightly; Corporal Leislip, Company B, in the hand; Privates Moore, Manney, and Smith, of Company B; and [Thomas] Shaughnessy, bugler. It is surprising the regiment got off so safe, but our tremendous fire prevented them from doing anything more than run.

NON COM., SIXTY-NINTH REGIMENT.

THIRTY-FIRST REGIMENT, N.Y.S.V.

ON THE BANKS OF THE CHICKAHOMINY RIVER

I now take this present opportunity of corresponding with you once more, and the pleasure of writing on a cartridge-box containing fifty rounds of Secesh pills, which, I have no doubt, will shortly be used in curing the rebels from using their legs so freely. Lately, the rebels have been showing themselves in larger bodies than usual. A few days ago, our regiment went out on the outpost picket. Throughout the day they were a little more quiet than they formerly had been. Just as soon as darkness came on, the rebel pickets could be seen advancing; we immediately sent our reserve back from the woods, where we were stationed, into the swamp, and the pickets advanced till they came up to the stream called, the Chickahominy River, but it looks more like some small brook rather than a river, although it widens as you go down the stream. Our pickets were on one bank of the river, while the rebel pickets were on the opposite side; every little while could be heard whispering between the pickets, but on account of their not firing on each other, everything passed off quietly until morning, it being wet and cold in the swamp. The men waited anxiously for the dawn, which came with the sun shining high, yet not a cloud to darken the sky; about 6 o'clock the pickets and reserve occupied their old positions, and at 8 o'clock there could be seen two or three squads of rebels on a large hill overlooking the country round, and after a lapse of about five minutes we ascertained that it was some field pieces that they had been placing on the hill, and they then opened fire on our men building the bridges, occasionally throwing a shell into our camps; but they did not do much damage, probably they had too many squints for gunners. Our batteries were then run down and placed in their respective positions, and opened a heavy and destructive fire of what sesech call rotten shot, which they did not seem to admire much, some of the shells bursting directly over their pieces, and when the smoke would clear away the guns could be seen minus the men. Presently two or three men came out with their horses, hitched them to the guns, and then vamosed. Since then, nothing has been heard of them or their guns. We have several rebel prisoners, and they assert that the South Carolina troops are desirous of going home, as the Governor of the State has ordered them to do so, and they also express their desires to open mutiny. Two or three regiments have thrown down their arms and refused to do duty for the Confederate Government. The prisoners also say that the army, as a general thing, is in a complete state of demoralization. There was quite a severe battle fought near here, at Hanover Court-House, not long since. The regiment was not engaged, yet we were ordered to hold ourselves in readiness to march at a moment's notice. We were waiting anxiously in this manner till dark, and we found out that our turn had not yet come for a fight, so we retired for the night.

Yours, respectfully,   HIGH PRIVATE.

FIRST REGIMENT LONG ISLAND VOLUNTEERS

CAMP NEAR RICHMOND, June 6.

Since my last writing, our boys have had some hot work. About 1, P.M., Saturday, May 31, our regiment, which lay next to Casey's Division, on the advance, were alarmed by sharp firing in front, which was almost instantly followed by the deep boom of artillery and rattling volleys of musketry. We were immediately formed in line, and went through inspection of arms. The din came nearer and nearer. Presently a couple of solid shot came whizzing into the centre of our camp, then the bullets came whistling past our heads. Hark! the batteries of Casey's Division are thundering forth their deadly welcome to the rebel visitors. Then a calm, but only for a few moments, for the rebels, who had been driven back at first, had received a re-enforcement, came rushing on, driving all before them. Bullets began to fly around us, and shell after shell exploded near. Our men had begun to fall, when the order came, "Down! every man". We fell flat on our faces; and in this position we remained for over two hours, under heavy fire. In the meantime, Casey's batteries had been silenced, and our brigade battery (Captain [Theodore] Miller's) [Co. E, 1st Pennsylvania Light Artillery] was pouring round after round of grape and canister over our heads into the rebel ranks.

Gen. Keyes rode up, and told the regiment to change position, which we did, by company into line, as coolly as if we were at our usual drill. Shortly after we had taken our position, the remnants of Casey's Division came running in, saying they were all cut up, and that the rebels were close on their heels. We were ordered to lie down, and not to fire until ordered to. First, then, the Eighty-seventh New York came rushing up in our front, cheering, and received the first volley of the rebels. They broke, but immediately formed in our rear. Then came the order from our gallant colonel (Julius Adams), "Up, and give it to them, boys!" And we did with a vengeance. Bullets flew thick and fast; volley after volley we poured in. Our men were falling all around us. Over our heads the grape was rattling among the branches of the trees. But the fire is coming from the right to left of us, as well as the front, and it is plain to see that they are outflanking us. The batteries had been withdrawn in safety. Then only did our colonel give the command: "Fall back, boys, but do it slowly." Making our grand rally around our glorious old flag, we retreated backward, contesting every inch of ground, until we placed it in safety.

That night, our regiment did picket duty.

Every officer and man did his duty. Our loss is heavy—probably 200 men out of the 500 we took into the engagement; but the rebels suffered as much as ourselves, for on the battle-ground won, lay the dead bodies of over thirty of them. We lost the most of our knapsacks; but I am weary, and close.

THE RIGHT GUARD.

June 22, 1862

SEVENTY-FIRST PENNSYLVANIA VOLUNTEERS

SEDGWICK'S DIVISION, NEAR RICHMOND, June 16.

Having been a frequent contributor to your columns before I doffed the pen and donned the sword—my name quite frequently appearing in your solid columns arrayed most effectually against traitors and treason—the inclination of transferring myself for a short space, in mind if not in body, from Sumner's gallant corps to a column under your generalship, has suddenly seized me, and hence the following narrative of facts.

Of course, you know all about the hard-contested battle of the "Seven Pines", and also of the subsequent engagement, on Sunday following, of "Fair Oaks", in which the rebel attack was so obstinately and successfully resisted. I do not, therefore, design to give you a full account of the battle, or a description of the scene throughout the whole of our three miles of line of battle, but only a succinct account of facts and events that came within the range of my vision while in the midst of as hot and incessant a torrent of musketry discharges as the imagination could possibly depict.

The repulse of Casey's division (about which I would like to say a word in digression, "farther on the advance" of "this scribbling") and the weakening or "worsting" of Couch's, reached our ([Gen. William W.] Burns's) brigade at about twelve o'clock, while leisurely eating our dinner in camp, about two miles on the south-east bank of the Chickahominy, near a place called Kid's Mills. In an instant, our brigade, which is composed nearly entirely of Philadelphians, with our regiment, the well-known "Old California Regiment", of which the lamented Senator Baker was the originator and father, in the advance—was in line, and in column by company, and on the road at a rapid and easy pace for the scene of action.

While on the road, Gen. Sumner and his staff passed our regiment at full gallop. The general looked excited and stern, and as he passed my company, he remarked, in quick tone, observing that several of my men had on old and light-colored grey overcoats, "Men, throw those off; they'll make you a target in this engagement"; and on he dashed to the front, and we did not see him again till we reached the battle-field; but we knew, without questions, that we had work before us. We marched on at a steady step over a very muddy road, and after the lapse of about an hour and a half, we crossed the now famous and swollen Chickahominy, over a bridge very badly constructed of pine logs lashed together, and the swift current sweeping in places for inches over and above them. We then passed over a marshy flat, up a green and beautiful hill-side, past a very comfortable and opulent-looking residence; saw many, to our astonishment, fat cattle in a large barnyard, and an old white-headed negro, leaning on the gate. As we passed, some of our men, hearing the sharp firing in the front asked, "Where is the fight, Uncle Tom?" "Not fah, massa; up dah, little space," and with renewed energy we hurried on through the clearing, then through a narrow road in a thick grove, then we plunged through a swollen brook, with water up to the waist; and at last, emerging into a large open field with a house on it, and thick woods surrounding it, the battle-field burst suddenly on the view, and in the most terrific earnestness. As we wheeled to the right into column, there seemed to be some confusion— several artillery horses had broken from their caissons and were dashing down toward us at a furious rate; but unheeded by our men, for by that time, having taken in the scene at a glance, they had, in their enthusiasm, become almost unmanageable, and were suddenly about to dash, orders or no orders, to the front, where [Lieut. Edmund] Kirby's Battery was delivering, with astonishing rapidity, shell after shell, interspersed with the condiment of canister, into a thick grove to the front and right of it, from whence the rebel infantry fire could be seen issuing in times of belching flame. Supporting this battery was John Cochrane's United States Chasseurs, and most admirably were they firing their fire by file into the ranks of "the homespun gentry."

Our regiment marched in perfect order to within about fifty yards (certainly not more) of the line of the then living fire, and in perfect order changed direction to the right—no, I forget; we changed direction by the right flank, and passed at this distance from the line several regiments moving up to the advance right, where, at about pistol-shot from a Massachusetts regiment (the Seventh, I believe), we halted, while the roar of the cannon was only relieved by the sharp, quick, snapping report of the Enfield rifle, the whole line being arranged along a high rail fence, directly in front of a thick grove. We halted in this fire, and came to a front in column by division, which was no sooner done than we heard the whistling and the screeching (if I may use such a word) of all kinds of bullets. For several minutes, perhaps five or ten, for you know minutes are divisions of time of much importance on a battle-field, we stood a perfect rain of balls. Our general perceiving that the bullets of the enemy were passing over the heads of the regiments then delivering their fire, and were falling directly in our midst, the order was given for "the men to lie down", and hold up their pieces, which they immediately obeyed. Several of the officers did not deign to stoop, and among them myself; and for one hour I paced up and down in the rear of my company, the men lying on their breasts and the bayonets vertical to the ground.

What freak of propulsion caused one bullet to whiz not quite near enough to strike my head on the right, or dart through my temple on the left, or splash through my brain at the front, I knew not; but this I knew: I stood there, and paced there, expecting every moment that the deadly fire of the Massachusetts regiment would slacken; that their cartridges would give out, and that we would be moved up a few yards to the fence, and give the rebels a specimen of our quick execution of firing by file, but the order did not come. The deadly, spiteful splashing of flame from right to left continued incessantly. Now and then I would see a man rise to his feet, deliberately aim—see the red flash, hear the report, and then see him sit down to load. For a second, now and then, the fire slackened, and then I knew that the rebels had been sadly cut up, and had fallen back to reform and renew the attack; but it was only for seconds. Again the sharp multiplicity of reports would ring in the ear; crack after crack, and a strange singing, shrieking noise of Minié balls, bullets, and buckshot, then shrieks of the dying, and the deep booming of the battery on our left made the very ground shake, and the flame as it issued in volley after volley felt warm on my left cheek, and the smoke in great folds passed over our heads, never concealing, and continually leaving bold in our front that immovable line of obstinate fire and flame. Twice I saw the rebels charge and mount the rail fence in the very faces of our men, but it was evident not a man got over. One bold fellow I spied on the top of the fence for an instant, and then a ball crashed through his brain, and it seemed as if the very ball carried him over the other side, for he did not fall, he swept out of view into the woods.

Twice the battery on the left was most desperately charged upon by the rebel infantry. They dashed out of the woods with a yell, reached within about three paces of the guns, and then at the terrific discharges of cannister, accompanied by the death dealing rifle balls of the Chasseurs, melted literally into thin air—the volumes of smoke disclosing to the senses naught but agonizing groans and short, stifled shrieks of the gory-wounded foe.

This battery [Co. I, 1st U.S. Artillery] was formerly Ricketts', and previously [John B.] Magruder's, who, it is said, was on the field in the wood beyond us. After the battle, a rebel officer—a prisoner, said that Magruder swore in the heat of the contest, and said: "That battery must be taken if it costs a thousand lives!" Two attempts were made, which I have above but partially brought within your imagination; and then the baffled general, in despair, with a deep oath, exclaimed, in a characteristic manner: "All hell cannot stand that fire!" and retired to the rear. I think he was right; and the comparison, though profane, just, for that fire was indeed devilish—hellish, if I may be allowed to use the term.

At last the firing ceased entirely, the gray of evening appeared, night set in, and at about 8, P.M., all was quiet, not even a groan or shriek was heard.

This was the part we took in the battle of Seven Pines, and certainly if I speak for myself I shall never pine for a repetition of that scene. I never fully realized before what an intensity of excitement my nerves could stand when in a passive condition, nor do I wish for a repetition of the test.

The California rested that night where it stood during the day, and before daybreak the next day the whole brigade was moved further to the left, and put in a different position in the line of battle. The second day's and the third day's fighting we were not in. Of course, we heard the violent raging of the battle, the booming of cannon, and the rattling of the musketry volleys.

Since then we have been doing picket duty in the woods. One of our lieutenants, from Philadelphia, was shot through the heart yesterday; and several of our privates have since fallen victims to the rifle practice of the rebel sharpshooters. Day before yesterday our regiment was shelled very briskly, some of the missiles coming very near, but none hit. One of our companies was flanked while in a rifle-pit before yesterday, and driven out of it by a battalion of the miscreants. And now while I am writing the rumor reaches me that Lieutenant-Col. [William L.] Curry, of the One Hundred and Sixth Pennsylvania Regiment, is missing, either shot or taken prisoner, for his horse has come in riderless.

And thus every hour of our time is engrossed with some new casualty and some deathful event, and before this reaches you I may be dead myself; but whether so or not, the remainder of our regiment, and our whole army, as an army of victors for the Union, will go to Richmond, and that very soon.

Yours, respectfully,   S. D. B.

First Lieutenant Stephen DeWitt Beekman, age 25, resigned his commission in the 71st Pennsylvania on July 25, 1862. He later joined the 2nd U. S. Cavalry and was commissioned a First Lieutenant on May 18, 1864. According to his service file, Beekman died on July 7, 1864 of "Phlegmonous Erysipelas" at City Point, Va.

FORTIETH (MOZART) REGIMENT, N.Y.S.V.

CAMP OF SEVEN PINES, June 12.

You will learn by this that I am still in the land of mortals (thanks to a kind Providence!), and not numbered with the dead. It is long since I scribed to you my last correspondence, which was at Alexandria, Va. At that time, I informed you that I should not again write to you until the Mozart Regiment had made its mark in the world of battle. I believe I have kept my word. But now it is with feelings of pride that I endeavor to lay before the public the part played in the late engagements by our brave New York regiments. The gain in praise and glory bestowed upon us by our brave and gallant generals, both of which I trust we may carry back to New York after we have concluded our part in the tragic drama of this vile rebellion. Yet, dear MERCURY, while it is with a joyous heart I chronicle below the particulars of our dearly-won laurels, it is with a sad heart I am compelled to place beside that laurel wreath the weeping wreath of cypress. But why should one mourn the loss of our brave companions?

"What strange circles in Time's wheel we trace in our life's onward way!" That is a true saying; and I might add thereto, that occasionally that wheel runs against snags, and knocks out of a seemingly-secure position an occasional spoke. To speak, as it were, in parables, I denominate the Mozart Regiment that wheel, because several of its spokes have suddenly and very unexpectedly, within the last four or five weeks, been wrenched from their apparently firmly-dovetailed sockets. Observe the precipitous workings of military law.

On the 31st day of May last, when the Mozart Regiment was ordered by its general to forward to the battle-field, it obeyed, and while it was directly in front of the enemy, General Kearny—one of the bravest of the brave—galloped up to the side of Colonel E. J. Riley, commandant of the Mozart Regiment, and ordered him to leave the field, go to the rear, and consider himself under arrest. Colonel Riley obeyed. The command of the regiment was then transferred to Lieutenant-Colonel Thomas W. Egan, who nobly led the regiment during its brilliant charge—in conjunction with the brave Thirty-eighth (Second Scott Life Guard) N.Y.S.V.—that drove the enemy from its position like sheep. This charge was a terribly grand affair, and has been highly complimented by the different generals of the day.

About the time the rebels were running from the points of our bayonets, Capt. [Chauncey] McKeever, Chief of Gen. Heintzelman's Staff, received a dispatch from the field, and, after reading it confidentially to himself, he passed over to the centre of the garden that surrounds the head-quarters of General Heintzelman, and there, in the midst of hundreds of wounded and suffering soldiers, exclaimed, at the top of his voice, that "General Birney's Brigade (of Kearny's Division), led by Colonel Hobart Ward, of the Thirty-eighth N.Y.S.V., had driven the enemy one mile at the point of the bayonet." This news was a great panacea to the wounded, and many a poor fellow, upon whose brow death had set his seal, could be heard faintly to exclaim: "Hurrah, hurr"—and then fall back exhausted.

In noticing the bravery of all the generals that have taken part in the late battles on the Peninsula, one of the foremost in rank is Gen. Kearny. Words are inadequate to express the daring and bravery of this general. He is always foremost in the fray; and many times was he observed with his bridle in his teeth, while his right arm (the only one he has), with a sword at the end of it, was cutting and slashing at a furious rate among groups of the enemy. The rebels style him the "One-armed Devil"; and after the battle of Williamsburg, I was told by rebel prisoners, during a conversation with them, that on the night of the fight he was closely watched by them and their officers, and that some of their most accurate sharpshooters were ordered to draw a bead on that "one-armed devil there"; yet they could not see him fall. Finally, a rebel colonel ordered his entire regiment (according to their statement) to withdraw their fire from everything else, and centre it upon that officer with one arm; his order was obeyed, and the entire regiment (the Fifth Carolina) belched forth a volley at that one-armed officer; but he was protected by a just cause and an all-seeing Eye above, and was not seen to fall from his saddle. Such men are too precious to their country and in the eyes of their God to fall by a rebel's bullet.

Our brigade lost many brave men, both officers and privates. Lieut.-Col. Thomas W. Egan, of the Mozart Regiment, and Major [Nelson A.] Gesner deserve the compliments bestowed upon them by their commanding general. Sergeant Joseph Conroy, Co. C, color-bearer of the Mozart, was shot down by the first volley of the enemy, and has since died. The colors were immediately picked up by Corporal [Charles H.] Graves, and carried triumphantly through the remainder of the fight. This corporal, after taking the colors, received through his clothes five balls, two of them grazing the skin. He deserves promotion.

We are encamped at Seven Pines, within six miles of Richmond. Mr. Jeff Davis has said that he will not permit McClellan to dig him out of Richmond; but if he keeps on talking, he will find little Mac and his Union boys rising out of the cellar of his capitol. We know how to dig, we do.

R. McW.

June 29, 1862
FROM OUR OWN SPECIAL CORRESPONDENT
ARMY OF THE POTOMAC

FIVE MILES FROM RICHMOND, June 23rd.

When I first stepped upon the peninsular soil, or mud, at the White House, the impression was made upon my mind that the Virginians were guilty of a horrible joke when they pronounced it "sacred". If sacred things are the things mostly damned by profane lips, then the soil of Virginia may be entitled to the name and all the honors. Certainly, there is nothing about it deserving of religious, or even gentlemanly, consideration. When McClellan would not attack Manassas because the "roads" were in such a fearful condition, many people thought it folly, and swore very hard at the general; but if the roads near Washington are comparable with those near Richmond, then, indeed, they might well appeal even as determined a commander as ours. Talk of mud! New Yorkers who once saw the mud amid which we exist here can even pray with religious fervor for Hackley and thank Heaven for the Five Points! Take Barnum's whale tank, fill it half full of water, dump in several barrels of soil, stir the two up, and call the whole a road, and even then your illustration of the thing will fall far short of the dread reality. Such has been my experience since first visiting the army of the Potomac, in this particular. To make the matter worse, there are but few fields in this neighborhood, the country being covered by heavy woods, which, of course, renders operations necessarily slow. But the huge trees bend before the axes of our volunteers, and the proud forests of the peninsula are slowly though surely being leveled to the earth. Thus has McClellan to fight a foe who outnumber him nearly two to one, and who know that everything depends upon the result before Richmond. We feel that much depends upon it, though not all, and, in consequence, will be slow to move, though powerful when we do move.

Thus much can the correspondent say, but not more. His eyes rest upon a multitudinous profusion of the most enticing items, and his ears drink in with the cannon's roar enlivening knowledge. But there he must stop. To disclose a word is disgrace, ay, even treason. Thus bound and hampered, the writer must lie upon his back, and dream of honors, until he hears the bugle note of battle. Then "Richard is himself again!"—the correspondent is in his glory. Around me are many of the gallant fellows who represent your city, and to speak of them, describe their position and condition, would be gratifying. But even the poor satisfaction of doing this is denied me, and the boys must submit to remain obscure until the great approaching struggle removes the disability. It will not be long, though, before things will have changed.

Of skirmishes between pickets, many little incidents might be written, but in the face of so great a struggle as that now approaching they would be too tame and insipid. The public mind greedily craves great events; it looks forward only to the clash of arms of half a million of men; of victory and re-assertion of our violated laws. Yet picket skirmishing furnishes many a victim upon the alter of Union, whose name is unheralded, whose gallantry receives no tribute. Poor fellows! Many a brave we have borne from the woods, half eaten by vermin, and consigned, uncoffined, to his last resting-place. Were the people who thirst for blood but to see what we see daily, their thirst for bloody triumphs might be allayed!

This letter is intended more as an excuse for not writing before, rather than to communicate information. I might add, that the First New York, Col. Dyckman; the Second Fire Zouaves, Anderson Zouaves (whose gallant colonel [J. Lafayette Riker] so bravely fell on the 31st of May), are in excellent spirits. When the last great reckoning with rebellion is made, rest assured that they will reflect no discredit on the city whose representatives they are in the army of the Potomac.

WATCHMAN.

SECOND FIRE ZOUAVES

CAMP ON BATTLE-FIELD BEFORE RICHMOND, June 19.

I suppose you are aware that I have passed through my second battle. During the last engagement, our company was on picket. We heard the roaring of artillery and the rattle of musketry, and we knew they were at it. As we expected, we were called. We had to shoot without anything but cartridge-boxes, leaving knapsacks and all. We had sixty-rounds of cartridges. We arrived there at dusk, and all was quite still. We, therefore, encamped. In the morning, the rebels came at it again, and in fifteen minutes, we were rushing at double-quick down the road, shouting as hard as we could. We were drawn up in line of battle, and ordered to fire. We poured in a tearing old volley in the woods (there were three rebel regiments there), and sent them skedaddling. We charged after them, and the poor devils were frightened out of their wits. That ended the fight that day. There were five rebel regiments in all—three in the woods (in front of us), and two others that tried to flank us; but the Iron Brigade ain't flats. We had quite a skirmish, on last Sunday [June 15]. We were on the outposts, and there came on a terrible thunder-storm, and the rebels came out sneaking on us, and drove us back aways. But it cost them a little. Captain [Thomas] Smith took about ten of us, and got behind some breastworks, about fifty yards from the woods, and soon the rebels came sneaking out, stooping very low. There was about fifty of them. I don't know how many more were in the woods. The captain would not let us fire until they got right on us. Then he suddenly jumped up, and shouted out: "Now give it to them!" We let drive; and they legged (what was left of them) into the woods. Then wis, wis, came their bullets, but the breastworks saved us. Our company lost three men—one wounded, and two missing. Our regiment lost forty-eight in all, I believe. They flanked Company G, and took nearly all of them. We played a right smart trick on them last night. We sent out a new regiment—a very large one—on a reconnoisance, and drove the rebels back as far as we wanted. The rebels got a large force and advanced; ours fell back to the edge of the wood, and fell flat on their bellies. The rebels came up in a hurry, and our cannon let fly a roaring old of grape and canister over our men's heads and into their ranks, which sent them flying at the rate of twenty knots an hour. They repeated it in quick succession; the woods were thick with them, but they got a double dose.

The coming battle is going to be a bloody one, and a hard one, too; but the sooner the better. We got knocked and hauled around awful. We have not over 200 men fit for duty, and have got to do picket duty every three days—twenty-fours hours on duty, and forty-eight hours off.

Yours, truly,   W. R. D.

July 6, 1862

THE SKIES BRIGHTENING.

As the details of the series of battles in front of Richmond begin to come forward, the gloom that followed the first vague accounts begins to clear away, and the conflict and its results present a more cheerful and encouraging aspect. The army is now in a position of safety; the brave men who have passed a harassing and terrible ordeal are resting from their heroic labors and recruiting their exhausted energies, and preparing, as soon as sufficient re-enforcements are sent forward, to resume their interrupted march upon the capital succession—this time with a force that will be irresistible, and under circumstances will preclude the possibility of disappointment.

The particulars of the series of engagements of the last ten days have appeared in the daily papers have been meagre and imperfect. Slight as they were, however, they revealed the bravery of the Union troops, which shines out through every official dispatch and every correspondent's letter. In the graphic account from our regular correspondent, which we give in the present issue of the SUNDAY MERCURY, something like a complete idea maybe be obtained for the courage with which the devoted columns of the Union army withstood the shock of superior numbers and the terrific onset of fire and steel, the mere description of which makes us shudder as we read.

Though under orders to retreat, and performing a retrograde movement, which always exerts a dispiriting influence, our troops resisted the overwhelming tide of rebel numbers which pressed upon them, and exhibited an unflinching heroism which finds few parallels in history. The record of killed and wounded furnishes a sad attestation of their courage, and still greater carnage suffered by their assailants measures the depth of indebtedness the country owes to those who sacrificed their lives in her defence.

Another effort is necessary, and it should be made promptly and without delay. What conscription has done for the South, patriotism will accomplish at the North. What we want is a man at the head of the affairs at Washington capable of comprehending the crisis and equal to its requirements. Armies have been sacrificed because the Government established a limitation, beyond which it would not allow their numbers to be swelled. Thousands have been allowed to waste their efforts in an unequal war, when a few additional hundreds would have snatched the victory which nodded to their grasp.

We have still men and means to retrieve the comparative reverses of the last few days and to drive the rebels from their stronghold, unless the criminal incapacity which has ruled the past is permitted to exert the baneful influence in the future.

The remnant of the gallant and indomitable army, now resting secure on the banks of the James River, should have its broken ranks restored by new men as rapidly as they can be mustered in. The war has been prosecuted as child's play. We seemed afraid to hurt the rebels. Babblers in Congress and sniveling dotards elsewhere, were more anxious for the safety of rebel property than the defeat of rebel armies. This policy must be reversed, and a sterner effort than has yet been put forth be made to retrieve the blunders of the past, and a success which those blunders have again postponed into the future.

July 13, 1862

FOURTH REGIMENT N.Y.S.V.

QUATERMASTER'S DEPARTMENT, SUFFOLK, July 8.

With difficulty I am trying to pen a few lines to you. This was one of the hottest days we have had for a long time, 120 degrees; but as I am writing, the band of the First Delaware Volunteers is out serenading General Mansfield, a gentleman and friend to all the soldiers—Music has its charms; it fetches Secesh; the music whispering the soul-stirring strains, "Star Spangled Banner", the flag they have outraged—it cuts them—it makes them feel miserable. The boys of our regiment raised another grand flag-staff, this makes the fourth one. It is at the railroad station and opposite our office. There was a gay old time when the time-honored flag was raised and some old-fashioned cheering. Times have changed. Secesh condescends to walk under it. The folks here expect their dear Southern soldiers back; two companies of fine young men, it is stated, have gone to the wars, and are now at Richmond awaiting their doom.

Our boys are getting wild; they have not had the first show yet; but before many days elapse they will meet the foe, face to face. We are under marching orders. Officers are sending their goods home, keeping just enough with them for necessary changes. The rebels are in force about twenty miles from here, and guerrilla parties all through the country. Why not send 20,000 men here and make one grand dash toward Petersburg? Here is a chance for fame and laurels for any general. By getting Petersburg we bag the rebels; if not, they will make another stand at Danville or Weldon.

Fourth of July was kept up here with some spirits, but there was no wasting of powder. It is our friend, and we cannot tell how soon we will want it for good purposes.

I must cork up. Taps!　　　　　　　　　　　　　G. R. L.

July 20, 1862
INVADING THE NORTH!
The rebel [Robert] Toombs, of Georgia, is said to have once boasted that he would one day read the roll-call of his slaves at the foot of Bunker Hill Monument. The rebel Secretary of War, just after the fall of Fort Sumter, informed his constituents that the flag of the Confederacy would soon float over Faneuil Hall. These promises have not been realized; but is a shameful and humiliating fact that now, for the first time since the war commenced, rebel marauders have crossed border, have seized villages in the free State of Indiana, and are threatening the chief city of Ohio. The guerilla-chief, [John H.] Morgan, is deprecating upon and harassing the loyalists of Kentucky; and in various localities we see an apparent attempt to carry out the threat contained in the address of Jeff Davis to his army after the late battles, that they should soon advance beyond the outer boundaries of the Confederacy.

Two thousand freebooters under Morgan have spread consternation in and around Cincinnati. There are tens of thousands of men in Kentucky alone who might be organized into an armed force powerful enough to hang each one of these bandits to a separate tree. The dainty opposition to the employment of darkeys as soldiers is about played out. We should fight the rebels with whatever weapon will hit the heaviest blow. These fellows violate the usages of civilized warfare every day of their lives, and to stand upon a punctilio such as the particular hue of the men employed to punish and resist their outrages, is an idea that could only be entertained by a traitor or an imbecile. We should fight the devil with fire, and Secessionists with the element which they have never hesitated to use in their own behalf. The slaves should be drafted into the service immediately, whether they belong to loyal or disloyal owners. We must use the means of overcoming the rebels in their own midst, if we would not transfer the scene of warlike operations from the South to the free plains of Ohio, or the streets of New York.

OUR OWN SPECIAL CORRESPONDENCE
FORTRESS MONROE, July 16.

The recent sweeping order of Gen. McClellan, excluding everybody not connected with the army for entering within the lines, is variously regarded. In its operation, especially, it is unfair and unjust; for, while correspondents with the army are allowed to remain, those who have just as good a right to be there are prohibited from performing their duties. But, the order will doubtless be productive of good results, for the following reasons among others:

First, It demonstrates that the commanding general is really in command. Even Secretary [Edwin M.] Stanton's passes are worthless.

Second, The sutlers, a nuisance, as all but themselves will admit, have no further chance of robbing the army by their excessive charges.

Third, Civilians, including Congressmen, who never had any other object than curiosity, can no longer interfere with the duties of officers, by claiming their attention and hospitality.

Should the order have excepted correspondents, an invidious distinction might have been claimed to have been made, and the reporters must patiently wait for a few days, when all may be right.

Let no one suppose that Gen. McClellan intends to rest for a very long while. His present position is a good one, but not so good as he might wish it; and after a few days pass, and re-enforcements have been sufficiently received, we anticipate more music of a stirring character. In the late actions he suffered badly—terribly, in fact, but saved his army. I have talked with generals who ought to know, and all agree that in his recent movement McClellan performed a feat that in nine times out of ten would fail of success. One hinted quite broadly that he anticipated a surrender or total annihilation of the army on the Chickahominy, owing to the vastly superior numbers of our rebel enemies, and that when the move to the James River was made he saw nothing but failure ahead. Of our own strength, the people have been shamefully deceived, and it is now time for an inquiry upon the subject, without arguing the question of McClellan's ability or not. Let Congress call for the facts, and then we may all know the truth, and know where to place the responsibility. Well do I remember, when at Fair Oaks, how the general would come darting around to examine the fortifications, and many a time have I heard him say to a general:

"By all means hold your position. Hold it, if every man falls. Don't pursue the enemy. Do nothing to bring on an engagement."

Six weeks ago, as the inquiry will show, McClellan telegraphed for men. He knew his forces were fearfully outnumbered, and that, with no succor, desperate means alone would save a desperate cause. The Fair Oaks fight took place. We were attacked on one wing by a force fully as numerous as was our whole army. We held our position, and again was the appeal made for re-enforcements. They were sent. But how many do you think? Hardly 12,000 men. It fairly covered the killed, wounded, and missing of Seven Pines and Fair Oaks, with the consequent sick; no more. The cause grew desperate. Every day we saw rebel divisions march in, and every night we heard their cheers of anticipated triumph. Daily they came nearer; daily we grew weaker. Then came a shock which only the foresight of McClellan, the power of our artillery, and the wonderful bravery of our men, prevented from effects the most fatal. We were forced back, but not into the swamps of the Chickahominy, as was anticipated. The James River was reached, and under the protecting care of our gunboats a wearied army received the rest so much needed. And it was a dearly bought triumph for the enemy, as the awful list of rebel dead tells most painfully.

Let no one think the army have lost confidence in their general, for he is a hundred fold more popular to-day than ever before among the rank and file. They know the number of the fierce foe who so terribly fought them for six successive days, and, whether justly or not, give to McClellan the credit of saving them all. And I have good assurance that President Lincoln is eminently satisfied. Of his visit here, you have already been informed. He went to head-quarters, and reviewed the army; he spoke to them, and took especial pains to say that the general had his confidence, as he should have his support. When the general had explained matters to the President, Abraham looked up and said:

"General, this reminds me of a story. When I was in the Indian wars (here he smiled); there was a fellow named Tom Jones, who was full of fight, and yet very careful. One night Tom went out to reconnoitre. He saw a redskin, and thought it better to give him a shot and then retreat to camp. Well, the Indian pressed Tom pretty closely, and the two blazed away at each other, until at last Tom got to camp with the Indian a prisoner. Tom had an eye shot out, a part of his nose shot off, besides showing other signs of rather rough treatment.

"Why, where have you been, Tom?" asked I, somewhat alarmed.

"Only had a little tussle over thar," he replied.

"Well, but you've lost an eye, your nose, and seem to have a pretty sore leg."

"Yes, thar you're right, but d—n him, I've got the copper-colored nigger!"

"So, general," said the witty President, "your case is similar. You've been knocked around rather roughly, but you have the rebels, unless I'm much mistaken."

It looks now as if the enemy intend to blockade the James River, and thus to starve us out. This morning they opened on the transport Daniel Webster, and put some solid shot right through her cabin. Fortunately, she escaped. But the gunboats under [Flag Officer Charles] Wilkes will stop this kind of work, you may depend. The iron clad captain is now here, getting his "house in order", and then look out for music.

Burnside has gone to Washington, but will return on an early day. He made a special request to be sent to McClellan, whom he regards as the ablest military man in the world. I have the best authority for saying, that Burnside insists upon giving McClellan supreme command of the army, and that the President is now considering a proposition to that effect.

Every day, a large number of officers from the army reaches this point, for some reason or other which needs explanation. Many are sick, and require kind medical treatment, but the large majority hop around quite lively, and seem quite ready for duty. They tell too, in many cases, such great stories of their bravery, etc., that one would think they could find more pleasure at Harrison's Landing, than here. The simple fact is, too many were engaged in this war, expecting it to be nothing more than a mere cloud which would give them a pleasant six months' excursion, and nothing more. They have been deceived, sadly deceived, and now wish they were home. The men are more stubborn, having fewer advantages of thus getting better satisfied with camp life.

We expect, ere long, to hear of an engagement at Yorktown, where our forces are at work strengthening the fortifications. The rebels know what kind of a place it is, and may be loath to attack it. Should they return to Williamsburg, we may lay it in ashes.

Expect big events before long. Think not that the postponement of the great struggle is for an indefinite period. It may come unexpectedly upon us all.

Your, etc.,   W.

FOURTH REGIMENT, N.Y.S.V.

SUFFOLK, VA. July 14.

Although much has been commented on the undue leniency with which rebellious citizens are treated in the Southern cities garrisoned by Federal troops, I do not think it amiss to state one or two of the many instances in which exaggerated protection is afforded to the inhabitants of the town. The many complaints which are constantly heaping on this subject must eventually attract the attention of the commander-and-chief at least, let us hope so. You will therefore, allow me to add my mite of experience and indignation to the well-founded complaints which find their way to the press, hoping that one day the North will awaken to the reality of the immense peril in which it is being hurled in a strife with a foe which shows no disposition to relent its hatred toward us, despite the child-like protection which we seem determined to exhibit toward our grateful "friends".

A sheep was recently killed by some of our pickets; it was found wandering in the woods alone, and away from any habitation. Their act was not prompted by wanton cruelty, no! the men had had no fresh meat for many days, and considered this (as all soldiers would in an enemy's country) a lawful appropriation. A part of the animal was brought to camp, but long before the captors had time to put it in their mess-kettle, it was communicated to the military authorities that some soldiers had committed considerable depredations on a neighboring farm. Would you believe it, the poor, exhausted men, after twenty-four hours of arduous picket duty, were summoned to return the meat forthwith to the place it had been taken from. Two hours later, a fine piece of meat was being sold to the colonel at a ridiculously high price. How great was the jubilation of the men on discovering that this leg of mutton was the identical one which had, once before, made its appearance into our camp, and how the Union man must have chuckled, when recounting to his friends—for every man is a "Union man" in Suffolk—the dodge he had played on the Yankee colonel. This is one of the many instances of the kind that have occurred since we have occupied this town.

I will, however, relate another one which occurred yesterday, far more serious and less amusing:

A slave girl—black, it is true; very black, in fact; but a girl, interesting and witty, full of devotion toward the officer in whom she had sought protection—had become the favorite of all who knew her. As if anxious to show how much she dreaded to return to the state of subjugation from which she had recently escaped, she endeavored by making herself indispensable (as she thought, no doubt), to remain in the employ of her new master, who would interpose in her favor whenever her owner—what a dreadful word, in its present acceptation—would detect her hiding place to drag her back into slavery. Poor child! Her fears must have prayed on her like an incubus, as the state of agitation into which she threw the whole camp sufficiently shows. Her owner had made his appearance at the lieutenant-colonel's tent (perhaps during his absence); and clothed with the authority which precluded all doubt of success (an order from the provost-marshal), had wrenched poor Topsy from her bright reveries and from the pure atmosphere which she seemed to breathe so freely, and dragged her away, amid the heart-rendering cries of the helpless child, to her gloomy prison. Let us not dwell on the tortures to which the poor creature must, at this present moment, be put for having stolen herself from her master. Let us not stop to inquire into the state of utter despair which must have taken possession of that aspiring soul, so happy a moment before. No, lessons of justice and philanthropy are yet to be taught a great many people, and it would be rash and unjudicious to develop in them lessons of high morality from which a deep chasm separates them yet. One doubts, sometimes, if society, as it progresses and perfects itself materially, develops in an equal progression the transcendental truths of metaphysics toward which all high aspirations centre. And truly, when studying human nature in all its ramifications, the future must appear gloomy to him who doubts the presence of a higher power among us. The word "Union" has grown old and obsolete; we all acknowledge tacitly that we are fighting for "something" besides the Union. We are afraid, in our lukewarm efforts, to recognize an evil. We blush to confess that we are fighting against slavery! O Topsy! May thy miserable and degraded life be offered as a holocaust on the alter of human freedom! may those like thee pining under the rod of abject subjection be an offering to the Almighty for the approaching freedom of thy ill-fated race!

X.

U.S. FRIGATE SABINE

NEW LONDON, July 17.

Once in a while, that is as often as I can, I get the SUNDAY MERCURY and eagerly read the contents, especially the letters department, as I think more is to be learned from the letters sent to you by our soldiers about their state and feelings, and about the condition of things generally down South than can be learned from any other source. Thinking thus, I have concluded to send you a few lines, which I should be glad to read in the SUNDAY MERCURY, but, of course, you will act your own pleasure about it. When I entered the navy, I did so under the conviction that I should be put into active service, and do my small share toward restoring our great-and glorious Union as it was; but I have been sadly disappointed, and what causes me to feel it more, is that I refused other occupation by which I could have made a great deal more money, if I had thought of compensation for my services as one of the objects for shipping in the navy. I can say honestly, that when I shipped I fully expected to be put into service, if opportunity offered, and I done my duty well, of course, I should be honorably mentioned, if not promoted; instead of this, we have made a little jaunt outside, with scarce a definite object, "cruising for the Vermont", came back, lays at the Navy Yard, Brooklyn, and off the Battery, New York, for eight weeks, and at this place now going on two weeks, with no prospect of getting away, and the ostensible reason for visiting this port was to recruit men for the navy. Well, since we have been here, we have shipped one white man, two white boys, and five negro men and boys, making a total of eight, and it would have been better for the two or three hundred on board if the new-comers had never come, some of them, at least. I do not think a man fit to be put among a clean crew, who has to be taken and scrubbed with tobacco juice, have head shaved, etc. I think our real object in coming here was to give the people of New England a chance to inspect a man-of-war, and to pay attention to our captain, Cadwalleder Ringgold, who so gallantly rescued the four hundred marines from the sinking transport,

Governor, last fall, for which he has been presented with a gold medal, a sword, which cost six hundred and odd dollars, complimentary resolutions, and other things perhaps that I know not of. The ship is thronged with visitors—men, women, and children—from morn till night. During the past day or two there has been a large float alongside, and a steam ferry boat has been running to and from the ship. The officers are busily engaged in escorting the ladies about the ship. One of them is courting a dislike from every one of the men in the ship's company. He makes use of such expressions as "This is where the common sailors eat", "and this is common sailor's bread", as he escorts the ladies along the berth-deck, where perhaps the men are at their meals at the time. I cannot write more; but if you see fit to publish this scrawl, I will soon send another.

ONE OF THE CREW.

July 27, 1862
SECOND FIRE ZOUAVES
CAMP NEAR HARRISON BAR, VA., July 19.

Not seeing anything of our regiment in your valuable paper lately, I thought I would address the Fire Department of New York with a few lines. My brother-soldiers in the habit of corresponding with your paper are now laid low in the late battle of Chickahominy. All our regiment numbers is 130 men fit for duty. We are still in the advance. It cannot be expected that our regiment, only numbering from 130 men, can hold the position of a regiment numbering from 800 to 900 men. I think if the Fire Department of New York wants us to uphold the laurels we have already won, I think it is their duty to try and fill the thinned ranks of our regiment, which fell in so noble of cause. We have no more confidence in ourselves, as we have not the men enough to stand by our colors. Is it possible the Fire Department of New York cannot produce men enough to fill up our regiment? We fought in every battle on the Peninsula under that magnificent stand of colors that was presented to us by the New York Fire Department. They never got stained by us yet, nor never will, I hope. When I left for the seat of war—that is twelve months ago to-day—I knew a great many young men who were very patriotic. I know them to be very anxious to meet the foe now. There is a chance for them to distinguish themselves. I hope they won't falter, and join the Home Guard. Arouse, boys, and lend a hand. Our next move will be "on to Richmond". There is not one moment to be lost. The boys are all getting along tolerably well, considering the hot weather. All we want is, to be recruited up to a regiment once more. We think we have been on the advance long enough. It was rumored in camp to-day that our regiment is to be relieved for a while to give us a chance to recruit up. I forgot to mention about our gallant colonel (William Brewster), who is now a prisoner in the hands of the enemy; also Capt. Michael Burns, Capt. [William] Fisk, and several of our sick. I am sorry to have to say it is discouraging to the boys to think we have neither colonel, lieutenant-colonel, major, nor adjutant. One good thing is, we have great confidence in our general—that is Daniel E. Sickles. He is as brave a man as ever rode at the head of a brigade. Capt. [Alfred A.] Donalds, of Company F, now in command of the regiment, it gives me great pleasure to say, acted and proved himself an officer and a gentleman. I will now close, for perhaps I have taken up too much of your valuable paper. Boys, come one, come all; we will soon crush this rebellion, and restore our glorious Union.

Your valuable paper comes pretty regular. There is no other paper suits the boys better than the old SUNDAY MERCURY.

Yours, respectfully,   COMPANY C, SECOND NEW YORK FIRE ZOUAVES

MILITARY MATTERS
LATEST ADVICES FROM RICHMOND—WHAT OUR RETURNED (PRISONER) CORRESPONDENTS SAY.—We have had conversations with several of the officers and men recently released from captivity at Richmond, and they agree very nearly in all their statements. It is the unanimous opinion of all that Gen. McClellan can take the rebel capital, but he must have at *least two hundred thousand men to do it*. They also concur in the belief that the Irish and German soldiers in the rebel army are true to the Union; and that if there were a few good leaders and a proper organization among them, they could give the traitors a vast deal of trouble—in fact, become a very fire in their midst.

The last visitor to our office was Charles B. Denny, hospital steward of the Second Fire Zouaves (Fourth Regiment Excelsior Brigade). He is known to our readers as the correspondent signing himself "Carolus". Mr. Denny is an intelligent young Irishman; was formerly head clerk in one of our large Broadway drug stores, and has studied surgery. He was taken prisoner at the battle of Seven Pines [Savage's Station] on Sunday, June 29th, being posted on the turnpike road leading from Bottom's Bridge, where Dr. John J. McGowen, surgeon of the Second Regiment, Sickles Brigade, himself and twelve assistants were left to take care of some 200 sick of Hooker's Division. These wounded were unable to be moved at the time the retreat commenced, and so fell into the hands of the enemy. Fearful of the shot falling along there, Steward Denny advanced to a breastwork near by and waved a white flag. In about two hours, a rebel sergeant and two privates entered the hospital line, and arrested all who were well. They were immediately taken before Gen. [Benjamin] Huger, and a detachment of thirty men sent down to the wounded. He speaks in the best terms of the treatment received at the hands of the rebels. They were taken to a large hospital fronting on Carey street and the James River, and extending the entire block, from Twentieth to Twenty-first street.

While in this hospital, an Irishwoman waved her handkerchief and also a small American flag to them from the upper window of some building in the vicinity. He says that an old American flag, used at one of the commissary tents to keep the flies out, and left behind, was paraded about through Richmond in great glee, where it was announced as being captured after a desperate fight, and that McClellan intended to raise it over the dome of the Capitol!

He also speaks of the daring valor shown by Father O'Hagan, Capt. Michael W. Burns, of Company A, Capt. Wm. M. Fiske, of Company E, and Capt. McCusley, of Company H, are all in prison yet. {Father O'Hagen is now released.}

Mr. Denny coincides with the others in stating that the Merrimac No. 2 [C.S.S. Richmond] is nearly ready for service; she is rather small in size, but heavily armed. There is also an iron gunboat or ram at Richmond, which is now ready for service, and two or three others are under way. He further agrees in the belief that an immediate draft should be ordered from all the States, and an immense army raised, and that all the re-enforcements possible ought to be sent to McClellan with the utmost dispatch.

A private of this regiment (named Smith), now in New York, lay in the woods from Sunday morning until Wednesday noon—his thigh shattered by a musket-ball—and he was compelled to drink his own urine in order to save his life.

These men show a devoted love toward McClellan, which seems to rouse them into new being. They declare that his army will follow him everywhere and at all times.

Charles B. Denny continued to serve as Hospital Steward for the Second Fire Zouaves until June, 1863, when on the march to Gettysburg he began to spit blood, and soon collapsed. He was diagnosed with Pulmonary Tuberculosis and discharged on October 1, 1863. Written in his medical record, the examining surgeon commented: "the disease was contracted in the service in the line of duty; improvement highly improbable."

August 3, 1862
NINTH REGIMENT, N.Y.S.M.
WARRENTON, FAUQUIER CO., VA., July 27.

Your paper is ever welcomed to us, and perused with great interest. The lucky ones who receive it regularly are sure to find plenty of listeners while they read it.

Much has been said in praise of our regiment; but we do not wish to be known as other than we are. We have been represented as being thoroughly drilled in the manual of arms; but night before last, and last night, have shown where we were slack. We have had three dress parades here, in town. The first one passed off very well—nothing could have been better. But the second one was made a complete balk of by our colonel (J.W. Stiles). Judge of our astonishment to see him undertake to put us through the loadings and firings. He has never given us a regimental drill in the loadings and firings since I have been with the regiment. Our major gave us one drill, while encamped one mile east of here. Never was the regiment so much displeased with the colonel before. He displayed his own ignorance and incompetency.

He knew perfectly well that we were not well drilled in it as a regiment, and ought not to have attempted it. The trouble is, that each captain drills his company his own way. By companies, we can't be beat at drilling. The colonel is at fault for allowing other than a uniform drill throughout.

There was a large crowd of citizens and soldiers to witness our dress parade. They seemed to be well pleased with our evolutions, but when we were going through the loadings and firings we felt mortified that it was done so poorly. It is no fault of ours. The blame rests upon the colonel and some of the officers.

We are here guarding the town and doing provost duty.

Our duties are very heavy to what they have been. Most of us go on guard every other day.

Some of the companies are so small that it takes nearly every man to make out the regular details. It is currently repeated here that General Pope is to take up his head-quarters in the Seminary just in the outskirts of town.

I trust this is so. He is a man we all like, and have great confidence in. This new order gives us assurance that he will prosecute the war in earnest; that no (rebel traitor) will receive protection from him.

Nothing is more galling to a patriot and Union loving man than to be compelled to guard the property of his enemies. We are glad this has been put a stop to. It is a very important step toward ending the war.

Until the rebels are made to feel the severity of the war, but little permanent success will be won by our arms. The citizens here are bitterly secesh.

Being asked by one of them if I was fighting for the abolition of slavery, I replied, "No, sir! That I was in the service of Uncle Sam, to aid in restoring the Union,—that if slavery was brought to an end in doing it, it could not be helped."

By restoring the Union, both the welfare of the North and South would be gained. "Never can the Union live divided." "Divided we shall fall," but, "united we stand."

The South is blind to this. They think we are fighting for the North alone; that the North seeks to conquer and subdue the South to her will. They begin to see now that this is not the case. May the time soon come when they may be brought back once more to the Union, and peace, and prosperity once more visit our now convulsed country!

Yours for the Union,   PLUMP

August 10, 1862
SECOND FIRE ZOUAVES
CAMP LINCOLN, HARRISON'S LANDING, VA., Aug. 2.

Seeing that none of our lads have written to you of late, I have taken it upon myself to act as correspondent, though perhaps I have undertaken a task which a green hand will find difficult to accomplish. Since the late retreat, our lads look rather the worse for wear. I have seen some of them washing a shirt in the brook while a friendly blouse protected their bare backs from the burning rays of a Virginia sun. One cannot look around among the lads without missing many familiar faces. There's no more ball playing; no jumping. The camp no longer echoes with "Dixie's Land" and "Glory Hallelujah", as of yore. Every face has a melancholy expression; every one has lost a friend. Our brave little colonel a prisoner adds bitterly to our sorrows. Our chaplain, Father O'Hagen, who was recently taken prisoner, has been released. The reverend father received rather rough treatment from the rebel officials. He was brought before the rebel, Gen. [John H.] Winder, who asked him what regiment he belonged to. On being told that he belonged to the Second New York Fire Zouaves, Winder assailed him bitterly, saying he had disgraced his cloth by ministering to New York thieves; and when Father O'Hagen asked to be allowed to retain his horse, Winder profanely replied:

"Damn you and your horse! You damn ministers come down here to raise hell."

Winder's better nature finally prevailed, and the next day he apologized for his harsh words. The reverend father is now in New York; and we hope he has the love and respect of all. A rumor that we were going to be relieved for sixty days, to return to New York to recruit, spread a ray of hope among us.

Yours,   GRAPESHOT.

TWELFTH REGIMENT N.Y.S.M.
HARPER'S FERRY, Aug. 8.

The Twelfth is still encamped on Bolivar Heights, Camp Morris, named after Col. [William H.] Morris (now brigadier-general by brevet), late in command of Fort McHenry, near Baltimore, and is still, in spite of the intensely hot weather, as assiduously and unremittingly engaged in drill as ever. We are excellently drilled now, having brigade drills—the brigade consisting of the Twelfth and Twenty-second Regiments, N. Y. S. M., and the Eighty-seventh Ohio—every Monday, Wednesday, and Friday; and battalion drills on Tuesdays, Thursdays and Saturdays; besides two company drills each day, and the evening dress parade. And, friend MERCURY, we are over-drilled; for with "police," duty, "fatigue" duty (very fatiguing, indeed), guard duty, "extra" duty, "volunteer" duty, and many other "duties" which those in command puzzle their brains to rake up or invent for us, "too numerous to mention" truly, we have a hard time of it. Our three months are up about the 28th of August, by which time we expect and hope to be in New York City. True, we have been stationed only at Harper's Ferry, but that was no fault of "ourn," for we would have marched on Richmond willingly, had we have been so commanded; and we can honestly say that we have endeavored to do our duty faithfully, and honestly. I understand that the Twelfth will, when re-recruited, go out again for a long period of service. Ours is a good regiment, and is with a few exceptions well officered. Our boys should be allowed to go swimming oftener than they are (once in five days), where we have such fine swimming chances as here in the Potomac and Shenandoah Rivers, as their health and cleanliness require, provided they behave themselves when out of camp. Now they have to march out in companies, under charge of a commissioned officer, to the sound of the drum, while heretofore they have had more liberty.

The whole regiment should not be made to suffer for the misbehavior of a few unsoldierly ones. Soldiers should try to be men and gentlemen, ever; should ever be cleanly, honest, polite; and never should shirk duty, lie, steal, gamble, get intoxicated, dissipate, waste, stray, quarrel, blaspheme, or talk obscenely.

Camp rumors are very many, various, ridiculous, and ever altogether unreliable. One day, [T. J. "Stonewall"] Jackson has beaten us, and is advancing rapidly on Harper's Ferry; the next, Pope has "whipped Jackson out of his boots", and is driving him—Mars only knows where! We were to march (per camp rumors) Richmond, Winchester, Gordonsville, Fort McHenry, etc.; and to Washington, Fortress Monroe, Annapolis, Manassas, and many other places. Our pickets, etc., have had (Othello-like), hair-breath escapes, deadly perils, daring, thrilling adventures (?) But enough of satire. Our health is quite good, we have had no deaths yet. We have soft bread as rations now (from ovens built by George W. Van Wagner, of Company I), half a loaf a day. There is fair fishing in the Potomac and Shenandoah Rivers here. Our water wells are played out, and water-carriers have to go a long way into Bolivar village, which is a great inconvenience. Our guards should be allowed to sleep or rest on their four hours off duty, and should not be made to go on brigade-drill. "Post No. 1, 12 o'clock and all's well!" cries sentry No. 1, and the cry goes clear around the large circumference of our camp every half hour. Berries of all sorts are ripe and plenty, and fruits are ripening rapidly, vegetation ditto. Riding stray or strange cavalry horses, is a game sometimes practiced here. I tried it, and was thrown, hurting myself quite severely. Milking cows is also a contraband game. I recently swam the Potomac River, about a half a mile wide here; also, I partially explored a very large natural cave here, and had my "fortune" told in Bolivar by a female fortune-teller. I am to get killed in battle soon, she says. The soil here is very fertile and productive; the fields are beautifully green, and fragrant with clover, and many with sown grass, and penny-royal, etc.; the air vocal with birds, and the sky of Italy's matchless cerulean hue. Destruction of any kind of United States property is very reprehensible. United States horses, etc., and other cattle, are branded "U.S." on the fore-shoulder. For a wonder, there's a barber-shop here. "Nuff ced." We have had divine service in the Bolivar church here, and preaching by the Rev, John Cotton Smith. For the first time since I left home I heard the sweet chimes of the church bells. Blessed, home-like sound; how soothing, and how pleasing! The beauty and glory of our sunrises and sunsets are sublime; our days are torrid, but our mornings and evenings are cool and deliciously bracing. There are many beautiful, cool, dark, and secluded nooks, and alcoves, and retreats here where a poet might dream on joyously. "Charge bayonets" on the "double-quick" in torrid weather is no joke. *Ennui*, listlessness, idleness, mischief-making, etc., are disgraceful. The MERCURY "special war correspondents"—a noble brotherhood—writing from the camps are indeed an efficient corps—larger than that engaged on any other paper in the United States. I wish them, one and all, all manner of success, and perpetual God-speed. In the rain or in the burning sun, the poor sentry suffers greatly; but 'tis the fortune of a soldier. Alone on his post, on a beautiful night, the sentinel dreams of home, love, fame, poesy. Numerous runaway contrabands are continually coming in here. A rebel major recently shot the daughter of a poor colored woman, living about eight miles from here. The poor woman is going about seeking redress. There is a large, intelligent-looking dog here that fairly haunts this regiment. On company, battalion, or brigade drills, he is as punctual in attendance as any officer; he reviews us at dress-parade, and he is emphatically a trump—"the Dog of the Regiment."

Double-quick races between the companies are hot and exciting affairs. By candle-light the posturings, attitudizings, etc., of the inmates of our camp tents are ever very grotesque, hugely funny, and particularly laughable. Clumsy marchers are necessary nuisances. Brilliant men (in a mental point of view) are often weak physically, and *vice versa*. Smart men don't always make smart soldiers. The mud and dust of the "sacred soil" beats all other muds and dusts all hollow; we get enough of both. We practice now at target-firing; we can boast of some very good shots, too. Washing our clothes and dishes is a necessary bore. Most of the talk here is of home and fight. We are all tanned and sun-burned, though strong and healthy. Letters and papers from friends and relatives are ever solicited. In haste.

Yours, truly,   J. S. H.

MILITARY MATTERS

NORTHERN NEGROES READY TO FIGHT FOR THE UNION.—Great excitement exists among the rapidly-increasing colored population of the North at the prospect of their services being needed to fight against the oppressors of their race. They confidently expect that, before white men are drafted, black men will, at least, be allowed to volunteer, as in the Revolution, to fight their own battle in defence of the country. Acting upon this principle, which [General] Washington recognized in his last great campaigns, and which General [Andrew] Jackson adopted in his fight with the Southern Secessionists, the Anglo-African newspaper, edited and printed by the colored men of New York, this week issues the following patriotic call to arms:

"The hour is at hand when the American government, realizing at last the stupendous strength and unrelenting hate of the slave power, and startled by the threatened intervention of the European courts, at whose feet its rebel emissaries have groveled, will awake to the imminence of the peril, and invoke the aid of colored Americans to save the life of the Republic.

"Lose not a moment, but be ready promptly to meet the call of our common country. Organize yourselves in companies at every convenient point. Obtain drillmasters. Practice the manual exercises and evolutions steadily and with a will. Accustom yourselves to the prompt obedience of military discipline. Arrange your affairs that you may leave home at a moment's notice. Appoint committees of correspondence and arrangement, that there may be no confusion or delay—that companies, battalions, and regiments may be speedily filled when the order comes for you to march.

"When this mad rebellion has been crushed by your assistance, a new day will dawn for America, and a brighter destiny for her colored children. Rouse to your new duties as American soldiers, serving under the flag of the Republic that no longer waves over the slave pens in our free capital, nor mocks the cargoes of despair packed between the decks of the slave-trader—swear allegiance to the purified banner that will soon wave again throughout the American continent, greeting the sun that in his course shall no more rise upon a master, nor set upon a slave.

"Remember your fathers, who fought under Washington, and sealed with their blood the independence of our country. Remember the brave men of your race when Andrew Jackson called to arms on the banks of the Mobile, and whom he afterwards thanked in a proclamation that perpetuates in American annals their heroic exploits and their noble ardor.

"Let the remembrance of the past, the great duties of to-day, and the hopes of a glorious future animate you to a holy daring. Let the historian record for distant centuries, that in the death-struggle between Slavery and Freedom on the American Continent, whoever were traitors, the blacks were true; that though their country at first declined their services, the instant she called they rushed to her support, and welcomed hardships, wounds, and death, to save her from destruction.

"Teach the men of the present generation to acknowledge the injustice they had done you, and fear not that your country will forget your services when the rebellion of the slave power is utterly vanquished, and its foreign abettors abashed—when the honor of the nation is vindicated, its supremacy established, its heaven-born principles of right triumphant, its Stars and Stripes shall command the admiration of the world, as the emblem of a nation alike powerful and free."

The darkeys are ready—let Old Abe sound the bugle.

August 17, 1862
FIFTY-SEVENTH REGIMENT, N.Y.S.V.
HARRISON'S LANDING, Aug. 10.

My last two letters created some little excitement here; the boys blame this one and that one, all but the right one.

The weather continues warm, and the boys almost begin to roast.

Some time ago [July 31], the rebels across the river became a little excited, and the first thing we knew when we awoke from our sleep, we heard the familiar old sound of shot and shell. It was almost dark as pitch, After awhile we were got in line, but we soon stacked arms, and back to bed we went. I took a walk next day near the vicinity that was shelled, but could not find out what damage was done.

Our drill continues the same. Our colonel is on the sick list at present, but just let him hear there is a prospect of an engagement, then see how quick he is up and in command. There is not a braver man on the peninsula than Colonel [Samuel K.] Zook, and I may say, in the army. I know the boys would like to see him our brigadier.

Last Wednesday night [6th], after tattoo, our regiment, with the rest of the brigade, and the Irish Brigade, and two batteries (as I was not out, being detained in camp by sickness, I will give you the details as given to me by a comrade), went on a reconnoissance. We marched to within a mile and a half of Malvern Hill. There we formed in line of battle—our regiment lying behind one of the batteries as a support. We stood there about half an hour, then marched back to our pickets, leaving the Irish Brigade to hold the place. We then lay behind a battery, almost within sight of the breastworks, till Friday morning. We then marched back to camp.

General French had command of both brigades—Colonel [John R.] Brooke in command of ours. He is a fine officer. Our worthy lieutenant-colonel commanded our regiment.

Our boys are glad to hear that the old regiments are to be filled up; and the sooner they do it the better, for we are anxious to get into the field again, and expect soon to take a meal in Richmond.

I agree with your correspondents in stating that the correspondents of the daily papers give an incorrect statement of things about this place, and the soldiers' camps, etc. I have not seen a correct account in a daily yet; and the only correct accounts we get are from the SUNDAY MERCURY.

I will write again.

Yours,   DIDO.

August 24, 1862
TWELFTH REGIMENT, N.Y.S.M.
HARPER'S FERRY, VA., August 15.

In despite of the really torrid temperature of the weather, we are drilled as much as we were in early June last; and, as a matter of course, we are nearly perfect in military drill in all its branches. A few days since our regiment was inspected and reviewed by Col. Marshall Lefferts, of the Seventh Regiment, N.Y.S.M. We made a very fine turn out, fairly excelling ourselves, and we could not have failed to have favorably impressed Col. Lefferts with our general appearance, drill, etc. The Twenty-second N.Y.S.M., and the Eighty-seventh Ohio were also reviewed the same day. The thermometer now ranges here from 100 to 105 degrees, but our mornings are delightfully cool and invigorating. We are all, for the most part strong and healthy, though sun-burned, etc. We had but little sickness, and I am pleased and thankful to record it; we have had no deaths as yet. We are under Major-General Pope, and we think he is a trump. May proud success attend his future movements. There is a rumor, I do not vouch for its reliability, that there are some 30,000 men (Union of course) coming this way very shortly. We expect to be in New York City by, or before September 1, and I bespeak for our regiment a kind, warm, and hospitable reception by New Yorkers generally; for though we've not been ordered further South than Harper's Ferry (a most important military and strategical military post), still we were ever ready, willing, and even anxious to "see service" and to fight; and while here we have done our duty faithfully.

The Eighty-seventh Ohio (a fine regiment 1025 strong) drill briskly; they arrived at their present camp on a rainy P.M., some time ago, every man fatigued and wet to the skin; the cook, of the Twelfth, with a very commendable and praiseworthy hospitality, etc., went to work and boiled the Eighty-seventh boys as much coffee as they could drink. And the entire regiment thanked the Twelfth for their kindness.

Two women (disreputable characters, I believe), after serving as "high privates" for a long time in the Second Maryland Cavalry, were recently "drummed out" of their camp near here. We have our scouting parties, who now go out several miles, and scour the country round about here. Our camp and picket guards are vigilant and active as ever. We have felt greatly (so have the crops) the want of rain; but as I write the skies indicate some. Peddlers infest camps, vending their trash at exorbitant prices. It's wonderful how these land-sharks and sutlers make their appearance when a regiment is paid off! Robert Johnson's tent-theatre has left here; he should have stayed a while longer. Our water is scarce—poor; and has to be carried a long way.

Small change is very scarce indeed. Letters and papers from friends and relatives are solicited, and ever welcome. The SUNDAY MERCURY is the great pet paper, and sole oracle of the soldier—his friend and vindicator. We have a regular regimental "bulletin", which often contains some very spicy reading. Soldiers should send their money home, and not squander it away foolishly and recklessly, here or elsewhere. The friends of the Twelfth, and most every other regiments in the war service, can learn of the whereabouts etc., of their friends or relatives in the columns of the SUNDAY MERCURY. Soldiers on the march should not over-pack their knapsacks with ridiculous superfluities. At our hospital here, a "gin-cocktail" is a castor oil and laudanum (ugh!); and "brandy-smash" is quinine and whiskey; a "mint-julep" is essence of rhubarb and something else, the doctors or the devil only knows what; "calves-foot jelly" is camomile pills, etc.; and so on to the end of the chapter. With Macbeth, I cry, "Throw physic to the dogs, I'll have none of it!" The very few typographical errors in your paper is a credit to you, and a pleasure to your readers, and a joy to your contributors. Fruit and vegetation is ripening rapidly and is very plentiful.

Camp life is generally very dull and monotonous; but we are continually kept doing one thing or another, and so time passes quite rapidly. We have some ball-playing here occasionally. There is an ambrotype gallery (wagon) here; so soldiers can have their handsome "picters" taken. We can see the Alleghany Mountains from a high hill here, away off in the dim distance. We have a very excellent, full, and efficient regimental drum corps, of which Chris. Sayers is drum-major, George Entricken and Wm. Sayers sergeants. These drummers have a fine tent of their own, live like princes, and are a first-rate set of fellows, every one of them. But, as the mail closes in a minute or so, until next week, *au revoir*.

Yours, truly,   J. S. H.

DETACHMENT SEVENTY-FIRST REGIMENT, N.Y.S.M.
CAMP COLES, August 20.

Although receiving communications from the regiment, I believe as yet you have heard nothing from this detachment. We are situated between Seventh and Fourteenth streets, some three or four miles from Washington, near a town called Brightwood. It is a fine place for a camp, as shady trees and woods are everywhere around us. The object in sending us here was, that we might guard these two entrances to the capital, and also act as a patrol-guard, scouring the country every other night. Being near the State boundary-line of Maryland, Secessionists are rather more numerous than were to be found near our old encampment. It was only the other morning that a cavalry company passed by our camp, after a night's scouting, with a man and about forty stand of arms, which they had captured. Toward the Maryland line, nine out of ten are as hot-headed in their devotion to Jeff Davis as the people of the Cotton States. They do not deny it; and it is quite curious to hear the reasons they give for their hostility to the Union. The majority of them saying that the Conscription Act extinguished their last hope for its restoration. It is my honest opinion that Virginia is fully as loyal as the District of Columbia.

Were we to stay here a greater length of time, our boys would make it their particular business to inquire a little deeper into people's business within this locality; for there is not the least doubt that contraband goods and contraband information are constantly being carried into Virginia.

There is a gentleman in this vicinity who says that, if any Union officer will come to him in citizen's dress, with a horse and wagon, he will go around with him and point out any quantity of men engaged in treasonable practices and intercourse. This gentleman is so well-known for miles around that his life would not be safe a moment, did he do so openly. There may well be uneasiness in Washington; they may well say the "Capital is in danger", when the people in such close proximity are so black-hearted and treacherous.

The romantic incidents of "Uncle Tom's Cabin" are not without their parallel so far North as we are. About six miles from this place lives as determined a Secessionist as any below the line. He has quite a number of slaves, and among them two or three handsome and intelligent quadroons. And, for simply holding conversation with a soldier, one of these girls was taken to a prison built for the purpose, all the clothes taken off her back, and whipped so unmercifully that she fainted dead away, before her master stopped. Since then (about two weeks ago) she has been kept in that place, with fetters and chains on her hands and limbs, with hardly enough food to keep life in her frame.

As a general thing, our boys enjoy themselves pretty well, scouring the country around for miles, in search of forage to satisfy the cravings of the "inner man", which is the soldier's second duty. Messes, as heterogeneous in their nature as the contents of an ostrich's stomach, and which would perhaps be repulsive to your very eyesight, are eaten by us with a relish which none but Delmonico's epicurean eaters can know. A rough life, open air, plenty of exercise, give an appetite which is not very fastidious as to its manner of being satisfied; and it is no matter if roast corn does taste rather smoky, or extempore apple-sauce is a little burned, there is still a flavor which reminds one of what we left behind.

Our dress-parades are witnessed by a great number of the people of Washington, as the roads between which we are encamped afford a very fine drive, similar in appearance to the Bloomingdale Road. The only fault to be found is, the great amount of dust, averaging two or three inches in depth, which the least irritation will cause to roll up in immense clouds, giving all who come in contact with it a miller-like appearance. Dust, like Death, is no respector of persons, and consequently, whoever of the *distingue* witness our evolutions, they are not distinguishable to us by their dress.

On Tuesday, we were mustered and inspected by our colonel, in accordance with the general order from the War Department to the whole army; the object being to get the exact number of men now in the service of the United States. How are you "skedaddlers"? Our regiment has not, as yet, lost a single man, either by disease, the bullet, or by accident—our camping-places having always been healthy in the extreme. We owe this good fortune as much to the good sense of our colonel as to the healthy food, water, and atmosphere.

The paymaster is anxiously looked for every day, and every strange uniform appearing within camp causes a fluttering among the boys, whose excitable imaginations see a close connection between him and "green-backs". And this is not strange, as our regiment has not as yet received a single cent from the Government since being out here, and our pocket-books are consequently pretty well drained.

Roast-beef has just sounded, and I fly to the rescue.

Yours, truly,   MORGAN, THE BUCCANEER.

August 31, 1862
THIRTY-SIXTH REGIMENT, N.Y.S.V.
CAMP NEAR YORKTOWN, VA., August 26.

I suppose you know by this time that the flower of the Union army has just finished its retrograde movement, and on the "home stretch" we wound up by occupying Yorktown and its vicinity. The three days of marching with light stomachs may be better imagined than expressed. But we did not complain, having the full assurance that at some future day we may be styled the "Preservers of the Union". Having finally accomplished our purpose, we halted, and looking back upon the ground, thinking it miraculous that such an army should escape uninjured. All along the line of our evacuation we laid in abundant supplies of grub. There was not an apple, peach, not even a plum orchard and corn-fields that was not ransacked by us poor "Yankee vandals". And such affections of the lovely and fascinating Virginia wenches, that they completely captivated our hearts. And they know, dear creatures, how to appreciate our affections, especially the bright quarters and fip-penny bits, before their own currency of shinplaster and brown paper notes. Headed by our sheet iron band we finally arrived at the gates of Yorktown, and the first appearance of any troops about the place was a member of ye gallant Eighth, N.Y.S.M., on sentry, and marching up and down the ramparts, large as life, and patriotic as a Virginian.

To the tune of "Gentle Annie", and four abreast, we promenaded through McClellan avenue, a fashionable resort of that Revolutionary city. Union blacks and patriotic militia-men with shoulder-straps welcomed us with a fraternal feeling—two white women being the sole residents of that renowned city. It is needless for me to say that it is a facsimile of our celebrated neighborhood of Park and Baxter streets. One would think that Yorktown was stereotyped from your Five Points. Arriving at our destination we rested our weary bones and quenched our parched lips by sipping of that delicious nectar, "swamp water".

Last Sunday evening [Aug. 24], our gallant and heroic major, James Raney, who by the by, went home on account of his being wounded in the hand, but now having returned. At the right of that noble and brave officer, applause after applause rent the air, which echoed and reechoed through the distant woods. Our cornet band having played many popular airs, among which were "Dixie", our gallant little major at last made his appearance to the assemblage. Cheers after cheers were given. Hats, boots, and shoes, were thrown up in the air, as tokens of respect for the gallant favorite; and in a nice little speech, he expressed his opinion:

"Boys, men, laddies or whatever I may term you, I thank you for this assemblage here tonight; and, boys, I will always remember, with deep gratitude, the patriotism of the Thirty-sixth New York. (Cheers.) Men, I love you as my heart's blood; and I shall always stick to you through thick and thin. There has been some ungenerous person in our midst, who sent anonymous letters to Newburg, New York, stating that I left Malvern Hill a day before the fight. (Cries of "false".) Men, you have a colonel [William H. Brown] who will lead you to victory; also, a lieutenant-colonel who is as true an officer as can be produced; and you have a major (cheers) who wants plenty of bread, and he will give you plenty of fighting."

After having alluded to the affairs of the country, and set forth some good hints for us to follow, he retired amid deafening cheers, first having welcomed the band into his tent to partake of some Bourbon, to wet their wizzeps and moisten the tubes of their many sheet-iron instruments. With "Yankee Doodle" from Mr. French's Musical Corps, the meeting dispersed.

Yesterday (Monday), about 300 men out of our brigade, armed, equipped, and with one day's rations, left our camp-grounds, thinking at the time that some blood was to be spilt. After having marched through Yorktown to the river, where we obtained shovels and picks (left-handed weapons of defense), we went to work leveling all the rifle-pits outside of Yorktown. With long shovels, long faces, and string haversacks, we went through our first day's work comparatively easy. Hereafter, I say, let the shoveling and digging *requiescat in pace*. Hark! What sound is that in the distance? Echo answers: The dinner-call! Feeling quite hungry, I must come to a close. Hoping I have not intruded upon your time and patience,

Yours, with confidence,   NUMBER TWO, OF THE REAR RANK

Major James A. Raney resigned on October 15, 1862.

THIRTY-FIRST REGIMENT, N.Y.S.V.

ALEXANDRIA, VA., August 26.

Once more encamped in Alexandria. My last letter to the SUNDAY MERCURY was dated at Harrison's Landing, where the army of the Potomac thought themselves in safe quarters; but the gallant McClellan thought it prudent to withdraw his little band from the James River, where they were of no possible use, and take up a new line of defense at some point where they will be near re-enforcements and supplies. I feel confident, yet, that the army of the Potomac will still take the head-quarters of Uncle Jeff., and the bogus capital. All the work on the fortifications at Harrison's Landing was of no possible use to us, but is left to convince the rebels that, if they had made their appearance before us, they would have met with a warm reception in the shape of lead, iron, and steel. We had one ration of bread, and then the splendid bakeries had to be destroyed. Our division left the landing on Thursday afternoon, the 16th and marched to Newport News, on the way encamping at Charles City Court-House, Williamsburg, and Yorktown. We then embarked on board the United States transport John A. Warner, and arrived at Alexandria day before yesterday. Troops are continually arriving here, and going to join the army of General Pope. At present, I cannot say where our division will go, but, most likely, they will go to General Pope. Several of our men that were wounded at the battle of West Point, and the seven days' fighting before Richmond, have returned to the regiment to have one more shot at Secesh. Some fifteen or twenty of our men have been exchanged from Richmond, and also returned to their regiment. They state that they had scarcely food enough to sustain life, but in other respects they were treated in the best possible manner. It is quite laughable to hear them relate incidents of their confinement, and especially the appearance of the Secesh while looking at our brave soldiers digging wells on Belle Island. While they were on the island, they saw the rebel rams Lady Davis and Richmond, which were then on the stocks, and receiving the iron plating that is to go under the water-line. They are of the same construction as the Merrimac, but of larger proportions, with two turrets resembling that of the Monitor. There are two or three other gunboats now in course of construction at Richmond. We expect our brave and gallant colonel, Calvin F. Pratt, to return to the regiment in a few days. The regiment is now under the command of Lieutenant-Colonel [Francis E.] Pinto, of the Thirty-second Regiment, N.Y.S.V. I hope the next time I write I may have something of more importance to write about. I will have to close, as I have to cook my supper of burned beans and salt junk. Good-bye for the present,

Yours, respectfully,   HIGH PRIVATE

PAROLED PRISONERS OF THE NEW ENGLAND AND MIDDLE STATES.

CAMP PAROLE, ANNAPOLIS, MD., Aug. 28.

Many of your readers have, I suppose, some friends or relatives of some kind in this camp and would be pleased to hear something concerning their welfare. This camp of instruction, as it is called, is not quite such a comfortable place as most of your readers have been led to believe. When we first arrived here, there were no accommodations whatever. However, things have somewhat improved since. The treatment is very harsh, especially on the part of the guards, who, more than in one instance, have used the boys belonging to New York regiments with all kinds of abuse. One young man, belonging to the Forty-second (Tammany) regiment, happening to be a little intoxicated, was arrested by half-a dozen guards, and (as always is the case with a man in such a state), made a slight resistance, when he was instantly struck in the head with a bayonet, and is now in the hospital, and is not very likely to recover.

Sick and wounded men have been sent from the hospitals on the Peninsula and other places to recruit their health, but instead of the health improving, their wounds break out afresh. It is as horrid a sight to see wounded fellows go to the doctor's tent to have their wounds dressed as if they had just come out of a battle. They are refused room in the hospital at this place, and it is not because there is no room in the different houses, but it is the general feeling towards us.

There are several incidents of importance connected with our camp, one of which is this: A patriotic young lady, a good solder, and an industrious and persevering wife, is here with us. Her husband enlisted in the Lincoln Cavalry [1st New York Cavalry], and went to the seat of war followed by his wife. They were side by side in the ranks, and side by side in battle. In the ever-memorable seven days' battles before Richmond, and in the fight at Savage's Station, the Lincoln Cavalry were engaged. The husband of this heroine was wounded, and was carried off the field by her own hand—she herself receiving a flesh wound—to the hospital. While there engaged dressing his wounds, the enemy drove our men back and took all in the hospital prisoners. She and her husband were among the first ones paroled, and are now here ready to do anything that the Government desires of them, as well as all the rest of us. Since our stay in this camp, there has been two deaths, otherwise the health of the place is excellent.

On the 22d inst. the members of the Fourteenth regiment N.Y.S.M., and the First Maryland Regiment were invited to attend the funeral of a patriotic young man, who recently enlisted in one of the Maryland regiments now stationed at Baltimore, and was scarcely gone from this place two weeks before his body returns a corpse to his dear and beloved friends. He was accidentally shot with a pistol in the head, and almost instantly expired.

Our duty at this place is very tedious, as we have nothing to do but lie around and pass away the time the best way we possibly can. Playing cards are the chief enjoyment of the camp. I am certain we are not doing our country any good in such a condition. We are all patiently awaiting our exchange, so as we can return to our regiments and again see active service. If this cannot be effected, the best thing the Government could do, would be to discharge us, and give us a chance to enlist over again. But there is a very short time now to, and if those young men at their homes do not come forward and volunteer, they will have the honor to be drafted.

The number of men now at this camp is from 1,500 to 2,000, and still arriving daily.

E. S.

September 7, 1862

GENERAL McCLELLAN AND THE ADMINISTRATION.

Once more the hopes deferred of the country rest on General McClellan, and spades and trumps. The partisans of the general averred that he would have captured Richmond, and terminated the rebellion, but that he was perpetually thwarted by members of the Cabinet, who feared his success would point him out as a candidate for the Presidency in 1864, who would command the suffrages of the people, in spite of all opposition; and, as they were after the same prize themselves, McClellan's prospects were to be nipped in the bud, if the destruction of the Union, the triumph of the rebellion, and national ruin, final and irrevocable, be the result. In proof of these assumptions, circumstantial statements were put forth to the effect that when

McClellan set out for the Peninsula, McDowell was to cooperate, and was to intercept the retreat of the rebels from Yorktown, and so place them between the upper and the nether millstone; that McDowell was prevented from carrying out the part assigned him by the President, or his advisers; and hence the escape of the rebels back to Richmond. Instead of the whole army acting harmoniously, and in subordination to General McClellan's ideas, different corps d'armée were sent hither and thither, under [Nathaniel P.] Banks, McDowell, and [John C.] Fremont, without any concert between them and McClellan, or between each other. Hence, Fremont was fooled and bamboozled by [Stonewall] Jackson, Banks cut off, and McDowell left to march and countermarch without effecting anything. Then when McClellan had actually invested Richmond, he left his right wing attenuated and exposed, because he relied on its being re-enforced by McDowell, and troops from Washington. But neither expectation was fulfilled; and hence, the rebels drove him back to seek shelter under the protecting vicinity of the gunboats. It is a matter of record, and abundantly confirmed, that rebel troops were dispatched from Richmond to give our side the idea that the troops defending Richmond were being reduced, and the ruse was successful; for the President publicly acknowledged that he had prevented re-enforcements from being sent on from Washington to McClellan, and the reason assigned was—besides the fear for Washington's safety—that a large number of rebel troops had been sent from Richmond to join Jackson's command, and that was equal to an equal number of re-enforcements to McClellan.

Now, if these allegations are well-founded—if it be true that McClellan was circumvented by a cabal; whether instigated by mere opinionative ignorance or engaged in political intrigue, the parties are guilty of a depth of traitorous villainy that has not yet been exceeded by any secessionist in Dixie. And if these allegations are not true, then why was McClellan practically deposed only to be again re-instated in his old command? That the army of the Potomac was capable of capturing Richmond and ending the war, if properly handled, is beyond dispute. It was prevented from reaching this grand devoutly-to-be-wished consummation by mousing politicians at Washington, we repeat that they ought to be smoked out, and their chances of expulsion from the scene which their presence pollutes not left to the vicissitudes of war, but made sure and sudden.

On the other hand, if the failure of the first year's campaign was the result of any incapacity on the part of McClellan, his restoration to the principal command of the Union forces is utterly inexplicable. The President, by his late action, has practically vindicated McClellan, and left the nation to conclude that the accusations chiefly leveled against Stanton, as the head and front of the opposition to McClellan's plans, are well founded. Under these circumstances, is the country destined to be edified by the spectacle of McClellan again at the head of the army, and Stanton still the chief of the War Department, so that the alleged jealousies which have driven the country to the brink of ruin may have free play to complete the wreck they have begun, and form another Golgotha of the new army, as they did of the old? We are almost prepared for anything; but this would be a fatal inconsistency, which is not to be believed in on any short or practical demonstration.

WILL MR. LINCOLN RESIGN?

It is idle to try and disguise the truth. The nation has lost faith in the ability of President Lincoln to bring this war to a successful conclusion. That he is honest, no one doubts; but honesty is not capacity. That he means to do what is right, is also granted; but the desire to do well and the ability to accomplish it, are two very different things. For ordinary times, Mr. Lincoln would, no doubt, pass muster; but, now that the very life of the nation is threatened, when the enemy, after eighteen months of war, is still thundering at the gates of the capital, the country requires, nay, demands, that the very best talent at its disposal should have the conduct of public affairs.

Mr. Lincoln, as a ruler, has two vital defects of character. He is unable to distinguish between merit and pretension, especially in the selection of generals in the field. Hence it is that, after eighteen months of war, there are only two or three generals in prominent positions whom the public regard as fitted for them. We are cursed with slow and incapable military leaders, because the man who places them in high positions is unable to distinguish genius and military skill. Another fault of Mr. Lincoln is his good nature timidity, which unfits him for war. As yet, none of our incompetent generals have been called to account, disgrace, or cashiered, as they should have been, for their repeated and wretched failures. They are continued in command, to the slaughter of our troops, and the destruction of the just hopes of the nation, because Mr. Lincoln is too tender-hearted to remove them.

This is no time for concealment. The press must speak out in thunder-tones. The obstacle in the way of crushing the rebellion is not the rebel armies, but Abraham Lincoln. It is the duty of all patriots—of all who have faith in the future of the country, to let the President know the truth. We believe that the honesty for which he is famed, the real kindness of heart he is known to possess, the undoubted patriotism of his nature, will prompt him to respond to the universal desire of the nation, as soon as he is made aware of it, and induce him to surrender the care of a state, the destinies of which he is unfitted by nature and education to wield.

Let Mr. Lincoln do this, and his name will be honored forevermore. This is a great sacrifice we ask of him, but his reward to all time will be commensurate with it. He will then rank in history with those heroes who have died that their country might live. Let him resign, and he will go down honored to his grave; but if, as President, he outlives his country, memory will be a curse and a shame to every lover of freedom in the myriad ages yet to come.

September 14, 1862
SECOND FIRE ZOUAVES
CAMP NEAR ALEXANDRIA, Sept. 9.

I write to you again, wishing to keep you posted as to our movements. Since we left the Peninsula (we left Harrison's Landing on the 15th, and marched to Yorktown, *via* Williamsburg, passing through the old battle-ground), the boys naturally recalled the ever-memorable 5th of May, when the field had resounded with the din and roar of battle. The graves of our comrades were still to be seen—the same rude piece of cracker-box at each of their heads, announcing their names, companies, etc. We arrived at Yorktown on the 21st, and embarked on the steamship Vanderbilt. Owing to the large number of troops on board, the passage was anything but pleasant. The issuing of rations to the men, during the trip, was sadly neglected, with the exception of coffee. We left the Chesapeake and entered the Potomac once more, and on the morning of the 24th we landed in Alexandria and marched to McCloud's Mills, where we stacked arms, and went to bed in the grass, and slept sweetly until morning. In the afternoon, we got aboard of the cars for the first time in over a year. A few hours brought us in the vicinity of Warrenton Junction. There we again stacked arms and remained all the next day and night, and on Wednesday morning, the 27th, we heard that the rebels had made a raid on the railroad, tearing up the track, and destroying several trains. We started down the track, taking with us three days' rations. We marched in the burning sun until about two o'clock in the afternoon, when we were startled by the crack of several muskets, which warned us that the enemy was near. Soon we heard volleys, and then we knew the fight had commenced, so we started on the double-quick through the pines. By this time the rebels were throwing grape, canister, and shell rapidly. In a few minutes we were at the scene of action, which was an open field, extending across the railroad. Several regiments were already in line and at work. As we came into line, the rebels received us with a murderous fire; the boys, however, began pouring miniés into the "rebs", making their nests in the pines extremely warm, so much so, that in less than an hour they were on the full run, with Hooker after them. In this fight Capt. Donalds, who was in command of the regiment, received a minié ball in his leg, shattering the bone, and causing amputation, from the effects of which he died. Poor Donalds! a braver or more generous soldier never drew a sword. Our hearts bled as we lowered his manly form into the grave beside his companions. It was pitch dark when we buried him, our only light being a tallow candle. The group around his grave offered up a prayer for the departed soldier and his bereaved relatives. Lieut. [Henry H.] Lewis, acting adjutant, was killed; also Lieut. [John] McAllister. Capt. [John P.] Short was severely wounded; Capt. Burns was floored by a spent ball, but came to time again. We lost, in killed and wounded, over fifty. At Bull Run, on the two following days [August 29 & 30], our boys did their duty, as usual. Although there are but a handful of them, they will never disgrace the Empire City. We are now encamped near Fort Lyons, and about three miles from Alexandria. Promising to keep you posted on anything that occurs, I will close,

Remaining yours,   GRAPESHOT.

September 21, 1862
PAROLED PRISONERS OF THE NEW ENGLAND AND MIDDLE STATES.
CAMP SANGSTER, ANNAPOLIS, MD., Sept. 16.

Thanking you for the insertion of my last letters, I now write to you, a great deal better prepared for the exercise than before. On the 4th instant, about 1,500 prisoners, who were taken in the battles of Cedar Mountain and the several skirmishes between that and the Bull Run fight, arrived in Annapolis, and were sent into camp about two miles from the city. They report the rebels in starving condition, and also that they received nothing whatever to eat from them for five days, save one small piece of meat; otherwise subsisting on green fruit. The rebels live entirely on green corn, which they call "roasting-ear", which is probably, the cause of the present raid.

The appointment of Major-General George B. McClellan as Commander-in-Chief of the army before Washington, was received with the greatest enthusiasm by the men, as they think there is nobody else fit for such a position; but "little Mac" (as the Army of the Potomac call him) is the right man in the right place, as he proved himself at the time of the Peninsula campaign; and had he been re-enforced at the time he asked for men, Richmond would, no doubt, have been in our hands at the present day.

The secessionists of this town call the redoubtable Stonewall, Uncle Jackson. The English man-of-war Racer, arrived in this port on the morning of the 5ᵗʰ inst., and fired the national salute as she neared the harbor. She took provisions on board, and weighed anchor, and left for some other port.

Many of the citizens of this town have skedaddled from Maryland to join the rebel army, and some of the leading men of this town have sent their sons to the South, in order to avoid the draft about to commence in the North. The quota of this town is 83, of which 52 have already enlisted, and the citizens think that a draft will hardly be necessary.

The young lady of whom I spoke in my letter of the 26ᵗʰ of August, and the wife of another soldier in this camp, have volunteered their services to tend to the sick and wounded soldiers belonging to the paroled prisoners. Such is the spirit of our Northern ladies, but I am sorry to say that it is not so throughout the North.

On the 14ᵗʰ inst., a dispatch was sent to our camp from Washington, and was read out at dress parade. It was an official account from General McClellan, announcing the success he had already met with. Three cheers were given for "Little Mac", three for Gen. Hooker, and three for the Army of the Potomac.

While I am writing prisoners are coming into our camp. 5,000 more from Belle Island, near Richmond, are now coming into our camp. A great many of them have no shoes, having sold them to get something to eat. Some of them have hardly any clothes on them at all, as some of them were furnished with them by the men already encamped here. At present they have no tents, but they will be supplied as soon as they can be received from Uncle Sam.

E. S.

FOURTEENTH REGIMENT N.Y.S.M.

Washington, D.C., Sept. 15.

It is so long since I have had any chance of writing to you, that I have almost got out of the hang of writing to anybody. Since my last, from Fredericksburg, it his been march, march, march, and we have had an incalculable amount of fatigue and suffering to endure, incident to the circumstances of the case, which have been of the severest nature. An order, about the 6ᵗʰ of August, came for a march to somewhere—we knew not where. We started at about 5 o'clock, on a very hot day, and had not gone far before Sergeant [Enoch] Stephens, of Company K, fell sun-struck. Many had to give out, in consequence of the intense heat. We marched on, and nearly till daybreak next morning, making about twenty miles, and, at last, bivouacked near Spottsylvania Court House. There we remained two days, and then returned to our camps, near Falmouth, opposite Fredericksburg. General [John] Gibbon's brigade was engaged with the enemy, and, I believe, a company of the Twenty-first Regiment, in [Marsena] Patrick's brigade also—as were the Harris [2ⁿᵈ New York] Light Cavalry, as usual. Some little incidents occurred; but I think, from all I could learn, the rebels got the best in the little skirmishes—or they took some of our men prisoners, and killed more than one of our brave Union soldiers. After resting just one day, we were on the march again, and started at daybreak Sunday morning [Aug. 10]—getting up at 1 o'clock. Passing through Falmouth some of the villagers showed their sorrow at our departure by many a tear-filled eye. It has been scorching, supporting batteries, hunting for, and retreating from the enemy ever since. On our way we had to ford the Rappahannock, marching about twenty-four miles and then sleep in our wet clothes on the wet ground. So on reaching near the battle-field of Culpepper (Slaughter's [Cedar] Mountain), and tired lay by our arms expecting a brisk time the following day; but the enemy had skedaddled, as seems to have been their secret and successful forte. A "rest" of a day or two after changing camp was allowed us and gratefully appreciated,—then were marched in front of the mountain of the battle-field, in which locality we were camped only one day; and it appears just as the whole army was moving backward, our regiment was sent for some purpose to the front on the Rapidan, and near where we were bivouacking, the Harris Cavalry had a skirmish, and lost a captain, killed by a man in some building firing upon him whilst the captain was watering his horse.

We returned to where our camp had been, and after the order by the right of companies to the rear into column of company streets, the order was promulgated and then 11 o'clock, to be ready to march at 1 o'clock, morning, and at that hour were off again. Since that we have passed through Culpepper, crossed the Rappahannock again, where we had three or four days of supporting batteries to do, and afterward through Warrenton, toward the Sulpher Springs—return, through and in action at Gainesville, Kettle Run, and Bull Run (No. 2).

While at the Rappahannock we learned considerable of the merit of our sharpshooters. They did their work excellently, picking off the rebel gunners and officers. The chaplain of this regiment—the Second United States Sharpshooters—is a regular fighting minister, as well as preaching. He has brought in his prisoners, and, I believe, has taken command of the company several times, and deployed them to skirmish, and then he fought like a hero himself, showing a good example to his men, and giving them plenty of engagement. When being under fire of shot and shell, or into action, it is not long before we find out who the brave and worthy men are. The colonel of the sharpshooters proved himself a good man, as well as the whole regiment of the sharpshooters. In fact, they speak well of our brigade—the Twenty-second, Twenty-fourth, Thirtieth New York, and Sharpshooters, who had never been exposed to such showers of shot and shell as they were on the Rappahannock; but no panic, no fright, or anything of the kind occurred, though some were killed, and others wounded.

Lieut. Colonel Edward B. Fowler in command, Major [William H.] DeBevoise, adjutant and our line officers acted with great coolness, as did the men. Too much praise can hardly be awarded to our commandant of the regiment—all eyes being generally directed to the "King Pin", who, of course, was "Big Ned", as we call him. He came riding along at one time saying: "There is a section of artillery on a hill near by, and we are going to take it. I think we can do it." For which he ordered us, as it were, to fall in. We most of us thought there was some rough work in store, which of course sure would have been; but every heart was resolved to follow where Big Ned led. Serious thoughts no doubt at that time were passing through our little regiment, but all were in earnest; and had we gone on such an errand, it would have cost the life of every member of the Fourteenth, rather than defeat in that object. However, the Fourteenth was not sent to take that section of battery, and the Fourteenth was not sorry, I can assure you, at least as far as I am concerned. Next morning, after changing positions, being roused from slumber at break of day—the order "Fall in", was given, and instantly every man was in line; we were immediately taken across a plain, and the general seeing our position was a dangerous one as we were marching, ordered us taken under cover, when we were ordered to double quick, and by the left flank taken out of range just in time to be saved from the enemy's shot and shell, which they poured over toward us, our brigade and batteries, in showers. Some few of the brigade were killed and wounded. On the third day, the 23rd, the enemy opened their batteries on us in force again, and one of our regiment, a young man named [William] Power, was instantly killed by a piece of shell.

The [16th] Indiana Battery, which we supported, worked pretty hard that morning. The enemy getting such close range on them, they began to be rather slow at last attending to the orders "Cannoneers, to your posts"; but they worked well whilst at it. It is said the Lieut. Colonel Fowler sighted a gun attached to this battery, with much success.

When the enemy's batteries had been silenced we were marched away, and time allowed us to cook coffee. After that we were on the march again, and went direct toward Warrenton, which we passed through early on the following morning. On Sunday [Aug. 24] we remained bivouacked in the woods, just outside of Warrenton, and early Monday morning we were on the march again, when we were taken toward Sulpher Springs, formed in line of battle, and then taken into the woods out of the hot sun. Here we remained (the whole division) until late in the afternoon of the following day (Tuesday), when we started back through Warrenton, and along until we came to Gainesville; and, by diverse marchings and counter-marching, we were at last thrown out so as to draw on the enemy, who got a little bit fooled that Thursday night [Aug. 28]; for they met with Tartars when they met with Gibbon's Brigade. A heavy firing was kept up for a few minutes, and the gallant Indianans and Wisconsin men just drove them, though the rebels came in very large force. It was encouraging to see how the rebels were pushed back and to hear our men cheer as they were scattering the traitors. Our brigade, Gen. [John P.] Hatch's, was ordered up, but that night were not used, except to resound the cheers for the splendid conduct of Gibbon's Brigade. Being ordered to lie on our arms, we availed ourselves of the chance for repose as soon as possible, and at about 1 o'clock the general came along and awakening us, told us to be quiet and ready to move right away. Our march from that hour was continued without any rest until we arrived at Manassas Junction—where, during the day, we marched backward to Manassas, and when nearing the scene of action received the order, "Double-quick", which, tired as we were, inspired us with new vigor, when knowing that we were then after the enemy. We soon came upon that well-known stream, Bull Run, which was as dirty as ever, but from which we were, as formerly, glad to drink. Up the road we kept, one moment a halt, and then off again double-quick, and when over Kettle River [Young's Branch], filed to the left, and up the hill to the top and commenced firing by file. The enemy were not in force in the direction we were firing; but, instead, were in the woods on our left, from which they raked us with their deadly volleys and charged upon us with a heavy force. Many of our own men, and, accordingly, were taken prisoners. That night our brigade suffered, particularly our regiment and the Twenty-fourth. It was, in appearance, to me, a very badly-managed fight on that night. Somebody was seriously to blame for taking our brigade in such a position, and allowing the rebels to have such a cover to use against us.

On Saturday [Aug. 30], blunders seemed to occur, as usual; but, of course, McDowell is not to blame, for he is a great general, you know, and the soldiers all know, and so does the public (?). We all (the whole army), and the public, too, have confidence in General McDowell, have we not? Echo—answers all but the confidence in his loyalty. It is terribly lamentable to see our best friends and soldiers shot down, and, at the same time, to think that those men who have charge of us should be so reckless and careless as to throw away so many lives which, by proper management, might be saved, and, instead of reaping defeat, obtaining victory. It seemed as though there were men enough to whip all the Secesh in America. I believe if our men had been handled right, or if we had such generals as [Franz] Sigel, or Banks, or Burnside, Bull Run No. 2 would have been a most glorious victory for the Stars and Stripes of freedom. By the good management of subordinate officers a tolerable and orderly retreat was made. It is to be noticed that there is almost an army of enlisted men, and many, very many cowardly officers as well, who will take good care they never get shot, for they are sure to be taken very suddenly with rheumatism, or pains in the stomach, when there is a fight immediately anticipated. Still, I suppose when the regiments return home, they will be on hand to receive the honors bestowed on the survivors of the war; while the brave men are lying beneath the sod forgotten. These shirks and leeches are contemptible in the eyes of their fellow men, for the good men have their duty to perform as well as their own, and, of course, on the field are in extra danger, by the lack of numbers. Passing through Centreville, it looked as natural as ever. The old cabins built by the rebels were hundreds of them still remaining. The Sunday after our engagement I believe, we were mustered, and there were present one hundred and fourteen to receive pay. Some then had come in who were not to be seen for days previously. The Twenty-fourth Regiment, which had four hundred and eighty to go into action, had one hundred and ten to answer their names. The entire division was very badly cut up. We at last started again, and marched to Upton's Hill, to our "old Camp Marion". Colonel Fowler was severely wounded, and is now home. Our best officers were killed and wounded. Company H lost its captain, [George R.] Davy, and first lieutenant, [Isaiah] Grummond—both dead; Captain [George] Mallory, of Company B, killed; Lieutentant [Charles B.] Tobey, Company C, severely wounded in the breast; Captain [Charles] Baldwin, Company D, killed [wounded]; and Lieutenant [William] Baldwin, severely wounded—same company; Captain [George S.] Elcock, Company E, now a prisoner; Lieutenant [William F.] Twybel, Company K, wounded, Lieutenant [William A.] Ball, Company F, wounded. There are now but about twenty-five of the old members of this regiment that are fit for duty, the rest are in this city, in the hospitals, wounded, sick, and unable to march. The recruits have come out to the number of about three hundred—they are a splendid-looking body of men—all in good spirits (not the ardent, you know)—but, at any rate, they have all received a good big bounty—to join the Fourteenth N.Y.S.M. The last fights have taken away the best men of the regiment. Since the battles, it seems as though everything had changed. We miss the friendly greetings of our best friends. It is a sad contemplation. I will close by remaining as ever your friend,

BROOKLYN.

THE TURN OF THE TIDE.

The events of the past week [Sept. 14 - 21] are of the most inspiring and reassuring in character. At no time since the war commenced did the cause of the Union look more dark and despairing than one week ago; at no time since the first gun was fired have the hopes of the nation seemed in such a fair way of realization as they do to-day. So much one eventful week can bring forth. When we last addressed our readers, we had to write of victorious rebel armies marching into free soil; of the sovereign States of the North filled with trepidation and alarm, preparing to defend themselves from devastation; to-day the rebel horde is broken and dispirited, driven back from the soil of Maryland where they expected to be received with open arms, and the grand scheme of a Northern invasion forever scattered to the winds.

It is hard to satisfy popular expectation. Many are disappointed because the whole rebel army was not totally annihilated, Jackson caught by the collar of his coat and the waistband of his breeches, and Jeff Davis suspended from the limb of a sour apple tree. But when we recollect what a transition has taken place, from the depth of despondency to the height of exultation, from defeat to glorious victory, we ought to rejoice over what has been done, rather than grumble because we have not accomplished everything.

In view of the splendid achievements of the past few days, it would be ungenerous to withhold from Gen. McClellan the meed of approbation which seems to be his due. His pursuit and defeat of the enemy was suddenly conceived and executed; there was no time for deliberation, or the elaboration of details. Yet with an army somewhat incongruous, and comprising many raw recruits, he closed upon the foe and routed him on his own chosen battle-ground. Of his scientific acquirements, or his ability in the construction of fortifications, and in conducting siege-operations, no one ever entertained a doubt. But many were undecided whether he possessed the rarer faculty of "organizing victory" on the battle-field; the quickness of decision, the fertility of mental resources, the ready expedients to deal with the fluctuating tide of battle, and pluck victory from the vortex of contending forces. His conduct in the late battles remove these misgivings, and establish his reputation as a thoroughly accomplished commander, both in aggressive and defensive war.

If no fatuity, such as we have too frequently witnessed in the past, should intervene, and the successes just achieved be followed up by the Government with energetic alacrity, the war will not drag its slow length along through many more lunar revolutions, but find a final solution in the dispersion of the rebel forces in Virginia, and the long delayed capture of Richmond. Not an hour should be lost in pressing on after the retreating foe, and finish what is so auspiciously begun. The fruits of our past victories have been permitted to melt away, by leaving the enemy time to recuperate. No such policy must be permitted to throw the prize, now fairly within arm's length, into the distant and uncertain future.

September 28, 1862

MILITARY MATTERS

SCENE AT A NEW YORK RECRUITING-OFFICE.—While walking up the Bowery, a few days ago, we noticed a small-sized crowd in front of the recruiting-office of the second battalion of Duryee's Zouaves, between Hester and Grand streets. Upon coming up to the gathering, we discovered the well-known face and figure of Horace Greeley, surrounded by some half-dozen red-breeched and turbaned soldiers.

"Come, Mr. Greeley!" exclaimed a strapping fellow, who stood six feet high, and was proportionably broad across the chest and shoulders. "Now's your time to enlist! We give $188 bounty to-day. Won't you go to the war with us?"

"Gentlemen!" answered the philosopher, "it's impossible. I am too old; besides, I am doing a great deal more service at home."

"Then, you won't go?" asked another Zouave.

"I cannot do it, my friend," replied Horace.

"You ain't afraid, are you? You don't know how well you'd look until you saw yourself dressed up in Zouave uniform," chimed in another.

"I have no doubt I should cut a pretty figure in your dress—"

"Especially if you wore a white coat," interrupted a waggish bystander.

"But that is nothing, my friends. Dress neither makes men nor soldiers. Principle, good character, good habits, and resolution is everything."

"O yes! that's all right; but that ain't enlisting," persisted the first speaker. "Uncle Sam wants soldiers, and talking or writing isn't the thing. There's lots of men older than you in the ranks, and any quantity of editors, reporters, and printers. If a few men like you enlisted, our regiments would soon fill up."

"That is true; but it is impossible for me to join you," continued Horace.

"You'd soon get a chance to wear the straps. Maybe you might sport a spread eagle," put in another Zou Zou, persuasively.

"No, no; gentlemen, I must leave you; but," turning around in a quiet manner, and eyeing the crowd, which by this time was considerable, "perhaps some of these citizens I see gathered about you will volunteer. If any will do so, I will give an extra bounty. Does any one wish to join?"

At this unexpected offer the crowd began to give way and scatter about, while several proposed three cheers for the white-coated philosopher. We did not hear whether Greeley secured any recruits by his extra bounty; but he soon after moved off, followed by the Zou-Zous, who laughed quite heartily at the attempt made to entrap Horace into the Union army.

EBENEZER HOSPITAL

WASHINGTON, D.C. September 25th

The object here is not how to make the most of time, but how to kill it. This is written more for the purpose of doing something, than with any expectation it will be deemed worthy of insertion, especially at a time when so much valuable and interesting matter must be seeking for admission. I believe when the daily routine of life in one military hospital is described, it answers for all.

When the body writhes with pain or becomes prostrated by sickness, the mind not only becomes correspondingly enfeebled, but any of its powers left seem to become concentrated in sympathy for the affliction of the flesh, or rather the latter seems to exercise a despotic power over the former in this respect, and in proportion to its ailing. Thus, it would seem, matter and mind go hand in hand to the grave, or rise in strength to life and action. Home, friends, country, or ambition would seem not to claim a thought from the afflicted; but with the first dawn of returning health, awakens all those passions, desires, afflictions, and sympathies which were only sleeping and controlled, but not extinguished or dead. I don't know whether my philosophy be just. Though, my hospital experience gives it some support. For days the patient may breathe not a word, or breathe it but for a drink. On the contrary, scarcely is a change for the better noticeable when such questions as the following are heard: "Any letters for me, lately?" "Any news from the regiment?" "Have you seen a paper lately?" "What about our armies, and what have they been doing?" Such questions cease as health increases; the questioner becomes a reader, and learns for himself. The invalid is now supposed to be convalescent and able to come down stairs; and now, sir, I may introduce you to the daily routine of hospital life.

The church basement is our dining-room, study, everything. At 7 o'clock, breakfast is ready, consisting of plenty of good bread and butter, or beans, or molasses, with very questionable coffee. All who can assemble on crutches, all of slight hand, body, or head wounds are present and ready for it. In fifteen minutes all is over, and from the onslaught made, we may infer that a ball through the arm does not injure the stomach. The next hour is given to washing, and then comes pipes. Of course, any very handsome fellow among us is sure to have a cigar, if worth five cents, though this is rather questionable at present. Then groups of fives and sixes find themselves together, as many as the old church-pews would contain, and soon the invariable topics of the day are introduced, viz., battle-fields and the incidents there of; their armies and generals, colonels and company-officers. Of our general, first in estimation of all stands McClellan. His name is ever spoken with love and respect. By those who have fought under him, he is regarded with admiration amounting almost to idolatry or infatuation.

I believe it is said of Pericles that, when thrown by Thucydidus, he made the spectators believe himself victor, though they witnessed his defeat. It is so with McClellan. If the whole country joined in fulminating even incontrovertible truths to his disadvantage, his soldiers would not believe them if disavowed by a single negative. And why? Because he rules in the hearts of his men. They believe all his reverses to be the work of his enemies, and all his successes his own. No wonder he should conquer. Such faith in the infallibility of a leader must make his army invincible. Sigel seems to stand next in favor; Burnside, Heintzelman, Hooker, etc. On the other side, McDowell is ever mentioned with doubt of his loyalty, with scorn, contempt, and anathemas, even by his own men. The hope is general that he will never be permitted to command an army again. Five men holding such opinions as these would not be worth one, if fighting under his command, because they would have no faith in him, and would believe every order is intended for their destruction. All this may be wrong, but the doubt exists, and can't be cured. Pope is deemed sincere and good in his own little place, but not qualified to step into the shoes of "Little Mac". But of all, company officers are subject to severe handling, and most searching analyzation. By some new process of anatomy, the very secrets of their hearts seem to be laid open to inspection. Not a bad or good quality but finds its debit and credit, and then the balance for or against is then commented on. If some lieutenants and captains could only hear their merits as men and officers put so severely to the test, I imagine they would not think themselves very highly complimented. On the other hand, many are mentioned with encomiums, respect, and esteem. This brings about one or half-past one o'clock, P.M., and dinner with it. The boys talk themselves into an appetite, and can revenge it on plenty of bread and soup with the beef that sometimes requires even the pluck of a soldier to handle with effect. The fight lasts some twenty minutes, and results in a complete victory, even the beef to the last morsel is put *hors de combat*.

From 2 to 5 P.M., is generally devoted to correspondence. Then parents, brothers, sisters, friends, and lovers are considered. This brings tea—very black indeed (there's a strong suspicion it is related to the coffee)—with mountains of bread and molasses, or green apple-sauce. There's no stint of food. From this to 9 o'clock is given to smoking, or reading anything we can pick up. Then the gas is partially turned off, and bed is the word—some to find sleep and refreshment, and others to roll from side to back till morning, thoughtful and unhappy. Such, sir, is the daily routine, down stairs, of the convalescents. But above, the scene is otherwise. Still, the moan and the groan tells of pain and suffering, and the eye can rest on nothing but the wasted form and attenuated limbs of the manly outline. The number is becoming daily less, and soon many beds will be vacant, awaiting new occupants. May the necessity to fill them with similar class never exist!

On yesterday I went out for the first time, and visited the city. I soon found myself within the precincts of the Capitol. In mute admiration I looked and looked at this beautiful and magnificent structure, this noble work of genius is consecrated to and by mind. My admiration was next drawn to the statuary. On the left of the northeastern entrance is a statue of Columbus with a globe in his hand, as if explaining the form and principles of the earth to an astonished and wondering Indian. On the right is a group which appears to represent one of the early settlers who has overpowered a hostile native; a dog stands ready to help his white master if called on. On the right of the group a mother fondles her babe to her bosom and looks up with unutterable anguish as if to scan the issue of a struggle which is to seal the fate of her child and husband. In the park is a magnificent bronze statue of Liberty nineteen and a half feet high, to surmount the dome when finished. I was told it was cast near to where it stands. By the side of this is another exquisite piece of art, in marble, representing the same goddess, and intended for the hall of the Senate Chamber. I am just as much a judge of the fine art of legerdemain, but these specimens appeared faultless to me, and I leaped to the conclusion, they must to all others. One thing I do know, I would rather my name should go down to posterity as the architect of the Capitol than be heir to a throne. There were some two hundred omnibuses there at the time, taking off the wounded—whither, I could not learn. Subsequently, I found myself in front of the post and Patent Offices, twin sisters, equally chaste and beautiful, their very simplicity giving them all their charms. If your correspondent's judgement only equal to his admiration for the grand and beautiful in art and nature, how thoughtless it would be! Here I felt as if I would retrace my steps, not feeling as if I would be quite able to pay a visit to the White House, as intended. I provided myself with a copy of the

SUNDAY MERCURY, and found my way to a seat in the beautiful little park, which incloses the southwestern front of the Capital, and before a revolving fountain of many jets.

During two hours in this cool retreat, I was lost, to everything, but the witchery of its pages.

On Tuesday, three batteries passed down this street, (Fourth), to the river, as if for transport by water. Surmise as to their destination gave us a new topic for an hour or so.

During the past week there have been five deaths, and little hopes are entertained for the recovery of a good many more. It is a low estimate to say that half of what came in here after the battle of Bull Run, will never bear arms again. What death will spare of this number, will be disabled for life.

The weather is very favorable for the wounded. I don't think I shall be able to scrape up materials for another letter, till some new feature in my life takes place.

A—, COLOR GUARD.

October 5, 1862
FIFTY-FIRST REGIMENT, N.Y.S.V.
IN CAMP NEAR ANTIETAM CREEK, VA., Sept. 25.

Allow me, through the columns of your widely-circulated paper, to make a few statements in connection with the taking of the Antietam Bridge by the Federal troops on the 17th inst.

I have seen in some of the daily papers of your city, correspondence purporting to give an account of the affair which is far wide of the mark. The facts are these: The First Brigade of General [Samuel D.] Sturgis' Division were ordered forward to engage the rebels at the bridge, which they did, but were repulsed. Then the Second Brigade, commanded by the gallant General Edward Ferrero, were ordered to advance and take it, which they did without ceremony. They went in under a galling fire from the enemy, and after exchanging the compliments of the day with the gray-backs, charged upon the bridge, and crossed it in fine style, making the "rebs" skedaddle in admirable disorder.

The regiments which compromise the Second Brigade are the Fifty-first New York (Shepard Rifles), Fifty-first Pennsylvania, Twenty-first and Thirty-fifth Massachusetts. The Fifty-first Pennsylvania and the Fifty-first New York were the first to cross the bridge—they went over together—and the colors of the Fifty-first New York were the first over the bridge. Our brigade, after crossing the bridge, took up a good position, and held it for about two hours, when we were again ordered into action, and remained there till relieved, when we retired in good order, and held the field till the next afternoon. This is a true statement of the facts as they occurred, by one who crossed the bridge with the colors.

I would here state, for the information of the friends of the Fifty-first, that our loss, all things considered, was slight. We deeply regret the loss of our late adjutant, [Andrew] Fowler, who fell a true and gallant soldier. Our officers, one and all, are good soldiers and true men, and while led by such men, with our gallant colonel, Robert B. Potter, on the lead, the Fifty-first know no such word as fail.

Yours, etc.,   ONE OF THE FIFTY-FIRST.

FIFTY-FIRST REGIMENT, N.Y.S.V.
NEW YORK, Oct. 1.

Having been in the battles of South Mountain and Antietam, and among the wounded, I take great pleasure in giving you some accounts of the Second Brigade, Second Division of General Burnside's army corps, commanded by Acting-Brigadier-General Edward Ferrero.

The regiments of this brigade are the Fifty-first New York, Col. R.B. Potter; Fifty-first Pennsylvania, Col. [John F.] Hartranft; Twenty-first Massachusetts, Col. [William] Clark, and the Thirty-fifth Massachusetts, Capt. John G. Wright, of the Fifty-first New York, commanding. This brigade, which has so often led to victory by the late General [Jesse L.] Reno, numbered before the late battles in Maryland about 2,000 strong. Before the battle of South Mountain, the men were all looking well and in fine spirits, eager for the fray. At the time of the advance, very few were lagging behind—most all being in their respective places. After we had reached the top of the mountain, we were ordered to support a battery, which we did for over an hour, when we were ordered in to re-enforce the division of Gen. [Orlando] Willcox. The Fifty-first Pennsylvania took the lead, with the Fifty-first New York close behind on a double-quick. The whole brigade was soon in line in an open field, when they had orders to lie down. Instantly the rebels opened fire on us, taking us by surprise; but in an instant we returned it with great effect. The keen eye of Ferrero convinced him that his men were not in right position, so the Fifty-first Pennsylvania were instantly brought in front, facing the enemy, where they poured in deadly volleys. After they had got fairly at work, the Fifty-first New York were brought up to the left, just in time to save the Pennsylvania boys from being flanked. The quick movement of Gen. Ferrero's is remarked as being one of the most masterly pieces of generalship ever displayed, and had a minute been loss then, all would have been up with us. The fight was kept up till after 9 o'clock, and then it ceased; afterward, it was quiet for the night. When morning dawned on us, the first thing we heard was the sad news of the death of General Reno, which caused every one to look sad and melancholy, and many to shed tears. It could hardly be realized by the boys, even for days after, and he was missed by all.

After this, everything was going on finely until Wednesday morning [Sept. 17], when we were shelled out of our position shortly after daylight, and were compelled to move further to our left. Here we remained but a few minutes, before we were ordered to advance on a double-quick. We remained in a corn-field a short time, and then advanced as far as the turnpike-road, and waited for orders. The word came for the Fifty-first Pennsylvania, and the Fifty-first New York to advance on the bridge; and we flanked to the right, and moved off on the double-quick, soon bringing up in line within a few yards of the bridge. The rebels were in large force on a small hill, a few yards beyond the bridge, and their fire was for a time very effective. Our boys were advancing steadily, step by step, until they carried the bridge, drove the rebels from the hill beyond, and occupied their position till night closed. Four stand of colors were taken that day by the different regiments. It is needless to add any further particulars, as they have been given before, but I would make particular mention of Col. Edward Ferrero, who had led the brigade so successfully through the late battles, also the recent battles in Virginia. He has every reason to be proud of his men, and they have every reason to be proud of him; and he, at their head, will undoubtedly lead them through the remainder of the campaign.

I also take great pleasure in mentioning Colonel R.B. Potter, one of the bravest of the brave, and one who is loved by all. Also, Colonels Clark and Hartranft, and Captains [R. Charlton] Mitchell, [David F.] Wright, [Samuel] Sims, and [Stephen W.] Chase, of the Fifty-first New York, who all distinguished themselves.

The men all went in the last engagement with more determined spirit than ever, and although at Roanoke, New Bern, Manassas, Chantilly, and South Mountain they distinguished themselves, they had a double duty to perform at Antietam. "General Reno must be avenged", was the cry throughout; and all through the fierce fight they never yielded; but pushed on with a determined spirit until they carried the bridge, charged on the hill beyond, drove the enemy from their position, and held their ground until their ammunition run out, and then they were relieved.

The total loss of the brigade in the two engagements was 560 in killed and wounded. The brigade is now with the gallant Burnside, near Harper's Ferry, Va.

Yours, etc.,   G. W. W.

Second Lieutenant George Washington Whitman, age 29, was the younger brother of poet Walt Whitman. After the battle of Antietam, on Nov. 1, 1862, Lieutenant Whitman was promoted to the rank of Captain. He was captured at the battle of Peeble's Farm on Sept. 30, 1864, and spent nearly five months a prisoner of war. Captain Whitman was paroled on Feb. 22, 1865, and was afterwards breveted Lieutenant Colonel. He died on Dec. 20, 1901.

October 12, 1862
FOURTH REGIMENT (FIRST SCOTT LIFE GUARD) N.Y.S.V.
BOLIVAR HEIGHTS, HARPER'S FERRY, VA., October 4.

It is now over three weeks since I wrote you my occasional record of things in this regiment. Since then, our movements have been so stirring that I certainly should have written to you sooner, had not the unforeseen circumstances—such as a slight sickness, and the loss of my writing materials at Antietam—prevented.

On the evening of the 8th of September last we received marching orders, and the following morning we bade farewell to Suffolk. A rapid train soon whirled us down to Norfolk, and from that city we took passage on board the old North River boat, J.P. Warner, for Washington. Newport News, Craney Island, Fortress Monroe, etc. were soon passed, and we woke up the next morning just in time to catch a glimpse of Mount Vernon. The scenery along the banks of the stately Potomac was magnificent, and the crowded wharves of Alexandria made one think of the ancient queenly metropolis after which it is named. Our swift steamer surged on past all those, and soon the Capitol, looming grandly in the distance, showed that Washington was near, that night we slept in the "City of Magnificent Distances". We found the First Delaware, our companions at Suffolk, in Washington before us. The Fifth Maryland was added to form a brigade, General Max Weber taking the command.

On the afternoon of the 11th ult., we—the Fourth New York, First Delaware, and Fifth Maryland—started from Washington to re-enforce McClellan. Of our march I shall say but little. The distance we traveled up to the 16th ult., when we reported for duty to General Sumner in Antietam Valley, was about eighty miles. The country, the whole way, was a series of lofty hills. Marching over such a road was, of course, wearisome; nevertheless, all hands footed it without grumbling. Knapsacks, blankets, coats, etc., strewed along the route, showed that, on such a course, all would be light weight. Sleeping under the dew, without any warm covering, was not very pleasant; but, under the circumstances, it could not be helped, and we were very philosophically consoled ourselves with the adage, that "what can't be cured must be endured".

Rockville, Frederick, and other towns lately occupied by the rebels, we passed through. The sound of the cannonading near Boonsboro hurried our march, but our utmost haste did not enable us to be up in time to participate in the engagement at South Mountain.

As I mentioned above, on the 16th ult., the brigade was reported for duty to General Sumner at Antietam Valley. He assigned us to General French's division, to which we are still attached. The next morning, the memorable 17th of September—hardly recovered from the fatigue of the march—we advanced against the enemy. I shall not pretend to give a description of what must be now quite familiar in New York. A few features of the occasion, however, as they occurred near our position, it will not be out of place to mention. Fording Antietam creek we advanced rapidly under cover of the woods, till the fire of the enemy's skirmishers gave us sharp and sudden warning of their presence. There were no objections. With a cheer and a rush we reached the brow of the hill destined to be our position that day. Before us, concealed in a vast corn-field, which was defended by a ditch and stone wall, lay the rebels in great strength.

Our appearance they greeted with a heavy shower of bullets; the weight of their fire showed their number to be much greater than ours. To advance would have been destruction, retreat we would not, so down we throw ourselves behind the crest of the hill, and replied to their fire with all our power. Each man had been provided with from eighty to a hundred rounds of cartridge, and when these were spent, the boxes of the wounded and killed afforded a new supply. For from four to five hours this scene—decided by military judges to have been the heaviest fire of musketry ever delivered in any battle in this war—was kept up between both sides. The enemy failing to overwhelm us by weight of his infantry fire, and not daring to advance outside his intrenchments, now tried to get a battery in position. This was foiled immediately, for as soon as the horses were seen dragging the pieces up, a well-directed volley from our rifles put horses and artillerists *hors de combat*, and the attempt was then abandoned. Several rebel colors were seen to rise and fall like the waves of a sea, for their bearers were repeatedly shot and replaced so, was also one of our own. The distance between us was not a hundred yards, and this closeness prevented the batteries in their rear from hurting us, as they could not shell us without killing their own men. Our more precise batteries threw their shell over our heads, and did the rebels great destruction. The arrival of our reserves—chief among was the Irish Brigade—decided the day in our favor, the charge of the Irish Brigade being the signal for a general skiddadle of our opponents.

The accurate report given our loss (I mean of the Fourth Regiment alone) as one hundred and eighty killed and wounded. The published list, I suppose, will give their names, officers and privates.

General Max Weber had to retire from the field wounded. Colonel [William L.] Schley of the Fifth Maryland, now acts in his place as brigadier-general.

Our field officers, Lieutenant-Colonel [John D.] McGregor and Major [William] Jamison, though much exposed, fortunately escaped unhurt. Lieutenant-Colonel McGregor has had the command of the regiment for a long time; he and the major could ill be spared by us.

Of the Fourth, Captain John Downes and Lieutenant [Henry K.] Chapman were killed. Many other officers were wounded.

A look at the position occupied by the enemy during the action proved their loss to be five to our one. The rapidity with which the rebel corpses decomposed and their bloated blackened appearance twenty hours after the battle, was very remarkable. Our dead presented no such appearance at all. A dead nigger could only be distinguished from a dead white man by his hair and lips, so black were the bodies. Many theories have been advanced to account for the—what I may call—phenomenon. The most probable is, that it arises from their irregular way of living, excessive drinking of rum with gunpowder, want of salt, etc.

Many of the arms picked up on the field proved to be of the English pattern, and to have been manufactured this year (1862) in London. To come into the possession of the rebels they must have run the blockade.

The evening of the 17th, it must be confessed, was one of suspense. The enemy's batteries still whizzed their shells in our neighborhood, our right was reported to have been roughly handled; Burnside had to yet give the finishing blow. As I lay down that night on my pallet of straw, and looked at the crowd of wounded and wearied men around me, a verse of Campbell's accord to my mind—often had I repeated it at home, then little imagine I should witness such a scene:

> "Our bugles sang truce, for the night-cloud had lowered
> And the sentinel stars set their watch in the sky.
> And thousands had sunk on the ground overpowered,
> The weary to sleep, and the wounded to die."

On the 22nd ult., Sumner's corps left Antietam Valley, and we took up our march for Harper's Ferry. In a few hours, we reached the banks of the Potomac opposite the village. The bridge having been destroyed by the rebels, we forded the river. The tide was strong, and the water reached above our knees, yet the whole corps—infantry, cavalry, and artillery—got across without difficulty. We are now encamped on Bolivar Heights, Maryland, and Loudon Heights, both of which completely command Harper's Ferry, and are now being strongly fortified. Trusting too much to the natural defensives of the place, the authorities neglected to fortify these heights before. Once fortified, Harper's Ferry becomes impregnable.

The rebels occupy Winchester, which is about thirty miles from here. Their pickets approach within sight of ours. So close were they the other day that one rebel proposed to trade tobacco for salt. The pickets do not fire on each other, but if any observation-parties of the enemy come near our lines, then our cavalry and artillery go out and capture or skedaddle them back to Winchester.

The prisoners taken by the rebels at Harper's Ferry, Shephardstown, and other places are being rapidly paroled. The rebels find that to feed their own men, and make both ends meet, is as much as they can do, without feeding our men, so they get rid of them the best way they can.

The President, with a numerous and brilliant staff, visited us the other day, and reviewed the corps. The many riddled and torn colors of the various regiments must have given Mr. Lincoln a pretty good idea of the way the bullets flew at Antietam.

The force now at Harper's Ferry is very considerable. An advance may probably take place soon. In the meantime, we suffer much for want of clothes, tents, and pay. There is five months' pay due now. If we had it, we could relieve many of our necessities. Coats, blankets, and knapsacks were all lost on the march, or previous to the battle. We shall be in a bad way if the government does not provide us with these necessary things soon.

When anything of interest occurs, you shall hear from me again. Till then, *au revior*.

A. K.

October 19, 1862
NINTH REGIMENT, N.Y.S.M.
IN CAMP NEAR SHARPSBURG, MD., October 7.

Last night, Major Allan Rutherford, and several of our line officers, returned to the regiment after an absence, on account of sickness, bringing with them a large mail to gladden the hearts of the boys. As the arrival of a mail in the out-of-the-way camp we occupy at present is a rather unfrequent occurance, the boys were immediately on the tip-dash toe of expectation, and as the contents of the bags were distributed, our camp was a sight on which our home guards would have looked with astonishment. Letters and papers from home were torn open and perused with avidity, and SUNDAY MERCURY stock was especially buoyant. Had our friends in New York seen the clusters of men around the fortunate owner of a SUNDAY MERCURY, to hear him read aloud the "Army Correspondence", "City Items", and "Fire and Military News", it would have stimulated them to send us a larger and more regular supply of MERCURYS in future. Our boys were especially gratified by the perusal of your paragraph headed the "New York City Guard". For the interest thus shown in our favor, you have the thanks of every officer and man in this command, and those also, I have no doubt, of the thousands of our personal friends and the friends of our regiment in New York and vicinity. As we deemed it an honor to bear the name of "City Guard", so have we made it our study to preserve that name unsullied by an unworthy act on our part. We left New York nearly eighteen months ago as the "City Guard", and as such we have marched and countermarched through Maryland and Virginia, to the tune of nearly a thousand miles. As the "City Guard", we received our fiery baptism at Cedar Mountain on the 9th of August last. As the "City Guard", we took our regular daily installment of shelling at the Rappahannock River for several successive days. As such, we opposed the progress of the rebels through Thoroughfare Gap on the 28th of the same month; and again on the 30th, at Bull Run, we did our best to check the rebel torrent that swept around our left flank, and compelled our army to fall back toward Centreville.

As the City Guard, we assisted at the dislodgment of the enemy from the Hagerstown Heights [South Mountain], on the 14th of September; and as such we had the honor of being among the first to open the ball at Antietam, on the 17th of the same month.

As the City Guard, hundreds of our best and bravest have fallen dead or wounded on the battle-field; and, as the City Guard, those of our regiment who pass safely through this war hope to return to New York, proudly bearing aloft the now blood-stained, service-worn, and bullet-riddled flags presented to the Ninth Regiment, N.Y.S.M., by the Corporation of New York city.

Once we numbered over a thousand men, and now we can scarcely muster three hundred and fifty all told. Surely no honorable military organization would wish to fitch from us a name we have expended nearly two-thirds of our number to uphold and win fame for. If this new regiment must have our name, let them hurry up their organization and departure for the seat of the war. Let them get assigned to Hooker's army corps, and let "Fighting Joe" place them in the front of battle, and shove them ahead for one day, and I opine there will be about men enough left in the two commands to form a decent battalion. Then we could take them in out of the cold, and make *bona fide* City Guards of them. Until then, we hope they will seek elsewhere for a name.

Since the Battle of Antietam, we have been in camp recruiting our strength, and getting ready for the next move. Unless a movement is soon made, the equinoctial storm will come to render roads and rivers impassable, and then follows a long winter of *ennui* and inaction. We did hope to have seen our homes long ere this, and Government owes it to itself and the army to push ahead, and, if possible, finish this unnatural war before the coming of another spring.

Colonel [John W.] Stiles is, and has been, under arrest for some time past, and to see him walking around without sword or shoulder-straps, one would think he had lost his last friend.

Lieutenant-Colonel [William] Atterbury has resigned since our last battle. The noise and jar of the battle-field did not appear to agree with his nervous organization, if one could judge correctly from his behavior under fire. We have no doubt but that he will be the "right man in the right place" when he gets safely home.

Adjutant Charles E. Tuthill has also resigned, and "vamoosed the ranch". If you should hear of any new regiment that wishes a competent and reliable person as "knapsack guard", be kind enough to recommend for the parish. He can get a certificate from this regiment, that he is able and willing to remain behind with the knapsacks when the boys leave them to go into action, and that he will remain with them so long as the booming cannon, or the rattling of musketry can be heard in the distance, or there is a smell of villainous saltpetre in the atmosphere—unless he should be shelled from them, as he was at Bull Run, or he should be ordered to join his regiment by some heedless and heartless officer, as he was at Hagerstown Heights and Antietam. I am sorry I cannot send you his address; but you will doubtless see and hear some gay and dashing officer singing "Billy Barlow" and "Lord Lowell" in a very masterly manner, and if you do, you may feel morally certain that you have the late "Knapsack Guard" of the Ninth N.Y.S.M. before you in proper person.

We hear with sincere pleasure that our gallant little Captain [Eugene] Pickett of Co. A, and Capt. [Ralph] Lanning of Co. D (both wounded at Antietam) are fast recovering from their wounds. Both are good officers and greatly missed.

Yours,   MINUS.

THIRTEENTH REGIMENT, N.Y.S.V.

PHILADELPHIA, PA., October 14.

I hope you will give these few lines room in your most valuable paper. Having written several times to the leading newspaper here (Philadelphia *Inquirer*) without any attention being paid to my communications, I now write to you, knowing you to be the champion for the rights of both soldiers and firemen.

The Philadelphians are daily grumbling about having their hospitals filled with men of other States. I can assure you, in the name of two hundred New York boys, they would not object to leaving the City of Brotherly Love for the Empire City; for we are kept more like prisoners here than men who have been fighting in defence of their country and flag.

Some of us [have been] in this West Philadelphia Hospital-prison over four months. Army regulations only allow sixty days to be either fit for service or discharged. If any of us ask to be either discharged or sent to our regiments, we are immediately put in the guard-house, and fed on bread and water, until the surgeon in charge sees fit to release us. None of us have received any pay since we came here, and some of our families are in want.

The Pennsylvania soldiers in this hospital can go out when they please, and mock us because we belong to New York and have to remain in this hospital-prison. The ladies come in with dainties, and, with very few exceptions, ask the ward-masters for "our troops"—meaning the Pennsylvanians. They say they cannot be troubled with other State troops, and pass by as if we were worse than rebels.

Now, Mr. Editor, I would ask, through your columns, is this proper treatment for men who would willingly sacrifice their lives in the defence of our Union? Are we not fighting in the same cause as the Pennsylvanians, that we should be treated thus? Were we not wounded and stricken by disease in the same cause as the Pennsylvanians? Will our State not do anything for these who went forth to do battle for our dear and beloved flag?

Yours,   G. M. W.

October 26, 1862
FORTIETH (MOZART) REGIMENT, N.Y.S.V.

Ill-health, since the last battle of Bull Run, has prevented me from keeping you posted as to the doings and whereabouts of the once Mozart Regiment, with its thousand and one. Alas, poor regiment, how thy ranks are thinned! Yes, dear MERCURY, the Mozart Regiment is not what it once was; we have seen our comrades fall thick and fast. But they fell for the Union. Never since first our regiment entered the field has it dishonored itself. We have had but little rest for fifteen months: for being placed in what is called Kearny's

Fighting Division, with that brave general at our head, we were among the first to enter, and, on several occasions, the last to leave the field of battle. The Mozart Regiment has taken an active part in building all the principal fortifications in front of our national capital, was the first that discovered the famous "cow-bell" designs of the enemy, during its many skirmishes at Munson's Hill and Bailey's Cross Roads. The Mozart also covered the retreat of the Union troops after the first Bull Run fight. That is the troops that retreated by the way of the Alexandria & Orange Railroad. Our division was then commanded by the old war-dog, Heintzelman, who afterward received the command of a corps, and the daring "Phil Kearny" took into his hand the reins of Heintzelman's old division which he managed fearlessly until his death.

Our brigade was composed of the Third and Fourth Maine, the Thirty-eighth New York (Second Scott Life Guard), and the Fortieth New York (Mozart), and commanded by Gen. Sedgwick, afterward by General Birney, who is still our general, having led us through all the fights on the Peninsula, and the late fights at Bull Run and Chantilly, Va. After arriving on the Peninsula, the Mozart Regiment took an active part in the art of the "shovel and spade" during the siege of Yorktown—was one of the regiments that did the last night's picket duty in the intrenchments along the enemy's front at Yorktown, and was the first to plant the New York State colors on the battlements of Fort Magruder, which cost us the loss of two of our brave men, who brought their rifles to a rest on the top of a torpedo, which sent them to that "undiscovered country from whose beurne no traveler returns". So you see that the Mozart Regiment was the first of the Union troops that spilled its blood on the breastworks of the enemy at Yorktown. But that is not all; for the old Mozart has sprinkled its blood on the battle-fields of Williamsburg, Fair Oaks, seven days' fight in front of Richmond, battle of Charles City Cross Roads, Malvern Hill, the late battles of Bull Run, on August 29th, was in two engagements inside of seven hours; on the day following (30th), again entered the field; and during the two days' fight, our loss was 162 men, killed and wounded. On the 1st Sept., our regiment was ordered by Gen. Kearny to deploy into line of battle at Chantilly, Va., and hold a certain position at all hazards. No sooner had we got into line than we received a tremendous volley from the "gray-backs", which was returned with interest. We fought for three-quarters of an hour, the enemy "peppering" us and we "salting" them. Our regiment commenced the fight at Chantilly with three hundred men, including officers, and finished it with the loss of one hundred and sixty-three men, and our brave Gen. Kearny. By the by, I might mention here that the last words spoken by Gen. Kearny to Union soldiers was addressed to the Mozart Regiment. Just previous to our deploying into line he said:

"Now my brave Fortieth, I expect you to fight."

After thus speaking, one of his aides rode up to, and informed him that a brigade had fallen back from our left, and broken our lines, leaving that wing exposed to the enemy's flank movement. No sooner had he received this information than he ordered the aide to remain with us, and galloped off to our left, with the intention, I presume, of ordering the above mentioned brigade back to its position; but mistaking his road, rushed into the very jaws of death. We have since learned from some of own men that were taken prisoners that day by the Sixteenth [Forty-ninth] Georgia Regiment, that it was they who shot General Kearny, and bragged that they had killed one of our best generals. They gave the particulars of his death as follows: The Sixteenth Georgia regiment was lying in ambush, General Kearny rode up to within twenty paces of them, when he suddenly brought his horse to a check. The entire regiment arose to their feet, and leveled their pieces at him.

At this the general made the following characteristic interrogation:

"What regiment are you, God damn you?" To which they made no reply.

He again asked: "What regiment are you?" To which they answered:

"Surrender yourself a prisoner!" When the general cried, "Never!" And throwing himself down upon his horse's neck, started off.

They fired at him, and a ball entered his body, killing him instantly. The enemy took his body within their lines, and, after turning his pockets inside out, and taking his sabre, they sent it through their lines to us. So ended the life of the warrior Phil Kearny.

Our regiment, in all the battles since that of Williamsburg, has been led into action by Colonel Thomas W. Egan, who upon all occasions proved himself most brave and daring. He has ever attended to the wants of his men without delay, which, in connection with his leading them personally into so many battles, has endeared him to them. He has been of signal service to the Government in many ways, the last work being the capture of rebel General Longstreet's personal train, with valuable papers, etc.

Olive Oil,   R. McW.

November 2, 1862
FIFTY-SEVENTH REGIMENT, N.Y.S.V.
HARPER'S FERRY, VA., October 27.

Having a few leisure-moments to myself, I improve them by writing to your much-loved paper, to let you know what the veterans of the peninsula are about. We lay within four miles of the rebel outpost, and are exchanging shots every few days. We had quite a reconnoissance a few days ago to Charlestown city, in which we were successful in capturing a large quantity of wheat and several other stores; the wheat, I think for one, ought to have been ground up and made into bread for the men, for we have picket-duty every other [day], and have to do it with hungry bellies. We have given to us for a day's ration one pound of hard tack about five ounces of salt pork or beef, to last from 8 o'clock one day until 12 o'clock the next. There is not much of importance going on inside the lines, except fortifying the heights around the ferry. We expect to go into winter-quarters in a few days, and I will write you more particulars.

The weather is very fine out in these parts, but rather chilly nights and mornings. The boys are troubled a great deal with the rations what we draw from the commissary. The meat mostly what is drawn, if it was not tied fast, it would run away before the cooks could get it into the pots; and the crackers are some of the ones that Noah had in the ark with him at the time of the flood.

We have not been paid off in four months, and what is worse, we do not know when we will be. There are quite a number of sick men in the hospital that money would be the means of helping a great deal.

> BOMB SHELL.

FOURTEENTH REGIMENT, N.Y.S.V.
HAREWOOD HOSPITAL, WASHINGTON, D.C., Oct. 27.

Will you allow me a small space in your paper. Being an old member of the Fourteenth N.Y.S.M., and not having seen for a long time any correspondence from the regiment. I thought I would send you a few lines in reference to words used by the Hon. Moses F. Odell about the new recruits coming out, saying that the scum of Brooklyn came out first, but that the pride of Brooklyn came out last. Now, I should like to know what has brought them out. Nothing more that the bounty (two hundred dollars), more than we have received altogether for eighteen faithful months. Now, have we not (the scum, as he calls us) fought faithfully to keep up the reputation of the regiment? The Hon. Moses F. Odell knows that. Now, what has he done for the regiment so much? We have not seen anything. Being worn out with fatigue and exposures, we were compelled to come to the hospital, not only us, but a number of new recruits, and nothing was the matter with them, which we have found out since. Now, this is a perfect shame. Some do not intend to go back to the regiment. There is a full as many new recruits in the hospital here as old members. Some have never been to the regiment, but have come to the hospitals and have got to be nurses, or cooks, or anything, to keep out of the army. That is what he calls his pride of Brooklyn.

Can you inform me whether we are sworn in as two-years troops? If so, you will oblige

> AN OLD MEMBER.

November 9, 1862
ANOTHER CORRESPONDENT GONE—Every few days, we are called upon to mourn the decease of some one of our brave and valiant army correspondents. The last one is Edward Britton, First Sergeant of Company I, Sixty-ninth, N.Y.S.V. He contributed several letters to these columns over the signature of "Non Com". He was an intelligent man, unflinchingly brave, and highly esteemed by his brother printers in New York for his many personal good qualities. Peace to his remains!

TWELFTH REGIMENT, N.Y.S.V.
EBENEEZER CHURCH HOSPITAL
WASHINGTON, D.C., Nov. 5.

During the past five or six weeks this hospital has been the scene of several thefts. The Ward Master (Sergeant Gaskill) and several of the patients have had sums of money taken from them during the hours of sleep, or whilst insensible from sounds and sickness. More recently, one of the latter had his watch taken, and another a purse and fifteen dollars. Inquiry was instituted in these cases, but without any definite results, though suspicion was attached to parties which recent developments have proved innocent, and which have brought the crime home to those who should, and were thought the least capable of it—the female nurses, Mrs. Margaret Clements and Mrs. Catherine Dougherty. From their mock kindness, sympathy, attention, and qualifications, they stood high, not only in the opinions of those who were the objects of their seeming solicitude, but also those of the medical gentlemen of the institution. In fact, everything, apparently, was in their favor, and they were the last persons who, from acts and demeanor, could be deemed "wolves in sheep's clothing". Many a depraved nature and guilty conscience are cloaked from the world's view by studied appearances and the assumption of characters as foreign to their true natures as the antipodes. If we could only tear off the false mask from the world, what startling revelations would be made. Think you, if "Honest Abe" were omniscient only for a moment, how many faithful servants to the country and the exchequer could he count? I imagine a number less than the righteous persons of Sodom and Gemorrah. Four, I believe, were found in them; but I think the number here would be limited to the "Disbanded Volunteer". What other inference can we come in, when the homes of the sick and infirm are made the theatre of robbers, and when the articles necessary for their use and comfort become their prey. I don't intend to moralize, but I want to show those persons in their true light, and how they should, in future, be regarded by all who knew them—this conduct suggesting so broad an inference, that I found it impossible to pass it by without comment. I hope their shame and disgrace will prove a salutary lesson to others; and now, sir, I will explain how suspicion was excited, and culpability established.

One of the patients imagined he saw Mrs. Clements one day conceal something about her person. He reported the circumstance to the Steward (Mr. Ira Chase of Rhode Island), who brought it under the notice Dr. McKlin, Acting Assistant Surgeon—in the absence of Dr. Waters, Superintendent. The Doctor instructed Mr. Chase to arrest Mrs. C., if any future act of hers should tend to confirm the surmises of the patient referred to; he at the same time was advised to keep his eyes about him. The natural character will sometimes out, in defiance of all the restraints and guarded watchfulness. Soon again, Mrs. C. committed herself, and this time the Steward acted up to his instructions, and placed the guilty one under confinement. Also, Mrs. Dougherty, her conduct about the same time having excited the suspicions of the Steward himself. He, Mr. George Ferrin (Warden), and the Wardmaster—backed by the law in the form of a police officer, next proceeded to search the residences of these persons. In the house of Mrs. C., they found not only 119 pieces of hospital clothing, but cans of jellies, jams, etc., sent to the sick by friends or benevolent persons; also, the purse referred to, minus the $15, though a large quantity of money was found. Mrs. C. also acknowledged the theft of the watch, but accused her husband of having received it, and other things for sale. I may here remark that an investigation into the quantity of hospital clothing on hand established the fact that 200 towels and 140 sheets were not forthcoming. In the house of Mrs. D. was also found an assortment of hospital goods. There are extenuating circumstances in this woman's favor. Her husband was in the army, and sick at home for some time. She asserts that the articles found were sent by friends for his use and comfort. All the parties were brought before Mr. Justice Call, and held to bail; Mrs. Clements in $200, and Mr. C. and Mrs. D. in the sum of $300 each, to appear on trial to answer the charges. Inquiry was also instituted in the other hospitals under the superintendence of Dr. E.W. Waters—*en passant*, I am happy to inform you that this gentleman is on the recovery—which implicated some of the kitchen employees, quantities of groceries being found in their houses. The parties were discharged, it being impossible to prove properly in such things. Too much praise cannot be awarded Messrs. Chase, Turrin, and Gaskill, for the tact and perseverance displayed in the foregoing developments. Would it not be well if their conduct were imitated in the other hospitals in this and other cities used for Government purposes? Have we any reason to think the employees in other institutions of the kind less scrupulous than those here? Depend on it, a general similar proceeding would be the means of saving a few thousands to our poor defrauded and much injured Uncle.

A—, COLOR GUARD.

The "Disbanded Volunteer" was another favorite feature in the Sunday Mercury. *Written in a tortured Irish dialect, by humorist Joseph Barber, the weekly column served as a running commentary on the war and was immensely popular with the soldiers.*

<u>November 16, 1862</u>
TRIBUTE TO THE BRAVE—The following, from the pen of a fair lady, is written in memory of our late contributor, Edward Britton, who died from wounds received from Antietam:

As, day after day, news of the numerous engagements reach us, accompanied with their lists of killed and wounded, so each one, who has those they cherish in the midst of this terrible strife, gazes with tearful eye and palpitating heart, to see if the name of *him* is there; to see if he, who is perhaps their sole support, has been speedily called away. "Gone!" they exclaim, with faltering voice, as they read the fatal name—a name, to them, written in letters of blood—a name that ere long will cease to be remembered by the multitude, while it remains a saddened recollection to the sorrowful few.

To such a one we would now refer—to a patriot who has descended to an honorable grave, leaving his name inscribed on the nation's patriotic banner; one who has always been both an indulgent husband and father—a true friend. Now, however, this poor fellow who has served his country so long and bravely, has gone to be judged at that great tribunal which will decide his future destiny.

After being engaged in all the famous battles since the commencement of this war, he distinguished himself for the last time at Antietam, in which he received a wound in the right arm, proving fatal, carrying him away to "his last sweet sleep". God rest you, Edward Britton! O, can we not say with truth:

> "This world would be a happy world
> Had politics the power no more
> To drench this beauteous land of ours
> In pools of human gore;
> Had proud ambitions to submit
> To arbitration's rule,
> And glory's gilded rays he thought
> The playthings of a fool."

THIRTY-SIXTH REGIMENT, N.Y.S.V.

CAMP NEAR NEW BALTIMORE, VA., Nov. 11.

"I pitch my tent on this camp-ground."

All hail! "The glad tidings of great joy," the arrival in camp of the MERCURY. And if one has the good fortune to receive his before the others, he is "besieged," "flanked," and surrounded on all sides. And to try and break through the assemblage is next to impossible. But should he manage to escape through some avenue not guarded, he is immediately attacked by the reserve-corps. Therefor, the only resource left to him, is an "unconditional surrender", by reading aloud the interesting items, of which there are numerous. The first article that meets our eye is the "Army Correspondence"; and as the boys cautiously peruse them, each are eagerly waiting, expecting that a correspondent may appear from the Thirty-six. My last letter, I believe, was written at Berlin. During our stay at that place, we were all fitted out in a new uniform, and we presented a fine and soldierly appearance, even far surpassing our neighbors, the three hundred dollar men.

Again the tap of the drum brought to our ears the welcome news of "marching orders" for breakfast, and accordingly we struck our tents, and, with our household treasures packed up in a small space, and our haversacks filled with "iron-bound" pork and coffee, we put out into the world to try our fortune again.

A half-hour's walk brings us to the Pontoon Bridge that spans the Potomac, separating Maryland from Virginia. And this time, with light hearts, we wended our way to "Ole Virginny shore", different men, and with different prospects before us than when we first entered Virginia some eight months ago. One little disappointment we encountered. We had hoped and expected that our laurel-crowned band would have struck up the fitting tune of "Carry Me Back to Ole Virginny", to instill our hearts with new vigor, and make us feel that we were re-entering the Old Dominion to crown ourselves with new laurels. One genius had the cheek to whistle that popular melody, and doubtless he may wish himself out of Virginia before long. Does he remember "Bottom's Bridge" and the Chickahominy or the swamps of Fair Oaks, with the very delicate water to drink. After traveling some three miles (for you must know that Virginia miles are equal to York leagues), we entered the romantic village of Lovettsville. And I must acknowledge that the inhabitants, scarce as they were, were quite reconciled to their fate, for no less than three American flags were swung to the breeze; and the feminine gender were less haughty and proud than we had seen elsewhere.

The next place worthy of any note that we passed was Goose Creek—a small collection of wooden shanties, with a creek that bears the (fowl) name of Goose running parallel through it, from which the village derives its name.

Nothing remarkable is seen here, so we pass on to the next, which place we will call "Whiteplains". This, like other Virginia localities, was devoid of inhabitants, save a Secesh cobbler, who intended to mend our soles (souls) before entering kingdom come. The bull-gine during our stay here, commenced running, which brought our supplies nearer at hand.

I am bound by a sacred duty to make mention of the last rites of a noble hero, who has offered up his life to his Maker. There, in a solitary cluster of woods, with but few companions around, they permitted the remains of a departed warrior to be hidden from their sight. By the dim light of a camp-fire they dug his shallow bed. And with the ground covered with Southern snow, they lowered the sacred remains to their mother earth. Perhaps a kind and devoted father, who has left a family to mourn his untimely end; or, even a fond and beloved husband, or the idol of some poor maiden's heart, whose frail constitution will be prostrated by the receipt of this sad intelligence. God grant that they may have sufficient strength to meet this woeful news! and may a guardian's care protect the widow and orphan, and bless the declining years of his aged parents! Noble youth!—Warren McWilliams—a martyr in Freedom's cause! Thy memory shall become as sacred as the cause thou wert engaged in. May thy body *requiescat in pace!*

We encamped in White Plains about three days, during which time, eating and drinking was the chief programme. And it was here that a new and fashionable, and I may say rare dish, made its appearance. And should any of your fashionable city caterers wish the recipe, they can have it by applying to me. I think it would become a great favorite among ye gallant parlor and kid-gloved generals. It bears the honest name of "Lob-scouse", as the programme would have it. We marched again, and are encamped at present at the village of New Baltimore. Yesterday (Nov. 10) General McClellan, with his staff, paid a farewell visit to us.

Little Mac looked as fleshy and hearty as ever he did; and everywhere he was received with tremendous shouts of applause.

Gen. [Charles] Devens, our Brigadier, in the last Massachusetts election, was the Union candidate for Governor, and, I am sorry to say, was defeated, and that the nigger candidate, [John A.] Andrews, re-elected.

Yours, as ever,   NUMBER TWO, OF THE REAR RANK.

November 23, 1862
THIRTY-SIXTH REGIMENT N.Y.S.V.
CAMP NEAR NEW BALTIMORE, VA., Nov. 14th.

Again my heart swells with patriotism, and my pen commences its "scribbleism", to be permitted to have the honor of attracting your attention for a few moments.

We are fast recruiting to our original strength, and availing ourselves of every opportunity to "make hay while the sun shines".

Some imprudent person has whispered that we are to go into winter-quarters. If so, we are willing; for the winter is fast winding its way upon us, and with the pelting snow and Mr. Jack Frost to contend against, our progress would be very slow. Whatever military stratagem is to be accomplished must be done while we have this fine weather.

We have lately heard (though not a very reliable source) that our gallant little chieftain McClellan has been relieved of command. If so, all our confidence is at an end, and our castle-built hopes, fanciful in their gorgeousness, are blasted, and our imaginary laurels are crushed beneath the feet. The nigger-worshipers at the North have been "itching" for McClellan's removal some time. Is this a war for the salvation of the blacks or for the continuation of the Union as it was? Before I would fire one shot to liberate any black now in slavery I would (as a noted pugalist once said) roll myself in that emblem of liberty, and let the "paragraph of my existence be distributed". By the removal of McClellan, dissatisfaction and dissension you stir up in the breasts of the Army of the Potomac. No general, no matter how popular he may be, will have the love and esteem he had.

Yesterday, for the first time, we had a battalion drill. Not wishing to instill into the minds of my readers any military qualifications, or disapprove of any of the many tactics in which we are taught. Our battalion is commanded by a gentleman whose military genius none can dispute. Also, he is assisted by proficient field and staff officers, which goes greatly to harmonize a regiment and prepare it for active service in whatever field is a sure omen of success, which otherwise would be a total defeat and disgrace.

While writing this, cannonading is heard in front, and we infer from that that our troops have become engaged. As we are encamped in a splendid position (on a high bluff) to pepper our "audacious foe", I would say let them come, and we will greet them with fatherly feeling intermingled with leaden hail.

This little hamlet of New Baltimore was once (in the days of Nebechudnezzar) a very thriving locality. At present it is chiefly populated by Dutch and lager-beer, in the persons of General Sigel's command; and "You fight met Sigel, you drink mit me", is the language.

The election in New York as it was pending caused no little excitement in our camp, all anxious for the returns to be forwarded. I was disappointed when I heard of [Horatio] Seymour's election. I had hopes that [James S.] Wadsworth would have taken the palm.

As the news is unimportant it is difficult for me to say much. But allow me to thank you for your kindness. Pardon me for this quotation:

> "Here I lay me down to sleep,
> And all the vermin round me creep;
> If they bite me before I wake
> I hope to gosh their jaws will break."

So mote it be.   Yours,   JERSHUA JENKINS.

SECOND FIRE ZOUAVES
MANASSAS JUNCTION, November 18.

As I sit and write to-day in my little canvas house on the famous plains of Manassas, I can almost look straight into the tent of our indefatigable sutler, Billy Cutter and since "Grapeshot" told you all about the breaking up of camp and marching, I can find no more lively subject to write upon than the owner of the above-mentioned shop. Allow me, in the way of general observation, to say, that sutlers, as a class, are a much-abused race, and that they—to give their revilers a large margin—are, at least, a much needed incumberance. This fact is based on observation. Tobacco, you know, is a much-needed article to a soldier, and, in fact, to probably the biggest slice of all male bipeds, and where on a march could one think of deriving his ration of the weed from if not the sutler? Traders established in towns and villages won't fork over on "tick", and since Major [John H.] McBlair and his strong box have kept aloof from us for over five months, the "rhino" is feeling out of order. But Billy gives on "tick". That is to say, he gives you your tickets for a certain amount (alarmingly small of late), and you can buy, at liberty, whatever in his ever-ready-to-be-packed-for-a-march establishment takes your fancy. The prices are, of course—no! I "sign" for a dollar to-day; and far be it from me to do violence to a feeling of gratitude towards Billy, and go back on him. He—the jovial Billy—got mighty cautious of late—a feeling infused by our late experiments in changing bases of operation on the Peninsula, one of which experimental military evolutions encumbers the sorry side of Billy's ledger to a healthy sum total. The boys know that, and often make it the subject of a joke on him, which, however, he is not slow to return, with compound interest. He, in fact, accused them of aiding and abetting the enemy of our common country by not protecting his person and particularly his stock, in time of need, and intends to have us court-martialed. One of his prime witnesses is just returned from Richmond, he says, and as soon as he has time to transfer the matter to the hands of his council, it shall be attended to.

This was the talk overheard this morning on "Change", when your humble servant presented himself as a candidate for Billy's farther indulgence for another dollar in addition to the already swollen figures which will startle my ears and weaken my purse on pay-day. Demurely I handed over the Captain's indorsement—a sort of collateral security, which means, in the sutler's language, that if the man don't pay, the Captain is certain not to. In days gone by, the single act of mine, like Aladdin's lamp, would instantly bring forth the much coveted bits of yellow, green, red, and blue pasteboards, representing respectively Uncle Samuel's "though lost to sight to memory dear" white half and quarter eagles and ladies' dime and half dime. But, as I observed before, I think Billy's sense of caution is remarkably alive to danger, in whatever shape it may disguise itself. And so, taking my humble petition, and subjecting it to ask close a scrutiny as ever a bank-note underwent at the hands of a Dutch grocer, he prepared to cross-examine me as to sundry little items furnished at various camp grounds, displaying a range of vision truly astonishing, and for which I had never given him credit for. The mentioning of such places as Camp Lawrence, McClellan, Cheeseman's Creek, Yorktown, Williamsburg, Fair Oaks, Alexandria, etc., brought back pleasant memories of innocent indulgences derived from Billy's caravansery, while, at the same time, the fact remained of unyielding figures, menacing my nomenclature on his books in lieu of these various drawings from his stock. But by promising verbally, together with my quondam promising collateral, I secured my tickets and was just now feting on "bolivers" and cheese; for I must say, that we had of late so much of Uncle Abe's platform, *i.e.*, hard tack, as to rather surfeit us, and a change of diet, at all times highly commendable, was in this instance much appreciated.

My leisure time in camp has often been diversified by a trip to Billy's establishment, where I was always sure of finding the representative classes of the second F.Z.'s. Here is your cautious, over thirty, stout built, bewhiskered pater familias, who hardly ever buys any thing but smoking tobacco, a new tin cup, paper and envelopes, post-stamps, and on inspection-day a sheet of emery paper wherewith to inveigle his musket into a bright smile to avert the wrath of the inspecting officer, who, as a sort of standing terror, is invariably detailed from the "regulars", and therefore ever so much more to be feared than a volunteer. Next in order comes your aspiring private or corporal, perchance sergeant—a noble fellow and model soldier; brave as a lion, with no disposition to blazon forth his own deeds of heroism and daring, but waiting patiently and uncomplainingly for the time to arrive to engage again the enemy with no less courage than he has repeatedly done before. You will find his shoes blacked, hair combed, clothes neatly brushed, and well fitting. His demeanor is always gentlemanly and courteous; and, although it seems odd to say it, he never indulges in any of the slang of which camp-life is so prolific. He is a strict attendant to his duty, misses no dress-parades, or guard-duty, goes every morning to the Adjutant's office for his mail, and may frequently be seen talking on politics, military matters, and the state of society generally, in an unobtrusive mild way. Our aspirant to the shoulder-straps and bugle is sure to correspond with some fair damsel, and, therefore, always asks for note-paper, and fancy envelopes. He orders his cap from Washington, by Billy, as also his Oxford ties and paper-chokers. He is in excellent standing with the sutler, and can get all he wants, since he was never known to over-draw.

Last, but no accident or oversight, least, comes your real, harum-scarum, devil-may-care, out and out, New York born, Bowery-raised, dare-devil, Rebel-terror, fireman F.Z. He laughs at danger, and tortures a smile and joke out of hardships in any shape. He is at the same time the delight and terror of the sutler. It is him that wakes him up, perchance, before reveille in the morning, which puts him in ill-humor for the emerging day. He rallies around at opening, *en masse*, and calls for anything in the establishment, from cream candy to onions, from a shaving-box to ten-pennyworth of raisins, or shoe-strings. In the temporary absence of the captain, he condescends to manufacture his own order, signature and all, presents it with the nonchalance of a French cavalier, and ten to one, succeeds in the object of his desire. He considers his own order at least as good as his captain's, and is more likely to pay for what he draws on that than the other. Approaching the tent with no idea of what he wants, and only a vague notion of what he needs, he is in his purchases mainly guided by the goods displayed, or any freaks of fancy having temporary possession of him. He commits compound murder on the King's English, and swears double-breasted revenge on the first Rebel he meets. His inventive genius for adapting language to different situations and subjects is without a known limit. Dickens might, with profit, take lessons from him; and Hugo's description of the Battle of Waterloo is insignificant compared with his graphic narrative of battles fought and sights seen. You can always tell him by his loud talk, near the camp-fire, when he holds forth in true [Henry Ward] Beecher style, not unfrequently representing an unfortunate stump orator, perplexed criminal lawyer, or Dutch grocer. He can take the part of either with great credit to his imitative genius. No stranger ever passes through camp unnoticed by him; and if he happens to be dressed in citizen's clothes, "Come in out of the draft!" is sounded from one end to the other. He has his own ideas of our military leaders, and is not to be hoodwinked by any arguments the newspapers may advance. He is on familiar terms with all officers of this regiment, calls his company officers by their Christian names, and thinks that a shoulder-strap is not always a sure sign of courage. It is he who is the life of a bayonet-charge; and tell him to take that battery on yonder steep hill, and, by a desperate dash, he will either have it, or his torn and mangled body will bear witness to the fearful earnestness of the attempt. Hooker wants us in front. We are going to-morrow.

I remain,   N.X. MT.

November 30, 1862

TWELFTH REGIMENT, N.Y.S.M.

CONVALESCENT CAMP, NEAR ALEXANDRIA, VA.,

November 27.

Lately, life to me has had so much of a sameness as to present little, if anything, worth communicating. As I don't remember any of your correspondents having alluded to this camp, I mean to devote an hour to a description, etc., thereof, with the hope that it may not prove entirely uninteresting to the sum-total of your readers. It is situated about midway between Alexandria and Fairfax Seminary, or about a mile from either, touching on the Alexandria Reservoir and Fort Ellsworth on the south and west. Hither all persons are sent after being discharged from hospitals, as well as that unenviable class known as "stragglers", previous to being forwarded to their respective regiments. But whether it is intended as a place necessary for probation for convalescents ere joining them, or as a convenient rendezvous preparatory to that purpose, I know not. Perhaps for both. But one thing is certain, that it is hard to conceive any place so unsuited for men not a foot from hospitals, many of whom are but partially cured of their wounds or diseases. The result is, that in a day or two, numbers are again on the sick-list, and some even returned to the hospital. This may not be the case if retained a little longer under surgical care, or if they could be sent to some place more comfortable, after discharge from hospital. In all cases I don't think there is sufficient discrimination shown in the parties discharged and retained. In many, the reverse of the action taken in this respect would be the more just. The camp is on a hill exposed to the biting cold from every quarter. Our occupation of this place since the breaking out of the Rebellion has left this place without a tree or bush for miles around. The consequence is, that we are not able to have even a camp-fire. There was a hard frost last night. It is also very cold to-day. I am shivering whilst writing this, with my teeth at war in very audible knocks, and will, for the present, bid you adieu.

I remain, sir, yours truly,   A—, COLOR GUARD.

December 7, 1862

FOURTH REGIMENT N.Y.S.V. (FIRST SCOTT LIFE GUARD)

BANKS OF THE RAPPAHANNOCK,

OPPOSITE FREDERICKSBURG, VA., Dec. 1.

I dare say that, for the last few weeks, the good citizens of New York have been reading with absorbing interest the newspaper accounts of the movements of the Grand Army. The campaign commenced about the 30th of October. Since that time our army has not met with any serious impediment to its progress. Before our threatening columns, Rebel cavalry and infantry have scattered like chaff before the wind. The Rappahannock, lined on the opposite side by Longstreet's army, for the time has temporarily delayed our advance. To overcome this obstacle, our side has not been wanting in industry. Batteries have been put up, pontoon-bridges constructed, and ready to launch at a moment's notice. In short, nothing neglected that might help to our success. The enemy, also, have not been idle, and make a show of erecting powerful defences. Whether or not they intend to defend the place, remains to be seen; but there have been many signs, which indicate that they contemplate a retreat. All the cotton and tobacco has been destroyed or conveyed to Richmond; and it is pretty clear that, when we capture the town, we will find but very little of what could be useful to us. It seems to be understood that the town itself shall not be the theatre of any fight that may take place. What Rebel forces are there are stationed outside of the city limits. They will not dare to fire a gun from the town itself, as in that case our batteries would lay it in ashes.

Fredericksburg if one of the oldest towns in Virginia, founded in 1727. It was named after Prince Frederick, son of George II. Its distance from Richmond is sixty-two miles—from Washington, fifty-six. It is interesting to know that two of our Revolutionary generals—[Hugh] Mercer and [George] Weedons—were citizens of the town. The former kept a doctor's shop, the latter a tavern. A refugee from Scotland, Mercer must have been glad to be engaged in the struggle against his hereditary enemies, the British. How well he acted his part, history tells us, which recounts his death at Princeton.

After the above digression, it is time I should say something about the movements of the regiment. With the rest of Sumner's Corps, we left Harper's Ferry October 30. Nov. 2 found us supporting a battery at Snicker's Gap, then threatened by the enemy. Nov. 4, we entered Upperville, evacuated by [Gen. J. E. B.] Stuart's Cavalry. Nov. 7, at Rectortown, we had the first fall of snow this season, it augured badly for our winter campaign, that, fortunately, the weather since has been unusually fine for this season. Nov. 9, entered Warrenton—said to be the prettiest town in Virginia, and looked as if it might have been—is certainly in a splendid location, being on the summit of a hill; its church-spires are visible for miles around. At Warrenton we were unavoidably detained six days. On the 15th, we left the place; soon after not a Union soldier remained behind. It was then entered by a few squadrons of the ever active Stuart's Cavalry. It may, at first sight, appear strange that we should so soon abandon Warrenton to the enemy again. This can be easily explained. Our lines of communication being changed, provisions and supplies for the last few weeks coming by the way of Aquia Creek—a much shorter and more convenient way than the Warrenton road—the possession of Warrenton is no longer of any consequence to us. Besides, if the army were to garrison every town, we have passed through on our way from Harper's Ferry, then the Army of the Potomac would soon dwindle down to a corporal's guard. The whole force being kept together in a body, can capture the big places; those once taken, the little ones will surrender of themselves. If at any time we needed to regain Warrenton, the Rebel cavalry there would disappear wondrously quick if they but saw the glance of a Federal bayonet. Nov. 17, we halted in Falmouth, an old town coeval in antiquity with Fredericksburg, and lying opposite the latter, the Rappahannock rolling between. The second day we were encamped here, a squadron of Rebel cavalry got inside our picket-lines—the latter but lately posted, and probably not stationed at all the exposed points—and made a dash at a train of wagon that had gone outside of camp to search for forage. The teamsters, thinking "discretion the better part of valor", as it certainly was, the numbers being so disproportionate, did not wait to argue the right of possession with the Johnny Rebs, but did not make tracks without firing a few pistol-shots. The pickets, hearing the noise, arrived in time to make the hungry gray-backs disgorge their prey and skedaddle.

A. K.

THRILLING INCIDENT OF THE WAR

NOVITIATE HOSPITAL, FREDERICK, MD., Dec. 3.

On Thursday last one of the scholars belonging to the Convent Hospital, wishing to amuse herself, displayed a Confederate flag for about an hour, pinned to her breast, accompanied by several of the scholars, and walking up and down the spacious yard, in rear of the hospital, singing the song, "My Maryland", the song more than anything else aroused the attention of the convalescent patients, and on looking round they beheld the Rebel flag on her breast, rustling in the breeze as she was walking. They at once demanded it, but it was of no use, for she would not give it up, and it came to the surgeon in charge, Dr. Evans, who sent a very complimentary note to the Mother Superior, demanding the Rebel flag. The Mother at once found the girl, and took the flag from her and dashed it on the floor, stamping her foot on it, and would have tore it in pieces but for the order of the Surgeon in charge. She at once reprimanded her severely, and would have sent her to her home, only it happened to be in Georgia. The girl at once began to cry, and said she wished her two brothers would only come to the city again and she would go home with them. Her father and brothers are in the Rebel army, and the morning she was enjoying herself (Thanksgiving morning) our cavalry had a skirmish, about twelve miles from this city, with four companies of Rebel cavalry, resulting in the death of her father, and the capturing of forty prisoners, her two brothers among them. When the brothers were in the city before, they went to see her often; but not as prisoners of war, and the morning after Thanksgiving (Friday) her two brothers, escorted by two guards, went to the Convent to see their sister.

The Mother Superior learned who they were, and called up the young girl, not knowing who wanted to see her. When she came in the room, she did not know what to make of it, in seeing two guards, and such affection she showed toward these brothers would have to be seen to be realized. She embraced both of them for about ten minutes or more, and after that was done the brothers commenced to speak to her, and tell her how they came to be taken prisoners, and then told her father was shot dead yesterday morning, while engaged with our forces. All of a moment, she gave one scream that fairly shook the foundation, followed by shrieks and cries that would melt a heart of stone. The brothers, on seeing this, began to console her; but the poor girl was so distracted at the news of her father's death that she went into convulsions, and is in a very critical condition ever since. There was not a dry cheek in the whole room at this time, for as soon as the brothers saw that nothing would console her, they burst out crying. When the mother saw the brothers, she commenced crying, as also did the guards. The screams of the girl were so loud that we did not know what to make of it; and I rushed in to see what was the matter, and I found everything as described—the girl in convulsions, and the brothers, mother, and guards all crying. I never witnessed such an affecting scene in all my travels through life. I thought it was better to have the girl removed to her bed-room, where she now is, in a very critical condition, and not expected to survive. I told the brothers they had better call when their sister was better. The girl was so excited before the brothers came, thinking on what was said to her the day before, that the shock was too much for her. The brothers have since gone to Fortress Monroe to be exchanged, and the Mother has told me that she did not know what to do with the girl.

ASSISTANT-SURGEON, U.S.A.

NINETIETH REGIMENT, N.Y.S.V.

KEY WEST, Nov. 26.

The weather is now delightfully cool and pleasant, and with the return of those residents who fled during the epidemic, the streets begin to look lively again. When the Paymaster arrives, there will be considerable activity and bustle. Thousands here are anxiously awaiting his advent, for the citizen shopkeepers are as much interested therein as the soldiers. One wonders how they ever got along before our occupation of the island, for all the money in circulation was first started by the soldiers and sailors. About a score of shanties have been put up within the last month, for the dispensing of "cool drinks" and other refreshments, and as it appears to be a rule among the "conks" and "dagos" to arrange their charges for everything so as to realize cent. per cent. on all investments, and as six months' pay will be coming to us, a rich harvest is expected. Bad rum is still sold surreptitiously at enormous prices; but the dealers are mostly holding back for pay day. A rich thing about the whiskey question occurred here a short time ago. A shopkeeper, somewhat fond of the ardent, bought a fourteen-gallon keg of rum from the captain of a schooner. He paid five dollars a gallon for it, and it was brought ashore at the dead of night by the captain and left in the buyer's yard, his store being closed. But, somehow or other, there were others abroad that evening, and before morning Mr. Keg was spirited away. This deponent saith nothing; but for a week after, Jamaica rum was plenty and cheap among a certain coterie. Seventy dollars was a large sum to pay for a keg of liquor; but to lose the latter, after paying the former, was, to say the least "rough."

A boat expedition, in which the subscriber participated, was got up last week, and spent five days among the islands to the eastward. Captain [Jeremiah] Simpson was in command, and Lieutenants [John] Locke and [Charles] Smith had charge of the boats. We visited about a dozen "keys", and rowed about 150 miles. Most of them are inhabited by squatter families, and though somewhat frightened at so large an inroad of "Lincoln's hirelings", the people treated us well. No better officers could be picked out for the work, roughing it as they did with the men, and paying every attention to their comfort. Some of those "keys", or islands, are exceedingly fertile, and an enterprising man might make a fortune in a few years by cultivating a few acres, and raising vegetables for the Key West market. Cabbages (brought from New York) retail here for four and five shillings, while other vegetables are proportionately high. But the people about here dislike labor, and, on the islands we visited, live mostly by hunting and fishing.

Two rebel prisoners escaped from Fort Taylor on the 16th, and reached Havana in an open boat. They were forced to leave, however, and may yet be picked up by some of our cruisers.

A.

THIRTY-SIXTH REGIMENT N.Y.S.V.

CAMP NEAR STAFFORD COURT HOUSE, VA., Dec. 1.

Since writing to you last, we have changed our camp, as we were situated where, whenever it should rain, the mud would be over our shoe-mouths. Now we are encamped in a prominent place, on a high hill which commands all the surrounding country, and presents to the view a conglomerated mass of tents; and should a shell unluckily drop among the assemblage, queer old "skedaddling" would be the result. Happy I am to announce to my friends that our Division-General (John Newton) has been appointed to the command of the corps (Sixth). And as a matter of course, in respect to the general, our volunteer band made itself conspicuous on the occasion, by the manner in which their musical selections were poured forth, in strains of the most harmonious nature, which not only enraptured the mind of their audience, but added another mark to their scroll of fame. It would be rude for me to remark that the "black bottle" soon made its appearance.

Thursday being a day set apart by Gov. [Edwin] Morgan as a Thanksgiving, all drills and business not of a necessary character were set aside for the day. But, on account of our not having a chaplain, divine pursuits were left unattended to.

One thing I think has become a great evil in the army. It is the robbing of sutlers, which I am sorry to say has occurred several times, to my notice. It is a practice which totally disgraces our army, and, if carried on, will throw a slur and stigma on this glorious band of men that the whole civilized world would shun at. Give us an honest and upright war, to be carried forward on principles of integrity and right.

The regiment is in a healthy condition, amid such circumstances that surround us. Not one, I am told, in the regimental hospital—all owing to the humane and skillful attendance of our surgeons, [Edward] Dalton and [William] Hall, who have spared neither pains nor time in regulating the physical condition of the men in this changeable climate.

I do not wish to be personal, but I must say, that of all the promotions, that of Sergeant [John] Burns to a lieutenancy is well merited and hard earned. He gives full assurance of his worthiness and fitness. May his sword never be drawn save in victory! and may it never be sheathed in disgrace!

Another thing I would call your attention to is, the more prompt payment of the troops. Here five weeks are flying over our heads, and no sign of our paltry pay. How are our families at home to get a livelihood? The wages we get are barely enough to sustain them. But what must they do when the Paymaster does not show his ugly picture till he thinks fit? I ask you, are the wives, mothers, and children of our noble volunteer, who sacrificed their lives for this shattered country, to be left, this coming winter, starving? Or are they to seek for charity from door to door, to be the scoff of every person? Or must the menial quarters of an alms house protect them from the inclemency of the weather? I should think that when the Government fails to fulfill its contract with us, we ought to fail to fulfill ours. A hint from your editorial sanctum would be quite acceptable.

Yours, till I "kick the bucket",   JERSHUA JENKINS.

December 14, 1862

FIFTY-FIRST REGIMENT N.Y.S.V.

CAMP NEAR FALMOUTH, VA., Dec. 9.

Since writing last, the weather has been all sorts. For two days we had rain, which ended in snow to the depth of three inches or more. On Sunday last, it was too cold to remain outside for any length of time—the ground is hard frozen.

The Paymaster has at last made his appearance. This pay-day the clothing account for the year ending October 31, was settled up. Some of the boys had as high as $20 coming to them for clothing not drawn. The State clothing was not taken out in one case, Company B had all their State clothing charged, the Lieutenant commanding the Company said he was ordered by the Colonel [Robert Potter] to do so. Upon inquiring into the matter, I understand that the Colonel gave no such authority. The boys are satisfied with the tale that the other companies will be dealt with in the same manner on next pay day, but the other companies say they don't see it.

Our regiment was ordered off on picket duty along the Rappahannock shore last Tuesday afternoon, and were relieved Friday afternoon at dusk, in the midst of the snow and sleet. When they arrived at the camp-ground, they had to shovel the snow off of the place occupied by them before in order to put up their tents. Quite a number sat up all night shivering by the fire. What has become of all the contractors for clothing? There is a leak somewhere. Every man in the regiment is in want of shoes. A few have bought boots from the sutlers around; but every man is not able, especially men with families, on account of the enormous price charged by the sutlers. Boots that you can buy in New York for six dollars are asked twelve dollars for. When shall this public robbing of soldiers discontinue in the army. It is a real shame that such outrages are permitted to be made upon the soldiers.

The rations of the men being short at one time, the men grumbled much. Whether their grumbling did any good or not, I cannot say. Now it has become the turn of the poor horses to do without food. Some days, they have gone with nothing to eat and no shelter, but there they stand, tied to a post, looking as if they had been forsaken.

One question asked by the boys can hardly be answered, and that is, when is the express company going to send an agent here to open an office, so the boys can receive their boxes, which have been lying in Washington some three or four months? That is one point which should be attended to without delay.

Our Acting Quartermaster took charge of money from the men to-day; he is going to Washington, and will express it.

I will write you soon of some promotions made in the regiment from the rank and file.

Yesterday, the boys had a shindy—a regular set-to. I dare say on account of the greenbacks making their appearance. All that appeared this morning of the affray was a few black bottles and black eyes.

Yours, etc.,   J. B.

December 21, 1862

TWELFTH REGIMENT, N.Y.S.V.

BIVOUAC, NEAR FREDERICKSBURG, VA., Dec. 12th, 1862

Early on Monday, the 8th inst. [Col. T. B. W.] Stockton's Brigade—consisting of the Twelfth, Seventeenth, and Forty-fourth New York Volunteers, Sixteenth Michigan, and Eighteenth Pennsylvania, and Twentieth Maine—was ordered on picket duty to the left centre. At 1 P.M., on the 10th, an officer informed us we should stand posts till 2 P.M., and that we would not be required for duty again till 6 A.M., on the following day. My company went each night on duty at 2. A.M., coming off at 10 A.M. This arrangement was said to be in consequence of Butterfield's Corps being out on review, and that we would not be relieved until the next day. We were glad of this, for two reasons. First, as giving us a little longer to sleep; and, second, as avoiding a review in snow and slush. But we had not long to enjoy ourselves on what we considered good-fortune. At 1½ o'clock, P.M., Lieutenant-Colonel [Robert M.] Richardson, in command of the entire picket line, rode up and ordered us to get ready, and leave the post and close in on the front. No relief came to replace us, thus making evident that the army was advancing. On the way to camp we saw the pickets coming in also from other quarters. We got to camp about 4 P.M., but there were only rumors of an advance there. In an hour after, the official order came to be ready at 2 o'clock next morning (11th), to march in heavy order.

At 5 o'clock we were in line; at this hour we heard the first boom of cannon in front. This is music we all understood on this occasion, also the ball that was being opened. We left camp at 6 A.M., marching toward Fredericksburg. The firing was becoming more rapid and reports gradually more distinct. At 10 o'clock the brigade formed in close column by companies, one regiment behind another. Round was a host of armed men—infantry, cavalry, and artillery. Some moving to the right; others to the left, whilst column after column was still streaming on, going forward, or forming amid the reserve that covered the extensive plain. To look on that still and moving host, it was impossible to avoid reflecting that a deep responsibility rested on the man who had the handling thereof confided to him. The fate of a nation, perhaps, depending on the wisdom and good management. Victory is not so much the result of numbers as to have every man in his proper place at the proper time. Artillery firing increased to 11½ A.M. Then it slackened, becoming still at noon, and with occasional shots, remaining so till 2½ P.M. At this hour a report came in that the Twelfth Regulars lost two hundred in killed and wounded, whilst acting as a covering party to the Fifteenth New York Engineers, who were employed in throwing a bridge over the Rappahonnock. Shortly after, some wounded were borne to the rear on stretchers to the ambulances, a long line of which were ready to remove their human freight. I imagine they will have something to do ere Christmas Day. In the interval of quiet, between 12 and 2½ o'clock, Lieut.-Col. Richardson addressed the Twelfth New York thus: "Men of the Twelfth, at the battle of Hanover Court House, Gen. Butterfield said: 'Men, we have a reputation to make, and let us make it.' I have something different to say to you now. We have a country to save and a reputation to preserve; and, heroes of Malvern Hills, I ask you to save it and preserve it." Three hearty cheers were the response. Subsequently, Gen. Butterfield rode by, drawing forth cheer after cheer from all. Next to Gen. McClellan, I know of no man more popular than Butterfield. He is indeed a splendid officer, brave as a lion, and experienced as brave. But still, Mac is the darling and ideal of the American soldier, and ever will remain so. At 2½ o'clock, artillery opened again, and continued to fire for half an hour more viciously than ever, and extending more to the right, sometimes firing in volleys, and at others resembling file-fire by musketry. As day closed, all became still. The large reserve, the whole day under arms, were then marched about half a mile forward and bivouacked for the night in the woods which crest the hills on the right side of the city. A portion of it was in a blaze from our shells. We had coffee, made our beds on beech leaves, lay thereon, and committed ourselves to the favorable care of the drowsy god.

Friday, December 12th—Called to arms at an early hour, and marched forward to the east side of the plain on which Fredericksburg stands, and through which the now deathless Rappahannock flows. From the top of these hills the scene was magnificent and grand in the extreme. At intervals of about a quarter of a mile on the other side of this extended flat, long columns were marching by the right flank, which, when brought into battle line, would cover the intervals between. Down the parallel slope on this side corresponding columns paused. The eye could rest nowhere without meeting the bright sunlight of the morning coming in dancing reflections from the stainless polish of a bayonet. Artillery now opened in front, each report and explosion being repeated many times along the glens and hills, made you imagine twenty guns were fired at the same time. Echo seemed to be in ecstasies, and with a thousand tongues made you imagine the thunders of Vulcan continuance. Blend the senses of ear and eye together and formed the really sublime. The firing of the day was mostly by artillery. I should have said that the enemy evacuated Fredericksburg on the night of the 11th inst., and fell back about three miles, to the hills on the west side thereof. Their present position is very strong.

A—, COLOR GUARD.

THIRTY-SIXTH REGIMENT, N.Y.S.V.

FREDERICKSBURG, VA., Dec. 14.

Amid the din of war, and the rattling noise of artillery, I pen to you a few brief words. Perhaps they may be the last that I will ever write. On Thursday, Dec. 11, we struck our camp; and as everything was done in haste, rumors immediately became prevalent. "Onward to victory" was our aim. Marching some half-dozen of miles brought us within eight of the doomed city of Fredericksburg. But, by the by, the artillery had commenced its murderous work of shelling the place. We formed into line of battle in a valley, directly under the muzzle of our guns, and hidden from sight from the Rebel sharpshooters. The Fifteenth New York Engineer Corps had been all day trying to build a pontoon bridge across the river, but were, on several occasions stopped by the deadly aim of their foe. Meanwhile, our batteries kept a heavy fire of shell and shot, and at night-fall the first bridge was completed. I think, without the least fear of contradiction, that (our) [Charles] Devins' Brigade was the first to cross and plant our standard on the sod—that is of the troops comprising Franklin's Grand Division, on the left-wing of the Army. Other troops may claim the honor; but the members of Devins' Brigade will testify that his command was the first to cross.

I do not wish to praise ourselves, or paint the picture of reality any brighter than it really is. We (Devins' Brigade) crossed on Thursday, Dec. 11, and 6 o'clock, or thereabouts; and the gallant Second Rhode Island (Col. Frank Wheaton), being in advance, of course they deployed as skirmishers, and marched gallantly on; then followed the stirring Seventh Massachusetts, whose noses have never smelled the powder, or finger pulled a trigger; then came the gallant and brave Tenth Massachusetts, whose marching was a sequel of a triumphant event; then totteringly and squeamishly came the three-hundred-dollar men—the Thirty-seventh Massachusetts—by their own accounts are red hot for a fight. And last, though not least, came the dashing and cheering on, the Thirty-sixth New York; and without flattering you in the least, a more jovial or hearty set of boys never exist than they did; by their manner and mode of conduct, you would infer that some grand celebration was about to come off. We respectfully formed into lines of battle anxiously waiting to unload our rifles at some sneaking foe. Night began to grow fast upon us, and our brigade being the only one across, of course we were put on picket for the night. And such a night I never have witnessed before, or hope to again. Without the least smell of fire, and the atmosphere being of the most chilly nature, we cannot narrate to you how we passed the night. Morning arrived, and with it a ray of hope, and which to a weary wanderer is exhilarating. As daylight shone forth, troops in immense numbers immediately came across, which appearance indicate a speedy operation. To make a long story short, I will say that on Friday and Saturday severe shelling was done, also heavy musketry all along the line, and by appearances we have become engaged, and on the left we have gained considerable ground—by a stupendous mountain on which the "Rebs" are placed, deem it hard for us to drive them off. Our division [John Newton's] has been ordered to several positions, but as yet we have not become engaged.

To-day (Sunday), little firing has been going on. I suppose on account of Jeff becoming quite religious.

As I am penning this, Gen. Burnside has paid us a visit.

At some future time, if God spares my life, I will give you a minute detail of this affair.

Yours, near eternity,   JERSHUA JENKINS.

SEVENTY-NINTH REGIMENT N.Y.S.M.

FREDERICKSBURG, VA., Dec. 15.

It is so long since I wrote you that I suppose you had me numbered with the "dead correspondents" of your paper, although I nearly shared the fate of many of them, I must state that I am still in the land of the living, and having so far recovered from my wounds as to enable me to join my old and gallant comrades of the Seventy-ninth N.Y.S.V. (Highlanders). You shall hear from me occasionally unless laid out again.

Since the regiment left this place, on the 13th of August last, to join Gen. Pope at Cedar Mountain, we have had but one incessant march, and either fighting or skirmishing daily. We have taken part in all the fights that took place in Virginia or Maryland since that time. Lieut.-Col. [David] Morrison, who commanded us at Port Royal and James Island, S.C., is in command of the regiment here. He is one of the original officers who left New York with us, and having shared in all our dangers, is consequently much beloved by all of us.

Our regiment at the present time is in excellent condition, except for numbers, as we now count only about four hundred men for duty.

We are making an effort at present to get up our old uniform pants and Glengary caps, which I think and hope may be successful.

Our regiment has not been paid off since the 30th of June last, consequently the families of many of the privates must be suffering severely, as their national pride will not allow them to disclose their poverty. The position of the contending armies at present is very imposing, and reminds one of the siege of Sabastopol on a large scale, and the battle of Saturday of the battle of James Island, S. C., through a magnifying glass. Had [William H.] "Bull Run" Russell been here to see that fight, he would have seen a more desperate assault then carried the Malakoff or was repulsed at the Redan, but since he was not here, I hope some other pen will do us justice. Although our regiment was not engaged, still, we were held in reserve and exposed to both our own and the enemy's guns. We had but two wounded slightly. Meagher's Irish Brigade suffered most on Saturday and behaved gallantly. On Sunday the fighting was light; on Monday the same, and at night we evacuated the city, and have retreated to our own old camping grounds—I must say, very much crest-fallen.

Wednesday, 17th—There has nothing of any importance happened since we re-crossed the Rappahannock. The enemy have their pickets extended on their old lines on the banks of the river, and so are ours. What our next move will be, is yet a mystery, but I think that this is not the right road to Richmond.

I hope I will be able to report soon that we have discovered the right road to Richmond, and that by

ONE OF THE SEVENTY-NINTH.

December 28, 1862
FIFTY-FIFTH REGIMENT, N.Y.S.M. (Lafayette Guard)
NEAR FREDERICKSBURG, VA., Dec. 19th 1862.

The terrible struggle for which both armies have long been preparing for some time past has at last ended, and many a poor fellow—the pride of his relatives and friends, and perhaps the only support of a family—has gone to that other and better world, where dissension and strife are unknown, and peace reigns supreme. These are not so much to be pitied as those loved ones at home that mourn their untimely death, as well as the number of soldiers who are maimed for life. What a terrible responsibility rests upon those fanatical ultra leaders of both sections, who for years past have done everything in their power to bring on this war, and who wisely staid at home after it had commenced!

On Wednesday [10th], we received the orders to get ready to march at one hour's notice. The wagons were accordingly loaded, and only the tents left standing for the night. Next morning, at about four o'clock, we were awakened from our peaceful slumbers by the firing of two heavy siege-pieces. Immediately, a terrible cannonade ensued; which lasted the whole day. Men were set to work on the pontoon-bridge over which Sumner's Grand Division was to cross over to Fredericksburg. After they had twice been repulsed by the sharpshooters of the enemy, who fired at them from the houses of the city, it was found necessary to shell them out of the town. I rode to a high hill, from where I had a splendid view of the bombardment. Our shells and solid shot fell thick and fast in the doomed city; the sharpshooters were driven from house to house; and at last, about four P.M., I believe, our first regiment crossed over. They seemed to meet with considerable resistance in the city, as there was some heavy firing of musketry; but the Rebels were finally driven out, and fell back to their formidable fortifications in the rear of the town.

On Friday [12th], everything was comparatively quiet, both parties preparing for another desperate struggle. I rode over the bridge to Fredericksburg, of which we were then in undisputed possession. Found it crammed full of our soldiers. Every house of this once beautiful town afforded a convincing proof of the destructive power of our guns. I did not see a single one that was not hit, most of them had been hit in from ten to twenty different places, and a good many were burnt down entirely. Houses and stores had been pretty well cleaned out by our men, some of whom I saw with basketfuls of cakes and other eatables, others with boxes containing envelopes and innumerable other things. One of our soldiers sat in the middle of the street on an elegant red damask chair, smoking his pipe.

On Saturday [13th], our army made an attack upon the fortifications of the enemy, and a grand battle ensued, which raged along our whole line (the centre and left also crossed over on pontoon-bridges below the city), until the night separated the infuriated combatants. On the right our troops attacked several times, but the position of the enemy was too advantageous, and we did not gain any ground. The city was shelled for a second time during this day; this time by the Rebels, who wanted to drive our troops out of it. In the centre Hooker's Grand Division met with a better success. They drove the enemy back to the other side of the railroad. Our brigade [Ward's] was in the advance, and entered the woods to drive them further back, but met with such a terrible fire that our men had to fall back again to the open field on this side of the road. Our brigade lost about 670 men in killed, wounded, and missing. The regiments that suffered the most were the Fifty-seventh [Pennsylvania], Thirty-eighth, and Fortieth New York, and Fourth Maine. Our regiment and the Third Maine were detached on the right, to support a battery (our Colonel [de Trobriand]—being the senior colonel—commanding), and did not suffer so much. When the battery had to fall back, one of the cannon was left behind, on account of the horses having been killed. As soon as this was known, these two regiments went forward again, and the cannon was safely brought into our lines. Our regiment had only seven men wounded. Among them was Lieutenant [Chas.] Burch. His wound is not severe.

On Sunday everything was pretty quiet, both armies resting on their arms. A flag of truce was sent over by parties on our side, who wished to get permission to remove those of our men who had fallen in the wood, behind the railroad, during the battle on Friday, but was not accepted by the Rebel General Commanding. The poor fellows had to lie until 3 P.M., on the 14th inst., when another flag of truce was sent over by the General, and the Rebels gave us one hour to remove our dead and wounded. The latter had been well treated, the Rebels having covered them with their blankets, and given them crackers and water. The blankets and shoes of our dead had been appropriated by the enemy in most every case. Our brigade has suffered terribly, having been in the open field, right in front of the enemy firing, almost constantly at them. Last night, the Rebels were felling trees and making preparations to give us a warm reception, in case we should again attack them.

Col. de Trobriand came back to the regiment about fourteen days ago, as Gen. Ward took again command of this, his old brigade. He lost two splendid horses through the carelessness of his servant, who was asleep when the army evacuated the other side, and who, when he woke up and rode down to the pontoon bridge, found it already taken up. He crossed over in a boat. The horses swam over behind him, until they came to the middle of the river, when they turned and swam back to the shore, where they fell into the hands of the enemy.

Even in these hard times, a good joke may not be out of place. One of the Rebel prisoners we took during the battle of Saturday, when asked about our chances of getting to Richmond said: "You have a hard road to travel; first you have to get over two big 'Hills', then through a 'Longstreet', and finally over a 'Stonewall'."

                    Respectfully,   H. D.

TWENTY-FIFTH REGIMENT, N.Y.S.V.

CAMP NEAR FREDERICKSBURG, Dec. 21.

I write these few lines to let you know what I have went through since I wrote last. Last Thursday week [11th] we got orders to be ready for action at any moment. Our batteries opened on the rebels Thursday and Friday, and our troops crossed the river to Fredericksburg on Saturday morning. Our brigade went into the fight about 12 at noon Saturday. The Irish Brigade was fighting all the forenoon. When we went in it was on a charge: The Irish brigade gave us three cheers. Our brigade relieved them, with the gallant General Butterfield at our head, and Captain [Patrick] Connolly acting Colonel. A braver soldier never drew a sword. In spite of all the officers, every regiment in our brigade but one skedaddled. Only the Twenty-fifth stood its ground, just as if nothing was the matter. General Butterfield said he would rather have the little Twenty-fifth than the largest regiment in the corps. No person ever can say the Twenty-fifth ran away. We commenced fighting Saturday, the 13th. We fought that afternoon until darkness compelled us to give over. We lay on our arms all night, and Sunday were relieved. I hope I may never witness the same fight again. The cries of the dying and wounded, lying on top of each other, crying to Heaven for vengeance on the men in Washington who forced a brave army to the jaws of death. If General Burnside had three times as many men, he could not rouse the Rebels out of where they are. The place puts me in mind of Weehawken, and the Bluffs along the Hudson. We were so close to their batteries that they could not depress their guns low enough to hit us, but they gave us the devil from their rifle-pits. Our color-sergeant was the first killed. The colors were picked up and waved, the men hollering: "Go in, Twenty-fifth!" Loading and firing is hard work; the sweat was pouring from us like rain. I fired sixty rounds that were in my cartridge-box, and twenty I had in my pockets. I never got a scratch—thanks be to God! We lost about eighteen or twenty wounded, in Company F—some with slight scratches and holes through the clothes. After all the slaughter, we had to retreat back to our camps. Give us generals, and we will be victorious. Let us have military men in Washington. Our loss is twenty thousand, and that of the Rebels two thousand or twenty-five hundred. We captured about one thousand prisoners. I am afraid I will be laid up with rheumatic pains all over my bones, and a very bad cough, bad clothing, bad shoes, and bad sleeping, and worse, no pay in nine months. I got no MERCURY in two weeks, or letter from you. The MERCURY is the only paper taken in the Twenty-fifth. It is all the comfort we have when off duty.

                                                        H. C. H.

TWELFTH REGIMENT N.Y.S.V.

CAMP NEAR STAFFORD COURT-HOUSE, VA., Dec. 22.

Early on the morning of the 13th inst., the battle of Fredericksburg was inaugurated. Like all combats its commencement was fitful and unsteady. Now the deep, hollow boom of cannon would awaken the echoes of the hills, and be reverberated along the valleys. Then the sharp and vicious rattle of the musket would be heard at intervals by file and volley. Position is to be sought and range is to be obtained. At 10 o'clock, A.M., these steps must have been accomplished, for then the battle commenced indeed. At this moment the bugle of General Griffin ordered the advance of his division; that of General Stockton took up the expiring note, and repeated the martial blast. We, as Third Brigade, advanced, but halted as the heads of the regiment cleared the hills which obstructed the view of the battle-field. This was on the west side of the town, and about half a mile therefrom. From about noon till half-past two, P.M., we were quiet, but eager spectators of the mortal strife, which raged before us—of the steady advances of the relieving columns and the falling back of the relieved. On both sides, there seemed a desperate will to fight. The tide of battle alternately ebbed and flowed, and with a slight advance on our side, the contest may be said to have closed on the ground of the morning. Our men never fought better; they had to do so, too, under the greatest disadvantages. Whilst our advancing and retreating columns were exposed to a destructive fire from the enemy's cannon, we had none to reply to him till late in the morning, and then they were all but useless for want of favorable ground. It is hard to convey an idea of the feelings of an interested spectator. Your whole being is, as it were, a part of the side in which your sympathies are enlisted. The heart throbs with alternating fears and hopes; your side drives and shouts, and then the heart flies to the mouth in a wild rush of joyous exultation, silently shouting within itself. Your side is forced back, when the very blood becomes a participator—retreating from its advanced posts and curdling in a freezing mass around its shrinking home. Thus, sir, we saw till the hour named, swayed by alternate hopes and fears, equally anxious and overpowering. Then we advanced to within one hundred yards of the river. Here we fled to the right to allow the First [James Barnes'] and Second [Jacob Sweitzer's] Brigade to pass. The last man of these had scarcely done so, when we saw them returning by the left flank. We were at a loss to comprehend the meaning of this, and still more so, when we saw them again advance, as the last man had recrossed the pontoon-bridge over the Rappahannock. This time there seemed to be a purpose, and no more retreating.

About 3½ P.M., we were crossing the river up the declivity on the other side, through the town, to the railroad station, then half a mile to the left, over dead and mutilated men, half immersed in the mud, through a shower of aimless bullets, so far as we were concerned, and then we halted and lay some five hundred yards in front of the battle-ground. The leaden shower was so thick and ceaseless that it was almost certain death to raise the head. At 4½ P.M., the bugle of the Third Brigade sounded to advance, and on the Twentieth Maine, Eighty-third Pennsylvania, Sixteenth Michigan, and Forty-fourth New York rushed. Soon their every ball was spent, and they returned, relieved, leaving two hundred and sixty-two men on the field.

The buglers of the Twelfth and Seventeenth New York did not hear the brigade command, and, consequently, did not repeat it. Nor, therefore, did we advance on this occasion. It was admitted the blast from head-quarters was too feeble to be heard by them. Our buglers are blameless; for on such occasions men are all ears and eyes, and no officer or man in these regiments heard the note they would but too willingly respond to. Indeed, it is more trying to be quietly exposed to fire, than if an active participator. In the one sense you are cool and reflecting, and have too much time to look that death in the face, which you every moment expect, and which you know will open to our immortal kin that dark and mysterious future which we all, more or less, dread. On the other hand, you are excited and indifferent.

Toward night the contest seemed to grow more fierce, some of our men began to fall back in a little disorder. The timidity of a few may set an example which might have the most serious results. On this occasion, the last of our reserve went forward and checked any further tendency of this kind, if such existed; nay, drove back the enemy. Still I became anxious and solicitous. I knew we could not drive the foe beyond his defences this day, if at all, and I believe I shared a common sentiment in wishing for the night, in order that we might be re-enforced by the morning. Late in the evening two of our field-pieces fired from an opening in the town, but slowly, and without effect. The position being comparatively low, its shot would be as dangerous to us as the foe. About five, P.M., another battery opened from the north end of town, but also with an unsteady, uncertain, and ineffectual fire. At the same time a Rhode Island Battery [Battery C] pushed forward, and took up a position on the right of the hostile ground. It was greeted with shouts of welcome, and had no sooner unlimbered than two of its horses were killed by the first fire of the enemy. This battery could render the most effectual service, but it was meanly abandoned by the artillerists, but saved by the gallantry of the infantry, and safely brought off the field.

At last night came, but the combatants seemed anxious to protract the work of death, and for three-quarters of an hour after the earth was folded in the embrace of darkness, it continued. A gun on our right kept firing at our signal lights for an hour after. It was certainly awfully grand to see the fiery missiles springing through the air like demons on their message of death. The motion was not even and continued, but leaps, a momentary pause, as if seeking for prey, and then a forward spring, as if it sought, in its blood to quench its fiery and burning thirst. I have not witnessed a more hotly contested field than that of Fredericksburg. From ten, A.M., till its close, there was scarcely a moment's intermission of fire. There were splendid charges before which the enemy would fall back, but our advance would be checked by his numerous artillery, nor could we retain the advantage for want of similar support.

Sunday, the 14th, was born, and died without much worthy of record. The most important news of the morning was, that the enemy had thrown up a new line of defences during the night. We had but to go to any of the cross-streets to be convinced, if we doubted. His position now was most truly formidable. Things began to look blue. We had nothing but numbers and courage to oppose, but we could be met with numbers as great, if not greater. At 10, A.M., we began to remove our wounded beyond the river. Toward noon, blinds were used as stretchers, to accelerate it. At this time it became rumored that a truce of six hours was granted for that purpose, and that it would expire at 2, P.M., when the town would be shelled. Though everything seemed to justify this report, the shelling did not take place, nor had any of our officers seen or heard anything official in reference thereto. At 5, P.M., we marched to the northern end of the town, stacked arms, and ordered to lie behind them. Officers were ordered to keep their commands together, as there was reason to anticipate a night-attack, and after dark, that shelling promised at 2 o'clock. What the reasons were for such anticipations I know not; but I know the stillness of night was not broken by a single gun. We emptied the houses of feather-beds, sofas, mattresses, etc., and comfortably slept thereon till midnight, laying them in the streets. Thus, without violating orders, we made ourselves comfortable. The only tangible fact of the day was the driving in of our pickets, at 1 o'clock, after half an hour's hot fire. The last rumor of the day was that we were to make a general attack on the enemy at daybreak on the 15th, and carry his works by storm. I heard this from artillery officers.

The first acts of the morning seemed to justify this report. At 12 or 1 o'clock, A.M., we were summoned to arms, and, with a caution to observe silence, marched toward the foe, occupying the position of our Sunday picket-line. The night was dark, but the men would come forth at intervals, revealing moving columns in all directions, silently and stealthily taking up positions. A certain individual, more prying and inquisitive than his neighbors, thought he could prowl around with impunity, and learn what was going on; but half a dozen bullets whizzing past his ear brought him in double-quick time to his senses, and cautioned him to lie down. We did not long occupy this forward position, but fell back to another, some two hundred yards. Here for a quarter of an hour we plied the spade and shovel, as if intrenching ourselves. Everything seemed to confirm the report of the evening—that we were to make a general attack in the morning. We did not dig long ere we again fell back, without a word, and in obedience to whispered commands. This time we occupied the ground of Saturday evening. In another half hour we fell still further back to the railroad where it enters the city; and lastly, we marched for the river, re-crossing it about four o'clock in the morning.

Now we all understood that the different movements of the night were but a decoy to effect our retreat. If Gen. Burnside ever seriously entertained the idea of making the attack in question, one thing is certain—he acted wisely in changing his mind. The probabilities of success were against us. Granted that we would, by a *coup de main*, carry the enemy's outer works, there was a second, and I believe a third line of defences. These repeated obstacles would dampen the ardor of the troops, and that is but the first step to a panic, and the idea of such a reality is too painful even for speculative philosophy. As it is, all is well. Except our loss on the field, we have left nothing else behind, and we have inflicted a chastisement at least equal to what we received. If a simple soldier be allowed an opinion, I would say that the enemy before Fredericksburg will have to be menaced from some other quarter for he cannot be driven from his present position by an attack from the front.

Fredericksburg is a place that will long remember the Rebellion of 1861-62, and our occupation thereof. Plenty of flour was found and the troops lived on pancakes, etc., etc. For want of other fuel I saw the most costly furniture converted into such. On one occasion I saw a man dash a clock against the wall for its frame-work. Books, vases, drinking-vessels in glass and china, found their way to camp. It was a pity to see the finest works of modern and ancient times committed to the flames. My whole booty consists of a copy of Longfellow's poems, handsomely bound in cloth. Nearly all the inhabitants had left some days before we entered it. Many of whom, I learned were in the woods to the rear of the Confederate army; also that many children perished from cold and exposure during the recent snow-storm. Some of the more wealthy went to Richmond. When these unfortunate people return they will find desolation before them indeed. Much of the northern part of the town is burned. A Mr. Gordon is the chief sufferer, but as he is a man of great wealth he will not miss it. The tobacco destroyed belonged chiefly to Hart, Hayes & Co., and Hill & Warren, and valued at $100,000 instead of $150,000.

Fredericksburg is, as all know, one of the oldest places in the United States, being second only to Jamestown in antiquity. Like all towns in Virginia, it would appear that the original builders of each house became satisfied when the last stone was laid and the last nail driven, and then left it to look out for itself. But now to briefly finish. We had scarcely crossed the river when it commenced to rain. By 5 o'clock, A.M., we came to a halt, wet through, but even thus we lay, and slept till daybreak, with our rubbers over us, and the wet ground under. As soon as day appeared, we marched for our camp at this place, and reached it about 7½, A.M. Washing, cleaning, brushing, boiling, roasting, eating, we brought 7, P.M. about. Then we sought and found sleep and refreshment. We awoke invigorated, indifferent of the past and careless of the future. This, Sir, is the simple tale of an observer and participator in what he relates. It is long, but much could be added. It is a "round, unvarnished tale."

Yesterday, all the paroled prisoners from Annapolis joined their regiments here. If we are to have any more fighting, we want every man at his post. The country can't afford to pay skulkers in its hour of need. Send every one from among you to his place, and send us McClellan at their head. If anything turns up, I shall write you at first opportunity.

Yours, etc.,   A—, COLOR GUARD.

SECOND REGIMENT, N.Y.S.M. (Eighty-second, N.Y.V.)

CAMP NEAR FALMOUTH, Va., Dec. 20th.

On the morning of the 11th inst., in obedience to orders, our regiment was marched from this ground to Gen. [Alfred] Sully's head-quarters, and reported for duty, four hundred and thirteen strong, and eager for the fray. Opposite his tent assembled his Brigade, and just at break of day we joined our Division [O.O. Howard's] at a point near the Rappahannock, where the hollow ground sheltered us from the enemy's artillery, placed on the side of the river. The Pontooniers had commenced to throw a bridge across, and at the first peep of day our artillery and sharpshooters drove in their pickets, and the work soon went on again. Their riflemen then fired from the basements of houses that lay along the wharves, thus making the city a garrison and, according to the laws of war, liable to be fired on. This was done, and in a short time the city was all ablaze. It was a terrible sight. The roaring of artillery, the bursting of shells, the sky darkened with smoke, the massing of our troops on the river bank; the desperate exertions of the men at work on the river, amidst a storm of fire; the groans of the wounded and mangled corpses, as they were carried to the rear, as one set after another fell at the bridge, made it a novel sight even for us who have participated in every battle from Yorktown to Antietam. At near sunset, the bridge was complete, and the crossing commenced. [Col. Norman J. Hall's] brigade, of our division, crossed first, then came ours.

The decent to the river, where the bridge crossed, is very steep, and the enemy had by this time placed their artillery so as to have complete range of it. A little further down the bank of the river is a deep ravine, made by the rain, that turns the ravine into a river in rainy weather. Through this our troops passed, until we got to the river bank, and then went along the bank to the bridge, thus escaping a good deal of the fire that poured down upon us from the basements of the houses and entrenched artillery. This ravine is filled with brushwood, and at one part is very narrow, which made it difficult to get the men through rapidly, so that one regiment would be over the bridge before the other would be out of the ravine. The bridge was vacant when we got to it, and the shot and shell were falling thick and fast all around it. The most of us felt our ardor cooling, for it was like facing death itself; but there was no time to be lost, for every moment the bridge might be blown to pieces. Lieut.-Col. [James] Huston, who led us, was the first on the bridge, shouting and waving his sword: "Come on, boys!" That was enough. The Second Regiment was on the other side in five minutes. There was some tall walking across that bridge until we were safely sheltered by the ascending ground on the other side. On went the work of destruction, the rebels firing from their houses, behind sheds and under cover, while our men were racking and tearing all before them; it was actually "Root hog or die" with us. There was quite an excitement around there about that time, with the houses burning, the flames crackling and dancing upward and forward, the constant thunder of artillery, and just dark enough to make distant objects visible; altogether, it was a sight so dreadful that I shudder when I think of it.

We bivouacked that night on the river bank, and at daybreak on Friday [12th] morning advanced into the city. Every street was filled with soldiers, and every house that escaped the flames was pillaged. Policies of insurance on household effects could be bought at the price of old paper, and the way handsome furniture laid around loose would have made the eyes of a Chatham street Jew water.

At ten o'clock, Gen. Sully came to Lieut.-Col. Huston, and pointing out a rising ground a little in the rear of the city, on which stands an unfinished monument to Washington's mother, said: "Your regiment is to take and hold that ground." The enemy's intrenched artillery had complete command of it, and their sharpshooters were around it; but off we went, and by a half-crawling attitude we made the base of the ground. We sent out videttes, and soon had a line of them along the brow. This was on the extreme right of the army, and we were placed there to prevent the enemy from getting on the flank. The Second Regiment was highly complimented by having such an important place given to them. The "chivalry" soon discovered our being there, and commenced to shell us; but the rising ground and our extreme caution prevented any disaster until the afternoon, when we lost one killed and two wounded by a shell that exploded right over our heads.

We were relieved at 8 o'clock, P.M., retiring to a street, called Princess Anne street, where we remained until the afternoon of the next day, when the great battle commenced by our troops trying to take their entrenchments. We were marched to the right of the field, and had to take position amidst a regular torrent of bullets; and here we lost three men killed and a number wounded, but our brigade held the position, and prevented the enemy from outflanking our lines. At one o'clock that night we were relieved by the Fourth United States Infantry, and retired to the same street we left in the morning. This was Sunday, and we had little to do except hold the street. On Monday we again had to advance and protect the right of the army. This position had been forsaken by two regiments, the One Hundred and Twenty-seventh Pennsylvania and the New York Tammany Regiment. General Howard asked Brigadier-General Sully if he could give him a regiment that would retake and occupy the place. Sully replied, "Yes, sir, I can give you a regiment that will take it and hold", and then called Lieut.-Col. Huston and his veterans, and pointed out what we were to do. Two companies were to occupy a house that the enemy's pickets had had, and were trying to regain. They had command of all the avenues leading to it, but Lieutenant [Cornelius] Murphy, of Company I, and Lieutenant [Thomas] Huggins, of Company C, were told that we must take it, and we did, of course. Two companies were detached to protect a battery, and the other four to act as a reserve.

In this undertaking we had one killed and one wounded. We remained in those positions until about eleven o'clock, when we learned that our General had concluded to re-cross the river. Next day General Howard and General Sumner came to our camp, and General Howard made a speech to the regiment. He thanked them for their brave and gallant conduct, and said we were a credit to our State. General Sumner shook hands with our brave leader, Lieutenant-Colonel Huston, and said: "I can depend upon you, sir, and your regiment. God bless you all!" This was extremely flattering, I assure you, and was sufficient reward for all the danger we went through. It was a proud day for the Second Regiment, N.Y.S.N.G.

We are all well, thank God, and during all the trying circumstances of the past week, we were all as cool and ready as if we were in New York.

Yours, truly,   A. S. A.

NINTH REGIMENT, N.Y.S.M.

IN CAMP NEAR FREDERICKSBURG, VA., Dec. 22.

At last I have a leisure-hour to myself, and I will avail myself of the opportunity to send to you and your readers another chapter of our "accidents by flood and field".

On Thursday week [11th], reveille beat at 4, A.M., and getting our breakfast, and into line as soon as possible, we marched to the music of a very heavy cannonading, to within a few miles of Fredericksburg, and lay down in a piece of woods, and waited for the engineers to throw pontoon bridges across the river. This we did, and after marching a short distance we were halted, about-faced, and ordered to return and bivouac on the ground we had just vacated. On Friday, reveille at 4, A.M. Formed in line at 6. Marched to river, and crossed on the pontoon bridge. Reaching the opposite bank, we halted until our position in line of battle was determined, and then our (Gibbon's) Division moved off to the extreme left, and our brigade ([Nelson] Taylor's) in the first line of battle. The Thirteenth Massachusetts were thrown forward as pickets, and took position in a road about sixty or seventy yards in advance of our line. Immediately, facing the Massachusetts boys, and about 300 yards distant, was the picket line of the Rebels. Their line stretched across an open field, and the pickets could be seen walking their beats as leisurely and confidently as if they were engaged in a laudable business, and had no expectation of being interrupted. Shortly after dark they set fire to some stacks of hay and forage, and as the red flames rolled and surged upward, casting a lurid light for miles around, the pickets and the advanced lines of the opposing armies stood and gazed silently upon each other, or watched the burning stacks as they melted away before the devouring element. The "fireworks" being over we returned to our line, and lay down on the cold, damp, ground, with our arms by our side, to await for the coming of the morrow's dawn.

We were in line at earliest daylight, but a heavy haze or fog that had filled the atmosphere during the night prevented any immediate movement from taking place. By eight A.M., the fog had considerably dispersed and we commenced to move on the Rebel position. The Thirteenth Massachusetts went forward as skirmishers and were closely followed by the remainder of the brigade in line of battle.

Slowly and steadily we advanced across and open field, the damp clayey soil of which adhered to our feet in such masses as to seriously impede our progress, while the Rebel skirmishers poured a galling fire into our ranks, and slowly fell back before us toward the woods. The place was growing uncomfortably warm for so slow an advance, when whiz, bang, came a shell from a Rebel battery on our right, passing through two men, and then exploded, prostrating our colors and the whole color-guard. An instant after a storm of grape in and around us admonished us that there were several courses in the entertainment prepared for us. "Halt! Lie down!" was the order, and the skirmishers and a couple of our batteries went to work on the Rebels. But they did not appear to better matters much, and we had evidently got in a hornet's nest. The hills, the woods, the railroad line, were literally swarming with gray-backs, and our batteries could not be got in proper position to effectively shell the Rebel strong-hold and cover our advance. Our men were being slaughtered as they lay idly on the field, and a charge was at last decided on, to help us out of the scrape.

On our left the Pennsylvania Reserve [Gen. George G. Meade's Division] swept gallantly forward, and drove the advanced Rebel line to cover in the woods. Our brigade tried to follow suit, but as we passed the brow of the hill, we were met by such a withering fire that our advance was brought to a stand-still. Our regiment appeared to melt away before the leaden storm that was poured into us, but bravely and nobly did our boys stand up to their work, until the second line of battle relieved us. Many a brave "City Guard" fell dead or wounded on that dreadful field. We went into the fight with about three hundred men and eleven officers; we came out minus one hundred and thirty-two men, and seven officers. Our acting Colonel, Capt. [John] Hendrickson, of Company G, was severely wounded. While lying on the field, unable to stand, his cheering crying of "On to glory, boys," rang high above the din of battle. Lieutenant [Felix] Hart of Company H, and Acting-Adjutant [Thomas] Leighton, of Company E, were killed. Capt. March, (Acting Major), Capt. [August] Cameron, Company F, Lieut.[Thomas W.] Quick, Company A, and Lieut. [George E.] Allen, of Company I, were all wounded.

Capt. Hendrickson has since had a foot amputated. After being relieved, we left the hotly contested field, and went a short distance to the rear to rest, while the human tide was rolled time and again—uselessly and murderously—against the foe concealed on the wooded hill—behind railroad cuts and embankments, behind standing trees, felled trees, stone walls, and almost everything else that could cover a human head and body from the deadly flight of a bullet. Resting for a short time, we were again ordered up to occupy the same ground we did before the fight. Reaching the place, we formed again in line of battle, and lay down "wearied" and "worn", to get a little sleep, but even this was denied us.

At midnight we were routed up to draw rations, (we had nearly starved for a day or two), and at two P.M. Sunday, we were ordered to fall in, and take position on the extreme left of the line of battle. The Rebs had evidently been detected in an attempt to turn our left flank, and our presence in that quarter was deemed necessary to prevent the success of that to us unpleasant operation. As no open demonstration was made, we lay down again on the ground, and munched our raw pork and hard tack. Bright and warm the sun rose, and as the day advanced neither party appeared disposed to open the ball for a general engagement, although cannonading and skirmishing was going on all day along our lines. Just before night the Rebs aroused themselves by shelling our lines pretty severely, but as their range was not good, it did us very little harm. Again we bivouacked on the field. Monday [15th] would have been a very-pleasant day if it had not been for the unpleasant proximity of our dear gray-backed friends, who would ever and anon send their leaden and iron compliments so carelessly in our direction. No great harm was done by them, however, and during the day we collected lots of straw on which to have a good snooze when darkness set in. We did not get the sleep, though. Shortly after we had "laid out" we were ordered to "fall in quickly and quietly", and batteries and troops coming from the front told us plainly that a skedaddle was in progress. Soon we commenced to move toward the pontoon bridges, and in a few hours the Rappahannock rolled between us and our chivalrous cousins. Once out of Johnny Reb's clutches, we lay out for the night near the river bank, and got completely soaked by a copious rain that came to fill up the cup of our troubles. Tuesday we moved to the ground we now occupy, and as I cast my eye over our used-up Division, and crowd up to the fire to keep myself from freezing, I cannot but ask myself, "Why don't the army move *now?*" That's the question.

Now, Messrs. Editors, we do not feel particularly inquisitive in this locality but, then, there are tens of thousands of brave and loyal men down here who want to know who ordered that move of Saturday? We are slightly anxious for this information.

Yours,   MINUS.

January 4, 1863
SECOND FIRE ZOUAVES
CAMP NEAR FREDERICKSBURG, Dec. 29, 1862.

Allow me to indicate a little in the general feeling of "virtuous indignation" now possessing the most part of the army.

Shall I write you of the unfortunate catastrophe upon the Heights of Fredericksburg? Others have done it more ably, and in tones, I hope, that will make the marrow shiver in the bones of those that are responsible for it. That monument of graves of brave Union soldiers will stand a reminder of burning shame to those through whose unpardonable acts the flow of precious Union blood was caused. Why waste lives for naught that sacrifice everything for the preservation of the country, whose institutions they believe sacred? Why weaken the confidence in new leaders, a confidence so necessary to success in a soldier? Ten thousand gallant fellows are led against the enemy's breast-works of stone and earth. His guns have been tried, their range ascertained; everything ready to scatter death among us. Our troops, knowing all, like martyrs advance and meet their fate. Those batteries must be stormed in spite of death and mutilation. Attempts upon attempts attest, by the fearful carnage, the valor animating all hearts. Terrible gaps fill up in an instant; the torn remains of a brother in arms lie unheeded, to be trampled under foot by the rear column or covered by the dead body of a comrade. The enfilading fire of musketry, steadied by a sense of security, becomes more and more deadly as we advance. The concentrated aim of the gunners sent the balls and shells of their artillery with terrible effect into our lines. Our very footsteps are implanted in blood and gore. The deafening roar of cannon, the paralyzing shriek of shells, the all-enveloping smoke of powder, making the very air almost too heavy and thick for respiration, the incessant cracking of musketry, the wailing in agony of rent and mutilated bodies, make the scene one of the most terrible to those even used to sites of carnage and slaughter. Howling with rage—for it is beyond the power of man to inflict the deserved punishment on the enemy—we were forced back only to repeat the attack a second and third time.

> "Say, did you hear the voice of Death!
> And did you not mark the paly form
> Which rode on the dark-grey smoke of the heath
> And sung a ghostly dirge in the storm?"

The attack on Fredericksburg is one of the bloodiest pictures in the book of Time. And for what? If in its train, this deplorable disaster, will produce that radical change in our military management to whose repeated blunders have been owing numberless similar ill-fated consequences, not a man in the army but will say; "Cheaply bought." There is not a voice raised here impeaching our Chief; but there is ill-management somewhere.

Next in my catalogue of complaints comes the very great remissness of our Paymaster, who was to visit us monthly, but whose ruddy face has been away so long, that the remembrance of it seems like a thing of antiquity. We are six months in arrears, and the sufferings of numerous families can testify to the heartless neglect to which we are subjected at the hands of those in power. It is useless to see that we are deprived of many comforts which only ready money can procure; but our little wants dwindle down to mere nothingness when compared to the deprivations to which our dear ones at home are exposed. Next to being home, certainly comes the satisfaction of knowing that those at home are provided for. Most of our notes to them are prefaced with the four-months' old stereotyped phrase: "No Paymaster yet".

Hoping that my next will bear a more cheering tone, I remain, with a "Merry Christmas",

Respectfully yours, N.X. MT.

MILITARY MATTERS

ANOTHER WAR CORRESPONDENT GONE.—We have lost our war correspondent (Lieut. Robert McWade) attached to the Fortieth (Mozart) Regiment, N.Y.S.V. After going through twelve engagements, he has determined to risk another, but leaves the field of Mars for the court of Cupid. In short, he is going to get married. We hope that Wade may be able to swim through it. Out of the 1,040 men of this regiment alive and well one year ago, but thirty-eight now remain. Such is war!

Chapter III

<u>1863</u>

by
Dr. James M. McPherson

The year 1863 opened darkly for the Union cause. Despite the optimistic claims of the first letter published in this chapter, Northern morale was depressed by military setbacks in the latter half of 1862. The battle of Fredericksburg had been a grievous blow. When Lincoln heard the news of Burnside's defeat, he exclaimed: "If there is a worse place than Hell, I am in it." The infamous "Mud March," when torrential rains bogged down the Army of the Potomac in the mud as Burnside tried again to cross the Rappahannock in the third week of January, plunged morale in that army to its lowest point in the war. Captain Oliver Wendell Holmes, Jr., of the 20th Massachusetts, recovering from the second of three wounds he received during the war, wrote home that "the army is tired with its hard and terrible experience. I've pretty much made up my mind that the South have achieved their independence."

News from the West initially seemed little better. Ulysses S. Grant's first effort to capture Vicksburg had come to grief in December when cavalry raids in his rear by Confederate commanders Nathan Bedford Forrest and Earl Van Dorn had destroyed his communications and supply base, while William T. Sherman's attack on Chickasaw Bluffs upriver from Vicksburg had been easily repulsed. The only thin gleam of cheer came from Tennessee, where the Army of the Cumberland under William S. Rosecrans staved off repeated assaults by Braxton Bragg's Army of Tennessee at the vicious battle of Stones River on December 31—January 2. "I can never forget," Lincoln wrote to Rosecrans, "that you gave us a hard-earned victory which, had there been a defeat instead, the nation would scarcely have lived over."

The nation scarcely did live over the winter of 1862-1863. Even Joseph Medill, the staunchly patriotic editor of the Chicago *Tribune*, succumbed to despair. "An armistice is bound to come during the year '63," he wrote in a private letter. "The rebs can't be conquered by the present machinery." The Emancipation Proclamation, signed by Lincoln on New Year's Day, did not help matters, for it initially had a more divisive than unifying impact on Northern opinion. In the West, Grant appeared to be floundering in the swamps and bayous in his second campaign against Vicksburg as his troops suffered alarmingly from dysentery and typhoid. Rosecrans' army licked its wounds for six months after Stones River.

Joe Hooker succeeded Burnside as commander of the Army of the Potomac in January. Hooker restored morale through a more liberal furlough policy, better food, more efficient administration of the army, and the creation of insignia badges for each corps. Having rebuilt what he was pleased to call "the finest army on the planet," however, Hooker froze when his opening moves in the Chancellorsville campaign did not compel Lee to retreat. Hooker then yielded the initiative to Lee, and took his own army back across the Rappahannock after several days of hard but futile fighting at Chancellorsville. When Lincoln learned the details of this defeat, his face turned "ashen," according to a reporter who was present. "My God, my God," the president exclaimed. "What will the country say?"

It said plenty, most of it negative. The "Copperheads"—Northern Democrats who opposed the war—stepped up their campaign for an armistice and peace negotiations with the Confederacy. They attacked the Emancipation Proclamation as a "wicked, inhuman, and unholy" provocation of slave insurrections that would only make Southern whites fight harder against the Union. Efforts to restore the Union by war had failed, they declared; it was time to put an end to this fraternal bloodletting.

But these events proved to be the dark before the Northern dawn. Grant finally got his army across the Mississippi below Vicksburg at the beginning of May. In a stunning campaign during the next three weeks, he defeated Confederate detachments in five separate battles, penned most of them up in the Vicksburg defenses, and settled down for a siege that would force their surrender on July 4. The Confederate garrison at Port Hudson downriver capitulated five days later. Rosecrans finally got off the mark in middle Tennessee, and in a campaign of swift maneuvers he forced Bragg to retreat all the way to Georgia by early September.

The events that mesmerized most of the media in both North and South, however, occurred in Pennsylvania. Hoping to capitalize on the momentum generated by his triumph at Chancellorsville, Lee invaded that Northern state with the hope of striking a knockout blow that would force the Lincoln administration to sue for peace. The Army of the Potomac, whose revived morale was not crushed by Chancellorsville, raced northward to intercept the invaders. On the eve of battle, Lincoln replaced Hooker with George Gordon Meade, who skillfully parried Lee in three days of desperate fighting at Gettysburg. The battered Army of Northern Virginia retreated to its namesake state while a thousand miles to the West, Grant accepted the surrender of 30,000 enemy troops at Vicksburg.

The momentum of war—and morale in both North and South—turned 180 degrees. "Copperheads are palsied and dumb for the moment at least," wrote a New York Republican after Gettysburg. "Government is strengthened at home and abroad." In Richmond, Confederate Chief of Ordnance Josiah Gorgas lamented at the end of July that "events have succeeded one another with disastrous rapidity. One brief month ago we were apparently at the point of success. Lee was in Pennsylvania....Vicksburg seemed to laugh at Grant's efforts to scorn....Now the picture is just as somber as it was bright then."

Confederate prospects temporarily brightened in the fall. Bragg counterattacked Rosecrans in north Georgia and won what seemed to be a smashing victory at Chickamauga in September. Lee began a campaign of maneuver in Virginia that compelled Meade to pull back toward Washington. But Grant went to Chattanooga, took control of the reinforced Union armies there, and drove Bragg back into Georgia in a pell-mell rout at the end of November. In Virginia the Army of the Potomac drove Lee south of the Rappahannock again in a series of smart actions as winter came on. In November a Confederate official in the War Department wrote a discouraged diary entry: "I have never actually despaired the cause...[but now] steadfastness is yielding to a sense of hopelessness." In Washington, by contrast, President Lincoln's annual message to Congress on December 8 noted that although the year had begun with "dark and doubtful days," now "the crisis which threatened to divide the friends of the Union is past."

Lincoln's statement turned out to be overoptimistic. The year 1864 would bring more dark and doubtful days. But the great battles of 1863, particularly the victories at Gettysburg, Vicksburg, and Chattanooga, proved to be major turning points in the war. They also helped to turn the tide of Northern opinion powerfully in the direction of emancipation as a war aim. As Lincoln said in his dedicatory address at the cemetery for Union soldiers at Gettysburg on November 19, 1863, those brave men had given "the last full measure of devotion" so that "this nation, under God...shall not perish from the earth" but instead "shall have a new birth of freedom."

James M. McPherson
Princeton, N. J.

January 4, 1863
MILITARY MATTERS

ONE YEAR AGO.—It is quite unusual for superficial speakers and careless writers to assert that the Rebellion is at the present time much nearer a perfect success than it was in November, 1861. It is also frequently stated that the Union armies have made but little, if any, progress during the last twelve months. Let us see how the case stands:

One year ago, the Rebels held the southern shore of the Potomac from a point not far below Washington, with Norfolk, Yorktown, and that portion of Virginia which lies on the eastern shore of Chesapeake Bay. Now, all this is in the undisputed possession of the Unionists.

One year ago, they held Centreville, Manassas Junction, Leesburg, Harper's Ferry, and the south bank of the Potomac *above* Washington for fifty or sixty miles, whence they inflicted on us the sad disaster of Ball's Bluff. Now, these are all in Union hands, and our main army threatens theirs across the Rappahannock and renders their possession of the Shenandoah Valley impossible.

One year ago, we stood on the defensive in Eastern Virginia, holding only a diminutive crescent over against Washington, and a little patch under the guns of Fortress Monroe. Now, we hold at least one third of the area of the Old Dominion, and are likely soon to hold still more.

One year ago, Kentucky was more than half in Rebel possession. Their main Western Army under Sydney Johnson lay strongly intrenched at Bowling Green, while Bishop General [Leonidas] Polk barred the Mississippi against us from his strong and well-maintained fortifications at Columbus. Now, Kentucky, though repeatedly traversed and ravaged by the rebels, is virtually deserted by them.

One year ago, Southwestern Missouri was given up to Rebel marauders, with most of the Southern part of the State. Now, scarcely a guerrilla band, and no formidable force of Rebels, remain within the State.

One year ago, Arkansas had not seen the Federal flag waving since treason expelled it from her soil. Since then, several bloody battles have been fought within her limits, every one resulting in a Union victory, and a Union army has traversed the State from the Boston Mountains to the Mississippi, without serious opposition. Arkansas has had very nearly her fill of rebellion.

One year ago, no Federal flag waved in Tennessee, though one-third of her people were loyal to the Union cause. To-day, we hold her capital, Nashville, her only considerable port, Memphis, a large portion of her territory, and all her navigable waters. Alas! for the fatally, the imbecility, which have thus far precluded our penetrating and liberating that home of persecuted, butchered, but unfaltering Unionism, gallant, glorious East Tennessee!

One year ago, the Mississippi below Cairo was exclusively in Rebel hands. To-day, the Union flag floats over every mile of it, and is probably at this time waving over Vicksburg; while New Orleans, the chief mart of the Rebel empire, the emporium of the Great Valley, has been undisputably ours for more than half a year.

One year ago, we held no part of North Carolina but Fort Hatteras. Now we hold New Bern, Washington, and two thirds of her coast, and control the waters of Albemarle Sound.

One year ago, we held no part of Georgia, save it may be some little sea island. Since then, we have captured and firmly hold Fort Pulaski, shutting the port of Savannah against blockade-breakers and privateers.

One year ago, we held not a foot of Texas. Now, Galveston, Sabine Pass, and other ports, repose peacefully under the folds of the Federal flag.

One year ago, a Rebel expedition from Texas had overrun the greater part of New Mexico, worsted our little army there in a pitched battle, and threatened to annex the whole vast territory to Jeffdom. Arizonia was already in the possession of the Rebels. Since then they have been whipped, routed, chased home (where but a disorganized remnant arrived); and New Mexico, with Arizonia, is now completely restored to the Union.

One year ago, the Rebels held Pensacola and nearly all the ports of Florida, threatening to capture Fort Pickens. Now those ports are nearly all in Union hands.

Our blockade of the Rebel coast is far more effective than one year ago, mainly because the ports to be closed have been reduced fully one-half.

Such are the auspices under which our strongly re-enforced and reorganized armies are about to advance for a final struggle with the half-clad, half-shod, ill-fed, shivering, "poor whites", who are forced by a relentless conscription, to fight the battles of Aristocracy and Slavery—the battles of a privileged, bullying caste—against their own rights and those of mankind.

January 11, 1863
U.S. GUNBOAT LOCKWOOD

PLYMOUTH, N.C., January 2.

As there is a great deal going on on board of those gunboats in Albemarle and Pamlico Sounds that the public never hear anything about, I make bold in stating some few facts that have transpired on board the U. S. gunboat Lockwood, Acting Master George W. Graves in command.

Some five months ago, the Lockwood proceeded from Plymouth to Bull's Bay, having Captain Hasser on board, who landed with two boats' crews, and arrested three notorious Rebel sympathizers, who were at that time strenuously and energetically aiding the Southern Confederacy. Shortly after our return to Plymouth, these men, for want of other place of confinement, were kept on board. During the following week, Capt. Graves treated them more like invited guests than as prisoners of war. The second day they were aboard it became necessary that the Lackawanna should go to Roanoke Island, to coal up.

On the passage down the Sound from Plymouth, we overhauled a small sailboat, bound in the same direction as ourselves, on board of which there was one white man (the owner of the vessel) and five darkeys, who had ran away from their masters, and were then on their way to Roanoke Island. Judge the surprise of the poor negroes when they recognized in some of our prisoners their former masters. The latter soon made it known to Capt. Graves, that the darkeys belonged to them, and, after a short consultation with Capt. Graves, they were allowed to get into the boat and bind the poor darkeys hands and feet. The Captain then had the white man provided with fire-arms. One of the prisoners then asked the owner of the boat how much he would charge to take the darkeys to Columbia, and have them lodged in jail in that place, until he (the prisoner) called for them? The man said he would do it for twenty dollars. The cash was immediately put into his hand, and the boat shoved off. All this happened in the presence of the whole crew, nearly one half of whom were blacks. Do you think this was right?

As a general thing, in these Sounds more darkeys have left their masters for fear of being driven further South. They have been known to roam through the swamps for weeks, subsisting on roots, until some of the Federal gunboats would be passing close to their place of concealment. They then show themselves with a flag of truce, and are taken on board. They very often bring valuable information concerning the movements of the enemy. They are mostly sent to Roanoke Island and New Bern, where they are put to work on the fortifications and breast-works. A great many of them have also been kept on board of the different gunboats, where they have proved themselves very useful to the Government.

Shortly after the taking of Plymouth by the Federal gunboats, under command of Lieut. [Chas.] Flusser, the steamer Lockwood, Capt. G. W. Graves, was sent to Edenton. At a point or turn in the land, a few miles from the latter place, one of the Quartermasters saw a darkey emerge from the swamp. Capt. Graves immediately had a boat lowered, and the darkey was brought aboard of the Lockwood. Poor fellow, he thought that he had fallen amongst friends, who would at any rate protect him from the tyranny of his cruel master.

He was doomed to be disappointed, for Capt. Graves, as soon as he arrived at Edenton, took the poor fellow ashore with him in the boat, and his master being sent for, was soon at the landing. He bound the poor negro's hands behind his back, and putting a halter around his neck, made him walk ahead, his master and Capt. Graves following after. How much Capt. Graves made by that operation your correspondent does not know; but he does know that Capt. G. W. Graves spent the remainder of that day and part of the night ashore in the company of as mean a band of traitors as ever tried to upset the Government of our great and glorious Union.

J. J. H.

SEVENTY-NINTH HIGHLANDERS, N.Y.S.V.

CAMP NEAR FREDERICKSBURG, VA., Jan. 8.

All is still quiet on the Rappahannock, and the weather, since the beginning of the year, has been unusually fine, making it pleasant to drill and do picket duty. The officers of this regiment inaugurated the new year in modern military style. On the 31st of December they issued cards of invitation to all the officers of the Ninth Army Corps, of which I send you an original copy. It reads thus:

"Officers of the Seventy-ninth Regiment N.Y. Highlanders, at head-quarters from 9 o'clock, A.M., to 4 o'clock, P.M., January 1, 1863."

Every provision was made for their reception that could be done under the strict surveillance that officers' boxes and baggage are subjected to. However, whether by running the blockade, or by some under-ground railroad that the provost-marshal is ignorant of, enough and to spare was procured; in the shape of roast turkeys, chicken, quail, and other fowl, also beef, roast and corned, and boiled ham, and sandwiches in abundance, with all the necessary bread, cakes, etc., to replenish the inner man, accompanied by the purest article of "mountain dew" and cogniac procurable in the country, and in quantity to suit the occasion. The Committee of Arrangements (Captains [Henry G.] Heffron, [William S.] Montgomery, and [John] Windsor) procured and erected a spacious tent in which they had set a large, covered table (with all the delicacies above enumerated), assisted by several waiters, late of the Fifth Avenue Hotel, New York, who happen to be members of this regiment. The day was fine, and everything passed off beyond expectations. But I must leave it to the visitors themselves to say whether or not they received a true "Highland welcome".

The end of the tent was decorated with the tattered and bloody colors of our regiment, which, although on this a festive occasion, reminded us that, although in the midst of life, we are also in the midst of death. However, appearances indicated that every one "felt good". Col. [David] Morrison presided at the table for the most part of the day, assisted by Major [John] Moore and Capt. [Alexander] Graham. Amongst the first visitors were O. B. Willcox, Brig.-Gen. Commanding First Division, Ninth Army Corps, who were all accompanied by their respective staff-officers, and who seemed to enjoy exceedingly what to them must have been original Highland hospitality. There were many other field-officers who made calls, also line-officers to the number of one hundred and fifty, being most all who were not on duty that day belonging to this corps, also most of the officers of the Fourteenth Regular Infantry, all of whom very pleasantly left their autographs, as a memento of the calls received by the officers of the Seventy-ninth Regiment, Jan. 1, 1863, and which document, comprising as it does nearly four pages of foolscap, it is hoped will be preserved and yet adorn part of the history of the Seventy-ninth and this Rebellion. The first toast was, Gen. Willcox's health, to which he nobly responded in one of those soul-stirring strains suited to the occasion, only equaled by a Bruce's address, with a Burns to give it a finishing touch. Amongst the other toasts were: "The President of the United States", "General Burnside", and "McClellan", which were all heartily drank. Among the healths of other prominent officers that were drank, I cannot omit Lieut.-Col. [Duncan] McVicar's of the Sixth N.Y. Cavalry whom it will be recollected made that splendid dash with 100 of his command on the 13th of December last at Barret's Ford, Rappahanock, where he encountered the enemy's pickets, driving them in under their batteries and to their reserve, which was 3,000 strong; they were taken so completely by surprise that Col. McVicar returned without losing a single man after killing and wounding quite a number of the enemy, with two prisoners of the First S. C. Cavalry. He is a native of Islay, Argylshire, Scotland, and served, before leaving his native country, five years in H.M. Royal Regiment of Artillery; he is a genuine Highlander, and takes as lively an interest in the prosperity of this country as any native born American.

We had a review to-day of the Ninth Army Corps, by General Burnside in person, accompanied by his Staff; the turn-out was not so large as might be expected, several regiments not numbering more than 300 to 400 men, being reduced by the casualties of war; still, the General must have felt proud of his "old corps", as cheer after cheer "three times", by each regiment in succession greeted his ears, which he most politely acknowledged. The camp-rumor of this corps says that we are to be relieved by those regiments in Washington and guarding the railroads in Maryland, so as to give them a chance to hear the whistle of the minie-ball and the crack of shells, so "familiar to the ear" of the Ninth Army Corps. Sickness, to some extent, prevails in several of our regiments, but so far the health is good of the one called the

SEVENTY-NINTH HIGHLANDERS, N.Y.V.

Lieutenant-Colonel Duncan McVicar, age 36, of the 6th New York Cavalry was killed in action on April 30, 1863, during a skirmish with Jeb Stuart's cavalry. He left a widow and five children.

FIFTY-FIRST REGIMENT
CAMP NEAR FALMOUTH, VA., Jan. 1st, 1863

Of late we have had beautiful weather. Last night the wind blew a little cold. I must say that I never saw more beautiful weather at this time of year. The last three or four days has been a busy time, making out pay-rolls, monthly reports, etc.

During the last week a few officers have tried to obtain a short leave of absence, but it was of no use. Furloughs have to go through the regular channel: from the commanding officer of the regiment to the officer commanding the brigade, to the officer commanding the division, to the officer commanding the corps, and to the officer commanding the great division; at the latter place it is disapproved, and sent back through the same channel, and reaches the regiment about five days from the day it was sent.

The sick and wounded of the late battle are nearly all removed to Washington, the accommodations at this place being quite limited. It is very disagreeable for a man when sick to remain in camp, for there is little or no change in diet, and camp food is not, in my opinion, fit for a sick soldier.

Our Chaplain (Rev. Porter Thomas) deserves credit for his exertions in aiding Surgeon [George] Cutter for several days after the battle, in caring for and helping to supply the wants of the wounded, burying the dead, and making himself in many ways useful.

The Mackerel Balloon makes frequent ascensions. One of the boys was relating a circumstance yesterday to an inquiring party, an incident that happened the day of the fight. The balloon had ascended in its usual way, for the occupant to take notes (the balloon generally rises near the railroad), when, "all at once", a shell came from the Rebel batteries, and passed between the balloon and car. One of the party wanted to know which car, the car of the balloon or the car below on the railroad track. The fellow caved in; he couldn't answer.

Early in the morning of the 13th ult., a mounted band came to the northern bank of the Rappahannock, and commenced playing pieces quite patriotic, when a shell from the enemy's batteries struck near them. As they just commenced playing "Leg of a duck", they didn't stop to finish.

It being tattoo I will close by bidding you good-bye.

J. B.

January 18, 1863
TWELFTH REGIMENT, N.Y.S.V.
CAMP NEAR STAFFORD C.H., VA., Jan. 14

On the 8th instant detachments from the several regiments which compose Butterfield's Division—in all 1500 men—left camp to relieve General Sickles' old Excelsior Brigade on picket. We returned on the evening of the 11th, being relieved in turn by Gen. Ward's Brigade. Our reserve was formed in one of those seemingly virgin woods which had never been invaded by the woodman's axe, but ere we left not a single one of those hoary and regal oaks, or of the towering and stately pines which composed it, was left standing in our bivouac, or for a considerable circuit around it. I mention this to show how great is, and must be, the destruction to this species of property in the neighborhood of a large army's camp. The only remarkable circumstance connected with the duty on this occasion was the arrest of Gen. [Turner] Ashby's body-servant. He was taken whilst attempting to pass our lines and delivered over to Col. [Henry A.] Weeks, of the Twelfth N. Y., who was general officer of the day.

The same day that we went on picket, Gen. Burnside held a review of the Centre Grand Division. Not being present, I am unable to give any particulars. I understand it was chiefly significant from the dumb silence which prevailed, not a single shout greeting the General-in-chief. An officer, in alluding to the subject, figuratively and forcibly characterized it as resembling a funeral or a field of mourning. Had McClellan been the reviewing General, acclamations of greeting, that could not be controlled, would burst forth wildly and spontaneously from every man present. This is scarcely fair to Burnside. He has not yet had a fair trial. From all the evidence adduced in reference to our repulse before Fredericksburg, it would appear that the real cause of failure cannot be attributed to him, but to those who neglected to aid him promptly in the carrying out of his plans. It is a matter of the greatest importance that soldiers should esteem and have confidence in their generals. They will not generally take the trouble of inquiring into the cause of defeat or disaster. They know how well they fight, and if victory does not smile on their arms, they leap to the conclusion that the general in command alone is to blame. Public writers should spare no pains in trying to disabuse the minds of the soldiers of any erroneous opinions they may entertain on this head.

There are rumors of active operations again floating around camp. Some of my authorities on this head are so respectable, and should be so well posted in what is passing behind the scenes, that it is hard to discredit their affirmations on the subject. If I credit them, the tocsin of war may again be heard any day. And yet it is hard to reconcile such statements with the fact that nearly all our high officers are absent from their respective commands. The only general at present with the Corps is General [George] Sykes. The Division is in charge of Colonel [James] Barnes, and the Brigade in command of one of the junior Colonels thereof—Col. Weeks, Twelfth N.Y.S.V. It is not likely General Burnside would permit the absence of so many of his officers if he intended immediate active hostilities.

Major [Henry A.] Barnum—once of the Twelfth N.Y.S.V., but now Colonel of the One Hundred and Forty-ninth N.Y.—paid us a visit on yesterday, on his way to [his] new command. He is one of those gallant, dauntless, and cheerful characters, who carry hope and confidence wherever they go. He was, and is, a great favorite with the Twelfth. He was severely wounded at the battle of Malvern Hills, and now returns to duty not as our Major, but as Colonel of the regiment specified. After the men came off dress-parade, they formed, with side-arms, in square, to hear an address from him. As his words are complimentary to the regiment, I am sure all its members would feel both proud and thankful for their insertion. He spoke, in part, substantially as follows:

"Gallant comrades of the Twelfth New York! It is one of the proudest and happiest days of my life, to meet and address you once more. On many a bloody and well-contested battle-field, you have immortalized the name of the Twelfth New York Volunteers. Some of you have been in the first battle of Bull Run, and all of you equal and similar participators in a common glory, from that to the present time. Yorktown, Hanover Court House, Chickahominy, and Malvern Hills, are fields of imperishable fame to you. I fell at the latter place, severely wounded, and was made prisoner. When one of General Hill's Aids asked my name, rank, and regiment, I proudly and distinctly answered, Major Barnum, of the Twelfth New York Volunteers; though from loss of blood I was scarcely able to speak. Subsequently General Hill visited me in person, and said, that they all had but too much reason to know the Twelfth New York, and could respect a brave foe. He desired me to command any thing I required, and that he would see my wishes were attended to. I found particular favor with the Rebels, and from no other cause than being of the Twelfth New York. 'We succeeded,' said General Hill 'to pierce your right, at Chickahominy, but we could not carry the position held by your regiment, till we came down on your rear. We led a brigade against you at Malvern Hill, with similar effect.' (I will here say that General Richardson sent special thanks to the Twelfth New York, for 'saving the left of the army' on that memorable occasion.)

The absence of pay is creating a very hard and bitter feeling in the army. Now that they have received none for seven months, they think the country has no claim on their services. Tell a man that, irrespective of all pecuniary considerations, his country claims his best exertions, or even his life, on her behalf, and you will probably be met by such arguments as the following: "Country be d—d! Why should I sacrifice or jeopardize my life for a country which has no sympathy for me or my family? How do I know but my family is starving now; and if not, 'tis not my country I need thank," etc.

The absence of pay is the cause of much of the straggling that takes place in the army. Cannot Secretary [Salmon P.] Chase or our Legislature do something to remedy this growing evil, or to put a stop to this pernicious state of things?

A—, COLOR GUARD.

FORTY-SECOND (TAMMANY) REGIMENT, N.Y.S.V.

NEAR FALMOUTH, VA., Jan. 3.

While reading your paper of the 28th December, 1862, I noticed in a letter from a correspondent in the Second Regiment N.Y.S.M., relative to the battle of Fredericksburg, stating that they (the Second N.Y.S.M.) had taken a position which had been forsaken by the New York Tammany Regiment. Gentlemen, I must state that the Second Regiment N.Y.S.M., or any other regiment, did not take the position that the Tammany Regiment were forced to leave, or as the correspondent says, "had forsaken". The way it was: part of my regiment, that were on the brow of a hill, were forced to leave their position by a battery which the enemy had opened on their right flank; the fire of it nobody could stand. This battery was put in position before our eyes, and we reported it to the General, who could have prevented the enemy from placing it there by throwing a few shell from our artillery. The ground which the Tammany Regiment were forced to leave was not held or retaken by any regiment after they left; and as for the house, the men who were posted there did not leave their post until they were properly relieved. Gentlemen, I am respectfully yours,

JOHN I. FERGUSON, LIEUT. CO. G.
FORTY-SECOND (TAMMANY) REGIMENT, N.Y.S.V.

January 25, 1863
TWELFTH REGIMENT, N.Y.S.V.

CAMP NEAR STAFFORD C. H., VA., Jan. 18.

In mine of the 14th inst., I intimated the probability that this Army would soon again be actively employed, though scarcely reconcilable with the fact of so many of its superior officers being absent. Though Captains and Majors command regiments, and Lieut.-Colonels and Colonels, Brigades, the fiat went forth at 2, P.M., on yesterday, to be ready to march to-day with three days' rations, and sixty rounds of cartridges to each man. Therefore, "forward" is the word, and ere you receive this, we will probably have tried strength with the enemy again. God grant with better success than that attending our last passage of arms here, or with more than lately seems to favor us. The darkest hour is before day. I hope our night is nearly spent, and that the dawn of a glorious and brilliant day is about to break upon us. As usual, rumor has been busy among us during the past week. All seemed to know a move was about to take place, but none exactly knew why, whither, or wherefore we were to march. Some one told some one that some one told him that we were going somewhere for some purpose. This was about the extent of everyone's information. Though the object of a move may fail to be discovered, yet the boys will divine that such is to take place many days previously, and that from signs and causes which would appear to the uninitiated as the common routine of military bustle and activity. They would divine it with a sense and perception as mystic as that by which the raven or vulture seeks and finds its prey. At first, this corps was to be relieved by the Eighth, and we, in consequence of being so badly cut up, and having done so much duty, etc., were to take its place. Our wagons, ambulances, etc., were all transferred to the Eighth, and everything settled for going into comfortable quarters in Baltimore and Washington to do fort and garrison-duty for the winter. Our sick were put on the cars to go down to Aquia

Creek on last Wednesday [Jan. 14] and this was looked on as a certain confirmation of the foregoing arrangement. But the sick, late in the evening were returned to regimental hospitals, and remain here, and all who deemed themselves unable to march were subjected to a surgical examination—the feeble to stay behind, the rest to go forth. Thus the idea of spending the winter in forts and garrisons is explored, and all now take it as granted that the din of battle will once more soon awaken the slumbering echoes of the Rappahannock. The order to march at 10 o'clock this morning was countermanded late last night, till the same hour to-morrow. We have the "grub" all stowed away, and every man has his sixty rounds of ball about him. The present order is, "The bugle will sound 'Strike tents' at the hour specified." The men seem hopeful, and if we are to attack the enemy, I feel more sanguine of success than when we first did, on the 13th ultimo.

I am tired of reading and writing of defeats and disasters. The health of the country now requires a change in the course of things. Joyfully would I act as her prescribing physician, and I hope Burnside will this time supply the needful medicine.

I have little else to communicate. The weather is now very cold, and should we have much bivouacking, it would certainly be very trying on the troops. One thing, the roads are in excellent order. From the recent severe frosts, they are as hard as if sheeted with iron.

A—, COLOR GUARD.

THIRTY-SIXTH REGIMENT, N.Y.S.V.

CAMP NEAR WHITE OAK CHURCH, VA., Jan. 18.

I suppose I owe you an apology for thus being silent these couple weeks back. But without mincing matters, I should say that on account of very arduous duties relative to the formations of a camp, and the regulation of our "sleeping apartments", have detained me from writing sooner. No doubt you are aware that our army lies in an inactive condition, and fears are entertained that it will be likely to remain so for some time. For at present there is nothing to indicate an active demonstration on our part, that is, as far as my opinion and eye will penetrate. On Friday [Jan. 16], our regiment, aided by the Tenth Massachusetts, was ordered on picket; and after a winding and wearisome march, we were posted along the bank of the Rappahannock, opposite that murderous ground where so many of our boys lost their lives for no gain. And it was quite singular to see the pickets of the two contending armies within gun-shot distance of each other. We stuck our rifles on the ground with the stocks upward; a sign that the picket knew no such thing as to fire on each other. The "Secesh" picket also stuck their muskets in the ground, and whenever we grabbed ours, they sprang for theirs. And as far as the eye could reveal to us, we could discover new made rifle-pits, which they threw up to stay our progress, in case we should attempt to cross at the same place.

But no sir-ee; they are mistaken this time. We remained on picket some three days, when we were relieved by the One Hundred and Twenty-second New York.

The weather to-day is quite soft and mild, although last night we had a heavy shower of rain, which, I fear, has placed the roads in an impassable condition.

In this communication to you, it is a good idea for me to make mention of the injustice of denying the bounty to disabled and wounded soldiers who cannot serve out their term of enlistment. I think—and I guess you will agree with me—a soldier who is prevented either from wounds or disability from serving out his time (provided he is not a $300 man) is entitled to his bounty; for, I think, it is worthy a dozen of bounties to have a person's constitution shattered, or lose a limb. The Good Book says, "If a limb offend thee, cut it off." I think if justice was meted out to all that deserves it there would be a great many cripples in the public institutions at Washington. It would be a regular one legged party. In fact, somebody must be blamed for our bad luck. I think if they would always rectify their mistakes, and guard against their recurrence instead of wasting valuable time in recrimination and mutual blaming, things would go better. But the best man wins, so say I.

Yours, truly,   JERSHUA JENKINS.

February 1, 1863
NINTH REGIMENT, N.Y.S.M.

CAMP NEAR BELL'S PLAIN LANDING, VA., Jan. 25.

Home again—once more back to our old camp, yet when we left it on Tuesday last (20th), little did we dream that we would once more again behold our comfortable quarters of log-huts, etc. We received marching orders at daybreak on the 20th inst., and left camp at 12½ o'clock, marching all the afternoon and night, up to 11 o'clock, when we halted within one mile of the river, four miles above Falmouth, through a drenching rain. Our regiment lay until 6 o'clock on the morning of the 23rd, when orders came for us to return to our old camp; so we marched back to our old quarters, through mud knee-deep. Such sights I never beheld—wagons, cannons, caissons, ambulances, all stuck up to the hubs in mud. I saw sixteen horses on one caisson. Over two thousand horses and mules lay dead on the roads. Never were the roads in such a condition, and thanks to a merciful Providence that it happened as it did, or else the grand Army of the Potomac, if they had gone across, would have been slaughtered worse than at the former battle, and two-thirds of the Army taken prisoners.

Why is not McClellan or some other good general (say [William S.] Rosecrans) put over us, so that we can be the Army of the Potomac again. We are discontented, if not demoralized. If the Government insists on taking Richmond by the way of Fredericksburg with this army, it is and will be sadly disappointed. You could not get one-half of the old veterans to cross the river; those that would go across would fire one volley and run. The Pennsylvania Reserves swore it; and our old Brigades would do likewise. As for the new troops, they are not worth all their salt; they straggle all over the country, and some New Jersey regiments do not know hardly how to drill. Such a state of affairs is perfectly alarming.

The only feasible and proper way to take Richmond is to take the old used-up regiments (such as ours and many more) to Washington to man the forts, fords of the Potomac, and defences around Alexandria, etc. All the two-year full regiments, nine-months men, batteaux etc, should be quickly transported to Yorktown, Suffolk, and North Carolina, and then make a combined movement, and fall upon the enemy's flank and rear. By good weather and quick marching, Richmond will be ours! In no other way can it be taken.

The Rebels are fully prepared to meet us over the river, for new rifle-pits and intrenchments for miles are seen with the naked eye, and they make no bones in helloing out to us: "Come across, you Yankees, we have a job for you this time." They have rafts built, to fire, to float down the stream and carry away our pontoons. Richmond can never be taken, as I said before by way of Fredericksburg; and the sooner our generals give up the idea, the better for the nation and our soldiers.

Now, we will let the papers discuss this subject, and I will turn to our own affairs. The night before we left our camp, our old Colonel, J. W. Stiles, took his final departure for home, his resignation having been accepted. We number 172 men all told, only 129 fit for service in the field, and here the Government keeps us in the front, making us do outer picket duty all the time, hard marching, and even had the impudence to put us in front line of battle with 129 men, non-commissioned officers included, and full regiments are in forts, fortifications, fords and doing provost-duty around Alexandria, Washington and other cities. While we who have so faithfully served our country for twenty-one months, are kept here to the front with only a corporal's guard. The Government owes us seven months' pay, and, when we get paid, if we ever will, the Paymaster only has four months' pay for us. I assure you this is the state of affairs out here, and we call upon you to aid us, and the Government to call us out of the field or else the Ninth Regiment will be with the things that were. No one knows at times how we suffer out here, and we look to our friends for help and protection.

                                                                                                MINUS.

February 8, 1863

THE NEGRO SOLDIERS BILL.

Those who believe in rose water warfare, and like the Hibernian Chesterfield prefer "amicable hostility and gentlemanly animosity" to hard knocks are not reliable prophets, though always dealing in dismal prognostications. They foretold disaster as sure to follow every act of the Government which failed to meet their approbation. The Emancipation Proclamation was to have thrown the Border States into the arms of Secession, produced a mutiny in the Army, brought about immediate foreign intervention, and realized the predictions of the Millerites by smashing up creation in general. The arming of the negroes was denounced as fraught with still more direful consequences. But the Bill is on its passage in Congress to arm and equip an army of contrabands, and no earthquakes nor terrestrial convulsions disturb the intestines of the globe; and the Bill will become a law without throwing the sun off its axis, or disturbing the equilibrium of the planets. In fact, any opposition which existed to the use of negroes as a part of the "war power" has simmered down, and if the Government can only redeem itself from the miserable lack of energy on land and sea which has permitted the war to drag its slow length along as if it was to stretch out to the crack of doom, by indicating an adequate though tardy punishment on its authors, no one not in full sentimental communion with the Rebels will object to the means employed, provided they are adequate as proposed.

Separation—the final and eternal—is the announced purpose of the Rebels. Nothing less than the destruction of the Republic and the dismemberment of the Union will satisfy their ambition. This is a consummation to which the American people will never accede while they are capable of preventing it; and the public enemies, who avow such an intent, should be foiled of their traitorous designs by every means within reach of the Government. Negroes should be allowed to fight and made to fight. They are parties to the contest, and their interests are bound up with its issues more intimately than any other class. The North has sacrificed hundreds of thousands of her brave and generous sons. No further drain can be made on the white population without withdrawing from society its chief pillars of support, and leave the social fabric to topple into ruins. It would be preposterous to draft white men to fight, while hosts of the sable sons of Africa are ready to be transformed into soldiers, and whose services the Government has a right to claim. Negroes have repeatedly displayed good fighting qualities, and history proves their adaptability to military duty and camp life. If they can fight we have as good a right to use them as the South, where no fastidious predilection in behalf of a transparent epidermis is allowed to prevent the darkeys from being put to any work that will help their Rebel masters to break up the Union and destroy its gallant defenders.

SEVENTY-NINTH REGIMENT, N.Y.S. (HIGHLANDERS).

January 27.

Never once did we imagine that Burnside would attempt another attack before spring weather had set in. He did, though—and so, pursuant to orders, we arose at an early hour on the morning of the 17th instant, packed up all that we could possibly carry, sighed over those things that we were forced to leave behind, resigned ourselves to our fate, and sat down and waited patiently for the orders to march. The day was dark and threatening, and many an anxious glance was cast to the murky heavens, and many an aspiration ascended that the weather would "clear up", or that the orders to march would be postponed. Our prayers were answered. No orders came that day, nor the next; and we began to dream of settling down again, when, toward the evening of the 20th, a long string of pontoons, artillery, and infantry made their appearance on the crest of the hill opposite our camp, and filed off in the direction of Falmouth. They were part of Franklin's Division. The "on to Richmond" had again commenced, and we knew that the time had come when we must once more encounter the dangers, exposures, and hardships that always await the soldier in a winter's campaign.

As darkness settled over the earth, a terrific storm of wind and rain arose; and while we felt grateful for still having the shelter of our huts, we felt heartfelt pity for our poor brothers-in-arms, who were exposed to its merciless fury. The storm continued for over forty-eight hours, and still we were allowed to remain unmolested in our camp. No news was received from those that had advanced to the front, until the evening of the 22nd; when straggling parties of soldiers repassed our camp, in the direction of Belle Plains. They were pitiable-looking objects. Faces covered with dirt, hair unkempt, clothes bedraggled and bedaubed with rain and mud, and arms and accoutrements looking a *leetle* the worse of wear.

By questioning some of them, we ascertained that they had intended crossing the Rappahannock some ten miles up, but the rain had vetoed all their arrangements. The roads were converted into quagmires, in which the artillery, horses, and wagons stuck fast. It was impossible to get the pontoons forward to form the bridges, and, even if they had got them laid down, after the first night of the storm, very few men could have been got together to have crossed them. The poor devils had sought shelter from the fury of the elements, here and there, wherever they could find it, and it would have taken a week to have gotten them into fighting trim again. Burnside's second attempt was like his first—a failure. Poor General! his unlucky star was in the ascendant. All day, Friday, the 23rd, the worn-out, demoralized Army of the Potomac straggled past, on their return to their old encampments. They presented a miserable appearance—looking worse, in fact, than I have ever seen them, even when flying before a victorious enemy. Talking with one of the Anderson Zouaves, I learned from him, among other things, that some of his disgusted comrades had erected a placard on the banks of the river, on which was inscribed in large characters: "Burnside's Army Stuck in the Mud!" "And this is the Army," he remarked, bitterly, "that is to break the backbone of the Rebellion! Why, there is not spirit enough left in us to break the backbone of a mosquito, nor never will, until we have generals over us that are capable of leading men into action."

We are now settled down again, and everything indicates a stay here for some time. Ovens are being built, and we have hopes that, at no distant day, we will once more enjoy that rare luxury to a soldier—a loaf of soft bread. Our Colonel—A. Farnsworth—who was severely wounded at the battle of Manassas, paid us a visit last week. He staid but a few days, and then returned to New York. His wounds still disable him so much, that he is unable to move without crutches.

Since I wrote to you last, the *rara avis*—the Paymaster—made his appearance, and "forked over" for four months. We expect him back again soon, as there are three months more now due us.

COLOR.

TWELFTH REGIMENT, N.Y.S.V.

CAMP NEAR FALMOUTH, VA., Feb. 3.

The past week has been productive of little worth communicating. There has not been such a dearth of news among us since the birth of the New Year. During the short period of its existence it made a great effort to distinguish and immortalize itself, but failing in this, it would seem to have become completely crestfallen and lifeless. Not even a camp rumor floats around, to give a little excitement to the monotony of its life. The earth, for a few days, has been wrapped in a winding-sheet of snowy whiteness. A shroud so emblematic of purity and innocence ill-becomes a corpse whose life was but a scene of blood and devastation; and whose resuscitation will most certainly be but a repetition of its past life. Yet, with all her vices, the men seem to mourn the inanimate appearance of their mother; confining themselves most assiduously to quarters. Since we returned from our late foiled expedition, we have had no drills nor dress-parades. Bugles and drums alone give signs of life to the camps, and of these there is a never-ending blast and beat. The year is but yet in its infancy, a stage in life from which we can expect but little. Maturity is the age for action and deeds, and that's to come. Old age for wisdom, council, and peace, and I hope that will be its end.

A snow-storm set in here this night week, continuing through next day and following night. Thursday and Friday we had hard frost, with every sign of its continuance on the evening of the latter day, and that the snow would, in consequence, be protracted on the ground. But the weather changed by Saturday morning to the wild and genial, ending in rain on Sunday evening. That inveterate enemy to its soft and downy predecessor had nearly expelled it before morning, causing it to desert to its own ranks—a movement more hostile to us than that barrier which the fleecy particles alone presented. From the seas of mud created by these combination of causes, pedestrianism was out of the question, only when necessity rendered it imperative. Last night commenced with frost and ended with snow. To-day, a breezy, dry, strong wind prevailed, resembling March weather. Should it continue, the place would soon again be in walking condition.

General Hooker has his staff formed, but as all appointments are long since before the public, it is needless to notice them now. Maj.-Gen. Butterfield is chief of staff. This is one of our New York men, but generally, if not unexceptionally popular. He is one of those officers whom I have never heard spoken of but with respect and encomiums, and he must be indeed near akin to perfection who has no enemies. Your correspondent has been under his leadership since he became a member of the Twelfth, and when he says that he is sorry to lose a commander whose presence ever brought hope, confidence, and willing action, he but reflects the sentiment of every man, and, he thinks, officer in his division.

Gen. Hooker has issued a circular granting furloughs to two officers from each regiment at the same time, and also to two enlisted men for every 100 in the regiment for ten days. To certain Northern and Western States, the period may be extended to fifteen, but in no case to more. Now, if Gen. H. intends to make his sobriquet good, and give us winter work, I think it is too many to permit to be absent; but if no more winter fighting be intended, the proportion is too small. Every man twelve months absent from friends and home, naturally yearn to see them—a yearning increased from a sense of the dangers passed through, and the probable ones yet before us. Twenty to the hundred could as safely be permitted the indulgence as two; but if the favor were extended to half the number at the time, the whole wishing for furloughs could be gratified. As it is, there's the greater number of applications already in, and as the records of all are equally strong and questionless, the eighteen who must be refused will naturally feel jealous and hardly dealt with. Two at the time would only permit eighteen to the hundred to be indulged by the 1st of May next. It is as unlikely as it would be unwise that we remain idle, should the weather permit action, to that time; and it is ungenerous of Gen. H. to be so niggardly of his favors, when he extends them at all. If the presumption be that we cannot possibly do anything for the next ten or fifteen days, why, the same observations hold good. Ten may as well be absent as two; and then, if an opportunity for fighting should present itself, there would be no grumbling, as all would know the maximum of favors was extended whilst they could without injury to the public service.

The camping ground of the whole Army is to be changed, in consequence of the difficulty of procuring fuel, or rather from the difficulty of carrying and carting it to the camps. Two months ago and I thought the supply around here was inexhaustible. Now, for miles around, scarcely a tree stands. Here and there may be seen a few shivering in the cold because unfit for firing. Virginia is certainly being shorn of its natural value and ornament. But this is but one of the many bitter souvenirs she will have of the Rebellion. She can yet justly apply the words of the Roman historian to us—"They created a waste and called it peace"—and she can justly apply their aptness to her own foolishness and treason. General Humphreys' Division, of the Fifth Corps, removed camp about two miles to the front yesterday. The forests of its new abode will soon bear the impress of the stranger, and heaps of ashes alone remain to tell the tale of their existence.

Since the boys got paid, hard-crackers have become a drag in the market. Cooks can't induce the men to take them off their hands, and boxes of them lie about at the option of any one who'd be so kind as to take them away. The boxes are useful in many ways, but will not be taken, as contents should be taken into the bargain. Before the poor and much disrespected representative of money made its appearance, it was as hard to see a sutler as a swallow in winter; but it no sooner came than they flocked as thick as a cloud of hungry and devouring locusts. Every trash and bauble found ready and contending purchasers at any price. 'Twas only necessary to have change to pocket tens as readily as cents. Certainly, a soldier is a curious animal; when he has no money he whines till he gets it, and when he does, gives it no peace till all is gone. Then pork, crackers, and salt-junk, are once more welcome, and Uncle Sam unmercifully anathematized if he does not furnish a full and ready supply. A soldier is a soldier, and that's all. Twelve months' active life in camp and field have a great effect on most men—in habits, ideas, sentiments, etc., almost transforming them into new beings. Though we may fail to detect any such changes in ourselves, we cannot help noticing them among comrades and associates.

The night threatens to be wild, cold, and stormy.

A—, COLOR GUARD.

FOURTH NEW YORK CAVALRY

CAMP IN TWO FOOT OF SNOW, NEAR ALLOCK, VA.,
January 31st, 1863.

Notwithstanding my present difficulties and troubles, I have the privilege of writing to you once in a while. Our regiment were paid day before yesterday, two months' wages. We have three months' pay due us yet. O, it's a "big thing" to get money, but a bigger thing when you can't buy anything after you get the money. That's what's the matter. Plenty to pay and nothing to eat. We are getting no coffee or sugar now-a-days, which goes against us like a dose of salts. People may think the Monkey Rifles are a lot of natural-born fools but it don't make some difference. We can answer for our incapacity. There is no whiskey for us here to take a "smile", as all the sutlers are stuck fast in the mud and can't get here. It is hard for a man to be exposed to cold rain and all sorts of weather, without a drop of the good stuff, far from home and friends, and no one to wish us success.

I hold correspondence with a dear little chickabiddy in the town of M—n. She tells me to be of good cheer, and that she should despair if she should lose me now. She allows my presence diffuses, a calm and holy glow through her soul. How pleasant it is to have a friend to counsel and advise with us when darkness has settled on the fair face of nature! He who has a friend to whom he can go in the hour of adversity can never be cast down, can never be driven to despair. I would have written to you before, but I have been so incessantly occupied that I could not command the necessary time. We are now in the woods of Virginia, and likely we'll stay here till the war is over, contending with numerous outlaws who infest this section, committing all sorts of depredations murder, rapine, arson, robbery; and meeting plunder with philanthropy. Such as may be properly termed fleet-footed robbers and human butchers to whom we give prisons and parole. It is unsafe for a small party to go two miles from camp, as the infernal Rebels lie in ambush.

ROUNCE.

SIXTH REGIMENT, N.Y.S.V., WILSON'S ZOUAVES

NEW ORLEANS, LA., Jan. 5.

The boys enjoy themselves finely in the city; it puts one in mind of home. Gen. Banks arrived here a short time since, with 30,000 men. Something is to be done. [Col. William] Wilson is in command of the First Division, under Gen. Sherman.

On the 18th of November we left New Orleans bound up the Mississippi River. The boys are in fine spirits, in hopes of getting a chance to show themselves. On the 20th we arrived at Baton Rouge city, La. Had a sad affair some thirty miles below here, at a place called College Point. It happened that the boat had to stay at the above named place to take six companies of the Twelfth Maine Volunteers on board; some two hundred of our men got on shore and into an old distillery, and were enjoying themselves drinking sugar-cane rum. They were all jolly in less than half an hour; one gill makes a man drunk. The Colonel dispatched Lieut. James Entwistle, with a guard, to send the men on board the boat. Lieut. Virginius Van Geison, hearing this, followed the guard. Lieut. Entwistle succeeded in getting all the men on board, except five or six, without any trouble, when he came across two more, the sergeant-major of the regiment, who was trying to get a sergeant by the name of Andrew W. Ekens on board the boat. By this time, a captain by the name of Daley had joined the party. I afterward learned that Lieut. Entwistle told them that he did not want them, but all to no purpose. They came up to Ekens and told him that they wanted him to go on board the steamer. They had some words; a scuffle ensued between Entwistle and Ekens, when Lieut. Van Geison snapped his pistol at Ekens three times. Entwistle told him to go away and not to shoot, as he could manage Ekens alone; but Van Geison came up again and placed the barrel of his revolver against Eken's head and fired. Ekens fell dead on the ground. Ekens was beastly drunk at the time.

Lieutenant Van Geison was placed under arrest on the 28th of December. He has not been seen by any of the men. The Sergeant-Major has been reduced to the ranks, and placed in confinement in the State Prison in this city. The general opinion among the men is, that certain officers of the regiment are trying to get Van Gieson clear, by trying to make it appear that Wood was the cause of his going on shore, as he was found with and trying to get him on board.

We had a large fire down town the other night. The State House was completely destroyed. Our boys had fine sport working the engines, which were three in number. It is supposed that the capitol was set on fire by some Rebel prisoners who were confined in the building. Several shots were fired at our men from the crowd on the sidewalk. It is said that three shots were fired at Colonel Wilson, supposed to come from the citizens of this place.

We have not received any news from the North since the 12th of November. There is some talk of our going on to Port Hudson. The troops here are in good health. Have a report that Burnside had fought another battle, and lost twenty thousand men.

                                                                                                J. W.

U.S. STEAMER R.R. CUYLER
OFF MOBILE BAY, Jan. 28.

Finding a stray copy of your Sunday issue of the 14th ult. in our mail this morning, I greeted it as an old acquaintance, and hastened to confiscate its budget.

You may rely on it that Mobile will not fall readily, every preparation that science or experience could suggest being already made for its defence. In fact, neither money nor labor have been spared in rendering it impregnable; but, thanks to the intelligence of various deserters, and the results of several reconnoitreing expeditions, we know just where to expect, and how to avoid, hidden dangers; while perhaps the greatest impediment to our entrance, next to Fort Morgan, and which will render that fortress doubly effective, is a triple row of spiles, blocking the Western or Old Channel, and obliging us to enter by the Eastern or Swash Channel, which will carry us within one-half mile of the fort, which must annoy us terribly, and with perfect impunity, with their casemate guns, while we will have those spiles and a heavy armed fleet of seven sail to contend with and destroy ere we can pass into safety beyond the fort. In fact, we rely upon a land-force, to carry Fort Morgan by storm—but this is *sub rosa*—or it would be folly to venture an attack under existing circumstances. Once inside, I, for one, look for the bloodiest portion of the battle, the approach to Mobile being lined with heavy sand-batteries, and the channel partially blocked by spiles, through which we must slowly pick our way, exposed to, and returning at random, their murderous fire, delivered at "tested range", until we reach shoal water, when we must effect a landing of troops, and cover their advance by light-draught mortar-boats and long-range rifled-guns from the fleet, dispatch a strong force in boats to aid and co-operate with the troops.

Such is a sketch of the task before us, though by no means an authentic sketch of our plans, which, of course, are secret. Having the "Bobbin Boy" [N. P. Banks]—who never yet failed—to aid us, we rely confidently upon him for the execution of a victory that will more than offset recent blunders in, and defeats upon the field.

Rear-Admiral [David G.] Farragut has moved up the river, with a heavy force, leaving Commodore [Robert B.] Hitchcock in command here of an aggregate of sixty guns off Mobile. Some of them heavy rifled Parrott's and other shell-guns of the largest calibre, while a large squadron are rendezvoused at Pensacola and daily augmenting.

Ere closing, I should add, the English steamer Vesuvius arrived on the blockade Saturday, and communicated with Fort Morgan, on Sunday, Monday, their visit was returned by the steamer Crescent, under a flag of truce, and the English flag. She remained some four hours, when the Rebel steamer Gaines, mounting one one-hundred-pound rifle and one thirty-pound, do. ventured out under a flag of truce. We then weighed anchor, and ran down for the Commodore, for orders, suspecting some foul movement: but on came the Reb. into short range, and, under our guns, officially communicated to the Commodore the fact of their communication with the British.

Be assured we viewed her with any other than friendly feelings; but the "white flag" must be respected.

                Truly, yours,   AL.

February 15, 1863
NINETY-NINTH REGIMENT, N.Y.S.V.
FORTRESS MONROE, VA., Feb. 6.

Since my last (dated from Newport News), not much has transpired here worth notice save the little excitement at Suffolk a few days since, which, as you of course are aware, resulted in the total defeat and discomfiture of the "Rebs".

On Friday, the 23rd ult., a German teamster suffered the extreme penalty of the law, on the Rip Raps, for shooting a colored man at Camp Hamilton, Va. The culprit seemed to be conscious of his fate, and evinced much repentance. This, I believe, is one of the first cases of the kind that has yet been carried into execution, and very naturally aroused much indignation. The affair, of course, caused the darkeys around the

Department to be more bold. Accordingly, one stalwart African, intending to display his prowess and equality, attacked the Forage-Master at this post, and, on being remonstrated with by a sentinel of the Third N.Y.S.V., whose beat was near by, he turned upon him also. The latter not being over-curious to take the insolence, although on duty, he was under the painful necessity of breaking his musket on the cranium of the darkey, and only regretted that it had been rendered perfectly useless by the first blow. The contraband was taken to the guard-house.

A very heavy snow-storm prevailed here on Tuesday last. Many schooners went ashore, but as far as can be ascertained, no other losses were sustained.

Newport News is about to become once more a place of rendezvous for a portion of the Army of the Potomac, the Ninth Corps d'Armée having just commenced to arrive. The busy, exciting scenes attendant on such an occasion, and the lively bustling of the vessels passing to and fro, reminds us of the warlike scenes experienced last spring. Their destination is unknown.

The appearance of several paymasters in this department, a fortnight ago, was hailed with much delight. On their arrival, they proceeded forthwith to their respective stations to dispense Uncle Sam's "greenbacks", and I have heard of no one case where they were not fully appreciated.

I perceive by this morning's paper a contradiction of the announcement made a few days since of the capture, sinking, and total dispersion of our fleet off Charleston. I very much wonder if the gentleman is sane who was pleased to promulgate such an infamous falsehood.

Let us hope that with the aid of our Monitors we shall reduce that Rebel stronghold to submission before they can have again the audacity of setting forth such absurd rumors for the perusal of our deluded friends on the other side of the Atlantic.

Alas! poor Beauregard, when wilt thou be through?

Very respectfully,   GOV.

NINTH REGIMENT, N.Y.S.M.

CAMP NEAR FLETCHER'S CHAPEL, Feb. 8, 1863.

Since my last, nothing has transpired. In the way of moving; things remain in *status quo* with us; the only thing worth mentioning is that the Army is made up of Corps now, Grand Divisions are done away with, per orders read to us last evening.

Joseph Hooker, the Commander-in-Chief, is trying to immortalize himself. Orders, to the amount of bushels are being sent in, and us poor soldiers have to wade up to our knees in mud (evenings) to listen to these documents read.

The fact of the matter is, there is too much red tape in the Army. Colonels of Regiments, acting Brigadiers, do nothing, from morning to night, but send orders and inquiries, calls of extra details to bury dead horses, etc.

We are doing the extreme left Grand Wing Picket Duty and we have furnished forty men every three days, and last week, on one occasion, two days hand-running, because Division Head-quarters saw fit to alter the picket. We number scarcely 200 men, and we have to do everything these would-be Brigadiers require of us. No remedy or redress can be had.

Furloughs are now all the go; a man who is down number seven for a furlough will stand as good a chance to get home as one would of climbing up to the moon—red tape the cause. Two privates or non-commissioned officers are entitled to a furlough for ten days, but no one is allowed to go until the other two return. How are you return? The soldier who gets away now, I tell you, he is for himself, and takes the chances of being brought back. I believe the Ninth Regiment N.Y.S.M. is well represented in the Empire City.

Why is it that 271 men representing the Ninth Regiment N.Y.S.M., in our city, do not recruit up their full standard and volunteer to take our places and let us come home, or let the U.S. Government let us come home like the Seventh Maine Regiment did and fill up the Ninth Regiment N.Y.S.M., No. 2?

We can furnish any quantity of officers, all able and talented, and have seen hard service. Those that would best be fit to come out again let them remain at home.

No one knows how we suffer out here. If one is sick, he must remain out here; if he gets well it is a miracle. For instance: a surgeon attached to our Brigade says that there are men now lying in the hospitals that would never recover, and as their complaints did not come under a certain set headings they could not get a discharge! Men in our own regiment have applied again and again to the Board of Examiners on the first of every month, and have been rejected on the above plea, and no less than forty men have died at the General Hospital at Acquia Creek in one single day. Laconically speaking, one of our hospital nurses says we carried forty stiffs to-day. To make things worse, all the good brandy, wine, and refreshments that are sent to the poor wounded and dying soldiers never reach them. They are drank and ate up by those rascally butchers of surgeons, hospital stewards, and nurses. I have known myself a certain hospital steward to sell the patients' liquor; but there is no redress. A poor soldier is thrown in the hospital, and his friends at home thinks he is receiving the best of attention, while the poor fellow is being robbed of food and drink; and the poor fellow dies, and is thrown into a hole and covered up. One half of our wounded soldiers who receive wounds in action are horribly butchered by a set of would-be surgeons, volunteering their services from the city.

It is no wonder, Messrs. Editors, that we of the Ninth Regiment are desirous of seeing our good old city as soon as possible; yet we do not want to come home until our time expires; but we ask of the United States Government something, that is, a little bit easier place than we have now.

FERRIS.

February 22, 1863
FIFTY-FIRST, N.Y.S.V.
NEWPORT NEWS, VA., Feb. 15.

We received orders to have three days' cooked rations, prepared to march at an hour's notice. This was on Friday, 6th instant. Sunday evening, orders came to strike tents early next morning, which was done in double-quick time. I might say triple-quick, for fear of the order being countermanded.

Early on Monday morning line was formed, and we proceeded to the depot, taking the cars, and arrived at Acquia Creek about 3, P.M. ; thence on board of a steamboat, which conveyed us to a schooner. There were on board of the schooner one-half of the Eleventh New Hampshire, besides our regiment. We were packed, or stowed away, like so many dead pigs—not live ones; for live pigs would not submit to such quarters.

At daylight, Tuesday morning, we "hev anchor" started for an unknown destination, being towed by the Louisiana. On our passage each one would form some opinion as to the point to which we were going; and from these opinions, or suppositions, one could hardly dare to surmise, but let time bring the required knowledge sought after. At any rate, Wednesday, 2, P.M., found us in Hampton Roads, anchored; but did not remain so long, orders being received to the effect that we were to go to Newport News and land. Then you ought to have seen the smiling faces around on the deck; for the boys were acquainted with the lay of the land hereabout, having been here last summer, and knew that it was far superior to our mud camp opposite Fredericksburg.

Our camp is a beautiful spot—such capacious grounds for company, battalion, and division drills, (base-ball included); this is no more than could be expected, but we don't mind a little drilling, but do mind the heavy guard-duty, and cannot see any good arising from it. Out of the brigade there is detailed every day between 150 and 200 men for guard; in the daytime it is all very well as long as the sun shines, but when night comes on, to have to remain on your post without any fire, and even when you are relieved having no fire to warm one's self by—besides all this there are the regular police and fatigue details, which are indispensable; this alone is sufficient without tiring one down with those monotonous drills.

Our corps is now commanded by Major-General [William F.] Smith; Brig.-General Ferrero is in command (temporarily) of the Second Division; Col. Hartranft, of the Fifty-first Pennsylvania Volunteers, is commanding his brigade.

Since our arrival here we have received fresh bread every other day; this, with fresh meat, onions, potatoes, beans, rice, and other articles, would not go amiss if they would keep it up. Gen. Hooker issued an order concerning the men getting furloughs of the period of ten days, allowing two out of every hundred to go at a time. Since our arrival here the affair is hushed; but what is the use of going home to see his relations and friends?

O Rewar!   GREENBACK.

TENTH REGIMENT (NATIONAL ZOUAVES), N.Y.S.V.
HEAD-QUARTERS PROVOST GUARD, GEN. FRENCH'S DIVISION,
NEAR FALMOUTH, VA., Feb. 17.

Nothing of special interest has transpired since my last, and we are still quietly domiciled in the little habitations which we have erected with our own hands upon lands donated to us for that purpose by the benevolent Uncle Sam. These habitations, though rude in their appearance, present an air of comfort to the soldier, and, considering the limited facilities for constructing them, reflect much credit upon the ingenuity and skill of the builders. The only materials used being mud, logs, and the ordinary Shelter tents for roofing. They are usually dug from two to three feet under ground, with a capacious fire-place, which affords ample heat in the severest weather. The furniture consists chiefly of shelving, made of cracker-boxes, placed upon which may be seen numerous tin cans, bottles etc., relics of the sorry dishes of preserves, pickles, jellies, etc., which they once contained. Some of the huts are supplied with bedsteads, constructed of poles, and being softly covered invite the soldier to Nature's calm restorer, "balmy sleep". The number of occupants to each hut is from two to four persons, these mutually perform the agreeable offices of cooks, wood-choppers, laundress, chambermaid, bottle-washer, and kindred employments. The great proficiency we have made in these attainments, would, in the eyes of the fair sex, be refreshing to behold; and I should not wonder if our knowledge does not lead to some great revolution in the domestic affairs of life. Young men, after the war, will be in great demand by the girls, for they "will be so handy to have in the house," particularly on cold mornings. An unfortunate Benedict, who is at my elbow, threatens to punch me if I say too much on the subject, for his wife reads the SUNDAY MERCURY, and the consequences might be fatal to him when he gets home. A crusty old bachelor, however, is in dudgeon, and says it is now demonstrated, to a certainty, that "man can live alone". Well, says "young man", let him live alone who will; but, for my part, I shall add a rib to my side, for the absence of lovely woman for the past two years has convinced me, more than ever, that two are better than one, particularly when those two are "made one flesh"; but he further adds, that he will leave all his knowledge of domestic affairs behind him. A few days since, in passing Sergeant S—, I observed before his fire, a large pan of beans undergoing the process of baking; they were most beautifully browned upon the surface, the centre of which was gracefully adorned with a neatly-cut piece of juicy pork. I thought it very creditable to the good taste of the Sergeant; but, as he did not invite me to dinner, I will say no more about it. As he is already married, the girls need make no inquiries concerning him.

We will now change the subject of eating to clothing. Not a little dissatisfaction is expressed by the men for charges made for clothing furnished them after the Seven Days' Battle, in place of those lost in action. In many cases, the men were ordered to destroy their clothing, which order they implicitly obeyed, and now for the Government to deduct from their monthly pay the amount for the articles furnished does seem rather inconsiderate. But it is done, and there is no use in groaning about it.

The weather is still inclement, and decidedly unfavorable for movements of any description hereabouts.

Yours,   G.

SIXTY-SECOND REGIMENT N.Y.S.V.

CAMP NEAR FALMOUTH, VA., Feb. 16.

On the 2d we received two months' pay, and there was a good deal of murmuring, as five months' were due. There is a rumor around camp that our corps is going to remain here while the rest of the Army goes to the South and Southwest. But Dame Rumor is a fickle jade, so we don't place any reliance in anything she utters. Thursday, last we started for picket on the river, in a heavy snow-storm. It wasn't bad enough to be out in the storm, but, as we passed the Reserve Post, we had such epithets as "Cracker Hunters", "Coal Heavers", etc., thrown at us. But it was through a mistake, they thought we were the One Hundred and Thirty-ninth (Persimmons) Regiment. We were on the reserve, at an old mill a little distance from the river. Very few of us slept that night, as the rain came down in a continual stream. I lay down under my rubber blanket to sleep, but I didn't sleep long, as the water began to get a little too deep for me. I don't mind a couple of inches, but hang me if I can lie in it six inches deep! Friday night, a scared corporal being on guard at the river, and thinking he heard the "Rebs" crossing, aroused the whole guard. Out they tumbled, with their rifles in one hand, their shoes in the other, and put themselves in a listening attitude. The moon now appeared, it having been obscured by a cloud, and revealed to their anxious gaze ten or twelve large musk-rats sporting on the ice. There was a general laugh at the Corporal, and the boys turned in to snatch a few hours more sleep.

Yours,   S. S.

March 1, 1863
FIRST REGIMENT CAVALRY, N.Y.S.V.

WINCHESTER, VA., Feb. 21.

For some months past, our regiment has been anxiously looking for the Paymaster, expecting him every day to come and pay us off our hard-earned few dollars. We have not been paid since we were at Fredericksburg, under General Burnside, in August last. But, the other day, the glad tidings came that the Paymaster was coming, with a squadron of cavalry as an escort. Yes, he did come; but what do you think he paid us? He paid us four months' pay, out of eight months' due us, and stopped our clothing-bill. This caused a great deal of dissatisfaction among the men; for they expected that the Government was going to settle up with them. Some men, who have large families depending on them, had only about $20 to receive. There was a good many who would not sign the pay-roll at all; for they do not think it is fair for them to pay for clothing that was lost in the Seven Days' retreat on the Peninsula.

Last week, a new Major presented himself to us, appointed by Governor Seymour, stating that his name was Tim Quinn, from New York. He is to be Major of the First Battalion. He promises to be a great disciplinarian; for, already he is making the officers pay more attention to their duty than they did heretofore.

I suppose you have already heard of a few Rebel cavalry paying a visit between us and Martinsburg some evenings since. As we were about going to bed, our Captain came to our tent and ordered us to saddle up immediately. We did so, and in about three minutes we were passing through the streets of Winchester, and then struck the Berryville pike. There were only about forty men of us in all, out of two companies (A and K), under command of Captain A. Jones. We had not proceeded far when we struck the Millerwood road, and, in making our way through the snow, our advance met a body of cavalry. One of our boys cried out, "Who comes there?" when the answer, "Friend", came back. "Stand fast, or I will blow your brains out," cried our fellow. By this time the main body of our fellows came up. Then we could see four or five men getting out of the way. Lieut. [William] Laverty charged on them, and received a pistol-ball through his leg; but he instantly shot the man who wounded him, through the heart. He fell, and never opened his mouth. There was another wounded, who, I learn, has since died. The very man we took prisoner handed over the mail. We recaptured the Assistant Adjutant-General and the driver of the stage, and others that were taken by the Rebels. You would have pitied the Adjutant; for they had him on one of the stage-horses, without either saddle, overcoat, or hat. He fell from the horse, and was run over by one of our men in the charge. It saved me about $8; for I captured a pair of fine blue pants, two fine shirts, and five pairs of woolen socks.

This week, there has been opened here an exchange office. And what do you think is pasted in glaring letters on the window? "Southern money bought here."! What do you think of that? We are all highly indignant at it, they will be under the necessity of opening it on a larger scale. I was speaking to a citizen of Oldtown, Md., yesterday, and he said to me: "If you ever are compelled to leave this hole, for God's sake, burn it to the ground, for it is the greatest den of Secessionists in Virginia." The people in this section of the country are very destitute, for starvation is nearly staring some of them in the face. Our duty is very hard on us now. We are out scouting every other day. The last scout that we were on, there was a considerable number of our boys frostbitten. There were some eight or ten in our company who had their feet and toes frostbitten pretty bad. I escaped with my right ear slightly touched.

"A'l.

March 8, 1863
THE RESPONSIBILITY OF THE PRESIDENT.
President Lincoln is an absolute dictator over the whole people of the United States. Not Imperial Caeser, in the palmiest days of Rome, ever wielded a more absolute sceptre than that which Congress has placed in the right hand of Mr. Lincoln. The purse and the sword are his; the liberty of the citizen is subject to his will and pleasure; and "from the centre, all round to the sea, his right there is none to dispute." Only the undisputed mastery of Selkirk in Juan Fernandes furnishes a parallel to such unlimited power. The responsibility in such a case is equal to the trust conferred. If the Government now fails to grapple with the Rebellion, it is not because any single iota of the power and resources of the nation has been withheld from it.

The liberality of the past, when the national pulse was at the first fever-heat of inexperienced enthusiasm, has been surpassed, and the future has been anticipated, so that the Government has had the means supplied for conducting the war for a year ahead. If, therefore the war is not now pressed forward, it is the President who will be responsible. It is incumbent upon him to use the unlimited powers conferred him, promptly and with all his might. If he is not seconded by his advisers, let him dismiss them, call around him those who will respond to his wishes. There can be no divided responsibility now. As the President will reap all the glory of success, so will he have to bear the undivided load of the obloquy which will result from mismanagement or failure. He has the power of a giant in his hand, and he must use it as a giant.

The war spirit of the North is again aroused; and it is in the power of the President to keep it up at its present pitch. A proper use of the means now placed at his command, will induce the people to back him up in solid phalanx, and cause dissension, if it exists, to hide its diminished head, and steal off, like Hamlet's Ghost at daybreak, before the glare of popular enthusiasm. All parties are again wheeling into line, and nothing but renewed mismanagement and new disappointments can chill their ardor or produce discord and dissension.

TENTH REGIMENT (NATIONAL ZOUAVES), N.Y.S.V.
HEAD-QUARTERS, PROVOST GUARD, March 2.
But little of interest has transpired, since my last writing, relating to Army movements, and, should the inclement weather, which has greatly retarded the plans and prospects of the Commanding General for some weeks past, continue, I fear it will be a long time before "Old Joe Hooker" will have an opportunity of gratifying his fighting propensities. In the meantime, however, he is putting his soldiers in first-rate marching and fighting trim, realizing, no doubt, to the fullest extent, the truthful maxim of a celebrated military chieftain—that "an army moves upon its belly". The order which he issued, a few weeks since,

allowing fresh bread four times a week, with the addition of potatoes and onions, has been implicitly complied with, and I am informed, upon the most reliable authority that whiskey will be served daily to the troops during the prevalence of the present inclement weather. Indeed, our Army has never at any previous period been better fed. Now let the Paymaster be prompt in his visits, and there will be but few complaints among the troops.

The provost-guard here, under command of Captain Charles D. Stocking, has been untiring in its efforts to suppress all unlawful practices. They have recently brought into camp quite a number of stragglers and deserters, and only a few days since made an important arrest in the person of a noted Secessionist in this vicinity, who was discovered by one of the guard to have a considerable quantity of commissary stores in his possession, which he alleges to have received from a Division Commissary. Captain Stocking immediately ordered his arrest, and sent him to the Provost-Marshal Gen. [Marsena] Patrick. If the stores referred to were obtained surreptitiously, the party charged will be promptly punished; but if it should be fastened upon the commissary, he will have a grave offence to answer for. Evils of this kind have long existed in our Army, and it is high time they were ferreted out and stopped. Captain Stocking and his guard are wide awake, and will not be slow to bring to justice all offenders against military law and order.

An amusing scene transpired in our camp a few mornings since. One of the guard was the recipient from a fair-one of New York of a valentine of huge dimensions. Chancing to be asleep when the letters were distributed, he was not present to receive the precious billet. Accordingly, it was placed upon a hand-cart, and a procession, headed by the Orderly Sergeant, having been formed, conveyed it to his tent, and duly delivered it, much to the amusement of all who participated. Not a little anxiety exists among the three years' men, as to their prospects of going home with the two-year men. Now, there are three classes of men to be mustered out of the service. Those who came out when the regiment was first organized; the old recruits who came out a few months after them, and the new recruits, or bounty men, who enlisted a few months ago. It appears that the old recruits were given distinctly to understand that their enlistment was merely intended to fill up the regiment, and that, beyond a draft, they would be disbanded with the regiment. Under these representations, many were induced to enlist who would not have joined a three-years' regiment. For the first few months they were even mustered for their pay as two-years' troops; but now they are required to sign the pay-rolls as three years men. Now, the question is: Are these men to be responsible for the errors of the recruiting-officers, and are they to be deceived and held for service? If so, dissatisfaction and discontent will be the inevitable consequence. I am sure a majority, it not all, of our officers view the matter as I do, and if the old recruits are not discharged with the regiment, the fault will not be with them. It would be the source of great gratification to our gallant Colonel, John E. Bendix, could he bring the entire regiment to New York; for justice, honor, and fairness to his men, toward whom he is devotedly attached, have ever been his constant aim. But should the Government see fit to separate his command, the decree must be submitted to. While speaking of Colonel Bendix, I may, with truth and justice, say that but few commandants of regiments in the service have drawn so largely upon the affections of their men as he. And this separation from them, which will soon transpire, will doubtless occasion many regrets. His name will ever live in their memories, and they will always be found ready and will sustain him in any position in life he may be called upon to occupy. How gratifying to the feelings of every military commander must be such evidencing of the esteem of his men! To him it is a rich reward for the services he has rendered his country.

Yours, etc.,   G.

THIRTY-FIRST REGIMENT, N.Y.S.V.

AMONG THE HILLS AND HOLLOWS OF VIRGINIA, Feb. 28.

You are probably aware of the fact that the regiment has been placed in a "light, flying division", under the command of General Calvin E. Pratt, our former Colonel. We have done no "flying" as yet, as there has been such an extreme dampness in the air, and so clinging a fondness on the earth for us (being afraid, I suppose, that we might get hurt in the operation), that we could not get a start, so that, since our last "three days' picket duty" (as High Private of Company I calls it) on the other side of the Rappahannock, we have not been rejoiced by any balls or Fourth of July celebrations.

We are very well contented as it is, for here we are, "reveling in luxuries" that nobody but some correspondent of the penny dailies ever saw or tasted.

On the 22nd, it was snowing as though the spirits of our Revolutionary forefathers had made a big haul of Confederate geese, and were working away might and main to get them plucked ready for dinner. Notwithstanding the storm the booming of artillery along our lines, about noon, showed both of us and the Butternuts that the memory of the patriot was yet green among us, in spite of the blasting sirocco of war, and, worse than all, party prejudices. I wonder that some persons did not want to know what party Washington belonged to before they would help celebrate his birthday, don't you? Would that we had the guidance of his wisdom and firmness now; would that the people would think and talk less of who is Republican, and who

Democratic, and would close their ears to the whining cry of "the President has broken the Constitution, and invaded State rights". You never hear a word of who invaded United States rights, thereby exceeding State rights, and settling an unconstitutional example. Not at all; oh, no! that would not fit; the shoe would pinch tender toes. I would like to get a choice collection of "copperheads" and "butternuts", train a battery upon them, and send them to "kingdom come". Any man that says "President Lincoln has had no right or need to issue his Proclamation", is rather soft, or too far gone in party prejudice to be cured. I think it was both politic and just; it will fight Rebellion with its own weapons, and if it is unconstitutional, it is better to save the Union unconstitutionally, than lose it in precisely the same manner. Were I to see an assassin about to strike at the heart of my mother, is it even supposable that, instead of rushing upon him at once, I would run for a policeman, because it was more lawful, and, coming back, find her weltering in her blood, and the murderer gone? So far as my poor judgement goes, I think the two cases are alike, and the people, rather than stop to argue about what is legal, thus creating divisions, ought to frown down all such twaddle, and unite for the Union and liberty; for, if the "chivalry" should ever get the better of us, God help us! We certainly have not much to be proud of in our Cabinet; but that is no reason why we should abandon the Republic to a pack of aristocratic "chivalric" traders in human flesh. I, for one, pray that the day is far distant; so distant, that it will never come; and I, will not only pray, but, as long as I am able, I will fight, thus proving the sincerity of my prayers. There is some talk of our regiment coming home next month—all talk, I am thinking. All our detailed men are ordered in to the regiment anyhow, and the boys are continually talking of "marching up Broadway", and other themes of as wild a nature. Hoping "your shadow may never be less", I remain,

SOL ID.

SEVENTY-NINTH REGIMENT, N.Y.S.V.
NEWPORT NEWS, March 2.

The Ninth Corp d'Armée has "changed its base"—from the Rappahannock to the James; from the mud, muck, misery, gloomy atmosphere of the one, to the crystal waters, silvery sands, brighter prospects, and purer air of the other—in a word, from the scene of everything that was humiliating in the past, to the starting point for victory and exultation in the future—is the change it has made; and that it is one for the better, "nobody can deny".

Six months ago, the Ninth Army Corps left Newport News for the Rappahannock. In numbers strong, and in *morale* healthy when it started, after undergoing the vicissitudes of three campaigns—under Pope, McClellan, and Burnside—it returns to its old places to-day, a mere skeleton of what was, its constitution shattered and its spirit—well, the "spunk" of the old corps isn't all dead yet, as the country will find when the hour of sacrifice again arrives. Six months ago, the country looked forward to a speedy crushing out of the Rebellion. To-day, it looks back, and sighs with a keen regret that Rebellion still stalks triumphant through the land, and that, of all the changes which have taken place, in the interim, none have been for the better, but all, politically, financially, and socially, for the worse. Let us hope, however, that the successes of the next six months may atone for the blunders and reverses of the past, and pray God that our hopes be not in vain.

The last of the corps reached Newport News on the morning of the 18th of February, the Seventy-ninth bringing up the rear. We came down in an old North River boat (the North American), and were two days and nights on board. A pretty set of transports the Government has in its employ! If a storm had been raging, I very much doubt whether any of us would have ever set foot in "Ole Virginny" again. Not much matter, I allow; but still, Virginia, bad and all as it is, is preferable to the somewhat humid dominions of Sir David Jones. By good luck, the weather, though rainy, was far from boisterous, and the asthmatic old boat managed to safely perform in forty-eight hours what she should have done in twelve. We are encamped about three miles out of the town, on a beautiful plain, within a hundred yards of the river. We are well pleased with our encampment, and will willingly stay here the remainder of our term, if circumstances will allow it.

A No. 1 tents have been furnished to the First Division, and we are now a little more comfortable than when in the shelter-tents. There is a rumor going the rounds that Gen. Burnside is to have command of this Department, but I don't know how true it is. Gen. Wilcox is back again in command of the First Division. We have busy times now—drill, drill, everlasting drill, four times a day. God help us! we have scarcely time to wash our face, and—but there beats the drum for dress-parade; so *au revoir* for the present. Yours,

COLOR.

March 15, 1863
SIXTY-THIRD REGIMENT, N.Y.S.V. (IRISH BRIGADE).
CAMP NEAR FALMOUTH, VA., March 9.

Since the death of your talented correspondent, "Non Com", of the Sixty-ninth, the people in New York hardly know how we are getting along in this land of trouble and mud. The shattered remnants of the Irish

Brigade are lying quiet in their camps, anxiously waiting for the order, not, as somebody says, "Onward to Richmond", but to proceed to Washington or New York (according as Secretary Stanton wishes) to recruit both in men and health. The three old regiments of the brigade, the Sixty-third, Sixty-ninth, and Eighty-eighth, do not now number more than 250 men fit for duty. This is a sad falling off from three full regiments that left New York scarce sixteen months ago 2,500.

The boys seem to be very well pleased with General Hooker's administration of affairs, which is no doubt owing to his kind and thoughtful orders in relation to issuing "soft tack" and granting of furloughs to the enlisted men.

There is nothing to bar the monotony of camp life except an occasional raid of Stuart on our right wing, and the regular routine of picket and guard.

It is the general opinion among the men that we will be on the move very soon.

R. G. H.

ONE HUNDRED AND SEVENTIETH REGIMENT, N.Y.S.V.
CAMP SUFFOLK, VA., March 8.

It seems very strange to the men to see so many officers sending in their resignations. We have but very few of our old officers remaining here, most of them, after being in the Army five or six months, think they have enough of soldiering to last them for some time to come. It is amusing to hear the men speaking of those same officers—the latter gentlemen saying that they would stand to their regiment and men until the war is over. I think it is far better for them to be at home than in the Army.

We have plenty of rain here at this season of the year; but, taken altogether, the weather is pretty favorable, considering the country we are in. Our boys are expecting the Paymaster every day, but yet he comes not. We are now over four months without any money. Some of us have not enough money to buy a newspaper. We get the SUNDAY MERCURY. The high-privates have plenty to do in the line of digging in the forts and trenches, besides picket-duty.

A HIGH PRIVATE.

March 22, 1863
THIRTY-EIGHTH REGIMENT, N.Y.S.V.
STONEMAN'S SIDING, VA., March 16.

Since my last, which was written from the vicinity of Poolesville, Md., our regiment has been engaged in a variety of exploits, too numerous to mention, but chiefly marching over a new (to us) field of duty, in another portion of Virginia than that in which our previous operations have been carried on in this State. I think our regiment, I think I may say all regiments, in the vast Army of the Potomac, have left their footsteps on many an inch of the virgin soil. After various marches and bivouacs, we camped near this station, and with Birney's Division (late Kearny's) were engaged at the battle of Fredericksburg, where, with our usual good fortune, we lost 135 men killed, wounded, and missing.

Some two weeks back, we moved our camp to the vicinity of Potomac Run as there are better facilities at that place for fuel and water. It is surprising how the vast pieces of woodland, that covered the face of the country when we first arrived here, have disappeared, leaving in their places an open country, like a blasted heath, shorn of all its forest grandeur. The desolation of war's footsteps is manifest at every point. Everything seems to be a prosperous condition in the Army since the gallant General Hooker took command of this Army, and he has won the love and the esteem of his command.

There was quite a happy affair came off the other day in the Seventh New Jersey Regiment, on the occasion of the nuptials of a young lady from Washington, whose name I have not been able to ascertain, with Captain [Daniel] Hart of that regiment. The event in which the ceremony took place was used at night for dancing, and was splendidly decorated; it was ninety feet long and forty feet wide—quite a tent. Outside tents were turned into dressing-rooms, and a large tent converted into a pavilion, in which a sumptuous collation was spread. In fact, as the song has it, "The tables groaned with the weight of the feast". There were some thirty guests present, a portion of whom came from Washington with the bride. Among the most prominent guests were Generals Hooker, [Hiram G.] Berry, [Joseph B.] Carr, [Alfred T. A.] Torbert, and [Joseph W.] Revere. In the afternoon, rustic sports were the order of the day, and at night a superb collection of fireworks illuminated the night-hours through. In fact, 'twas quite the night of the season.

On the night of the 13th, the party were invited to General Sickles's head-quarters; and the next night they were the guests of General Joseph Hooker. Bully for them.

There have been several raids made lately by the Rebel General Stuart, but luckily have not amounted to much.

E. H. R.

FROM GEN. MEAGHER'S BRIGADE
March 18, 1863.

Yesterday being the natal day of Ireland's patron saint, it was throughout the entire encampment celebrated in a truly jolly manner, especially among such as claim "Erin is my home".

It was left, however, for the Irish Brigade, under General Meagher, to get up the star performance, and that they succeeded admirably well, none who participated in it can deny. For more than a week had they been engaged in perfecting the arrangements; special invitations were issued to the *distingue* parties who are among us, while a general invitation was extended to all and everybody to come and partake of that jollity which is proverbially characteristic of the Irish.

The day opened bright, clear, and pleasantly warm, and so it continued until nightfall. At the time stated in our invitation we repaired to the spot designated as where the ceremonies were to be held, near to General Meagher's Head-quarters, and where round not only an immense assemblage, but discovered that every arrangement had been made by which the programme could be carried out to its fullest extent.

At the point from where the races were to start a judge's stand had been erected, and from which a clear and unobstructed view could be had of the entire field to be gone over. This was occupied by the judges, General [John C.] Caldwell, Colonel [George] Von Shack, of the Seventh New York Regiment, together with the three H's, Generals Hooker, Hancock, and Howard, and a whole host of Major and Brigadier Generals, too numerous to mention.

Near to this structure were two other raised platforms, one occupied by the band, and upon the other was some forty ladies, who had honored and enlivened and gave zest to the entertainment. The first upon the programme was a grand steeple chase and hurdle race, open to the officers, best two in three heats, for a purse of $600, being the amount of the consolidated entrance fee. When the word "go" was given, the horses started off fairly, and followed by some three or four hundred horsemen, all splashing through the mud. The heat was won by General Meagher's horse, ridden by Captain John Gossin; time made, three minutes and five seconds.

The second heat being won by the same horse, in three minutes, he was declared the winner. Two-thirds of the money was then handed over to the owner of the winning horse, while the balance was given to the second best, Major [St. Clair Agustin] Mulholland's horse.

The next scene enacted was another race over the same track, open to all officers, entrance fee five dollars, the winner to take the pot. In addition to the purse so contributed, the stakes were materially added to by the Major-Generals contributing a sum, in all amounting to over one hundred dollars. There were five horses entered for this race, time made by the winning horse, belonging to Colonel Von Shack, and ridden by Count [Gustav Von] Blucher, a Prussian officer in our service, and attached to Captain Thomas' Battery.

After the races were over, the ladies and Generals adjourned to General Meagher's Head-quarters, where for an hour they indulged in the agreeable pastime of a nice lunch, and potations of Irish whiskey punch. After this was over, the party again visited the track and witnessed the comicalities attached to a mule race. After this was over, greased pig, and other sports, were indulged in. When we left the premises early in the afternoon, the latter sports were in progress, all lookers-on as well as immediate participants, seemed to be enjoying themselves to their hearts' content.

Nothing occurred to mar the peace and harmony of the occasion. It is safe to say that there are none but will remember with pleasure their St. Patrick's Day in camp. We should not forget to mention that early in the morning a grand mass was celebrated. The priest upon the occasion, Father Dolan, being clothed in a surplice of a truly gorgeous and splendid appearance; this relic being presented to the brigade by some generous parties in New York City.

FOURTEENTH REGIMENT, N.Y.S.M.
LOWER BELLE PLAIN LANDING, VA., March 18.

A new system of things seems to pervade the army. Mules are being used to pack oats, corn, etc., upon— rather a new thing here in Virginia, though we've read of "pack-mules" being used anterior to the date of this Rebellion. Oxen, also, are to be used for the hauling of siege guns, and other heavy matter. Deserters are returning, according to the President's order, to their respective regiments. Convalescents are being returned from the different hospitals, and other members, who are on details or detached service, doing duty as oatlers, cooks, etc, etc., are also to report back, and negroes are to be substituted as soon as possible.

The system of furloughs have had a very salutary effect; for different modes are adopted to dispensing the "happy privilege". Some receive it by the most soldier-like bearing; others by favoritism, which is nothing new in the Army—the true soldier having learned to put up with such things without even murmuring. In the great majority of cases, the furloughed men are on time returned to their camp, so as to give the next turn his happy privilege. Occasionally we see in the papers accounts of the Army of the Potomac being so demoralized that it is not to be expected they can be successful. Now I will just give you the facts, viz.: The Army of the Potomac is in good condition, and ready to try old Jackson, Lee, or all the Rebel hosts that dare to come in their way. There is a feeling of confidence existing that even surpasses that which the Army had in Burnside. The Army knows the man, and is satisfied of his devotion and courage, and that if he once gets them going, he'll never stop until the Rebel Army of the Potomac is numbered among the elements that were. The precautionary steps that have been taken for the purpose of facilitating army movements, and adding to its strength, has also had the effect of producing greater confidence in the minds of the soldiers. The Conscription Act also shows the Army in the field that there still exists a real bona fide "Uncle Samuel", who is determined that the Rebellion shall "simmer down".

The continuous cry of "We're fighting for niggers!" is getting played; and many in the Army who thoughtlessly joined in that monody, are satisfied it is right to wield any power we can bring to bear, so as to weaken the enemy in rebellion against our laws and country.

Yesterday, cannonading was heard on our right wing. The Rebels have dared to cross the Rappahannock. There'll be a lively time if they only persist in staying.

                                                                                J. J.

TWELFTH REGIMENT, N.Y.S.V.
CAMP NEAR FALMOUTH, VA., March 17.

Stoneman's Switch was the scene of a sad and tragical occurrence on Thursday last, 12th inst. A member of the Forty-fourth Regiment, N.Y.S.V. rode up to a news-office on a mule, and purchased a paper. As he turned to leave, he was seen to spur the animal, which sprang forward; at the same time, the left stirrup-leather broke. The rider, in trying to regain his balance and command over the animal, fell to the right, the foot becoming entangled in the stirrup. The half-tameless creature which he rode, like all its kind, galloped madly towards Gen. Meade's head-quarters, at every spring lifting the unfortunate man from the ground, but only to come dashing on it with desperate violence. The locality over which the mule ran is covered with the stumps of felled trees, and the victim being dragged over and through these, made his chances of escape worse. Capt. [William] Fowler, of this regiment, happened to be riding by at the time, and through his means and exertions the run-away animal was secured; but the man was quite discolored and speechless. He was promptly removed to the division hospital, but breathed his last a few minutes after being got there. I did not learn his name.

The brigade went on picket last Wednesday, returning on Saturday, Col. Weeks of the Twelfth New York being general officer of the picket line. There has a great improvement been effected in the systematic arrangement and general details of this important duty. The sentries are posted within sight and call of each other, the outposts being similarly connected with the reserve. Thus should anything occur at any point of the line, a message to that effect become necessary to transmit to the general officer of the day, or to any other point, the first sentry sings out to the second, he to the third, and so on to destination. This verbal mode of telegraph is nearly as quick as lightning. Written communications are similarly sent. The first sentry runs with it to next post, and soon from the first to last. In this way, too, a message is sent through very quickly. I happened to come by one thus transcribed by Captain [Joel O.] Martin, Seventeenth N.Y.S.V., which came from right to left of brigade—a distance of four miles—in twenty minutes, and which shows not only a good officer, but really is too rich to send you a copy.

> "The sentry walks his lonely round
> Upon this cursed Rebel ground;
> And if a Rebel shows his head,
> I'll take the curse or shoot him dead."

There's one thing, sir, that I have often thought could be introduced into our army with the most beneficial effects, medals for battles engaged in, or some badge for distinguished bravery, good conduct, etc.

Another tragical occurrence happened in Griffin's Division—the first of this corps—this morning. The Ninth Massachusetts Vols. appointed this day for gymnastic and athletic exercises, horse and bag-racing, etc. The programme of the day commenced by efforts to get to the top of a greased pole; the successful one to be rewarded with ten days' furlough, the document giving that privilege being placed on top. Next some horse-racing came off, when the Doctor [S. Watson Drew] and Quartermaster [Thomas Mooney] of the regiment entered the list to test the relative speed of their nags. The starting-ground was the winning point, the contestants being obliged to turn round a pole on the way home. The Quartermaster had turned this pole on the backward run, when his horse came plump into contact with the Doctor's. The concussion resulted in the death of both horses, the riders being thrown violently forward. The Quartermaster was taken up lifeless, and the Doctor insensible, and it is thought mortally injured. Of course this unhappy catastrophe cast a gloom over all, and put an end to the sport.

                                                                      A—, COLOR GUARD.

FIFTH REGIMENT, N.Y.S.V. (DURYEE'S ZOUAVES).

CAMP NEAR HENRY HOUSE, VA., March 18.

We have (with the exception of three days picket duty every twenty) remained quietly in our camp near Henry House, since the last forward movement into the mud.

The men, however, have been very actively discussing the question, "Will the recruits go home with the regiment?"

Being a recruit myself, the question to me is an important one, and although J. B. Stonehouse, Assistant Adjutant-General, State of New York, says "recruits cannot be enlisted for the unexpired term of a regiment, but must serve the whole time for which they were mustered", I differ with him in his first decision, and therefore, in the cases of "recruits for regiments in the field" (as they were styled last summer and fall), I also differ with him in his second. My reasons for this difference of opinion are the following: 1st, a bulletin was issued by the War Department signed by Secretary Stanton, by and under the authority of President Lincoln, stating that all those recruits who enlisted for those regiments already in the field would be discharged with the regiments. This was published some time in July, about the 15th or 20th, and is, I have no doubt, the "proclamation" to which a great many of the interested so often refer.

This bulletin was issued, I believe, in consequence of the dullness in the recruiting business—to stimulate enlistments, and also in consequence of a communication from Gen. McClellan, informing the President that it was of more importance that the ranks of the old regiments should be filled up than that his army should be augmented by the addition of entire regiments of raw and undisciplined recruits.

For a few days the enlistments still continued to be but few. As soon, however, as the purport of the said bulletin became generally known, the recruits, so to speak, flocked around the several standards, and continued to do so through August, September, and October, all eager to do their country what little service they could, and all expecting from it (the bulletin) to be discharged in May, 1863, when the time of the several regiments expire.

My second reason is, that if the Government retains these recruits in the service, they cannot be held for "the whole time for which they were mustered", but can claim their discharge on the plea, "They were enlisted under false pretences". And if the matter were brought before the civil courts, I think there would be little doubt of the decision being in favor of such discharge.

It has been argued that the Government being much in want of men, these recruits should be retained in the service—they being well disciplined and accustomed to the sound of the conflict, would be of more value than raw recruits; and that by consolidation we could thus obtain several regiments of well-trained and acclimated soldiers. If my former reasons are good, the manifest unjustness of the above argument will constitute my reason for differing with Mr. Stonehouse.

3rd. It is true we have been under fire; have suffered much on the tented field (we passed the whole winter in shelter tents), and have been well drilled, but having been, as it were promised, our discharge in May next, we naturally expect it. If this should not be granted, we shall feel that we have been deprived of our rights—and when in addition to this we shall be consolidated, thus losing in addition to their anticipated personal liberty their regimental individuality, I doubt very much if the arguments of those who wish to have us so retained will hold good as to our being of more value than raw recruits.

In addition to this, the Conscription Act, recently passed, does not exempt a man who possesses an honorable discharge from the United States service. And should the war continue (as perchance it may) beyond the time for which we are retained, we, even then, are liable to be drafted for another term.

We are liable, under the same Act, to conscription in May or June next, and if we receive our discharges when we are, in my opinion, entitled to receive them, I have no doubt but that many of the men would re-enlist immediately, and those who were drafted would gladly serve their allotted time; they at least, would, if drafted, feel more patriotic than if treated as many suppose they will be when the regiment returns to New York.

Be the decision as it may, however, I think, for myself, that, although I am not receiving my "just rights", I shall still do whatever duty may be demanded of me, in camp or in the field. There are, however, only about six or seven thousand of us, and I doubt not but that we shall receive our discharge, even if they draft us again immediately—in which case, I think all will serve with pleasure, having been discharged, as per agreement.

Hoping to hear the reasons of the other side of the question, I remain,

Yours, etc.   J. T.

John Tregaskis, age 20, was born in England. He enlisted on Aug. 23, 1862, in Co. K, 5th New York Infantry, with the understanding that it was for the unexpired term of the Regiment, which was due to be mustered-out on May 5, 1863. He was not discharged with the regiment, but was transferred to Co. K, 146th New York Infantry and mustered out on June 27, 1865. After the war he was a reporter for the New York Herald. He died in 1924.

March 29, 1863
MILITARY MATTERS
The Soldier's Prayer.
{For the N.Y. Sunday Mercury}

Our father, who art in Washington,
Uncle Abraham be thy name;
Thy victory won, thy will be done,
Make Sister South loyal again.

Give us this day our daily bread—
Our crackers, pork, and beans—
And we'll shoot all the Rebels dead,
If you'll provide the means,

Forgive us our trespasses,
And we will surely go
To clean our guns and brasses,
And keep them always so.

Keep us from all temptation,
And give us all we need.
Then we can stand inspection,
And look quite clean indeed.

Deliver us from evil,
And pay us off in gold;
Then we will be quite civil,
And do not as of old.

We know you have the power,
The will, and also the greenbacks;
But some grapes are sour,
And we don't fancy hard tack.

Give all these wishes, Uncle Abe,
And give us victory, and then
United will be every State
Forever and ever, amen!
                    J. R., JR.

SECOND REGIMENT, N.Y.S.M. (EIGHTY-SECOND N.Y.S.V.)
CAMP ON THE FIELD, NEAR FALMOUTH, VA. March 23.

I cannot tell you how pleased every officer and man is out here with the turn events are taking in our own loved New York. The speeches of such gentlemen as James T. Brady are read around our camp-fires, and commented on with a pith and acumen that would do credit to Kit North, and are giving hope to the boys that they have still the sympathy of the good and talented, who, in common with the multitude, encouraged them first to go to the war. I never lost hope that this would be the case. "Excelsior", the motto of our flag, is the destiny of everything mortal, white or black; and every he, she, or it, National or State, that tries to impede this tendency to elevation stands in the way of destiny—tries to blockade the infinite, and will be crushed into nothing just as sure as God reigns. Lying politicians, "policy" pimps, and bloated huxters in human degradation, may make a fuss for a time, and may be used as a scourge to punish an ungrateful people; but they cannot retard the progress of humanity, or its approximation to the Infinite. They are less than naught—instead of being an obstacle they will be made a motive power on the onward track of the race, like the rubbish that becomes fuel. This is apparent in many incidents of the war already; and ere it is ended there will be much accomplished that was never designed by either those who originated it or opposed it.

Our regiment is still in the same place, and we are still doing the same kind of duty—picketing the Rappahannock.

Gen. [Alfred] Sully is again in command and in excellent health, which has a good influence on the men, for when he is with us we know there will be no *faux pas* on the field. The General has only to speak, and the boys will obey with a hurrah, for they have never been put in a wrong position by him yet.

J. H.

FORTIETH REGIMENT, N.Y.S.V.

CAMP NEAR BELLE PLAIN, March 22.

There is no news to transmit from our locality, nor even rumors of war; but there is one thing certain, that active preparations are going on for an early movement of the Army of the Potomac, and whatever may be the result, failure cannot be attributed to publicity, secrecy appearing to be inviolable, so far. How unfortunate it could not be kept so with McClellan's campaign, and what subsequent disasters avoided! The disaffection that reigned throughout the army some time ago has in a great measure subsided. A little improvement having taken place in our diet, and not, indeed, before it was needed; but the furloughs, in particular, have given, great satisfaction, and in no instance in this regiment have they been broken; so that with the growing confidence in General Hooker, it is very probable that you will soon have the news of some great achievement by the Army of the Potomac, to record.

Our Brigade now consists of the Fortieth and Eighty-seventh consolidated; Thirty-eighth and Fifty-fifth consolidated; Third and Fourth Maine; Ninety-ninth Pennsylvania (largest regiment out here), and the Twentieth Indiana; thus taking the remains of eight regiments to form a brigade only about half the strength of the original four regiments. I have only spoken of this brigade, as I can speak with more accuracy; and one-third of these, at least, are of the Celtic race.

We want no flattery; but still it is gratifying to the soldier occasionally to see his regiment mentioned in the paper, as well as to his friends. New York has been very remiss in this from the commencement of the war. Articles can be written on every subject, but the suffering soldier appears to be lost sight of. An occasional encomium passed on his service would cheer him and stimulate him to greater exertions.

The health of the army around here is pretty good generally speaking, considering the state of the weather for some time past; but now that the sun is once more beginning to establish his power, we look for more pleasant and cheerful times, and the roads will become a little drier as the Army of the Potomac once more takes its position for victory or annihilation.

Yours, WATERFORD.

April 5, 1863

MILITARY MATTERS

A WARNING TO BAD SOLDIERS.—Some three months ago, as will be recollected by our readers, Lieutenant Van Gieson, of the Sixth N.Y.S.V. (Wilson's Zouaves), shot Sergeant Andrew W. Ekens dead, at or near College Point, La., because the man was disobedient, disorderly, and mutinous. A few of this man's comrades have since attempted to take the life of the Lieutenant; no less than seven of them entering his boarding-house at one time for that purpose recently. Instead of killing him, however, one or two of them came near going to kingdom come themselves. In order to show that young Van Gieson was justified in what he did, the following copy of a special order issued in reference to the matter is published for the benefit of parties interested, and as a warning to obstreperous, hot-headed enlisted men who may be disposed to get into trouble.

HEAD QUARTERS FIRST BRIGADE, GROVER'S DIVISION.

CAMP NEW YORK, March, 1863.

SPECIAL ORDER

First.—At an inquiry into the death of Sergeant Andrew W. Ekens at the hands of Lieutenant Van Gieson, at or near College Point, La., on or about December 20th, 1862, it was found that Lieutenant Van Gieson shot the said Sergeant Andrew W. Ekens in the performance of his duty, and that the said Lieutenant V. Van Gieson is therefore justified in the act.

Second.—Lieutenant V. Van Gieson will return to duty with his company. Inasmuch as several attempts have been made on the life of Lieut. Van Gieson, the Brigadier General commanding the Brigade finds it necessary to make the following remarks:

It was necessary to kill this Sergeant, and it is a proper warning to all soldiers that their only safety is in strictly doing their duty. Good soldiers will rejoice that the officer did his duty firmly.

All officers and all good soldiers are directed to use the utmost vigilance to apprehend or to kill on the spot any of those lawless and bad soldiers who attempts to take the life of any other officer. The Brigadier-General commanding the Brigade desires to hear of the death of such wretches at the moment he hears of their apprehension. Extreme cases must be met by extraordinary means. This order is no reproach upon the soldiers of this Brigade, but calls on them to purge themselves of those who are unworthy the honorable name of "soldier".

By command of   Brigadier-General Dwight.
                                 Wm. B. Hunt, A.A.A. General.

NINTH NEW JERSEY VOLUNTEERS

FALMOUTH, VA., March 29.

"The winter of our discontent" is past. The sorrowful memories of Fredericksburg are yielding to high hopes and confident expectations of a brilliant campaign, and a successful termination of the contest in a few months. My spirit is astraddle of the highest henroost of glory. The men all around are eager for a fight. The general dissatisfaction that existed a short time ago, is nearly dissipated. Soldiers who wanted to go home on any terms, a few months since, are now red hot to try their luck in another great battle, that they may go home like men, if they ever go.

I like to hear the music of the cannon, it sounds like business. Give us another fair field, and I believe the tide will turn in our favor. Sooner than go home, as the case now stands—sooner than see the glory of the great Republic depart forever, I would sink to my eternal rest, with the roar of cannon, the crack of rifles, and the shouts of charging heroes, ringing in my ears. If the old flag must fall, let it go down in flame, with a jar that shakes the universe.

The beginning of this letter is a spontaneous outburst of feeling, the inspiration of the hour, and might have gone on indefinitely, but was brought to a dead halt by an order to turn out.

You will be glad to learn that my religion is proof, against awful temptations. A "widow" lady, whose husband is in the Rebel army, undertook to marry me last Sunday; but I passed through the terrible ordeal pure and virtuous, as Joseph in the Bible—had for the same reason, too, I expect; the lady was homely enough to turn a pail of hot water into ice, forty rods off, by looking at it. It is astonishing how virtuous men can be, when they can't help it. When I was a small boy, my father spanked me with the Bible, and my entire system was so thoroughly filled with doctrinal points, that I never fairly got over it. Religion is a great thing in a city, where you can't keep a cow. I do hope those poor, misguided "seceshers" will see the error of their ways, and come back, as the prodigal son spoken of in Scriptures did, and in imitation of the prodigal father, we will kill the old shanghai rooster and get up a Jersey dance. It is perfectly natural for a genuine Christian to look with compassion on a backsliding sinner, and that is the reason why I sympathize, in a certain way, with the deluded natives of Dixie. But they never had and never can have my consent to make such fools of themselves as to tear down the flag that our grandfathers fought under at Yorktown. It would do you good to hear me preach the Gospel to the prisoners, and explain to them the difference between boots at six dollars a pair in our camp, and boots at sixty-five dollars a pair in their camp, and ask them how many pairs of boots they can wear out while they are saving money to pay for one pair.

Yesterday was washing day, and I had two fine linen, white woolen, red flannel shirts washed, and Providence, as usual, had a fit of the tantrums, and wouldn't let the sunshine come out. There was no help for it, but to use myself for a clothes-pole, and put on a wet shirt, and let it dry when it got ready. This morning, the wind blows from the north, which is a great novelty here; for it has blown from that point only six weeks, without winking. The snow is falling fast, and we shall probably have to keep in our holes a few days again. If the weather permits, we shall, in all human probability, be under motion in a short time for some place. We have been furnished with new shelter-tents; we shall be very likely to leave this place now, we would rejoice for it is desolate and barren, and there is nothing to draft into the Union. We are now looking forward, and not back, and are determined to rise above the awful memories of the last year, and follow the old flag, with a light heart, head and tail up, wherever it leads. If I live to come home, I shall devote the rest of my life to the service of the church, smoking cigars, comforting widows, and going up and down, on a bender, as the devil did, in the time of Job.

S. M. P.

FIFTH N.Y.S.V. (DURYEE'S ZOUAVES)

CAMP AT POTOMAC CREEK, VA., March 26.

We came off picket last Tuesday, and found the SUNDAY MERCURY of the 15th instant in camp, containing the Report of the Military Committee of the Legislature of New York State. You cannot conceive the excitement and enthusiasm which existed when we found that the "two-years regiments" would not be consolidated. It was, also, a great gratification to learn that the people at home remember us, and are looking after our rights.

The copy of the SUNDAY MERCURY I spoke of having come to hand, was the only one in camp, and, I can assure you it was the best-read paper I ever saw. It opened at "Military Affairs" of its own accord, and you could tell at any time in what company it was in use, from the repeated cheers to be heard at the sentiments and arguments of the Report in question.

There cannot be the slightest doubt of the correctness of the deductions adduced by the honorable Committee, and the change of sentiment in this regiment alone, since the receipt of this Report is a sufficient guarantee of the triumphant success of the movement should it be put into execution by the War Department. If you could hear the hurrahs and comical cries daily put forth in this camp, you would agree with me that the gentlemen comprising the Military Committee of the State of New York understand human nature pretty well, and are doubtless shrewd observers.

From morn till night, nothing is to be heard but "How are you Thirty day Furlough?" or "Remember the fifth of April!" "By file right up Cortlandt street!" and innumerable other suggestive phrases. Again, the impromptu songs about going home are really amusing. Just as I am writing, a little knot of vocalists have struck up:

> "We'll all go home the ninth of May—
> We'll all go home the ninth of May—
> We'll all go home the ninth of May—
> As we go marching up Broadway";

and there is scarcely any popular song that has not been parodied to suit the occasion. Poor fellows! I am afraid the anticipation of going home is the best of the two, for after they have been home a few days they will long for the excitement of the midnight patrol, the advance picket (where you get so many orders, and the repeated one "to shoot any one not answering your challenge, and then call the corporal"), they do not seem excitements now that we are in the midst of them, but when talked over by the family-circle they assume new aspects, and then the thought of going back presents itself. Then will the wise forethought of the Military Committee be apparent. Let us hope that the War Department will adopt the suggestions of the honorable gentlemen.

While we are rejoicing over the prospect of going home, we are suffering great injustice in the transmission of our packages. I know of several cases where boxes were received by the boys, of which half the contents had been abstracted. In one case a pair of shoes were taken, in another all the tobacco (an inestimable treasure out here) and some pairs of socks were gone, in others underclothing, knick-knacks, etc., were missed, and nobody can find out who does it. It is understood that the Provost Guard open all packages in search of liquors, and it is noticeable that everything in the shape of glassware is broken, no matter what the contents. I saw a box yesterday which contained a couple bottles of extract of ginger, some black current jam, and other preserves, pleasant and useful in their several capacities, but distributed as they were over towels, shirts, drawers, writing paper, etc., you will readily believe that the "mixture" was more promiscuous than agreeable. There are so many Provost Guards that it is impossible to find out the thieves as we have to grin and bear. In the meantime, let all thoughtful mothers and loving sisters put up everything of a liquid nature in tin.

The weather is the same old story, lots of rain and plenty of snow, and consequently no "forward movement". To tell you the truth, no one bothers themselves about moving forward, but when it comes, all hands will move with alacrity. I speak thus, for I know that people up North think the Army do nothing else but wish for "fight". We are too old in the business to do anything of the sort, and take after "Fighting Joe", as you folks will persist in calling him. I see by the papers that we are getting fresh bread every day and are living on the best of everything. It is astonishing what news one finds sometimes in the newspapers. It is true that we are better provided in the way of rations since the advent of Gen. Hooker, but there is considerable room for improvement yet.

Affairs out here are very quiet, but we leave very strong pickets on duty in anticipation of another raid, but we have seen nothing as yet of Johnny Reb.

With many kind wishes for the future welfare of the MERCURY, the live newspaper. Good-bye.

FEZ.

SIXTY-SEVENTH REGIMENT, N.Y.S.V.
NEAR WHITE OAK CHURCH, VA., March 31.

Our regiment numbers now, 365 men, rank and file. When we left the Peninsula, we were reduced down to about 250 men; but we have received over 100 men from Allegany County. Our regiment has a great deal of duty to perform. We are on picket-duty every three days, besides daily drills; the biggest feature being a brigade drill, nearly every afternoon, under the auspices of Colonel Alexander Shaler, who is now in command of the brigade—an able and efficient drill-master.

There are active preparations going on for a move, the officers having received orders to turn in all their superfluous baggage and tents. General Hooker has made arrangements for each regiment to have two pack-mules to carry the officers' baggage and ammunition, in place of wagons, as they want the wagons to carry enough rations for the Army. Since General Hooker has been in command of the Army, it has improved greatly.

Professor Lowe makes excursions daily in his balloon, near our camp, and the opinion here is that the Rebels are evacuating, or trying to induce Hooker to make an advance.

We had quite a fall of snow last night; but it changed into rain, and the weather is at present quite wintry again. Your paper is more sought for in the Army than any other paper printed. It is like a friend from home.

DOZEN.

April 12, 1863
TWELFTH REGIMENT, N.Y.S.V.
CAMP NEAR FALMOUTH, VA., April 7th.

The President of the United States is down here with us, and seeing for himself the condition of that Army on which so momentous a future hangs. It is not saying too much, that he, on no former visit, ever saw it in finer condition or better fighting trim. Nothing has been neglected to render it as effective as possible, and every regiment bears a marked impress of this care and attention. Mr. Lincoln, I think, could not help being most favorably impressed with the general appearance of the men, and to augur therefrom the happiest results from the forthcoming campaign.

A salute of twenty-one guns announced his arrival at General Hooker's Head-Quarters, on Sunday last [April 5]. On Monday he reviewed the cavalry, and to-day the Fifth Army Corps, riding by each regiment drawn up in respective color grounds. It was at first thought the Army would be reviewed *en masse*, but this, I understand, is to take place to-morrow. He was to be at General Meade's Head-Quarters at noon. I think it was Charles X. of France who said: "Punctuality is the politeness of kings." Mr. Lincoln, I dare say, thinks the same of Presidents, for he arrived shortly after that hour. He was escorted by a troop of Colonel [Richard H.] Rush's Lancers, and received at Gen. Meade's by the Twenty-fifth N.Y.S.V. (Kerrigan's Regiment), as guard of honor, with the fine band of the Second U. S. Infantry on its right. General Meade, with Col. [Frederick T.] Locke, A. A. General, and Col. [Alexander S.] Webb, Inspector-General of Corps, rode forth to meet our worthy and amiable President, and tender him their respects. The entrance to Gen. Meade's quarters was draped with a splendid United States flag. Opposite to this entrance stands the General's tent; and between them was formed another arch, of which fell to the ground on either side in graceful, wavy folds. Mr. Lincoln was accompanied by Judge [Edward] Bates. On his right rode, I think, General [Alpheus] Williams, and on his left, General Meade. Among the Presidential cortege, I noticed Generals Hooker, [Charles] Griffin, Sykes, and [Andrew A.] Humphreys. All was silence until he approached to within some twenty yards of the guard of honor when the word "Present arms!" was given by Col. [Charles A.] Johnson, of the Twenty-fifth. Simultaneously, the band struck up a martial quickstep, whilst loud and prolonged vivas awakened the slumbering echoes of the surrounding hills. Mr. Lincoln did not stay many minutes in Gen. Meade's quarters ere he set out on the business of the day. The Twelfth New York was the first regiment reviewed. The men, holding their arms at a present with the left hand, waved their caps with the right, accompanied by three hearty cheers and a stunning tiger. The Forty-fourth New York came next under review; and here I may say, *en passant*, that this gallant regiment has lately received the new uniform of the Ellsworth Zouaves, such as worn when organized by that young and patriotic martyr to the Rebel Jackson's treachery. I have heard of Mr. Lincoln becoming fleshy, but to me he never appeared so cadaverous, or so like one lately from the tomb. It is hard to expect otherwise of one who, of all on earth, has, perhaps, the most care and anxiety resting at present on his shoulders. Mr. Lincoln, after his review, paid a visit to the division hospitals—an act of kindness and attention that none can more fully appreciate than the invalided soldier.

'Tis sweet to be thus delicately remembered in the hour of adversity.

A—, COLOR GUARD.

FOURTEENTH REGIMENT, N.Y.S.M.
CAMP REYNOLDS, NEAR BELLE PLAINS LANDING, April 6.

It is one year ago since we pulled up stakes and started on the spring campaign, confident then that it would be the last one of the Rebellion. Now we are preparing for another, with the same sanguine hope, trusting that this time it may prove a delusive one.

On Thursday last [April 2], our Division was reviewed by General Hooker, and every available man in the regiment was on parade. In heavy marching order, with overcoats rolled—for said coats had seen a whole winter's service—was certainly the best manner in which the regiment could appear to advantage in point of dress; but I think the addition of white gloves was quite unnecessary, and only served to mark a more glaring discrepancy when we were in a position of about-face from the front, for the Quartermaster, or somebody, has been very remiss in his duty, as our pants, when we are in the above-mentioned position, will sadly attest. Altogether, we acquitted ourselves in a very creditable manner. If we do not soon become "regulars", it will not be the fault of our worthy Colonel, for his zeal is untiring, and, I presume, his faith abiding. On the 10th instant, there is to be a general muster throughout the Army, in order to ascertain the strength of the various regiments, with a view to filling up their ranks to the maximum standard. We are decidedly adverse to a consolidation of this regiment with any other; but then we can have no voice in the matter. The Government assumes the authority of changing us from the Fourteenth N.Y.S.N.G. to the Eighty-fourth N.Y.V.; and our new officers humbly accept their commissions as such. The regiment, however, does not recognize the number; and wherever we are known, it is still as the "Fourteenth Brooklyn".

The pack-mule system of transportation works admirably, and is well calculated to facilitate the movements of the Army by keeping the supplies apace with the troops, however bad the roads may be. Occasionally, some very amusing scenes occur among the trains when one of the animals lies down for a roll, wholly unconscious of the contents of his pack, and which, in one instance, proved to be crockery-ware, and was attended with fatal results—to the ware, I mean. While returning from the review the other day, I saw a train of these mules carrying ammunition. They were at a halt, and three of them, at the end of the line, were gratifying their natural propensity (though they did not succeed) in turning over, owing to the size and strength of the boxes. Presently the train started, and as the chain tightened (for they were all attached to each other) the head of the first prostrate jack lengthened. A temporary check was the result, when each mule braced himself for the long and strong pull; but just before the second move, and while the teamster was rushing to the rescue, we descended a hill, and the scene was lost to view, leaving me in an agar of suspense. I am firmly convinced, however, that when the head of that train started, the chain broke, or that mule's head came off—and the chain was a strong one. With a heartfelt wish for an early, determined, successful, and final campaign, I subscribe myself, yours,

C.

NINETIETH REGIMENT N.Y.S.V.
KEY WEST, March 26.

Last week a certain place was accidentally left open during the night, and various cases of brandy and gin carried off to the beach and drank. About break of day one of "ours", whom I shall call Mr. Riseitbarry, was seen staggering up the road under the weight of a box. On finding himself discovered, he enjoined suddenly, and invited the crowd to follow him and help him discuss the contents, which he asserted contained the "real stuff". A glance at the label satisfied all of us as to the kind of "stuff" it was, but we kept dark and followed. After about an hour's travel Riseitbarry at length arrived at a spot which he thought sufficiently retired, and throwing down the box proceeded to open it. I will not attempt to describe his look of surprise and bewilderment when, instead of nicely packed bottles of Schiedam or Hennessey, he started back with horror at sight of symmetrically arranged bars of—Colgate's soap! With a yell he started for his quarters, and since then, if any one wants to be posted in language he has only to whisper "soap" in Riseitbarry's ear. Indeed, from his appearance since the event, I doubt whether he has used any saponaceous compound at his ablutions. He was going to kill one of the cooks the other day because when he asked him what was for dinner, he (the cook), by a slip of the tongue, answered: "Soap" instead of "Soup!"

What a miserably tedious life we have here! We are not allowed to leave the barracks, and the only chance we get to go into the city is when we are detailed for provost-guard. Our duty there is to stand on the street-corners and salute the officers as they pass, and fill up our time when "relieved" by arresting drunken sailors. Don't you think that a dignified and noble occupation for our "gallant volunteers?"

By the way, your department of Military Correspondence is a "big thing", but bad for the old paper dealers. By the time a copy of the SUNDAY MERCURY goes the rounds now, it is worn so thin, by constant handling, that a million of them would not weigh a pound. Fifty cents were offered and refused for a copy of a recent number—my excessive modesty forbids me to specify the precise date.

In my next, I will relate to you a little story about "Whistling for Yellow Girls", in which a certain Captain shouted, "Pat, you're well", in answer to a whistle over the fence, when—

But I must not anticipate.

It's a rich thing, and will be all the richer for a little embellishing from

Yours, truly,   T. K.

U.S. STEAMER STARS AND STRIPES.
ST. MARK'S, FLA. March 28.

Let me ask you, "What is the duty of a U.S. gunboat at this present time?" Does it consist of merely running about from one port to another always giving a wide berth to those places supposed to contain

Rebels? Does it consist of going into neutral ports, and giving entertainments to Secesh ladies and their English protectors? I will suppose, for instance, that you are appointed to the command of a Union gunboat. I say, suppose you should run your boat into (I will say) Nassau, and while there (with Stars and Bars floating defiantly all around you, and English niggers circumnavigating your vessel, singing "Yankee Doodle" in derision), you should invite several ladies and gentlemen (of more than doubtful sentiments) on board your vessel to dine, and also invite the American Consul to meet them—and when the Consul comes on board, and finds the company he has been invited to meet, he should naturally feel himself insulted, and tells you plainly that you are entertaining Rebels, would you become very indignant, and tell the Consul to leave your ship? and if he did not, you will confine him in irons. At this the Consul may get slightly incensed, and again tell you that he will inform your Government of your conduct. Still more, he calls you opprobrious names, says you are a disgrace to the American colors, and furthermore, he challenges you (in the presence of your crew and officers) to meet him on the beach. Would you go on shore and meet him as becomes an officer wearing the uniform of the U.S. Navy, or would you remain on board your vessel, only venturing on shore after nightfall, when it was safe for you to do so? Again let me ask, do you think that you would be doing your duty by the Government in using your vessel to freight oysters for private individuals?

Still another: If you received orders to lay in on a particular place, and keep a bright look-out that no vessels ran the blockade, do you think that the mere sight of some half dozen mounted guerrillas would be a significant excuse for your leaving your station and running your vessel so far out to sea that it would be necessary to have a good glass to discover a vessel in the channel even on a bright and clear day, and, consequently, a matter of improbability at night.

Now, respected Sirs, you may, perhaps, think that it is not at all necessary that those questions be answered. If so, I wish you would give them one insertion in your widely-circulated paper, and perchance they may meet the eye of some one who will make it his duty to see that they are answered in the right place. At all events, something of the kind is needed down this way.

Yours, etc.,   UNION.

April 19, 1863
TWELFTH REGIMENT, N.Y.V.
FALMOUTH, VA., April 13, 1863.

This morning, our cavalry, under Gen. [George] Stoneman, to the number of 10,000, struck tents, and commenced their march to Culpepper. The men carried three day's rations, and were followed with pack-mules, carrying five days' more. The cavalry is supported by a strong infantry force. The precise nature of the movement is well known. Should this force be successful in its object, I am given to understand that the entire Army will act in concert. Ere this appears in print, it is probable there will be something worth communicating, and the motives for secrecy at an end. The ball now may be said to be opened.

The Regulars are to get a uniform to distinguish them from the Volunteers. The Second Division of this Corps is mostly composed of them. They were paid off to-day and yesterday; so that we soon expect a similar favor. The past week has been warm, indeed, so much so as to render it a little uncomfortable, some finding it necessary to adopt means to woo a cooling current of air through their tents. The weather seems to have regularly taken up, and in a short time mud will be a thing of the past.

Rather a curious story is going the rounds of the camps lately. In the One Hundred and Eighteenth Pennsylvania Regiment—known as the "Corn Exchange Regiment"—is a supposed young man, who was promoted a Corporal for meritorious conduct at Shepardstown—being no less than saving the colors of the regiment. This individual was taken sick about a week since, and not being able to leave the tent, the doctor attended the patient there. When the Son of Esculapius retired, it was found he left behind in that tent two, where he found but one on his entrance. The second was a young soldier some minutes old. The young fellow gave notice of his arrival in camp with huzzas that would not be hushed.

Conformably to General Orders, No. 25, a muster of this army was held on the 10th inst. So far as this Regiment is concerned the following facts were elicited, viz:—Strength of Regiment when it left Upton Hill, March, 1862, 1,040; present strength, including recruits since received, 585; of latter number, absent, sick and wounded, 268; present for duty, 317. These figures include officers of line, staff, and field, and are almost equal in two and three years' men. Capt. [James] Cromie, one of our best officers, has received an honorable discharge in consequence of wounds, and Lieuts. [John] Scanlan and [John P.] Stanton discharges of another kind.

Every day lately brings more or less men from the convalescent camps. Some deserters, too, are coming in, many under the idea of being discharged with the honor of those who have been true to their flag and engagements. But those who have not come forward before the 1st of April will find the scales turned. Two who reported to this regiment behind the days of grace were sentenced by court-martial to serve a future period equal to that absent, and without pay. We wanted examples and stricter discipline, and we are going to have both. Some others, who refused duty, were fined each $50. This is the way to render the army effective and to put down insubordination, desertion, straggling, and running.

A—, COLOR GUARD.

Throughout the Army of the Potomac, rumors were rife about the "curious story" of a soldier giving birth in camp. Understandably, no mention of this blessed event was ever recorded in the regimental records of the 118th Pennsylvania Infantry. But, curiously enough, there is only one soldier—James Pickens of Company K—who could be suspect. Pickens, age 21, five feet seven inches tall, enlisted in Philadelphia on Aug. 11, 1862, and was promoted to color-corporal following the battle of Shepardstown. According to his service record, Pickens caught a cold while fording the Rappahannock River and was discharged by order of Gen. Meade on March 7, 1863 for "dropsy."

THIRTY-FIRST REGIMENT, N.Y.S.V.

AMONG THE HILLS AND HOLLOWS OF VIRGINIA, April 10.

The reason I locate the regiment as above is, that we are camped on such extremely debatable ground, that I cannot tell, for the life of me, whether we are nearer to Falmouth than to Belle Plain, or White Oak Church, or *vice versa*. I know we are among the hills and hollows, and somewhere near all three of the above, mentioned localities—that is as near as I can get to it. The last three days here have been, most unaccountably, three days of fine sunshiny weather—the forces of the Sun have completely put to route the rear-guard of Old Winter, and if Sol only holds his ground, mud will soon surrender to dust, consequently, "mudsills" will be in the ascendant. I have no news worth telling, still, out of the meager material I possess, I will try and extract a little gossip with our home authorities.

Last Wednesday the President, accompanied by General Hooker, reviewed our corps (6th), which is commanded by General Sedgwick. The President appeared to be gratified by the appearance of the troops, but he must have noticed the entire absence of that clamorous enthusiasm which the appearance of "Little Mac" always elicited from us; the absence of this enthusiasm is no sign of any decrease in our love and devotion for the Union, or any want of confidence in Gen. Hooker, or respect for the President; but, we loved McClellan, and we do still love him, and were he to return to us, we should go crazy with delight; we should absolutely fight, with pleasure, our Southern enemies, but, would rather let our Northern ones alone, as our "oil factories" are rather sensitive, in fact, almost as much so as the chivalrous noses of our Secesh brethren who cannot stand copperhead perfumery at all. It was generally noticed, by the troops present at the review, how thin and care-worn the President looked, poor fellow! I don't wonder at it; the cares of his office, the pestiferous political hyenas who worry him, are enough to waste him to a skeleton. Many were the words of sympathy spoken by his truest friends as he passed along their lines; and if we did not cheer as we used to, our sympathy was none the less warm for him.

There is quite an excitement among the men of our regiment, who were enlisted after the two years' service was abolished, as to whether they will be discharged with the regiment, or be retained till the term of three years is served.

The regiment is in the enjoyment of good health, if we except colds, which are, I think, contagious. It is really laughable to hear the regiment, when on parade or drill, croaking and barking like an assemblage of over grown bullfrogs discussing an exciting subject.

Our time is pretty well divided between drilling, reviews, and the like; the drilling is more for some of our ready-made officers than any others, I guess; one or two know enough for an awkward squad, that is about all. They have been sent here from that military hot-house, Albany. We have a "slap-up" Colonel Frank E. Jones. Were he not with us I don't know what would become of our military here. Wishing success to the Union, and the MERCURY, I remain, for Civilization and Liberty, at all times,

SOL ID.

April 26, 1863

CHARLESTON EXPEDITION

PORT ROYAL, April 17.

I had the misfortune to be a spectator at the humiliating drama in Charleston Harbor, and as you have, no doubt, been thoroughly posted in regard to it, I will merely advert to one or two incidents which happened there, and may prove interesting.

The Weehawken led the van in the attack, and as we well knew she would be the first under fire, every eye was fastened on her with an anxious, fascinating interest. When she had got within easy range, a small flag showed itself above the parapet of Sumter, and immediately the broadsides of Forts Sumter, Ripley, Moultrie, Beauregard, Cumming's Point, and Battery Bee were literally rained on her. For an instant our gallant little Monitor was so completely deluged by water (thrown up by the falling shot) as to be completely invisible, and I can assure you it was an instant of breathless anxiety to us. The spray subsides, and now, instead of water, she is enveloped in a cloud of smoke, and the boom of her "fifteen incher" hurls defiance and destruction to Secesh, and brings a cheer from our side, such an only a sailor can give. "Well," remarked a veteran at our elbow, drawing a long breath, "if she can stand that weight of metal, Old Galena can steam straight into hell, and shell the devil out of his den." The Weehawken fired the first and last shot.

The Keokuk still remains in the position in which she sank, and no efforts have been made to raise or destroy her. Four Rebel deserters came into our lines on the 15th, from Savannah, and gave information to the effect, that the first shot fired by the K. had entered one of the ports of Fort Sumter, and mortally wounded twenty men. They also state that the report was current in Savannah that the morning after the attack, Gen. [R. S.] Ripley transferred his head-quarters from Sumter to Moultrie.

It is not generally known, that Mr. Faron, Master-Machinist at Port Royal, advised the testing of the Keokuk's powers of resistance by an eleven-inch broadside from the Wabash. Had this been done, we would have been saved the recording of the most disgraceful affair which has occurred during the Rebellion.

Hurried preparations are being made for another grand combined attack, and Mr. McCleary, Engineer-in-Chief, has orders to have the Monitors ready for sea in two days—pretty conclusive evidence that nothing is the matter with them. Comment is unnecessary and motives of pride and patriotism compel me to restrain from saying more on the subject.

Yours, ever,						MARINERO.

FIRST NEW YORK MOUNTED RIFLES.

NEAR SUFFOLK, VA., April 18.

The silence of my reports for your paper will be, I doubt not, satisfactory accounted for, when I inform your readers that I have been an involuntary visitor to the Libby Prison, in Richmond. On the 2nd of April, our troop was detailed to build a bridge across the west branch of the Nansemond River, at a point known as Reed's Ferry. On the 4th, I was sent about ten miles from the camp to bring down a small scow-load of lumber to the bridge. Starting down the creek with four men. I had proceeded about five miles, when a most portentous halt! accompanied with the presentation of eighteen or twenty pieces of fire arms within ten feet of my nose, gave me a not very agreeable surprise. In fact, the "Rebs" had me. While loading the lumber at the mill, the very gentlemanly proprietor thereof, knowing that a squadron of North Carolina Cavalry was at a point about three miles from us, sent an invitation to them to come down and "bag" us. They arrived too late to get the Lieutenant, with his ten men and our horses, and so resolved to have us anyhow. So, proceeding down the road, he passed us as we were making our way through the sinuous windings of the creek, and ambushed us very handsomely. They treated us to a ride of some ten miles on the crups of their horses, and then, getting within their lines, handed us over to the care of the Fourteenth Virginia Regiment, of Longstreet's Army Corps, who received us very kindly. I parted with my captors with no regret save that of having been jockeyed out of a pair of buckskin gloves by a high private in a gold-laced cap and shocking bad shoes. As they (the gloves) bore the name of our good Captain, however, I have no doubt he has long ere this pronounced me a captain disguised as a "non-com", which so far as the Captain is concerned, and as appearances were, is far more complimentary to me than the Captain.

Shortly after, we crossed the Broadwater, and I was politely introduced between two soldiers into the presence of General [George E.] Pickett, who, I doubt not, was much better pleased to see me than I was to see him. He questioned me very kindly as to our forces, etc., to which he received respectful answers; but I think the information he got was very limited. From thence to Ivor Station, on the Norfolk & Petersburg Railroad, and we were permitted to rest our weary limbs for the night. We were treated very kindly by all whom we met, and received double rations before we slept.

The next day we were sent to Petersburg, through the streets of which we were followed by a crowd of half-grown boys, who appeared to act as though Yankee prisoners were a great curiosity. Having been presented, in due form, at General Longstreet's headquarters, we were conducted to the City Jail, and there remained until Tuesday morning, when we started for Richmond, and were sent to the Libby Prison, remaining there until Wednesday night when having been paroled we were started in the night for City Point, and at 11, A.M., of Thursday, were on board the flag-of-truce boat State of Maine, and under our dear old flag. That night we were, by arrangements of Major—, the Confederate Agent, and Col. [William] Ludlow, Agent for Exchange of Prisoners of United States, declared exchanged; and, having received no papers, waited until Sunday before starting for camp, when, receiving a certificate of our having been declared exchanged, we started for camp, and reported for duty on the 14th, having been made prisoners, paroled, and exchanged in the short period of ten days. Here we found intense excitement at the investment of Suffolk by the very forces through whose lines we had passed but a few days before. Before proceeding to other subjects, let me say that we were treated with kindness and good feeling by all whom we met; but the fact, was staring us always in the face, that the men who seemed so little like our enemies, and who questioned us so eagerly as to the signs of peace, were battling against almost starvation, and deprivation of every comfort, with a blind fanaticism almost inconceivable in men of such intelligence as many of them showed. Not an insulting word was spoken to us or of us in our presence, and yet the thought that they were in arms against the Union, seemed to harden us against them. The soldiers told us freely of their intended crossing of the Blackwater, and a probable "big fight", and yet, with the sound of artillery ringing in my ears while I am writing, I cannot believe, and venture (at the risk of being laughed at) to predict that the entire movements of the force under Longstreet has been made to cover the evacuation of Richmond; and, further, that when the force now before us has fallen back, it will be found that they have gone to the Southwest, there to hold out during the summer months, and until their grain can be harvested and let disease assist them against our armies. Another singular fact is, that the Government of Jeff Davis will permit its supporters, and even its officers, to depreciate their own currency by offering $3, or $4, of Confederate money for $1 in greenbacks—and yet these offers were freely made by some parties whom we met. They are the best allies we can have at the South, as they are toppling their whole base of finance in thus decrying their own money.

And now to later matters. Our regiment has been very busily employed, in picket and other duty, during the seven or eight days' siege; and on the days before yesterday, Troop E, under Capt. [Lemuel B.] Gregory; our own troop, under Captain [Cornelius S.] Masten, and one of our little howitzers—the whole under command of Major [Alexander G.] Patton—were ordered by the General Commanding to make a reconnoissance on the Edenton Road, feel the force of the enemy, and drive the force as far as possible back upon their reserves. Starting before daylight, they were joined at Fort Dix by a small detachment of infantry, under command of the gallant Col. [John E.] McMahon, of the One Hundred and Sixty-fourth (Corcoran's Zouaves), consisting of companies from his own and the One Hundred and Seventieth and One Hundred and Fifty-fifth. Having proceeded about two and a half miles out from our intrenchments, they came upon the pickets of the enemy and drove them a short distance back upon an entire regiment of Rebel Infantry. Major Patton ordered the howitzer to open the ball, which it did in a very neat manner by pitching a twelve pounder shell among a knot of them who skedaddled further back. Troop E then charged down the road, supported by our own troop, and, falling back, deployed as skirmishers, and some lively practice took place. Gradually we drove them back, the infantry cheering and pushing forward, and here another charge was made by a portion of Troop D, who being on picket, had come in for a share of the fun. This, with the effective fire from the howitzer, and the rifles of the infantry, forced the Rebels into a pell-mell retreat for some distance, when they advanced an entire brigade against our little force. Slowly we fell back under the guns of the battery, having succeeded in sweeping the Edenton Road clear of "Rebs" for a distance of over five miles. The loss on our side was very light; but from the continued musketry fire, we lost many horses. Our own men have to regret the wounding and taking prisoner of a Sergeant and Corporal of Troop D—one them a man not easy to replace, and the highest encomium I can pass upon him is, to say he was, in every sense of the word, a soldier. To those of your readers who knew Sergeant [John] Kane, this is well known. The reconnoissance was conducted throughout with admirable skill, and its success, with such slight loss, it truly gratifying, while it is not less pleasing to know that our Major gives the credit to Col. McMahon and the infantry, while the infantry say it was all done by the Major and his cavalry, and both agree that the little howitzer in charge of Corporal—was "a big thing". Since then, the old routine of picket-duty and an anxious waiting for the attack (which, as I have said above, I don't believe will take place) are all I have to chronicle; and I can only say, as I said to a Secesh in Norfolk, the other day, when the attack does come, if it comes at all, that by the time Gen. Longstreet does get into Suffolk, he will be sufficiently tired out to wait some time, before moving further. Of events, as they progress, I hope to keep you further advised, and trust soon to date my letters from within sight of the Libby Prison, but with the Stars and Stripes floating over me.

TROOP M.

SIXTH ARMY CORPS (BROOKS DIVISION).

WHITE OAK CHURCH, VA., April 20.

You are doubtless well aware, that, since the failure at Fredericksburg, we have occupied this portion of the sacred soil of Virginia as our winter quarters, with the exception of once (on or about the 20th Jan.) that we took a promenade for the purpose of trying how many inches we could sink in the mud, and then escape without the loss of our boots. Since the advent of Joseph into head-quarters, a new system has been adopted, to prevent the possibility of getting out of ammunition and supplies. We were to make a movement the other day, and each man was to carry 120 rounds of cartridge, and in place of clothing in our knapsacks, five days' rations of hard tack, etc., were to fill up the place—besides three days' provisions in our haversacks. Nobody can accuse us of being proud; for we do not rob our stomachs to cover our backs. But I do not approve of the plan; for Joseph will find, by the end of the summer, that however fast we may march and fight, we will be but slow coaches, in fact, only creeping. Whether the blame of our not moving this week is to be laid to the clerk of the weather, or [Samuel F.] Du Pont's non-success at Charleston, I will not pretend to say; but, as the old saying goes, "it's an ill wind that blows nobody good"—so it has turned out in this case good, for within the past few days we have had a visit from those whose visits are like angels, few and far between—the Paymasters. It is little enough that we get as individuals; why should it not come more regular? or ain't that press at Washington in good running order? Can't you lend them your "Hoe's Lightning" some day when they get bothered? or won't it answer the purpose? And now let me speak of something which is doing a great deal of injury to our cause, viz., the papers saying that the best men are coming now. Suppose we had all been best men, and remained at home, enjoying the comforts and privileges that are denied us here, where would our capital have been. Long ere this it would have been numbered with the things that were; and perhaps the North would know by this time what war is. Do not let these Copperheads go too far. A coward is the only person who would talk of peace now. Our division has many a debt to pay ere this war is ended. The dead of Ball's Bluff, West Point, Gaines' Mill, Fair Oaks, Malvern Hill, Bull Run (second), Antietam, Crampton Pass, etc., call to us, and tell us not to let the sacrifice they have made for us be in vain. We came at the first call, in May, 1861, from purely patriotic motives, and however the aspect of affairs may have changed (nigger or no nigger), our country still claims our undivided services. Do not let us be called to the rear, to keep rebellion down at home; for our men think more of a full grown Rebel, who has the manliness to come out in the ranks and stand by his colors, than of those cowardly curs, who keep up a running fire in our rear. We would rather have them in front of us, across the Rappahannock; then we would know what their designs are. As it is, we do not. As it is nearly time for the two-year troops in our division to think of going home, I would say, give them a good welcome. Let all good and loyal men grasp them by the hand, and thus show them that there are men in New York who, although not with us in person, are with us in heart. They are worthy of credit for the services they have rendered; and I hope it will be accorded to them. I would not be surprised if they met with friends who will do all in their power to deter them from joining again, if they felt so inclined. I would advise the Copperheads to be careful of their remarks; for you know the boys have been under military restraint for the past two years, and when they reach New York they will be kind of loose, and may hit somebody.

How the boys will parade themselves, as the song goes:

> "When we get back to old New York,
> Won't we go into beans and pork;
> Our friends we'll cheer
> And in lager beer,
> Drown times in Old Virginia."

I hope they won't forget the old Division entirely, and their rough but kind old General, [William T. H.] "Bully Brooks", but drink to the health of the remaining ones, not excepting us of the one-armed Kearny Brigade.

EMPIRE HOSE.

FOURTEENTH REGIMENT, N.Y.S.M.

LOWER BELLE PLAIN, VA., April 20.

The Fourteenth is now (after its thinned ranks being filled up again), nearly, if not quite, in as efficient a condition as when we were at Upton's Hill, or Falmouth. Twenty-six regiments of cavalry started off a few days ago, in search of something, but we have not heard anything definite. It is hardly probable they have effected what they went for, on account of the sudden rise in the Rappahannock River, from the rain which came on soon after they started. Great preparations seems to be made preparatory for some kind of a movement.

General Hooker's "orders" are to the point. Every soldier is expected to do his duty, and any lack of which (the offender) is to be severely punished.

The officers' tents and superfluous baggage are all being turned in, to be taken care of. This depot is filled with all kinds of "paraphernalia" of war. This afternoon, three balloons were up, at one time, with a range of about six miles, near the Rappahannock.

Each corps is designated by a peculiar form of badge; as for instance, the first corps has a round piece of cloth attached to the cap about the size of a half dollar (of ancient times, you know, previous to the days of green-backs and postage-currency), the second corps have an ace of clubs; the sixth corps, a [Greek] cross. The first, second, and third divisions of each being designated by the three colors, respectively:—red for the first; white for second; blue for the third divisions. This badge is a good idea, and will enable commanders of regiments, brigades, etc., to assign soldiers to their respective commands, as well as enabling soldiers to know each other, and their whereabouts on the march. Orders have been promulgated, that each man shall have eight days' cooked rations on hand, in haversack and knapsack, ready for a march at a moment's notice.

Quite a large squad of detailed men left this landing for their regiments, belonging to the One Hundred and Thirty-sixth Pennsylvania, and the Twenty-sixth New York. They left very comfortable quarters. There is still a little squad of eight representatives of the Fourteenth N.Y.S.M., Thirty-seventh Massachusetts, Ninetieth Pennsylvania, and One Hundred and Seventh Pennsylvania, all occupying one large tent, and under the guardianship of one of the most gentlemanly officers of the Army, Capt. J. D. Crittenden, of Missouri.

The soldiers throughout the Army seem to enjoy themselves well, playing ball, and other healthful exercises.

The roads are in a very good condition, but it is to be hoped when Gen. Hooker moves it will be at the right time. The Army if on the *qui vive*—in no hurry, but, as far as I can judge, ready to respond to the "long-roll".

There is considerable fishing done in this Potomac Creek, and we have had some good feasts of the finny tribe. We had a grand time eating shad, which are caught near the Maryland shore, across the creek.

J. J.

May 3, 1863
SHALER'S BRIGADE
ON THE FIELD, NEAR FREDERICKSBURG, VA., April 30.

This portion of the Army broke camp at 3 o'clock Tuesday afternoon. The Sixth Corps, General Sedgwick, moved toward the Rappahannock, the Third Division, General Newton, being in the advance.

To the five regiments composing the first brigade of the third division, was assigned the arduous duty of carrying the pontoon boats and placing them on the banks of the stream. This was a difficult job. These special engineers had to be thus detailed, as the pioneer brigade had duties similar to perform elsewhere. The regiments were divided, each with a given number of squads; these unslung their knapsacks, slung their rifles on their backs, and tackled the pontoons about a mile and a half from the river bank, along the line the boats would have to be taken. This was to obviate all noise, and the halloing of tipsy teamsters. A guard was left over the knapsacks, in which were stored seven days' rations. During the entire night we pulled, hauled, lifted, laid down, took up, and carried along these huge pontoons. Before the morning began to dawn, we got the last of them to the river side. So quietly had the movement been conducted, that it is doubtful whether the pickets of the enemy mistrusted what was being transacted on the Federal shore.

I have before described a crossing of the Rappahannock at evening. We are now to consider the operation performed in the first gray of morning. The mist was so dense that an object could not be distinguished from one bank to the other. There were not now, as formerly, many guns in position to protect the advancing column. As soon as it began to dawn, the One Hundred and Nineteenth Pennsylvania jumped into several of the boats, pushed boldly out into the stream, and sculled away. The movement was witnessed with breathless interest by the few soldiers on our side. The Forty-ninth Pennsylvania was approaching at a distance. Battery D, Second U.S. Artillery, was coming up, but would consume some time in getting into position. A half mile in the rear were the different brigades of the corps. The gallant Pennsylvanians reached the Rebel shore, jumped from the boats, many going to the waist in water, and charged up the embankment. The Rebel pickets were taken altogether by surprise; the shore was lined with rifle-pits, manned with Rebels, but the onset was so sudden, bold, and dashing, that the Butternut dogs, after firing a few ill-aimed volleys, fled in dismay. We poured into them a murderous fire, and charged home to the first line of rifle-pits, killing and capturing a large number of men, and two officers. Skirmishers were deployed to the right and left, and advanced with only slight opposition. We lost one man killed and eight wounded. The Colonel of the Forty-ninth and General [Henry W.] Benham, of the Engineer Brigade, were wounded—the former quite seriously. As yet, there was no bridge across—nothing but loose boats in the river. The details of the first brigade, with their rifles slung, endeavored to peer into the fog and mist from the other shore, and knew that the infantry already over stood a good chance of being taken by the enemy. At this moment, General Benham (the only general officer, and one acting Brigadier-General, Shaler, to be seen) rode up, exclaiming to the first squads he met:

"What troops are these?"

"Chasseurs!" replied Captain [David] Milne.

"Then fill the boats! fill the boats! Go to the rescue of your comrades! My staff, to the right, this way!"

And then a bullet struck him near the nose, just biting out a chunk of flesh. Two full regiments came to the bank at the same time, and in a twinkling were in the boats and across. The work was now complete. There was no cheering, no noise; the deed was done between the light of day and the darkness of night. Then other troops crossed. Guns were got into position, whole divisions hove in sight, and we had got a second time upon the battle-field of Fredericksburg.

The above is only one point of crossing. The telegraph must inform you of the others, for I could not be in two places at once. But yesterday the most serene quietness reigned all along the lines; to-day, the stern panoply of battle marks every field for miles. The heights in our rear have all been mounted with heavy guns. Three balloons are up. There has been no firing up to this time, save an occasional shell from the Rebels on the left. We are lying in line of battle, ready for the word. The sun has emerged from behind the clouds, and it is very hot. The entire scene from the adjoining heights is magnificent in the extreme. We are utterly ignorant of what is to take place, but look for the commencement of the engagement at any moment. This note is written in the midst of the field, surrounded by the general hubbub.

SERGEANT DRILL.

SECOND FIRE ZOUAVES
ON THE MARCH, April 29.

Yesterday, at 2, P.M., the Brigade left camp, taking almost a straight line of march toward the banks of the river. The sky threatened rain, and promised a disagreeable march. As we appeared on the little plain just ahead of our camp everything seemed to be in motion. Long lines of Ambulances were in sight, moving, apparently, in all directions. Columns of soldiers, half-hidden by the fog, went before and closed in behind us. Everything quiet and noiseless as possible. Hooker seems bent on crossing the river to-night or early to-morrow morning. We camped last night near the river, but not in sight of it. The fog is very dense. I think the enemy's outposts have no notion, as yet, of what is going on. They are but a short distance from us, but cannot see across the river.

Before closing, the news reaches us that our Division (Brook's) crossed this morning without resistance. To-day, we shall, in all probability, meet the enemy, for an attack. Great secrecy prevails, one of the best and least-practiced features during this war.

We expect to move momentarily, and I have to close this to be ready to march.

P. S.—2 o'clock, P.M.—I open this to add: Four corps across. Our troops massing on the other side for an attack. Skirmishing took place, costing us some men. A number of prisoners have just passed us. Balloon up in front of our Brigade. Third Corps on the reserve.

N. X. M—T.

TWELFTH REGIMENT, N.Y.S.V.
ON THE MARCH, April 28.

The Army of the Potomac is once more in motion, and ere this meets the eye of the public another page of its history may be written in blood. I have no positive information of any corps marching on yesterday other than the Fifth, though some say that the Twelfth also did. The enemy is on the *qui vive*. Our march, I hear, is toward Kelly's Ford; but, this, I understand, is merely a decoy, and that the real attack will be made at a point where it will not be expected. I am cautious of giving information on this head, even to the limited extent of what I possess. The weather was very fine when we left camp, but a rain-storm set in about 10 o'clock this morning.

A—, COLOR GUARD.

May 10, 1863
LETTER FROM NED BUNTLINE.
SUFFOLK, VA., May 5.

After a little over three weeks of investment by a largely superior force of Rebels, under the command of Major-General Longstreet, the advance of General Hooker has suddenly drawn away the Confederates from before us, and the forces who have held their own here, and participated in daily skirmishes with the enemy, are free, if permitted, to follow the foe or to give him trouble elsewhere.

Our losses in killed and wounded, in all this time, have been small, not over 300, I think. The enemy acknowledge, in killed and wounded, prisoners, and deserters, near five times the number. Our cavalry are now busy in picking up stragglers from the reach of the enemy—watching their movements, etc., etc.

The "Siege of Suffolk" is over. Viva! Viva! On Sunday, the enemy, leaving a strong force to cover their retreat, gave us the toughest battle of all. Col. [Benjamin] Ringold, of the One Hundred and Third New York, and several of his officers, were killed. His men suffered severely. The Chaplain [Francis E. Butler] of the Twenty-fifth New Jersey—since dead—was mortally wounded while carrying water to the wounded of his regiment engaged in front.

I enclose to you a paper in pencil, signed by "A Little Sesesh Georgian", which was found pinned to a tree near a spot where pools of blood and fragments of flesh and bloody clothing told of great havoc. The best of it is that it was taken from the tree by a big Union Georgian—Lieutenant Frank Boudinot, of the New York Mounted Rifles, well known in your city—a gentleman standing over six feet two in his boots, and well liked by all who know him. He is a Georgian by birth, married in New York.

IN LINE OF BATTLE, May 3, 1863

TO THE YANKEES:—You cowardly rascals, for one month we have dared you to come out of your boasted Sebastopol, but you were afraid. We will soon leave you to your robbery and pillage. *We go but to return.*

Did you ever take one sober thought? Why are you fighting us? Have we ever done you a wrong? You have pillaged, robbed, and devastated our soil. All we ask is our rights. Go home; no longer be led by the Ape whom you honor as President. Then you may live in peace. Persist, and we will fight you until the Millenium. You can never whip us. Our brave and glorious women will take the field ere that disgrace befall us. We are better off to-day than when the war began. "Perish us out!" Turn O fool! from your folly; we have provisions in abundance.

I guess you have found your thousands of Unionists!! Ha! ha! ha! Where do they live? Thank God, we are united and will wed death or victory.

Good-bye. I hope you may enjoy your life. We part friends, and are friends, save in battle; there we whip you.   A LITTLE SECESH FROM GEORGIA.

That the large force gathered here will be left idle, while the gallant Hooker is moving on, is not to be supposed. We have some work before us, undoubtedly, and I will let you know what it is when it is going on, or is done. Anticipation is not one of my faults in this war.

And now, friend MERCURY, Au revoir,   NED BUNTLINE.

Edward Zane Carroll Judson, writer, adventurer was born in Philadelphia, Pa., in 1822 and is credited with being the first of the dime novelists. In many of his nearly 400 stories, mostly penned under the name of "Ned Buntline," he was his own hero. In 1853, Judson organized in New York, the "Know-Nothing," or "Native American" Party. On Sept. 25, 1862 he enlisted in the First New York Mounted Rifles and became a sergeant in Company K. He was reduced in ranks and transferred to the 22nd Veterans Reserve Corps, and finally discharged on Aug. 23, 1864. On his return to New York, he announced that he had been "Chief of the Indian Scouts with the rank of Colonel." In 1869 he went to Fort McPherson, Nebraska, and made the acquaintance of William Frederick Cody, and claimed to confer on him the name "Buffalo Bill." Then Ned Buntline began a series of dime novels in which Cody was the ostensibly historic hero. Judson died in Stamford, New York on July 16, 1886.

MARRIAGE IN CAMP—Sketches by a Lady

WASHINGTON, May 4.

Did you not read in the papers of a wedding in camp? I was fortunate enough to be one of a late bridal-party. On Wednesday morning [March 11], we started from the Washington wharf, on the mail-steamer John Brooks, our party composed of a number of ladies and gentlemen, friends of the bride-elect—a merrier company could hardly have been found. Arriving at Aquia Creek about twelve o'clock, we remained there until one, when we were provided with an extra car by the gentlemanly Provost Marshal of that place, Lieut. M—.

The train reached Stoneman's Switch about half past two, where we were met by an escort of officers. The remainder of our journey was performed either on horseback, or in ambulances, more commonly called in the Army, "Uncle Sam's coach and two". Our road lay through every variety of Virginia land; over hills, dales, and desolated cornfields—the soldiers meantime keeping up an astonished gaze at the sight of so many females, thinking, I suppose, we intended going through the Fredericksburg campaign with them, and wondering, from the size of our trunks and amount of luggage, how we would compromise with their commander-in-chief about the twenty pounds of baggage allowed to each.

Upon our arrival at camp, every one proceeded to enjoy themselves as suited their fancy—eating, singing, walking, viewing the camp-ground, which had been tastefully decorated with evergreens; and the rapid completion of the dancing and dining saloon, that also being built of cedar, with canvas roof. The first night spent in camp! Well, girls, you should have been there to enjoy the sport. For my own part, I did nothing but laugh until daylight. Soldiers, you know, don't indulge in feather-beds, nor are bedsteads built for one well calculated to hold two, making it necessary to give warning when you wish to turn over to spare your bedfellow a disagreeable descent on the floor. Many were the cries. "Oh! girls, don't make me laugh so; I shall spill out of bed". Just think of it—the Staff head-quarters—three tents thrown into one, and ten girls in it. Of course, being females, we were reproached by all the heavy eyes next morning; as if we had kept any one awake! Twelve o'clock being the time for the marriage to take place, the feminine portion of the party were miserable from breakfast time. At exactly the appointed time the tent was thrown open, and the bride in white silk, with puffed illusion overdress, pearl tiara and bridal veil made her appearance, attended by two bridesmaids, dressed in our national colors, white, with red and blue puffings, and black velvet tiaras, bearing thirteen silver stars. The groom, with the handsome and agreeable Colonel and Lieutenant-Colonel of his regiment as attendants, joined them, in full uniform. The party, preceded by General Hooker and Staff, and followed by the parents and friends of the bride, made their way through the pavilion to the parade-ground, where the regiment had been drawn up in hollow square, or three-sides of one. The ceremony was performed by the Chaplain of the regiment, which added another one to the Army. Time will not permit me to speak fully of the reception, which lasted till four o'clock, and the cry was "still they come." Surely all the officers from the Army of the Potomac must have been there. Dinner came next; and such a one, O ye lovers of good eating, look, feast your eyes, for surely seldom are such tables set in the city, all cooked in camp, even to the bride's cake. Ask me what was not there, and I will look for a deficiency, but ask me what was, and the task of repeating the different courses would be too difficult. Take a look at the arrangements, two tables, so long you can scarcely hear from one end to the other; General Hooker at one end, with the bride and groom to his right and left; the remainder filled with ladies and officers; the Colonel, Lieutenant-Colonel, with their committees, seeing that all are served and enjoying themselves. At night comes a ball, which lasts till the gray dawn, then followed a day of receiving calls, at night, a ball at corps head-quarters, and so on through a week, visiting, dancing, riding, till we began to wonder if we were down to the "Front," in what many called a "perfectly demoralized army". Never was there a greater piece of slander given to the world. The slightest look, word, or order of the old chieftain is obeyed promptly and cheerfully. But everything must have an end; so did our visit. Bidding good-bye with many sighs to the spot where we had spent so many happy days, and thanks to the officers who had so charmingly entertained us, we left and returned to W., to pray for those we left behind, and that there might be *many* more such scenes.

N. G.

May 17, 1863
THE HOSPITAL DEPARTMENT

MANSION HOUSE HOSPITAL, ALEXANDRIA, VA., May 12.

The SUNDAY MERCURY, for some cause or other, don't come to us in time for Sunday morning breakfast-table, but comes good as sandwich between breakfast and dinner; and I assure you, that were it not for its relishing propensities, Sunday would be to us a lonesome day. There is now in this hospital twelve of the Rebel [John S.] Mosby's men, who were wounded in their late engagement with General [Julius] Stahl, at Warrenton—among whom is Captain [S. P.] Dushane, of General Fitz Hugh Lee's staff; also the redoubtable dare-devil, Dick Moran, is among the number. The Captain complains bitterly of the unmerciful manner in which our boys killed his horses, as he had four shot under him in his endeavor to escape. He also states that he was worth two millions of dollars previous to the Rebellion, and all he is now possessed of is a roll of Confederate scrip. The rest lies trembling in the balance.

Last week a soldier was admitted to this hospital suffering from rheumatic pains (contracted while in the line of duty, of course); and, being unable to walk, he was carried to his room on a litter. After undergoing the usual bath, he was carefully put abed. His legs seemed to be powerless; and, to use his own words, "Van legs bes vaser un t'other". The extremely-attentive and skillful surgeon, Dr. K—g, after a careful examination, pronounced the amputation of one leg necessary, in order to save the man's life, and gave orders to the Steward (who was at that moment vainly endeavoring to get the patient to swallow one spoonful of wine), to have the necessary instruments in readiness of the following morning; but, strange to state, and to the astonishment of all concerned, "Hans" disappeared during the night, and the only means of escape was over a fence twelve feet high. He was, of course, reported as a deserter, but has since turned up with his regiment, ready to take the chances of battle under "Fighting Joe". So, you see, Uncle Sam's surgeons are not all quacks, as some would have us believe.

Yours, considerably, P. C.

THIRTY-SIXTH REGIMENT, N.Y.S.V.

CAMP NEAR WHITE OAK CHURCH, May 9, 1863.

After considerable marching and counter-marching along the bank of the Rappahannock we finally crossed over. After delaying some two hours in resting and other military necessities, we marched to the front. (By the by, the pontoon bridge that our division crossed on, lay some two and a half miles below Fredericksburg.) And by the right flank took the Fredericksburg road. We were unmolested in our progress till within half a mile of the city, when the insolent foe became engaged with our pickets that had been previously posted. It took a short space of time to get the numerous batteries into position, and ere the bright Sabbath morn' dawned upon us, the "ball was opened" and the various instruments of death were on their deadly errand. We finally "arrived in town" at day-break, meanwhile cannonading was going on with a wonderful effect.

Now and then might be heard the faint report of some Rebel muskets, then the crashing report of our advancing skirmishers. About ten o'clock we were ordered to the interior of the city (for it leaked out that the Thirty-sixth was among the number to storm the hill.)

At eleven o'clock, everything being in working trim to resume our murderous work, with nothing with us but our rifles and belts (beg pardon; I don't wish to be vulgar, but I must say that we had our clothes on, too), we marched with a steady step down Hanover street to our day's work, confident of victory or a glorious death. As soon as we arrived at the foot of the hill, the Rebels opened their battery with grape and canister upon us, which told with woeful effect.

The Seventh Massachusetts and Thirty-sixth New York took the narrow road and ascended by the flank, while the remainder of the storming party took to the green field, and advanced in line of battle. Instantaneously, musketry, intermingled with plenty of grape, fell upon us. The Seventh Massachusetts, being ahead (although an old regiment, still new to fighting), having lost its Colonel, broke and fell back upon us, which, as a matter of course, compelled us to give way to the sudden pressure that came on us. But the brave and undaunted Lieut.-Col. [James J.] Walsh rallied us together, and showed heroism scarcely equaled in the annals of war.

The Rebels at first showed a stubborn and stern resistance; but so deadly was our fire—the righteous and sacred cause that we have espoused gaining the precedence over all our fears—that, with one superhuman-effort, we carried the hill, although the prize cost us most dearly.

Time and space will not permit me to give you a minute description of the fortifications; but, suffice for me to say, they are Nature's fortifications, and, if properly and carefully managed, could never be taken by any power on earth. There are three hills, each having fortifications independent of the other, while strong and impregnable rifle-pits stare us in the face.

Among the numerous trophies captured were several pieces of artillery; also, fair examples of Southern horse-flesh, and an abundant cargo of Confederate soldiers—all more or less seasoned from hard use. No sooner had we taken possession of the hills, when the cry became "on, still on"; and, without leaving any force to protect the hills or even guarding our left flank, we pushed on, reckless of all coming consequences, and finally halted, fetching up some three miles from the hills. Here we met the enemy, engaged him, and drove him to the adjoining woods. Night coming upon us, we bivouacked on an empty stomach. Next day (Monday) nothing was done, save now and then our skirmishers would exchange shots with those of their opponents. Toward night some severe cannonading was kept up, and the Rebels, during the preceding night, had so worked themselves as to get in our rear, re-capture the city and the hills, that we had left unguarded, and, by sundry flank movements, completely hemmed us in. Our only hope now was to fight; and, after a very severe engagement, we fell back to save ourselves from being all captured. All along the line of our retreat might be seen large and plump knapsacks that were thrown away, and I am not afraid to say that the Rebels picked up clothing and food enough to last them all spring and summer. We recrossed the Rappahannock at Bank's Ford about one o'clock Tuesday morning. We encamped about two miles from the river for three days, and finally started for our old quarters at White Oak Church. So here we are situated at present, not exactly in our old locality, but about half a mile distant.

In my opinion, should we have held the heights we captured instead of advancing, and fortified the position we gained, things would have went better.

Do not entertain for a moment the thought that we were whipped. We were only "out-generaled."

JERSHUA JENKINS.

May 24, 1863
THIRD DIVISION—SIXTH CORPS.
HEAD-QUARTERS SHALER'S BRIGADE
WHITE OAK CHURCH, VA., May 18.

The Third Division of the Sixth Corps, General Newton commanding, was this morning reviewed by General Sedgwick, Commander of the Corps. The weather was unusually pleasant and the display was remarkably fine. The regiments in succession cheered the General as he sped along the front, and their unbounded enthusiasm was indicated by the hurling of hats high in the air, and by the savage demonstration of the Stentorian "Tigers". Many of the fluttering banners were rent as though in a holy war, and some of the commands, in their thinned ranks, gave token of having stood, the brunt of the hottest contest. The shattered division fronts of the glorious Andersons' would almost draw from the beholder a tear for the brave sons of New York who are with them no more; but the cheers of the valiant remnant were as full of fire as of yore, and the Empire State have done Herculean deeds in the cause of the Union, but none can inherit a higher renown than the Sixty-second N. Y., the veteran Anderson Zouaves.

And the sons of Long Island—the First Regiment—who won imperishable glory on the Heights of Maryland, they were on the field to-day, nothing daunted, not shorn of their brilliant prestige, but rather with many laurels in their evergreen crown. There, too, with diminished fronts, glittered the gallant Chasseurs, confessedly the pride of the First Brigade. I have been in the Army two years, and never till to-day felt that exalted martial pride that was born while reviewing these grand movements at a distance. The solid divisions of old Keystone, the proud tramp of the Empire State, and the martial bearing of Rhode Island, the thrilling airs of the band, the time, the associations, all were fraught with events of the highest moment. All inspired the liveliest sensations of martial delight.

After the general review, the regiments of the three brigades were successively inspected in quarters by Gen. Sedgwick. The different camps are conveniently located among the pines; the streets cleaner than Broadway; the quarters neat and commodious, and nothing can be met with to mar the health of the soldiers. The General, at the conclusion of the exercises expressed himself to the different regimental commanders as more than satisfied with the general appearance of the troops on the field, and highly gratified with the aspect of the quarters.

"I don't care which side whips!" said a citizen of these parts to an officer—"I'm doin' a good business—it makes no diff'rence to me". This stuff was addressed to an officer of the First Corps—a burley hoosier, who clutched the wretch by the throat ere the words were uttered; but seeing that his dignity would be monopolized by giving way to passion, he had the fellow put under arrest, and the Provost looked after him. The Indianian had a brother killed across the river, and he was of the opinion that the man who didn't care "which side whips" deserved a home on the Rip-raps. The citizen has been making piles of greenbacks all winter, and was doubtless delighted at the pleasant prospect of amassing more. In the touching language of Smith, "There's a few more left of the same sort".

A new edition of infantry tactics has been issued for the special benefit of stragglers—those of the First Corps found in and around Fredericksburg, also the "beats" of the Sixth Corps, were organized under the vigilant eye of the Provost Marshals, each man was furnished with sixty rounds, and as many as were needed during Monday, 4th, were deployed as skirmishers, and had to stand the pelting of the Rebels as the latter gradually advanced toward the city. Some of these cowardly stragglers learned a lesson that day which they will not soon forget. They skulked from the companies in time of need, but did not the less escape the peril in store for them. Some ingloriously fell while actually compelled to resist the enemy.

SERGEANT DRILL.

ONE HUNDRED AND SIXTY-FIFTH REGIMENT N.Y.V.

New Orleans, May 18.

Since my last letter, we have moved from Camp Parapet to the lower part of the city of New Orleans, directly opposite Algiers, the depot for Rebel prisoners who are nearly every day arriving in the hundreds from up the river, where General Banks is driving all before him in the Teche country, scattering to the four winds of heaven the Rebel troops of [Gen. Henry H.] Sibley and [Gen. Richard] Taylor, who were concentrating around New Orleans, for a dash to regain the city once more for Rebel rulers. In this, General Banks has woefully disappointed them; for, as one of the prisoners remarked the other day, when landing, "General Sibley promised us we would be in New Orleans in six weeks, and here we are." But on the wrong side of the river. And such a miserable God-forsaken set of gray backed wretches you never saw. Texans, Mississippians, and Louisianians, but all alike wretched and miserable looking, with the true Southern belief that one Southern man can lick his five Northerners any day. But before they are long here, they will, like their Confederate soldiers (who are taking the oath of allegiance every day), find out that the Yankees are not such a demoralized rabble as their generals had led them to believe we were. Nor will they find the city of New Orleans in such a defenceless condition as they had expected, nor as some Northern letter writers here are in the habit of representing it. General Sherman knows his duty, and does it—he cannot be caught napping—his vigilance is sleepless. The city was thrown into quite an excitement by the news from Baton Rouge, that a brigade of cavalry had arrived there, footsore and dust-covered, with prisoners and booty of every description, after having cut their way for three hundred miles through swamps, creeks, and tangled woods from distant Tennessee; tearing up railroad tracks, destroying telegraph stations, burning Rebel stores, taking prisoners, and last, but not least, whipping the Rebels everywhere they met them, and spreading terror and dismay throughout the length and breath of Mississippi. They consisted of detachments of the Fifth, Sixth and Seventh Illinois Cavalry, and some artillery, amounting, in all, to about 900 men, under command of Col. [Benjamin H.] Grierson, a true son of Illinois. For seventeen days and nights they were in the saddle, with but one night's rest. Talk of the exploits of Stuart's, Morgan's, of [Gen. Joseph] Wheeler's Cavalry, why they sink into mere insignificance, when compared with this, the most daring of modern times. They had a bloodthirsty enemy in front and rear, and on each side of them, and yet they cut their way through all obstacles. All honor to noble Illinois, the valor of her sons has been proved on many a battle field in this war! The only exciting news in our regiment is the arrival, in New Orleans, of our old Colonel, who was and is beloved by nearly every man in the regiment—Col. H. D. Hull. Company A escorted 300 paroled

Confederates up the river, to near Port Hudson, this week. On the voyage they expressed themselves perfectly sick of the War. So they should, poor devils! for they were a miserable set. The good work of reclaiming New Orleans to loyalty still goes on. Nearly all the public schools have the Stars and Stripes waving over them. Gen. Banks's orders, that all registered enemies must leave or take the oath of allegiance before the 15th, is doing good.

KAPITA

May 31, 1863
THE MILITARY SITUATION.
There has been scarcely anything talked of, or thought about, during the past week, in connection with war matters, except the siege and capture of Vicksburg. All the information conveyed to our readers on Sunday morning last has been confirmed; and the final possession of the city—a thing no great consequence, beyond securing the soldiers, and arms, and supplies therein—is doubtless, by this decided upon. We must not be too sanguine about the victory until it is completed, every Rebel flag flying about the place removed, and every Rebel head respectfully bowed in humble submission. As a strategist, Gen. Grant is the superior of many of our Army commanders. He covers his lines, from front to rear, in the order of close column, and moves all his Army together by such advances as circumstances may require, pushing forward the centre, left, or right, to feel and engage the enemy. His tactics are of the order of Lee, the only difference being that one moves on offensive, the other on defensive principles. Grant does not allow his Army to be broken up into half a dozen small armies, like certain Union generals in Virginia, and then permit one or more of these detachments to be beaten in detail.

There is, however, one circumstance decidedly in Grant's, as it has also been in Banks and Rosecran's favor. That is, he is at a respectable distance from Washington. We begin to believe that if the Army of the Rappahannock, with its present commander, Hooker, could be transferred to Texas, and the Rebels, under Lee, would only follow him there, the latter, would be swallowed up in victory. If the troops scattered about on the Potomac, and on the Peninsula, as well as these in North Carolina, were gathered on board of transports, and carried within a few miles of Savannah or Mobile, they could land and take those places some morning, before the Red Tape had got through his first cup of coffee, or while he was wiping his spectacles.

In the latest rumors about Lee moving away from Fredericksburg, so as to make a grab, and dash somewhere else, may be relied upon, and it turns out to be true that the Rebels are advancing into Maryland or Pennsylvania, it may throw the grand chess-board operations at Washington into a series of chills and fevers, and before it is possible for them to recover, or find out which way he has gone, Joe Hooker may fall upon the Rebel rear like a sharp-toothed terrier, and have the rat of this Rebellion in a tight place.

Let us hope and pray that Washington may, for once, be so stupified by the chloroform of fear, that, while in temporary trance, our armies everywhere may accomplish Vicksburg victories.

FIFTEENTH REGIMENT, N.Y.S.V. (ENGINEERS).
CAMP BEFORE FREDERICKSBURG, VA., May 23.

We are sorry to learn from the papers that such a Secesh feeling exists in the Empire City. I think if our regiment had been home on the night of that Copperhead meeting in Union Square, somebody might have found us square on the Union, and certain D. B. C. would not have answered roll-call the next morning. We would have routed them very easy. There are very few men in this regiment but would a great deal rather march on that meeting of traitors than cross the river again; and the latter is their dearest hope, in order that they may show the world that the Army of the Potomac can and dare meet them at any and all times notwithstanding the faults of the Eleventh Army Corps. There is no doubt in our minds at all, if Halleck had stayed in Washington, the Army would have re-crossed on the left, as all our bridges and everything was in readiness for throwing them in the same place as at first. But Mr. Halleck came up and stopped the move, and there was not more than one brigade occupying those heights for two days after we recrossed.

Now, from present appearances we will be here the balance of our term, as the order to keep eight days rations of cooked grub on hand has been revoked, and head-quarters is moved off in the woods somewhere, to get out of the sun.

We have brushed our pontoons all over, to keep the sun off them. It is getting pretty warm down this way. Some fools talk about demoralization. Why, the Army of the Potomac don't know the meaning of the term. They never were in better humor, and certainly never wanted fight more than they do now. They will follow Hooker when or wherever he leads. All complaint is on account of the inactivity shown by our heads of the War Department in the prosecution of the war. Johnny Reb may whip us at every point, but we won't stay whipped. We can stand more defeats than any other army ever known.

Transportation has been spoken for us on the 10th of June, so we will muster out about the 12th. We will muster about 460 men, rank and file, and expect to make a good show, as the boys have mostly all drawn new clothes for the purpose.

Yours, as ever,					WOODSEY.

June 7, 1863
U.S. GUNBOAT "TAHOMA"
TAMPA BAY, May 10.

A few lines from this part of the blockade may not be uninteresting to your many readers. We are lying in a very beautiful bay, where the disciples of Izaak Walton can satisfy their pleasure to the greatest extent, as it abounds with some of the finest fish, such as mullet, blue-fish, redfish, sheep-heads, and hundreds of others that I know nothing about, more than when they are cooked they make a delicate mess.

Basking under the bright blue canopy of a Southern sky, gazing at times upon the wonders of the mighty deep, contemplating with wonder and amazement the vast and mysterious treasures that must forever lie concealed within its briny bosom, I am involuntarily bound to exclaim, in the language of Cowper:

> "There lives and works a soul in all things,
> And that soul is God".

And so manifest is the assertion in the universal laws of Nature:

> That e'en the wild Indian, with untutored mind,
> Sees God in clouds and hears Him in the wind.

The dreariness and monotony of a life at sea we try as well as possible to destroy, and hundreds are the ways we rig to get up a little fun. However, we have a violin and a first-rate violinist on board, and many a weary hour he whiles away for us. In the evenings he comes on deck, when we gather around, some forming a set for a cotillion; but, Mr. Editor, we miss the kind and loving embraces of those fair friends from whom we parted in New York and with whom we used to lead in the happy festive ball to gay and mirthful measures. To supply the deficiency—if it were possible to do so—we represent, in turn, our once gay partners; so that it is nothing uncommon to see young men, who sport moustaches and imperials, personifying respectfully Miss Moore, Miss Murphy, Miss Magennis, and Miss McCann, etc.

There are many abuses in the Navy, of which I would like to inform you; but I think I hear the cries of merciful critics shouting, "What does an old 'shell-back' know about such things?" And, believe me, Sir, we are not permitted to know anything of such matters. If we were, "a man could be a man for a' that", and not what he is at present—a slave to every whim and caprice of his superior officer; and if he dares to lift his voice to expose his wrongs, he is at once impeached as a mutineer. I feel it my duty to speak of the majority of the officers of the Tahoma, especially Captain Semmes, in terms of the highest respect and regard; but the screw is loose in other vessels, and it is for them that I would speak.

We have lately captured a little schooner, loaded with cotton and turpentine. She is rigged out of one of Francis' patent metallic life-boats, and, in herself, is quite a curiosity. Her captain says he ran out of St. Marks; but I think he came out of Clearwater. It is a noticeable fact the Secesh will not risk large vessels now, the way they have formerly. They know that our blockaders are on the alert, and, of course, they naturally calculate, if they fit out a large vessel, the chances are against her getting clear, so that the loss is too heavy on their side, while our gain is increased; and, by sending out little vessels, if one in five gets free, it about pays their expenses, and with this they are content.

LARRY MOORE.

MILITARY MATTERS
A HEAVY LOAD.—In the year 1862, the U. S. Army used up 16 tons of bullets. What a pity one didn't hit Jeff Davis.

June 14, 1863
FOURTH NEW YORK INDEPENDENT BATTERY
CAMP NEAR BELLE PLAINS, June 8.

During the past week, the dull routine of camp-life was interrupted by stormy rumors of work ahead. Orders soon followed, and the Army was put in readiness for a move—a quick one, if necessary, judging from the way surplus clothing, etc., was turned in. Speaking of clothing being turned in—of clothing lost on nearly every march—one treats of an item which, being considered in a pecuniary light, is a matter of considerable interest to our men. In camp, inspectors and company officers are exceedingly anxious to have the men look well; and then health, etc., makes it almost imperative for each man to have at least two complete changes. Orders came to move, and the soldiers are ordered to carry so many pounds of baggage;

and the amount will in no manner allow of the extra clothing being transported with the troops, hence the rest amount of clothing which marks the path of the Army of the Potomac, and which the soldiers are obliged to pay for. I see that strong inducements, in shape of bounty, are being held out to returned soldiers, to induce them to re-enlist. A stronger inducement could be offered, by establishing a liberal system of furloughs. No man who has a family or loved ones at home, cares about banishing himself from their presence for three years or during the war. One-half the dissatisfaction and two-thirds of the desertions in the Army can be traced directly to this despotic-system of holding men. Considerable fault has been found against certain officers for stealing soldiers' packages, which have been sent from home. Of late this plundering has been carried on in the most barefaced manner possible. We are on the track of several of these miscreants, and as soon as sufficient evidence has been obtained, will give the benefit of a notice, free gratis.

This battery is at present commanded by Lieut. Wm. McLean, an efficient and gentlemanly officer. Orderly Wm. Sands has been promoted, and will make a popular officer. We are at present pleasantly encamped on the edge of an oak wood; and by discussing the news in the papers, playing ball, exercising horse, praying for the paymaster, breaking up hard tack—our most laborious work—can manage to wait for "something to turn up".

PRONO.

June 21, 1863
U.S STEAM GUNBOAT KANAWHA
OFF MOBILE, ALA., June 3.

There have been a great many prizes gobbled up by this fleet with the last two months, we having the good luck to grapple on to five of them. Besides these, we have shares in four others, and last year we took seven (but we have not been paid for some of them), making in all sixteen; which, is not a bad seventeen months' work. Hereafter, the prize-money is to be put to our accounts and paid us on our discharge; so when we boys get home, we will have quite a pile of money due us. "So stand clear, or we will knock you down with a roll of greenbacks." Who wouldn't be on the blockade. "Dat's what's de matter."

We were in Pensacola last week for coal. We heard a rumor there that the Monitors are coming around here to take Mobile. The only foundation it has is, that the steamer Thames is there, loaded with fifteen-inch shell. I will not believe it until I see them here.

The forts in Pensacola harbor are garrisoned by the Seventh Vermont and Fifteenth Maine. All the contrabands are employed in digging a ditch outside off Fort Barraccas. A great many of them run back to their masters. They had been living on Uncle Sam's rations for some time; but when he wanted them to work, they thought it about time to "cut mud". Some of the officers of the Fifteenth Maine are organizing a colored regiment. Very near all the white men in the place are working in the Navy Yard. They seem to be very good Union men.

The Rebels sent out a flag of truce the other day. The gunboat Kennebec has been sent to New Orleans, to communicate with Admiral Farragut, who is at that place. I was unable to learn its purport.

The following vessels are blockading this port, viz.: Colorado, Lackawanna, R. R. Cuyler, Pocahontas, Arostook, Kennebec, Kanawaha, Pembina, Pinola. The two last-named are being repaired—the former in Pensacola, and the latter in Ship Island.

Billy Travis, of Hose No. 55; Billy Andrews, of Engine No. 30; and Jim Douglass, of Engine No. 21, send their respects to the boys of their companies.

Yours, truly,   JOHNNY HAULTAUT.

June 28, 1863

THE MILITARY SITUATION; INCOMPETENCY OF HOOKER.

It is not necessary to wait for the final upshot of General Lee's present movements to estimate the character of Hooker as a military commander. It was clearly anticipated here at the North, several weeks ago—indeed, immediately after the Battle of Chancellosrville—that Lee would soon make an offensive demonstration northward. Not only was this case, but the correspondents of the English papers writing home expressed the conviction that the next move of the Rebels would be an invasion of the North. The reduction of our armies by the casualties of war, the expiration of the term of enlistment of so large a number of the soldiers, and the contempt entertained by the Confederate General of Hooker's abilities, all conspired to warn our authorities that an aggressive demonstration might be expected. The probability that Vicksburg will fall, also rendered it necessary for the Rebels to set off the disaster by a show of carrying the war into the Northern States. Moreover, their necessities required a foray into the fertile and hitherto unmolested valleys of Pennsylvania, now waving with the riches of a golden harvest. But all these premonitory considerations were thrown on Hooker, who conducted a vigorous war in the newspapers, while he left Lee to pursue his plans at leisure.

An outcry was raised against McClellan, when he drove back this same General Lee at the battle of

Antietam, because he did not gobble up the whole of his army. But McClellan met him on the threshold of the Northern invasion he had planned, nipped it in the bud, and, in promulgating the result, announced, as one of its consequences, that Maryland and Pennsylvania were safe. If it was considered a lame and impotent conclusion on the part of McClellan, what can be said of Hooker, who allowed the North to be invaded without interposing a solitary obstacle to protect it? His incompetency has been proved by events too serious to allow of repetition. The fate of the country may be decided by the events of a day, and this is not a time to stand upon a ceremony. Let the Government remove Hooker at once and place the Army of the Potomac under command of Heintzelman, or some General in whom the soldiers and the people will have confidence. Unless the change is made, at once it may very soon be too late.

THIRTY-SIXTH REGIMENT, N.Y.S.V.
CAMP NEAR FAIRFAX COURT-HOUSE, June 23.

With the audacity of Paul Pry, I would exclaim: "I hope I don't intrude?" In my last letter to you I thought, ere this, I would have dissolved partnership with Uncle Sam and retired from the public arena, contented with my active life for the last two years back; but, by some mismanagement on the part of the ruling officers of the regiment, our term of service is, most unfortunately, prolonged till the fourth day of July. Without any further introduction on my part, I may again resume my correspondence, which has always afforded me unspeakable joy to communicate at all times.

Without going into minute details of our operations on the Rappahannock, I will merely remark, that we (Sixth Corps) crossed without much opposition. Gen. [Albion P.] Howe, of the Second Division (white cross), led the advance, and drove Mr. John Reb from their useless rifle-pits. The Second Division was relieved by the First (General [Horatio] Wright), who remained over for three days; and they, in return, were relieved by the gallant Third Division. They had Major-General Newton commanding. The impregnable rifle-pits and well constructed redoubts were thrown up by this gallant division. The Third Division, formerly commanded by Gens. Buell, Keys, and Couch, is everywhere recognized as the flower of the Army of the Potomac, and, with such a disciplinarian as Newton at its head, it will be able to challenge the whole military world (although we must soon take leave of it).

On Saturday night (June 13th), we recrossed, for the third, and, I hope, the last time, that memorable river. During the first part of the day the rain began to descend, both on the just and the unjust, and by the time we were to assume the defensive (for it is insubordination and disloyal to say skedaddle) the sacred soil was pretty well "kneeded". But patience is a good thing. We halted for the night near Falmouth, to rest our wearied bones preparatory to defensive movement. Sunday morning, bright and early, we took up our line of march, which was very pleasant; that is, considering the way we are steering our course.

Some persons who had more wit than talent very cleverly remarked: "that as our term of 'sogering' was nearly up, that the whole Army of the Potomac, with Hooker as Chief Marshal, and the other corps generals as his assistants, were escorting us to the cars."

It was well put—but I can't see the point.

JERSHUA JENKINS

FOURTEENTH REGIMENT N.Y.S.N.G.
BIVOUAC NEAR THE POTOMAC
TEN MILES FROM LEESBURG, June 23.

On the night of the 11th inst., positive orders came to Camp Wadsworth for a march at three o'clock the following morning. At about eleven o'clock, I was relieved from guard, when I went to my quarters and prepared for the march. I got about one hour's rest, and was aroused, and at the appointed hour, the regiment was on the march. The morning air was pretty close, and when the sun came up, it told pretty heavily on the energies of the trampers. Soon blankets, overcoats, and other articles, even to writing materials—in fact, everything that the soldiers could at all dispense with—were thrown away, until the road was literally strewn with the paraphernalia of a soldier's camp necessities.

During the march, after having made about twelve miles, the unfortunate deserter, Private Wood, was shot according to sentence from a general court-martial. From this sad scene, we were marched on our journey, and instead of the joke, the song, or the merry laugh as we wended our way, all eyes were cast down, and not a word seemed to be spoken. It really was the stillness of death, and showed that each heart was touched.

We halted after a very tedious march at a mill-site on a stream—a well known bivouacking locality. Here was a general bathing-time, and after cooking our coffee, we had a rest, which was much needed for we had marched twenty-two miles that day, having been on the go since three o'clock, A.M.

Next morning, we were aroused at three o'clock, and Company I acted as rearguard. The weather was very warm, and the roads were dusty; and as usual in our marches through Virginia, there was a great scarcity of water. Toward night, we were encamped near Bealton. We had very heavy marching next day and the following night; and on the afternoon of the 15th, arrived at Centreville Heights, worn out, where we remained until three o'clock, A.M., of the 17th, during which time we recuperated our energies and feelings considerably—having had sufficient time to wash our clothes and eat substantial and properly-cooked food. We started at about three o'clock, and this day being about the hottest, and besides being marched the roughest, it resulted in hundreds of this small corps being left behind, from exhaustion, sickness, and sunstroke. Water was very scarce, and our rests very short and seldom—it would seem without much regard for humanity. Several have been laid up from the effects of the march of the 17th of June. Captain [Adolphus W.] Gill, of "I" Company, fell from sunstroke, and is reported that several have died from the effects of that march. The day afterward, ambulances were sent out to pick up the men thus affected.

For the past two or three days, considerable cannonading has been heard as within a very short distance from here. We have had considerable rain this last day or two, and the boys have been nearly drowned, to escape which many went up in the middle of the night to the top of the high R. R. embankment, while the rain was pouring down in torrents. Many have had to pay pretty dear for their persistence in striving to keep up on the march, and in throwing away their overcoats and blankets, because they have deprived themselves of covering, which is necessary in this climate of heavy fogs and cold nights. The weather is now quite warm.

J. J.

NAVAL ITEMS

THE FAMOUS WEEHAWKEN, THE CAPTURE OF THE REBEL RAM, ATLANTA.—As the famous iron clad steamer Weehawken has gained imperishable fame under her gallant commander, Captain John Rogers, and his officers, we subjoin a brief outline of particulars respecting this indomitable iron clad Ericsson vessel, which have not already appeared in print.

The Ericsson iron-clad-steamer above referred to was built at the extensive iron clad yards of the Messrs. Secor, the contractors, in Jersey City, some seven months ago, where she was successfully launched, and, after the turrets and other armament were completed, to the perfect satisfaction of the Government-Inspector of Iron-clads, she was sent to the Brooklyn Navy Yard, and shortly afterward put in commission by the Government.

Captain John Rogers was appointed to the command of this far famed war-vessel, and rather than to let her be taken in charge of another vessel to act as a guide and safeguard in taking her to Port Royal, that gallant officer at once declined, taking upon himself the charge of his favorite war-pet iron-clad, and desirous of testing her seaworthy capabilities, set out for Port Royal. During the trip he encountered a terrific storm, which shook some of the strongest ships of war, disabling some; but in no way deterred at the tempestuous sea, he bore her safely through, without sustaining the slightest injury. The fact Captain Rogers rejoicingly telegraphed to Captain Ericsson at the time.

In the attack upon Drury's Bluff, Captain Rogers was present with his favorite Monitor iron-clad, and the noble vessel there came off uninjured.

More recently, when the blockading squadron of the South Atlantic, under Admiral Dupont, was summoned to share in the naval attack against the forts of Charleston, the Weehawken was pitched upon, with her gallant and distinguished commander, to lead the entire fleet; and although subjected to the destructive shot and shell of the enemy for some time, she stood out in her majesty in the Charleston waters, in bold relief, as an impregnable barrier against all the dreadful cannonading that was leveled against her from that tremendous battery, and came off unmolested.

The last great service which Captain Rogers and the Weehawken have rendered to the country, has been the capture of the iron-clad Rebel ram Atlanta, a triumph which shall long redound to the honor, the renown, and the bravery of Captain Rogers; for, although this herculean ram persuaded herself that she had little to do, only show herself to the Weehawken, for a speedy surrender of her captain and brave crew, yet the contrary was the case, as already reported.

To those who were opposed to the erection of these Ericsson iron-clads, the scenes which the Weehawken has already passed through tell of their great use and service to the country, and the Messrs. Secor, who were her builders, having employed the well-known talented gentlemen, Mr. George Birkbeck, Jr., feel confident that the three others which they have now in hands for the use of the Government—namely, the Mahopac, Tecumseh, and Manhatta—will be in no way inferior to the Weehawken, as they will be built according to the specification of Captain Ericsson, the master inventor of these formidable ships.

July 5, 1863

THE BATTLE OF GETTYSBURG.

The official announcements from President Lincoln and Gen. Meade, and the dispatch, big with tidings of triumph, received from our correspondent at Washington at a very late hour last night are worth, to a country painfully eager for authentic tidings from the battlefield of its best-loved Army, a score of such murky telegrams as previously heralded and followed the events of the past week. Silence in Washington has so long been synonymous with disaster in the field that the brief statement of the President would be entitled to attention from its novelty, even if the modest dispatch of General Meade did not confirm it in every line. The additional advices in our possessions show the victory of the Army of the Potomac to have been even more decided than its commander's words would indicate.

The career of that Army, under its new leadership, has been a scarcely-impeded march of triumph. Not a dissonant word interferes with the record that, up to the close of its Friday's engagement, it had been led so ably, and had fought so well, as to have shattered Lee's audacious plan of invasion beyond hope, and crippled his army to a condition which was certain to ensure us a decisive triumph in the final battle, which was yesterday expected. General Meade tells us that the enemy, who had been driven back with severe loss in Thursday's battle, were repulsed on Friday in two terrific assaults on our left centre, after having directed upon our line a concentrated fire from one hundred and fifty guns during three preceding hours. "The world", says a correspondent, "never saw so much fighting." We may conceive, with a pang, that the world has seldom witnessed such slaughter. Experience has shown that rebel infantry do not charge like men, but like demons. Twice hurled by their officers against the line of an opposing army, and the fire that causes them to give way must be like a scythe, that sweeps all before it. What human harvest went down before the "left centre" of the Union Army on that day is yet to be told, alike to the glory and the sorrow of our cause. Night came welcomed, we may be sure, by an enemy whose ranks were too decimated, and whose position was too insecure to make him wish to prolong an engagement wherein his every attempt had been fruitful of disaster. His loss in prisoners alone, including general and other officers, must have been seriously felt; nor can the Army of the Potomac, deprived, by death and wounds, of such leaders as [John F.] Reynolds and Sickles, dare to regard its advantages without abundant sadness.

The position in the field on Friday evening was such as to preclude the probability of Lee voluntarily renewing the battle on the morrow. The honor of opening the closing engagement therefore belonged to General Meade. How he opened it—how the soldiers that he led, stung by the recollection of recent defeat under incompetent leadership, and nobly mad with thoughts of the past and the future of the Great Day on which they were called upon to struggle for the perpetuity of the nation's life, fought and hurled the Rebel legions back, let the dispatches tell. Should the statement that the expedition from Bloody Run to co-operate with Gen. [Benjamin F.] Kelley succeeded in cutting off Lee's retreat, prove true, his Army, routed already, is lost to treason and gained to the Union!

TWENTY-THIRD REGIMENT, NATIONAL GUARD.

FORT COURT, HARRISBURG, PA., July 1.

Since last writing, our boys have had a slight taste of a soldier's life. About dusk, on the 26th inst., our regiment was pushed to the extreme advance, and posted as picket to watch the approach of the Rebels, who were reported to be advancing in strong force.

We were all posted in concealed positions, and instructed to fire and fall back on the reserves, as soon as the gray-jackets made their appearance. But, in spite of sharp eyes, we were unable to discover any Butternuts; and the long night dragged on without anything unusual occurring to alarm us. As soon as morning broke, we began to look around for something to eat; and they had not long to look, for soon we had a nice meal brought to us by the fair maidens of the vicinity. The day stole away much pleasanter than the preceding night, for many of our picket-posts were enlivened by the presence of the aforesaid young lasses.

And it was with sad countenances that we saw the companies of the Thirtieth Pennsylvania marching to relieve us. Well, some poet has written, "To meet! to know! and then to part, is the sad, sad tale of many a heart". And as I suppose the Twenty-third cannot be excepted from the general rule, we put the best face possible on the matter, and bade our kind friends good-bye.

As we were marching in, our ears were somewhat startled by hearing the long-roll beat. We started on a double-quick, arriving at the reserve just in time to behold the Seventy-first and Eighth New York come running in, reporting the Rebs in close pursuit. We stacked our arms, and slung off our equipments, and commenced felling trees, building barricades, and obstructing the road, so that they would have "a hard road to travel". We worked until midnight, when we were relieved by a Pennsylvania regiment, much against our will, for the boys were all anxious for a brush.

Yesterday forty of our boys went skirmishing, and have not yet returned; but, judging from the constant discharge of musketry in their direction, I imagine they are having warm work. The regiment has been drawn up in line several times, expecting an advance on these fortifications by the Rebs.

But their goes the drum again, so I must stop scribbling, and fall in.

Yours, truly,   Co. H.

ONE HUNDRED AND THIRTY-NINTH REGIMENT, N.Y.V.

ON THE MARCH NEAR RICHMOND, VA., June 29.

Here we are in Dixie, and with [John A.] Dix. While the Rebels are evidently getting themselves into "a scrape" in Pennsylvania and Maryland, our forces are pushing on toward a flank movement on the Rebel Capital. Our scouts bring us news to the effect that the garrison of Richmond numbers from 40,000 to 50,000 men, who-are ill-assorted, and many of them the poorest troops in the whole Confederacy. The North Carolina and Louisiana troops, it is reported, cannot be depended upon at all. Quite a meeting occurred among them recently within the lines of the Rebel Capitol, and but for being overpowered by a superior number of Virginia soldiers, there must have been a complete upset of affairs, right under the nose of the conspirators.

Our columns are very strong. As it is contraband news to allow you to publish our actual strength, I send an estimate of the forces we possess in a private dispatch. One thing is very certain, we have probably more men than is supposed, and our leaders are thoroughly competent. The Regulars make a splendid appearance, and are thoroughly determined for the work before them. We have also with us a few of the Union boys, who were recently amusing themselves in catching some of the miserable butternut renegades who infested the line of the Blackwater, etc.

The good people of Brooklyn will be pleased to hear that the One Hundred and Thirty-ninth N.Y. Vols. (Colonel Anthony Conk) is in the advance, accompanied by Berdan's Sharpshooters, skirmishing ahead, who every now and then bag Secesh farmers (murderers) prowling about to decoy our scouts.

The Richmond defences are commanded by [Henry] Wise (not Bragg). Adjutant-General [Samuel] Cooper acting as sort of Major-General. Jeff Davis is quite sick, and there is considerable mortality of life in and around Richmond. After cutting off all the telegraph communications and destroying the railroads leading northward from the Rebel capital, we expect to attack it in a direction least expected. We possess the key of their defences, and shall enter at some point or other. Therefor, do not be surprised if the Stars and Stripes is floating over Capitol Square on the 4th of July, and the hated Libby Prison is in ruins.

There is just now a perfect stampede among the citizens of Richmond. They are making great haste to reach Lynchburg, Staunton, and Charlottesville, villages to the west of the place.

It is impossible for me to write more, as I am ordered to ride twenty-five miles through a pouring rain to express some $6,000 belonging to the regiment. As I close, several brigades are moving forward, and a special courier waits for the mail. Good-bye.

EAGLE.

NINETIETH REGIMENT, N.Y.S.V.

PORT HUDSON, LA. June 21.

We have now gone up to this place, having returned from Barre's Landing, about 130 miles above this point, whence we started, some days ago, to convoy a train of contrabands that had come in from above, and, after one of the most extraordinary marches on record, succeeded in the object of the expedition. When we started from Barre's, the negro train extended about four miles; but, every few miles, teams of all descriptions fell in, so that, by the time we reached our destination, our procession of "persons of African descent" stretched out over seven miles, from front to rear. To protect this immense train, about 4,000 men were brigaded under the command of our Major Nelson J. Shaurman. Everything passed off well, until we were about to encamp for the night—about seven miles from the city of Franklin—when the order was given to fall in again, our rear-guard being attacked. We had marched twenty miles that day, over a hot and dusty road; nevertheless, the order was obeyed with alacrity, and we started off at double-quick. We couldn't keep that up long, however, with our blistered feet, but relapsed into a quick step, till we had nearly reached Franklin again, where the attack had been made. Secesh could not be found; consequently, we marched back again, and had just lain down for a rest, when up we had to jump, a large force being reported advancing rapidly in our rear. We might have waited for and fought them, but the immense train to our charge, consisting of nearly 3,000 men, women, and children, with a large drove of horses and mules, could not be risked, the object of the attack being mainly to recover them. We marched till daylight, and were then allowed to rest; and, having but a dozen miles further to go, our mission was as good as accomplished. As this was our first experience in campaigning, it is wonderful that we stuck it out so well. As for myself, I am so rare all over; my feet are blistered so that I shall not be able to walk for a week. But I'll hobble around somehow.

This, and other expeditions of a similar nature, show that Gen. Banks knows where to strike at the vitals of the Rebs. Take away the niggers, and the land is profitless; take away the means whereby the enemy lives, and he must succumb or perish.

Your correspondent has just left Port Hudson, and the regiment, being detailed to remain a few days in the Crescent City, and, as this is my first visit, everything is strange and novel to me. I go wandering about through the streets, like a veritable New Zealander. New Orleans is still a gay and lively place, despite the War; but the great warehouses are mostly closed, and the sidewalks are sprinkled with lounging soldiers, and the military patrol meets one at intervals. As I write this, a crowd is collected before the Era office; an "extra" has just been issued, and the boys are rushing with them among the anxious multitude, in genuine New York style. News from Vicksburg and Port Hudson is given in these "extras" every day, though no communication is allowed between these points and New Orleans. This is paradoxical; but so long as the extras aforesaid sell, I should be the last one to find fault.

I shall write you as soon as the fate of Port Hudson is sealed, which, I think, will not be delayed many days. They are doing nothing now but getting heavy siege-guns in position, and, when the regular bombardment commence, there will be lively times. A few assaults had been made, but they were merely to gain certain positions. The place will soon be ours.

T. K.

NEW YORK REGIMENTS AT PORT HUDSON

NEW ORLEANS, LA., June 20.

I arrived in Port Hudson upon the evening of the 10th inst., and pushed my way forward to the front, where the New York regiments were stationed. I found upon the extreme right Gen. [Cuvier] Grover's Division, which is composed of all New York regiments, with one or two exceptions. The First Brigade of this division was commanded by Colonel [Joseph S.] Morgan, who is acting Brigadier-General.

Upon my arriving at the front, I was informed that that night (10th inst.) an advance would be made upon the enemy's works by the right of the line. This included the Ninetieth, Ninety-first, One Hundred and Thirty-third, One Hundred and Thirty-first, and Seventy-fifth New York, and one or two Maine Regiments. At 11 o'clock, the movement commenced. The advance was led by the Ninetieth Regiment, under command of Major Nelson Shaurman, of Brooklyn. The charge was a most desperate one. The sight of that moving column in the glare of the muskets and cannon fire was most grand. The Ninetieth moved forward, and succeeded in capturing the rifle pits of the outer works, which they held for some hours, expecting re-enforcements, which did not come, and at daylight they abandoned them, and made a successful retreat to their own works—a distance of some two hundred yards. The night was dark, and the march through the ravines dangerous and uncertain; deep pitfalls had been dug by the Rebels, and trees put in such shape that it would seem almost an impossibility to pass from one point to another. Two companies strayed from the regiment, and were obliged to remain in a ravine until the following night, within six yards of the enemy's rifle pits. The object of this advance was to learn the strength of the Rebels, which I believe amounts to some five or six thousand. But one man in Port Hudson is a thousand of himself. The loss experienced in this engagement was small. All got back safe, and remained quiet until the morning of the 13th instant, when a general bombardment took place. I was informed that we threw 3,600 shells into Port Hudson in one hour. The Twenty-first Indiana Battery and five Monitors, in charge of Lieutenant [William E.] White, of the Ninetieth New York, were engaged upon the right, the gunboats from the river side, and other batteries along the line. After shelling these poor wretches for one hour, a flag of truce was sent to General [Frank] Gardner, commanding officer of Port Hudson demanding his immediate surrender. His reply was brief and to the point: "My duty as an officer, and soldier is to hold this place as long as I can. I await your attack." All remained quiet during the remainder of the day and night until the morning of the 14th inst., when an advance was ordered, and a general movement took place along the line from right to left. The right again took the advance and Col. Morgan's Brigade was in front. This was composed of the Ninetieth, Ninety-first, One Hundred and Thirty-first, Seventy-fifth and One Hundred and Sixtieth N.Y.S.V., and two Maine Regiments. The advance was made steady and with coolness. Our regiments marched some two hundred yards under the direct fire of the Rebels, but none flinched, notwithstanding they were cut down by hundreds. On they marched, and at last gained the intrenchments, when for a time they escaped the fire of the enemy's guns. Our loss was heavy, both of men and officers. Col. [Leonard D.] Currie of the One Hundred and Thirty-third New York received a wound in both arms. General Banks seems to have great confidence in New York troops, as he gives them nearly all the duty to perform in this department.

It is stated that our loss was some 1,500 killed and wounded, and the Rebels must have lost much more. We took the outer works, but did not deem it of importance to hold them. A large number of men desert from

Port Hudson daily, and come within our lines, all telling the same story, giving the same account of scarcity of food, etc. All the corn has to be ground by hand; one of our shell having set fire to their mill and burnt it. Quite a number of wealthy Southern ladies are in Port Hudson, and live in caves under the ground, to protect themselves from shell. A day or two since, a shell burst and killed two, and dangerously wounded two more of the ladies. Our informant also states, that our shell kill hundreds of soldiers daily. It is also reported, that desertion is so very common, that to prevent this the officers stand on picket at nights instead of the men.

New Orleans is quiet to-day. Some little excitement prevailed yesterday, from a report that a force of six thousand, was marching up on New Orleans, but it appears to-day that his force is much smaller, and that the only danger as yet done is the taking of the New Orleans & Opelousas Railroad, which cuts off communication with Brashear City and the famous Teche country. There is also another strolling band of Rebels up the river, near Donalsonville, who have burned two small river-boats, and still continue to annoy passing boats; but a force has been sent from New Orleans which will, no doubt, succeed in either capturing them or driving them out of the country.

The wounded from Port Hudson have been sent to this city. What was formerly the St. Louis Hotel, on St. Louis street, has been taken for a hospital, and the wounded men receive the best care. Gentlemen and ladies of New Orleans call daily, and administer to their wants.

E. S.

FIFTY-FIRST REGIMENT, N.Y.S.V.
HAINES BLUFF, NEAR VICKSBURG, MISS. June 24.

We received orders in our last camping place, in Kentucky, to pack up our surplus clothing; having done so, it was shipped to Hickman's Bridge. This was taken as an omen that our summer-campaign was near at hand. The point we would aim for was a mystery soon to be solved.

On the morning of June 4, we left Hustonville, Ky., passed through Stanford, and arrived at Lancaster before evening, in time to witness the school exhibitions, where there was a large attendance of the ladies, and a fair proportion of the members of the regiment, including Frank Butler, who was requested to sing a song. He, after a while, complied, by singing: "The Sexton!". Early next morning we left Lancaster, arrived at Nicholasville by 3, P.M., having received quite a lift in the shape of empty hay wagons, which were seized by the Colonel, and appropriated to the use of the regiment. While lying here, the boiler of a locomotive exploded, killing five and wounding several, all soldiers who were employed in loading cars on the adjoining track. On the morning of the 6th, we left Nicholasville by the Kentucky Central Railroad, arrived at Covington at 9, A.M., the next morning, crossed over to Cincinnati, got breakfast in Fifth-street Market-house, started from the city at 12, M., and arrived in Cairo at 9, P.M., the 8th inst. On the route through Ohio, Indiana, and Illinois, the ladies were very enthusiastic. At every station, bouquets of flowers would be thrown into the cars. To several, if not more of these bouquets were appended small pieces of paper with the address of the giver. At Seymour, Ind., we received coffee. At Centralia, Il., we received ditto and fried fresh pork.

At 3, P.M., June 9th, we embarked on the steamer Rocket, Capt. Wool. Stopping at Columbus, Ky., Gen. [Alexander S.] Asboth, the noted Hungarian, presented himself and was addressed by Col. [Charles W.] Le Gendre, after which he was heartily cheered. The General responded in a few words. We arrived at Memphis on the evening of the 10th, and had fresh bread and eight days' rations of salt meat issued. We left Memphis on the morning of the 12th, and went ashore at Sherman's landing, where there is to be found the site of "that contemplated canal". On the morning of the 15th, we proceeded to Warrenton and crossed the river below Vicksburg, remaining there a short time, re-crossed, and returned to where we started from. We could see the mortar-boats shelling the city, but saw no return-shots from the enemy.

On the morning of the 16th we embarked on steamers, directing our course up the Yazoo River some ten miles, and landed near to what is called Snyder's or Haines' Bluff; marched four miles, and encamped.

It appears that all of the extra baggage shipped in Kentucky is still with us, and has had to be stowed and re-stowed in the holds of the different vessels, instead of being left in Cincinnati. No doubt, if we move inland we will have to carry all or throw them away, and then draw again next winter.

Very little firing is heard in the vicinity of Vicksburg. It is the general opinion that the city is totally surrounded. We thank Heaven that Vicksburg is out of reach of the Capitol by telegraph, for Grant can do his own planning and work to his own advantage.

As General Grant has enough troops to hold Vicksburg, our part in the tragedy must be to keep Johnston out.

I think General Grant's plan of starving them out is a very good one, and saves the slaughter of a number of lives, which would inevitably happen were he to charge the Rebel intrenchments.

Yours,   GREENBACK.

NINETIETH REGIMENT, N.Y.S.V.

PORT HUDSON, June 28.

At midnight of Saturday last [June 20], that portion of our regiment not on picket, numbering 206 men, were again called up, and forming quickly and noiselessly, were marched through the woods some three miles from our camp, and there took position at the right of a brigade, under Col. Morgan, who is still Acting-Brigadier. We soon got the order to forward, and about daylight, came in full view of the battle-field, where a brigade was already fighting fiercely to drive the Rebs from their rifle-pits and intrenchments. Resting here on our arms, we awaited orders, which at length came, and our whole column advanced down a newly-cut road direct on the enemy's works. Col. Morgan, a short time previous, had been assigned to take the place of Gen. [Halbert] Paine, who had been seriously wounded that morning; and the command of our brigade devolved on Col. [Richard E.] Holcomb, of the First Louisiana. In front of us, at the bottom of the road, was a steep ascent, at the top of which was a formidable intrenchment of earth and cotton-bales, and as we sprung up the side-hill, we were met by a murderous volley, and one half of our First Company, including Col. Holcomb himself, who was shot through the forehead, went down. Major Shaurman, acting-Colonel of the Ninetieth, ably assisted by acting-Major [John C.] Smart and Adjutant [Conrad C.] Ludiker, shouted to and encouraged the men to continue advancing, which they did till the entire Ninetieth were up the hill, while a continual shower of bullets thinned them off. A glance showed plainly that charging up the hill would be useless, as their breastworks were impenetrable, except with scaling-ladders; and the next thing was to seek shelter from the unseen foe at the top of the hill. Every one has heard of the curious topography of this part of the country, and the friendly gullies and ravines now saved our regiment from annihilation. Here we remained till evening, within sound of the Rebels' voices, when the remnant of us crept out, bruised, wounded, and choking with thirst. Our killed and wounded, while passing through this *feu d'enfer*, amounted to about one out of every four, while many whom we thought would recover, have since died. Among the latter are Orderly Sergeant Dennis Shea, than whom a better soldier or braver man did not exist.

Thus our friends at home will perceive that the Ninetieth will not disgrace the colors they bear, for though most regiments would have become effeminate and demoralized by such a long period of inactivity, our men went where they were ordered, through a storm of death, and remained in imminent peril and under a hot sun, racked with hunger and thirst, until permission was given them to retire. Veteran troops could do no more.

Our leader in both these affairs, Major Shaurman, has endeared himself to the men and won their confidence since our expedition from Barre's Landing. He is a thorough soldier, and will not send his regiment where he will not go himself. The mail has just arrived, and I have two letters, and *laus Deo*, a SUNDAY MERCURY.

Yours,   T. K.

THE ANTI-DRAFT RIOTS.

The riots which raged in this city during the week assumed proportions which even those who anticipated trouble did not expect to witness. Originating among those who dreaded being conscripted, and had not the means to effect a pecuniary compromise, it soon degenerated into the hands of the thieves and vagabonds to whom public disorder is a harvest day, and who never neglect an opportunity to make hay while the sun shines. Once the movement fell under the control of this class, it was directed to the accomplishment of purposes of indiscriminate plunder and outrages of the most revolting character. Such is ever the tendency of mob law. To whatever end it may be originally directed, there are always reckless characters to change its courses into the direction that promises to give them opportunities of pillage and outrage. No one can foretell, when a mob arises where it is going to end; for its originators themselves soon lose control over the turbulent elements which they put in motion. Hence, all such methods of righting wrongs, real or imaginary, are to be deprecated by all interested in the stability of society and the good order of the community.

But we should not allow our hostility to riot and disorder to close our eyes to the fact, that the idea of an enforced conscription is odious in the eyes of the people. There was among the rioters, who spread wild commotion throughout the city, a degree of desperate determination that showed them to be ready to risk any consequences. And as these are the classes upon whom the conscription, if enforced, must chiefly fall—as they could not command the necessary sum to secure exemption, while other classes could—it is worth while to inquire what sort of an army such men would make, even if actually forced into the service. We have urged the Government all along to dispense with the draft, and rely upon the voluntary patriotism of the people. Liberal bounties, and some provision made for the wives and families of the soldiers, would swell the ranks of the Army beyond the necessities of the Government. More property has been destroyed in this city during the last few days that, if converted into bounties, would have brought forward more volunteers than the quota of the city. It is right enough to suppress disorder and preserve the public tranquility by all means; but when difficulties can be avoided, it is the part of the wisdom to do so. The ultimate ascendancy of law and order is always certain; but it is better, whenever feasible and proper, to avoid the cause that lead to their temporary infraction.

Nor do we consider the draft necessary at the present time. The series of brilliant victories on the Mississippi which have bisected the Rebellion, would have given a new impetus to recruiting, and secured all the men that can be necessary. No call for men was ever made by the President that did not elicit a full and spontaneous response; and now, if ever, an invitation to enlist, with the additional incentive of adequate bounty, would enable the Government to dispense with a measure that can never cease to be repugnant to the popular sentiment. Were the President to issue another call for as many men as he requires, there would be enough respond to it among those whose avocations or condition of life will enable them to go to war without their absence interfering with the progress of industry and peaceful enterprise, or swelling the ranks of pauperism by leaving dependent families behind them. This would be a better method of raising an army than dragging the mechanic from the workshop and the farmer from gathering in the fruits of the earth.

It is a well-known fact, that within the past six weeks more volunteers have been enrolled in New York City for the same amount of time for a year previous. Why there is such haste just now about a draft, puzzles military men not a little. There cannot be less than 150,000 Union troops at the present time in a state of inactivity. The immense army of Grant, as well as the troops under Banks, and Meade, and Dix, are, with the exception of men required for garrison service, quite unemployed. Richmond and Mobile will fall in autumn, in the same way that Vicksburg has. What more troops are needed for at all, is something we cannot understand. The raid is over in Pennsylvania and Maryland, and 125,000 men called for the five States are ready by this time. With these additional troops, and those relieved from siege-duty, the probable return of Louisiana and North Carolina to the Union, and the constant daily accessions of volunteers, not only in New York City and State, but all over the Union, there is not the slightest cause for a draft, and its insane advocates cannot produce one single argument to contradict what we assert.

FOURTEENTH REGIMENT, N.Y.S.N.G.

BIVOUAC NEAR ANTIETAM, July 12.

With some difficulty, I have obtained paper and pencil with which to give you a few lines in brief of what has transpired since I wrote last. The marching has been of the severest character, and we have suffered all that human beings could in our endeavor to keep up.

On the 1st of July, the ball was opened by the First Division, First Corps. I think the First and Second Brigades were the only ones engaged for about an hour; after which some of the rest of the Corps came up; and toward the very close, after the First Corps had been fighting over five hours, the Eleventh Corps (two divisions, I believe) was brought up and posted on our right. During all the six hours, we were kept fighting without any relief, and at every point, we seemed to be successful, being continually changing direction, and scattering the Rebels at each attack. I never was so completely exhausted; for it was cheering, yelling, double-quicking, and loading and firing from the very commencement until we fell back to the other side of town.

The Sixth Wisconsin, of the First Brigade, fought well, and took a number of prisoners. The Fourteenth and Ninety-fifth did not do so bad; for in one of the charges made, we took a gun and again a number of prisoners, besides a set of Rebel colors.

At one time, while the regiment was in line, a movement was observed on the brow of the hill, which proved that a whole brigade of graybacks were not more than a hundred yards in front and moving forward; and in a very short time, another view showed that we were being flanked, and that this same body was still moving upon us, with large bodies on each flank and our little force completely encircled. We fell back, and soon were placed to support the noted Battery B, which we have so often supported.

Soon we saw on our right large bodies of the Rebels moving upon the railroad, and you may judge it was hot when Battery B had to retreat. The Eleventh Corps (the two divisions) were flying pell-mell, which made it necessary for the little force of the First Corps on the left and front to fall back.

I never have felt disposed to say a word against the Eleventh Corps, but when reading in the papers that it fought well, and that the First Corps ran, it makes me feel it my duty to state that the facts are just *vice versa*. That little remnant that is left of the First Corps stood the brunt, which their losses in killed and wounded on the first day prove, and the Eleventh—the flying Eleventh—flew. The propensity shown by the gallant Eleventh in this case was proverbial with the Rebels, and some that we took prisoners in the following fights say that they were told that they had the Eleventh Corps only to fight, and that made them feel secure of success.

The loss in the division I cannot state, but all lost heavily. The Fourteenth, in the first day's fight, lost 109 killed and wounded. We have not now more than a hundred rank and file for action. We lost some while fighting the second and third days. The breastworks are a big thing, and the majority felt safer in them and fighting than when relieved, for it seemed as though we were in more danger when away resting—at which times some of our men were hit. On falling back to the other side of town, we soon had positions assigned, and through the night of the 1ˢᵗ, intrenchments were thrown up, which showed sagacity and foresight by the result of events that followed. The roar of musketry and booming of cannon, with the whirr and whizz, banging of shot and shell, and singing of the little Minié warblers, was somewhat interesting, though not very pleasing. Dead men and horses, broken gun carriages, shattered buildings, with the wounded besides, is no very pleasing sight to contemplate—let alone realize—as a sight. The morning of the 4ᵗʰ of July declared a victory by the retreat of the Rebels. Their dead and wounded lay over the slopes, up which they charged. Behind each rock, and many places where little piles of stones had been formed, lay the unfortunate Rebel dead, here and there in groups. They fought desperately, as the close proximity of some of the bodies prove, being within ten feet of our breastworks in places. One daring deed was attempted; and that was by one of the Rebels crawling through the darkness of night, reaching the breastworks of one of the Wisconsin regiments to where stood the regimental colors, which he grasped; but had no sooner done so than he was shot dead by the men in the trench.

I never saw our men in better spirits than during the fight around Gettysburg. The retreat of Lee has caused it necessary for us to do more marching, which, though hard, is cheerfully done, in the hope that we shall soon have the work accomplished, viz., that of closing this cruel war, with a restoration of our glorious Union.

We crossed, day before yesterday, one of the highest mountains in the country. It was hard traveling. We are all suffering to some extent for want of shoes and socks—our work causing a necessity for supplies to remain in the rear, and walking is wearing away our shoes and socks very rapidly.

Yesterday, we passed through Belleville and Middletown. Our cavalry has been fighting for two or three days. Some of the Rebel prisoners were brought up past us as we were approaching this locality yesterday. We have, I believe, most of the important positions about here. Troops all along are in lines of battle. Fifteen hundred prisoners were taken by our cavalry, and the work is still going on favorably.

I don't see in any of the accounts of the first day a word or mention regarding the movements of Colonel Fowler's regiment, which resulted in preventing the Rebels from capturing or demolishing our brigade, which calamity would certainly have occurred but for his quick perception in timely movement of our regiment.

J. J.

July 26, 1863
TYRANNY IN THE ARMY—THE ERECTION OF A MONARCHY.

An army officer, who constitutes himself the historian of his own exploits, writes a letter to the *Tribune*, the statements in which involve considerations of such importance, that we here produce the main portion of it.

"I was compelled to speak to the troops along the route—speaking one day some seven or eight times. During my tour, I met with an Irish regiment—the Nineteenth Illinois, from Chicago—men who read the Chicago *Times*. After talking to them awhile, I proposed three cheers for the President of the United States. These were given heartily. Three cheers were then proposed for the settled policy of the United States with regard to the negroes. This was met by cries of 'No!' 'No!'. The Colonel was absent, and Lieutenant-Colonel was in command, I inquired what such conduct meant? The Lieutenant-Colonel endeavored to excuse the men by saying that they had no opportunity of thinking over the matter. I replied, 'You are not telling the truth, Sir. I know they have been discussing this question for a week past. I know that fact, if you do not.' The officer was considerably mortified. I ordered those opposed to this policy of the Government to step forward, and said I knew the regiment had seen considerable service and fought well; but I also knew that there was but little discipline observed among them; that I wanted a distinct recognition of this doctrine—that was the point with me. Several stepped forward. They were instantly seized and sent to the guardhouse. I then left the regiment, telling them I would give them a week to consider what they would do. At the next station, I met the Colonel of the regiment, who begged that I would leave the matter in his hands, and he would see that the men were taught the duty of soldiers. I complied with his request. When I reached Memphis, I was taken sick. When I got up to Louisville, I was shown a long article from the Chicago *Times*, written by a Captain of the Nineteenth Illinois, who was not on the ground at the time of their insubordinate misconduct, but who saw fit to write a very insubordinate article in reference to what he heard I had said, and in which he terribly distorted the facts. He was, of course, dishonorably dismissed the service."

We have earnestly sustained the policy of the Administration in liberating the negroes, and allowing them to aid in fighting the battles in whose issue their own interests are involved as much as those of any other class; but to compel the soldiers to express concurrence in it where their feelings are the other way, is an act of despotism which converts the soldier into a slave. If this were an isolated instant of petty tyranny and insolent impertinence, it would be simply a disgraceful absurdity; but if it be part of a system of coercion, by which the will of the people is to be overborne by the enforced action of the military force of the

Government, then it forebodes perilous consequences to our liberties, before which the individual features of the case sink into insignificance. The soldiers owe prompt obedience to their superiors in all military matters; but beyond that, the humblest private is as much entitled to exercise unrestrained and freely, according to his own judgement, the prerogatives of an American citizen as the Commander in Chief. To subject privates to punishment, and officers to disgrace under such circumstances as those above described is calculated to "discourage enlistments" and provoke opposition to the draft more than any other cause.

If the army is to be coerced in this way, and its vote and influence secured to elect an Administration ticket, the next Presidential election will be a farce like that by which Louis Napolean constituted himself an Emperor, and our hitherto free Government be converted into a monarchy or an empire. There are supporters of the Administration who avow themselves in favor of such a *coup d'etat*, and facts are not lacking to corroborate the avowal. At the late election in Iowa, the anti-administration party had over 4,000 majority on the home vote, but it was overcome by the vote of her citizens who had joined the Army. There were 9,000 citizens of the State in the Army, and of these, 7,000 votes the Administration ticket. That this was a free and voluntary expression of the real sentiments of the soldiers, it would be preposterous to assert. Never in any American community did such unanimity as this exist; not in Vermont, where hardly any live political issues divided the people. Of course, if it was entirely and absolutely unanimous, the result would be too shamefully glaring and self evident, and a show of a minority was kept up.

August 2, 1863

FIFTY-NINTH REGIMENT, N.Y.S.V.

IN THE FIELD, NEAR BLOOMFIELD, VA., July 22.

The Fifty-ninth Regiment left New York City in October, 1861, numbering over eight hundred men. Since then, it has received about six hundred recruits. The first general engagement it was in was the memorable battle of Antietam, this was followed by the battles of Fredericksburg and Chancellorsville, and these again succeeded by the battle of Gettysburg, where the Second Corps, to which our regiment is attached, greatly distinguished itself. We, however, have lost a great many men, and a short time since, were consolidated in a battalion of four companies. It can now only muster about eighty men fit for duty. Our loss at Gettysburg was severe. Our Lieutenant-Colonel, Max A. Thoman received a serious wound in the shoulder from a piece of shell, from the effects of which he has subsequently died. His last words were, "Bury me as near where I fell as possible." Our Adjutant, Wm. H. Pohlman, received two bad wounds, from which he is slowly recovering. I mention these officers particularly on account of their well known patriotism and bravery, both at home and in the field. After the wounding of Col. Thoman, Capt. Wm. McFadden took command, doing credit to himself and battalion by his bravery during the rest of the battle. But six officers are present with the decimated but plucky battalion, fit for duty. It is now commanded by Capt. Horace P. Rugg, the senior officer remaining, ably assisted by Adjutant George H. Crawford, formerly in the Regular Army. Its Company commanders are: Second-Lieut. Wm. Kelly, Co. A. Capt. Wm. McFadden, Co. B. First-Lieut. Henry N. Hamton, Co. C; and First-Lieut. Edwin F. Richards, Co. D. Three of these officers are awaiting orders to proceed to New York for the purpose of bringing out drafted men. Company B deserves especial mention in the fight at Gettysburg, capturing two stands of colors, one belonging to the Eighteenth Virginia and Forty-eighth Georgia Regiments. The reason I am particular in addressing you "New York" SUNDAY MERCURY is owing to the expulsion from camp of all vendors of the Philadelphia *Sunday Mercury*, on account of its treasonable publications. Hoping that the honest advocate of all classes may continue to prosper, I remain,

Yours, etc.,   KAOD.

Lieut.-Col. Max Thoman died on July 11 and was buried on Schwartz's farm, near Rock Creek. He later was removed to the National Cemetery (A-70 New York Plot). Adjutant William H. Pohlman died of his wounds on July 21, 1863.

August 9, 1863

FOURTEENTH REGIMENT, N.Y.S.M.

WEST SIDE OF THE RAPPAHANNOCK, VA. (near "Rappahannock Station"), August 6.

Since the fight at Gettysburg, we have marched considerable, having recrossed the Potomac, and passed through towns that have been visited before by us. We expected very strongly when at Funkstown or near Hagerstown, to have had another fight. Our forces were drawn up in line of battle, and our skirmishers were driving the Rebel skirmishers in. On the following day we raised breastworks, and were again "invincible". But we had not the fight. We were marched to Williamsport, and on the morning following returned back and marched on, passing through Maryland and across the Potomac, and through the greatest little Union town of all we had yet seen. Nearly at every house, on the porch or stoop, and on the sidewalks, were the beautiful ladies, passing water, and bestowing their real cheering words and blessings for the soldier-boys; smiling such sweet smiles, which none but real Union ladies know how to smile. Flags and white handkerchiefs were waving at nearly every house—such is the picture of the Union town of Waterford, Va.

We had, some days, very light marches; but when the sun came out in earnest, especially as it has been this last few days, it is really exhausting to have but a few miles to march. When passing through Middleburg, we noticed the effect of strong Secessionism on that place and its suburbs—windows closed, stores shut, and, where we chanced to meet the gaze of a female hiding behind her window-curtains, the same sour look met us. In marching to Warrenton, a portion of our little regiment skirmished in. Nothing in force was found of "Johnny Reb" there. The Fourteenth were placed on duty for Provost, Lieut.-Col. Jourdan, Provost-Marshal, our Colonel (Fowler) acting Brig.-Gen. of Second Brigade. The morning after our advent, twenty-one Rebels were brought in, having been captured by the cavalry. The cavalry has had a great deal of work lately, and have done pretty well. Night before last, we reached the locality of one of our former spirited engagements, and where, while supporting the Sixteenth Indiana Battery, the Rebs were pouring their shot, shell, shrapnell, and even railroad iron at us from batteries on our right, left, and centre, from hills across the river, when formed a splendid position, but which are now occupied by us. The reasons for our movement across the river is very suggestive, and will, in time, speak for itself. We are now well intrenched, and expecting each hour to bring us in contact with the Rebel advancing hordes.

Since my last, I have collected further particulars and facts of the part the Fourteenth, with our gallant Brigade, took in the action of the first day at Gettysburg, and which the friends of the regiment, I feel, will be interested with knowledge of. So to begin, and as brief as possible. The Fourteenth, with the Second Brigade, consisting of the Fourteenth and Fifty-sixth Pennsylvania, and Seventy-sixth, Ninety-fifth, and One Hundred and Forty-seventh New York, from camp four miles north of Emmitsburg, about 7:30, A.M., marched July 1. The First Division of the First Corps led. The advance of the Division being the First Brigade, composed of Wisconsin, Indiana, and Michigan boys; the Second Brigade following, and then a section of rifled battery. Arriving within one and a half miles of Gettysburg, the report of artillery was heard, and we saw the shells burst over a woods half a mile to our left and front, denoting the presence of the enemy. The head of the column immediately filed off in that direction across the fields, passing to the left of the seminary, which is situated on the crest of a hill, about half a mile west of the town. Our brigade (the Second) was advanced to the crest of the next rise, about a quarter of a mile distant, and formed line of battle. The Fifty-sixth, Seventy-sixth, and One Hundred and Forty-seventh Regiments forming to the right of a farm-house, and the Fourteenth and Ninety-fifth, by order of General Reynolds (very shortly afterward killed), forming to the left of that house. Still further on, our left was the First Brigade, but out of sight from us, as our left was covered by a wood running up inside of our line. We were prevented from seeing the right of our brigade (the Second now) by the farm-house hiding it from our view. Before we were fairly formed, our cavalry came rushing out of the woods to our left, and gave us notice that the enemy were coming. They opened fire from a strong line of skirmishers in the woods to our left in front. We drove them back, although with severe loss—the Fourteenth and Ninety-fifth being divided. The command of both regiments devolved on Colonel Fowler, of this regiment. We could now see a strong line of the enemy advancing to our left, but a volley from the First Brigade compelled them to turn back. After finishing those up in our immediate front, we saw, with consternation, the enemy's line of battle advancing steadily to our right and rear. One of our guns was in our front, deserted, except by one man, a brave fellow, who fired the piece when the enemy were close upon him, and retired. It appears that while we were busily engaged, the enemy had driven back the portion of the brigade on our right.

It was at this time that Colonel Fowler displayed his military skill, and saved us from capture. It was plain that had we attempted to retreat, hardly a man would have been left; the only chance was to charge them. He at once forced the two regiments' rear, and retired until on a line with the enemy, when he changed front perpendicularly to meet them, the enemy at the same time performing the same manœuvre and firing rapidly. At this time the Sixth Wisconsin came bravely to our assistance and formed on our right (the Ninety-fifth being in the centre, and the Fourteenth on the left), then came the order to advance the line and "charge" them. The boys rushed forward with a will, the enemy fell back to a railroad cut in which they took cover, showering their bullets on us, our brave boys dropping at every step. On, on they advanced, and retook the lost gun. When nearing the cut, the Sixth Wisconsin was directed to flank the position by advancing the right, which they did. With a tremendous cheer the boys advanced to the cut. The enemy rose up, threw down their arms and surrendered. It was Gen. [James J.] Archer's Brigade.

After this, the regiments were ordered to join the Brigade, and superior numbers compelled us to fall back beyond the town. It was at about this time that the noted Battery B had to leave. Many of our men were captured or shot by the grand skedaddle of the flying Eleventh, two divisions of "half moons" still to our rear. Through this day's fight many long-cherished incidents occurred worthy of remembrance. In one instance, the form of an old man of over seventy years could be seen—with some odd citizens—loading and firing—gallantly defending their homes and their country's honor. In passing through the town, bullets whizzing rather fast and promiscuously, I remarked to a young lady, who handed me a drink of water, that I thought it unsafe for her to expose herself outside of the door so while so many bullets were striking about her. She said she did not care; she was going to help all she could to a drink, and was not afraid of the Rebels; did not care enough for them, etc. The credit of the capture of Archer's Brigade should be awarded to Colonel Fowler. He not only fought the force that had driven back three regiments and the Sixth Wisconsin, not only drove back the same enemy, but captured them all. I've had so little chance to write before, that I hope you'll excuse my delay. When anything occurs, the MERCURY shall be speedily informed.

JENKINS.

SECOND FIRE ZOUAVES
BEVERLY FORD, ON THE RAPPAHANNOCK., VA., Aug. 3.

It is time to write and let you know how we have lately been putting in our three years' time.

We left our camp, near Falmouth, on the 11th of June, and up to the present time we have traveled upward of 500 miles through a country almost impassible. Our corps acted as rear-guard for the Army, guarding all the fords and mountain-passes on the march to the Potomac. We are now on the reserve until there is a fight. We are then the first into it. We started from Gum Springs on the 19th of June, for Goose Creek, and we struck the Potomac. The mistake was a pleasing one, and we halted with joy the prospect before us of civilization, and setting our feet on Northern soil.

We were well received in Maryland and Pennsylvania, but not a bit too well. We marched rapidly through these States and pressed forward on Gettysburg where we encountered the enemy's pickets on the night of July 1. We captured one of their sentinels. He was much surprised, as he took us for their re-enforcements. We told him it was all right, but he could not see it. Next morning, we opened the ball, and fought the biggest and hardest fight of the whole war. We were on the field at 10 o'clock A.M., formed in line of battle, and advanced to support our skirmishers. A few minutes before the battle, Gen. Sickles passed along our lines and said: "Be careful, boys; we must whip them to-day."

They opened on us with their artillery, which appeared to be massed, and under cover of that fire their infantry advanced in solid column, to break our lines, but were repulsed. Again they assayed to drive us, but again they were driven back, with greater slaughter than before. It was at this critical moment that good men were needed; and we had them. It was here, as on several occasions before that the noble Burns and the fearless and brave Purtell showed what good men could do when they were tried; and I can assure you the trial was a severe one. Capt. [Thomas] Smith also acted well, and so did all our officers, not forgetting the renowned Capt. Jack Downey, who was always at his post.

Major Burns was in command of the regiment, Capt. Purtell was acting Lieut-Colonel, and Capt. Smith acted Major, and all three had their horses shot from under them. Capt. Purtell's veteran little bay was struck with a round shot, which passed through her; but, fortunately, without touching the Captain.

But, while speaking of the living, let us not forget the gallant dead. Captain [Eugene C.] Shine fell, with his face to the enemy; he was a general favorite here, and deeply regretted by all the officers in the brigade. Lieut. [James] Marksman, he, too, was beloved by all who knew him, and, like his Captain, he knew no fear. Lieut. [William L.] Herbert was not with us long, but he has, while with us, behaved like a soldier and a gentleman; and poor [Second-Lieutenant] George Dennin, I understand, is no more. He, like his brother Tom [killed at Chancellorsville], was as brave as a lion. The three first-named were buried like soldiers, next morning, on the battle-field.

On the morning of the 5th, we learned that the bird had flown. They left, in great haste, for the Potomac, so we immediately gave chase. We made for the old Antietam battle-ground; we thought they would make a stand there. When we got there, they were reported to be at Williamsport, and fortifying themselves. We advanced to the usual distance, and threw up some rifle-pits. We did expect to fight them here; we would have certainly whipped them. Why we did not attack them is a mystery to me, and to many others. The whole Army was sure of victory. If we attacked them, we would end this cruel war at Williamsport, on the Potomac.

But, as you are aware, they made good their escape, and, at this date, they are in the vicinity of Culpepper and Gordonsville. We are at the Rappahannock. Before coming here, we caught up with them at Manassas Gap, and we gave them fits. They tried hard for the possession of the Gap. They drove in our cavalry in the morning (I forget the date) [July 23]. When we arrived, Berdan's Sharpshooters were skirmishing with them. They do it well. We were then ordered to charge them. We did it with a will. General [Francis B.] Spinola acted like a veteran. He said: "Go in boys; give them h—l under their shirts." It was a splendid charge—but a foolish one—as we did not have any artillery to reply to theirs. They had a battery playing on us, at point-blank range; but they did not move us. Next morning we drove them across the Shenandoah River, and we instantly took up our lines of march for this place, where we arrived yesterday, in good trim, but few in numbers. We have about 145 men in the regiment fit for duty, and about 700 in the brigade. There was a cavalry fight here yesterday. It resulted in our favor. The whole Army is now on the north side of the Rappahannock.

GLADIATOR.

ONE HUNDRED AND EIGHTEENTH ILLINOIS (MOUNTED INFANTRY)

BIG BLACK RIVER RAILROAD BRIDGE, MISSISSIPPI, July 31, 1863.

It has been a long time since I have written to your paper. My excuses are few and short. The first reason is that I, with the rest of the Army of the Mississippi, have had no idle hours for a long, wearying period. When I have had a few spare moments it was necessary to devote it to rest, else it has been so warm that I became so languid that I could hardly find energy enough to write a short note to a friend. The climate here exerts a very strange influence over our men. When lying in camp they become so dull and indolent that they can hardly be got out to attend roll-call; but, on the march they all become invigorated with energy and endurance as becomes a Northern soldier, and when the skirmisher's gun sounds in their front, Southern langour and lassitude gives way to all the hardy energy of our invigorating climate of the North, and their superior power is felt and acknowledged by the Rebels, in their hasty flight, when "our boys" are ordered "forward". There is no power that can resist their sweeping advances. The battles of Thompson's Hill, near Port Gibson; of Raymond, near Raymond; of Champion Hill, near Edward's Depot; of Big Black Bridge, and the siege of Vicksburg, and the two engagements at Jackson—one before and one after the capture of the Gibralter of the South—are sufficient proof of the truth of my statements.

You, of course, have had minute descriptions of those engagements long ere this, but, would a brief recapitulation of the whole be uninteresting? Perhaps not; therefore I will give you a brief sketch of our whole movement. Of course, I can give personal accounts of only the Division with which I am connected—the Ninth of the Thirteenth Army Corps, under Brig.-Gen. Joseph Osterhaus.

On the first of April, our Division was on the circuitous route that finally terminated in the city of Vicksburg, via Grand Gulf and its rear. At Richmond, fifteen miles from the Bend, we had a skirmish with the enemy. The Second Illinois Cavalry drove them from the place, and wounded and captured several of their numbers. Here we delayed some time to build pontoon bridges and repair roads, and this was the most formidable enemy we had, as the bayous were many, deep, and often their currents swift. The Ninth Division did the whole of this work. We neared Carthage, twenty-five miles below Vicksburg, and here met opposition from the Rebels, they moving about us in the bayous and swamps in their skiffs, having a more perfect knowledge of the country than we. Several chases were made in skiffs and small boats—one by a few members of the Second Illinois Cavalry lasted half-a-day, and their arms being more hardy and their guns of longer range the Rebel boat finally surrendered. It was loaded with officers alone. One colonel, one lieutenant-colonel, and a major were among the prizes of this miniature naval engagement.

We were within a mile of Carthage; Rebels were there, and we had swift-running bayous and overflowed land intervening. Artillery could not be used, as a heavy swamp timber obscured the locality from view. Reconnoisance was made in skiffs; Rebels were soon on a levee and a small space of dry ground. Our troops had but a narrow levee to land upon, and that was commanded by a Rebel six-pounder. But the indefatigable Osterhaus was not at a loss to find means to get into a fight. A large flatboat was constructed and planked up on each side, and one end with heavy plank. Through these planks were cut loop-holes for muskets, and port-holes for a "pivot-gun" on the bow. To complete the "Flying Dutchman's" *gun-boat*, the boys painted over one of the port-holes the imposing name "Opossum". She was launched, and steadily wended her way down the bayou. The Rebel picket saw her coming, and whether thinking an iron clad had got down below Vicksburg by way of the Lake Providence Canal or Yazoo Pass, or that we had started a ship-yard in Louisiana, I know not; but he took to his heels after discharging his musket in the air, and had gained the Rebel horde by the time the Opossum hove in sight. The Rebels were confused at first, but began to adjust their piece, when the Opossum was enveloped in smoke, and shell alighted in the midst of the Rebels. Their confusion was complete, and, limbering up their piece, away they went in search of glory down the Mississippi River levee.

Now other divisions came up of our corps and we again pushed on the Perkins' Plantation, where we waited the arrival of the gunboats and transports that so successfully ran the blockade. Our troops were crowded on the boats and conveyed to Grand Gulf; but the gunboats, failing to reduce the place we marched below it, where our transports once more reached us by once more running the blockade, and we were again floating down the great river. Landing at Bruinsburg, we took up a line of march for Port Gibson, and met the Rebels at Thompson's Hill. Whoever has got the honor of this first victory after crossing the river, Gen. Osterhaus has not been justly dealt with. [Gen. James B.] McPherson's Corps was crossing the river at the time this battle opened, and Sherman's Corps was marching through Louisiana, laying waste, with fire, scores of plantations. His was then the rear of the Army.

Gen. Carr's Division of our corps was engaged nearly the whole day; but his casualties were insignificant compared with that of the Ninth Division. Just as the Rebels were hastily retreating, Gen. [John A.] Logan, of the Seventeenth Corps, came up, and his division fired several rounds at very long range. This was the first time any of the Army came up with Gen. Osterhaus's Division, though, from some motive, I learn Gen. Grant has, in his report, placed the Thirteenth Corps on the left and rear. I know nothing of the merits of Gen. [John A.] McClernand, though we all liked the farmer-like, shrewd "Old John A.", as he was styled by our boys, and the little affair of "complete Rebel bagging" at Arkansas Post is indicative of military skill and power.

But, let that pass for what it is worth. We have been completely victorious and I cannot believe that the bold plan of Gen. Grant's could have been so completely carried out without some disaster if every man, from the humblest private up to the major-generals, had not done his duty in soldier-like style.

Gen. Logan was the first to cross the Bayou Pierre and passed over the stream on a pontoon-bridge, while the suspension-bridge was still in flames, having been fired by the retreating Rebels. Here he took one road in pursuit, and Gen. Osterhaus another, and, at Rock Springs, Gen. Osterhaus was in advance of the whole Army. Here Logan turned to the right, toward Raymond; Sherman still farther to the right, and moved to the capital of this State, Jackson. Osterhaus moved directly toward Edwards' Depot. Logan met the Rebels at Raymond and defeated them, after a few hours' fight, and some few hundred killed and wounded. The Raymond hospitals showed that the Rebels had sustained much the heaviest loss. When the battle at Jackson was fought, Gens. Sherman and McPherson's Corps were in that region; which enacted the greatest part, I know not. Both did their duty, no doubt.

The engagement took place during a heavy rain-storm. Afterward, Gen. Osterhaus advanced toward Edward's Depot, but soon came on the enemy—composed of the greater portion of Gen. [John C.] Pemberton's Army. Not wishing to draw on an engagement while the larger portion of our Army was at Jackson, out of aiding distance, he made a detour to the right, passed over Gen. Logan's recent battle-field and entered Raymond at midnight having marched all the night in rain and mud with his weary and poorly fed division; for our line of communications was long, we having been in advance all the time, our division suffered on account of scarcity of provisions, while other divisions had a plentiful supply of hard bread and bacon. Our division at one time took possession of a one-horse corn-mill, ground meal, which they mixed with water and baked on coals by some who had no skillets, and ate with mouldy sides taken from Rebel smoke houses. This experiment terminated in a prevailing diarrhea, while every one was hungry and more fatigued than when they began. They were not used to hoe-cake.

Next day, we lay in open fields and a few old sheds at Raymond, during the heavy rain of that day, and on the following morning took up our line of march toward Bolton; but soon were checked by finding Pemberton's whole force in our road. Leaving a part of his command in a favorable position for defence on this road, General Osterhaus took the remainder, retraced his steps to the forks, where a road branched off toward Edward's Depot. At quick time he advanced on this road till again near the Rebel lines, where he posted his troops on a favorable ridge, with an open field in front, on Bonner's plantation. His skirmishers were thrown out, and his orderlies dispatched to the rear to inform others of his position. All that day, while Gens. McPherson and Sherman were coming up from Jackson, Osterhaus was skirmishing with Pemberton's main Army. Many rounds of cartridges were expended by the skirmishers, showing that they were in earnest. Was the Thirteenth Army Corps on the left and rear at the time he was skirmishing with Pemberton's Army, and the remainder of our Army coming up from Jackson?

We chased the Rebels till beyond Edward's Depot that night, and opened the fight at "Big Black Bridge" the next morning [May 17]. Here Gen. Osterhaus was wounded. He received a pretty painful though not serious contusion of the thigh from a piece of shell. Giving his command to Gen. [Albert L.] Lee, he left the field, yet he kept his aids and orderlies engaged in keeping him posted as regarded the Ninth Division. It was a source of great trouble to the soldiers of his division when they learned of the accident. But the fight soon terminated here by Gen. Sherman outflanking them, he crossing the river on our right, and the Rebels retired in great haste to their works at Vicksburg, having fired the railroad bridge and several buildings containing stores and arms, before retreating.

The next day, we crossed Big Black, and, on the 19th, began the siege of Vicksbug. For six days—at a time when, of the whole siege, our loss was the greatest—the Ninth Division pressed up on the left, and its loss in killed and wounded will speak for the energy of officers and men. On the first day of the siege, and each remaining five days, Gen. Osterhaus was on his horse and in charge of his favorite troops.

Joe Johnston was making demonstrations in our rear, and our Division was ordered to the Big Black River, where the energy of Gen. Osterhaus was such, in making demonstrations, and watching for any show of attack, and quickly preparing for defence at every point the Rebel force pressed upon, that an attack, which might have proved disastrous with Joe Johnston's augmented forces, was delayed till it was too late, and Vicksburg was past assistance. An advance was now ordered on Johnston, and were there an advance to be found in a better position than General Osterhaus? He was in the centre, and the 6th of July, met the Rebels with his cavalry and mounted infantry. Other forces from Vicksburg pressed up, and Rebel Joe was forced to believe that Vicksburg was on the outside of the fence, surrounding his loving and cherished "C. S. A."

He fell back to Jackson, where he had been fortifying. Our troops closed up, and after a few days' desperate fighting, he evacuated the place silently at dead of night, leaving his artillery behind him, as he took his way across Pearl River.

General Sherman is now Military Governor of this State, and occupies Jackson, its capital, with his corps, while the remainder of the troops will seek glory elsewhere. Whether they will be allowed rest, or whether we again are put on the tramp, none know, and few care. They are willing to do anything if it will honorably depose of this new broken-backed Rebellion; for it must be acknowledged that the "back bone of rebellion" is broken at this present time. But like many other vipers, it must be beheaded before it dies.

N. N.

August 16, 1863
CONCERNING THE INVALID CORPS
United States Army Hospital,
Corner Fifty-first Street and Lexington Avenue, Aug. 12.

I desire very much to obtain some information respecting the Invalid Corps , authorized by Orders 105 and 130, current series of War Department. I have not seen either of these orders; but believe the object is, to take all those men who, from sickness and trifling wounds are rendered unfit for field-duty, and substitute them for those doing garrison-duty, and who are variously employed in the hospitals, abundantly able to perform the arduous duties of the field. Looked upon in that light, it is a capital institution, and the soldier ought to feel, and no doubt does, highly favored in being allowed thus to save the balance of his time. As far as those are concerned who have been discharged on account of the loss of a limb, or the entire use of it, and who feel inclined to re-enlist—in this case the Invalid Corps is a fine thing; for very often the person so unfortunate finds it impossible to obtain employment, and his pension, insufficient to support him, he is taken in the Corps, and receives $13 per month and rations, with little or nothing to do. But it seems to me that a man so crippled ought to be discharged, if he so elects, and in no case have they a right to force him into the Invalid Corps.

Many men there are whose mutilated bodies presents the most ample and substantial evidence of their having served the country well and faithfully, and who by their honorable wounds, disqualified for the exciting and glorious duties of field, have too much ambition to be contented with earning a paltry living in a hospital, with its unpleasant associations; but, on the contrary, would much prefer to make the most of their disabilities, and qualify themselves if possible, for something more lucrative, and if a man of not blunted sensibilities—something more congenial.

I know of instances in the hospital of which I am at present a patient, where men have lost a limb, and notwithstanding were retained for the Invalid Corps against their will. One case I will mention particularly. A young man had lost his arm, and was waiting in the hospital for the stump to get well, intending then to get his discharge. Shortly after the order for organizing the Corps, he was ordered before the surgeon in charge, Dr. Mott, and without being allowed any voice in the matter, was given to understand, in the most authoritative tones, that he might consider himself in the Invalid Corps; his arm at this time was unwell, and he is a resident of this city, his family being also in comfortable circumstances. I mention the last facts in order that you may know that in his case it was no charity.

I have understood that in one of these orders the conditions which exempt a man were specified.

HENRY SMITH, Co. D, Second N.Y.S.M.

{The Invalid Corps is comprised of wounded and disabled veteran soldiers, divided into three classes. Their duties are confined to the garrison and hospital, and in guarding deserters or conscripts. It is considered to be a great honor to be attached to this corps, and instead of forcing men there, we believe it requires some trouble and influence to get into it. At least, we are so informed; and only those faithful who have seen actual service can become members of the "Corps of Honor", as it is called. We cannot doubt our correspondent's statement of facts as presented, but there is a woeful mistake made somewhere, as it is generally feared the Invalid Corps will become too large without forcing anybody into its ranks.—ED.}

ONE HUNDRED AND THIRTY-NINTH REGIMENT N.Y.V.
CAMP WESTMAN, WILLIAMSBURG, VA., Aug. 19.

Our regiment is under the influence of the weather just now. Nearly all in camp are complaining of a sort of marsh or low nervous fever. This Peninsula is one of the unhealthiest places in all Dixie, and with "a heated term", of course, is made much worse. Your correspondent is, however, in good health. We have nothing of a warlike nature on hand. The village of Williamsburg is filling up rapidly with people returning to their homes. The Rebel Conscription is picking up every one that does not wear crinoline, and of course, drives into our lines lots of deserters and disgusted traitors anxious to take the "oath of allegiance". A boy came in the other day, direct from Richmond. He says they were going to make a soldier of him; but he couldn't see it.

The ladies (?) of Williamsburg are intensely secesh. They curse our boys morning, noon, and night, who plague them in return with monstrous stories of dreadful battles, in which thousands of Rebs are reported killed, cities burned, etc. The nigger regiments are a complete stunner to them. These feminines say: "Is it not enough to have the scum of the Northern cities spewed among us, without sending an army of runaway slaves to complete our destruction?" Despair makes these "ladies" mad, and the boys coolly tell them they are going to kill all their husbands and lovers, then marry the widows and forsaken sweethearts, and improve the race.

To show you how the F. F. V.'s get along just now, let me relate an incident or two. Some days ago, while in the village, I sat down to dinner in one of the finest and largest houses hereabouts; was waited upon by one of the fair daughters of the hostess; and both mother and daughter felt very ready to accept of our greenbacks to save them from starvation. In fact, these beauties were glad to "keep a hotel". Another whilom wealthy lady of Virginia now peddles pies, cakes, etc., around our camp, sitting on her behind in the bottom of a mule-cart looking round for a customer as eagerly as a clam-boy in New York, but with not half his independence. The contrabands have decidedly the best of it, taking the boys' greenbacks for washing, indigestible compounds, odd chores, or anything to get money of which they seem to be as craving as a Chatham street "old clo' man". Speaking of old clothes the wenches appear to have laid violent hands on mistresses' wardrobes. The other day, there was a darkey funeral near here, and you should have seen the darkeys, how they spread themselves—their trails extending as consequentally as that of a Fifth Avenue belle. If not as fair, they are a good deal frailer; for chastity among these wenches is rather the exception than the rule. Poor devils! nothing seems to trouble them but the dream of their old master catching them again.

Last week, I went to see a regiment of negroes at Fortress Monroe. If they fight as well as they look, the enemy had better keep his eyes skinned, for a more muscular body of men or more obedient soldiers I have never seen—all young, and evidently pleased with their position. They were "off for Charleston afore the broke of day", and doubtless by this time are kicking against the gates for admission.

Our regiment is undergoing some changes. Colonel Conk has resigned. Also Major [Andrew] Morris; ditto Captain [Thomas] Lunny of Company B; ditto Captain H. W. Phillips of Company E. There is a great speculation in camp as to when and where this war will end. I see by the papers New York is now getting a healthy draft, and your amusements are comprised of ghosts and hobgoblins. There is nothing like quinine to steady your nerves, the dose with us is a full one, three times a day—it is awful stuff.

How is it our mail comes so slow and irregularly?

EAGLE.

NINETY-NINTH REGIMENT, N.Y.V.
FORT RODMAN, Aug. 17.

Your correspondent (Gov.) lately stated in part how we are situated here, but he made a mistake in saying that Capt. D. J. Bailey had command of this post which is not so, as he was sent from here to take command of his company at Yorktown, leaving First Lieutenant Jas. A. Fleming in command, and a Second Lieutenant by the name of [John] Walker, belonging to the One Hundred and Thirty-second Regiment, N.Y.S.V., being second in command. We have fifty men of our company here at present doing garrison-duty at this post. We have splendid quarters, and we are every bit as comfortable here as if we were home, with the exception of friends being absent, victuals, and the guard-duty. When we first came to this point, from Suffolk, two of our men went out on a scout, and came back each with two possums, which they had captured from a contraband. They immediately went to work, and dug a hole in the ground, about six feet long and two feet wide, and boarded it all round, put the four possums in it, and left them there; they had fed the little things (which are quite tame) on toads, frogs, corn bread, and all sorts of fruit. They were growing quite large, when the other night, while I was on post, they escaped out of their cage and got prowling around the quarters (I was thinking they were rats all the time), when one of them went in a Lieutenant's quarters and run across his face. He sang out for his sword and revolvers, also singing out, "Where are you? we are attacked!" also crying out, "Pompey, Sam, Jack, you black devils! where are you? hurry and bring me my arms, and arm yourselves at the same time" I went over to the harmless thing, when one of them taking a bottle of hair-oil, fired it at the possum, the Lieutenant singing out, "D—n you for an ignorant contraband, what did you break that for? After fighting for about one hour, they put up their swords, reeking with the blood of the terrible animal, and lay down exhausted with the strife they had gone through.

JUNE.

ARMY OF THE POTOMAC.

ALEXANDRIA, VA., August 17.

Last summer, about this time, I was corresponding to you from the Forty-seventh Regiment, N.Y.S.V., from Hilton Head, South Carolina. I thought then, that the weather was terribly hot, but I found it not much worse than Old Virginia, during the past few days.

Last Sunday morning, I embarked on the cars at 4 o'clock, and started for Warrenton Junction and the front, to see what was transpiring. I arrived there about 7 o'clock A.M. I found the Junction to be quite a lively place. Heavy trains, loaded with conscripts, troops, and provisions were constantly arriving, and were then forwarded to the different corps of the Army of the Potomac encamped in the neighborhood.

The Military Railroad runs out regularly to Warrenton Junction, a distance of thirty-nine miles. Irregular trains are then sent out to Warrenton town, over a branch road nine miles in length. Other trains are sent up on the main road, to Bealton, and to Rappahannock, distant fifty miles from Alexandria. The United States Military Construction Corps have rebuilt the railroad bridge over the river; so, whenever our Army advance, the trains can be run through to Culpepper without much delay.

From present appearances, it does not look like as either Army were very anxious to make a move, or engage in another battle, very soon.

General Meade's Army holds a good position, and are ready for Lee and his followers at any time. Our cavalry force extends for several miles along and beyond the south side of the river, watching any movements the Rebels may make.

I called at Warrenton Town, and found it to be a very pretty little place, somewhat deserted; yet there is a number of the old residents living there, and among them a few pretty girls; they are, of course, the strongest kind of secesh, and would not, for the world, condescend to speak to us "Yankee Mudsills". I stopped in front of the Warren Green Hotel, and found it occupied by our soldiers. It looked as though it had seen better days. The old sign hangs out over the street the same as ever. I saw everything there in about an hour, and then started back to the Junction, where I was well taken care of by Messrs. Edwards and Graham, of the United States Military Telegraph Corps. They are quartered in a car on a side-track, and have everything comparatively comfortable for such desolate country. Their wire connects direct with the War Department. The greater inconvenience from Warrenton Junction up to Rappahannock, is the scarcity of water; hardly any can be procured without a walk of a quarter of a mile or more, and then it is so muddy and unpleasant that it can hardly be used—a man wants to be very, very, thirsty to drink it. A pontoon bridge is still stretched across the Rappahannock just above the railroad bridge. Cavalry in small bodies are constantly crossing and recrossing. No Rebs are visible within five or six miles of the river at that point. The heat is terrible, especially as you cross the bridge, for then you get the full strength of the sun.

All along the road, just before coming to the river, soldiers beat out and unable to march are lying among the bushes, to regain a little strength and to get cooled off. Nary drop of water; so they must suffer until they arrive at the railroad station.

I do not know what the Army would do if it were not for the railroad. It is only a single track, but as much business is done as on any double track road of the same length. Messrs. Devereux and Lord, the Superintendent and Assistant, are entitled to considerable credit for the energetic manner in which they forward troops, supplies, sick, wounded, and prisoners. Our Government may well be proud of their military railroads, for they have the finest motive power and some of the best railroad men in the country.

Your correspondent is under many obligations to Mr. James McIntosh, the storekeeper, and to the railroad-men in general. I expect to go out to the front again soon, and will keep you informed as to what is transpiring there.

The SUNDAY MERCURY is eagerly sought for all through the Army, and cannot be dispensed with, in fact, it is part of the soldier's rations.

Mosby and his gang have been, of late, doing a flourishing business robbing sutlers, between Alexandria and Fairfax. Night before last, Mosby captured a lot of sutlers within ten miles of Alexandria. Where is our cavalry? Why cannot they capture him? Something should be done soon.

"HA FELLERS."

AN AMAZON—The Gettysburg correspondent of the Detroit *Tribune* gives the following account of a female soldier:—"I talked with Mary Lippey [Tepe] this morning. She is the French woman who has followed the One Hundred and Fourteenth Pennsylvania Regiment since it entered the service. She is an interesting character. She wears the regular Zouave uniform; the only one thing indicating her sex is a short skirt. She wears red pants and top boots, carries a revolver, and sometimes a musket, if one of the boys gets too tired to carry his. She is the idol of the regiment, and they have good cause to revere her. She gave me an amusing account of her arrest by the Lieutenant-Colonel in command here a few days after the fight. Mary was coming in from camp for supplies for the wounded, and was arrested and taken to jail. She said he was a militia Colonel, and did not know his duty. She showed her pass, but it would not do, and he was about to search her, when, with a pistol in hand, she ordered him to 'stand off'. 'I am a woman,' said she, 'but I can teach you your duty; lay a hand on me and I will shoot you.' The Colonel soon saw he had made a mistake, and ordered her release. She is known as Mary all through the camp, and has saved the life of many a poor fellow. She had followed the French Army seven years, went through the Crimean campaign, and has served nineteen months in this war."

August 30, 1863
MILITARY MATTERS
GENERAL GRANT A GREAT SMOKER.—Nearly every general in command of an army has a peculiar habit, which he exhibits only on the battle-field. In civil life, wine frequently develops traits of character never revealed in a state of sobriety. In military life, battle takes the place of wine in this respect. Men who are noted for their observance of the Second Commandment in camp, exhibit signs of profanity while the skirmish line is being formed, and get to swearing vigorously before the battle is fairly begun.

You cannot read in General Grant's countenance how a battle is going. Whether the enemy is driving him, or he is driving the enemy, he wears the same placid features—neither a smile nor a frown. You look in vain for hope, fear, or anxiety, depicted in his facial expression. But there is one key by which some idea may be formed as to how he feels while the struggle progresses. The General is, in camp, addicted to the "use of the weed" to a moderate extent; but on the battle-field he indulges more than usual. The more desperate the battle, the more extravagant the use of Cubas and Principes. When his men are pushing forward, and the enemy giving way, the blue smoke ascends at regular intervals in small and scarcely perceptible curls. When the ground is being contested, his face is lost in Cuban exhalations. When there is a prospect that the day will go against him, he ceases to smoke, and commences to punish his innocent exotic by vigorously biting the end of it. When he rides along the line without a cigar, there is no enemy in front except a small body of Rebel cavalry, and he knows it.

General Sherman is an inveterate smoker on the battle-field, also. When he was wounded at Shiloh, he wrapped his pocket handkerchief round his hand, lit a cigar, and became more earnest then ever.

September 6, 1863
FORTIETH REGIMENT, N.Y.V.
CAMP FORTIETH REGIMENT, N.Y.V.
SULPHER SPRINGS, VA., August 29.

This regiment is, as you are probably aware of, composed of five New York regiments viz.: the Fortieth, Eighty-seventh, Fifty-fifth, One Hundred and First, and the recruits of the Thirty-eighth N.Y.V., which makes it one of the strongest veteran regiments in the service.

We took into the battle of Gettysburg about 600 able men, and lost there about 200 in killed and wounded, among whom were our gallant Adjutant, William H. Johnson, killed; and our Major, now Lieut.-Colonel [Augustus J.] Warner, and several other officers, wounded. The regiment behaved well—better than could be expected from so many consolidated regiments, representing almost all nations of the world. But it could not be otherwise with such a gallant and heroic commander as Colonel Thomas W. Egan. Brave almost to daring, he led us on. After his horse was shot from under him, he swung his sword and cried: "Come on, Fortieth, to victory!" and he led us close to the Rebel ranks, which position we maintained for one hour and a half, until relieved by a brigade of the Fifth Corps. The regiment was highly praised by Generals Birney and Ward.

We are encamped in a beautiful grove near the celebrated Sulpher Springs, at present the Head-Quarters of Major General Birney, our Division Commander, who is as good and brave a man as we wish to serve under. Our duty at present is not as light as it might be, as we have to do picket by detail, sending out fifty men every day. We picket along the Rappahannock River. There have been no large bodies of Rebels in this vicinity since we came here. Scouting parties are sent daily to scour the country on the other side of the river. So far, they have had no brush with the enemy.

We have had a change in our food since we came here; we occasionally receive rations of vegetables and dried apples, and we get soft-tack every day. We are said to be the best regiment in the Division, by all the officers that inspect us. White gloves are furnished by our Colonel, and the men take pride in keeping their clothing and equipments in first-rate order; and I think that there is no volunteer regiment in the service that makes a finer appearance than this. We have only nine months and a few days to serve, and during that time we will try and maintain the good name that the old Mozart has won, but at the cost of many lives that we hold most dear. We have company and battalion drill every day, and brigade drill twice a week, all the maneuvers are executed well, as veterans only know how to do them.

We have a splendid drum-corps, consisting of thirty drummers, five fifers, and ten buglers, under the leadership of Drum Major [Michael] Erb, formerly of the Regular Army, and I may safely say it is the best drum corps in the United States.

Last Sunday, we had divine service which was attended by a large number of staff-officers, accompanied by their ladies. The Seventeenth Maine Volunteers and our own regiment attended. The exercises were very fine and impressive; they were conducted by the Chaplain of the Seventeenth Maine Volunteers and our own Chaplain, Rev. Mr. Guilder. The pulpit was made of a pyramid of drums, covered with the National Flag, and on each side of it there was a stack of arms and our regimental flags, which gave it a very fine appearance.

It pleases the boys of the Fortieth to see that our old comrades of the Twentieth Indiana and Third Michigan Regiments have at last some rest from their weary labors and hard-fought battles in Virginia; and we hope that they will do nothing to dishonor the red patch while in New York City. We hope they will have good times, and that diamonds may always be trumps.

FILE-CLOSER.

The 20ᵗʰ Indiana and 3ʳᵈ Michigan Infantry Regiments were among the units temporarily sent to New York City to quell the draft riots.

September 13, 1863
NINTH REGIMENT, N.Y.S.M.
CAMP PAROLE, ANNAPOLIS, MD., Sept. 7.

I was taken prisoner at Gettysburg, July 1. Although over two months ago, the terrible battle which was fought on that day must be still fresh in the minds of the readers of the MERCURY. Being one of your correspondents while in camp, I now take the pleasure of giving you a short record of my captivity, being the first chance which has offered since my release from Rebeldom (last Friday a week ago). On the 1ˢᵗ of July our corps, after fighting for several hours, with no support whatever, and no signs of reenforcements, were compelled to give way, for two reasons, viz.: first, the melancholy death of Major-General Reynolds; and, second, the running of the Eleventh Corps (the flying half-moon). In losing the former, we had no general to command us, and in the latter were even allowed to be outflanked; and I must mention as disgracefully running, was the Forty-fifth New York. Eight of these men with muskets surrendered to one Rebel. The whole regiment is in Dixie yet. We were completely outflanked by these fellows running, and were marched to the Rebel rear, and by the fourth, there were 3,650 non-commissioned officers and privates, and some 182 officers, the Eleventh Corps having the majority. We were marched off to Williamsport, guarded by Pickett's Division, *i. e.*, what was left of them. They treated us well. We reached Williamsport July 7, passing through Hagerstown. The people cheering us, and just in time to be too late to be rescued by our cavalry.

The whole Rebel Army could have been captured on the 4ᵗʰ of July, as they were all stuck in the mud, disabled, and, worst of all, the most miserable and poor defeated creatures I ever saw in all my life. Our boys hallowed out, "How are you Baltimore, Washington, and pontoons?" The former cities on the 1ˢᵗ they were bound to take, and the pontoons were destroyed by our cavalry.

At Williamsport, the people baked us 4,000 loaves of bread, but a rascally quartermaster of the Rebel service took them, and sold them to us for fifty cents a loaf. On the 9ᵗʰ, we were taken across the river and were promised plenty of rations in Virginia. On the 10ᵗʰ, we reached Martinsburg, and the ladies of this place (God bless them!) gave us bread, milk, etc., as far as they were allowed to; for in one instance a brutal officer cut at one of the boys with his sabre for trying to get a loaf of bread a young lady offered him. We were guarded now by [Gen. John D.] Imboden's Cavalry, and some of them were regular brutes. We encamped about two miles from Martinsburg on the 10ᵗʰ, and the ladies sent us all the bread, which they cooked all night long. We were nearly starved, and all the piety of rations which we were to get did not come, and did not reach us until we reached Winchester, July 12. Here we got a pint of flour and some fresh meat. We simply mixed the flour up with water, and baked it on tin plates, stones, wood, and every imaginable way. We left the following day (13ᵗʰ), and reached Edenburg, marching twenty-three miles this day; 15ᵗʰ, New

Market; 16th, Harrisonburg. During these three days' marching we were nearly starved, only receiving a pint of flour during the whole three days' march. All I kept up body and soul was by chewing tobacco, which I never did before, eating peppermint, pepper grass, and green apples as big as plums, and once in awhile a few blackberries.

The men could hardly be got along and a great many had fallen out exhausted. The guards would hallo: "You, Yanks, go along dare! get in ranks! doggon, you Yanks!" On the 17th, we reached Mt. Sidney, and on the 18th, Staunton; having marched in thirteen days 168 miles, over a turn-pike, the majority of the men barefoot, no blankets, and no hats in some cases. At Staunton, they took all the India-rubber blankets from the men, and on the 19th, we took the train for Richmond, arriving there on the morning of the 20th. Daylight, they marched us to Libby—700 of us—and kept us three hours. While here, we got a ration of bread and meat (rather small), and one of the chivalry shot a Kentucky soldier, who was deaf, in the arm—since died— for looking out of the window. After this, they searched us; took all our money, writing-paper, haversacks, etc., allowing us only our blankets and caps. We were then marched over to Belle Island, a miserable, hot place, an acre of ground, about 4,000 men in it, and full of lice and vermin. Here we lived on ten ounces of bread and two ounces of fresh meat per day. Breakfast at 9, 10, 11 and 12 o'clock, just as it suited the Quartermaster; dinner at 3½, slop rice soup and bread. Almost two and three times a week we were turned out and counted, and put in messes of a hundred each. On the 10th of August, they played a sharp game upon the Yanks. A citizen came over from Richmond, and offered $8 in silver for $10 greenbacks. A great many of the boys having large bills—10's and 20's—got them changed; and I suppose, $500 so exchanged. The next day, the men were all turned out and searched, and the silver confiscated. On the 14th, they deliberately murdered a member of the Ninety-first Pennsylvania. He had just come in, and was sitting near the bank inside, when the guard ordered him up. He simply asked him, "Where will I go? I have no tent." "You Yankee son of a b—" leveling his piece, and shot him dead, wounding two others. The brute and murderer was taken before the officer in command of the post, nothing was done to him, and the Union soldier lies buried on Belle Isle unavenged. A great deal of trading with the guard at nights was done. They seemed perfectly crazy for greenbacks, offering $10 of their money for $1 of ours; for $7 of our money would buy as much as $10 of their money. Those that had money speculated considerable, and, I must say, a great many of our men completely robbed the boys by selling a small five cent loaf for $1; pies they would buy for twenty-five cents a-piece, they would charge $1 for; tobacco, a plug for fifty cents, worth 10 cents; and a canteen full of whiskey, $5—cost them $1! The camp had any quantity of these speculators, who would sit up all night, buy off the guards, and sell to our own men, some realizing a small fortune—one man having $1,000 in greenbacks.

We were subjected to all kinds of treatment while we were in the Rebel clutches and thank God we were released from their hands on Friday, August 28, leaving Richmond at daylight, August 29, stopping two hours at Petersburg, arriving at City Point at 11, delivered upon the flag-of-truce boat City of New York. Once more under the good old flag, the Stars and Stripes, we arrived at Fortress Monroe at 4½ P.M., and reached Annapolis Sunday morning, August 31. Upon the free soil of the United States, we received our clean clothes, of which we were very much in need, got our dinner, wrote to our friends and relations, thank Almighty God for our safe deliverance to our homes and firesides. We are now in the new barracks, Camp Parole. I will drop you a line, in my next, about this place. It is under the control of Colonel [Adrian] Root, and all we want is Uncle Sam to pay us two months' pay, give us a furlough until we get exchanged, which, by the way, is very doubtful, as the Rebels will not exchange negro soldiers. However, I hope that this will find you well, and I remain yours truly,

J. F. W.

P.S.—I forgot to mention what I have seen of the inside of Rebeldom. The bogus Confederacy is nearly played out; then, provisions they have none; their large, boasted armies are all fudge. Vicksburg and Port Hudson stunned them; Charleston, Mobile, and Savannah, will kill them; and our Government ought and can take Richmond any day, if they have a mind to; no soldiers around there nearer Fredericksburg. The city militia does not amount to anything, and the people of Richmond will help us as soon as our forces near the city.

J. F. W.

John F. White, Jr., age 28, enlisted in the 9th New York State Militia (83rd N.Y. Infantry) on Sept. 18, 1861. He was promoted to corporal on Oct. 21, 1863 and served until his discharge on Jan. 10, 1865. In 1867, he enlisted in the 31st U. S. Infantry and was discharged at Fort Stevenson, Dakota Territory in 1870. He died in Kansas City on February 8, 1902.

September 20, 1863

ANOTHER STOP TOWARD DESPOTISM.

Were we to say that the recent Proclamation of President Lincoln places it in the power of any officer, and or military, in the service of the United States Government to arrest and incarcerate in a dungeon any citizen, and that the person so dealt with was without redress, and no Court in the land dare inquire why he was held in durance, we might be deemed guilty of exaggeration. Yet such is the condition imposed upon American citizens by a literal interpretation of the edict of the President suspending the writ of Habeas Corpus throughout the length and breath of these United States. The Proclamation confers the power to arrest and retain any person in custody upon "the military, naval and civil officers" of the United States—which includes every Government employe, from General Halleck and Secretary [Gideon] Welles down to a tidewaiter or a collector of the internal revenue. And these arrests are authorized to be made for no specified offence; for, after enumerating the cases of prisoners of war, spies, aiders and abettors of the enemy, and men belonging to the land or naval forces who have enlisted into either branch of the service, and exhausting every conceivable case covered by municipal or martial law, the Proclamation goes on to include "any other offence against the military or naval service"—not any law or regulation governing either, but anything that any irresponsible official may choose to consider an offence. We have not exaggerated, therefore, in describing the scope of this Proclamation, which absorbs all the laws of the land and the rights of the citizen, as the rod of Aaron swallowed up the wands of the Magi.

It requires no argument to show that the power conferred upon Congress by the Constitution to suspend the writ of Habeas Corpus when, in case of rebellion or invasion, the public safety demanded such action, was intended to apply only to the immediate scene of hostilities; and the idea that the power to suspend the writ here, in New York, because there might be a rebellion in Georgia or California, is granted by this Constitutional provision, is an absurdity. But, passing that consideration, the question arises—Does the public safety require the suspension of the writ?

It is said that persons enlisted into the Army and Navy were being discharged by State Courts; but this could only happen in cases where the parties were not legally enlisted, and their number were too few to have any appreciable effect on the strength of the armies. But if it was only intended to reach these cases, why was not the necessary restriction observed in the phraseology of the Proclamation? But we have distinct and positive evidence, emanating directly from the Government itself, that the public safety did not require it. Mr. Seward has just addressed a circular to foreign nations, in which he recapitulates the victories which have crowned the Union arms within the past year, showing that the Rebellion has been cut in two, one-third of its territory recaptured, and, in a word, that it is on point of final extinction, and that, should the aforesaid nations desire to render it any aid, they will find themselves too late. Now, if this be so—and it is the Government's own statement of the case—from what source does the appalling danger arise that renders it necessary to sweep away the laws and the liberties of the people "at one fell swoop"? And what a commentary will this edict be on Mr. Seward's circular when it reaches Europe! It will give their rulers an opportunity to assert either that the boasts of the weakness of the Rebellion are groundless braggadocia, or Mr. Lincoln assumes absolute power, without even the tyrant's plea of necessity.

People seek in vain for a reason for the issuing of such an edict, and fail to find any object to be effected, unless it be intended to operate on the approaching State elections, to be used as an engine of terrorism in the hands of the Administration party. But this can assuredly not be so; for the President cannot be so infatuated as not to know that the endeavor to wield any such despotic machinery for such a purpose would incite the people to rebuke the usurpation almost unanimously. And we can only attribute the edict to that fatuous fatality which has led the Administration on more than one previous occasion to tamper, unnecessarily, with the liberties of the people. Its only effect has been, and will be, to cloud the lustre of our military achievements, and injure if not disgrace us in the eyes of other nations.

September 27, 1863

FROM A PAROLED PRISONER

CAMP PAROLE, MD., September 21.

It is now three weeks since I left Richmond, Va.; since which time, I have devoted myself to the recruiting up of my health by eating any quantity of Uncle Sam's rations; and rest assured I have improved considerable, together with all of us. I wrote you of our travels in Dixie, which appeared in the SUNDAY MERCURY for September 13; and I now will, according to promise, give you, as far as I know, about things in general in Camp Parole.

When we arrived at Annapolis, we were put in College Ground Barracks, under the charge of Major Daniel Evertts, Eighty-ninth N.Y.V. Here the paroled prisoner is ordered to wash and clean himself, and put on new clothes; then the Major, a fine man, says: "Now, boys, when you get clean, go and get your dinner. Keep the barracks tidy, and you have the privilege of going into town. I have no guard whatever; every man must be his own guard. If any of you should happen to get inebriated the boys will duck you." We remained here but two days, when all the New York, New Jersey, Maryland, and Delaware troops—about 450—were marched to this place, our new barracks, two miles from Annapolis. Here we found about 3,000 paroled prisoners, some that were taken as far back as Chancellorsville.

The camp is well laid out, on the banks of the Annapolis Junction Railroad. Fifteen well-aired and built barracks, cook-houses in the rear; but, alas! no cooks. Every one of us is now our own cook; and we are led to believe that our victuals should be served up to us, which they ought to be; but beyond gross neglect of the Quartermaster, who does not understand his business, we have to cook in all shapes, kinds, and manners, and draw five days' rations, the same as if we were on the march.

The camp is under the control of Colonel A. Root, Ninety-fourth N.Y.V., who was captured at Gettysburg, subsequently paroled on the battle-field, taken to Carlisle, and from thence ordered to his regiment (the parole is not being recognized), but the Colonel threatened to resign, and the Government finally sent him here. He is pretty strict with the boys, and I must say he is not liked by all—unlike Major Evertts. He could have many warm friends.

The Provost-Marshal of the camp is Captain A.N. Briggs, a fine officer, who does his duty satisfactorily to us all.

There are four battalions under the command of paroled captains and lieutenants, and each barrack averaging 120 men, having a sergeant, who sees about drawing rations, issuing passes, cleaning up, making out reports, and calling the roll every evening at sundown.

There are all sorts of troops here, infantry, cavalry, and artillery, and the three militia regiments of New York are represented—the Second, Ninth, and Fourteenth, N.Y.S.M. About seventeen of the former were taken at Gettysburg; twenty-seven of the Ninth, and seventy-seven of the Fourteenth.

All sorts of rumors prevail from day to day, and the exchange of prisoners is the subject which now engrosses the minds of all. The Commissioners, it seems, meet every week; but they meet with no progress, and arrive at no definite settlement, the stumbling block, it seems, is the negro. Some 200 of these ebony soldiers have been taken prisoners, and the Confederate Government turned them over to the State of South Carolina, saying that they were runaway negroes, and their masters claiming them, and it was now decided never to exchange them for one of their white soldiers. They would rather die than put the negro on an equality with their white men. This was the talk in Richmond. Now, the demand has been made for these negroes by our Government, and the only way to obtain them is by taking Charleston and breaking up the nest of traitors at Richmond, and then we will have an exchange, and not before.

We have sent a petition to Governor Seymour to ask the War Department leave to allow us a few days' furlough to visit our families, but with what success remains to be seen; but I am afraid the Governor not being very popular with the Administration, his prayer and our petition will meet with a refusal. Now, why ought it? We have served our country faithfully for over two years, and not one of us here to-day has seen our wives, mothers, and families. Having yet nine months more to serve, some a year, it is not more than fair and right that us veterans should see our homes. The Government has allowed the Maine paroled troops to go home; and, rumor says, Ohio and Pennsylvania will go also; if so, New York should not be neglected. Can you speak a good word for 1,200 New Yorkers?

I must speak of one thing before closing, and that is in regard to pay. The broken-down and thieving hordes of Rebels robbed us of every cent of money which we happened to have about us when taken prisoners; since which time we have heard that the Army of the Potomac has been paid twice since the 1st of July, and not one cent have we been paid. Our families are greatly in want, and we are without anything; the sick are without luxuries to recruit themselves up, and nothing to eat but salt junk and pork, and without articles which we are very much in need of. They have always been prompt in the payment of paroled prisoners every two months, but why this gross neglect we cannot account for? This kind of treatment to the old troops rather discourages them, and a great many take French leave and go home in disgust. Just this alone accounts for having so many deserters in the Federal Army, not paying promptly the men, and not granting furloughs to the soldiers.

J. F. W.

October 4, 1863

SECOND FIRE ZOUAVES (FOURTH REGIMENT EXCELSIOR BRIGADE)

CAMP NEAR CULPEPPER, VA., Sept. 26.

We had quite a wet time crossing the Rapidan. Those that had taken the precaution of stripping their lower extremities were all right. The rest suffered the penalty of a wet skin for some hours afterward, which, I can assure you, is not very pleasant early in the morning. As the boys say it is all in our three years, we are satisfied.

We do not fare as well as we ought to at present, considering our close proximity to Northern markets. The entire absence of vegetables here is the cause of a large attendance at the doctor's calls in the morning. Had some enterprising firm (as the Government does not take notice of it as it ought to) got permission to supply us with vegetables, it would realize a fortune, and improve the health of the Army more than all the doctors we have among us.

I understand, by a letter received here yesterday, that our old and valued friend, Captain Purtell, is convalescent and rapidly improving in health. It was feared here by his friends that the severe attack he sustained would terminate fatally. But thanks to an All-wise Providence and the care he has received at his home, he has been spared, and will be with us again. He is our favorite, and the oldest officer in the regiment. Col. Brewster ought to be a brigadier. Justice would be done to a good, honest, and deserving officer.

It is reported here that Gen. Sickles is coming back. We are all anxious to see him. The whole Corps is unanimous on that point. We never had a general we liked as well. Stanton may try to give us another; but we will have none but General Sickles.

It is the source of a great deal of pleasure to me to state that Lieut. Mathew Stewart is again with us. Our mail comes slow and irregular, which fact disappoints a great many. Fears are entertained here for the safety of the officers and men who went for conscripts. It is suspected that they have gone in out of the draft, as we have not heard from them since they left here. I don't believe our decimated ranks will be much improved by their absence. But we are here to fight or play, and we will do it to the last.

Lieut. [Thomas] Manning is getting his band together; he expects by the middle of next month to have them in full blast. He requires a few more volunteer recruits, with their instruments. They have been shooting deserters all over the Army; we had none in our corps yet, and I hope we will keep so. We are now waiting for Lee; if he comes, we will give him as warm a reception as possible.

Truly, yours, etc.   GLADIATOR.

October 11, 1863
FORTIETH REGIMENT, N.Y.V.
NEAR CULPEPPER, VA., Oct. 4.

We left our camp at Sulpher Springs, September 15th, and after two days' march reached this place. Nothing of interest has transpired since my last, in the war-line. We are at present going through our usual routine of camp-life.

Last Tuesday, the Paymaster paid us a visit, and also paid us some "greenbacks". On Wednesday night last, a grand masquerade ball was given by the drum-corps and some of the members of the regiment. Among the characters on the ball-ground we particularly noticed an Indian chief and maiden, a colored dandy and his lady, clown, landlord, sailor, Irishman, and peasants, male and female. The belle of the ball was a handsomely dressed young lady (*a la* Fifth Avenue). There were many other characters also worthy of notice, but I will not enter into details. The affair was well conducted, most of the officers were present and tripped the light fantastic toe with the damsels. The dresses were very good, considering the limited means they had of getting the materials to make them. The ladies were personated by the younger drummers, and looked charming. The music consisted of two violins and a flute. During the intermission, Larry Finekenour, of Company H, sang several comic songs, which were received with great applause. Contraband "Ben", formerly of the Twelfth Miss. Vols., danced Jim Crow and a hornpipe, which was also loudly applauded.

This morning we had a division review by Major-Generals French and Birney. The whole division looked very well; many of the regiments have been filled up with conscripts. We have received no convicts (conscripts) yet, although we have a detail at Riker's Island, in charge of Captain [James R.] Stevens, Company D, who, I am sure, will endeavor to use them right, as he is a gentleman and a good soldier.

The health of the regiment is extremely good, very few attend surgeon's call in the morning, and I am happy to say, that we have had no death from disease in the regiment for over seven months.

I am very glad to say that the "SUNDAY MERCURY" has a very extensive circulation in the regiment, and is always eagerly sought for in the mail.

We had a very heavy rain-storm which commenced on Thursday night, and continued all day Friday, during which time we got a nice shower-bath in elegant shelter-tents; but the sun is out again in all its splendor, making the fine old woods and ripe cornfields look bright and green.

FILE CLOSER.

October 18, 1863
SECOND REGIMENT COLORED U.S.V. (CORPS D'AFRIQUE).
PORT HUDSON, LA., Oct. 3.

The officers of this regiment were selected principally from the Army of the Potomac, and were of those number of officers that reported to General [Daniel] Ullmann at 200 Broadway, New York. After leaving New York, we had a pleasant sail of some two weeks, arriving at New Orleans; we there were ordered to Baton Rouge. We remained there for some time, and obtained 350 able-bodied negroes. At first, it was trying to our patience to attempt to teach these men to drill, but having once got started, I was surprised to see how rapidly they progressed. They did far better than was expected by any one, and better than a certain class of white soldiers, a great number of which can be found in old regiments.

While the siege of Port Hudson was in operation, we were ordered up there, and did a great deal of hard service, working day and night in digging trenches, rifle-pits, approaches, and in building batteries. The prompt manner, and the vast amount of work, together with the cheerfulness of the men while at this work, before Port Hudson, was the wonder of all who witnessed it, and they were made the recipients of some very flattering remarks by officers high in command. We now are hard at work drilling our men, and with the exception of one or two companies who have not proper officers to command them, I will put them against any company of white volunteers, in company drill, that have been in the field for the same length of time that we have. There is no use in saying that negroes won't make soldiers, as every one who has been among them in this department can testify.

We all look anxiously for the appearance of the SUNDAY MERCURY in camp, and no one is satisfied until he has read and re-read its columns through and through.

NEW YORK BOY.

October 25, 1863
FORTIETH REGIMENT, N.Y.V.
CAMP NEAR FAIRFAX STATION, VA., Oct. 18.

You know by this time that we left near Culpepper. On the morning of the 10th, we received five days' rations; we had them on hand three days, making eight days altogether. All sorts of speculations were made in regard to where we were going, very few thought that we were coming back as far as this. We "took in" our roofs, put our beds (blankets), and clothing, and extra "provender" in our bureaux [knapsack], put on our harness, "grub bag", strapped the whole of our wealth on our backs, took our trusty "fire-locks" in our hands, and bade adieu to the land where all the fence-rails were burnt up, and which Stuart and the Yanks never held any length of time. We went only a short distance that day, and bivouacked in an old camp. Next morning, we were up and off by 6 o'clock; it was 12 o'clock that night before we halted at Freeman's Ford. On the way, we came near having a brush with the Rebel cavalry. We were drawn up in line across a road leading to Culpepper, the Rebels came to a fence out of range. I concluded that it was unhealthy to come any farther. Captain [James C.] Briscoe, on Birney's staff, made a dash out alone, and captured one of their scouts. On Monday, the 11th, we lived all day in the woods near the ford. We heard heavy firing all day on both on our right and left, but no enemy made his appearance in our front. We received two days' rations while there. On Tuesday morning we were off at about six o'clock, and about three o'clock the head of our column, the Third Michigan Volunteers, at a small place called Auburn, ran against a small body of Rebel cavalry and two pieces of light artillery. Quite a brisk little fight ensued. The Michigan skirmishers charged through the woods, and then you ought to have seen the Rebs "take out". Our regiment lies in line as reserve for the other regiment. We had three men wounded and one killed, although we did not fire a shot. One dead Reb was all I saw, although more than one was killed; we buried him in the woods just where he fell; he met a traitor's doom, and deserves no monument. We bivouacked that night at a small town called Greenwich. Most all the houses were deserted, but were in pretty good order, but they did not long remain so, for we were tired and hungry. I felt ugly. I could not find many rails, so rip went the boards off the houses, and we soon had cheery fires. (Rebels' houses furnish good wood for Union soldiers' bivouack-fires.) On Wednesday morning, we were off again early, and marched all day with the music of artillery in our rear. When we came in sight of Bristoe Station, we halted, and drew up in line, went on again, crossed the railroad at Manassas Junction; also the plains of Manassas; forded the Bull Run stream, passed over a portion of the Old Bull Run battle-ground (first battle); bivouacked, near Centreville, in line, expecting that the Rebs would come up; but nary Reb came. From where we were, we could plainly see the shells from the guns of ours, and the Reb artillery (at Manassas) burst in the air; the cannonading was very heavy, and toward evening it grew more distant; so we knew by that that "our fellows" whipped them. All along the road was one continual line of ambulances, wagons, and artillery. The object of the Rebels appeared to be to cut off our train (wagon), but nary a cut off. The fighting was near Manassas. We took five pieces of artillery, and several hundred prisoners. Those whom I have seen are very well dressed, and don't look much like starving. On Thursday morning, we got under the wing of Washington, by coming inside of the defences. We came to this place, "set" ourselves down, and here we are now. We are within six miles of Alexandria, and about two miles from Fairfax Station, on the Alexandria & Orange Railroad.

General Sickles arrived here on Thursday night, and a right hearty reception he got. We all like him as well as we did Kearny, and that is to almost worship him, as a general. We all hope that he will be able to remain with us. General French is not liked at all. He may be a good general, but the boys call him "blinky".

On Friday, we were witness to a very painful scene—no less than shooting one of our soldiers, belonging to the Fifth Regiment, Michigan Vols. Only our division was out. We were formed in four lines, two lines at an about-face, making two aisles; the prisoner was marched through the lines handcuffed, accompanied by a band of music playing the Dead March; the guard were in front and behind him; his coffin, carried by four men, preceded him. After they had passed through the lines, they halted on our left, on a small hill, near the side of the grave. The sentence of the court-martial was then read to the division; the prisoner, in the meanwhile, was praying; he was then blindfolded, and seated on his coffin. The firing-party took their position a short distance from him; at the signal, they all fired together, and he fell into his coffin, pierced with ten balls, all in the region of the heart. He made no speech before he died. He was buried where he fell. The circumstances, as far as I can learn, are as follows: He deserted from his regiment a long time ago, and went home to Michigan. He re-enlisted in several other regiments while home, and received large bounties. He remained there a short time, and then went to Canada; he remained there a short time, and then went back to his home in Michigan, where he was arrested, sent to his regiment, tried by court-martial, condemned, and very justly shot. His name was Judson, and he belonged to Company D, Fifth Regiment, Michigan Vols.

The weather here, for the past week, has been quite cloudy, and on Friday it rained all day and night. It has been excellent weather for marching.

SAMUEL.

November 8, 1863
FOURTEENTH REGIMENT, N.Y.S.N.G.
BRISTOE STATION, Oct. 29.

It is a long time since I wrote you, but we have been on the tramp so much, and so utterly deprived of the time and means for writing, that I have been unable. To-day is a most beautiful one—we have had very pleasant but cold weather lately. Since leaving "Rappahannock Station" we have marched to the Rapidan, and performed picket-duty for some time, changing camp every few days. There has been little rest for the regiment since the battle of Gettysburg. It has seemed as though the little squad of our regiment had to perform as much duty as regiments of two or three times the number—but every regiment has been well taxed in that way. If there was not quite so much "red tape" humbug, it would be much better for Uncle Sam as well as for the soldiers. Patriotism is not at all at a discount, it still swells the bosom of the Union soldiers, but re-enlistment where so much humbug is practiced by staff officers with men going to their duty, or on the march, rather tends to create a feeling of disgust at some of the shoulder-straps that are mounted on horseback. On the 8th of this month, it was observed that the enemy were making movements of a suspicious character. The picket-line was being weakened very much. At night, they had their brass band playing just opposite where I was picketed, on their reserve, and such a rattle they kept up with their drums and music was worthy of remark. Their fires soon went out that night, and early next morning, the same pickets were to be seen in the cornfields and on the hills, but the smoke along the ridges of hills had disappeared, General Newton and his staff were down, and occupied the house near our reserve at an early hour on the morning of the 9th. Orderlies were going backward and forward to the different head-quarters; and when night came, we of the picket having been relieved by a fresh detail the same afternoon, we were with our different regiments ready for a march, and got started at about 9 o'clock, P.M. It was a dark night, but we marched until we reached near Culpepper. The halt was very acceptable, for it was very cold, and we were anxious to get under our blankets from the cold and heavy dew. We soon got coffee cooked, and lay down for about two hours, when we were aroused again, but did not start off until about 10 o'clock that morning, when we started as a guard for the ammunition-train, and remained with it that day, arriving at Kelly's Ford, crossing the river, and shortly afterward proceeding into camp a short distance back, where in the woods we halted by a stream, and remained with the train (marching with it) till we arrived at Centreville on the 15th. Troops at this time are occupying the defences; and as the enemy were fighting our rear-guard, composed of a portion of the Second and Third Corps, with other troops, and cavalry, we naturally expected hourly to be brought into action, and accordingly made the best use of our time, while in position, getting our clothes washed, cooking, etc. We remained at Centreville until the morning of the 19th ult., when our line of march was taken up amid a rain-storm, our tents packed soaking wet. After two or three rests, we at last reached Haymarket, of which village nothing but the charred ruins of a once thriving place was left. Got camped at about three or four o'clock; butchers went to work killing beef, and just got it ready for delivery to the different regiments' company-servants, when an alarm was sounded of pack-up, and to the rescue. Just think of a body of men marching about twelve miles, through rain and mud, fording streams, getting up at four o'clock to cook breakfast, amidst a perfect hurricane of storm and rain, carrying sixty rounds of ball-cartridges, musket, with equipments, blanket, his change of clothing, tent, and eight days' rations of hard tack, coffee, and sugar, and after getting snugly ensconced from said march, to be greeted all at once by the exciting stream of "pack up! pack up!" from an old bugle, supposed to be troubled with bronchitis very badly. Then think of the "patriots" on the go double-quick, with the said load, after the enemy, who are supposed to be advancing upon us with their war-horses, charging with their sword in one hand and rifle in the other; and if the strength of the patriot flags under the jackass load of eight days' rations and double-quick—said patriot to run the risk of court-martial for falling out—you will readily see that a man that succeeds in being up to time through all this, and successful in the fray, is worthy of a badge, inscribed "Phenomena".

On the night of the 19th, I believe, a number of the First Brigade were captured, but the Rebel cavalry did not dash forward to us. After remaining in reserve for some time, and the cannonading from our batteries had nearly ceased, we (of the Fourteenth) were ordered forward, but it was only to strengthen the picket-line. We were placed at a distance of about five feet apart, and there, on duty all night, without the slightest relief, hardly daring to risk taking our blanket off the knapsack, or even taking our knapsack off, well knowing that if we lost anything, we must suffer the consequence and expense, which, to a soldier camping in swamps, and at this season of the year, besides being allowed but $42 a year for clothing, we could not very well stand it. (Query.—What has become of the two million dollars appropriated by Congress as a contingent fund for soldiers' clothing lost in battle, or thrown away, by orders, on a march?) The soldiers do not seem to get any recompense for their persistent efforts in keeping up on the march to the battle-field, or for their efforts in action. It is all very nice for men on horses to look at those on foot; but the double-quick, with all the necessary fixings, and eight days' rations, of a soldier, is too much for any one to expect a very determined fight from. If anyone doubts, let them try their hand at it by merely running one mile with such a load.

On the morning of the 20th, the Seventh Indiana relieved us, and we were taken back to near where we had camped on the previous night. Toward evening, we were on the march again, and passed through Thoroughfare Gap. We remained at this locality until the 25th, when at six o'clock we were off again, and passing back the Gap, the rain coming down throughout our march, and soaking us. After marching all day, we arrived at this place, and soon had our tents up, fires built and our clothes drying, supper over, and then in the arms of Morpheus—the soldier's great friend. A great many graves mark the scenes of the late battles here. The railroad being in ruins, and everything waste. Shot, shell, and fragments of such, lie around plentifully. There is hardly a spot in Virginia (and this regiment has been about it considerably, "I reckon a right smart heap"), but has been either a camp or battle-ground. Graves of soldiers are almost undiscernible in many places. The little pine slab, or stick, or other marks, having passed away like the memory of the departed soldier from his friends. Passing over the old battle-fields of Manassas and Bull Run, skulls of human beings were not unfrequently seen above the surface of the earth, lying around—probably exposed in that manner from the effects of rainstorms and the wind, or dug up by animals.

While we were at the Rapidan, a proposition was presented to the men of the regiment with a view to the members signing it. This proposition referred to three years' troops, and as it seemed to be expected that our regiment would get the privilege of going home to re-organize as the order read, providing we would re-enlist as a matter of course, we take it now for granted that we are acknowledged by the War Department as being a three-year organization (sworn in for the war). At any rate, we rely upon the fact of being one of the first regiments in the service and that we did not have the bounty-inducement before us. And as it would not seem proper to keep men for an indefinite period, thereby making slaves of us, we accordingly look to next spring giving us a release from the service, having served three years faithfully. I believe ovens are being put up so as to give us a continued supply of fresh bread. We had fresh bread to-day for the first time since we were at Rappahannock Station, in camp. There are not much prospects of a move for some days. Lately, a number of the paroled prisoners have returned, besides many of those who were so severely wounded at Gettysburg.

Yours,   J. J.

November 15, 1863
ONE HUNDRED AND FIFTY-EIGHTH REGIMENT, N.Y.V.
MOOREHEAD CITY, N.C., November 8.

As I write, the boys are cleaning up for inspection to-morrow. Our muskets are to be inspected, for the purpose of condemning them, I believe. We are to have the Springfield rifle. Our little band is sadly decreasing. I have another sad affair to relate. On Sunday night last [Nov. 1], Michael McCue of Company H, while on post at the sutler's house, was accosted by a man named John Mullen, of Company A. McCue hailed Mullan, when he (Mullan) said he would not halt, as McCue did not challenge him properly, and, with that, tried to force the musket from the sentinel—and the sentinel struck him with the musket, which so irritated Mullan, being under the influence of liquor, that he went to his tent, put on his accoutrements, loaded his musket, fired at the sentinel; one of the buckshot striking him a little below the cap of the left knee, the ball and the three other buckshot entered a post about eighteen inches from where the man stood. Mullan is at present confined in Fort Macon awaiting his trial, which will speedily take place.

We were mustered in for pay last Sunday, and are all anxiously awaiting the appearance of that good old soul, Major [George B.] Simpson, who is such a liberal dispenser of Uncle Samuel's green paper. How about them conscripts? We sent home some officers and men about three months ago, to bring us conscripts, but I see neither officers nor conscripts. Our regiment is very small, there not being 150 effective men in the whole regiment. When we left Brooklyn, fifteen months ago, we did not number 650 men, and with deaths, desertions, and discharges, we are quite decimated.

SLINGSHOT.

Irish-born John Mullen, age 33, five feet nine inches with red hair and blue eyes, enlisted on July 1, 1862, for three years in the 158th New York Infantry. On Nov. 7, 1863, six days after he shot the guard, Mullen wrote a letter to Lieut. Col. W. H. McNary apologizing for his drunken act: "Sir, I do not remember what I have done I was exhausted from Liquor. I hope that you will forgive me this time…I promise that during the remainder of my enlistment that I will keep clear of all trouble…" In Jan. 1865, Mullen was found guilty and sentenced to five years in the penitentiary at Albany.

Pvt. Michael McHugh survived his wound and was discharged; no further information is available.

November 22, 1863
FORTIETH REGIMENT N.Y.V.
NEAR BRANDY STATION, VA., Nov. 18.

Having been encamped in the vicinity of Warrenton Junction some time, a detail of our corps being employed repairing the railroad, which had been destroyed by the Rebels after our last countermarch to Manassas, but which is now in good working order, on Saturday, the 14th of November, we once more slung our packs on our backs, having received marching orders the night previous; and certainly, since Gen. Meade has had command of our Army, to secure the development of his plans, we have to march, I think, as an army never marched before. But although it may be distressing and fatiguing for the while, having to carry such heavy loads, we have now several times had ocular demonstration of the signal success which has crowned the celerity of the movement. Between 1 and 2 P.M., our corps arrived in the vicinity of Kelly's Ford, although finely screened from the enemy by the natural screens of the country, such as rising ground, woods, etc. We had but rested a short time when the pontoons arrived, having followed close in the rear. We fell in and marched to a fine, open place of ground, the front of which commanded the river and south bank, having two batteries brought in position at the front, where I can assure you they were not idle, shelling vigorously the woods about a mile back on the south side, assisted by a battery on the extreme left, firing at long range. We now formed line of battle, when Berdan's First U.S. Sharpshooters were ordered out to the front as skirmishers; and too much praise cannot be awarded to them for their conduct on this as well as on other occasions. When they commenced to ascend the slope facing the river, the Fortieth New York advanced; and when we came to the crest of the hill, orders were given to press forward to the other side of the river, not across pontoons but through the water, when, setting up a yell peculiar to the Fortieth, heedless of every obstacle, the goal once in sight, on we dashed, General Ward and Birney (the latter commanding the corps) cheering us on by their presence and inspiriting influence. By the time we got to the river the sharpshooters were across, and we immediately dashed over, some up to the waist, and some to the hips; others, more fortunate, up to the knees, but having crossed, we immediately started off double-quick, most of the pickets surrendering, and coming in our lines near to the woods, in front of which were deployed skirmishers along the whole line, the remainder of the First Division having crossed by this time, when some lively firing took place. Our regiment was very fortunate; but one member, although lost sight of by the daily sheets, ought to be mentioned here, and he is Sergeant [Jonathan] Sproul, who warily advanced from the whole line of skirmishers, and crept to the woods, being all along an object for the concentrated fire of his concealed foes, having fired a number of shots, he was at length pierced through the thigh by some fiendish rifle, and has been obliged to undergo an amputation. So completely were the enemy taken by surprise, that some were washing in the river, others playing cards, and Ewell's corps to the rear of the woods in our front, were out drilling, and their artillery horses grazing around the country, so that from the first alarm, before he could take a position and form line, we were across the river and checkmated him. Next morning, they had all disappeared. So we advanced to the neighborhood of Brandy Station, where we are now encamped.

Yours, as usual,   WATERFORD.

Sergeant Jonathan Sproul died from the effects of amputation on December 7, 1863.

November 29, 1863
THE ACHIEVEMENTS OF GENERAL GRANT—THE CROWNING VICTORY OF THE WAR.

The rout and dispersal of Bragg's Army is the heaviest blow yet received by the Confederacy. There have been many abortive victories and inconsequential defeats gained and suffered by us in the great contest between North and the South, and many of the engagements that should have been decisive have failed to bear the expected fruit because bunglers in the Cabinet have coiled their red-tape fetters around the limbs of heroes in the field. But in the great national duel which has been going on, as in a combat between individuals, every knock-down, if it does not end the fight, brings the weaker party nearer to a surrender. Every new round finds him more exhausted, less prompt to come to the scratch. The South may endeavor to cover the consequence of defeat with braggadocia, but the efforts to keep a stiff upper lip under the repeated defeats they have suffered, is more than the facial muscles of Secession can accomplish. Each successive concussion with Grant's forces splits up new rents and gaps in the Confederacy, like powder in a rock.

This victory crowns Grant as the hero of the war. Whether regard is had to the ability he has displayed or the importance of the triumphs he has achieved he occupies a proud pre-eminence among the foremost generals of the Union Army. He fought his way through the enemy's country to Vicksburg, and captured that stronghold, in pursuance of a regular plan adopted in advance, and adhered to throughout, until it eventuated in final victory. He disentangled the Army of the Cumberland from the mesh of difficulties into which the discomfiture of Rosecrans led it, and changed what had been a grand disaster into one of the crowning victories of the war. The opening of the Mississippi was the first event which demonstrated the vulnerability of the Rebellion, and put an effectual extinguisher on European intervention, which has not been heard of since; and the defeat of Bragg is a gigantic stride of the Union Army on its march to penetrate to the Gulf of Mexico—as the fall of Vicksburg opened up the international highway of the Mississippi. Such have been the Herculean achievements of General Grant.

REBEL TREATMENT OF OUR PRISONERS—The evidence multiplies that the Rebels deliberately starve and maltreat the Union prisoners in their hands, and treat them with a barbarous inhumanity only worthy of savages. This is a state of things that will not be permitted to exist. Either let our Government renew the exchange of prisoners; or, failing to do that, compel decent treatment of ours by an application of the *lex talionis*. Much as we should abhor the introduction of barbarity into the arena of military operations, the Government must secure protection to its captured soldiers speedily, and at all hazards. This is a duty from which it will not be permitted to shrink.

INDEPENDENT BATTALION, N.Y.V.

MORRIS ISLAND, S.C., Nov. 16.

What the next move on the board is, we are looking anxiously for. We think, by the cut of the embrasures, that Sullivan's Island will be the next object of our guns. To-day, one of our Sergeants, from a Parrott, shot away the last flag the "Rebs" have hoisted on Sumter—that pile of impregnable brick-dust. Sullivan's Island batteries have been amusing themselves, as well as us, by throwing ten-inch mortar-shells at our Monitors, while they, apparently unconscious, still bang away, with all their fury, at Sumter. Our regiment is well camped at present, if any one can be well camped on such a barren island as this. At good high tide, we have all we can do to keep from being floated away by the surf, which reaches the very threshold of our door, and threatens to carry us all captive to Charleston by way of the channel.

A few nights since, a Captain of our battalion—Captain Thaddeus C. Ferris—visited the ruined fort (Sumter) under the fire of our own guns. After remaining and perambulating nearly the whole fort, he was discovered by the accidental discharge of his revolver, and was forced to retire, amid a shower of Rebel bullets, brickbats, and hand-grenades. He, however, escaped to our lines without any serious injury, and with a great deal of satisfaction to himself.

The day after the above occurrence, General [Truman] Seymour received a present in the form of a brick, one of the many he very probably saw during his stay in that fort. We believe he is about to make that brick the "nest-egg" of all future bricks from that fort and Rebeldom in general. May he have a nice "batch".

Everything is in readiness to open a severe fight on the city in a few days. The Navy is hard at work; not "taking in ammunition" or "tinkering", but closing decks for the grandest naval bombardment the world has ever seen. Everything is being pushed forward with a vigor never before seen in this department. The Ironsides, instead of going to New York "for repairs", is soon to moor herself along side of the Charleston docks, or else sink to the bottom of Charleston Harbor, which latter we doubt. For the especial edification of that learned correspondent of the Charleston *News* (Rebel), we will here state that instead of dismounting one of our guns at "Gregg", they only cleared the sand from one of their own old guns which we had buried after taking possession of it, not thinking it worth the while to take up the place of a 300-pounder with such a piece of smooth-boreism.

Speaking of buried objects, you should see the way the gray-backs' shots tear up their dead on Cumming's Point. The other day, I assisted in reburying a Georgia captain; I forget his name. He was buried into then two feet below the surface, and was disinterred by a mortar-shell from Fort Moultrie. It would be interesting to have some account of these poor Georgians published, as probably they, more or less, have friends or relations in the Northern States. Captains, lieutenants, non-commissioned, and privates are all mixed indiscriminately together.

We have just received the news that above four hundred conscripts will be here in a few days. They, of course, will help to augment the strength of our battalion.

By our next, we hope to have some stirring news for your numerous readers. Until then, I am,

                    Yours respectfully,   XAPHED.

December 6, 1863
DOES THE ADMINISTRATION REALLY MEAN TO PUT DOWN THE REBELLION?

When we intimated, last week, our apprehension that the victory which promised such important consequences, should, like so many previous displays of heroism, prove to be but Dead Sea fruit that turns to ashes on the lip, we had no idea that our misgiving should, meet with such an immediate realization. As we then stated, it was only necessary for Meade to follow up Lee, and put the rival forces maneuvering on the soil of Old Virginia to test the battle, to end the war before the close of the present year. But the past history of the war gave us too much reason to fear that Grant's success would be allowed to stand alone; that no effort would be made to second the impression he had made on the fabric of the Rebellion, and to strike the vibrating structure and cause it to topple over; but rather that it would be allowed to settle back into its old perpendicular posture, and regain the equipoise which had been disturbed at Chattanooga. One week after Grant's splendid achievement in Georgia and Tennessee we find that Meade, after playing bo-peep with Lee in Virginia, had given up the amusement and retreated to the vicinity of Washington, where he is to go into winter quarters. No more work is likely to be done before spring sets in, and our half-starved and wretched prisoners immured within the dungeons of Richmond, who ought to and should have been released by this very Army of the Potomac, long before now, are kept waiting in suffering and anguish. Why, we may ask, did Meade retire without throwing down the gage of battle to his adversary? We are told that he found Lee strongly posted and thought it would not be prudent to meddle with him. In other words, that the Army of the Potomac—which was the first great body of troops organized at the commencement of the war, to oppose and overthrow the rebellion—after three years' contest with the Rebel Army, organized and maintained from the scant resources of the rebellion, in which it has generally had the worst of it, when it ventures to follow up the Rebel general, is either drawn back or skulks back of its own accord. What a confession is this, of the grand Army of the Potomac, organized for years and reinforced ad infinitum, dreading to force its adversary to a contest and retiring for security behind its own intrenchments. But it is not the fact that it is unable to cope with Lee's arm; or, if it is, it is because the Administration had not used the means at its command to strengthen it sufficiently to defy every soldier Jeff. Davis has got under arms in the entire South. If the Army of the Potomac has been unable, or, being able, has failed to scatter the Rebel forces in Virginia, it is the fault of the War Department; and if it is unable now, what hope have we what it ever will be? As hostilities have been carried on for three years in Virginia, there is no reason and why they might not be conducted for twenty years, and the Rebel Congress still held its sessions in Richmond.

People are beginning to doubt, and with reasons, the earnestness of the Administration in putting down the Rebellion. Wendell Phillips has publicly denounced the President and his Cabinet as having constituted themselves into an electioneering committee for the next Presidency, and using the power and patronage of the Government to this end; and it would seem as if they wish to keep the war going on for another year, as so to have a larger Army, not to suppress the Rebellion, but to coerce doubtful men into voting the Administration ticket next year at the point of the bayonet! If these insinuations are not based upon truth, and the authorities at Washington really wish to end the war, they must show some other evidence of their determination than the retreat of Meade, and the aspect the "military situation" in Virginia presents to the country and the world.

INDEPENDENT BATTALION, N.Y.V.
MORRIS ISLAND, S.C., Nov. 28.

Yesterday there was great rejoicing in our camp, on account of the arrival of the MERCURY among us. The good old messenger comes to us full of everything that is good—brimfull of those things that we most require; and was received, not exactly with any of the "out-pourings of enthusiasm", but with a serious determination to peruse it to the end. Sumter has been catching thunder ever since my last; and although the One Hundred and Forty-fifth Pennsylvania Volunteers do not garrison that Rebel stronghold, there appears to be not much of anything to prevent that, or any other regiment, from doing that same.

Yesterday we sent a few shells into the city. We could see them explode; and after a while, down came the report, telling us how well our messengers had done their duty. They appeared to fall about the centre of the city; and I firmly believe that all that had anything to "pack up", might have been seen doing that very necessary job at about that time.

Our casualties of late have been very small, owing to the effective manner in which our engineers have built their batteries on this island. Gen. [John W.] Turner is always on hand to point out the proper objects to fire on, and to give that encouragement to our men which they so justly deserve. The Rebs attempted to throw grape at us, at about two miles and a half range; and succeeded, much to our satisfaction, in not reaching us, by nearly a mile. They must "up and at it" some new way; for, as their last ditch is gone, and "spades" are trumps, they have lost the "stake"; therefore, we advise them to "draw out", on their present "losings", and allow us to "rake the pile".

Last night another attack was made on Sumter by infantry. Some say they failed, and while we see our mortars firing into it, the same as before, I am inclined to believe they did. It appears the Rebs had a dog on the fort, to raise the alarm in case of an attack from the Yanks. It is impossible, at this early hour, to say what was the cause, but at the least approach of danger the dog might give the alarm, when the Graybacks could rush out and shower all kinds of destructive missiles on the storming party (which in some measure they did). The attempt was made chiefly by volunteers for the occasion; some funny things may yet be said about this affair.

We were visited yesterday by Adjutant-General Sprague, of New York State, and we were made to feel a thrill of gladness at his attention; for that he has come to benefit us we were certain. He visited our good old brigade commander (Col. W. W. H. Davis), and we were certain he received a good account of the Independent Battalion. It here becomes me to speak of our dear old (Acting) General; his command has full confidence in him, and are sure he is the right man in the right place; his efforts for our welfare are not disregarded, and for that reason we call him "our dear old brigade commander". Beautiful weather here; warm as June weather North; heavy dews at night; scorching during the day.

XAPHED.

December 13, 1863

THE CONTRAST—NORTH AND SOUTH.

The Legislative machine at Washington is once more in motion under a full head of steam. The head of each Federal bureau has rendered an account of his stewardship; and although their reports are long and dreary, they exhibit the country in a flourishing condition; the Armies of the Union going forward, conquering and to conquer; the greenbacks continuing to keep up a respectable proximity to gold and silver; our foreign "relations", behaving rather better than usual, and everything going on quite as well as we have any right to expect. The Richmond engine has also been placed on the track, and the Rebel authorities are all aboard for another trip. The prospect of the company as set forth by their chief engineer to his new prospectus, are such as must make the stockholders despair. In a word, the exhibit of the affairs of the Confederacy, contained in the Message of Mr. Davis, must satisfy his most sanguine followers that their hopes of establishing an independent empire were built on sand, and are rapidly crumbling away. It must be admitted that the Rebels do not attempt to conceal from themselves or others the condition of their causes, which would indeed be impossible. They face the music, and admit the force of all the disasters that have befallen them, and the melancholy aspect of affairs at home and abroad. Davis, for the first time, admits that the Rebel soldiers showed the white feather during the late battle at Chattanooga, and broke and fled while holding positions of great strength. It is also admitted that the Rebel Armies in the Southwest are weakened and demoralized; the failure of the conscription is acknowledged, and the utter breakdown of the finances, so that the Government currency is hardly worth the paper spoiled in its manufacture. No wonder that Mr. Davis loses his temper in view of his prospect, and accuses, not merely the United States, but all Europe and the rest of mankind, of being engaged in a conspiracy against the rights of the Confederacy. To make headway against all this odds must be uphill work; and the hopelessness of the task must here become manifest to the Southern people, if not to their leaders. To continue the unequal contest further, would be the very acme of midsummer madness—particularly when our patriarchal and benevolent Uncle at Washington has given them a chance to retrace their steps and come back on the easiest terms ever held out to repentant sinners. All they have to do is to leave Old Abe to deal with his colored proteges as he sees fit, and make an affidavit, each and every one of them, to that effect—duly acknowledged before a notary public with a five-cent revenue-stamp on the corner-and place the documentation file with the Secretary of State , and the thing is done. We have no hope of the Rebel leaders coming in—for they are excluded from the terms of the amnesty, and saltpetre can't save them; but we do expect to see the masses of the Southern people come up and kiss the book, and reinstate themselves as good and true citizens and supporters of the Union. Now or never is the time for them to come to terms. As army of "three hundred thousand more" is getting ready, and will be armed and equipped in a very few months, or weeks rather; and once it commences its triumphal march, it will be too late for them to avail themselves of the clemency now extended to them.

FOURTEENTH REGIMENT, N.Y.N.G.
NEAR THE RAPPAHANNOCK RIVER, Dec. 8.

Again we are along the banks of the Rappahannock River, just arrived back from another of those visits *en militaire*, to Johnny Reb. The second one since my last letter to you. It would seem, as though it were most time that the great game of chess was dispensed with, at least for the winter; for such marching and countermarching as the Army of the Potomac has been proverbial for doing, would seem a slow way of going to Richmond. Yet we all know it is for the best; and each time we skedaddle we console our lucky selves with the assurance that it is strategic, and old Lee has got too much Meade, and is apt to lose his equilibrium if he plays with our present Commander too much. The last trip we had and fell back, Lee followed our Army up and got badly drubbed, and had to make a skedaddle himself. This time he has not followed Meade very closely. Lee, it would seem, is acting a little bit more cautiously; but whether he will get any advantage over our brave and cautious General is yet to be seen. When our Army got back the previous time, the troops were put to work on the R. R., and soon the road was pushed through as far as Brandy Station. Orders next came to "pack up"; but, on account of the weather, were countermanded. At the first indication of fine weather we were off again, "Thanksgiving-day" being our starting-time. Up at 3 o'clock, and off at daylight, and crossed the Rapidan at Culpepper Ford at 12 o'clock the following morning. The weather cold, and roads cut up badly. We halted for breakfast near Chancellorsville, at a locality where are graves of some Rebel soldiers killed last year at the battle of Chancellorsville. We cross a little run by the graves of still more of the Rebel dead. Soon we hear the reports of musketry and also that of cannonading, which subsequently proves to have been an attack upon our train by guerillas, who killed one man and wounded another of ours. They left one of their dead by the side of the one of our men they had killed, and in the very spot (a fork of roads, one of which runs to Orange Court House) where the Rebel General Stonewall Jackson was wounded. The guerillas destroyed some of our train and killed several of our mules that they had not time to take along with them. Cannonading was to be heard all that day, and we were marched along to the Rapidan, again halting at about ten o'clock, I think, that night. At three o'clock were aroused again, morning of the 29th, and soon reached to where some sharp-skirmishing had been done by the Second, Third, and Eighth Corps the day before and soon the different troops were formed in lines of battle, and at about 10 or 11 o'clock the order came to advance. The Fourteenth was in the second line, and forward went all hands, Colonel Fowler commanding the regiments of the Second Brigade. The Rebs kept falling back as our skirmishers advanced. They left their breastworks for better positions across the river or creek—called, I believe, Robinson's Creek. Our batteries played a few shells; but there was not much reply from the enemy. They seemed to wish us to cross the creek. Soon lines of battle were formed with our troops in a wood on the slope of a line of hill opposite to the enemy. Our position was a pretty good one; but commanded, I think, by the hills opposite, held by the enemy. We will long remember Locust Grove as one of interest, for we really expected some terrible and bloody scenes being enacted in this locality. Our skirmishers kept at work pretty busily, and the Rebels wounded many of ours.

On the 30th of November, the Fourteenth is ordered down and across the creek, for the purpose of feeling the force and locality of the enemy's skirmishers, etc. Col. Fowler sent the right wing across; up the hill they advance, and there find, just over the brow, the Rebel skirmishing line, very strong, and coming up on the right flank. Our boys, seeing them, fire at them; shots are pretty freely exchanged and Col. Fowler having noticed the flanking movement, sends for further orders and the boys are called in, without one of the skirmishers being hurt. Orderly Sergeant [Henry] Cookson, of Co. C, was struck in the foot by one of the chance shots, while with his company in the reserve. Soon after we came in, the Ninety-fifth N.Y.V. went and lost some. The Seventh Indiana was afterward sent on the same errand, and lost thirty in killed, wounded, and missing. During this day our batteries open upon the Rebs, but only two or three shots were fired from their batteries in reply. Fighting was going on to our left and we heard that the Third Corps had crossed the river. On the morning of 1st December the rifle cannon were displaced by our favorite Battery B, Fourth Regulars. When we saw them we suspected what was in the wind, and that we were going to fall back; for Battery B is always used for close quarters, and on a retreat many a hundred Secessionists have been made to bite the dust from those brass howitzers. At about 4 o'clock, orders came to fall back, and soon we are on the return-march. A very large tannery and leather factory was destroyed; many thousands of beautiful skins and hides were burned, and still hundreds remained in the vats, too wet to burn. Such is the havoc of war.

On the night of the 30th of November, five men of the Fifth Corps froze to death, and four sick men died in the ambulances, very likely from the intense cold. We march all night of the 1st of December, and halt after recrossing the Rapidan, bivouacked till we march on again at about eight o'clock on the morning of the 2nd December. We halt on that afternoon at close of day, and bivouac in a piece of woods. The Ambulance Corps drew rations, and are more content. Many of the troops ran short of food, and great prices were paid for hard tack in many cases. In one case I saw a soldier pay $10 for ten hard tack to a party who was mean enough to receive it for them. The troops are now putting up log cabins and winter-quarters. The regular camp rations are now being issued again, and I expect some of the lank, cadaverous-looking Yankee soldiers will get filled up again. It has been a pretty trying march; for the weather was very cold, particularly at night. The water freezes in our canteens through the day with the sun out. So you may judge it is cold at night for men when having to lie, as they did, on the march with but one blanket under the open canopy.

The Ambulance Corps (in which I am now serving) are at work putting up winter-quarters, logging up.

J. J.

December 20, 1863

SEVENTY-FIRST REGIMENT, N.Y.V.

CAMP NEAR BRANDY STATION, VA., Dec. 15.

We are now in our winter-quarters. We did not have much trouble in building them, because the Johnny Rebs had them nearly finished when the poor fellows had to leave them in our hands. I must give them the credit of building good log shanties. There is a great deal of talk about our brigade going home to re-enlist as mounted infantry. I think it would be a good plan for the Government to let the brigade go home and come out again; I believe we are the oldest brigade in the service, therefore I think we are entitled to it, and we have only six months more to serve. In fact, the time of the whole division will be up in summer. The weather is now changeable. It looks as if winter had come in earnest to-day. It is raining so hard that it won't do the roads any good for marching. It would be a good plan for General Meade to stop where he is, and to go no further until spring. His last move was a failure, and it ought to learn him a lesson, to stand still awhile. We have done more marching since he has had command of the Army of the Potomac than any other two generals put together. Furloughs are now all the go, yet ten days is a very short one. The work has commenced very early this season, and no doubt before next June every enlisted man in the Army will have a chance to go home. It would be better to send a company at a time, so as to give them all a chance. In the late battle our regiment lost one killed, and six wounded. That was very small for the time it lasted; the one that was killed (Sergeant R. A. Eastaby) was liked throughout the whole regiment; he was a true soldier, and he died without a struggle—may he rest in peace!

GUARDIAN.

SEVENTH REGIMENT CORPS D'AFRIQUE

PORT HUDSON, LA., Dec. 2.

We still continue to rest in peace, as the Rebs have not, as yet, made any demonstrations toward retaking this place, although General [J. L.] Logan (Rebel) boldly asserts, as has been reported by persons coming from outside the lines, that he (Logan) will eat his Christmas dinner in Port Hudson, which I have good reason to doubt, unless his dinner consists of something heavier than hard tack; for the old fortifications, by a great deal of labor, and under the management of Colonel I. I. Zalensky, the efficient engineer, have been repaired and altered, so that they are as efficient as new and much stronger than when the Rebs held them. Besides this, there is in operation, and nearly finished a new line of works half a mile back and inside of the old ones, and which are far superior to any impromptu fortification that I ever saw—the credit on which is due to Lieutenant-Colonel [S. H.] Long of the Fourth Engineer Regiment, and to the soldiers and officers of the Corps d'Afrique, who have been constantly at work on them every day for the last two months, from 6, A.M., to 6, P.M.

The fatigue that these colored troops undergo, the cheerfulness with which they work, and the quality of the same, is deserving of remark, and not only in their work, but the interest taken, and advancement obtained in their drill, for already, although not having had much time for practice, they are superior to a great many white troops that have been in the field the same length of time. They are always obedient to their officers, merry and happy by themselves, and very anxious to learn to read and write, which accomplishments they are rapidly attaining under the instruction of Mr. Seymour (regimental instructor), who although quite a young man, is very talented, and undoubtedly understands his "biz". Punishments in the Corps d'Afrique is a very rare occurrence; the men can stand anything but that; for to be punished for any misdemeanor in their regiment is a disgrace, and when a man is so disgraced, it takes a long time for him to obtain an honorable standing among his associates.

On Sunday before last, our regiment (Seventh) was the recipient of a magnificent stand of colors, presented to the regiment by a number of prominent citizens of New York City, through Chaplain Conway of the Seventh, who brought them on here from New York. The colors were presented at dress parade by Chaplain Conway, who read a speech prepared by the citizens of New York for the occasion, after which he made a few spirited remarks, which were very appropriately responded to by Col. Clark, of the Seventh. Speeches were also made by General [George] Andrews and Ullmann, with the usual amount of cheering, etc.

It would be a great benefit to the service if the officers, particularly the field-officers of the Corps d'Afrique, could be picked out with more care; for it is generally known that, in all the Southern States, the negro is accustomed to look on the class of "poor whites", which imply ignorant and vulgar traits, as persons beneath even their respect, and in fact, below the level of the nigger. Of such officers some of the regiments of this corps are more or less composed, and it would not be a bad idea if General Andrews would take the trouble to pay a little attention to this fact, and get rid of such kind of officers as I mention. If he would take the trouble to glance at the officer second in command of the Seventh Regiment, he would perhaps give the matter a little thought, and therefore benefit the service of the removal of those leaders who sport the straps.

Your paper is regularly received in camp, and enjoyed by all. Au revoir.

C. d'A.

December 27, 1863
THIRTY-NINTH REGIMENT, N.Y.V.
CAMP NEAR STEPHENSBURG, VA., Dec. 17.

Again I am permitted to write to you these few lines. During my two years' campaign, I have been a frequent visitor to your list of Army correspondents. I have again enrolled myself under the banner of freedom, becoming one of the members of that noble band, the Army of the Potomac. Apparently, the Army has gone into winter-quarters, and the boys are resting upon their late won laurels; eager on the approaching spring to resume offensive operations. The hardships and struggles of camp-life came rather natural to my organic nerves. Old "hard tack" seemed to me like a bosom friend, whom I welcomed with a fatherly affection; and my downy and "Shanghai" feathers, soft as a pine plank, found a cordial welcome in my wrinkled body. I suppose you will hint that the big bounty had a tendency of causing me to re-enlist. If you harbor such an idea, let me inform you that you are laboring under a great mistake. It was love, and a strong patriotic devotion to my native land, that caused me to become a "veteran". And I intend, as long as armed traitors North or South remains on our soil, to help to suppress them. My first duty is to my country, then to the "Emerald" backs.

I have become attached to the best corps (excepting the Sixth) in the Army. And I have full confidence that when the veteran Second is called to do battle for freedom and justice, that she will give a good account of herself. The Veteran Sumner, the undaunted Couch, and the intrepid and patriotic General [Gouverneur K.] Warren, have each, in their turn, commanded us.

It is not usually my habit to praise or condemn any officer, whether field or line; but necessarily there must be exceptions. During my connection with the Thirty-ninth (Garibaldi Guards), I have found the majority of the officers gentlemen, and every inch a soldier. Prominent among the number, I may mention—omitting all names—the captain commanding the battalion; the adjutant, surgeon, captain of Company D, and the ensign of Company C, all, in my humble opinion, are a credit and honor to the battalion.

Everything continues lovely; all being quiet on our right, nothing happening to mar our pleasant and comfortable quarters. Should Johnny Reb see fit to leave us alone this coming winter, we can pass an agreeable time, and live as happy as a king, and as contented. But should Lee have the audacity of forcing a winter-campaign upon us, my word for it, he will find that "the Army still lives".

Yours,   JERSHUA JENKINS, VETERAN.

SECOND FIRE ZOUAVES
BRANDY STATION, VA., Dec. 18.

Since my last letter to you we have been busy marching and countermarching. We have crossed and re-crossed the famous Rappahannock and Rapidan Rivers. During this time we have frequently tried to draw the Rebels into a fight. On four different occasions we have offered them battle, but they "could not see it". We actually went up to within a few hundred yards of their works, and dared them to come and knock the chip off our shoulder. We were prepared to charge their works, and only awaited the signal from General Warren, who had command of the assaulting column, but they fell back and fired scarcely a shot. For the first time in our history as a regiment, we were detailed to guard the wagon-train of our division. The duty was not as easy as might be imagined, for the Rebel guerillas tried all sorts of dodges to harass our flanks and rear. We got along tip-top, and did not lose a single wagon. The Sixth Corps were not as lucky; they lost about 200 mules and 27 wagons. The Johnnys took the mules to the mountains and burned the wagons. Our old friend, Captain Purtell, is with us again; he looks as gay as ever. Captain Phelan is also here; he don't look as well as he used to; his wound is not yet healed. Lieutenant-Colonel Burns was on General [Henry] Prince's staff in the last fight, and Captain Purtell was in command of the regiment. Right well did he sustain his old reputation. There is a report here that we are to go home and recruit for mounted infantry. I hope it is true. The majority of the men would enlist again for three years if they were allowed the privilege to go home for a few weeks. There is no doubt but we would make a good mounted brigade, for we are all used to the saddle, and know the country to add. We are all anxious to see General Sickles back again. Colonel Brewster is still in command of the brigade. There is not a man in the brigade but would like to see him have what he deserves—the star on his shoulder. There is some likelihood of going into winter-quarters here. We are all briskly preparing for old King Frost. We are now quartered in log huts the graybacks built for their winter-quarters; but, alas! for human calculations, they were disappointed. We are preparing for a grand time at Christmas and New Years. Adams' Express is to furnish the Army with packages from dear friends at home. We are to have a new commander, if reports are true; some would have it General [Alfred] Pleasanton, others Warren, but the majority say: "Give us McClellan; he is just the man for this Army." The order to grant furloughs has just come into camp, and all hands are in high glee at the early anticipation of a visit home. We have very cold weather here at present. Living in shelter-tents is not very comfortable. We are not yet ordered to go into winter-quarters.

Yours,   GLADIATOR.

INDEPENDENT BATTALION (LOST CHILDREN) N.Y.V.

MORRIS ISLAND, S.C., Dec. 20.

Morris Island is not the most desirable place in the world during the winter months. Comfortable winter-quarters, with a tight roof overhead, and a good warm fire to thaw frozen fingers and toes, or dry your clothes after a pelting rainstorm, are what we know nothing about; but we have to grin and bear it, and rub our shins, until Gen. [Quincy A.] Gillmore furnishes better quarters in Charleston. The dry and marrow-less bones of Boneyard rattle frightfully in these furious northeasters. On the morning of the 11th we opened our eyes, and to our great astonishment found that we were actually pickled in salt water. The tides had risen during the night and taken us by surprise. The first notice we had of our ticklish position was by the surf dashing over and around us while in our watery beds. I found my shoes floating around inside my tent as graceful as a duck, and invitingly requesting me to jump in and take a ride to dry land; which request was readily complied with without further ceremony. The weather here is quite emblematic of South Carolina. It is contrary, and to extreme both ways. To-day, it may be cold enough to freeze a Russian, and the water in the kettles may be transformed into ice; to-morrow, the sun comes out, and the atmosphere is as calm and serene as a summer's night; in fact, so warm and pleasant, that you see men along the beach bathing in the surf.

That ever welcome and important official, the paymaster, made his appearance in camp on the 3rd, and "came down" with two months' pay. Since we have been on this island, our pay is never allowed to run longer than two months; an arrangement that we will never get tired of, and hope that it will be kept up during the future.

The loss of the Monitor Weehawken, is a subject much talked of and regretted, as she had proved herself to be one of the most efficient of the whole fleet—always the first into action and the last one out. But now she has gone down to Davey Jones' Locker, to keep company with the ill-fated Keokuk, which lies out in front of our camp, and is plainly visible at low tide. The smoke-stack of the Weehawken can be seen at low water; and probably will be raised at some future time by the Government, with the consent of the Rebels on Sullivan's Island; for she lies in a position commanded by the guns of Moultrie.

The siege of Charleston still lives, and barely lives at that. Shells have been thrown into the city almost daily for some time past. On Cumming's Point you can plainly hear them explode, and see the smoke as it rises among the buildings. It is a continual boom, boom, boom. The cannonading has been actually terrific and often grand. The heavy roar of artillery is sounding in our ears day and night till we hardly notice it. Sumter, Johnson, Simpkins, and Moultrie, all receive their share of iron compliments almost daily. Slowly and steadily our mortar batteries pelt into the ragged walls of Sumter, which one naturally would suppose was dead, and it is unchivalrous to pound a dead body; but still that heap of mortar, brick and rubbish is held by the enemy, and is yet known as a formidable barrier to the movements of the fleet upon Charleston.

Fort Johnston occasionally practice ricocheting shot and shell into and around Sumter in anticipation that our troops may soon be posted in that fallen and shattered citadel. The Old Moultrie House, which was always a landmark of this harbor, has at last entirely disappeared, and a new mortar-battery has opened from behind its site. This is the only visible existence of activity among the Rebels, and every day of delay on our part renders the task before us the more difficult to accomplish.

What the next step in the siege will be, no New England Yankee can conjecture with a certainty. We heartily wish the crisis would arrive, and let us off this cursed and barren sandbank. We are tired of the monotony of digging in the sand like muskrats; tired of the moan of the breakers; tired of the thunder of cannon, and the screeching shell.

E. L. B.

January 3, 1864
SEVENTY-FIRST N.Y.V., SECOND REGIMENT, EXCELSIOR BRIGADE
CAMP NEAR BRANDY STATION, VA., Dec. 28.

Re-enlisting is now all the go in our brigade. Veterans, as I may call them, who have been through all the dangers and trials of war, are now re-enlisting over again for the short period of three years. It is hoped this cruel war will not last so long. In our regiment re-enlisting goes on very slowly at present. All we want is, some patriot from New York to come out here and make a stirring speech. It seems as though our brigade is not going to be filled up, either by volunteers or conscripts. We have to do the duty of a brigade, whether we have 5,000 or 1,000 men. It comes very hard on us for picket-duty; but that is nothing—we can stand it for six months more for Uncle Sam. Christmas passed away the same as any other day, in the Army, with our fat pork and hard tack for dinner, with a little bean soup, to satisfy our appetite, and a half gill of whiskey for a break-down. Instead of a quill for a toothpick, we use our bayonets for that purpose. Your city will be full of veterans in a week or so from our brigade. The Second New York Fire Zouaves have all re-enlisted over again. That is a credit to the New York Fire Department. May they have the same success in putting down this war as they have had in saving the public property at home! They go into a fight as coolly as they go to a fire. The sound of a cannon is as the sound of a fire-bell to them out here. It is not a pleasant sound; but it strikes terror into the hearts of the enemy.

GUARDIAN.

FIFTY-FIRST REGIMENT, N.Y.V.
CRAB ORCHARD, KY., Dec. 30, 1863.

This regiment is expecting daily to make tracks for New York. I don't want to prejudice the minds of those having relations or friends in the regiment, and to lead them once to think that the members of our regiment have not been of late used to high living—at least, if the living was not high, the pay was. Any one concerned, that wishes to doubt my word, will please, if ever out this way, commence at Cincinnati, Ohio, and examine the records of the different hotels, likewise the would-be-hotels through Kentucky.

We are coming to New York, "and for what?" A number of New York's peaceful citizens will murmur, (only murmur, dare they do otherwise?). I don't consider myself competent to foreshadow the future; nevertheless, grant me the liberty to say that the regiment is expected to re-organize and recruit, and that in New York. So if the people of New York want the war to close, they must fill up the ranks of our regiment, and that will be doing a share toward it. They must not think of the privations, etc., of camp-life. Do any of you, for a moment, think that we thought of privations or such things, when we held up our right hands for *another* "three years"?

In this manner you become noted; you are absent from home and acquaintances, it is true, but on returning home, you will appreciate them the more, and they likewise appreciate you as much as is possible. This is what I want the people at home to do. When they see our thin, veteran ranks, when we parade Broadway on our return, and also during our short stay, to appreciate us—that's the word. Do not fear that we will not appreciate our many friends, etc., we left behind in October, 1861. If we are welcome, let it be shown on the day we arrive, which will in time be made known.

Those members that did not re-enlist were left at Camp Loudon. Our Colonel (Le Gendre), before coming away, made a short but appropriate address to them, stating that it may be painful for them not to have the privilege of parading with the regiment in New York under their old banner, with which they have been connected since our advent. He was pained to do so, but the exigencies of the service would not permit them so to do; and it may be that they would be detached from the regiment during the rest of their time of service. It will not be possible for us to spend our New Year in New York, still we can appoint a day and observe it.

UNO.

ONE HUNDRED AND FORTY-SIXTH REGIMENT, N.Y.V.

BEALTON STATION, VA., Dec. 28.

The Fifth Corps is now employed guarding the Orange & Alexandria Railroad. The Second Division is encamped at Bealton Station. There is at present but two brigades in the division, the First and Third. The First Brigade is composed entirely of regulars whilst the One Hundred and Forty-sixth and One Hundred and Fortieth N.Y., and the Ninety-first and One Hundred and fifty-fifth Pennsylvania, comprise the third.

The One Hundred and Forty-sixth has been in the service some fourteen months. Brigadier-General [Kenner] Garrard was formerly Colonel of it. The regiment is now commanded by Colonel [David] Jenkins. At the present time, the regiment numbers some five hundred men, nearly two hundred are conscripts. The three-year men of the old Fifth (Duryea's Zouaves) were transferred to this regiment last May; there were some two hundred of them then, but at the present time there are not more than fifty of them with the regiment. They were a splendid body of men, and deserve better treatment at the hands of the Government than to be consolidated with any regiment, after the term for which they had enlisted had expired.

The keeping of three-years' men belonging to two-year regiments, was a great blunder of the War Department and about as mean a piece of business as the National Government has been guilty of. Men enlisting for the unexpired term of a regiment, with the full understanding that they should go home when the regiment did, and then to be kept and shoved into another regiment (as the old Fifth was on the battlefield of Chancellorsville), has been enough to extinguish all the patriotism that a man is capable of holding.

Orderly-Sergeants [Hugh] Chalmers, [Lawrence] Fitzpatrick, and [Peter D.] Froeligh, of the Fifth, have all been promoted to lieutenancies in this regiment.

Everything remains perfectly quiet round these parts, though, now and then, a few of Mosby's men show themselves, but are generally driven off without loss.

TYPO.

Chapter IV

<u>1864</u>

by

Dr. Richard J. Sommers

"Some people seem to think that we will have no fighting this year," wrote a soldier of the 40th New York on April 9, 1864, as published in the *Sunday Mercury* on April 17. "It cannot be so. I know we will have some hard battles to fight during the coming campaign, and may be more severe than any we have had to fight during the two years and a half we have been here." His prophecy proved correct. Although the 40th had already seen much action, from Yorktown and Williamsburg through Chancellorsville and Gettysburg to Kelly's Ford and Mine Run, the fighting in 1864 would indeed prove severe and seemingly ceaseless. Seven weeks of virtually non-stop battles, May 5—June 23, gave way not to months of respite as earlier in the Civil War but to siege at Petersburg: daily sharpshooting and shelling, punctuated every few weeks with flare-ups of fierce fighting.

The situation was similar in Georgia, as William T. Sherman's armies spent four months fighting their way into the heart of the state and finally captured Atlanta on September 2. They squandered October in futile pursuit of the Confederate army. In mid-November, however, they cut loose on their devastating March to the Sea, which culminated in the capture of Savannah on December 21.

Until Sherman erupted onto the Atlantic coast, that theater had seen relatively little fighting in 1864, because General-in-Chief Ulysses S. Grant had transferred most of the troops from the Carolinas and Florida to Virginia. The Trans-Mississippi Theater comparably quieted down after the failure of the Red River Campaign, as Grant shifted forces to more important fronts: Memphis, Mobile Bay, and the Middle Military Division.

The selection of letters from the *Sunday Mercury* reflects early operations in West Louisiana and East Florida, garrison service in New Bern, Port Royal, Decatur, and Nashville; blockade duty off the Atlantic coast and on the high seas, even prison guard at Johnson's Island and Elmira. But overwhelmingly the letters describe the fighting and campaigning in the main war zones: central and southside Virginia, the Shenandoah Valley, and Georgia. Bermuda Hundred, Petersburg, Third Winchester, Cedar Creek, and Atlanta are especially well covered.

One letter came from a soldier in the 16th Wisconsin. Another penman was in the 12th U. S. Regulars. Several other writers belonged to the U. S. Navy. The vast majority of correspondents, however, served in New York units. There were ethnic regiments, such as the German 45th and the Irish 170th. There were State Militia regiments long in service, such as the 9th and 14th (83rd and 84th Volunteers, respectively), and National Guard regiments called out just in mid-1864, such as the 77th and 84th. There were units whose service was drawing to a close, such as the Independent Battalion and the 71st, and units which first experienced the full rigors of war only in 1864, such as the 16th Heavy Artillery and the 25th Cavalry. There were outfits which had heeded the call for "300,000 more" in 1862, such as the 146th and 165th. And there were the Boys of '61, who had volunteered in the beginning and who would still be there when victory was finally won: such regiments as the 3rd, 17th Veterans, 40th, 47th, 48th, 51st, 56th, 61st, 65th, 68th, 73rd, 81st, 90th, and 95th Infantry and 5th Cavalry.

Not all the individual correspondents survived that long. The correspondents, after all, were officers and soldiers, who wrote with the authenticity of experience. Wartime experience includes the risk of death.

Sunday Mercury correspondents suffered that fate in 1864: Sergeant Albert Kennelly of the 17th Veterans, killed at Jonesboro on September 1; Lieutenant John Smith of the 47th Volunteers, killed at Port Walthall Junction, on May 7; Captain William D'Arcy of the 48th Volunteers, killed at Second Deep Bottom on August 14; and Sergeant William Doak of the 84th National Guard, drowned in the Potomac on August 23.

Another casualty of 1864 was McClellanism. Its death came hard for the editor of *Sunday Mercury*, who had grown increasingly angry with Abraham Lincoln and who championed George B. McClellan for President in the November 8 election. Many letters which the newspaper published, not surprisingly, also supported "Little Mac" and claimed that the writer's entire regiment backed him as well. Such claims, one suspects, were exaggerated. Lincoln received the vast preponderance of known soldier votes. Although ballots by Empire State soldiers cannot be identified within that state's total electoral returns, scholars generally presume that New York soldiers, like those from Pennsylvania and Ohio, voted overwhelmingly to support Lincoln and the war. Even the editor had calmed down by late autumn. Five days following the election, he promised to support the President in a program of "peace and re-union on the basis of gradual emancipation....Only give the nation peace, Mr. Lincoln, and the nation will keep you in the Presidential chair, if you so desire, to the end of your natural life."

The "natural life" of both the President and the Confederacy would not extend much beyond 1864. As the year closed, Northern prospects shined more brightly than they had twelve months earlier. The soldier-correspondents rejoiced in the great Federal victories in the Valley, in Georgia, and at Nashville. They expected to "make ourselves as comfortable as possible" through the winter and then to resume campaigning in the spring.

And all the while, the correspondents and their fellow soldiers enjoyed reading the *Sunday Mercury*. "On Monday evening last," wrote a soldier of the 61st New York on November 18, "the *Sunday Mercury* came as usual. If it did not, we would miss it very much...." Two months earlier, on September 20, a soldier of the 65th New York expressed himself more positively: "The health of the regiment continues good, and there is nothing that adds so much to their happiness as the arrival of the mails, and the *Sunday Mercury*." Reading the newspaper with all its tidings from the armies helped Federal fighting men endure the rigors of the 1864 campaigns. Reading that newspaper today helps students of the Civil War better to understand those campaigns and the individual soldiers who experienced them.

Richard J. Sommers
Carlisle, Pennsylvania

January 17, 1864

Sunday Table-Talk

The best explanations of the following received poem, will be found in the author's note, which is as follows:

"I had in my mind at the time that section in the in the 'National Cemetery' at Gettysburg which is set apart for the burial of those unrecognized bodies collected on the field."

UNKNOWN.

All side by side they lie interred
And at their heads a single stone
Which speaks for all in one sad word,
  Unknown.

They calmly rest, the good and brave,
Who came when war's wild blast was blown.
And nobly won an honored grave,
  Unknown.

They came from homes with plenty blest,
Where peace and joy were all their own.
And now, afar from friends they rest,
  Unknown.

How many hearths are bleak and bare,
How many hearts the loss bemoan
Of those who sleep serenely there,
  Unknown.

Perhaps some watch and hope, though vain,
For one whose spirit long has flown,
Who perished on that bloody plain,
  Unknown.

But soft above each manly breast
The tender springing grass is grown,
The cloak 'neath which so many rest
  Unknown.

And at th' Almighty's final call,
Their glory that in blood was sown
Will reap reward with Him, where all
  Are known.

      —MERCUTIO.

January 24, 1864

INDEPENDENT BATTALION (LOST CHILDREN) N.Y.V.

MORRIS ISLAND, S.C. Jan. 18, 1864.

According to the General Order, the troops on this island, notwithstanding the heavy duty already being done, are compelled to form upon the beach, whenever the weather permits, and drill in the evolutions of a division. The result of the above order is a great amount of hard feeling and plenty of grumbling.

During the evening of the 6th inst., seven deserters, belonging to the Confederate Navy, landed at Gregg. They were from the large three-masted vessel lying behind Castle Pinckney that is being iron-plated, but used at the present as a receiving-ship. These men were detailed for picket; and while near Fort Johnston, the officer in command concluded to quarter himself within the fort, where he would be more comfortable, for the night—the weather being very cold and stormy, leaving the tars to do the picketing in the harbor. This proved to be the opportunity long looked for by these rebellious sons of Neptune; and as soon as the Lieutenant was out of sight, they pulled their boats for Morris Island shore. Upon landing they were blindfolded and taken into Wagner, and from thence escorted to the Provost-Marshall's, where they were provided with safe lodgings. Their song is the same old tune, so often heard and repeated, dissatisfaction and starvation; and, since the proclamation of Jeff Davis, compelling soldiers and marines to remain in the Rebel service until the end of the war, their howl of dissatisfaction has been almost mutinous and hundreds would accept the pardon offered by President Lincoln, and desert to the bosom of Abraham, if they could but get the chance.

Also that another sub-marine arrangement is completed, and almost perfect in its construction, for the purpose of blowing up the Ironsides. Attached to it are three monstrous torpedoes, each containing 500 pounds of powder; and the first trial of this machine cost the lives of sixteen men, it being a little too perfect; it went under water, and was not seen for three days. When it was picked up, the lifeless forms of its suffocated occupants were found shut up in its water-tight compartments.

They also tell us that our shells are creating sad havoc in the city. Nine persons were killed on Christmas, and a large number wounded, including men, women, and children; and ten or twelve houses were burnt to the ground. We could plainly see the fire from our batteries, and it is needless to disguise the fact that Parrot shells are not entirely harmless. Southern newspapers may boast of their invulnerable powers of resistance until doomsday, but to resist the force of a 100-pound Parrot requires an article more substantial than newspaper puffs. The smouldering ruins in the city speak for themselves; and, if the buildings were capable of dodging, then their chances of escaping the dangers of Yankee shells would be more perfect. The destruction of the city is certain; time will tell what virtue there is in the destructive powers of powder. Slowly and steadily our batteries hurl forth their missiles of death, and almost daily the Charlestonians are receiving our iron compliments. At all hours of the day they are liable to be treated with shells for breakfast, and shells for dinner and tea; shells at twilight and shells for supper.

The holidays passed very quietly. We masticated our New Year's dinner, consisting of salt horse and sandbag pudding, and wonderingly inquired, "When will this cruel war be over?"

E. L. B.

January 31, 1864
SEVENTY-FIRST REGIMENT, N.Y.V.
(SECOND REGIMENT, EXCELSIOR BRIGADE).

CAMP NEAR BRANDY STATION, VA., Jan. 25.

>Welcome them home from the battle-plain gory,
>Bringing the banners all war-stained and torn,
>Which they on many a red field of glory
>Proudly, defiantly, bravely have borne;
>Honor and praise are due
>Unto the tried and true
>Who from the camp and battle-field come,
>Our starry flag beneath
>Crowned with the laurel wreath
>Of glorious victory! Welcome them home!
>
>Send sounds of welcome from hill-top and valley,
>Out o'er the land let your sweetest notes swell,
>Fling out the flag with the breezes to dally
>Which they have fought for so bravely and well,
>Where firm they met the shock
>Of the foe, as the rock
>Meets the old ocean's wild billowy foam,
>There where they fought and bled,
>By Right and Freedom led,
>Struck they for Liberty—welcome them home.

Yes, the brave veterans from the Iron Brigade, who have nobly stood in the ranks fighting for their country's honor for nearly two years past, are coming home on a furlough, having still further proved their devotion to the flag, by re-enlisting, showing by this act on their part, that they are really in earnest and determined to see the finishing up of the work which they have been so zealously engaged in, since leaving their homes to become soldiers; yes, who are really war-worn veterans of the Army of the Potomac, men who have stood by the cannon's mouth, have heard the sharp crack of the rifle; and the groans of their dying comrades, men who have suffered on the march by day and night, in sunshine and storm, in winter's cold and summer heat; men who have stood shoulder to shoulder in many a bloody fight, are now waiting for their furloughs, which are promised to them by the Government, if they should re-enlist. The officers of our corps are going to have a grand ball at General Carr's headquarters. Now is the time for young ladies to come out here, and have a grand hop with our shoulder-strap gentlemen; when the dance is over, if there is any not married, I would advise them that this is the chance to get a vet. No feminine with Copperhead sentiments need apply.

GUARDIAN.

FIFTY-FIRST REGIMENT, NEW YORK VETERAN VOLUNTEERS
NEW YORK, January 25, 1864.

By the aid of steam power and telegraph we have managed to get, at last, by strenuous efforts, to the city of our homes, having been trying so to do since the 18th of December, 1863.

Great enthusiasm (?) was shown along the whole route, especially at Buffalo and Albany. We were not many days coming from Cincinnati to Buffalo, yet, to a great number, it seemed as many weeks; for this reason, that they were anxiously awaiting the time when they would arrive in New York.

Through Ohio we had first-class accommodations, but, indeed, things assumed another aspect upon arriving at Buffalo, where emigrant-cars awaited us, and this when, before leaving Cincinnati, the agent of the New York Central Road promised us first-class accommodations through.

The boys did not murmur at this. They thought surely they would be repaid in a bountiful supply of provisions, ready for storage, as our coming had been announced by telegraph. We waited an hour or so, when, behold! eighteen loaves of bread—no more—and about three gallons of coffee. This supplied the deficiency of the fishes. All this to be distributed among 225 men. We thought we had a good joke upon several of the boys, as they hailed from B.; but they denied their country. Can't blame them for it.

Upon arriving at Syracuse the tide seemed to change in our favor, for we dined at the principal hotels. This was more than we really expected. I noticed a piece in one of the city papers, announcing our arrival at Syracuse, and the doors of the hotels thrown open to us, thereby leading our folks to think that we had been living in the best style the whole route. It would have looked a great deal better if they had inserted under this paragraph an account of our arrival and reception at Buffalo.

"It's all right," says the boys, "the Governor will make up the difference when we get to Albany." He did! We arrived about two in the morning; remained in the cars till daylight. Upon the right officer being found (the officers having dispersed in the meantime, no doubt to make an early call on the Governor) we formed in line and marched through the principal streets to the Arsenal—some call it a jail—situated in the suburbs of the city. A grand reception awaited us there, in the shape of coffee, bread, and cold meat; and after this, to be dragged off to attend a funeral, having nothing to replenish our stomachs till night—with the same as the morning. There were bunks to sleep upon, but they were built of slats, for straw mattresses, and as there were none, a large number slept outside.

Directly after our arrival here, an officer was dispatched to New York; no doubt to see if they had made similar arrangements.

After a delay of two days we crossed the river upon the ice, and took cars on the Hudson River Road.

This is a slight sketch of our return. Is it not given in order to find fault, etc., but to let our friends at home know that a soldier does not live in clover. Those acquainted with the incidents upon the route home will verify the above statement.

More anon, when the regiment is re-organized and returns to the seat of the war.

UNO.

February 7, 1864
INDEPENDENT BATTALION (LOST CHILDREN), N.Y.V.
HILTON HEAD, S.C., Feb. 1.

The career of our battalion is being brought suddenly, though not unexpectedly, to a close. The day following our arrival here an order was read to us from the Secretary of War consolidating our battalion with the Forty-seventh and Forty-eighth Regiments, N.Y.V. The organization known as the Lost Children is to be wiped out, and in the future will be known as among the institutions of the past.

On the 20th we received marching orders and bade farewell to Morris Island, hoping never to return; for certainly it is the most desolate, God-forsaken and worthless desert of sand that ever white man, or black man, or any other man, set foot upon. God formed Morris Island at the end of creation, when he probably ran out of seed, and left these naked pinnacles of sand for General Gillmore and his beseiging army to decorate with trees and shrubbery; but our impetuous chief has neglected the cultivation of the sturdy oak and wavy pine, and has busied himself in planting siege-guns in their stead, which brings and sends forth bitter fruit for Rebels. Snakes and lizards, that are so plentifully found on the adjacent islands, scorn to populate this sterile drift of the ocean, where there are no mysterious hiding places, and where Nature affords them no shelter; and the only original native that Morris can boast of is the inevitable flea, that kicks, jumps, bites, and dances in a manner to suit the most fastidious. There is no forest to ramble over, or broad fields of grain to wave like a sea of green; no blue-top mountains to gaze upon, or shadowy oaks and lofty pines to shake their plumes in pride; no gentle breeze to kiss and fan, and all that sort of thing, but the wind kicks up the devil, and whistles as if delighted with its wild pranks, sprinkling the flickering sand into kettles of beansoup and gratuitously peppers our salted pound of "junk". We are choked with the crazy clouds that fills our ears, eyes, nose, and mouth with pulverized morsels. The birds do not sing—there is nary a bird, nothing but the lank, long-legged marsh hen and turkey-buzzard that croaks and pipes its notes in ceaseless tones of sadness, and hovers over our camps, flapping its wings in disgust. It never rains, but pours down in torrents. The lightning hisses and tears through the atmosphere frightfully past our ears like a huge serpent. The thunder peals forth its ponderous salvos through the heavens, as if all hell and its satanic imps had broken loose upon us. Notwithstanding the heats and chills, and calms and fogs, and rains and gales, the siege operations of Morris Island has made it famous in all lands; and when the dust and smoke of this great conflict shall have passed away, then will be seen emblazoned on the annals of this Rebellion the dazzling deeds of blood and conquest; and generations yet unborn will listen, with breathless awe and tearful eyes, to the campfire tales, and heroic deeds of by-gone days in the trench and in parallel, over bastion and parapet, where a husband, father, or brother fought for the starry banner, and fell a mangled corpse by the screeching shell of Moultrie, or Wagner's wicked grape and canister. How many Northern home is made desolate! how many a sorrowful mother or loving sister is looking with tearful eyes in imagination for the lonely grave in the marsh, on the sand-hill, or in the trench, where the heroic dead reposes in peaceful slumbers. The summer-flowers will not write the unreturning heroes epitaphs in blossoms of red and gold, for the sod is yet moist with blood, and the guns of Wagner, Gregg, and Chatfield are avenging their death and peals their only requiem.

ED. L.B.

NINETY-FIFTH REGIMENT, N.Y.V.

CULPEPPER, VA., Jan. 29.

You may think the Ninety-fifth is no more, on account of not hearing from us. But no, in spite of the half day's rations stopped out of every three (we drew eight extra days rations in our last summer's campaign, and now have to make them good), we still live, yes, and going in for three years more. Most all the old members are just taking those thirty-five days furloughs, and the small sum thrown in. We intend showing the "Johnny's" that we are not pressed like them to stay in the service, but will stick it out until the last of the Rebellion (to use their own expression), is "done gone".

Well, here we are, boarding at Uncle Sam's expense, on the outskirts of that town we have so often passed (and once on a rather quick gait) through. We have a pretty good camping-ground, and by this time we are comfortably settled in our log houses. If it was not for these drills, what a bully time we would have; but a drill is part of a soldier's life. But there is our theatre. We can go to that one night in the week. Only think of a theatre way down here in Virginia! We do not have as dull times as one would think. The aforesaid theatre was opened for the first time on Saturday night the 23rd of January. It was crowded. Among the audience was our gallant General [James C.] Rice and lady. Colonel Fowler, and the Quartermaster of the Fourteenth, with their wives; also the commissioned officers of the different regiments of the brigade. The performance was splendid, and everything passed off nicely, to the satisfaction of all.

We are now having quiet times, only when a box comes to the company of Regulars in our regiment, or when some happy individual with four or five canteens slung under their coats comes slouching across the hills from the town. Then comes the big talk, the singing, a little squall, a file of men, and, for the rest of that night, the guardhouse. But it is not often this occurs with the men.

Since I last wrote, we have had some promotions. Our worthy Major, [Edward] Pye, who is liked by all the men, is now Colonel. Captain [James] Creary, of Company F, Lieutenant-Colonel, and Captain [Robert W.] Bard, of Company I, is Major. The latter looks out for the wants of the men, and is a good soldier, but he is rather strict for the Ninety-fifth, who are a sort of careless lot of chaps.

Hallo, there goes that bugle! and now I hear the drums. Good night.

Q.M.D.

February 14, 1864

THE PAY OF NEGRO SOLDIERS.

The question of the payment of colored soldiers was discussed in the Senate yesterday, but without any practical result being arrived at. We have advocated the employment of colored troops from the commencement of the war, preferring that they should help to fight the battles, in which they were as deeply interested as any other class, rather than the fighting population of the white race should become exhausted, and inroads be made by conscription on the classes necessary to carry on the industrial interests of the country, and prevent society from disorganization. And if these troops will fight, they should be paid. After the policy of employing them has been long adopted and acted upon, and when fabulous countries fall to stimulate recruiting to the desired extent, to quibble and wrangle about a dollar to two a month to colored troops is mere driveling imbecility, and worse than child's play. Let every man who does the work of a soldier, receive a soldier's pay, and let Congress cease to weary the public patience with dawdling patronage of the negro on one side, and petty caviling on the other. The work in hand is to raise soldiers, and this can best be accomplished by ending these discussions, and treating all soldiers as they should be treated.

FOURTEENTH REGIMENT, N.Y.S.N.G.

CULPEPPER C. H., VA., February 9.

The Fourteenth Regiment's Troupe of Minstrels gave their first entertainment last Friday night, and the performances were a perfect success. Stars were in the ascendant on more ways than one, and with them were their ladies and families. A grand galaxy of the fair sex were in attendance, lending, as they always do, a charm to the entertainments, as well as viewing in this case with the beautiful scenery and sketches from the brush of our "veteran" young artist, Freytag. The performances were raptureusly received—particularly the originalities and peculiarities adapted by the troupe to the Fourteenth Regiment. Evans' "Billy Barlow", a Fourteenth song, and "Shady", by De Graff, so appropriate to these days of contrabands; Richardson's "Essence of Old Virginny", Desmond's Plantation Jig, and our friend De Vere's Banjo Solos (the inst, by-the-by, is from our glorious fellow-militiamen, the gallant Ninth) brought down the house in raptures. Last night, the second concert was given, and was as complete and successful as any I ever attended in Gotham. The quartet, by McDowell, Warburton, Day, and Baker, beside the duet of "Larboard Watch", by Baker and Bowen, was good, Stevens and Coleman keeping all in good humor by their witty sayings and actions. Cole's "Marseilles Hymn" and Brett's song were both well done, and as well received.

Before the close of the performances, the word came that we must march at daybreak. The troops, at the appointed hour, were on their journey; and soon the work commenced, particulars of which I could not glean, farther than that the roads became dreadful, that there was continued cannonading the first day, and at night heavy volleys of musketry could be heard, supposed to be where the Second Corps were at work.

It is said that the Second Corps lost over 200 men killed and wounded.

The Twenty-fourth Michigan was sent, I am told, to burn the buildings near Raccoon Ford, which were being used as a protection or shelter by the Rebels whilst shooting down our pickets. The work was accomplished; and after being out thirty-six hours, we returned to our different camps. The night was very dark, and the mud very deep, making it very hard work for the troops to travel.

Well, as Johnny Reb, failed in his undertaking, we feel that we shall not be troubled again for a while.

Good-bye, for the present.

J. J.

February 21, 1864

THE CONTEST FOR THE PRESIDENT.

As the Presidential election approaches, the politicians are busy as bees, all working with an eye to the main chance, and with their noses on the scent of the loaves and fishes. The Republican Party is divided— one section clinging to the fortunes of Uncle Abe, believing that a bird in the hand is worth two in the bush, and that "possession is nine points of the law." It must be admitted, that for a simple-minded, honest, unsophisticated old gentleman, Father Abraham plays his hand shrewdly. He holds some heavy trumps, and in this respect has the better of his antagonists. The Army and Navy are both immense electioneering machines and are being extensively used for that purpose. In Louisiana and Arkansas rotten boroughs are being created to give electoral votes enough to give Mr. Lincoln a renewal of his lease to the White House. The expedition of General Gillmore to Florida would seem to have been undertaken for the same purpose. The bogus electoral votes thus created, together with the army vote, it is expected will secure the re-election of present incumbent to a dead certainty. Another influential section of the Republican Party is, however, working with equal zeal and assiduity for Mr. Chase. The Treasury Department is, of course, enlisted in the interest of its chief, and the whole greenback influence in working to the same end. There is, beside an outside independent organization, and whose members disclaim any idea of being the partisans of any candidate. These are the "unconditional Union men", whose shibboleth is "principles, not men", but who are secretly operating for Chase, and will come out as his avowed supporters, in due time. With all these elements and influences to back him up, Chase will be a formidable candidate, and will give Mr. Lincoln a sharp tussle for the nomination.

Besides these factions, there is an earnest and disinterested party attached to the interests of Fremont. They believe that he has been sacrificed by Lincoln, who stole his thunder after laying himself on the shelf. Fremont was the first to sound the call of emancipation, when he was snubbed and rebuked by Mr. Lincoln, who afterward proclaimed the very doctrine which he rebuked, when uttered by its original author. Fremont was the first to hold unequivocal ground, and go ahead of public sentiment, and his supporters can make out a strong case in his behalf.

So far as the Democratic Party is concerned, there appears to be less likelihood of a serious struggle for the nomination. It is understood that Governor Seymour is entirely out of the race, and although, in the West, there is some preference exhibited for General Grant, it is now very generally believed that General McClellan will be the choice of the National Convention that is to meet at Chicago on the 4th of July. He seems to be the only man under whose lead the Democrats would stand the shadow of a chance. The halting course of the leaders of the party on the war and slavery questions, drove most of the available men over to the other side, and McClellan will have no serious competition for the nomination. It's expected that his popularity with the Army will secure a considerable soldiers' vote, which no other Democratic candidate could expect to receive.

The contest for the Presidency will be one of the liveliest, and it need not be added, one of the most important, political struggle that has been taken place in this hemisphere.

SECOND NEW JERSEY CAVALRY

JACKSON, TENN. February 12.

As I have no doubt it interests many of your readers to hear of the doings of this regiment (the Second New Jersey Cavalry), I take advantage of a few leisure moments to write an account of our exploits since landing on the soil of Tennessee.

On the 23rd December, we left Columbus for the purpose of driving [Nathan B.] Forrest out of the State. After a series of marches, during which the men suffered severely from exposure, we occupied Jackson— General Forrest having left in great haste when he heard of our near proximity. Jackson was, in times of peace, a very flourishing business town; but now, thanks to the vandalism of the Rebels, all business is stopped, the stores destroyed, and the court-house nearly a mass of ruins. We had the pleasure of taking our Christmas dinner with a noted Rebel sympathizer, who had laid in a large store with the intention of feasting a party of Rebel officers, and his chagrin may be better imagined than described, when he found himself playing the host to a party of Union officers. After remaining in Jackson four or five days, we received orders to return to Paris (a small town between Columbus and Jackson), which we occupied, and commenced scouring the country for guerrillas, and succeeded in capturing a large number in the immediate vicinity of Paris.

The Colonel of the Regiment, Joseph Kargé, captured a Rebel Colonel, after pursuing him a distance of two miles. The Adjutant took a Captain, and Lieutenant [George A.] Hewlett, Company M, captured two guerillas, after chasing them over a mile.

So far we have done pretty well, having traversed a large portion of Western Tennessee, and cleaning it thoroughly of Rebels and guerillas. The people complain bitterly of the depredations and marauding acts of the guerillas, and everywhere we find a large amount of Union sentiment very clearly expressed. The memory of Andrew Jackson still lives in Tennessee, and it only requires the protection of our forces to have the State prove herself loyal both by deeds as well as words. Within the last six weeks a battalion of cavalry has been raised in the neighborhood of Huntington and Dusden.

The weather has been colder here this winter than it has been for thirty years, and although the men have suffered very severely from the effects of frost, still, for a new regiment, we are in very good condition, and under a more popular colonel, we may yet rival the First New Jersey Cavalry.

VIATOY.

ONE HUNDRED AND THIRTY-SECOND REGIMENT, N.Y.V. (INFANTRY).

NEW BERN, N.C., Feb. 15.

Since writing my last to you, we have had some stirring times in this vicinity, although your correspondent still lives to write one more letter to the SUNDAY MERCURY. The scene of ball opened on Monday morning, about 3 A.M. The picket on our out-posts on the Neuse road were surprised by an advance-guard of the Rebs. They were challenged by the men on post, when the Captain in charge of the Rebs ordered them to fire, wounding one of the men on post in the foot, while the others fell back on the reserve, firing as they retreated, until they reached the Block House, at the Neuse Bridge, where the Rebs were held at bay until re-enforcements were sent up from camp. After they arrived, we kept the Rebs in check for five long hours, and during that time, many a daring Rebel was made to bite the dust that morning, by our little band, placed behind the breastwork, and in the Block House, and from this position, kept them on the opposite side of the bridge. About 6, A.M., re-enforcements from Newbern came to our assistance, consisting of three companies of the Seventeenth Massachusetts Regiment (who were at the time doing provost-duty at Newbern, but when sent for, were gallantly relieved by the Newbern firemen, who shouldered the musket, and patrolled the city in the capacity of soldiers as well as firemen). General [Innis N.] Palmer also sent one section of artillery, which did very good duty in keeping the Rebels from crossing the bridge. Our entire force at this time consisted of about 950 men, infantry and cavalry, besides two pieces of artillery. At the bridge, Lieut. [Arnold] Zennette, of Company A, who was acting quartermaster, was killed while attending the serving of ammunition. Lieut. [William A. C.] Ryan, of Company G, was wounded severely at the bridge, but he dropped three Secesh in the creek, while attempting to cross on a log. Lieut. Ryan is in the hospital at Newbern, doing as well as can be expected. We also had three privates killed at the bridge. About eight o'clock we were ordered to fall back, having discovered the enemy had placed trees across the creek. We captured four prisoners, who stated that there was a large force, consisting of Generals Pickett and Hoke's Division, besides cavalry and fifteen pieces of artillery—in all about fifteen thousand men. But our men bravely disputed every inch of ground between the Neuse Bridge and the railroad station. The woods seemed literally swarming with them—the Rebs. The famous Louisiana Tigers were very conspicuous among them, with their red caps and red jackets. Many of them came no farther than the creek. The regiment retreated toward Newbern in good order, finding there was such an overwhelming force to contend with. Colonel P. J. Classen and Lieutenant Colonel G. H. Hitchcock were conspicuous throughout the whole of the engagement, and conducted the retreat in true military style. The Rebs followed us until within three miles of Newbern, where they halted in the woods for the night. The next day Forts Totten and Rowan shelled the woods, when it becoming too hot for the adversary, he took up his line of march for Kinston, their band playing "Over the hills and far away", "Bonnie Blue Flag", and "Dixie". While the band at Fort Totten struck up the "Star Spangled Banner", "Yankee Doodle", and "Rally Round the Flag".

We had a small force of about eighty men stationed at Beach Grove, in charge of Lieutenants [Samuel] Leith and [William L.] Bath, consisting of a detail of one man from each company of the regiment, and one company of the Second North Carolina Union Regiment. The Rebels besieged this place two days, and they were compelled to surrender. We left the breastworks in front of Newbern on Friday, Feb. 5, and arrived here at 5, P.M., to find our beautiful camp burned. Everything was destroyed excepting a few of the officers' quarters, the theatre, and sweat-box, or familiarly known as "Fort Henstein". The regiment has been furnished with new tents, and all are engaged pitching them to-day. Almost every man in the regiment lost all his clothes, and everything they possessed, keepsakes and all, stolen by the Rebs, and the inhabitants around the vicinity of the camp.

Yours, etc.,   V. J.

One of the soldiers mentioned above is Lieutenant W. A. C. "Wack" Ryan, who, in 1873 almost single-handedly started a war between the United States and Spain.

After his wounding at Neuse Bridge, Ryan was eventually sent to "Ladies Home" Hospital in New York City to convalesce from his wound. While recovering there, Ryan wrote a letter to the Sunday Mercury *detailing the poor conditions and incompetent staff at the hospital. As a result he was court-martialed and found guilty for "Conduct prejudicial to good order and military discipline," and summarily dismissed from the service. Ryan was later reinstated by the President and honorably discharged.*

After the war, "Wack" Ryan became an adventurer and soldier of fortune. He served briefly with the Fenian movement, and later became a general in the Cuban Rebel Army who were then fighting for independence from Spain. While running guns in October 1873, Ryan was captured by the Spanish navy onboard the Virginius—an American-registered ship. Ryan was quickly tried and executed by a Spanish firing squad and beheaded; his head was then mounted upon a pike and paraded through the streets of Santiago. The resulting "Virginius Affair" brought the United States and Spain to the brink of war twenty-five years before the sinking of the U.S.S. Maine.

SEVENTY-FIRST N.Y.V., SECOND REGIMENT, EXCELSIOR BRIGADE
CAMP NEAR BRANDY STATION, VA.., Feb. 16.

Since I wrote to you last, we have been on a mud expedition to look after some Rebs, and to support the Second Corps, which was fighting at the same time, but it was rumored around that a Georgia Brigade wanted to come over into our lines to give themselves up, and to take the oath of allegiance, and they sent out our division, and a part of the Second Corps, to see whether it was so or not. But when we got there was soon found out what was the matter. It turned out to be a hoax, but the boys enjoyed themselves by cutting down trees and hunting squirrels, and we were preparing for a good night's lodging, when we got the order to fall in, and to go back to our old camp, without taking the Georgia Brigade.

The Second Fire Zouaves started for home the day we marched off. They cheered each regiment in the brigade, and the whole division. They have left a little band of heroes behind them, to represent them in the next fight, if we should have one before they come out again. Perhaps our regiment will be in New York before their time is up, and I do believe we would have a fine time together. "Fall in for your high hats and petticoats."

We had a Division Review to-day by General Prince and some young ladies. I think the latter found it to be very cold—in fact, it was very unpleasant; the wind was sharp, and a little snow blowing into our faces, and we were in heavy marching order. Our Major (Rafferty) was promoted to Lieutenant-Colonel last week, and well he deserves it. He is just the right kind of an officer to have command of a regiment, and we feel proud of him.

GUARDIAN.

February 28, 1864
FIFTH REGIMENT, NEW YORK (Ira Harris) CAVALRY
STEVENSBURGH, VA., Feb. 17.

The evening I received your spicy sheet, I turned into my "virtuous couch" with the intention of having a "soft thing" "until daylight did appear". About two o'clock in the morning, we were awakened by the cry of "Saddle up! the Johnnies are driving in the pickets!" The steeds once saddled and the armor buckled on, we sallied forth in quest of the graybacks. Over hills and hillocks, ditches and mud-puddles, and the outpost was at last reached, and we had the gratification of seeing the "Last of the Mohicans" describing a 2:40 gait to perfection around the corner of a barn, for the benefit of his health. But this affair of the "Johnnies" was the cause of our having a six-days' scout, in which nary a "Johnny" was to be seen. Upon our return to camp, after a seven days' scout, we hardly had the saddles off the "frames", when we were again ordered to "saddle up" for a five-days' picket.

Well, here we are once more in our winter-quarters, but how long we are to remain idle, time alone will tell. I hear that there is a grand raid on the programme, to come off shortly.

Gen. [Hugh J.] Kilpatrick has erected a pretty little theatre in the village of Stevensburgh, which he intends to open this evening. The first week will be devoted to the lovers of negro minstrelsy, the second week to "ye spouters", the third to lecturing, etc. I would have secured the position of "bones" had I made early application; but I had a long conversation with "Old Kill-cavalry", who is a boss-beater of the show, and an old English spouter in the regiment and myself are to be stage-managers when it opens. Aside from stage-managing, Jack and I intend to give Kil, and his staff, together with numerous "beats" who wear the bars, a touch of our spouting abilities.

As the mail leaves in a few minutes, I must wind up.

LITTLE LUMP

March 6, 1864
FORTY-SEVENTH REGIMENT, N.Y.V.

My last letter was dated from Barber's Plantation [Florida]—to which place we had fallen back from Sanderson—and in it I stated that we were perfectly ignorant of what the next move would likely be. We have since ascertained all the knowledge required, and greatly to our regret, as the thinned ranks and sad hearts of the regiment abundantly testify. But I might as well give you all the particulars without further preliminary.

On Saturday morning [Feb. 20], our brigade (Forty-seventh, Forty-eighth, and One Hundred and Fifteenth N.Y.V., under Col. [William B.] Barton) took up the line of march forward. We soon heard that re-enforcements had come during the night, and so imagined that we were bound for Lake City, a place of some importance, about twenty-five miles distant. Passing through Sanderson, we pushed on at a quick march, and by 3:30, P.M.—having accomplished a distance of nearly twenty miles—heard artillery-firing a short distance in front, soon followed by the rattle of musketry. But little attention was paid to the matter, as it was thought that we were merely driving in a picket thrown forward from the town of Olustee, where it was rumored the enemy would make a stand. At this time, our brigade was marching in three parallel lines—the Forty-eighth on the road, the Forty-seventh on the left, and the One Hundred and Fifteenth on the right—both the latter in the woods. We received orders to close to our place in line (One Hundred and Fifteenth on the right, Forty-eighth in the centre, Forty-seventh on the left), and after marching a short distance came into line of battle by the left flank, moving forward to support a battery already in action. Most of us thought we were thrown in to relieve another brigade, but to our surprise, found that we were directly in front of the enemy. His position was a strong one, for he had full choice of the ground, and was further protected by rifle-pits and artillery. The line advanced steadily until within short range, when both sides opened briskly. From this time until we covered the retreat from the field, a space of over two hours, we were always in the advance, except when, for a brief space, a negro regiment (First North Carolina) took the front, and finally moved at once off the ground. The enemy attempted to flank us on the left, and actually planted a battle-flag within 200 yards of the left company (C), but a forward move checked them. Our men were dropping fast on every side, but still we kept up the unequal fight—now falling back slowly when pressed too hard, and again advancing the colors and holding the ground for a time. On the right of the brigade, the One Hundred and Fifteenth were pushed very hard, the enemy also attempting a flank movement upon them. Our New York and Brooklyn boys, of the Forty-seventh and Forty-eighth, seemed to have the greatest confidence in each other, and that they made a good, steady, and gallant fight, even when they knew success was impossible, is heartily acknowledged by the commanding general and those in a position to judge.

It was near 8 o'clock when we finally started the retreat. The Rebels, when we first retired from the field, made a motion as if to follow, but our brigade was again used to check them. Facing by the rear rank, we would march some fifty or a hundred yards, then halt and about-face, answering their cat-squalls and coon-squeaks by hearty New York cheers "and a tiger". It appears they had received information to the effect that we had received large re-enforcements, and cheering they took as an indication of the arrival of fresh troops. This may account for being undisturbed while forming and marching as a rear guard.

As I intimated above, the Forty-seventh has lost heavily. Captain Henry Arnold, Co. K, First Lieutenant Charles C. Evry, commanding Co. D, and Second Lieutenant F. T. Hunting, commanding Co. I, were killed; Colonel Henry Moore, Captain Joseph M. McDonald, Co. H (acting field officer), First Lieutenant W. Scott Duffy, commanding Co. H, and Second Lieutenant George L. Schioenderff, Co. B, were wounded, but will recover. The company losses, giving them as they stood in regimental line, are as follows; the proportion of wounded only being unusually large: Co. G, 32; Co. D, 20; Co. I, 24; Co. E, 32; Co. H, 31; Co. B, 40; Co. K, 28; Co. A, 40; Co. F, 38; Co. C, 28. The total of officers and men killed and wounded, amounts to 314. Captain Arnold was first shot through the shoulder, but refused to leave the field, and was again struck in the thigh; Lieutenant Evry had his brains dashed out by a piece of shell, and Lieutenant Hunting was struck in the left breast by a rifle ball.

The "narrow escapes" were in some cases almost miraculous. Major [Edward] Eddy (for some time back, on General Seymour's staff, as Assistant Inspector-General, and who assumed command after Colonel Moore and Captain McDonald were wounded) was, with his horse knocked down but escaped uninjured, although the horse was hurt. Adjutant [Charles] Huggins received three balls through his overcoat, one in the saddle, and another in the blankets strapped behind the saddle. Lieutenant J. A. Smith had the throat-button of his overcoat cut off by a rifle-ball, and was twice struck by a spent ball. Captain [Abijah S.] Pell came near losing an eye by a piece of lead; and, I might go on to any length, in mentioning like cases. All the officers acted in the bravest manner. Captain Tom Sawyer, at one time running the colors near a hundred yards in advance of the line, calling on the boys to "rally round the flag". The gay Captain, in the thickest of the bullet-storm, very energetically expressed his opinion that he could "lick" any Rebel on the field. Most of the non-commissioned officers behaved most gallantly, as the heavy loss among them testifies. One company (G) took three sergeants and six corporals on the field, and all but two corporals were struck.

I must here mention the cool and heroic conduct of our Color-Sergeant, James Cox. Although he had received a ball in the body (hardly an inch from the heart, as it has since been ascertained), and another in his thigh, he never let the fact be known but remained bare-headed, facing the enemy, advancing and then slowly falling back with the colors, as ordered from time to time. Once, when struck, he fell, but the colors were instantly grasped by Orderly-Sergeant Michael Reder, of Co. B, who likewise conducted himself nobly all through. The enemy never saw Sergeant Cox's back, and he stuck by his flag until we left the field, when Sergeant Reder had the honor of carrying it home.

Colonel Moore was struck in the left fore-arm, immediately below the elbow; the ball passing out at the wrist, without breaking the bone. Captain McDonald, who then assumed command, had a ball pass through the fleshy part of the right thigh. Major Eddy's conduct in bringing off the regiment, and aiding and covering the retreat, is the theme of universal admiration. He rallied the men in splendid order, and under his command they formed, marched in regimental line, about-faced, and acted as coolly as if on battalion-drill at Hilton Head. The Major, by General Seymour's permission, and very much to the gratification of both officers and men, has since remained with the regiment—Colonel Moore having been sent to Hilton Head for quiet and rest.

It has been ascertained, almost to a certainty, that with a force of not more that 6,000 men, we fought a force numbering at least 16,000, said to be under command of General Franklin Gardner. Whether it was right to fight, under the circumstances, is not my province to determine; neither need I allude to the many wild rumors in relation thereto now circulating here. Suffice to say, the men have all the confidence in General Seymour, and expect to go back again for another brush.

Hurry along the veterans, who are now regaling themselves with the fat of the land in New York.

I remain, as of old, yours, etc.,   MUTUAL

SIXTEENTH REGIMENT, N.Y.V. ARTILLERY

FORT KEYES, GLOUCESTER POINT, VA., Feb. 18.

The Sixteenth Heavy Artillery is the most extraordinary organization that has ever left New York for the seat of the war. We have no colonel, lieutenant-colonel, or major, and are at present commanded by Captain [Eugene W.] Sheibner, of the Third Pennsylvania Artillery.

We are finishing a new fort here, and are engaged at present in sodding the sides of it. There are seven large guns mounted on the parapet, and the place wears a very formidable appearance.

The Post bakery-loaves at Yorktown are growing "beautifully less" every day, and it would take a microscope to magnify them to anything near the size of the twenty-two ounce loaf that "Uncle Sam" is supposed to give his men. There is a big thing made somewhere. We never get the dried apples, potatoes, molasses, or rice that we should get, and I think it is high time that the Government should look after this and see that the soldier should receive the food that is allowed him by regulation.

Sometimes the boat does not bring our bread from Yorktown, and some laughable scenes ensue among the men for want of bread. In the next tent to us, the following funny scene occurred the other morning. One of the men went to his haversack for a piece of bread, he had left there the night before, and found it was missing, and accused the others for stealing it, but they all steadily denied it, except one. "Arrah, drink your coffee," said he, "and I'll tell ye about the dhreams I had last night."

"An what has your dhream to do with my loaf," said the loser of the bread.

"Hould on, bedad, till you hear it," cried the other. "You see, I dhreamed Captain Sheibner bucked and gagged me. An' put me in the guard-house, the spalpeen, for twenty-four hours. An' I was very hungry. Well! a beautiful lady came to me, and relased me, an' sint me to my tint. 'You'll find bread in the haversack,' says she."

"Well?" said the loser of the bread.

"Well?" said Pat, "I got up in my sleep, an' ate your loaf."

The roar of laughter that followed, drowned the complaint of the loser, who to use his own words, "had to drink dhry coffee that morning."

The Army around here is lying in slothful idleness. This war appears to be, to me, interminable. It looks as if we were trying to prolong instead of trying to crush the Rebellion. The spring will be half gone by, before there is another onward movement made; and it will be time to return to winter-quarters ere anything great is accomplished. So wage the war its slow length along. Two years ago I was with McClellan here, and now, although the prospects are brighter, still we should not let the golden opportunity slip through our fingers, but strike at once, and crush out the last relics of this fratricidal Rebellion.

T. M.

<u>March 13, 1864</u>

ONE HUNDRED AND FORTY-SIXTH REGIMENT

WARRENTON JUNCTION, VA., March 10.

We are now encamped close by Warrenton Junction, some ten miles from the town of Warrenton.

I visited Warrenton a day or two since, and found it fast going to ruin and decay; many of the finest buildings in and around town being either burnt or torn down. Warrenton, before the breaking out of the Rebellion, was considered one of the prettiest, as well as the most aristocratic town in Virginia. But all its wealthy residents have long since left it, and those who remain are now fed from Uncle Sam's Commissary.

Indeed, the whole of Fauquier County is now nothing but one vast waste—a perfect wilderness—where food for either man or beast has long since ceased to exist. Throughout the whole county may be seen the ruins of magnificent *chateaux*, which have been destroyed generally by the Confederate soldiery if owned by Unionists, and by our men if owned by Rebels. Fauquier Co. has, I think, suffered far more by this war than either Stafford, Prince William, or Culpepper.

The Ninty-first Pennsylvania Regiment, of our brigade, which went home some two months ago to recruit up their thinned ranks, returned to us three or four days ago. They don't number even now more than between two hundred and three hundred men. A band of guerillas, known as the Black Hawks, who, before the Third Brigade came here, were the terror of these parts, have all disappeared. There is not a more safe spot on the Alexandia & Orange Railroad than from Warrenton Junction to Bealton station.

Lieut. Hugh Chambers was the recipient of a magnificent sword, sash, and belt, yesterday, which was presented to him by the members of Co. E, in token of their high esteem of him as an officer and a man. The presentation was made by Orderly-Sergeant John Kenny, on behalf of the men, who, in a few, brief patriotic words tendered the sword to Lieut. Chambers. He in turn spoke a few well-timed words of thanks. Lieut. Chambers is one of the most popular officers in the regiment. There are several men in Company E who belonged to the old Fifth (Duryea's Zouaves) among whom are [Cornelius] Lane, [John] Hayes, [Robert] Cornell, [Aaron] Muckridge, and others.

There is great rejoicing now among the men on account of being allowed the privilege of voting at the next Presidential election. McClellan would be the soldier's choice if he should run. In fact, the Army of the Potomac fairly idolize the name of McClellan, and I doubt if the hero of Marengo and Austerlitz was half as much loved by his soldiers as he who won the bloody fields of Malvern Hills and Antietam.

TYPO.

March 20, 1864
FORTIETH REGIMENT, N.Y.V.
March 15.

We left Brandy Station on the afternoon of December 31, arriving at Elizabethport, N. J., at 11 o'clock, A.M. We came home the same way we went out in 1861, by the Northern Central Railroad. We took passage on the steamer Red Jacket for New York City—the same boat that took us from Yonkers to Elizabethport—and I am sorry to say we returned as we left, unnoticed and unknown.

On the night of January 29, the members of Company H gave a ball at the City Assembly Rooms, which proved to be a very pleasant and agreeable affair to all present.

After our furloughs expired, we were taken to Fort Schuyler to wait for the regiment to assemble. We thought to have a soft thing for once, and stay for a while in the vicinity of New York City, but we were glad to be relieved. Our fare there was worse than here in Virginia. We received salt-water coffee and spoiled meats. The treatment in general was more fit for slaves than soldiers. Our regiment complained, and the consequence was, that General [Harvey] Brown took us out on the ramparts—out of sight of our barrack—while the guards took our arms away. That affair gave us a bad opinion of so old a soldier as General Brown. We received our arms again when we left on February 16th. We went on board the steamboat John Romer, which brought us to the transport Mississippi, at the foot of Canal street. Many went home that night, and were left behind—at half-past six o'clock next morning, the steamer sailed. Those that went on the transport had a rough time of it. We arrived at Alexandria on the 19th, and stopped in the Soldiers' Rest. I must say that this is the best and cleanest place I have yet found. We started for the front on the 21st, and arrived at Brandy Station at sunset. We had to bivouac for the night, and next day we went into camp near our old place.

February 28, the division started on a reconnaissance. We went as far as James City, a small village about ten miles beyond Culpepper. We remained out until the morning of March 2, when we returned to camp. The roads were in a bad condition returning, on account of a two days' rain. We reached camp at 4 o'clock, P.M., tired and hungry, the boys cursing at what they term a "regular nuisance" (reconnaissance).

The weather during the past week has been very stormy, so that there is a good supply of mud on foot.

To-day, we had a division-review, by Major-General Birney. A large number of ladies were present.

It is rumored that General Grant will review the Army next week.

Taps are beating, so *au revoir*.

MILLIE O'RYLIE.

March 27, 1864
FORTY-SEVENTH REGIMENT, N.Y.V.
PALATKA, FLA., March 18.

Our moving days, of late, have been quite numerous. On the afternoon of the 9th we received very sudden orders to pack up and prepare to make tracks, with one day's rations, for a new field of operation. We were soon on board the steamer Delaware, and about 9 o'clock in the evening left the wharf at Jacksonville, and were soon under full headway steaming up the St. John's River in the darkness, destined for Palatka, eighty miles inland from Jacksonville, and, as we supposed, occupied by the Chivalry. All hands were quartered on deck, for the purpose of returning the fire in case we were attacked; but the hellhounds of destruction were silent, and daylight found us quietly disembarking at the docks unmolested; not even a sable monk or a friendly dog to welcome our advent into this deserted and war-stricken town, which formerly contained about 2,000 inhabitants, and is beautifully situated on the St. John's, 125 miles from its mouth and 100 miles from Lake City. Only three families were found remaining, and they were of the poorer class of women, whose husbands, fathers, and sons were dragged from their homes by the merciless Rebel Conscription Act, while their families were left to the tender mercies of the uncivilized Yankees, and to starve.

Scouting parties were dispatched in different directions, and soon afterward returned with numerous specimens of the old gray-haired and down-trodden white slaves of the South. The blacks were all run off, previously, into the interior of the country by their masters. The old men, and frightened women and children soon began to flock into our lines for protection and food. Their stories are indeed frightful. To describe their sufferings your correspondent will not attempt; but you can imagine their joy when they found that the Yankees were civilized and humane, and not barbarians, as they had been told by the tyrannical and we hope extinct chivalry.

Wheat flour has been sold here for $300 per barrel, and not to be had at that price. Coffee is an article that has not been seen here for the past two years. Deserters are coming into our lines every day. They all tell us they are tired of fighting for the slaveholder and his niggers. Jeff. Davis's game-of-bluff in Florida is certainly played out among the poor whites.

We are now fortifying Palatka, which will be the grand starting point in the future operations against the Rebels. An advance from this place would cut the enemy's communications and force him to retire from before Jacksonville.

E. L. B.

NINTH REGIMENT, N.Y.S.M.

CAMP NEAR CULPEPPER COURT HOUSE, VA., March 20.

The past week has not been marked with anything extraordinary in this Department, yet what has transpired has been somewhat varied. Last Thursday [March 17], we had a brigade-drill, by General [Henry] Baxter, walking two miles, wind-blowing a cool breeze, and the dust in the road heavy. The drill was a complete success as far as it went, it being short and simple; yet two regimental commanders did not exactly know the simple moves, and the General remarked that it would be well to have a change of officers. Our brigade is now composed of the Twelfth Massachusetts, Ninetieth Pennsylvania Volunteers, Ninety-seventh New York Volunteers, and Ninth New York State Militia, at present—the Eighty-eighth Pennsylvania Volunteers are away on furlough, having re-enlisted for three years longer.

Yesterday afternoon, we had a scare. A reliable contraband came within our lines and reported that the enemy was advancing; so the order came to pack up and be ready to move at a moment's notice. We were having a battalion-drill by Colonel Joseph A. Musch, the wind was blowing a perfect hurricane, and the clouds of dust arose in pyramids. Nobody was frightened, however, and at six o'clock the order was revoked, and we were relieved of a great deal of anxiety about leaving our comfortable quarters.

All the talk is the 8th of June and the gallant Ninth. After three years' trials and hardships their term then expires. Twenty-six have re-enlisted, mostly recruits who had nine months to serve; they thought they might as well get the large bounty and the war would be closed by that time. Do you think it right to hold a few men who enlisted in September, 1861, receiving no bounty and recruited to come home with the organization by Lieut. Jas. Wickan (now deceased) authorized by Col. Stiles? They took the oath for three years, but the mustering officer had to give all recruits at that time the same oath—why, because there was no other—all other oaths had expired—but assured them that the Government would let them come home with their regiment. Now they say they will have to remain. Is it just and right?

CORPORAL.

April 3, 1864

SEVENTEENTH REGIMENT, N.Y.V.V.

CAIRO, Ill., March 28.

There is at the present time a peculiar interest attaching to the Seventeenth. Composed of men who have fought in every action of the Army of the Potomac, from Manassas to Gettysburg, they are looked upon here in the Southwest as fitting models of those troops of whose deeds before Richmond they have so-often heard and envied. The contrast between the discipline of the Western troops and the Eastern (as represented by the Seventeenth), is certainly not to the advantage of the former. The great attention paid by the officers of the Seventeenth to the enforcement of strict discipline, shows how conscious they are of the fact that the men of this regiment have to uphold before the men of the West their reputation as soldiers from the "Army of the Potomac".

The experience of this regiment since it left New York, five months ago, has been a changeful one. Constantly moving—often gliding down the Ohio, the Tennessee, or the Mississippi, and as often marching over roads by turns rugged and muddy, into the heart of the Secesh country, as for instance our last expedition to Meridian. It would take columns to describe half of the interesting events and features of the campaign. I shall not, therefore, attempt such a difficult task, but confine myself to the affairs of the Seventeenth alone. We were barely allowed a week's rest after returning from the expedition sent in pursuit of Forrest, in West Tennessee, when we received orders to report at Vicksburg in order to engage in the expedition to Meridian. In Virginia it would be considered a great hardship to send men sore-footed and frost-bitten, as our men were, on a march of near two hundred miles, but here in the West it is thought quite a matter of course, and as matter of course we went. The regiment was put in the Second Brigade, Fourth

Division, Sixteenth Corps—the brigade commanded by Colonel [John H.] Howe—the Division by Brigadier-General [James C.] Veatch, and the Corps by Major-General [Stephen A.] Hurlbut. General Veitch admiring the efficient way in which the Seventeenth did guard-duty, detailed the regiment to guard a part of our very large supply-train. The train was too much for Rebel cupidity to stand, and the guerrillas accordingly violated their usual prudence by making a lively attack on the train just as we had passed through the town of Decatur. Their attack, sudden as it was, did not by any means disconcert the men on guard, who readily returned their fire. The firing very soon brought our regiment to the scene of action, but the Rebs not liking our appearance, concluded that discretion was the better part of valor, and retreated to the music of Springfield rifles. Our line of march—owing to the dryness and abundance of long grass, and the carelessness of some regiments in building fires—was lined with fire and smoke. Novices would imagine, when they beheld the fields covered with fire, that they beheld the veritable "prairie-fire", and would feel disappointed on being told that it was nothing but the grass on fire. Often having to march till 1 o'clock in the night, we found this general conflagration no less useful than magnificent, as it enabled us to pick our steps through swampy places which would have been the graves of many of our mules but for the friendly light which I have mentioned. There was not much fighting to do, although we ascertained that the force that was fleeing before us was quite a considerable one; a random volley now and then would occasionally mislead us into the belief that they were going to make a stand at last, but our infantry would barely reach the ground where our cavalry (which was always in advance) were trying to hold their own with the Rebs, when off the gray-coated gentry would go, again to repeat the same useless performance perhaps the next day. The Rebels in this State are not of the same fighting stuff as the Virginians. A force from which in Virginia we would expect nothing but hard blows and knocks, here awaits an appearance but to fly. While the very free use they make of gunpowder shows their familiarity with "villainous saltpetre", yet the great care they take that we should not get inside of musket range betrays their extreme sensitiveness

"—to the dangers that environ,
The men that meddle with cold iron."

It must be confessed that this judgement is based upon but a limited experience, and their apparent cowardice may be owing more to want of discipline than want of spirit.

We reached Jackson, the Capital of Mississippi, on the 7th of February. Leaving Jackson behind us, and passing through Brandon, Hillsborough, and other towns, we camped near Meridian on the 13th. While other regiments at this point were engaged in tearing up railroad tracks, the Seventeenth, in addition to its ordinary duties, had to take charge of about a hundred Rebel prisoners-of-war. The expedition had now crossed the State of Mississippi from the border-line of Louisiana to that of Alabama, bringing the war home to people that had never seen a blue uniform since the commencement of the war; had also destroyed many miles of the different railroads that intersect the country, and done incalculable damage in many other respects to the cause of rebellion. Why General Sherman, now in the full tide of success, did not keep carrying the "war into Africa" till he reached Mobile, is a question I shall not pretend to discuss, but from Meridian we went no further. On the 22nd, we commenced our return-march, encamped a few days at Canton, really a very pretty town, and on the 4th of March pitched tents on the hills of Vicksburg. I should have stated before that our Colonel, William T. Grower, was a part of the time acting as Brigadier-General. Colonel Grower being a tactician of a very high order, was well fitted for the command; and one who so unmistakably bears the stamp of a gentleman, could not but favorably impress all those who came in contact with him. I mentioned above that we reached Vicksburg in the 4th of March, and that this ever-moving and active regiment has participated in another dash at our old foe, Forrest, in West Tennessee, but that wily guerrilla escaped again. We are now at Cairo, waiting for our corps (the Sixteenth), to proceed on another expedition. It would seem that the Seventeenth Regiment is going to be kept on expeditions till we have visited every nook and corner of Uncle Sam's territory. To give you an idea of the traveling that this regiment has done since it left New York, five months ago, I will give you the names of the States we have passed through—come, as we followed the course of the Ohio, the Tennessee, or the Mississippi, on board transports; and some as we tramped with our feet at the rate of twenty miles a day—Maryland, Virginia, Ohio, Kentucky, Indiana, Illinois, Arkansas, Tennessee, Mississippi, and Alabama.

Yours,   A. K.

April 10, 1864
SUGGESTIONS FROM A SOLDIER
NEW YORK, April 8.
To my old Friends and Comrades in the Army of the Potomac:

As I presume you have all heard of the noble acts of the loyal women of the North and South in their present heavenly undertaking—the Metropolitan Fair for the benefit of the Sanitary Commission. It is unnecessary for my enlarging on the subject, but this I will say: From their noble exertions they will realize a large amount of money, which, expended in the cause which it is intended for, will cause a great alleviation of suffering and sorrow, both in the hospitals and on the battle-field. My object in addressing you is this. Among the many wonders and curiosities to be seen at the Fair is a sword which is to be presented to either General George B. McClellan or General U.S. Grant, as the majority of votes for either person will decide. The voting is done in this way: a person by paying one dollar can have the privilege of voting for either of their favorites. The race at present is very nearly even, Little Mac having the advantage of a slight advance. The sword is to be presented to the victor, and the proceeds of the voting is to go with the other receipts of the Fair.

I wish to exhort you to rally to the aid of your old, tried, and beloved commander, as I have seen you do at Williamsburg, Fair Oaks, Malvern Hill, etc., and show his enemies that, though they tore him ruthlessly from you, they can never obliterate him from your hearts, and, at some future day not far distant, we will, with raptures delight, hail him back to his old command.

There will be no obstacle to your voting, for have you not that right now? But should there spring up one before you, just drop two or three files to the rear from the right and left, and deploy (employ) skirmishers at home by furnishing them with the required greenbacks to vote for you. So now once more, "Rally round the Flag", and send your contributions with your names, regiment, and company-letter, to some friend on whom you will agree. If you have not got the dollar to spare, let two or more of you club together and make up a vote.

You might send your contributions to the office of the soldier's friend, the New York SUNDAY MERCURY, 113 Fulton street. Hoping soon to hear from you all as with one voice, I remain, with much pleasure,

MARION BOY,
An old Veteran of the Excelsior Brigade.

FOURTEENTH REGIMENT, N.Y.S.M.

CAMP NEAR CULPEPPER C.H., VA., April 4.

As you see by this we are still at Culpepper, and the Fourteenth still does provost-duty for the town. Gen. Grant's arrival here among us is a source of considerable stir, particularly among the shoulder-straps. An order was promulgated authorizing officers to use one side of the street, and enlisted men the other, but I presume Gen. Grant got wind of the idea and put a stop to it, for I believe it no longer exists. A grand review took place, the other day, and passed off pretty well. The rain somewhat hurried matters, and after the Generals and staff passed, we were allowed to proceed to our different camps without going through the formality of marching in review.

The concerts by the "minstrels" of the Second Brigade still continue a success, and concerts are still given at the Fourteenth Regiment's Concert Hall. A grand serenade was given last night to Generals Rice, [James] Wadsworth, and [Lysander] Cutler, at this (Gen. Rice's) headquarters. The music was really splendid, and without doubt was a great treat to our much-loved commanders. The arrival of Gen. Wadsworth among us is hailed with joy, for he has endeared himself in the affections and memory of all under his command. The same affection and respect exist for our late Corps-General (Newton), and our present Brigadier-General (Rice), not forgetting Gen. Cutler. At these head-quarters we have had a very gentlemanly set of officers—from the General to his Aids. They all invariably make it a point to look to the interest and comfort of the men under their command—and the result is the love and respect of subordinates in return. The time is fast approaching when the Fourteenth may be expected home, at least eight companies; and Companies I and K, though but a very few left, still hope to come home with the regiment. At any rate, they will not have but about five or six weeks longer to serve to make up the three years, if retained.

A squad from this guard arrested some citizens—one on a very serious charge: that of inducing men to desert from our Army to the Rebels. We were out to the picket front, where we brought these citizens (?) from. The day was a very stormy one, being cold, windy, and rainy. Some refugees came through the lines, about twenty-four persons in all, on the same day. It was a pityful sight to witness the females trudging over the muddy roads through the cold sleeting rain, with little children, and see them suffering so. The young men were soldiers of the Rebel Army, who, having succeeded in getting with their families again, concluded it better to try and get among the Union people rather than serve Jeff Davis any longer. They suffered a great deal trying to get to us. The young men belonged to the Tenth Virginia Infantry (Rebel)—a regiment that accidentally got to our rear at Gettysburg.

The re-enlistment fever is quite high.

It is now raining pretty fast, and the roads are in a bad condition.

J. J.

ONE HUNDRED AND TWENTIETH N.Y.V.

NEAR BRANDY STATION, VA., April 6.

There is no stirring news here at present. The weather is very bad, and we have had constant rain for nearly a week. Virginia mud is now in its worst possible condition.

Both the officers and men in our brigade (Excelsior Brigade) are justly indignant at the recent alterations in the Third Corps, or, rather, the breaking up of the Third Corps. They nearly all say they will not fight in any other corps than their own; for which (were everything known of the circumstances by the public) they cannot be blamed.

It is the opinion of nearly all, that the breaking up of the Third Corps was occasioned by malice on the part of General Meade toward General Dan Sickles, the hero of Gettysburg. It is universally acknowledged that General Sickles won the Battle of Gettysburg, contrary to orders, and wholly on his own responsibility, after orders had been given by General Meade to retreat. Consequently, General Meade is jealous of him, and everything connected with him. No other reason can be assigned for breaking up the largest and best corps in the Army of the Potomac.

The Third Corps fought, alone, the first battle (Williamsburg) and the last battle (Locust Grove) that the Army of the Potomac has been engaged in. The most distinguished generals this war has produced have served in this corps. Under such leaders as Heintzelman, Hooker, Kearny, Prince, Birney, and others nearly as good, the Third Corps was always the first in battle and the last to retreat.

It is true, this corps has had a commander for the last six or eight months who was not fit or competent to command a brigade; but he could have been relieved from command of the corps very easily. It is an easy matter to relieve a general not competent to command. Why, then, was not General French relieved, and some good general placed in command of the Third Corps, instead of breaking it up? The men that have fought under the red, white, and blue diamond of the corps are now dispirited, gloomy, and sullen, and do not feel that enthusiasm they did while members of their old organization.

The Second Corps—to which we are attached—(Gen. Meade says "temporarily") is a good corps, and has a good leader, in the person of General Hancock. Our division (formerly known as the Second Division, Third Corps) is now called the Fourth Division, Second Corps. Our three brigades have been consolidated into two—the Excelsior Brigade and the Second Jersey Brigade.

We are yet in our winter-quarters, but expect soon to pack up and move after the Johnnies.

We have the utmost confidence in Lieutenant-General Grant, and think that, under his supervision and leadership, the heretofore-defeated Army of the Potomac may be able to conquer General Lee, and take the immortal City of Richmond; thus conquering treason, and once more restoring our beloved country to its former peace and happiness.

Yours, respectfully,   PRIVATE.

April 17, 1864

FORTIETH (MOZART) REGIMENT, N.Y.V.

NEAR BRANDY STATION, VA., April 9.

We are still in the land of the living (though it is some time since we spoke to you), and living very well at last. A few days ago, two of our old tent-mates (Veteran Volunteers), arrived, their furloughs being up (Wm. Firdon and T. Harvey), and as our hotel here was full and overflowing, we had to take them to board in our "mansion"; which being rather small for its size—say about ten feet long and seven feet wide—with five regular occupants, we were therefore obliged to give our boarders a "layse" upon the floor when they wished to become lodgers. Fortunately, the three "down-stairs" tenants had to "go to the front" (on picket-duty), so that the returned V. V.'s found themselves a little better accommodated; and we are quite happy, and "R spirits R lite and ga." So we composed a new song (Samuel and I did). For fear you will not understand my "ritin" I will "transport" it for the benefit of the (un)—inlightened people who, every Sunday morning, make such a "scrabble" after the MERCURY:

Our (R) spirits are (R) tight and gay.
So said the horse when he had no hay;
And that is what the "sogers" say,
When the "greenbacks" come and they get their p-a-y.

When you read this "poick" (pork) effusion you will find that it is a piece which would have done great (in)justice to the great and original Bard "Mathusala", and I don't want him to know that I "rote" it, but you may "print" if you think proper, and I will shoulder the "responsibility". Our Corps, the Third, I suppose you have heard, has been consolidated with the Second Corps Fourth Division. We were very sorry to have the corps broken up, for it had a good name, and has been considered one of the best in the Army. General Birney is to remain in command of our division. One brigade (first) of the division has been broken up, and consolidated with the second (Ward's) and third ([Alexander] Hayes'). Ward is now the first, and Hayes the second.

Last Thursday, we moved camp about three-quarters of a mile nearer the station. We set to work, six of us, and built us a first-rate "palaise"—the largest, but, not the most comfortable, we have had yet. It is about 15 feet long, 8 feet wide, 4½ feet high, ridge-pole 10 feet high, and a fireplace occupying one end, with a three-cornered chimney to it. It has two bunks. Brother Gus [Titus] Harvey and self occupy the up-stairs (second story); [William] Ferdon, and [Dennis] Brannon the downstairs (kitchen). We have had some talk of having it papered, but the great difficulty in procuring suitable artists from New York (we would not let any others do it), and the extravagant rise in the materials for making paper, may cause us to be "quiet on the Potomac" in regard to that matter for awhile. We have plenty of room for two more; so send on your conscripts, and we will learn them in short metre (saltpetre) how to "rake oysters", and such other details as belong to "ye army in ye field".

The whole Army was to be reviewed by General Grant on Wednesday. We got ready, and marched near to the reviewing-ground, but had to turn back, on account of the rain. We have worked so much in the water that our hands are chapped in the inside. That is something new to us. We are getting fat. Cause why? We live upon the fat of this land, or "sacred soil".

I will give you a description of the dinner we had last Sunday, and I think you will believe what I have said about high living. Sausages; yes, Uncle Sam dont issue them, but the sutler does, at five cents per sausage, thirty cents a pound. We had three pounds, ninety cents, or three sausages per man. Ain't that cheap? We think it is, for we have seen them sold for sixty cents per pound out here. We also obtain from ye sutler, for our table, prime old cooking-butter for only sixty cents per pound; and it is also, mind you, "worry" cheap, because we can't eat much of it, and the brine is so strong that it nearly takes the "hide" off our mouths. Talk about Sampson being so strong, why, I have seen butter out here strong enough to knock chain-lightning out of your Sampson. We often get up some messes which "causeth great rejusting of ye jackets and ye vests". It is composed of pork (salt hog), and fresh beef corned (not horse), hard tack, bread and flour. It is "tiptop", and answers out here, for "poiple". Tell our good mothers that if we ever live to get home once more, we will storm their flourbags and capture them to make paste with. To make crust for potpie, take "dumps" gravy (paste) and flapjacks.

Many of the men are now chopping away, putting up shanties, but I think we will not bother putting up another, If we have this. We ought to know something about building huts by this time, for this is the fifth we have put up this winter.

The weather has been quite changeable along bank. One day we had a very hard snowstorm (twelve inches deep), the deepest I have ever seen in Virginia, and Tuesday we had two sunshines, one hailstorm, one big rainstorm, and to-day we have had one long sunshine.

Some people seem to think that we will have no fighting this spring or summer, if so, they make a great mistake. It cannot be so. I know we will have some hard battles to fight during the coming campaign, and may be more severe than any we have had to fight during the two years and a half we have been here. All is "quiet on the Potomac" at this time.

It is laughable, sometimes to hear the "speeches" of those who have had no experience in war. On our late reconnaissance, a new recruit, belonging to the Third Michigan Regiment, and who had not been in any "forward movement" before, asked an old soldier, one of his comrades, "Where are we going?"

"Out reconnoitering," replied the Vet.

"Out raking oysters?" exclaimed the recruit, with astonishment. "Good heavens! What does the General want to take the whole corps out to rake oysters for? I should think a brigade could rake all the oysters he wanted to eat!"

I rather guessed at the time that he thought it an awful long distance to where the oysters were. We did not get quite to the spot where the raking was taking place, and believe there were not many found; but the "shells" were around us at one time pretty thick, and our recruit had a taste of them for the first time.

SAM.

Of the three occupants mentioned in Sam's "palaise," two became casualties in the upcoming campaign. Titus Harvey was killed on May 8, in the battle of the Wilderness. William Ferdon was wounded in the foot in the Wilderness and wounded again at Petersburg on June 16, and again at Hatcher's Run on Oct. 27, resulting in the loss of both eyes. Only Dennis Brannon escaped unhurt; he was mustered out on June 26, 1864.

ONE HUNDRED AND SEVENTIETH REGIMENT, N.Y.V.

DEVERAUX STATION, VA., April 12.

Although several weeks have elapsed since I had last the pleasure of writing to the SUNDAY MERCURY, still I fear I must plead guilty to the trite excuse of not having any news of interest to impart that could interest our friends. But (as Dan Bryant says in his celebrated political speech on the "situation") to return to our subject.

We of the One Hundred and Seventieth New York still maintain an unbroken front, and hold our own along the line of the Orange & Alexandria Road, notwithstanding the incessant and heavy rains of the last two weeks, which have swollen Bull and Pope's Head Runs to such an extent as to overflow their banks, carrying away Bull Run Bridge and innumerable smaller temporary structures of the kind, besides sweeping away a few of our picket-huts, at midnight on Saturday last, from which our boys had to beat a hasty retreat, as the water burst suddenly in on them.

The same night, as the officer of the day was going the rounds, he essayed to cross one of the torrents (formed by the freshet), in order to visit the picket-post, when he was carried down the stream, though a good swimmer, and narrowly escaped with his life; assistance, fortunately, being near at the time. Twenty four hours' constant labor of the Construction Corps, from Alexandria, who came up immediately, sufficed to erect a bridge in place of the one swept from Bull Run, so that the cars are again passing to and fro.

Of course, the roads are in an awful condition; "mud to the hub" is the cry of the teamster, as desperately he urges his jaded team forward, slashing the flanks of his "unfortunate critters", jerking vehemently at the lines, in his almost fruitless attempts to get through the sacred soil. A warm sun and fresh winds for three weeks or thereabouts can alone put the roads in a fit condition for a forward movement of our armies. When that comes, we shall see.

Wagonmaster Emerson and one of his men, who have been engaged in hauling timber to this station, was captured at the home of a farmer named Buckley, about two miles from our line, yesterday morning, under the following interesting circumstances: It appears that Emerson and his friend were intimate with the family, in which there are two young ladies, to whom they had presented, the day previous, two silk dresses. The fair ones, being grateful, no doubt, for so handsome, and by no means, unwelcome a present, invited the gentlemen to spend Sunday at the house, which kind invitation they accepted most graciously, and yesterday morning, being well mounted on two fine little horses, they proceeded to Mr. Buckley's. That was the last seen of them within our lines. About noon, old Mr. B. came in out of breath, to inform Lieut.-Colonel [Michael C.] Murphy that Emerson and his man were taken by four Butternuts while, posted in his house, in social converse; the horses were taken, of course. A scouting party was immediately dispatched, but returned minus success. Let this be a warning to all susceptible wagoners and others to keep within the lines; and, above all things, not to fall into the meshes of Cupid when, the attraction is located within the enemy's country. Exit, ye victimized Emerson!

Colonel James P. Molver has been in command of this brigade for the past two weeks, and the Lieutenant-Colonel in command of this regiment and post.

Duty is very heavy, consisting of picket, guard, and escort; besides scouting, and fatigue duty, but we, old campaigners though not "vets", stand it very well as our sicklist will show.

If Congress could but settle this matter about the increase of the soldiers' pay, which has been so long harped upon by them without coming to our decision, we might ought to look for Major Greenback, P.M., who now owes us nearly four months' pay.

An order has been promulgated in this Department, regulating and providing for the transfer of soldiers from the Army to the Navy. This order has caused such a commotion among the "sailors" in our ranks, of which there are several. Some of them will embrace this opportunity of getting afloat again, while many prefer to see it out ashore—that is, their three years.

Some twelve or fourteen "Butternuts", captured at the front, passed through on the cars en route for Washington to-day; they were well clad in the Secesh course homespun gray uniform, and did not appear to have suffered much for food, as they were rather robust and healthy in appearance. They expressed themselves as tired of fighting in a hopeless cause, as one of them said: "Old Lee would get h—l this summer." They appear to fully appreciate General Grant's fighting qualities, and the gigantic military machine in operation for the opening of the greatest, and, we sincerely trust, the final campaign of the war.

Yours truly,   A. O. P.

FIRST U.S. CHASSEURS

JOHNSON ISLAND, SANDUSKY BAY, OHIO, April 9.

At present we are engaged in the responsible duty of guarding Rebel prisoners, who are confined here to the number of 3,000. They present such an appearance in their various costumes, that they baffle my powers of description. Suffice to say, a more miscellaneous crowd eye never beheld. Among the notables (who are sojourning here for the benefit of their health, and also that that their heated passions might have time and opportunity to cool), we may mention Generals [Isaac R.] Trimble and Archer. I assure you, they have not a very exalted opinion of this style of a hotel.

Our Colonel, who has been absent from the regiment for a week, returned the other day, and his return was hailed with delight by the boys, who have unlimited confidence in him, for he has endeared himself to every man of the regiment by his soldierly qualities and gallant bearing.

It would be an act of injustice, as well as a breach of etiquette, did I fail in recognizing the many kindnesses we have received at the hands of the fair and loyal ladies of Sandusky. By the excellent sanitary regulations, which are strictly enforced, sickness is a stranger, and "Surgeon's Call" might well be dispensed with.

Your invaluable paper arrives here regularly, and is eagerly read by the boys, who always hail it as a welcome messenger.

F. G. T., Co. B.

Private Francis G. Thompson, age 22, was five feet eleven inches with sandy hair and grey eyes. He enlisted on Aug. 20, 1861 in Co. H, First U. S. Chasseurs (65th New York Infantry) and was later transferred to Co. B. His occupation before the war was waiter. After the battle of Gettysburg, he served for three months as a cook in Camp Letterman. Thompson was a frequent contributor to the Sunday Mercury *using the pen-name of "Franconi."*

April 24, 1864
FOURTH REGIMENT, EXCELSIOR BRIGADE
NEAR BRANDY STATION, VA., April 19.

Since my last, nothing of any importance has transpired here. As usual, we are under orders to march; it is proverbial with the Army to move in April. We cannot do so at present, but will some time next month—rain permitting. We had very stormy weather for the past few weeks; we are sorry (very much) for it is impossible to have our regular reviews while it lasts, which, by the way, don't improve the Army a bit. A good, thorough inspection would do more good than a dozen of them; this is the opinion of military men high in authority. Picket-duty, as I said before, is severe with us; we catch it on stormy weather.

We are now in the Second Corps, which is an excellent organization; but we believe (and always will) that the Third Corps never ought to be broken up; our two old Divisions (the pride of Generals Hooker and Kearny) ought to be a distinct organization in themselves; but as politics rule the hour, we will have to submit. We are but machines to be moved when wanted. If it is for the general good we are so mixed up, we will be satisfied! give us the pride of the Army (Little Mac) among us, even as a guest, and we are satisfied to stay three years more, or end the Rebellion. Adjutant [George B.] Doris has just got here, looking in excellent health, after a short visit to New York. He reports everything quiet there.

We are daily expecting Captain Purtell, who is on a visit to his family. The performers on the Indian clubs and dumb-bells don't meet as frequently at the Captain's marques as they were wont, and ball-playing is played out. In a word, our sports are not as well patronized as when the Captain is present.

Lieut. [Thomas] Manning is as jolly as ever. He is all right now; his band is in full blast—the air is vocal (nightly) with the sweet sound of their mellow voices. Such a combination of talent is not often found in the Army. My candle is almost gone, so I will have to finish.

Yours, etc.,   GLADIATOR.

SIXTEENTH NEW YORK HEAVY ARTILLERY
GLOUCESTER POINT, VA., April 18.

At last we have indications of a considerable movement from this point toward the enemy; but whether the Sixteenth Heavy will have an opportunity of participating actively in the spring campaign is a mooted question. When the raid on Richmond, to relieve the Union prisoners, projected by General Butler, was made known, our boys were on the *qui vive*; and as soon as they received marching orders,, the alacrity shown in getting ready told well. The River of York has been considerably ruffled of late, by the continued rains and high winds, causing considerable washing away of the banks, and also by the appearance of several large transports, crowded with troops from Hilton Head, Beaufort, Folly Island, and other points on the South Carolina coast, whose places have been supplied by the dusky warriors claiming descent from the renowned Hannibal.

The Tenth Army Corps will soon be assembled on this Point; the Fifty-fifth Pennsylvania, Fourth New Hampshire, One Hundredth New York, and Seventh Connecticut are now here, with several light batteries, and the beautiful green plain is now covered with a multitude of white tents, presenting a most cheering contrast to the view. They have two excellent brass bands, and the exquisite strains produced on dress-parade this afternoon were most enlivening. It is expected that General Gillmore is to have command of the corps. If so, we may presume that a long and heavy siege is to be commenced against Richmond, when the Sixteenth Heavy, who are industriously engaged drilling on the columbiads in the citadel, will be called upon to perform that duty they owe to their Government, in battering down the defences raised by the traitors to defend the Capital of their bogus Confederacy; and most cheerfully will they respond. Long ago, a connection should have been made with the Army of the Potomac across the Rappahannock, which is distant only about forty miles, with the intervening territory almost destitute of Rebs. By occupying it, we could have direct telegraphic communication, and the facilities that would give in making a simultaneous movement would be invaluable. Perfect co-operation from this department by General Butler would insure success for General Grant; but General McClellan would be the best man to lead the army up the peninsula. We wonder greatly at the obtuseness, or petty jealousy, of the Administration in not availing themselves of the talents possessed by this latter officer. It is astonishing what love for him exists in the breasts of the old veterans.

A part of our regiment is now at Fort Magruder, near Williamsburg, and two companies at Yorktown. At the latter place, there was a military execution on the 16th, of two bounty-jumpers belonging to the Second New Hampshire. One of them had been taken out the day before, but a telegram from Fort Monroe, staying the execution, arrived just in time, as he was descending from the wagon.

Yours,   JACKSON.

FOURTH NEW YORK HEAVY ARTILLERY
CAMP NEAR BRANDY STATION, VA., April 17.

It is just three weeks ago to-day that I remember well, we left our comfortable quarters, at Fort Ethan Allen, and reported to Brandy Station, where we halted for the night, and at sunrise next morning we resumed our march to Stephensburg, and along the route we were greeted with shouts from the old Army of the Potomac, such as "How are you, Heavy Artillery?" and "How are you, Defences of Washington?" which we took with a very good grace, and pitched our tents near the Irish Brigade, Second Militia, and the old Tammany Regiment, where we remained for over two weeks, when the First Battalion were ordered to the Sixth Corps, where we are guarding ammunition-trains for the present.

I hear of a great many rumors as to our grumbling about being sent into the field; but among the privates I hear of none, as all the lads appear to like it tiptop, as we had a plenty soft thing on Uncle Sam, for more than two years, around Washington, and by next fall we expect to perform the same duty in the fortifications around Richmond.

While looking over a late number of your paper I saw the closely-contested vote between Little Mac and General Grant for the Army sword, when a number of us concluded to give a vote to General G. B. McClellan, hoping that he will soon be restored to his old command, and wear that blade he so nobly deserves.

Yours, with respect,   ALL OF CO. F.

SIGNIFICANT CHANGES—Three years ago, a colored man dared not open his mouth in Baltimore. Had he shown himself in uniform at that time, it is certain some white brutes and cowards would have assassinated him. On Monday last, three regiments of negro troops passed through the streets of that city, *en route* for the seat of the war. They were loudly cheered! The same men and boys who stoned the Sixth Massachusetts in this same Monumental City, on the 19th of April, 1861, now pronounce the troops from there to be among the best volunteers in the service.

A commodious armory on Talbot street, Portsmouth, Va., formerly occupied by the aristocratic "Junior Cadets", now in Rebel service, is at present used as a school-room for colored children.

May 1, 1864
THE SWORD-CONTEST QUESTION
NEW YORK, April 27.
To the Editors of the Sunday Mercury:

I wish through your paper to thank the noble Army of the Potomac for their prompt answer to my suggestion in your paper of the 16th instant, soliciting from them a vote for the army-sword in favor of their old commander, Gen. McClellan.

On Wednesday night, the 20th inst., while I was standing guard at my old post, beside the two swords (army and navy), patiently waiting for the appearance of the Army of the Potomac (I was confident they would come, for when have they ever failed to do so when Little Mac was before them?), I was greatly surprised to observe springing up beside me, as if by magic, an old and well-known friend, in the shape of an imaginary battle-flag of the Old Iron Brigade, who were the first to enter the field, being led by the indomitable Second Fire Zouaves, who came in on the double-quick and discharged 104 volleys (votes) for Geo. B. Mc, and 2 for U.S.G. I felt so delighted I could not suppress a cheer of welcome for my old comrades, who arrived just in time to turn the scale, for a majority in favor of U.S.G. was accumulating quite rapidly; but the tide had turned; the Army of the Potomac was in motion, and I was in hopes they would meet with success in this enterprise, not of war, but of love and esteem. But, alas! it was not to be, for the same death-shadow that haunted them through the Peninsula Campaign defeated them in this undertaking. What I mean by the shadow is, the jealousy manifested by the authorities at Washington for the nation's idol, Geo. B. McClellan.

The Excelsior Brigade were quickly followed by the following regiments: Fortieth N.Y.V., 81 votes for Little Mac; Tenth Massachusetts Regiment, 48 votes for ditto, and the Twelfth U.S. Infantry (Regulars), 32 votes for ditto, besides a number of others, the regimental numbers of which I was unable to obtain.

But for all the Army made such strenuous efforts to obtain the sword, it was to no purpose; for, at the eleventh hour, when they had certain victory within their grasp, a change of base was evident, or, in other words, swindling commenced; and then the Government obtained the victory over the volunteers, not in votes, but in greenbacks. And why shouldn't they? for, while the Army were pinching themselves to forward their little mite for the great cause of their heart, the nation's great financier, Secretary Chase, was quietly fingering a pile of greenbacks, which were borrowed for the purpose of defeating them, from the Sanitary fair, or of the United States Treasury. That little word "If", has to be brought in use once more. If the Executive Committee of the Sanitary Fair had but abided by their former rules in regard to the voting for the swords, General George B. McClellan would have obtained the Army sword by an overwhelming majority; and that majority was principally composed of votes from the Army, who, although they had two difficulties to face, faced them manfully. The first difficulty that arose was a detriment to voting, by placing under arrest two voters, one commissioned and one non-commissioned officer. This was done by a Colonel in the Second Corps, who must understand that, by a law settled by the ballot-box, his men under his command, as well as that of the rest of the Army, have a perfect right to vote as they please. I know his name; and should he not be careful in future and not strive, by buying and imprisonment, to influence the men's votes, he will hear from me personally. The other difficulty of which I spoke is the Government and Union League swindle.

The Army and public are now informed that they will not be denied the pleasure of presenting a sword to their most worthy favorite, and General; for the proprietors of the New York SUNDAY MERCURY have, at the suggestion of a number of highly-eminent citizens, kindly opened a subscription-book at their office, for donations from $1 and up, and I presume anything less will not be refused; so now, that you all have a chance to show your regards for Little Mac, with no chance of a defeat, come forward, or send your contributions to the place designated, 113 Fulton street, and show some people that, although we didn't borrow money to vote with, our large number of votes did not break us. Hoping you will read this with approval, and that I will hear from you favorably,

I remain, with pleasure, yours, etc.,   AN OLD VET. OF THE EXCELSIOR BRIGADE.

FOURTEENTH BROOKLYN REGIMENT
CULPEPPER COURT HOUSE, VA., April 23.

It is Saturday night, and as there seems to be such a strong probability of a move soon—not knowing when I may get another letter to you—I just concluded I could not devote my leisure-moments to a better purpose than in writing a few lines; so here goes. The roads are drying pretty fast, but there is a likelihood of a storm again soon, it being very blustering. There certainly is something very mysterious going on, which, I hope, is best known to our General-in-Chief. The Fourteenth are now quartered as comfortably in their new camp as ever they have been, and I think the shanties we have built reflect credit upon the great majority of the regiment, being spacious and comfortable in nearly every respect. To-night, a full supply of cartridges are being dealt out, in anticipation of an attack from the Rebs to-night.

There was some excitement in the regiment on the 18th instant, caused by the fact that one of the old members of Company A, William Burns, who had been transferred from this regiment to the Regular Cavalry, being discharged. The said William Burns was sworn in as a member of the regiment on the 18th of April [1861], at precisely the same time and place with the eight first companies in the city of Brooklyn, and his muster-rolls for the United States service date back to that date, while the rest of the regiment, at least those who are out here to the front, are being retained till the 23rd of May. The men of the regiment, as a matter of course, thought that if one man can be mustered out from the date of his first oath the rest should receive the same privilege. But red tape is a curious article; it certainly takes a longer time to unwind from one "bobbin" than it does from another. One being a Regular "bobbin" and the other a "Volunteer". Perhaps this being a "Militia" bobbin, makes all the grand difference. How are you militia-privileges in United States service? Perhaps when the regiment gets home it will have the opportunity of enjoying some of the privileges; Echo answers, Perhaps. Time, it is said, works many changes, and wondrous ones, too; so we shall see what we shall when we see Brooklyn once more.

A reorganization of the different departments of the service has been going on for some time. The First Corps—what is now remaining—is merged into the Fifth Corps, and I believe now forms just one division, viz., the Fourth. We still wear our old corps badges, as a mark of distinction, I suppose, in honor of the old First Corps. Pioneers are now differently organized, being brigade, division, etc., instead of guard for headquarters, or Regimental Pioneer Corps. All, I believe, are now to be mounted on horses or mules, for greater expedition. All the sutlers are gone, and most of the civilians, who were usually camp-followers. The Sanitary Commission are, as a matter of course, excluded in the order. It is very gratifying to learn that New York is doing so well for the sick and wounded soldiers, and to alleviate the sufferings of those on the tented field. It is to be hoped a strict lookout will be kept, to see that the soldiers, sick and wounded, gets his rights. In some hospitals, such cases have occurred of men dying of starvation by not being able to eat the horribly gotten-up dishes of Government food, when, if they had been so liberally bestowed by societies or friends for that purpose, they would have lived. Beware of the chief cooks, hospital-stewards, and over-zealous parties attendant upon the unfortunate sick and wounded soldiers. Wines and liquors, as well as other luxuries, often find a different channel for consumption than to the cots of the disabled defenders of the country.

Yours, truly,   J. J.

FORTIETH NEW YORK REGIMENT

NEAR BRANDY STATION, VA., April 24.

Nothing important has occurred since my last.

I am very sorry to record the death of our Chaplain (Rev. W. H. Guilder). He had been sick for several weeks with the smallpox. He expired on the evening of the 15th. The body was sent home on the 17th. The regiment escorted the body to the station, Company D, Captain James R. Stevens, being the guard of honor. A large sum of money has been subscribed to raise a suitable monument to his memory. His son (Adjutant W. H. Guilder) accompanied the corpse to his home, "*Requiescat in pace*."

On the 13th, the Paymaster paid us a visit, but paid us very few greenbacks, as we had to pay for everything we lost on our late trip to New York.

On the evening of the 17th, the non-coms presented Colonel Thomas W. Egan with a magnificent gold medal, set with diamonds. It was received by Colonel Egan with one of his neat little speeches, after which a visit was paid to the sutler's ale-vaults. The sutlers have all since left, so that officers and men have to come down to Uncle Sam's grub.

On the 23rd, we had a corps review by Generals Grant, Meade, Hancock, and most all the generals in the Army. The day was fine, and the red-patch division turned out in good style, and made a very fine appearance.

We have had any quantity of brigade-drills and inspections, but they are of no interest to the general reader, so we will say nothing about them.

We will probably have to move in a short time, when we expect to give the Johnnys a little trouble. We want General Grant to make a sure thing of it this time, as we don't care about staying in Virginia more than three years longer.

We have a regimental court-martial sitting every day, consisting of one officer, for the trial of light offences. About three dozen cases were read out on parade last night. In each case the sentence was five dollars fine, "two-thirds of the court concurring in the verdict". The boys call this "the shirt-sleeve court-martial". O discipline, "thou art a jewel!"

Last Monday night, Companies D and E subscribed eighty-one dollars for votes on the great sword contest, at the Sanitary Fair, New York City, in favor of Major-General Geo. B. McClellan.

The weather has been fine during the past week, but a rainstorm has set in, and is coming down pretty heavy now.

The buglers have blown "Lights out", so *au revoir*.

MILLIE O'RYLIE

MILITARY MATTERS

FEMALE RECRUITS.—A Washington correspondent says the official records of the military authorities in that city show that upward of one hundred and fifty female recruits have been discovered, and made to resume the garments of their sex. It is supposed that nearly all of these were in collusion with men, who were examined by the surgeons and accepted, after which the fair ones substituted themselves and came on to the war. Curiously enough, over seventy of these martial demoiselles, when their sex was discovered, were acting as officers' servants. In one regiment there were seventeen officers' servants, in blue blouses and pants, who had to be clothed in calico and crinoline. Even a General, who has won many laurels in the war, had a handsome, "detailed man" acting as his clerk, whose real name turned out to be Mary Jane G—, and who has parents in Trenton, who are estimable members of society. She said, in excuse, that she "wanted to see the world", and we think she has seen it, to a considerable extent. But wearers of blue coats and brass buttons will fascinate the fair sex; 'tis a way they have, the wide world over.

May 8, 1864
ONE HUNDRED AND SIXTY-SECOND REGIMENT
GRAND ECORE, LA., (RED RIVER), April 25.

We are now resting ourselves beneath the shade of the mighty pines of Louisiana, after two days' conflict with the enemy at the cross-roads, near Mansfield and Pleasant Hill. The first day's fight took place on the 9th inst., and the next on the day following. The first fight was interrupted by darkness, after skirmishing the whole day—the Thirteenth Army Corps being engaged, with a portion of the cavalry division. The Nineteenth Corps was held in reserve until 5, P.M., when the order came for us to fall in; and, after a double-quick of six miles, we arrived in ample time to check an overwhelming force of Rebels that intended to show our boys no quarter at all. We remained in line of battle until 1 o'clock the next morning, when we took up a line of march back to Pleasant Hill, a distance of fifteen miles. Here we remained until 4, P.M., our skirmishers being driven in. Our brigade (Third), under the command of Colonel Lewis Benedict, was in the advance. The Rebels got within a good range of us, when we gave them a good volley, and fell back, at the same time keeping up a galling fire. Here our brave Colonel (Benedict) met his fate. The Sixteenth Corps took the advantage of us, drawing the Rebels out of the thick woods, when they advanced upon the Butternuts in a style that will be long remembered by the Third Brigade. Our boys were in great confusion for a spell, but they soon rallied again, and participated in the bloody conflict. I have since learned that the Rebels captured, on the first day's fight, [Ormand F.] Nims' Battery and eighty wagons, with 50,000 rations. If this is a fact, it is indeed a bad start for our campaign in Louisiana.

Our regiment met with considerable loss. Captain [Frank T.] Johnson, of Company H, and Second-Lieut. [Theodore A.] Scudder, of Company D, are known to be killed. Second-Lieut. George W. Gibson, of Company G, was wounded, and is supposed to be in the hands of the enemy; First-Lieut. Henry P. Fisher is slightly wounded, and is in our hospital, doing well. Among the enlisted men there are a great many missing, and the general impression is, that they are in the hands of the Rebels. The friends of those who are missing may keep up their spirits for awhile, as I am confident that a great many missing fell into the hands of the Rebels as prisoners. Our brave color-bearer, James Ball, formerly of the Second Precinct, Metropolitan Police, in your city, now slumbers in a soldier's grave. He was killed in the first volley from the enemy.

We have been busily engaged fortifying this place, and we now defy the Rebels to advance upon us, as they did from the crossroads to Pleasant Hill.

The weather is quite cool as yet, and the river is falling pretty rapidly, and it has a tendency to create some alarm among the military scions on account of the future operations.

In this campaign we have captured quite a host of prisoners. The Rebel Generals [Alfred] Mouton and [Thomas] Green are dead, so the Rebel prisoners say. I have reasons to believe that such is the case.

SHANGHAI.

FIRST UNITED STATES CHASSEURS
BRANDY STATION, VA., April 30.

There was recorded in the New York journals, a few days since, the death of Wm. M. Guigan, Drum-Major of the First United States Chasseurs (Sixty-fifth N.Y.V.). The sad event deserves more than the frigid statement of fact in the mortuary column. The deceased had an extended reputation in the Army. He was, in fact, the acknowledged superior of all the musicians in the Army of the Potomac. Brought up in the rigid school of the Regulars, he was a purist in his peculiar sphere. His instrument was the fife, upon which he discounted notes that charmed all ears. He was a musician of undoubted genius; and whether as Fife-Major on Governor's Island, or as Bandmaster in the Army, his distinguished ability everywhere asserted itself. The First Brigade of the Third Division, Sixth Corps, to which he belonged, was last winter ordered to Johnson's Island, near Sandusky Ohio. Soon after arriving there, Guigan was taken ill. Application was made for furlough. The papers came just time enough to pass him home to die. Two days after his advent in New York, he breathed his last, in the arms of his mother. They had not met during nearly three years. In all that period her noble son had proved himself a gallant soldier. He knew his every duty, and was faithful in its performance. He was no luke-warm loyalty. When the original 75,000 marched forth, he was enrolled in the ranks of the Twelfth New York. He won the friendship of Colonel Butterfield, as well as the highest regards of every comrade; for his musical talent was allied with the more superior qualities of the head and heart. The war literally wore him away. Spared on numerous fields, he fulfilled his destiny beneath the domestic roof. The intelligence cast a sorrowful pall over the minds of all his associates. For him they cherished an affection lasting as truth, and true as the magnetic needle. He left a vacancy which will not soon be filled. Indeed his place can never be supplied while the Chasseurs are banded as a regiment. Art may accomplish much; but genius shines effulgent above all art. What others did by the aid of art, Guigan did by genius. They might do well; he did the best possible. We have tears for his memory; sympathy for his mother; and kind words in his praise. Thus we leave him to rest in peace, followed by the blessings of all the Chasseurs.

SHORT.

ONE HUNDRED AND THIRTY-SECOND REGIMENT NEW YORK INFANTRY
BACHELOR'S CREEK (NEW BERN, N.C.), May 3.

The regiment is still at the Creek doing the outpost picket-duty, and holding the key to Newbern. We are, and have been, expecting the Rebs down to pay us a visit ever since they made the assault on Plymouth, N.C., which is located about sixty miles from here on the Tar River. They have succeeded in capturing that town, but it cost them more men and stock than the whole town was worth. I understand their loss was very heavy. They afterward made an attack on Little Washington, located thirty miles from here, where they met with a still warmer reception. There was the Fifteenth and Sixteenth Connecticut, Fifty-eighth Pennsylvania, Seventeenth Massachusetts, Ninety-ninth New York Volunteers, First North Carolina Cavalry, and a part of the Twelfth New York Cavalry stationed there, and they all fought bravely. The North Carolina Cavalry, and women and children, were all sent out of the town to Roanoke Island.

The Twelfth New York Cavalry and a battery started for Newbern by land, and were intercepted at Swift Creek by the Rebs, under Col. [John] Whitford, thinking to cut our boys off; but after getting our battery and the howitzers to bear on them, they soon skedaddled and left the cavalry boys and battery-boys in possession of the field, and companies D and B of the Twelfth are now here, having arrived on Saturday in camp, and are doing picket and vidette duty in conjunction with the brave One Hundred and Thirty-second.

On their way down from Little Washington they captured a Lieutenant [Hardy] Whitford, a son of Colonel Whitford, who was at the time in a schoolhouse making love to the schoolmarm; and also another Lieutenant whose name I did not learn; and also four privates, one of whom they took from a chimney where he had secreted himself. He said if he was treated as a prisoner of war he would come down. He was ordered down by one of the cavalry, and he came, and is now a prisoner with the rest at Newbern. Our infantry-troops evacuated Little Washington on Saturday, after laying the town in ashes, and they are now concentrated in Newbern, ready for an attack from the Rebels, unless they are called back toward Richmond, where they will be most likely wanted. The Rebel Ram Craven, constructing at Kinston, in this State, should have been destroyed last summer, as also the one that came down at Plymouth, and destroyed the gunboat Southfield; but I am inclined to think, that when the Craven comes down toward Newbern, that she will get more than the Rebels calculate on; she will have a right smart chance of not going back again. Our iron-clad Monitor (car) stands sentinel, at the bridge that crosses Bachelor's Creek. She has good metal on board her, and she is in charge of Lieut. [John] Walker of Co. A. Our regiment has at last been furnished with the Springfield rifle-musket which are far superior than the clumsy, heavy, Vincennes rifles we left New York with—every one seems to be satisfied with the change. The regiment is in splendid condition, there being very few attending surgeon's call mornings, but very many attending the grub calls. The regiment was again mustered in on Saturday, April 30, and the Colonel P. J. Classen, made the boys a short and neat speech, complimenting them very highly for the neat and soldierly appearance, a reputation that this regiment has borne for a long while in this department, and we intend keeping it. The regiment has not received one cent since the 31st of December, 1863. We have now four months pay due us; and with the high price of provisions at home, what are our families to do? It is really too bad that we have to wait so long for a few of those greenbacks. The weather here is beautiful. Hurry along the Paymaster.

Au revoir.   V. J.

May 15, 1864

THE STRUGGLE IN VIRGINIA.

The contest going on in Virginia is the subject which is uppermost in every mind and on every tongue; its vicissitudes hold the absorbed attention of the country in breathless suspense, and rivet the attention of the civilized world. Never in the history of the human race did a struggle take place involving more important and far-reaching issues, or exhibiting more desperate energy or unflinching bravery than that displayed on both sides. It will stand alone in history without a parallel. The circumstances already adverted to, the numbers engaged, the appliances of destruction brought into requisition, the determination to conquer or perish; give to the contest a character different from any hitherto recorded. The further the combat deepens, the more evident does it become that on it hangs the fate of the nation. Each side is hurrying forward its reserves from all quarters. From every section to which the Union armies have penetrated they are being recalled, so far as their absence is compatible with the retention of the advantages hitherto achieved. And we may well imagine that the Rebels do not fail to bring to the aid of Lee every man that can be spared from other quarters. The dogged persistence of Grant to move straightforward to the goal he aims to reach, regardless of the obstacles in his path, finds it's counterpart in the resolute stubbornness of Lee, who rallies his retreating columns whenever the topography of his pathway offers a vantage-ground for either attack or defence. It is only in a civil war like this that such fighting could take place. In a contest between foreign nations, half the engagements that occurred would have decided the fortunes of the campaign; for no Army, in such a case, could be held together, and hurled again and again at the enemy, as Grant has dashed the Army of the Potomac against the works and the hosts of his antagonist; nor could an Army be induced to retreat and fight alternately, and suffer such terrific and continuous punishment as he has inflicted on the Rebel troops. But in these two Armies, in addition to the pride of the soldier, and the bravery which is his creed, each man fights for an object which elicits the highest enthusiasm of his nature. The citizens composing Grant's Army fight for the unity of the Republic, and to determine whether it is to have a future; whether America is to be a great nation or a chaotic nebulae of petty and discordant communities, without influence and without a place among the nations. The South when it took up the sword, cast its fortunes on the "hazard of the die", and struggles with the tenacity with which mankind, in the mass or in the individual, resist the prospect of annihilation. The contest is therefore marked by a ferocity equal to the depth of the passions animating the combatants.

The defeat of Lee, if accomplished, will be the end of the war. Not only would a victory over him go far to extinguish the Confederacy under any circumstances, but now that he has called to his aid the great body of the Rebel military forces from all quarters, his discomfiture would leave the South without any formidable armed power. That Grant will defeat him in the end is the confident hope of the country. The ten days' fighting that has already taken place, though varying from day to day, and pregnant in instances of material disaster, leaves a balance in favor of Grant sufficient to place the ultimate issue beyond the regions of doubt. The preponderance of the forces, which must outnumber largely those of the enemy, his own resistless determination, the capacity of the subordinate generals of the Army and the unwavering heroism of the troops, all tend to give assurance of final triumph. What further encounters are to be met, what additional sacrifices may be necessary, the future only can reveal. That there is more desperate fighting to be done is beyond question, and a considerable time may elapse before the capture of the Rebel capital is consummated. But its fall is regarded as certain; for its fate has borne somewhat of the relationship toward the existence of the Confederacy which that of the Coliseum was supposed to bear to the density of ancient Rome—"While stands the Coliseum Rome shall stand—when falls the Coliseum Rome shall fall". In this expectation the country awaits the close of the gigantic contest that has already cost such a frightful sacrifice of human life.

ONE HUNDRED AND SEVENTIETH N.Y.V. (Detachment).
TWENTY-SECOND CORPS
OUTPOST DEFENCES OF WASHINGTON,
KETTLE RUN, VA., May 10.

Thinking that a few notes from my diary may not prove uninteresting at this exciting and anxious period of our national crisis—of the greatest Rebellion the world ever witnessed—of the advance of the finest Army on the planet into the heart of the enemy's country, to conquer or lose all on the issue—I enclose the following brief extracts of what we have seen and heard during the past eventful week:

At Devereux Station, Va., May 2.—Marching-orders have arrived, and we leave here for "elsewhere", on the 4th inst. Fewer trains pass front, "and they return with non-combatants" and "other useless baggage"— useless to a moving army. We have had the first heavy thunder-storm of the season this evening.

May 3.—To-day is beautiful and brilliant with spring verdure and clear sky, cool atmosphere, and the warbling of birds. All "extra" baggage being prohibited in our removal, the boys are lightening their kits by the disposal of such articles of clothing as can be possibly dispensed with. This is the first anniversary of the Battle of Nansemond, during the siege of Suffolk.

May 4.—Immediately after reveille this morning, packing knapsacks, filling haversacks, buying out the sutler (the latter appears to be a very important preparation for all movements), and striking tents began. Good-bye to comfortable quarters, fresh tack, and other army-luxuries known in permanent quarters, but strangers to the field. Where the former is replaced by the little "shelter-tents" and the latter by the "hard tack". Companies A, E, and H having joined the regiment from Bull Run Bridge, Union Mills, etc., where they had been stationed, at about 10 o'clock we formed in line on the parade-ground, stacked arms, and unslung knapsacks, and patiently awaited the coming train, which was to afford us transportation. At 11 o'clock, they had arrived, and we were piled in, only as soldiers can be piled on railroad cars. For my part, had I not been a second Hanlon (acrobat), I don't see how I could have managed to reach this point of the road at all, so nicely was I compelled to balance myself on the left leg at the edge of the car, from the crowded state of its freight, during our transportation from Devereux to Kettle Run. At Manassas, we passed General Ferrero's division of negroes, belonging to the Ninth Army Corps, Companies D and G got off the train at Cannon Run, where they are located under the command of Maj. J. B. Donnelly; A, C, H, and K, at Bristow Station, which is the headquarters, Col. [James P.] McIvor in command, at Kettle Run; B, F, and I, debarked and remain under command of Lieut.-Col. [Michael C.] Murphy.

May 5.—During the whole of last night troops passed front, principally consisting of Ferrero's Division (colored), of Burnside's Corps. They sang merrily, and tramped through the Run knee-deep, in the best possible humor. The Third New Jersey Cavalry also broke camp at this place, and have gone off to parts unknown, to us. The passing of this army enlivened the night—our first at Kettle Run. We learn that the advances of the grand old veteran Army of the Potomac crossed the Rapidan yesterday, at 4, A.M. Cannonading could be heard this evening. But one train went front to-day. Mails are restricted to the Army for sixteen days. This we think a greater curtailment than our rations. Breastworks are being thrown up around our little camp, and an abatis of trees placed outside of them. These defences are very necessary—our position one of great importance, our position one of responsibility and trust. The country is open and level, affording great scope for cavalry-operations, and the operations of Old Sol, whose scorching rays play on our devoted band in a most unmerciful manner, for nowhere can a bush or tree be found under which to seek shelter in our camp. Kettle Run is a small narrow stream, and like most runs in Virginia, of no importance except for drainage and washing purposes. On the slope of the bank is a blockhouse of octagon form, recently built for the defence of the railroad-bridge which crosses the run. When we have it provisioned with five days' water and bread, we could, if compelled to take shelter in it, stand quite a siege. Of course, it is loopholed, and musketry can keep an enemy at bay, from any point of attack, for a long while. There is a new organization at present infesting this section of the country, known as Pine Rangers. We have not heard from them yet, however.

May 6.—No train up or down. Heavy artillery firing could be heard, though very distant—a squad of stragglers—sick men, known, in military parlance, as deadbeats, arrive, and report a battle at Germania Ford, and other skirmishing. All is quiet here. To-day has been a long, hot, sultry, and anxious one—anxious to learn of triumph of our Army. Here our little command is isolated, I may say, it being many miles from our Army.

May 7.—A squadron of the Sixteenth United States Cavalry, from Aldie, halted here at noon, en route for the front on a scout. They were accompanied by two British officers, who appear to be on a tour of pleasure. A wounded soldier from the Army reports Grant within a short distance of Fredericksburg. The Assistant-Secretary of War [Charles A. Dana] passed up on a special train this morning, and returned again to Washington. We learn that General Grant would not allow him to cross the Rapidan. It is a self-evident fact, that Grant is determined to command the present great movement, to the utter exclusion of all intermeddling and incompetent political interference.

May 8.—Still another warm, sultry day—a Sunday of anxiety has fled past on the "wings of Time"—and in its course many a spirit has winged its way to eternity. The distant reverberations of artillery, borne to our ear on occasional sultry currents of air, tell us that the Angel of Death reaps his harvest, from the war-path— as onward, still onward, toils our brave army. At noon, a telegraph-office was opened here, but was subsequently ordered to Nokesville, a mile and a half up the railroad. When the operators reached there they found the wires cut, and three lengths of it carried off. It had been accomplished in the interval which elapsed from their departure from here to their arrival at Nokesville—about twenty-five minutes; thus showing a proximity to guerrillas. At retreat, this evening, an order was read from corps headquarters, from Gen. [Christopher] Augur, ordering and authorizing commanding officers to shoot all deserters and stragglers from the Army that may come into our lines, on sentence of drumhead court-martial. This is a very stringent, though doubtless necessary order. So far, be it said to the credit and honor of our Army, none have made their appearance, and thus we are saved from the unpleasant execution of this order. Some fifteen trains pass up—it is said for wounded. None have passed over this line as yet.

May 9.—A cavalry scout, from Fairfax Court House, went by this morning. The trains which went up yesterday passed down to-day; they contained a few wounded; they were officers. From what scout-news we can glean, the "star of the Republic shines brightly", as the Stars and Stripes will float o'er the walls of Richmond ere many days! God grant our prediction may be right! More anon.

Truly yours,   A. O. P.

ONE HUNDRED AND SIXTY-SECOND REGT. (METROPOLITAN GUARDS), N.Y.V.

ALEXANDRIA, LA., May 4.

We have had quite a lively time since my last, and my promise to you of important news for the future is, to some extent, realized.

We left our breastworks at Grand Encore on the 29th inst., and commenced our "grand retreat", as it may be termed, which will be considered a great achievement to General N. P. Banks—one that will surpass his retreat in Western Virginia ten to one. We marched unmolested until the morning of the 23rd, and Johnny Butternut took a strong position on the Cane River. We halted for a spell, and our artillery opened the ball; but we found it necessary to use the flanking idea. We had to ford the river, which was composed of more mud than water. After going through our toilet—that is, washing and arranging our "shoddy socks", and taking off the mud from our "gunboats" (shoes)—we marched through a dense forest, under the supervision of a brave and intelligent contraband. We at last struck a real tough swamp, and the boys grumbled at the idea of having wasted time in washing off mud at the river; but the skirmishers soon drove the thoughts of mud from their brain. The brave son of Africa told the General ([Henry W.] Birge) to come on; that there were not more that 20,000 of them about here, which made the boys feel a little nervous.

As I stated before, the skirmishers' fire became warmer and warmer. The Rebels ran up and took a position on a hill 130 feet high. But now comes the tug of war! To charge up a hill that a human being could scarcely walk up, without laying hold of the shrubbery with one hand, and carrying a knife in the other, is, indeed, one of the most daring charges that has been made since the breaking out of this Rebellion. New York City can now praise the One Hundred and Sixty-second New York Volunteers, and say that her sons are pervaded with the same courage and spirit that her sons of '61 were—that is, the three-years' men of that year, as we are the three-years' volunteers of '62. The whole brigade (Third), consisting of the Thirtieth Maine, One Hundred and Seventy-third New York Volunteers, and the One Hundred and Sixty-fifth Regiment New York Volunteers (Duryea's Zouaves), deserve great credit in supporting us in leading the "charge" that will be recorded in our country's history. We are, to a great extent, sorry that the season has been so dry, as the Red River is lower now than it has been for years past, and it has prevented us from taking Shreveport. The expedition will disappoint a great many; but it cannot be helped. We are ready to strike at any point to drive the "graybacks" from the land that we love the best, and shout the battle-cry of "Freedom".

Our regiment left Franklin, La., about six weeks ago, 600 strong, but many rest in their graves in the Red River country. We muster about 240 fit for duty, at the present time; but we earnestly hope that our regiment will be filled up again, and add more fame to our old Empire State. We are in hopes that the State will furnish us with an ensign, as our flag has seen so much service that it cannot be adjusted to the staff. There have been two color-sergeants killed while bearing it in action, and two wounded.

The prospects of $16 per month seems to please the boys very much, as the sutlers charge enormous rates in this Department. Adieu!

SHANGHAI.

U.S. STEAMER "GRAND GULF"

AT SEA, May 8, 1864.

At 4:30, A.M. on the morning of the 6th, we sighted a steamer steering nearly south, which we stood for; she proved to be a veritable runner, apparently affected with "Nassau" on the brain. Her evident uneasiness in her position, and her increasing anxiety to get away from the sight of an "honest Lincoln gunboat", but served to augment the inquisitiveness natural to a Yankee, to know who she was, where she came from, and where she had been all night.

At 6, A.M., we had gained on her, and at 7:30, A.M., it was apparent the bird begun to be frightened as we begun to pass "King Cotton" in the shape of bales riding King Neptune's borrowed throne, instead of quietly continuing his journey. At 9:30, A.M., we fired our first shot from our 100 [pounder] Parrot pivot, but the distance was too great to allow us to do more than cause her to yaw to, and pitch over her cotton bales the faster, of which there seemed to be a continued line for nearly thirty miles; but our speed did not slacken; and at 11:10, A.M., after finding our shot and shell too uncomfortably near, she hoisted a white rag and turned toward us, lat. 32:10 north, long, 78:19 west; thus ending a hot and well-contested chase of six hours and forty minutes, and proving conclusively that the "Grand Gulf" is yet in good wind for some of the bold "Confeds". On boarding her, at 11:25, A.M., we learned she was the side-wheel steamer "Young Republic", of Nassau, N.P., commanded by Captain Frank U. Harris, C. S. Navy.

In her track and about her, for the space of a mile, the sea looked thick as with the fragments of a wreck. Stools, chairs, sofas, boxes, and barrels, hencoops and sextant-boxes, trunks of clothes, books, and papers, scattered in confusion over all the ocean, told plainly the chagrin and despair caused by the capture. On board the steamer, the same scenes of wanton destruction were everywhere visible; boats' falls cut, and the boats adrift; boxes stove, and the contents wasted; in fact, every movable thing spoiled, even to the captain's chronometer and charts. Many of these which were light, were afterward recovered; but the weighty, like the future of the Confederacy, sank into oblivion. In the cabin, which gave evidence of having been splendidly furnished and occupied by lady passengers, mirrors were smashed, windows broken, and lamps thrown about, the whole exhibiting a reckless fury which it is not our fortune to often witness. The boat herself and engines were entirely uninjured. So having put on board a prize-master and crew, and taken forty prisoners on board the Grand Gulf, we turned back, and leisurely picked up the cotton. Before night we had secured 110 bales (mostly Upland). On the 7th, we picked up about 257 bales more, making in all 367. How much she contained is a question to be solved. Captain Harris reports 60 tons of tobacco and 1,300 bales of cotton, mostly on account of the Confederacy. Whether this is reliable or not, it is certain she has some hundreds of bales of cotton on board, if she has not that quantity of tobacco, as her lower hold is full to the hatches. The sum of half a million is esteemed a very low estimate for the prize and her cargo, and it is very evident that much had been risked on her, making a safe passage to Nassau. It may appear a strange assertion to state that she is a New York boat, but such is a fact. She was built in the fall of 1863, has a powerful beam engine, in excellent condition, with a splendid outfit of tools and stores of every description for the engineer's department, which happily escaped the fate of the movables above-decks. Her length is 210 feet; breadth of beam, 30½ feet; depth of hold, 18 feet; is about 1,150 tons. It may readily be surmised that she has not always borne the name of Young Republic. A month ago, she was called the Conqueror, and hailed from New York; and her register with her present name only dated back to April 23, 1864. Now for the web, which I leave you New Yorkers to unravel. When the Grand Gulf left New York, February 23, the Conqueror lay at Marston & Power's coalyard, loading with coal; her log shows she sailed for Matanzas partially unloaded, and thence to Nassau, N. P., where she changed her name from the "Conqueror", of New York, to the "Young Republic", of Nassau, N. P. Now, who shipped anthracite coal for a neutral port frequented by the Confederacy and their allies? And what became of it after it arrived at its destination? We venture to say that the one who shipped that coal left the wharf in New York; and her change of name and her sale are so plainly traitorous, that if Government overlook such a transaction, it has no right in future to say a word against England. The vail is so flimsy that comment is superfluous.

It is a curious circumstance, that two months had elapsed between the capture of the Mary Ann and the capture of the Young Republic, with the difference of only eleven miles north and thirty-eight miles east, sighting them both about the same time in the morning, but gaining on and capturing the Clyde-built steamer in less time than the American.

Since writing the above, we have discovered that they threw overboard $175,000 in specie.

FEND.

May 22, 1864

SEVENTEENTH REGIMENT, N.Y.V.V.

DECATUR, ALA., May 14.

In behalf of himself and many comrades of the Seventeenth Regiment, New York Veteran Volunteers, the undersigned begs leave to protest against the late wholesale slaughter of the garrison of Decatur by the New York Press. Said slaughter was committed by means of certain telegrams, and other detective dispatches, which, as we understand, did most summarily dispatch us, in hot blood, on or about the—day of May, 1864.

The canard about the "capture of Decatur, Ala., and murder of the garrison", (what news for anxious mothers) we presume to have originated in Nashville or some other enterprising Western city. In the West they are a fast people—in some cases, as in this last, perhaps a little too fast; and on hearing of the attack on Decatur, the go-ahead Western telegraphists and news venders jumped to the conclusion that Decatur was taken, and that, horrible to relate, the garrison was murdered! That their inferences were not sustained by their premises, arose probably from the fact that they forgot that a part (the most important part perhaps) of the garrison was composed of New York troops, to wit: the Seventeenth, a Regiment of veteran New Yorkers. In the southwest, it is too often the case that the biggest crowd and the loudest noise gains the day; but our boys have learned (no matter how small their number) not to retreat till they are whipped and not to be whipped as long as they are able to fight. The events of the morning of the 8th instant demonstrated to us very clearly the superiority of pluck and discipline over mere numbers. The Rebels have been in strong force for some time outside of the town, and on the morning of the 8th instant they advanced a strong line of skirmishers toward the town. Our cavalry-picket of Western troops disputed their progress a little, and then skedaddled. The infantry-picket was composed of details from the Seventeenth New York, and the Rebels expected that, as very often usual in such cases, the infantry would follow the cavalry, but in this case they did not meet with their usual adversaries, and, much to their astonishment, our picket, instead of retreating, advanced! A lively engagement took place, and resulted in the Rebels being handsomely repulsed. The early check disconcerted their plans, and their programme for taking the town by assault, of which we saw indications, was not carried out. Since that time they have been content with occasional dashes, and are fond of displaying their prowess, particularly in the nighttime. At such times they make a most needless and extravagant use of gunpowder. The happy issue of the engagement was in a great part owing to Colonel Grower, who was out on the skirmish-line encouraging the men. It would not be in good taste, perhaps, for me to mention any particular officers from amongst those who did well. No one, however, still begrudge to Lieutenant [Isaac] Menke, of Company H, the honor of being (to use a hackneyed term) "the hero of the occasion". I sat down to write this letter with the intention only of letting you know the men were all alive and well, despite the papers, and I fear I have scribbled into a narrative.

A. K.

FIRST BATTALION, TWELFTH INFANTRY.

CARVER HOSPITAL, WASHINGTON, D.C. May 14.

I take my pen in hand to give you an account of the way about three hundred of wounded men got away from the battle-field of last week.

All wounded who were able to walk were told by the surgeons to get to Rappahannock Station by way of Ely Ford. Well, we should say about ten or twelve hundred, perhaps more, started on Saturday evening [May 7], and got to Ely Ford at different parts of the night. Next morning, before daylight, we were told to go back to Chancellorsville, as the Rebels had possession of the railroad, and had torn up the track; so back we started for Chancellorsville. When we got there we were told that we were going to Fredericksburg. Down the plank-road for that city we started, but, when we got to the heights back of the place, we met some of our men who got there before us, coming back from the city in great haste. They said that some Rebels were in the place, and were taking our men as fast as they went in there, and sending them off to Richmond. Some of them told us that there were only a few Rebel cavalry there, but that the citizens were helping them. There were two officers—Lieutenants [Michael E.] Urell and [Thomas J.] Burrell, of the Second Regiment, N.Y.S.N.G. (Eighty-second Volunteers) with us; so we said we would do whatever they thought best. We had about a dozen muskets in the crowd, so the officers called them to the front, and told them to load; then we formed on the road and marched down into the city, capturing it without any blood being spilt. We then went down to the ford, opposite the ravine, between the Lacy House and Falmouth, but to our astonishment, there stood about a dozen Rebel cavalry, on the Falmouth side, who told us that we could not cross there. Their point was to keep us at Fredericksburg until more Rebels would come and capture us. Thinking, I suppose, that we would not cross, they went up to Falmouth and got off their horses, but kept watching us. Another squad of wounded, under Lieutenant [Charles H.] Zeilman, Forty-fourth N.Y., now joined us. The three officers spoke together for a while, and finally concluded to cross and make for Acquia Creek, and there be taken off by some gunboat. They called for volunteers to go across with guns and hold the heights above the river while the rest of the men were crossing. Edward Williams, Co. C, Tenth N. Y. Vols.—quite a boy—took a musket from some wounded man (he was sick himself) and went across. Three or four more followed him, but Williams was the first upon the heights. I think he takes down that drummer-boy of Barnum's who crossed to Fredericksburg with Burnside. When they got over, about 500 followed in their wake, but, when nearly or about 300 got over, the Rebels came galloping down to take us (almost 200 ran back into Fredericksburg and were captured) but our rifles flashed and two of their horses fell dead, and on "Johnny" went limping away. They then fell back out of range of our guns. We now formed again, put out flankers on each side, and advanced a rear-guard. The advance led by Lieutenant Burrel and Zeilman, the rear brought up by Lieutenant Urell.

We got on the Aquia Creek Railroad, and kept on it until we got to the burned dock, at the mouth of the creek. We arrived at the creek about eight o'clock, P.M. The distance we walked that day was about thirty-two miles. All the men lay down to sleep until daylight except a few who were put on picket, afraid the Rebels might make a dash on us.

Next morning (Monday), we could not hail any boat, so the officer told us to make rafts out of the planks of the docks. In about a half an hour there were three floating out on the broad Potomac, and got within hailing-distance of some schooner that was passing, but they would not come near them. We heard, after, that they were afraid our boys were Rebels. So all hands who were able, commenced and built rafts and floated out. Nearly all had left, when a Government transport, the Rebecca Barton, Capt. Baker, came along, and picked us all up, then sent boats to take the rest of them off. The officers were the last to leave. Capt. Baker did all he could to make the men comfortable. We had nothing to eat for over two days. The Captain gave us all he had on board.

REGULAR

MILITARY MATTERS

DEATH OF JOHN A. SMITH—We regret to notice the death of Lieut. John A. Smith, of Co., G, Forty-seventh Regiment, N.Y.V., who was killed in the recent battle of Chesterfield, Va., between Petersburg and Richmond. Mr. Smith was connected with this paper for several years, in the capacity of Fire Reporter. He served as an officer of Engine Co. No. 51, for a considerable length of time, and as a Representative had the reputation of being one of the best debaters in Fireman's Hall. The bills creating the Fire Commissioners, Board of Appeal Commissioners, and several other reforms, came from his hand. At the breaking out of the Rebellion, he joined the First Fire Zouaves, and remained with that organization until it was broken up. He then procured a commission in the Forty-seventh N.Y. Vols., and was with his command when killed in action.

The news of his death is communicated in a letter addressed to his wife by Capt. Chas. A. Moore, dated at the camp of the Forty-seventh Regiment, N.Y. Vols., at Bermuda Hundred, Va. He says: "He was killed at the same time, and by the same piece of shell that Lieut. [George L.] Stoendorff was, in a battle had with the enemy on Saturday, 7th inst., on the Petersburg Railroad. The piece of shell first struck Stoendorff in the head, and then glanced off hitting Smith in the breast, taking his left arm off, near the shoulder. He lived only a few hours. After his body was brought to the rear, the enemy advanced in great force, and we were compelled to fall back." His personal effects were after recovered; but his body remains within the Rebel lines.

May 29, 1864

EIGHTY-FIRST REGIMENT, N.Y.V.

BERMUDA HUNDRED, May 20.

We arrived at this point on the James River nearly two weeks since. Our sail here was delightful, we fully enjoyed the scenery of the country along the banks of the river, reaching Bermuda Hundred on the 5th day of May. We and the Ninety-sixth N. Y. V., were very fortunate in being on the large and clean steamboat John A. Warner. The following morning we marched six miles to the front and went on picket, the line of battle having been formed facing the Richmond & Petersburg Railroad; the Tenth Corps on the right, and the Eighteenth Corps on the left. During the succeeding two days our forces encountered the enemy, but were unsuccessful in reaching any good results, the Rebels maintaining themselves on the railroad.

Sunday[May 8], we lay quiet, feeling that the coming morning would be fraught with important events to us. No one could tell what might happen to him or his dear comrade. Orders came to march at daylight with three days' cooked rations. At 3, A.M., all was astir; silently we fell in and took our place, the extreme advance, and skirmished along through the swamps and thickets for two miles, until we came in sight of the Rebel rifle-pits and railroad, this battle ground of the two proceeding days. Here we were greeted with sharp volleys causing us to halt and study the best move. Nothing could be done except advance and charge over the works.

Over the field we went, a long line of skirmishers. On seeing our bold front, the Rebels fled up the railroad. [Gen. Gilman] Marston's Brigade followed close to us. We moved on a mile and a Rebel battery opened on us, but pressing on, we met their infantry. A hot fight ensued, the Rebels falling back. H Company pressing on too far, ran into the muzzles of a masked battery, which fired canister. Our skirmish line was broken, and came to a halt; the men hiding behind trees and logs. The Brigade then came up and a heavy fight took place, resulting in the defeat of the Rebels, the Twenty-fifth, S. C. Eutaw Volunteers charged the Twenty-fifth Mass. V., and were driven back, leaving 103 dead and wounded within a few yards of the gallant Yankees. The following day, we fell back to support Gen. Gillmore's right which was pressed by troops coming down from Richmond. Wednesday, we rested in camp enjoying a good night's sleep. Thursday we moved toward Richmond, having been placed under Gen. Gillmore during that day, and took part in a skirmish, in which the Rebels were repulsed. Spent the night in a cold rainstorm. At daylight we formed part of a flanking-party moving by a detour to the rear of a Rebel fort, which was charged upon and taken in part by a New Hampshire and other regiments. The work consisted of a breastwork, a mile long, with a fort at each end. The next day General [William F.] Smith's force took the remaining fort. That night we were on picket. On the 14th, we took part in another battle. The enemy fell back, one and a half miles, into his heavy works. At night we moved up to within one thousand yards of the works, and threw up rifle-pits. On Sunday, the Rebels shelled us, and the sharpshooters kept up a continual popping from the walls of the forts. A shell now and then came into the trench. Monday, the ball opens along the whole line. We are situated on the extreme left, and take good care to keep down in our pits. After shelling us for two hours, the Rebels move upon our trench, but fell back after receiving heavy volleys. The boys fired low, and the Rebels fell back in five minutes, without returning a shot, except from the walls of the works. Angry shelling now took place but the mist must have prevented them from getting good range. We now returned the sharpshooters' fire, and kept back the flanking parties who sought to turn our left. The Rebels having received heavy re-enforcements, burst in great force at 10, A.M., upon out center, driving it back. We are now within seven miles of Richmond, and have made a diversion for General Meade. General Gillmore placed the Eighty-first New York and the Fortieth Massachusetts Volunteers on the crest of a hill, overlooking the Rebel charge. The regiment went into line of battle cheering. A regiment was on our right and front, almost alone, fighting most gallantly. With such an example, how could we stand. The Rebels recoiled before the fire of that gallant regiment, turned to our left, and coming out of the woods in front of us, received a galling fire of grape from a battery on our left, and the full round volleys of the Fortieth Massachusetts Volunteers. As suddenly as they burst upon us they disappeared. Our loss is small, owing to the fact we fought behind the breastworks which our boys, although very tired, threw up during the two nights. We were on duty without a night's sleep for five days. Loss: killed 1; wounded, 25; prisoners, 4; total, 30.

I send you some papers taken from the body of the Adjutant of the Twenty-fifth South Carolina Volunteers.

C.

FIFTY-SIXTH REGIMENT, N.Y.V.V.

BEAUFORT, S.C., May 20.

Once more we tread the sands of South Carolina, after having been roaming around through the hills and valleys of our native State. In the month of February last, the most of our regiment re-enlisted as veterans, and were allowed to come home on furlough of thirty days. On the 13th of March we left camp, arriving in New York on the 14th, where we were met by the sons of Orange and Sullivan Counties, who gave us a grand reception at the Seventh Regiment Armory, and we in return presented them with our tattered colors, which they presented to us on our first entry into service, and which had been through a dozen battles. The strength of our regiment was 850 men, but 400 of them were substitutes from the last draft; so we had 450 men who were entitled to re-enlist, and we brought home with us 430, and left the remainder here. On the 20th of April, we were ordered to rendezvous at Middletown, but before that date an order was issued extending our furloughs ten days, as some of the counties had not paid the bounty, and the Colonel would not take us back until we had all received our County bounty. But on Saturday, May 14th, everything was in readiness, and we set sail for South Carolina, in steamer Arago, arriving here on the 18th. We found everything in good order, and the rest of the boys who had been left behind, very glad to see us. As soon as we arrived in camp, they came to meet us, and many were the exclamations that burst from their lips. We were about as glad to get back as we were to get home.

Military changes in this Department have been very numerous since we left. Our Major-General (Gillmore) has left us, and taken most of the Tenth Army Corps with him. When we left, there were five white regiments here, now we are the only one, their places being filled with colored troops. The climate here is delightful, everything being as forward as it is in June, in New York. We have had all the garden-vegetables that are to be found in New York markets, and are very well satisfied to remain here. If anything important turns up, you will again hear from

GUS.

June 5, 1864

A PROTEST AGAINST THE NOMINATION OF ABRAHAM LINCOLN FOR THE PRESIDENCY.

Abraham Lincoln stands at the bar of popular judgment; and the time has come when, to remain silent, must be regarded as either cowardly or criminal. The people must look facts straight in the face, and then decide whether it is safe to intrust the Ship of State another term in the keeping of the present incumbent of the White House. If the President has been false to the high trust reposed in him by the people, then it is time for the people to speak, time for journalism to denounce, high time for all honest citizens to rebuke the ambition, not of a patriot but of a demagogue. He has deliberately violated his sacred obligation to the Chicago Platform—nay more, he has proved recreant to the grand principles of human freedom; he has added rivets to the clinking chains of the slave; the freedom of the press and freedom of speech have been made a mockery and a farce; and the despots of the world have dared to smile approvingly on his acts of oppression and misrule. General Fremont looked upon slavery as the Gordian Knot of our troubles—he cut it asunder by his Emancipation Proclamation. Mr. Lincoln rebuked him, and in order to save to his Rebel relations the human chattels who cringed beneath the slave-driver's lash, he temporized, and thereby acknowledged the right of slavery.

The holy bond of our Union—that Constitution which Daniel Webster proclaimed the Government of the United States—has not escaped his sacrilegious grasp. It has been tramped upon even as traitors here dared to trample upon the flag of our country. In violating the Constitution, which he swore to obey and protect, Abraham Lincoln has virtually assumed the power of a despot, for the written law is the only safeguard of the people. It is the Constitution which says to the people in their moment of excitement, when headlong passion would overthrow the established maxims of reason., "thus far shalt thou go and no further"; and it is this same monitor which frowns upon the Executive who would infringe in the slightest degree upon the rights of the sovereign people.

At the time when the Republic fairly groans beneath the accumulating horrors of internal strife, and when the best and wisest of our citizens commence to fear lest the last days of freedom are at hand, Mr. Lincoln has not hesitated to send out brave soldiers to establish rotten boroughs for the purpose of securing his re-election. Who has forgotten the terrible Florida massacre, of all others the truest indication of Mr. Lincoln's cold-blooded, unscrupulous policy for his re-election? A Moloch could hardly do more. The senior Generals of the Army, men of valor and patriotism, our McClellans and Fremonts, have been shelved, one after the other—sacrificed to petty jealousy and unwarrantable ambition. Great generals may become popular candidates for the Presidency; all opposition candidates must be made way with, even if the Republic goes down in the whirlpool of popular commotions. Militia-men, such as the Banks and Butlers of the Army, are kept in command, because, being politicians they are safer in the Army than out of it; and, being but sorry dabblers in the art of war, there is but little danger of brilliant victories paving their way to the Presidency. Rather than sacrifice a petty feeling of pride, Gen. Grant is made to take the overland route to Richmond, because the better route had been pointed out by McClellan. The price of this obstancy has been a sacrifice of about 60,000 men; whereas, the Grand Army might have reached Belle Plain by the Peninsula route without the loss of a man.

Mr. Lincoln has not hesitated to strike at the dearest rights of freemen—he has recalled the horrors of the darkest days of despotism. Free American citizens, do you not blush when you look upon the frowning walls of the bastiles which disgrace your country? A touch of a bell—an order—and the most virtuous of our citizens may be thrown into a loathsome cell, to weep alone over the ruins of his guaranteed rights. Men, against whom no tribunal has pronounced judgement, have gone insane and died in loathsome cells, away even from the benefit of friend or clergy. We arraign Mr. Lincoln for these offences against the rights of the citizen and the great principles of human liberty.

Mr. Lincoln has dispensed more patronage than any other President, from Washington to James Buchanan; and instead of being satisfied with the vast fortune his family has already amassed, he is afflicted with the itch of office and the leprosy of greed. He has become a vampire that gnaws into the very bowels of the country—he is the nightmare beneath the horrors of which the nation groans in the agony of despair.

Give us any man but Abraham Lincoln, and we will support him, if he be true to the cardinal principles which ought to actuate an Executive in these disastrous times. The indorsement of Fremont will unite the Union Party—but under no circumstances will the friends of free soil, free speech, free press, and national integrity support Abraham Lincoln! We want a man for the Presidency. Let us light our lanterns and, Diogenes-like, go and seek one.

FUNERAL OF LIEUT. DAVID HAMEL—Lieut. David Hamel, of Company H, Sixth Heavy Artillery, who was mortally wounded on the 19th of May, at Spottsylvania Court House, died at his late residence, in Morrisania, on Monday last, and his remains were, on Wednesday, conveyed to Cypress Hill Cemetery for internment. The regiment in which the deceased was attached was stationed on the extreme left of the Army on the morning of the 19th, when they were attacked by the Rebels under Gen. Ewell, who was endeavoring to cut off the supply-train. Captain H. B. Hall, of Company H, was acting as Major at the time, and had charge of a battalion, while Lieut. Hamel was placed in command of both Company D and his own company. He was rallying his men to charge upon and drive back the enemy, at the time he was shot and felled to the ground; but recovering himself, he again pushed boldly to the front, and stimulated his command to push onward, when, overcome by fainting from loss of blood, he again fell, and was carried off the field. Upon examination of his wound—in the left arm, and, as was supposed, a flesh-wound on the left side—the surgeon pronounced his injury not of a serious character; and the deceased firmly believed that he would be able to return to active service in less than a fortnight. Obtaining a short furlough, he came home to see his family. He arrived at Morrisania on the 30th ult, able to walk about, though somewhat weak from loss of blood, apparently in good spirits, and full of hope of a speedy return to the Army. The anxiety of his friends induced them to call a prominent surgeon to examine his wounds, and then the discovery was made that the ball which wounded his arm must have penetrated his body. Lieut. Hamel died in three days after his return home; and on a *post-mortem* examination being made by Dr. Horton of Morrisania, the ball which caused the death of this brave and gallant soldier was found to have destroyed one lung, and had lodged under the other.

The deceased was well and intimately known to us. He was, as a man and a citizen, highly esteemed and respected by all who knew him, and a braver, more earnest, or a more devoted soldier was not to be found in the Army. The company of which he was lieutenant was raised in the town of Morrisania, through the exertions of himself and Major [Henry B.] Hall (who was badly wounded in the thigh at the same time Lieutenant Hamel received his wound), and the men all testify to the good qualities of their late commander.

The Fire Department of Morrisania, of which the deceased was a member, together with Company A, Seventeenth Regiment, N. G., attended the funeral of Lieutenant Hamel, on Wednesday last, and the most marked evidence of regret and sorrow for his untimely taking off was exhibited by his numerous surviving friends.

In addition to Lieutenant Hamel, we understand that some three or four privates of his company were killed, and quite a number wounded. Among the killed are Mr. Hutton and Mr. Sanguinette—two very worthy men. Maj. Hall's wound is improving slowly, but he is considered entirely out of danger.

The citizens of Morrisania propose to get up some kind of public entertainment for the benefit of the families of deceased soldiers from that town killed in the recent battles.

June 12, 1864
ONE HUNDRED AND SIXTY-SECOND REGIMENT, N.Y.V.
MORGANZA BEND, LA., May 26.

We struck tents on the 13th instant and took up a line of march toward the Red River. I am sorry to state that the torch was applied to a few houses in Alexandria before we left, although the commanding-general used every means in his power to prevent such infamous warfare. The impression prevails that it was the work of some of the contrabands who are so bitter against the Rebels. As I stated before, we took up a line of march, but met with no great obstacles until we arrived near Marksville. Here the rebs showed themselves in pretty strong force. Our cavalry had driven them three days. The infantry formed in line of battle on a prairie ten miles square; and the scene presented here was, indeed, magnificent. The Nineteenth Corps led the van, and the Sixteenth and Seventeenth Corps followed up our right, and the cavalry-division was placed on the right and left flanks; the wagon-trains came up in four columns, guarded on the right and left by a division of the Corps d'Afrique, and the rear was brought up by the Thirteenth Corps. We drove the Rebs down to a town called Big Bend; here they came to the conclusion to try our strength. Artillery opened upon us. Our artillery responded. The "duel" lasted five hours, in which the Rebels displayed practical gunnery. They made us suffer considerably, as the sun was extremely hot, and no water to be had, except participating with the sheep and drinking from these almost dried-up ponds.

Marksville and Big Bend are both fine villages, but are, like all other places in Dixie, "deserted", or, "contrabandly" speaking, "dun gone to Texas". (In making inquiries for the white folks in any of the towns in Louisiana, the contraband's reply is, "Dun gone" with the Rebs, or to Texas. The country, here and there, is cultivated, but there is plenty of room for settlement, *i.e.*,

"When this cruel war is over,"

and the property confiscated, why, we can all have a beautiful farm, and devote the remainder of our days tilling what was once upon a time considered King Cotton.

We had no difficulty, until within a few miles of Simsport; here a few guerrillas made a raid on the wagon-train. We were ordered back one mile; but, Mr. Reb knew we were on the alert, hence they skedaddled. After remaining a few days at the latter place, a bridge was formed of about thirty steamboats, side by side; we crossed the Atchafalaya and marched to our present locality. So ends the "Great Red River Expedition". I notice that the Western papers are out in full blast against General Banks, as well as the Western troops; but our corps (Nineteenth) has full confidence in him, and are ready to march against the foe at any time. He is hailed in this corps as the hero of Port Hudson, and is cheered very often by the boys.

There are a great many rumors in regard to our future movements. The principal rumor is, that we are to be formed into a marine division, to guard and patrol the Mississippi. If this should be so, it would please our old tried regiment much, as we have participated in all the movements in this Department since we have been here.

SHANGHAI.

June 19, 1864
ONE HUNDRED AND SIXTY-FIFTH REGIMENT, N.Y.V.
IN THE FIELD, NEAR MORGANZA, LA., May 29.

We have just finished a very long and hard campaign. General Banks marched us as far as Mansfield, La., and turned around and came back again. I say nothing, but if I was at liberty to speak my mind, somebody would suffer.

We are in the Third Brigade, First Division, Nineteenth Army Corps; and a fine brigade it is, commanded by a good and brave man, Colonel [George M.] Love, of the One Hundred and Sixteenth New York. The brigade will never want for anything while he is in command.

The Thirtieth Maine Veterans is in our Brigade. If you want sugar, go to the Thirtieth Maine, and for ten cents you can get any quantity. If they see a sugar-house, a general rush is made for it, and haversacks, towels, caps, and anything capable of holding sugar, is filled with it. If you see one of the Thirtieth Maine lying on the road, having fallen out with fatigue, search his haversack, and you will find it filled with sugar. It has got so, that when the boys find the Thirtieth giving out on the march, they sing out, "Sugar-house ahead!", which immediately revives them.

Our boys expect to be a marine corps, to be stationed on the transports from New Orleans to Vicksburg, in order to keep the Mississippi River open. The boys are delighted with the idea, and we are expecting every day orders for us to embark on board the transports.

Our camp is on the banks of the Mississippi, and the boys amuse themselves with fishing and swimming. We are getting plenty to eat, and not much to do.

Our regiment received a fine lot of recruits from New York; and, as we have lost quite a number, they were very much needed.

Our Quartermaster's Sergeant has received his commission as Quartermaster, at last. He deserved it long ago. The boys were all glad to see him promoted.

Yours, truly,   ZOUAVE.

July 10, 1864
TWELFTH U.S. INFANTRY
HEAD-QUARTERS, IN FRONT OF PETERSBURG, VA., July 2.

I was up early this morning, about break of day, and went almost about two miles to find a little water to wash my clothes in. I was obliged to be up with the lark, or somebody would have taken possession, and the water would have been too dirty for use. After washing shirts, drawers, socks, and pocket handkerchiefs, I took a bath myself, and finished off by emptying two canteens of cold spring-water over my head, and having a military shower-bath; after which, I returned to camp and cooked my breakfast, consisting of a piece of fresh beef, roasted on a stick, a cup of coffee, and a few hard-tack roasted on the ashes.

Our boys are in excellent spirits: they have had two or three days to clean themselves up, and our rations have been much better lately. Only fancy sour kraut and dried apples. We are encamped in a pine-wood, about three-quarters of a mile from our old position in the trenches—which position we expect we will have to take again, either to-night or to-morrow night. Our regiment is very small now, we have lost very heavily; a good many of the veterans have been knocked over. We have lost twelve officers since the campaign commenced. Brigadier-General [Joseph] Hayes has command of our Brigade now, and General [Romeyn B.] Ayres is in command of the Division, with Capt. Frederick Winthrop of ours, for his Adjutant-General (Capt. Winthrop, of Co. B, Twelfth U.S. Infantry). He is a brave and dashing officer; he had charge of our regiment after Major [Matthew M.] Blunt was wounded, and the boys think there is no one like him; in fact, he is the pet of the whole Brigade. The Volunteers think the world of him. Major Blunt is now commanding; he is a very nice officer, and much respected by the men in the regiment.

Picket-firing still continues, night and day, and there is some heavy cannonading going on the extreme right; it sounds like very heavy guns, it may, perhaps, be gunboats. Burnside is having a terrible hard time of it—his works are so near the Johnnys that they are obliged to fight. He keeps his niggers hard at work, either digging, chopping, or fighting, and if the Johnnys make a break on him, he opens upon them with artillery, and makes them hunt their holes in double-quick time.

We were mustered on the 30th for four months pay. It went rather hard to hear the names of so many comrades called who will never answer their names again. The company-clerks are busily engaged filling out the rolls; and all we want now is, the sutler and paymaster to make their appearance, and we will be all right. These are, indeed, melting moments; and our boys may be seen laying off in the shade almost in a state of nudity, striving to keep themselves cool; after sundown, they will be round brisk as bees, some playing cards, others reading, and some skylarking, and most all smoking. What is the reason why the Government will not supply the soldiers with tobacco? They could do it as well here as they do in the French Army; a French soldier can get his weed from his commissary at about thirty-two [cents] per killo, and the American soldier has to pay $2 to $2.50 a plug for the commonest of Navy tobacco full of molasses and stalks. I wish some of the big-bugs in Washington would take this matter into consideration, and confer a boon on the whole Army.

Our men are hard at work on the railroad from City Point to this place, and in fact the Army is getting comfortably settled, but I suppose by the time everything is in good working order we will be moved off to some other point, and I sincerely hope it will be to march into Richmond with trumpets sounding and banners fluttering in the breeze.   WILL.

FORTY-EIGHTH REGIMENT, N.Y.VOLS.

CITY POINT, VA., July 2.

My company was guard for a portion of the Eighteenth A.C. wagons. We started at 6, P.M., and marched through the woods, with nothing to cheer our lonely traveling but the occasional croaking of the bullfrogs, and screeching of the whip-poor-will. It seemed very lonely to me, as we marched through the woods, occasionally emerging into an open field, where the farmer had sowed his seed, and which was now flourishing, only to be destroyed by the onward tread of armed hosts. As we passed house after house, all of them deserted, leaving in them all their household goods, and the barns and outhouses were all supplied with every necessary farming utensil, which as we arrived were all destroyed.

We reached the Chickahominy River on the afternoon of the 14th, and crossed it on our pontoons. The wagons had but just crossed, and some two hundred head of cattle that were in our rear, awaiting their turn, when the Rebels suddenly pounced upon them and captured them, as also part of the guard. The larger part of the guard succeeded in getting upon the pontoons, and then cutting it loose, allowed it to float down the river, thus saving themselves from capture, and not allowing the Rebels to capture the pontoons. After crossing the river, we parked for the night near the house of a Dr. Robert Epps (now a surgeon in Rebel service). This house was the only brick one we met with on our route. In going through it, I found a great many medical works, and various documents belonging to the Doctor; among the rest was a paper, requiring his payment of taxes and tithes. Dr. Epps was the proprietor of 840 acres of farming land, which was accessed at twenty cents per acre, and he was required to send to the Commissary store at Richmond one-tenth of the products of his land. Close by this home lived Captain [James] Cooke and wife (formerly of the United States Navy). When we arrived here, we were asked to furnish him a guard to protect his grounds and houses, which were well stored. I asked him how it was that he had not been taken into the Rebel Army. His answer was, "When I resigned my position in the Navy at the outbreak of this Rebellion, it was with the understanding that I was to remain neutral." These are the kind of men whose property we guard as we go along. Men who received a magnificent education at the hands of our Government, only to desert her in time of need. Such men should be treated the same as all deserters are dealt with. They should not be allowed to keep what they have stored away, from our men; for I know that it is all shipped to Richmond as soon as an opportunity offers.

Going still further, we came upon several large plantations that had splendid orchards to them. Apples, cherries, and peaches were here in abundance, and the boys helped themselves to everything. The country through which our route lay is a very undulating one, the roads winding through the woods and over open fields, up-hill and down gulleys, with the dust flying in all directions; but there is one thing in Virginia which makes up for this—it is, that water can be obtained at almost every step.

On the afternoon of the 17th, we crossed the pontoon on the James River, below City Point, and continued our march toward Petersburg; heavy firing was constantly heard in our front. We arrived within four miles of Petersburg, when we were ordered to cross the pontoon and join General Butler's column at the Point of Rocks. We arrived there at 8 o'clock, A.M., of the morning of the 18th, having accomplished a distance of sixty-four miles in less than five days.

We were visited the other day by the President, who was enthusiastically received by the men. On the 19th, an officer was drummed out of the service, with the word "coward" on his breast and back. This is what should have been done long ago. There is no other cause to which can be laid the reason of men running, excepting that they follow their officers.

Our Lieutenant-Colonel [Dudley W. Strickland] was allowed to resign his commission at Coal Harbor, when, in truth, he should have been served the same way. It can truly be said of him, none so brave as he in camp, and none so cowardly as he in battle.   M. L. J.

<u>July 17, 1864</u>

WERE WE BETRAYED?

The Administration papers represented the President as cheering the troops and giving them confidence as they marched to the defence of Washington against the Rebel raiders. This is the most fulsome potion of news which the White House apologists have prescribed for us. It is an insult to the already indignant people, who know that Lincoln is personally responsible for the whole raid, and any attempt to palliate his guilt by painting him as a buffoon, waving his title on a cane, and crying "forward!" will fall this time. Had it been the first or the second foray, we might have been patient, but it was the thrice-told tale of murder, havoc, and configuration, with the added disgrace of the capital of the country besieged and completely isolated, while no preparations for defence had been made, and the exact routes traversed by the raiders twice before were left unguarded. This looks very like complicity between the White House and the Rebels. The SUNDAY MERCURY advised Lincoln of the purpose of the Rebels and General Grant added his timely warning. The facts which have transpired were clearly set forth by our always reliable Washington correspondent and the

President was implored to concern himself less with his own re-election and more with the border defence. But what to him was the integrity of the North, the tranquility of firesides, the safety of property and life? He has no wish to see the conclusion of the war, whereby himself and his servitors are fattening. Peace would be ruin to his rich friends, the contractors. Grant might capture Petersburg and compel the evacuation of Richmond. To counteract such Union successes, Lincoln left the back-door of the Capital open to the Rebel cavalry. They swept Maryland like a threshing-floor, they thundered at the gates of Baltimore, they stole oxen enough to feed their army for one year; they destroyed four railways, burned stacks, dwellings, and storehouses; shot Federal troops on the parapets of the forts of Washington, and calmly re-crossed the river with all their plunder, leaving the North panic-stricken, humiliated, and indignant. And all this time the guardian of our destinies was waving his hat in the suburbs of Washington, as if the whole episode of invasion was but a clever electioneering device to give him dramatic character. Perhaps he wished to appease the rising wrath of the people by moving their sympathies for his idiocy. Such subterfuges are played out. Nobody disputes that Lincoln is an ass, but many ascribe more design than weakness to his follies. Nero could jest while Rome was in flames and some people probably thought him only a weak, good-natured individual; but history accuses him of firing the city! In the same way, some people may be diverted by the picture of a grave Chief Magistrate waving his hat amidst the convulsions of a great nation in the pitch of danger, while on every hand the stern question of the grieved and thoughtful surges up "Were we not betrayed?"

The significant feature of this latest crisis we commend to the Administration for its careful attention. Twice before Southern armies gave battle upon Northern soil, and the people rose up, like the ocean, to overwhelm them. This time, the North was not so prompt. It demanded time for reflection. A change of rulers only will satisfy it that patriotism has any reward or loyalty any safeguard. Lincoln must leave his office. He is arraigned as an incompetent, bad man, and the people have lost confidence in him. He may receive the adulation of the thieves and contractors who listen to his stories, and perhaps share their pickings with him. But not even the effrontery of these can shield him from the just indignation of an outraged people.

NINETY-FIFTH N.Y.V.
BEFORE PETERSBURG, VA., July 9.

We are just now lying in the front line of our works on the right of the Fifth Corps. The Rebel line is distant about three hundred yards. Their position is naturally an advantageous one; and being made trebly strong by well-planted and constructed earthworks of a truly formidable character, it will render an attempt of ours to take them by assault red-hot work.

Not too far to our right (the left of the Ninth Corps) our line is advanced to within one hundred and fifty yards of the enemy. The church spires of Petersburg are plainly visible from this point; and for several days past they have served as targets for our artillerists, who play upon them at intervals.

The Ninety-fifth left Culpepper Court House on the 3rd of May, five hundred strong, commanded by Col. Edward Pye; since mortally wounded at Coal Harbor, June 2; died at Alexandria, June 12. His loss is deeply deplored by all of us, as he was truly a soldier's friend. On the 5th [May] inst., we deployed as skirmishers; found the Rebs at 1 o'clock, P.M., fought until 8, P.M.; renewed the battle at daylight on the 6th inst., and continued engaged throughout the ever-memorable battles of the Wilderness and the Po. In these engagements, we lost in the neighborhood of 150 killed and wounded. Companies A and E, officers and all, were captured on the 6th inst. We had hot work at Spottsylvania Court House, on the south bank of the North Anna, at Coal Harbor, and later still here. In the charge our division (Cutler's) made on the 18th, our regiment suffered severely. Among the wounded was Lieutenant-Colonel James Crusey, who, after being twice wounded, refused to be carried from the field, saying to those who were anxious to assist him, "Go forward, and take the enemy's works." I am glad to hear Colonel Crusey's wounds are doing well. We stack at the present time 107 muskets. Out of the ninety-odd men in my company who left Staten Island in March, 1862, I am the only one at present fit for duty.

The weather is very warm here just now; the ground so dry as to be well nigh blistered. Blue-tailed fleas, sandflies, and that fixed institution of ours, the Army "crumb", are as thick as humbugs. We are just in receipt of the news of the sinking of the Alabama by the Kearsarge, and another invasion of "my Maryland". We are glad to hear of the discomfiture of "Old Beeswax" [Raphael Semmes], and we hope that, ere long, the Rebel raiders who have lately crossed the Potomac will meet with an end as disastrous as that of the pirate "290". We don't see any greenback "about yer". Can't account for the non-appearance of the Pay-master, unless Chase took the pile.

Yours,   ALLEGHANY.

ONE HUNDREDTH AND FORTY-SIXTH REGIMENT N.Y.V.

IN FRONT OF PETERSBURG, July 16.

The One Hundred and Forty-sixth N. Y. Vols. (Garrard Tigers) have been getting along all sorts of ways since leaving Warrenton Junction, Va. Our ranks have been thinned pretty badly. In the first day's fight (May 5), in the Wilderness, there were swept off about four hundred men, with our Colonel, Major, Adjutant, and about twelve of our line-officers. We have felt the loss of our colonel, though he was not extremely well liked by rank and file, yet he was a man to depend on if in a tight place. He is reported killed, but it is not a certainty. Our next exchange of compliments with "Johnny Reb" was at Laurel Hill; we had to go in, after marching all night and no sleep, though just before 6 o'clock, A.M., we halted, times enough for the men to get water; had to advance under a heavy fire of shot and shell across a plowed field, and as it had to be done on the double-quick, the usual number of knapsacks strewed the road, leaving a good trail for any one to follow.

One part of the battalion went one way, another part another way; some swore they would not go into a fight with such officers as we had. In fact, a good many went to the rear. At last, one of the aides to Brigadier-General Ayres (like a good angel) came to the rescue; could see what was the matter. He turned to the men, and asked: "Will you follow me?—just for old friendship's sake?" "Yes!" was the answer. He did not look behind to see if we were coming. (But the Tigers were there.) He found a position for us, and we stayed there and held it, threw up breastworks, and that place got to be a pretty hot hole before it was left. Our next passage-at-arms with the Rebs was on the other side of the North Anna River, the Johnnys advancing on us in three lines of battle. We paid our compliments to the first line—the artillery attended to the third line, the first line breaking. The second could not help themselves, and all skedaddled in the confusion, leaving us masters of the field. We lost about sixteen in the regiment in this engagement. Our Color-Sergeant, George F. Williams, who was reported dead and buried, has turned up again in the hospital at Alexandria. He was wounded through both hips, taken prisoner, and was recaptured by our cavalry. Fifty in all were recaptured with him—all that was left in Locust Grove Hospital.

We are now lying in front of Petersburg, but on the reserve—for we have been in the pits since the 18th of June—and now relieved for a little rest, though ready to move to the front, no matter what work is to be done. The Rebs treat us nightly to a few bombshells, and of course we return the compliment. Now and then a rally, and then a volley of musketry resounds through the air, reminding us that Bobby Lee is still on our front.

The glorious Fourth passed over very quickly, though it was expected to open very warm with shot and shell, and so we were agreeably disappointed. The weather here is very hot, every one is wishing for rain; we have not had any since the 2nd of June, and water here is pretty scarce.

The Sanitary Commission still pursues its labors, relieving one then another of our sick and wounded, but, I am sorry to say, that eatables issued to this regiment by the Sanitary Commission, the majority of the articles are appropriated by the shoulder-straps, of course it creates a great amount of grumbling, among the men. Such things when issued should pass through the regimental Commissary's hands and not issued to the companies according to the number of men, but I suppose enlisted men have no friends, and have to put up with what is dealt out to them.

In hopes that my next will contain the capture of Petersburg, Va. I am,

POOR JOE MUGGINS.

July 24, 1864

TWENTY-FIFTH NEW YORK CAVALRY

WASHINGTON, July 18.

We started from City Point, Virginia, of the 7th instant, our destination being Baltimore, which city we reached on the afternoon of the 8th, and after considerable delay had supper at the "Soldiers' Rest" and then sat in the street for several hours, which time, some of the officers spent in horse-trading and whiskey-drinking. One patriotic citizen, whose name I regret that I could not learn, brought out a large basket of oranges and distributed them amongst the men. Toward midnight we were hustled on board a cattle and baggage train, with a number of other dismounted cavalry, and arrived in Washington at 6 o'clock, A.M. We then took up our march for our old quarters at Camp Stoneman, and arrived there about noon. A soldier experiences a feeling something like coming home, when he returns to an old camping-ground; and with that idea we had determined to take things easy, and make ourselves comfortable until we got our horses and equipments, which we were told would be very soon. But, alas, "the best laid schemes o' mice and men—"; and so it was with our visions of rest; for at midnight on Sunday the bugle sounded, and the regiment started on its way to Washington, through which city it passed and took the road toward Silver Springs. Here all was confusion, and white lips and pale cheeks were announcing that "the Rebels were right at hand in great force". Couriers dashed back and forth, frightened men and women were flying from their homes and crowding into the city, and everything betokened the complete surprise which the Rebels had succeeded in making at this point. This, by the way, is supposed to be the weakest spot in the chain of defences which surrounded the National Capital. The regiment was now pushed out to the front of Fort Stevens, and hardly had it taken position when the Rebels were soon coming down the opposite hill, a perfect cloud of skirmishers. The Twenty-fifth was immediately deployed in skirmish-lines, and ordered forward to check the advance of the Rebels, which they did in gallant style; and after two hours' hard fighting, drove them over the crest of the second range of hills, and held this advance position until they were relieved, the fire of the enemy being by this time completely silenced. The handsome manner in which the regiment behaved itself elicited the warmest commendations from all who witnessed it, and has set it in a high niche in the estimation of the people of Washington. The few officers of the regiment who went on the field behaved themselves in most excellent style, but on the line, where shoulder-straps should have been, there were many, many vacancies. Major [Samuel W.] MacPherson has raised himself considerably in the estimation of the men by his conduct during these few days, as they had supposed he was too much of a martinet in camp to show much fight in the field; but I am happy to say that he has belied this opinion.

On the next day (Tuesday [July 12]), we lay still, and on Wednesday were marched toward Fort De Russay, and pushed out in front of it on the skirmish-line, and hardly had we taken position when the music opened again in lively style, and the effectiveness of our Burnside rifles began to be apparent in the number of stretchers which the Rebs began to bring into requisition on their side of the field. We kept up an incessant fire until about six o'clock in the afternoon, when our lines of battle advanced, and attacked the Rebs in their chosen position, and after about three hours' hard fighting we drove them over three miles, the Rebels burning the farmhouses as they retreated. When daylight broke we advanced to the hills which the enemy had occupied in our front, and found their dead lying around in great numbers. The party detailed for that purpose buried about two hundred of them, and we have taken about four hundred prisoners, inclusive of 163 wounded, who were left in a house in charge of two of their own surgeons.

What they mean to do with this regiment, the Lord only knows. We have very few men; very, very few officers, and very d—d few of those who are with us will be found on the battle-field, although the regiment has some noble exceptions; but, as a whole, the line of shoulder-straps is exceedingly of the "dead beat" order. This will always be the case where money, not merit, is the keystone of the arch that leads to preferment.

The loss of the regiment in the two days' fighting was nine killed and seventeen wounded.

B. O. B.

SIXTEENTH NEW YORK VOLUNTEER ARTILLERY
FORT MAGRUDER, VA., July 17.

This has been a great day with the Sixteenth N.Y. Volunteer Artillery. The Colonel was placed in command of this post on June 30, and has been busily engaged—assisted by his able staff—in placing everything in order to resist an attack of the enemy, which is nightly expected, and has succeeded admirably; and now, though we have but a small force, we are rather anxious than otherwise that the Rebs may have the temerity to make a demonstration.

We were reviewed by Brig.-Gen. [Joseph B.] Carr, commanding at Yorktown. The review was most satisfactory, and we anticipate a good report from the Inspector-General, Captain M. G. Cushing, a most gentlemanly man and thorough officer. Our band acquitted themselves most creditably; receiving their instruments but three weeks ago, they have already acquired a proficiency little excelled by far older organizations.

The colors presented by the Board of Aldermen and Councilmen of the City of New York arrived a few days ago, and the presentation took place to-day. The speeches delivered on the occasion were in the most happy vein, and, being the outspoken feelings of the hearts of the utterers, were indicative of unswerving loyalty and patriotism, and evinced a determination to stand by and maintain our noble Government, and its glorious standard, under all circumstances, so that should we be fortunate enough to return at the expiration of our term of service, no stain but the honorable ones acquired on the battle-field will be suffered to appear on its folds.

The town of Williamsburg, one mile above, still retains, although in a ruinous condition, sufficient evidences of once being the resort of the aristocracy of Virginia. The College of William & Mary, the oldest institution in the country, the pride of Virginia, and in fact of the United States, is now a blackened ruins looming up with shattered walls at the end of the town a mute, but effective rebuke to the atrocities some of our soldiers commit without provocation. This college was burnt in a spirit of wanton incendiarism, long after the town was in our hands, and the immense library, the collection of two centuries, was almost totally destroyed. Many valuable private libraries have also been ruthlessly invaded, and rare editions of works rendered worthless by the sets being broken. The Eastern Lunatic Asylum however, contains a large number of books, carried there by their owners for preservation, being donated to prevent their destruction. Autographs of Washington, Jefferson, and Patrick Henry, are in profusion, especially among the papers of the Carter family, which are now scattered to the four winds of heaven. The statue of Governor Berkley, a splendid work of art, erected in 1761, is defaced; but, of course, outside of its merit as a piece of sculpture, it has no value in the eyes of the descendants of the Revolution.

Our picket-duty is very heavy, our line is about ten miles long, extending to a semi-circle from the James to the York. Every point is well guarded, and the men are vigilant. Being isolated, our mails are very irregular, and New York papers are sought for, but seldom found. We are in considerable excitement regarding the Rebel raid in Maryland. The plunder they may take, if allowed to get safely across the Potomac with it, will be invaluable to them—for fresh meat is a great rarity to the Richmond markets, and commands $25 per lb. Refugees frequently come in, and as they are generally communicative, whenever I happen to be on guard over the guardhouse, I hear how affairs are in the Reb capital. It is laughable to hear of the prices; coats, $1,000 to $1,500 dollars; boots, $250; flour, $350 per barrel; tea, $45 per lb.; felt hats, $25, and everything else in proportion; whiskey, $10 per drink. I wish to the Lord it was that price everywhere, and we might have more quietness North. Wages are high, ranging for laborers $100 per week, to good mechanics who command $500. They represent the people in Richmond as perfectly wild; anything able to walk is impressed in the service, and hundreds of girls in Rebel uniforms are drilling on the heavy fortifications around the city.

We are at present in some excitement, caused by a report brought from our picket-lines, that Rebel cavalry, in some force, are in the woods outside. The Colonel sprang upon his horse, and ordering the gun-detachments to their places, called for twenty-five volunteers to follow him, and has gone to the front. I anticipate that it is a party of our own, who went off secretly to capture some guerrillas who were prowling around, as they had a brush with them this morning, the result of which has not transpired. When the Rebel raiders leave Maryland, I should not wonder if they attempt to dislodge us; but they will find it another Fort Stevens affair. Two of our companies have gone to Havre de Grace, and I hope they will arrive in time to meet the Rebels. The Government farms worked by the contrabands are in prime condition. Cornstalks are now nine and ten feet high, and promise abundant yield. I think if they are permitted to harvest their crops, the yield will be sufficient to maintain them, as the incubus they are on the Treasury is a serious matter, and the question is practically put: "What shall we do with them?" I should say, from present appearances even, that the Peninsula was a perfect paradise for slaves. Very comfortable quarters on every plantation, and in the town of Williamsburg the negro-houses are scarcely inferior to the mansions of their masters.

Yours as ever,   JACKSON.

ONE HUNDRED AND SEVENTIETH REGIMENT, N.Y.V.

BEFORE PETERSBURG, VA., July 20.

My last letter from Kettle Run, Va., appeared in your paper on the 15th of May last. On the 13th of May, we took our departure from that place, and after considerable fatigue in marching and travel reported to General Grant's headquarters on May 15th, when we were ordered to the Second Division, Second Army Corps, which we, with the One Hundred and Sixty-ninth New York Volunteers—Corcoran Legion—formed the Fourth Brigade; we were afterward joined by the Eighth New York Heavy Artillery. On the morning of the 16th we opened the ball at Spottsylvania and suffered much in that desperate engagement, charging the enemy's works, which were carried under a terrible fire from their batteries. Long marches and trials incidental to this the hardest campaign in which even the veteran Army of the Potomac has yet been engaged, occupied the interval, to the 19th of May, when we again, at North Anna, advanced and occupied the enemy's works on the left of our line, keeping them back, and losing in our regiment some one hundred and nine in officers and men, until finally obliged to retire, leaving our wounded on the field. Remaining in the front line until the 26th, we again charged the enemy, driving them back, and carrying off the wounded of the previous attack, with a loss this time of two men wounded. By this movement we also covered the movement of the Army, which was about changing its base for that point of operations. On the second of June, while taking our position at the breastworks to relieve the One Hundred and Second Pennsylvania Volunteers, four of our men were wounded. During the terrible battle of the 3rd of June we supported [J. Henry] Sleepers' New York Battery. Ever in the front line on the march. June 15 found us in the assault on the enemy's works before Petersburg. One hundred and odd casualties were the losses of the One Hundred and Seventieth in that encounter. June 16th, we supported General [Gershom] Mott's Brigade in the charge, which, however, was repulsed by the enemy. Continually moving from one point to another, we advanced on the 22nd June, under a terrible fire of all conceivable deadly missiles, and occupied the line from which Birney's Division of this Corps had been driven, with a loss of some thirty-six officers and men. Marching and countermarching— occupying and breaking up camp again, doing picket-duty and fatigue-duty, occupying various points of the line, upon which an attack might be expected, has occupied our time to the present date, when we find ourselves resting inside shelter-tents on the left of the line, digging wells, building shady bowers of green pines and such foliage as can be procured in the vicinity of our present resting-place, which is rather exposed to the scorching rays of the sun. We have been especially blessed with a fine fall of rain within the last twenty-four hours and the sombre aspect of the heavens beckons a further supply of that really welcome and much longed for element. It is nearly sixty days since last we enjoyed such before. Cannonading has been quite brisk along our lines all day; yesterday—owing, I presume to the continuous rain—was remarkably quiet; but last night and this morning there has been a very brisk exchange of musketry between our pickets and the Rebels.

There are many rumors afloat, which, if true, betoken more very warm work around Petersburg. Both lines are very strong and equally vigilant. The return of Colonel Matthew Murphy, who was wounded at Spottsylvania, has released Colonel James C. Melver from his duties as commander of the Second Brigade. Colonel Melver is, therefore, again in command of the One Hundred and Seventieth Regiment.

The mortality among our wounded has been very heavy, owing, doubtless, to the heat of the weather. The Sanitary Commission and Christian Commission have been quite active, during the campaign, in the discharge of their highly laudable duties, administrating to the wants of our boys; but we think there is room for improvement and an enlargement of their generous labors, especially in that of the former commission, whose means are so enormous, and resources almost unlimited from the unbounded generosity of the people. Now with the Christian Commission it is different, we believe, as their resources are more limited, being confined more particularly to private contributions and religious beneficiaries. The Sanitary should come out more liberally with their delicacies, and the refreshments which they are provided with for the use of our soldiers. They should not confine themselves in their labors to the hospitals alone, but remember that there are many "in the front line" who are in need of care and nourishment as much as some who are to be found in the hospital-tent. Our mails have come to hand pretty regularly the last few days—though we had an interval during the Rebel raid into Maryland which caused their delay. Let every one who has a friend or relative in the Army write them, as no one can appreciate a letter from home as well as the soldier at the front.

A. O. P.

U. S. BARK FERNANDINA

OFF ST. CATHERINE'S SOUND, GA., July 2.

The 2d of this month will be a memorable day to this ship's company. While basking under the awnings, they were startled by the cry of "man on the beach", and what was more singular, there were none of our crew on that island. A boat was accordingly sent to pick up the stranger, whoever he might chance to be. The boat was not long before it was alongside, containing the only survivor of the gunboat Water Witch, captured by the Rebs.

He states that it was during the middle watch (12 to 4) about two o'clock, he went into the fireroom for some purpose or other, and while there, he heard the officer of the watch hail, "Boat ahoy!" and the answer, "Go to hell, damn you!" but not taking any notice of this, he next heard the rattle sprung, calling the crew to quarters. Before he could get out of the fire-room he was met by a Rebel, who demanded him to surrender. Not being armed, he was obliged to knuckle under. He could now hear the noise of the conflict on the deck, and, watching an opportunity, he left the fire-room, went in the water-closet on the port side, and jumped overboard. He struck out for the shore, which was about nine hundred to one thousand yards off. The tide running flood, he soon reached the marsh. He waited some time, and could hear the noise of the conflict still raging. He counted four launches alongside. At daybreak, he started for the plantation on Ossibaw Island, once the property of McAllister, the originator of the fort by that name on the Oghechee River. He arrived there, and got a cap and old shoes from the darkeys, and started overland for this vessel.

At first, we could not believe the story, for the reason that we did not hear any firing in that direction. A boat was started to Sapelo Sound, to notify the Ladona, lying at that place. All was now bustle and confusion, every one looking to their arms, to see that they were in proper condition for the fray, should it come to that, which no one doubted. We were at last to have a slap at the Rebs. A second boat was now called away, and sent to Squedunk Navy Yard, so called by the boys. She, however, soon returned, loaded to the water's edge with Georgia pine, cut small, so that it would ignite soon. This movement soon showed the plan to be worked upon. The pine was piled upon the magazine scuttle, ready to apply the match, and every one was ordered to have one extra suit of clothing near at hand, ready to leave the ship at a moment's warning.

At 6, P.M., everything and everybody being ready, the word was given, and a cloud of canvas was crowded on the old Fernandina; and away she goes, thump, thump, over the bar of St. Catherine's out to sea, and nary a Reb in sight, which has, no doubt, saved the papers the trouble of telling some more lies. Probably the Herald's reporter has forgotten the exact distance of a mile, to the Vermont. Big mile, that. "Forty mile, by the chart." Some of the big 'uns are getting up something of the ballad style, and as soon as I can lay claws on the document you shall have it in full. We have received a draft of contrabands from the main, but nothing new from that quarter. Dixie is now a "beat", and everything left to "de Sesechunists". Rather hard that; plums, peaches, figs, green corn, turnips, cabbage, potatoes, squash, etc., are all ripe and ready for the plate. You can look out for some stirring news from this quarter before long, but mum is the word with us at present.

Yours,   FRITZE.

July 31, 1864
MILITARY MATTERS
OUR CIRCULATION IN THE ARMY.—The circulation of the SUNDAY MERCURY in the Army exceeds that of all the other papers published. The soldier would sooner go without his rations than his favorite paper. Its influence is acknowledged to be most salutary, and the effect of its weekly visits in keeping up the spirits, stimulating the patriotism, and preserving a high state of discipline and good order among the troops, is equal to a victory over the enemy.

THIRD BATTALION, FIFTH NEW YORK ARTILLERY
MARYLAND HEIGHTS, July 26.

I have written to you once since our arrival on this side of the river, but suppose the epistle was burnt by the Rebs in their attack on the railroad outside of Baltimore. The first information we had of the close proximity of the Rebels, was on Sunday, the 3rd inst., when our scouts brought intelligence of a force of between six and seven hundred mounted men at Charlestown, which we supposed were Mosby's guerilla-party after the horses of the Twelfth Pennsylvania Veteran Cavalry. We were immediately under arms (our Company, M, was temporarily attached to the Second Battalion at that time), and advanced to meet them, but returned at night, without being honored by a visit from the "chivalry". On the following morning (4th) the assembly call was sounded, and the entire (Second) Battalion was under arms and behind the breastworks in less time than it takes to talk about it. Along came the line of the enemy's skirmishers, advancing boldly and our line was thrown out, when we quickly routed them, they taking refuge in the houses in and around Bolivar. We charged the town twice before succeeding in dislodging them. A party of twenty was immediately detailed to act as sharp-shooters, and advance and hold the Shenandoah pike and railroad, winding round the base of the heights, among whom was "yours truly". We reached the road just as a party of Rebs drove in the Twelfth Pennsylvania Veteran Cavalry, who retreated on a full run, and in great disorder. After these "veterans" had retired, we advanced and drove the Rebs, and held the road during the day. These cavalry are veterans, but a greater set of cowards never mounted a horse. They are a disgrace to their State. Early in the forenoon, rapid firing was heard by us in the direction of Martinsburg and we concluded that General Sigel had "gone in, hot and heavy"; but not being able to withstand the large force against him, he retired across the river into Maryland, then on to Maryland Heights. He saved all his cattle and wagon-trains. On Wednesday, 8th instant, we were re-enforced by Major-General Lew Wallace, from Baltimore, and we drove them back into Virginia, they making tracks down the river to Washington, with which accounts you are familiar. On Thursday, 14th instant, General [Jeremiah C.] Sullivan's Division—the advance of General Hunter's Army—arrived at Harper's Ferry, the entire force of General Hunter's arriving shortly after. But in such condition! Covered with rags, shoeless, dirty, and half-starved. The first battalion of our regiment, which has been with Hunter through the entire command, say their sufferings were intense, and that they will serve as infantry no longer. The come straggling into Harper's Ferry daily. We again occupied the Ferry on Friday, 18th instant, the Rebs leaving on the previous night, after destroying all Government property and plundering the citizens of everything of the least value. The railroad-bridge is repaired, and communications is open.

Yours,   HEAVIES.

EIGHTY-FOURTH REGIMENT, N.G.S.N.Y.
NEAR ARLINGTON, VA., July 26.

My last epistle was dated on board steamer Merrimac. Since that time we have been constantly on the move. To commence: we reached Washington on the 16th inst., marched across (via Long Bridge) to Arlington Heights, and encamped in front of Fort Richardson. On the 17th inst., struck tents and proceeded to Fort Lyon, about three miles below Alexandria, which the regiment garrisoned until the 20th instant, when orders came to proceed to Arlington Heights, the camp being five minutes from the Rebel General Lee's former homestead. On the 22nd inst. we pulled stakes and marched to our present camp, where we are likely to stay. What good the regiment has done, or is doing, to serve the Government, is more than a common soldier can determine; but one thing is certain, and that is, the regiment is being rapidly put through "a course of sprouts", which will tend greatly to improve its discipline and drill, and it is to be hoped will fit them, in case of any sudden call, for good and active service. Yesterday afternoon, about fifty men arrived from New York, and joined the regiment. I made a flying visit to Washington the other day, and noticed that the President's grounds were filled with citizen-clerks, in Government employ, who were being drilled in the manual by volunteer, invalid, and civilian officers. It was rather a comical sight. Old men, middle-aged, young, stout, thin, and extremely slight mortals, being mixed up indiscriminately.

Our regiment, thus far, has been remarkably healthy.

Yours, for the present,   K.A.O.D.

August 7, 1864
FROM AN OLD SOLDIER
WASHINGTON, D.C., August 3, 1864

I have just returned from the front. The fighting was going on at the time I set out from City Point, and I accordingly had somewhat of a view. After all was over, Captain [Henry H.] De Winstanley took me around and showed me the line of breastworks, and the ruins of the fort just blown up, in which there were a body of Rebels destroyed. Through some bad management or treachery, the position which had been gained was lost again. Talking to the men in the trenches, they informed me that, after the fort was blown up, and our mortars and guns opened upon the Rebel batteries, the fortifications were deserted completely in front of the Fifth Corps, and some of our men almost cried because they could not get the order to advance and occupy them. The colored troops fought well, but it is said that many of the officers in command over them acted cowardly. I saw one of our mortar-shells in front of the Second Maine—a one-hundred-pounder that did not burst. The Rebel and Union fortifications are very close to each other. The pickets of each contending army are within a very few feet—in fact, they sit and talk to each other; get water from the same spring, and are very agreeable, giving each other warning, or else shooting over each others' head until each can get away for a fair show. All speak well of the action of the colored troops, and say they could have gone into Petersburg if the Fifth and Tenth Corps had been allowed to support them.

On my return home from the Fifth, the boys being just paid off, I bring nearly $3,000 in money to their friends. I think that is doing well out of less than two hundred men now remaining of the Brooklyn Fourteenth, transferred to the Fifth N.Y.V.V. Inf. There was considerable whiskey in the camp, which created some pugnacity among the Fifth, or what the Fourteenth portion call the "Chinese" portion of the Fifth. Not one, I am glad to say, of the Fourteenth portion showed anything from the effects of the liquor. All without exception, take a pride in the remembrance of the old regiment (the Fourteenth Brooklyn). The officers of the Fifth are very much pleased with the conduct of the men of the Fourteenth transferred to the Fifth; and seem also well pleased with the new officers, Captains De Winstanley and [John F.] York, and Lieutenants [John T.] Taylor and [George] Osborne (Lieutenant [John C.] Brown being a prisoner, Lieutenant [James B.] Rich killed on the 18th ult. I felt sorry to leave the boys, when I thought how I had parted before, and many were killed or badly wounded since—though so short a time since. They are all in good spirits and patriotic; willing to undergo, without a murmur, all the hardships, in the hope of a speedy close of the war. To see the men in the broiling sun, working on these gigantic fortifications, and suffer as they do, and still cheerful, it makes me ask what cause any of us at home have of complaint?

Yesterday morning, we left City Point, on the John Brooks; and when about three or four miles down the river, we all at once saw the shells bursting. The Rebs had a battery planted and was shelling the S.R. Spaulding. The John Brooks halted and blew her whistle, after which one of the Rebel guns was opened on us. We fortunately did not get stuck, though several shots came very near, passing just over the bow of the vessel. The S.R. Spaulding was not so fortunate. She got one right through the wheelhouse, which killed five horses and did some other damage. I could not learn whether any human beings were hurt.

Yours, etc.,   J. J.

THIRD REGIMENT NEW YORK VOLUNTEERS
CAMP NEAR PETERSBURG, VA., July 30.

Since I last wrote you, our regiment has passed through most of the struggle of the campaign. It bore an honorable part at Procter's Creek, Cold Harbor, Drury's Bluff, and on the Heights of Petersburg. At this last place, our line charged and carried one of the enemy's strongest earthworks, capturing the guns and the battle flag of [John] Wise's "Rebel" Brigade, for which one of the privates of Company G was promoted on the spot to a lieutenancy in the regular Army. Since leaving Bermuda Hundred, over a month ago, we have been constantly under fire. This is called "the inactivity of the Army of the Potomac". If those correspondents who write these articles would but see the boys dodge the shot and shell of the "Secesh", they would think it anything but a life of "inactivity".

I see several accounts in the papers that the Sanitary Commission were actively engaged in sending vegetables to the troops here; but I think they must have met with some very serious obstacle, as the only place where we have seen vegetables were those served for the officers' mess. With one exception, then, our regiment was furnished with a variety sent, as we were told, by the "noble firemen of Gotham". The sutlers here, or as the boys style them, "Army Sharks", have become very cautious in their dealings. They will not accommodate any of the men with credit, unless their company commander will be security for them, as they (the men) are liable, at any moment, to "shuffle off this mortal coil", and close their accounts. This makes it very inconvenient for the privates, as pay-day has been long in coming. Most of our officers have been very obliging. All the companies, with but two exceptions, have been enabled to obtain their tobacco and other necessaries. The commanders of these two companies refused their signatures on the same grounds that the sutlers refuse to credit without them. The boys are looking eagerly for the Paymaster, when they intend to raise a sufficient fund, and place it at the disposal of their two officers to secure them against loss. All these things are only secondary to the political excitement. Through our camps our regiment seem to be all of one mind in regard to the coming election, nine-tenths of them being good Union-loving men, who are in favor of "free speech", "free press", and the "Monroe Doctrine". The man that advocates these principles will secure the numerous votes of the New York Volunteers.

Yours respectfully,   HIGH HAT.

ONE HUNDRED AND FORTY-SIXTH REGIMENT, N.Y.V.

IN FRONT OF PETERSBURG, VA., August 2.

Contrary to my expectations, we have not captured the Cockade City yet, though we have blown up some of the principal works of the enemy, and lost the ground we gained by the cowardice of the black troops. The sky toward the city was illuminated to such an extent that it was believed the whole place was burning. At the same time our mortars kept up quite a lively tune. Our two hundred-pound shell are not acceptable to Butternut. The One Hundred and Forty-sixth is continually on detail with pick and shovel, building and strengthening the works in our front; and all we wish is that Bobby Lee will give us a chance to show him how the "Tigers" can fight behind breastworks. A rumor was in circulation that Johnny Reb intended to make an attack on us. To hold ourselves in readiness to move at a moment's warning was our last order at retreat. For some reason or another, Johnny did not come.

According to reports from Petersburg papers, the Yanks are short of water, and have to draw it in barrels from the Appamattox River. The best advice to Johnny is to come over; we will show them plenty of wells, from fifteen to thirty feet deep, in every regiment in the Fifth Corps, and all full of good cool water.

The Clerk of the Weather has accommodated us with some rain, which has cooled the air to a considerable extent.

Can you inform us what has become of the greenbacks? Did Chase carry them all off with him, or is the Government waiting for this campaign to end, thinking, no doubt, that it would take less to pay off the troops then at the present time, as a good many of us have families depending on us for assistance. Hurry up the greenbacks.

The news of camp is, that Hunter has been whipped again, with Johnny at his heels. It is to be hoped that the "On to Richmond" crowd will now mass together and smite them hip and thigh, and drive them so far they will not think of coming back again.

We have had a good supply of vegetables from our Commissary and the Sanitary Commission; also, a pretty good share of tobacco. It is to be hoped they will be continued.

How is that last call, only five hundred thousand more? It has cost a big pile of men to get here, and yet have twenty-two miles to go to get to Richmond; plenty of works to get over; any quantity of room for this last pile to find a resting-place in Virginia. So they had better hurry up, or they will be too late for the fray.

I am, as usual,   Yours,   J. O. E.

IN CAMP NEAR FREDERICK, MD.

August 3.

On the morning of the 26th inst. we left Washington on the road leading to Rockville, on our way to Harper's Ferry. We arrived there on the 29th inst., and went into camp; and we thought that we should be allowed to stay here a few days and rest ourselves, but we were mistaken, for the next day we were ordered back to Frederick. When we passed through Harper's Ferry we were joined by the Eighth Corps, who came with us to Jefferson, when the Sixth and Eighth Corps took different roads, leaving us alone to proceed to Frederick by ourselves. We arrived in Frederick on Sunday, and encamped about three miles from it, on the road leading to Pennsylvania; but, yesterday, we struck our tents and moved to this place. We are now stationed on the Baltimore & Ohio Railroad. I do not know how long we shall stay here, but when we do move I think it will be toward Washington. We have experienced some hard times since we have been in this Department; we have been here nearly a month, and have been on the march every day except two; they could not let us rest quietly a single day, for last Monday, while we were in camp, they raised a false alarm that Gen. [H. G.] Wright's head-quarters were attacked, and we had to turn out and go "double-quick" nearly two miles, surprising everybody we met. When we got to head-quarters we found all quiet, and so we returned to camp; but not at a double-quick. It is all hills and very stony, and a good many men fall down on the road, and some even fall dead. Even yesterday, when we changed our camp we marched about eight miles. The General marched us so hard, that four or five men fell right down dead in the ranks, out of our Division. General [William] Dwight commands the division, and he has no more feelings for the men than he has for a lot of cattle. He marches us three or four hours without resting us at all, and then he marches us day and night. None of the men in the division like him. Sometimes, when we go in camp of a night, some regiments have about twenty-one men to stack arms; and if we should happen to meet the enemy after a day's march, the men would be too tired and worn-out to fight. We have been round here now for three days, and the stragglers are still coming into camp. I do not think it is right for the generals to march their men so hard when there is no need of it; but they are all mounted on good horses, and do not think of the men who have to march on foot, with his gun and equipments, and four days' rations in his haversack. When we are going to re-enforce any place, then it would be time enough to give us hard marching. But the citizens all along the road do all in their power to help us along. On Sunday, as we passed through Frederick, the citizens treated us very kindly.

CORPORAL.

ARMY OF TENNESSEE

NEAR ATLANTA, GA., July 29.

On the 20th inst., Decatur, six miles east of Atlanta was occupied by our troops, the Fifteenth, Sixteenth, Seventeenth and Twenty-third Corps, reaching the town, at the same time, by different roads. But little opposition was manifested; except toward evening, a Rebel battery commenced shelling the Sixteenth Army Corps, but the Fourteenth Ohio Battery soon put a quietus on them.

On the morning of the 21st, we moved directly on Atlanta, the Fifteenth Corps moved on the railroad, the Seventeenth Corps on a road south of and parallel to the railroad, the Sixteenth Corps moved in rear of the Fifteenth, leaving a portion of the Corps at Decatur. Of the disposition of the remainder of the Army, I cannot speak certainly. Our advance met with but little opposition until within three miles of Atlanta, when the Rebs commenced making a bold stand. Here our army was halted, our lines established, and the necessary preparations made to ascertain the exact position of the Rebel works. We have now a new man to deal with, Johnston having been relieved on the 18th inst., and [Gen. John B.] Hood placed in command of the Rebel Army. Hood has the reputation of being a fighting man, and we soon had an opportunity of testing his qualities in that respect.

On the 22nd inst., it was reported that a large force of the enemy were in the rear and on the flank of the Army of the Tennessee; and almost simultaneously with the report came the enemy, charging our lines with the full confidence of victory, thinking that at last they would drive back the horde of Yankee invaders; in the first onslaught, the Rebels carried everything before them; our men gave way, and battery after battery fell into the hands of the exultant Rebs; the prospects of the Army of the Tennessee looked dark and gloomy. McPherson soon ascertained the true position of affairs; and, riding to the front, personally rallied the men, and re-established the lines, being ably assisted by Generals [Grenville M.] Dodge and Logan. It was while thus engaged that McPherson fell, mortally wounded. He lived about fifteen minutes, but was unconscious. One of our men remained with him, for nearly an hour, until the body was removed from the field. Some Rebel soldiers took his watch and papers. They were also going to take the man prisoner who was watching the body, but he declared that he could not walk, so they left him.

After our lines were established firmly, the battle raged hot and fiercely; our batteries being served at short ranges, threw grape and canister with terrible destruction amongst the Rebel ranks. Slowly and sullenly the Rebel lines gave way. Our lines were pressed forward, until finally a charge was ordered; with a wild cheer our boys pressed forward, driving the Rebels in an utter rout from the field. The next day, the Rebels, under a flag of truce, requested permission to bury their dead; our men were already engaged in that task, but permission was granted to the Rebels to remove the bodies that were not buried; 3,220 dead Rebels were buried by our men, or turned over to the Rebels; 1,017 prisoners were taken, and 1,000 wounded Rebels were also taken—making a total of 4,227, dead and alive, that passed through our hands. Therefore 12,000 is a low estimate to place their total loss at.

Our total loss in killed, wounded and missing is 3,511; we captured seventeen stands of colors. When the Rebels succeeded in taking from the field ten of our guns, with a few caissons; six of these guns belonged to Company F, Second United States Artillery.

On the 22nd inst., Gen. [Lovell H.] Rouseau reached our lines, after making one of the greatest raids of the war. He started from Decator, Ala., on the 10th inst., and proceeding south, struck the Atlanta & Montgomery Rail-road, and destroyed the road for a distance of thirty-five miles, destroying many valuable bridges. At one time, they were within thirty-two miles of Montgomery, from the State-House of which floated a white flag for two days, in token of surrender, as the Governor wishes to save the town from destruction; but the capture of Montgomery was not included in the orders, so our troops returned to our lines with the loss of but a dozen men.

General [Kenner] Garrard also made a raid on the road running east from Atlanta. He proceeded as far as Covington, destroyed twenty miles of the road, burned three important bridges, one of which was five hundred feet in length. They also destroyed two thousand bales of government cotton, a large supply of commissary stores, and other Confederate property. Several thousand pounds of tobacco were captured, which General Garrard distributed throughout the Army on his return. But one road is left running out of Atlanta, and a large cavalry-force left the Army last night to tap that same vital point.

In the meantime, our Army is industriously at work for the capture of Atlanta. To give the position of our troops now would be contraband; but rest assured that all is well, and that Atlanta will fall in good time; for a city as well fortified as Atlanta is not to be taken in a day; and besides, the capture of Atlanta itself is not so much of an object with General Sherman as the capture or destruction of the Rebel Army within its fortifications.   N.Y. VETERAN VOLUNTEER.

August 14, 1864
SIXTY-FIFTH REGIMENT, N.Y.S.V.
NEAR BOLIVAR HEIGHTS, VA., Aug. 8.

We arrived at Washington on the 11th ult., and marched immediately to the vicinity of Fort Stevens, where we took the place made vacant by the Volunteer [Veteran] Reserve Corps, who went to the rear as soon as relieved. The Johnnies, finding their old foes in their front, retreated the same day, and we pursued; but all our efforts to overtake them, as you are aware of, were in vain. After we had crossed the Shenandoah River, and had reached a point within five miles of Winchester, we received orders to go back to the vicinity of the Capital. On arriving there, most of the corps received their greenbacks, and preparations were going on for our return to City Point, when the late raid demonstrated the great necessity of effectually guarding the line of the Potomac.

To-day, it is reported that [Gen. Jubal A.] Early, with no less than thirty thousand men, is crossing the Potomac at Williamsport and Hancock. If there is any truth in this, you no doubt know of it before now. It is the general impression that Early has received large re-enforcements from Lee, and that he intends, if possible, to transfer the war to Maryland or Pennsylvania soon. If he crosses the Potomac, he will have to fight almost as soon as his feet treads loyal soil.

We have a great deal of marching, and numbers of our men have been overpowered by the heat; so, if Early does cross, we hope he will stand and fight—for we greatly prefer fighting him than chasing him all over the country in this hot weather.

Those of our regiment who are left will soon be going home, so most of them have served out the specified time, three years. There is only a little band of them, between seventy or eighty; they deserve a warm reception from their fellow-citizens, for no regiment has stood with greater bravery than the Chasseurs. Those who remain, veterans and recruits, will probably be merged in the Sixty-seventh (First Long Island) Regiment. Most of our present officers return with those who go home. Captain [David] Milne, Co. F, has been appointed Brigade-Inspector on the staff of General [Emory] Upton, a compliment well-merited to a fearless soldier and a true gentleman. The health of the regiment continues remarkably good, considering the exposures and privations we are called upon to undergo. It is rumored that we are to have a change of commanders in this department; if so, were it left to the opinion of the rank and file, they would choose General McClellan.

We are content to acquiesce in whatever the Government sees fit to do, believing that what it does do is intended to crush the Rebellion and restore the Union.

Owing to some hitch in the mail, your paper has not been as prompt; but now, as we are near the railroad, we expect it regularly, for without the SUNDAY MERCURY we would all be adrift. Hoping that if the Rebels invade our soil that we will give them a good thrashing, I am, dear MERCURY, your happy reader,
                                                                FRANCONI.

SIXTEENTH REGIMENT, WISCONSIN VET. VOLS.

CAMP NEAR ATLANTA, GA., August 4.

We have seen some very hard fighting since July 13, as we have since that time crossed the Chattahoochee River. On that night we received orders to fall in line as still as possible, which we did, and marched continually until noon the following day; then we halted for two hours and drew our rations. Our line of march was then continued toward the left wing of the Army. As our men had rebuilt a bridge which the Rebels had burnt in their retreat, as soon as we had finished drawing our rations we resumed our march, crossing the river and camping four miles from it, where we enjoyed a good night's rest, and starting at twilight in the morning nothing of any note took place until the morning of the 20th, when we took Decatur, after a little skirmishing.

The Sixteenth Army Corps were in the advance, but stopped there to destroy the railroad, when our Corps, the Seventeenth, took the advance and soon commenced skirmishing, driving the Rebels before us until dark without much loss to us. After a good deal of maneuvering around, we were finally got into position in a heavy piece of timber, near the edge of a cornfield, in a deep ravine. Then we were ordered to lie down in line of battle, and not to take a thing off, and there we slept what little was left of the night. We all well knew that the Rebels were not more than forty or fifty rods from us, as we could distinctly hear them working all night making breast-works. So in the morning, as soon as twilight could be seen, we were ordered to fall in for a charge; but as the rest of the brigade were not quite ready, we did not start until nine o'clock, when we were ordered to fix bayonets, and forward, double-quick, which we did with a yell; and the moment we reached the top of the small hill which covered us from their fire during the night, we found ourselves on a level field, with nothing larger than a cornstack for protection, facing strong works, which were filled with double our number of Rebels; but onward we went through the most murderous fire that any men were ever in, cutting our men down by the dozens; but we carried the works, jumping right in among them, and charging some fifty rods after them; the Twelfth Wisconsin on our right. We captured three hundred prisoners. The Rebels fought desperately; worthy of a better cause. Hardly any of them left their works until we had got within two or three rods of their works, and many of the men remained in their position until we compelled them to surrender. After we pursued those who skedaddled, we returned and took possession of their works, and commenced fixing them to suit ourselves. Then we started with three hundred men in our regiment on the charge, and in less time than it takes for me to write it down, ninety-eight of the number were killed and wounded. Our Lieutenant-Colonel [Thomas McMahon] was badly wounded, and I helped to carry him off from the field. We now expected to have a little rest after such a loss, or at least have a chance to fight them from their works; so we did on the 22nd ultimo, which was the next day. We heard heavy firing in our rear and our left flank, so that it left our Rebel works entirely useless for a defence for us.

Then we hurriedly threw up a small work of rails and dirt facing our flank, but did not get half enough done before we saw our men coming and running in great confusion toward us with the Rebels close behind them, yelling at the success they had accomplished, expecting to drive everything before them; but just before they came in range of our guns, Gen. [Mortimer D.] Legget came riding up to our regiment, and said: "Sixteenth Wisconsin hold this position at all hazards"; but even if he had not said that, it would have been done at any rate. But on came the drunken rascals. We reserved our fire until they came within four or five rods of us, when we let them have it right in the bread-baskets, which turned them tail to in a hurry; but very few of that line got back to tell the tale. They did not expect such a sudden check until they run against the "Veteran Badgers". But it seemed that they were not satisfied with what we gave them; for, in about an hour after, we saw them coming in four solid lines of battle against our single line. We had no support, as our supports were sent off to re-enforce another part of the line, yet they did not scare us, nor could they even if they had been a hundred lines. We fixed bayonets, and double charged our guns, determined to die in the ditch before we would let them cross our little works; but we hadn't more than got ready to receive them, before their first line made its appearance, when we gave them the contents of our guns, cutting their first lines all to pieces, and serving the second same; but the others were a little more successful than them, for they charged up within fifty steps of our works, behind a small work that one of our company had built for flank-firing, but not occupied at the time; they planted three stands of colors on it, while others came closer up to our works, and were shot or bayoneted. They kept their colors on the little work until dark, until after having them shot down more than fifty times; but they always raised them up again, and we kept up a heavy fire on them all night, and they returned with a will, but what was left of them scrambled off before daylight in the morning.

Such a sight as that battle-field presented in the morning, it would be useless for me to try to describe. There were some eighty dead Rebels laying behind these small works which were not more than thirty feet long, while the ground around was covered in piles. We lost forty-two men during that day, and one hundred and forty-two during both days' fighting. We fought harder the second day and lost less men. We found that the fighting from behind works is better than to fight then in the open field. We are now within one and a half miles of the doomed city; the Rebels have a heavy battery planted within three-quarters of a mile from us; they throw a shell over us every once in a while; our skirmishers keep up a considerable fire all the time so as to keep the Rebel skirmishers from crawling up to us to shoot our men over in our works, but still they shoot a good many balls over for all, and kill a man once in a while. They killed one man of my regiment this morning, of Company A. He was a Welshman. This man was killed by a stray shot coming over the works while he was cooking dinner for his company. I did not receive a scratch in the fight, while my comrades were falling all around me. I can never see how I escaped in that desperate charge, where the balls flew like hailstones, without receiving a wound, or losing my life, but I may be like many others, spared for another time. I have received the SUNDAY MERCURY regularly, and I assure you that very good use is made of it, as all the boys read it until it is all worn out.

COUSIN TOM.

FORTY-EIGHTH REGIMENT, N.Y.V.
FOSTER'S PLANTATION, NEAR BERMUDA HUNDRED, VA., August. 9.

Since my last I have been on a visit to Portsmouth, and during my absence our regiment was in the charge on the Rebel works before Petersburg on the 30th ult., when the Rebel fort was blown up. If I had been there I would have written before.

Our regiment suffered pretty severely in the fight, and the next day we were relieved and marched to this place; the day was sweltering hot, and numerous cases of sunstroke took place, some of them dying; some twelve or fifteen died from the effects of the sun, others were disabled for a time, and are now returning to their companies.

In the fight of the 30th, we lost Major S. M. Swartwout, and Lieutenant [Jeremiah] O'Brien, and eight men killed, and thirty wounded; those that were killed were all shot outside of our works, and died while bravely doing their duty. Our Division ([Gen. John] Turner's) lost as many as the Eighteenth Corps.

I wish to say a word in regard to an institution kept by the Sanitary Commission at Portsmouth, called the Soldier's Lodge; here any soldier, on pass or otherwise, can always find a ready welcome at the hands of Mr. J. Alcooke (the superintendent), and during his stay he is made comfortable as he can ask for. I would wish through you, to thank Mr. Alcooke for his kind treatment of me, and would recommend all soldiers who may be in Portsmouth, to call on him.

There is nothing going on here. The pickets are within 150 yards of each other, and occasionally notes are sent across to each other, one of which I will give you, as near as possible:

"TO MY FRIEND ON THE PICKET-LINE:—Do not vote Old Abe; for if you do, it will keep the war up for four years longer, as our leaders will never give in while he is President. I kicked Old Abe once, and if he is elected again, I will go to Washington and kill him. I am your friend on the picket-line, but your foe in battle.
'SUGAR'."

The answer was sent in the following style:
"'SUGAR':—All right. I am your friend everywhere but in battle.
'SALT'."

I have no more to write at present, but will shortly have some news to write, as something in the way of digging is going on which will be a hard blow to the Johnnies, if successful.

LEO.

August 21, 1864
SIXTY-EIGHTH REGIMENT, N.Y.S.V.V.
EAST BRIDGE, ALA., August 9.

The comparative quiet of our camp has suddenly been interrupted by a bold dash of the Rebels and an attempt to cut the communication with the front.

At five o'clock on the morning of the 5th inst., word was brought into these head-quarters that a party of guerillas had cut the telegraph-wire near Taylor's Store, about three miles from here, and were tearing up the railroad. Captain [Otto Von] Fritsch immediately started out with a small force from this detachment, accompanied by Captain [George] Renneberg and Lieutenant [Otto] Mussehl.

This gallant little band pushed forward on the double quick to the scene of the Rebel depredations. The Rebs must have been apprised of our approach, for they fled in such haste that they left behind them four rifles and all their tools. Several spikes had already been removed, and fence-rails were placed under the track, ready to pry it up. Some five hundred yards of telegraph-wire were cut off and dragged a short distance into the woods, where it was found by the railroad-employees.

The Rebels were all mounted and of course we could not follow them to any advantage. Our boys returned to camp rather discontented at not being able to capture the Rebs, or at least give them a sound thrashing.

But another and more bloody tragedy remains yet to be told. Last week, a party of about eighteen guerrillas came to Jasper, Tennessee, which is about eleven miles from here on the other side of the river.

Going to a house about three miles from the town, they took therefrom two white men and a negro. The two whites were placed against a tree, face to face; no entreaties or prayers for mercy were listened to by the heartless scoundrels, and the unfortunate victims fell dead, pierced by fifteen balls, all the guerrillas having fired at one and the same time. The negro was then tied to a limb and met the same fate. The poor darkey was evidently aware that begging for mercy would be of no avail, and he calmly submitted to his terrible fate. Two women in the neighborhood were taken out and stripped of every particle of clothing, their persons violated, and beaten in the most inhuman and brutal manner.

It is hardly probable that this was the same gang that attempted to tear up the railroad, for there is no ferry or fordable point on that immediate vicinity. The two white men so cruelly murdered were but a few weeks since discharged from the First Alabama (Union) Cavalry, and their having been in the United States service is probably what prompted these fiends to do the foul deed. The negro was murdered simply for being a negro.

It is doubtful whether the farmers of this neighborhood are complicated in these crimes; but at any rate they should be narrowly watched, as there is no trusting people that change their sentiments to suit the times.

Large numbers of prisoners are passing here daily on their way to the rear, and at the front it seems that "everything is lovely and the goose hangs high."

But enough for the present.   Yours, truly,   BLUE JACKET.

ONE HUNDRED AND SEVENTIETH REGIMENT N.Y.V.

CAMP NEAR PETERSBURG, VA., August 10.

Since my last, nothing of special interest has occurred in this Department to interfere with the equanimtry of the Second Corps, or, in fact, with the Army of the Potomac, further than now and then some brisk exchanges of musketry on the part of the pickets in front of Petersburg. Yesterday, however, the writer was at City Point, hunting up some contrabands to take charge of a portion of our culinary department, and he had not been more than fairly seated with [Col. Walter] Van Rensselaer, commanding the Twentieth New York Militia, enjoying a beautiful glass, or should I say ten, of ice-water, than one of the most fearful reports of, as it appeared, of shell, grape, canister, and musketry that ever vied with the elements in their hissing sounds, took place, dealing death and destruction in every direction. The greatest consternation that ever affected white or black men spread far and near; negroes, male and female, rushed in every direction; white men—the majority of them veterans of many hard-fought battles—stood aghast; officers, who commanded many a fierce charge, and whose scars betokened many a hard struggle with the enemy, stood almost petrified. In fact, so sudden and so terrific was the explosion, that description is impossible.

Quiet being partly restored, we emerged from our canvas shelter to learn the cause. We were not more than two hundred yards from where the explosion took place, and on casting our eyes around, we found the ground literally covered with shot and shell, and near where we stood, we picked about twenty as beautiful specimens of man-annihilators as Jeff Davis can boast of. Thank Providence! none of them came in contact with our craniums. From here we proceeded down to the scene of the catastrophe, and what was our astonishment to find houses, docks, boats, tents, in a state of perfect wreck! dead and dying strewn among the ruins; bodies torn to pieces; an arm here, a head there, a leg and other portions of the human frame mangled to pieces, at some places a distance of two hundred yards; muskets and rifles bent into every imaginable shape; ordnance-stores, including almost everything in the vocabulary, lying helter-skelter; and ammunition, of all sorts and sizes, covering the ground as far as the eye could reach. Detachments from the different regiments stationed there soon arrived on the ground, and immediately set to work removing the ruins about the barge which had exploded, and quiet reigned once more. Body after body was extricated—some dead, others dying, mangled in the most fearful manner, and the groans of the poor fellows who had any life left were pitiable in the extreme.

Colonel [Theodore] Gates, commandant of the post, and Van Rensselaer, commanding the Twentieth New York, having now arrived, everything went on like clockwork; and, indeed, too much praise cannot be bestowed on both these gentlemen for the manner in which they exerted themselves to restore order and relieve the wounded. We proceeded from here to the camp and houses in the village, and found about every tent more or less perforated, and the interior of the houses divested of their plaster—some of them not having a solitary pane of glass left—yet, strange to say, very few were hurt; although from the appearance of the ground, it was very evident that there was ample cause for considerable mortality.

After an hour or so, we visited the scene of the explosion again, and found that some twenty dead bodies, principally colored men, had already been extracted from the ruins, besides several who were fearfully wounded—many so badly, that amputation had to be resorted to. It was impossible to learn the exact amount of mortality or damage done, but, on a rough guess, we should think that one hundred covers the number of killed and wounded. The damage done to Government-property cannot be much less than half a million of dollars. All sorts of rumors are afloat as to the cause of the explosion, but are merely surmises. There is very little doubt but what it was purely accidental. So far as we were enabled to learn, a large barge was lying alongside of the wharf, loaded with ordnance and ordnance-stores, and was being unloaded, when suddenly an explosion took place, resulting in what I have already stated. It is very probable, and I do not see anything more likely, that as the barge was being unloaded at the time, some colored man, who was ignorant of what he was handling, dropped a percussion-shell, which immediately exploded, and hence the fearful catastrophe that followed. It is nevertheless a matter which requires thorough investigation; for, if proper care was taken, no such accident could have happened. I forgot to mention that the steamtug (fire-boat) Chilli was on hand immediately after the occurrence, and got eight streams of water playing on the ruins, which was the cause of preventing any further disaster, for another barge lay quite near the scene, also loaded with ammunition.

The regiment is in the best of health and spirits, encamped in a wood near Petersburg, waiting orders. We are expecting some active work again in a few days. Do advise Uncle Sam to allow us an opportunity to recruit. A regiment that has fought so manfully, and lost over two-thirds of its number in this campaign, and that has never been beaten, should have its ranks filled up.

Yours, etc.   A. O. P.

The Aug. 9, 1864 explosion at City Point, Va., was indeed the work of a saboteur named John Maxwell, a captain in the Confederate Secret Service. Maxwell rigged a bomb of 12 pounds of powder and a timing device and had placed it aboard an ammunition barge. In all, 58 were killed and 126 wounded.

NINETY-FIFTH REGIMENT, N.Y.V.

NEAR PETERSBURG, VA., Aug. 14.

Since I last wrote you, nothing of importance has transpired with us. We expected a brush with the Johnny Rebs the day Burnside sprung his mine, thereby forever emancipating a pretty tall number of our woolly-headed brethren of African descent; to those unfortunate colored individuals, "the whip is undoubtedly lost, and the shackle broke" forever. With something of the same feeling that prompted some one in the long-ago to exclaim: "Lo! the poor Indian!" I might cry: "Oh! the poor nigger!" or any other man who fights with him. Yet, at times, I cannot help feeling, when reading this, that, or the other proposed plan for the darkeys' salvation, that it will be a large economy to save the like, as Byron said of the soul of George III.

Our division, the Fourth (Fifth Corps), was under arms and in position to charge, but we were not put in; therefore we cannot boast of any laurels won in the brilliant move in question. The niggers can—that is, the few whose heels were sufficiently clean to enable them to regain the shelter of our friendly works. As it stands, we cannot say that we particularly envy Sambo the glory he has won on the 30th of July last, although he will doubtless reserve a place in that history of the Great Rebellion by Horace [Greeley] or some other philosopher. We have lately received some fifty substitute-recruits, and enough of our old wounded have come back to swell our number up to two hundred. Maj. Robert W. Bard is, at present, in command; Col. [James] Creney's wounds still keeping him absent. We have a very pleasant camp, good water, and if that man with the greenbacks would call and settle with us, we would all be as jolly as "clams at high tide". I hear no talk of re-enlisting for one, two, or three years—the one, two, or three hundred dollars bounty being considered by the boys generally not worth the taking. All of us old soldiers (and most of the new ones, too), are hoping that 'Little Mac' will be nominated for the Presidency upon a Democratic *war* platform. If he is, he can count upon our hearty support.

Yours, truly,   ALLEGHANY.

BAD REPORTS ABOUT GENERAL GRANT— It is useless to try and keep from the country what is notorious in the Army, East and West, as well as here at the capital. Gen. Grant is a victim to intemperance. He is not a tippler or drunkard in the ordinary sense of the term, but has recurring fits of drink-insanity. For three months on a stretch he is the most sober of men, never touching or tasting liquor of any kind—then the fit comes on him and he is no longer a free agent. It sometimes lasts for three weeks at a time. It is reported that he kept sober from the Rapidan to the James, but that he got one of his "fits" after the first repulse from Petersburg, which accounts for his long inactivity. Of course, no one likes to repeat these stories of the weakness of a great general, but it is due to the public that they should be made aware of the reason of the failure of our main Army.

August 28, 1864
FORTY-EIGHTH REGIMENT
DEEP BOTTOM, VA., August 21.

On the 13th, we received orders to take three days' cooked rations and be ready to go at a moment's notice.

At 11, P.M., we started for Deep Bottom, and at 5, A.M., on the 14th, we crossed the pontoon and marched to the front. At 7, A.M., the ball opened, and shortly afterward the One Hundredth New York, Colonel [George B.] Dandy, captured one of the Rebel forts containing four guns and two mortars. Our regiment was to be the supporting column; we marched to the right of the line, and as we reached it, we were greeted by a shower of shot and shell, which killed Captain W. E. D'Arcy, (one of your former correspondents) and wounded five men. We afterward marched to the extreme left and went on picket at night. Next morning (15th) we marched across the country in the direction of Malvern Hill; during the march a great many men were obliged to fall out, in consequence of the heat; the idea of marching a distance of four miles with knapsacks and three days' rations, in sweltering sun, was beyond the strength of men. We lay in the wood all night; and on the morning of the 16th, we were ordered into an open field to support some batteries stationed there, but afterward, the first division of our corps (the Tenth), charged the main works of the enemy, and carried them, capturing some three hundred prisoners and five stand of colors, two of which were captured by the Eighty-fifth Pennsylvania Volunteers. Our brigade was shortly afterward ordered to advance, and we went in on the double-quick, amid a shower of bullets, and gained the works and held them for some time, when, by somebody's stupidity, a space of about fifty yards on our left was allowed to be unoccupied; and not more than fifteen minutes after, the troops were withdrawn from it, when the Rebels had their colors planted on the parapet and they poured a heavy fire into our flank, which caused the regiments on our left to break, and that was the signal for every one to go. It was almost a rout, and no sooner had we left the works than the Johnnies had occupied them. We rallied in the woods, threw out skirmishers, and held our ground.

On the next morning, we were marched to this place, and immediately went on picket, relieving two regiments of negroes. They went to join their brigade. Since we left the front, all that was wanted had been accomplished, and last night they all withdrew across the pontoon, and are now on the way to strike a blow in some other direction. Our loss in the several engagements amount to fifty-four.

LEO.

HAREWOOD HOSPITAL
WASHINGTON, D.C., Aug. 21.

I suppose some of your readers would like to know something about the Harewood Hospital. It is situated on Corcoran's Farm, about one mile from the city of Washington, on Seventh street, and it is kept nice and clean—everything in good order and ready for the sick and wounded, who come in daily from the front. Great care is taken of them by the doctors. They work night and day, looking after the comforts of their patients. Some of them are badly wounded, and there are a great many cases of diarrhea.

The Hospital is divided off in wards, five tents in each ward, and each tent contains eighteen beds. One doctor has the charge of two wards. Doctor Briggs, of my ward, is all the time at work, and he knows how to handle the wounded so as to bring them up to their proper state, so as to be fit for duty in a few weeks to return to their regiment. Dr. Benteen has the full charge of this hospital, and he sees that every thing is in good ship-shape. There are about two thousand sick and wounded here. We have had a good shower this forenoon, which will help the wounded along. It drives away the bad smell which comes from the wounds. There are between four and six die here every day. At soon as they die, they are taken down to the dead-house, and afterward put in an ambulance, with the flag of our country spread over their coffin. Finally, they are laid to rest in a neat graveyard at Fairfax Seminary. This place has about eight thousand graves in it. Each noble sleeper has his name, and company and regiment to which he belonged, on his head-board. A great many are taken home by their friends. What a sacred spot that will be after this cruel war is over!

GUARDIAN.

FORTY-FIFTH REGIMENT, N.Y.S.V.V.
NASHVILLE, TENN., August 20.

It is now some time since last I wrote to you. Until lately, our regiment has seen some times that is only known to a soldier. On the 8th of July, orders came for the regiment to go to Nashville to relieve a regiment that has been two years in service, and never in the front, and was anxious to get there. When we left the rifle-pits, we could plainly see Atlanta in the distance. We left the brigade, [Col. James S.] Robertson's, of Hooker's Veterans, and took up our march for Marietta, which was fourteen miles. We arrived there at 3 o'clock on the afternoon of the 9th. There we got transportation for Nashville, where we arrived on the 13th inst. We marched to the outskirts of town, and there we struck our camp to await orders, which came the next day. Company F was detailed to the Capital. Companies B, C, and E are doing guard-duty at the State Prison. Companies H and A take Rebel prisoners and deserters to Louisville, Kentucky.

The weather here is fine for a country like this, the only fault that we find is that it is very hot, but the boys stand it well. Last week one of our men that was home on furlough got love-struck, and went and hung himself out in the woods, where he was found the next day by one of the drummers belonging to the regiment. He was a flat.

Our old dog "Sport" is no more. He got killed last week by some other dogs with whom he got a skirmishing, and he being well advanced in years, could not stand the fatigue; he might have got the best of them had they not attacked him from the rear and flank with too strong a force. The consequence was, poor dog "Sport" got killed. He was the favorite of the whole regiment, as he was with the boys in all the battles of the Potomac and Cumberland Army, and that the Eleventh, now the Twentieth Corps, has been in. Old dog "Sport" was always behind the regimental colors, and took to catching the bullets after lying on the ground.

I am now going to Chattanooga with some deserters.

OLD WAR HORSE.

FIFTY-SIXTH REGIMENT, N.Y.S.V.V.
ADVANCE PICKET, PORT ROYAL FERRY, S.C., Aug. 16.

Since our last expedition we have remained very quiet, with the exception of moving to the advanced picket-line on this island. The reason of our being ordered there is on account of several regiments having been ordered to Virginia. General [William] Birney with a large brigade has gone to re-enforce General Grant, and what troops are left in the Department of the South are enjoying a period of quiet repose.

The unhealthy season has commenced, and there is a great deal of sickness. The sick report of our regiment is about one hundred and forty. We have lost quite a number of men lately, among whom was First-Sergeant Jacob B. Dewitt, Company G. His time was nearly expired, and he soon expected to go home and meet his friends, but alas! in three short days he was carried away.

It is a very dull life on picket, and were it not for the flags of truce which come over every few days, we would almost die of ennui.

The Colonel, Adjutant, and a Lieutenant, went over to Rebeldom a few days ago, and made arrangements for Major [John] Anderson, of General Foster's staff, to meet Major Long, of General Sam Jones' staff, in regard to the exchange of some prisoners. This morning, the meeting took place, and there was some prisoners exchanged, among whom was Lieutenant-Colonel [Henry M.] Hoyt, Fifty-second Regiment Pennsylvania Volunteers, who was captured last month. The Union men who were exchanged looked very rough, and were almost starved. They said that they were picked out of fifteen thousand on account of their looking so well. If they are a specimen of the best, there is no telling what the rest are.

The most important event now is when the mailboat arrives with our weekly mail, and brings us letters and papers from our friends; the most welcome of all is our favorite MERCURY.

We are looking with great interest on the campaigns of Grant and Sherman, and continually pray that they may succeed, and this winter see the end of the war, and we be allowed to return home.

When anything important occurs, you will again hear from

GUS.

DEATH OF MORE CORRESPONDENTS—Since the commencement of the present war, no journal published in the United States has ever been able to approach us in our feature of "Army Correspondence", either as regards variety or reliability. Among the writers contributing to our weekly budget, we can enumerate many whose professional pens gave the reader both an attractive and interesting recital of this or that regiment's doing. It afforded us pleasure to receive their letters weekly; but a pang of pain came every now and then, as the sad tidings of death of some esteemed correspondent reached us. We have, in this way parted with many a noble-hearted friend. It is not for us, however, to alter the fate of a wonderful Providence. As the leaves fall and the flowers fade, we can but gather their remains together, and treasure them up among the bright and beautiful things of the Past.

During the last week, no less than two of our correspondents have died. One is Captain William D'Arcy, Company F, Forty-eighth Regiment, Volunteers; the other, Sergeant William H. Doak, Company F, Eighty-fourth Regiment, N.G.S.N.Y. The former was killed by a piece of shell—the latter was drowned at Great Falls, Md. Young Doak was well known in New York. He gave up a situation in the Custom House, and went out with the Eighty-fourth from pure love for a soldier's life. His remains are to be buried to-day from his late residence, No. 261 West Fifty-fourth street.

THIRTEENTH N.Y. CAVALRY

CAMP NEAR FORT BUFFALO, August 28.

Last Sunday [Aug. 21] night was a busy one around camp, preparing for a grand scout that was to leave on the following day. The cooks in all the companies were busy most of the night cooking three days' rations for the men, the blacksmiths were also kept to work steady shoeing the horses, and the men working with a good will, to be in readiness at any moment the next morning at the sound of "boots and saddles" on Monday morning. The sutlers were also kept busy dealing out crackers, cheese, cakes, etc., to all those that had tickets or greenbacks.

Every man that could be possibly spared was obliged to go on the scout, such as teamsters, blacksmiths, buglers, clerks, and even some of the men belonging to the band, which would leave all the picket-duty to be done by the Sixteenth N. Y. Cavalry, we having done the same while they were on a scout.

Our boys returned on Thursday morning last, having captured forty horses and six prisoners; they also brought in saddles, wagons, guns, etc.

During their absence, the Rebs, under Mosby, took advantage to attack the stockade at Annandale, where there is a detachment of the Sixteenth Cavalry. Our boys fought bravely, and drove the Graybacks, killing and wounding many of them. One sergeant and two of the Sixteenth's men were captured; a demand of surrender was made three times by Mosby, each demand being preceded by shots from his artillery. The demand was obstinately refused, and finally the Rebs were forced to retire. During the small hours of Thursday morning last, some of Mosby's men made a raid on our old camp at Falls Church, capturing ten sick and disabled slaves and two men who were doing picket there, also shooting one of the pickets in the breast, which will no doubt prove fatal. The man belonged to the Sixteenth; our scout had just come in, and had hardly got the saddle off, when the bugle sound to arms reached their ears, although pretty well fagged out. The boys were up and ready, and had the Johnnies made an attack on our camp, they would have had a good reception in the way of cold lead. Of late, Mosby and his men are getting very daring, as our old camp, where they took the horses from, is not over a quarter of a mile from our present one. The boys are awaiting anxiously for the paymaster, as they are running out of greenbacks; but I am afraid they will have to be easy until the middle of next month, as they will be mustered on the 31st, for four months' pay and will not be paid until then, when for the first time they will receive their pay at the rate of $16 a month. Although getting more pay, the boys' rations seem to be getting smaller; which, no doubt, makes up for the extra three dollars, for the past month we have not had either potatoes, molasses, or apples allowed to us in our rations. Has Uncle Sam stopped it, or is there some underwork about it? Probably the Brigade Commissary can inform us.

For the last three nights, our men have slept with their arms and equipments, in case of an attack from [Elijah V. (Lige)] White's or Mosby's men. Their horses have been kept saddled all night, so at a moment's notice they would be in readiness. Last night, the whole camp was alarmed by hearing two shots fired, when "to arms" was sounded, and the boys turned out double quick, but it was a false alarm, as one of the pickets mistook a large stump for a body of Rebs, and fired; the next picket hearing the shot, also did the same.

I see by all the papers that there is considerable talk of peace, and I say, let us have peace by all means, if we can come to any terms with that arch-traitor Uncle Jeff, as I know that the boys—I mean the privates who do all the fighting—are tired of this long war; and it is the truth, that most of the officers in our Army will still insist that the men under them wish to still keep fighting, but such is not the fact; as long as the officers, from general down, can haul in Uncle Sam's greenbacks, they will talk fight; but I am afraid if Grant does as he said he would in regard to fighting it out if it takes all summer, had better put in the clause ere it is too late, and all winter too, as summer is departing fast. Hoping I have not intruded too much on that valuable sheet, the MERCURY, I will close.

Yours respectfully,   EUPHCANISTIFICAN.

SEVENTEENTH REGIMENT, N.Y.V.V.

BEFORE ATLANTA, GA. August 19.

A spell of idleness and an irksome confinement in a trench, a confinement enforced more by Rebel bullets than by any military order, has thrown me upon my own resources for to kill time and ennui; and the best way of doing that at present, it has occurred to me, would be to drop you a slight sketch of the events in this regiment for the last few months.

On the 27th of May, our brigade, consisting of the Seventeenth New York, Thirty-second Wisconsin, and Twenty-fifth Indiana, as also a force of cavalry, started from Decatur on an expedition to Kortland, a town about twenty miles from Decatur, and which has always been occupied by the Rebels, and been the head-quarters of [Gen. Philip D.] Roddy or whatever guerilla-leader happened to be in command of that section of

Alabama. Three miles outside of Decatur, we were fired on by a Rebel force of observation, which had always pretended to keep on a mock siege of the place, and from thence to Pond Spring, a running fight was kept up between our advance (cavalry) and their rear; they taking advantage of all the inequalities of ground for to contest our progress. Near Pond Spring, about three miles from Kortland, we were brought to a stand by Roddy, with a force estimated to be between one and two thousand. Our force must have been near this latter number. Two guns, posted on a commanding position, greeted our arrival. We were immediately formed into line of battle, and waited for our artillery to return the Rebel compliments. While our three guns were getting into position, our boys had their coolness tested severely by the well aimed shots of the Rebel battery, which threw its shell a few yards before and behind our motionless line, and scattered fragments of iron into our ranks. Singular to say, no serious hurt was given to any one. Our guns once in position, soon silenced Johnny Reb. Our lines advanced; and the battle, apparently so imminent, sunk at once into a skedaddle on the part of the Rebs. That night, we slept in Kortland. Private property was respected, and the citizens treated with courtesy. A great deal of Confederate stores fell into our hands, and other advantages gained by the expedition. We returned to Decatur with a number of prisoners the next day. The loss of the expedition consisted only in a few wounded. The Rebels had several killed. A Major Williams, of the Alabama Regiment, was killed during the running skirmish on the road.

An interval of one month now took place before the next expedition of importance. During that interval the Rebs had returned to Kortland, and were reported to be concentrating for an attack on Sherman's line of communication. General Rousseau had taken away nearly all our cavalry on his great raid, and the Rebs consequently expected they could perfect new plans without fear of surprise. Colonel Pattison had his regiment of cavalry encamped at Pond Spring. To surprise that regiment, Colonel Grower, Acting Brigadier-General, planned an expedition and conducted it himself. The force under his command consisted of the Seventeenth New York, Twenty-fifth Indiana, Eighteenth Michigan, a detail from the Thirty-second Wisconsin, and a few cavalry. The regiments being all small, and not in their full strength, did not, perhaps, clubbed together, make more than one thousand men; if anything, the number was less than that figure.

June 28, the expedition left Decatur, marched all day along the bank of the Tennessee River, in the shade of the trees, and apparently bivouacked about 10 o'clock, P.M. Three hours afterward, we were roused from our sleep, and kept on again toward our destination. The night was dark, not a moonbeam gleamed through its somber stillness; myriads of glittering fire-flies, however, seemed determined to substitute their evanescent light for that of the missing luminary. The appearance of our line of march was, therefore, singularly fantastic and pleasing. At daybreak, we were one mile from their camp, and were congratulating ourselves on being about to make a complete surprise, when we heard a bugle-sound ring through the air. That sound shook our confidence as we hurried on; we reached their picket-lines and burst through it toward their camp, and then for about twenty minutes there was a grand scare in Rebeldom. A company of their cavalry were just about proceeding to ascertain our whereabouts, when we saved them the trouble by appearing ourselves. They fired and fell back, we fired and followed up; a few volleys in front seemed to indicate a stand on the part of the Rebels. Our bugles sounded the charge, our men cheered. The word was given, "double-quick", and forward we went like an avalanche. This vigorous onslaught disconcerted the Rebs, who gave way at once, and we entered their camp at one side as they left by the other. I have not space here to give the details of Col. Grower's plan, which was an excellent one. It failed in its chief object, because we could not march our men through the clouds and so drop on the Rebs unexpectedly; for to surprise the Rebels in their own country is like surprising a rat in his hole, or a weasel in his burrow. As it was, we came within twenty minutes of bagging the whole lot.

When we started from Decatur, they, of course, received speedy information of it. Col. Grower's line of march, however, must have considerably puzzled them, as we could not be found on any of the roads. On examining all the roads, which of course took some time, they would come to the conclusion that we were in the bed of the river, in the sky, or in the woods—the latter was the correct one. That would still leave them uncertain, as the woods here are large and numerous. They expected us, but did not expect us too soon, and did not expect us from the direction we came, which was in their rear.

On summing up the events of the expedition, I have concluded that the whole affair was a mutual surprise. We surprised them in their rear by coming so soon, and they surprised us by being so ready to run away. The proof that we came sooner than was expected, is pretty substantial; being in the shape of a Rebel commissary train, the good things of which our Quartermasters duly appreciated, and also some sixteen or seventeen gray-clad individuals, a part of whom we caught napping or putting on their scanty clothing. Those who do not want to be caught by the Yankees must get up earlier in the morning than these gentlemen did. The camp destroyed, all that was useful in it conveyed to Decatur, we turned our backs to Kortland itself; whose garrison, if they knew our real strength, would have come out and gobbled us up without ceremony.

For want of space, I have not mentioned the doings of any regiment in particular, from that of others; each did equally well. The *éclat* of the whole affair, perhaps, attached to the Seventeenth, who charged with an ardor quite new to the more sedate Western troops.

We are now, as you have perceived by the heading of this letter, in front of Atlanta. We left Decatur on the 5th inst., and arrived here on the 7th. The trip was a very interesting one, as there are many beautiful landscapes along the bank of the Tennessee River, which cannot be surpassed even in classic Italy. Chattanooga, Lookout Mountain, and the numerous fortifications around were, of course, objects of great interest; and from thence to Dalton, and on to Marietta, along the railroad, were the numerous and powerful lines of earthworks thrown up by both armies in their different positions. That spades were trumps, we had here ample testimony, especially so when they are played on the Union side. If those works could be preserved by law, for the benefit of our curious posterity, they would last for many generations. Each battle-field would thus have its own monuments to celebrate the events that transpired there; each rifle-pit and battery speaking more to the heart of the spectator than would whole volumes of history. Since our arrival here, we have had our full share of duty—one day putting up breastworks, while exposed to the fire of sharpshooters; another day, on the skirmish-line, exchanging shots with our Rebel foes in the rifle-pits; and the next day perhaps building a fort, and supporting its battery when it has been established. As our lines approach Atlanta, our shelter-tents follow them—we have consequently been the whole time since we came here within range of the guns of Atlanta. While putting up breastworks near the skirmish-line, we had one man killed and five or six wounded. While camped behind our works another day, a shell from the Rebs tore through our tents, almost decapitating a man of Company K, killing him instantly, and wounding several others. Company K seems to be peculiarly unfortunate, and have lost more men since we came here than all the other companies of the regiment together. Every shell, solid shot, or musket-ball, traveling in our direction, seems to have a special inclination for the quarters of that company.

Our approaches to Atlanta, if slow, are steady. We are now within rifle-shot of their works, and have not stopped advancing. Atlanta itself is not visible from our camp, on account of intervening trees and declivities of ground; but the town itself, is known to be so near, that I have only to stand upon the place I am now writing and fire my piece, to drop a musket-ball into the town. The ball, it is true, would be pretty well spent near the end of its flight, but nevertheless, its contact with a Rebel's skull would be apt to give one of the colliding substances a headache, and I hardly think the suffering substance would be the bullet.

We have not had a mail from home for several days, for reasons best known to Forrest, Roddy, Wheeler, or some other enterprising Reb; but our letters are now arrived, the trains coming in yesterday. Cutting our communications is a thing often talked of in the Confederacy, but seldom done. The individuals who ought to don't, if they were able, seem to be very well aware that stopping travel from the North very often expedites their own journey to Federal prisons.

We are attached to the Third Brigade, Fourth Division, Sixteenth Corps—Corps Commander, General Dodge; Division, [Gen. Thomas] Ransom; Brigade, Colonel Wm. P. C. Grower, Acting Brigadier-General. Major J. O. Martin is and has been in command of the regiment for several months.

The health of the regiment is good, and its discipline and morale are excellent.

There have been promotions and other changes in the regiment since I last wrote to you. I am not just at the present moment, posted well enough on these changes to state them.

Au revoir,   A. K.

September 11, 1864
THIRD REGIMENT (INFANTRY) N.Y.V.
IN THE TRENCHES, BEFORE PETERSBURG, Sept. 5.

Since writing my last, we have had a short visit to Butler's lines, at Bermuda Hundred; our brigade holding the works, while the rest of the corps were with General Hancock at Deep Bottom. On their return, an order from General Birney was read to them, complimenting their gallant conduct during the campaign. It would have been well if he had not given of the negro as an example for white veterans to follow. If they had followed their example on the 30th of July, the disasters of that day would have been still greater.

While at Bermuda we had a very pleasant time. The duty was fatiguing, but not dangerous, as there was no firing on picket. A regular exchange of courtesies were kept up among the privates on both sides; where they allowed, the Rebellion would be settled without the aid of peace conventions. It was nothing uncommon to see them meet half-way between the lines, shake hands, exchange papers, and have a general chat over the national affairs. The Rebs appear very anxious that little Mac should be the next President, as they think it will end the war satisfactorily to both parties. This peaceable state of affairs was too good to last long; for, about 2 o'clock on the morning of the 25th of August, a detachment of our regiment was hastily called out to re-enforce the picket-line, as our friendly Johnnies had made a sudden attack on the weaker part of the line; and we were just in time to take a hand in a brisk skirmish, which lasted two hours, and resulted in the capture of fifty prisoners, while our loss was one officer and two privates, who were captured while trying to rally a detail of another regiment who broke on our left.

When we returned to camp orders were to pack up and leave for Petersburg, where we now are, in the trenches. This makes our third visit to this place; the men are all familiar with every part of the line, for they have done duty on every front.

Our regiment is now very small; we only have about ninety privates and two commissioned officers. Capt. [Jay M.] Wicks is in command, and Lieutenant [James] Reeve Acting Adjutant. Both are good officers.

Five of our best and bravest lieutenants were dismissed the service by General Butler for offering their resignations in front of the enemy. Although the men think they had just cause in so doing, I feel proud to say it was not cowardice that caused them to resign; for their bravery had been tried on many a battle-field.

The boys are all anxious to hear the news from the Chicago Convention. If McClellan is the nominee, he will command the almost unanimous vote of the New York Volunteers.

HIGH HAT.

NINETY-FIFTH REGIMENT, N.Y.V.
YELLOW HOUSE, WELDON RAILROAD, Sept. 4.

Again has the Ninety-fifth passed through the ordeal of terrible fighting. On the night of the 18th of August, our Corps (Fifth) moved from the position near Petersburg, advanced toward the left, and took possession of a good portion of the Weldon Railroad, but not without resistance although the enemy was not there in force, as General Grant had maneuvered the Second Corps and other troops on the right, and by so doing caused the enemy to draw his force in that direction. As soon as we held the road, up went the breastworks, and our brigade got in readiness to give the Johnnies their due if they attacked. Attack they did. On Sunday morning our regiment was on picket. Down came the Rebels in line of battle. Our picket-line, owing to the persistency of Major Bard, who was in command, kept them in check until they were actually on top of us, and then, with their fire and the fire of our men in the works, we were in rather a tight situation. We got in, however, but left about seventy men on the field, most of whom were taken prisoners, the rest wounded or killed. The Rebels, in the meantime, had charged up to within twenty feet of the breastworks from which our brigade were pouring in a deadly fire; in fact, it was too hot for them. They threw themselves on the ground, and held up their hands in token of surrender. A few went back, but very few. Our brigade took those who were not wounded prisoners and during the fight also captured three stand of colors. It was indeed a bright day for the old Second Brigade. Colonel Hoffman, who was in command, was highly excited at the success his brigade had won on that memorable Sunday. But, alas! the Ninety-fifth lost some of its best men, who stood the brunt of the morning's fight on the skirmish-line. Major Bard received a wound in the knee.

At the time of writing this, notwithstanding the close proximity of the Rebs, we are enjoying the comforts of camp life.

Yours,　　　　　　　　　　　　　　　　　ALGIERS.

FORTIETH NEW YORK VETERAN VOLUNTEERS
BEFORE PETERSBURG, VA., Sept. 4.

Our brigade is now occupying a position in the front line of works firmly held by the Fifth Corps previous to their never to be forgotten *coup de main* on the Weldon Railroad. Our works do not exceed five hundred yards from those of the enemy, the intervening space being occupied by the pickets and videttes of both parties, thus bringing us within convenient speaking-distance; and as there is a mutual understanding existing between both parties (and one which I think ought to be more generally observed, on their side in particular), or, at least, in our immediate neighborhood, that is, no picket-firing, it leaves us very quiet and easy, comparatively speaking, although the close vicinity of the Southern chivalry call for our constant presence and immediate service, should any demonstration take place. Thus every one is on the alert, the works being manned through the night by reliefs, which, with the picket-duty, and continued watchfulness, render it more fatiguing and severe than would be at first supposed. Occasionally we have fierce artillery duels between the forts in our immediate neighborhood, in which some excellent skill is shown in the art of gunnery, and which is enjoyed as quite a treat by the rank and file. It is amusing to hear, when a good shot has been fired on either side, making a visible demonstration on the works, the loud exultant yell which will be set up by the active party, but beyond this firing, we are on very good terms with the Johns, and a continual system of exchange and barter in small wares is carried on, the parties meeting half way. The troops in our front are Floridians, and are sadly tired of the war, and anxious to get back to their own State; and from their accounts, our maintaining possession of the Weldon Road has encroached considerably on their commissariat, and raised things to an enormous price in Richmond. Our Army is lying quiet and resting now. In fact, as far as a soldier's opinion will go, I do not see how we can do any more, without re-enforcements. Give Grant the men, and he will complete the work he has commenced; it is well known that without the material he cannot succeed.

The weather for the past two months has been intensely hot, causing the Army generally to suffer a great deal; but the heat is now beginning to moderate, and the nights are getting to be cool. So now, whilst we are thus resting on our arms, all cares and anxieties are forgotten, and every intervening subject cast aside, for the great political struggle that is now, and about to take place in the North. If the vote could be taken throughout the Union Army, to decide between Little Mac and Lincoln for the Presidential Chair, how soon it would be settled; true, we have an Abolitionist now, here and there rearing his solitary rabid head, and occasionally we hear some one crowing for our reigning President. Oh! how our hearts exult, our bosoms swell with joy, and our confidence in the people begins again to be restored, as we read the proceedings in the Convention at Chicago. And the successful nomination of the long-neglected, maligned (and despised by the Administration), George B. McClellan, the prayers and jubilees of his old Army—of the Potomac will follow every movement that is made in favor of his election, and pray for his success and although we have not the slightest doubt that he is the choice of the people, as he has such particular friends in power, there is no telling yet, but bribery, patronage, and treachery may stultify the efforts of honest men; and, as in the one of the sword at the Metropolitan Fair, his interest was shamelessly and clandestinely bought out of the affair. But let the matter terminate as it will, he will have the satisfaction of knowing that he is the man for the people, and enjoys their confidence; while the contrary may be painfully plain to his opponent. We wish you every success, Geo. B. McClellan. I have enclosed the Richmond *Examiner* of to-day, just for what it is worth, but the price of subscription is rather startling. There are printed orders passing round too, inciting aliens to desert over to the Rebel lines, who find themselves unfairly enlisted in the Union service, and they will furnish them with transportation to any place they may desire, out of the United States. The order is signed by [Samuel] Cooper, the Rebel Adjutant-General, but I do not think the bait will take.

WATERFORD.

FORTY-EIGHTH REGIMENT, N.Y.V.

NEAR PETERSBURG, VA., Sept. 4.

Since my last, we have again come back to Petersburg; but this time we are farther on the right of the line, occupying the place of the Eighteenth Corps.

We left Bermuda Hundred on the 28th of August, and marched during the day until we reached this place. As we arrived here, we were greeted by a shower of shell from the Johnnies, giving us our old welcome. They seem to know the Second Division of the Tenth Corps, and whenever and wherever we appear we receive a warm reception, but I dare say the Johnnies think that the boys give as good as they receive, for many a Rebel has fallen before the gallant boys of Foster's (formerly Turner's) Division.

There is nothing going on here at present. Occasional artillery-duels occur once in a while; and if our fire does not do more damage to them than theirs to us, I think it would be better to stop this waste of ammunition. One thing I see is, that our shot falls into the city of Petersburg; and when the mortar Dictator, mounted on a platform-car, comes up the tracks, and sends a shell into the ill-fated city, we can see the dilapidated appearance of the place.

The all-engrossing topic of the day here seems to be the Chicago Convention, and who is going to be the nominee. The soldiers all want peace, but do not wish to have it upon the "Vallandigham and Wood Peace Platform"; to make a compromise with the Rebels than make any other terms with the South than make the restoration of the Union as it was, we will show Jeff and his myrmidons that we are not yet tired of fighting them, and that we will do it to the bitter end. But we want another Administration. The bungling of Lincoln and his Cabinet should not be tolerated for another term; give us a live man, who will take the reins of Government in his hands and teach the Rebels that they have another person to deal with besides the blundering old fogies who are now the powers that be.

Little Mac seems to be the favorite with the men in the Army, and he will receive the solders' vote, at least, the largest share of it, and it is hoped by all that he will be elected.

There is a movement on foot here that will shortly tell on the Rebels; it is to be another explosion. Where it will be I dare not tell, but the mine is nearly ready for springing.

LEO.

MARTYRS TO THE ADMINISTRATION

{We add the atrocious experiences below to our indictment of the Administration. It requires no comment, being a plain narrative, sworn to before the law, of the condition of the Union volunteers in the camp of Andersonville, Georgia. Thirty-five thousand starving, insane, and invalid men are existing in the direct misery there, and the callousness of an Executive in their behalf has enlisted the indignation even of the Rebels.

The authors of the annexed were exchanged on the 16th of August, and, with three others, were appointed by their companions in prison as a deputation to see Lincoln in their behalf.}

I am a private in Eighty-second Regiment N.Y.V., Co. G. Was captured with about 800 Federal troops in front of Petersburg, on the 22nd of June, 1864. We were kept at Petersburg two days, at Richmond, on Belle Isle, three days, then conveyed by rail to Lynchburg. Marched seventy-five miles to Danville, thence by rail to Andersonville, Georgia. At Petersburg, we were treated fairly, being under the guard of old soldiers of an Alabama regiment; at Richmond, we came under the authority of the notorious and inhuman Major Turner, and the equally notorious Home Guard. Our ration was a pint of beans, four ounces of bread, and three ounces of meat a-day. Another batch of prisoners joining us, we left Richmond 1,000 strong. All blankets, haversacks, canteens, money, valuables of every kind, extra clothing, and, in some cases, the last shirt and drawers had been previously taken from us. At Lynchburg, we were placed under the Home Guard, officered by Major and Captain Moffett. The march to Danville was a weary and painful one of five days, under a torrid sun, many of us falling helpless by the way, and soon filling the empty wagons of our train. On the first day we received a little meat, but the sum of our rations for the five days was thirteen crackers. During the six days by rail to Andersonville, meat was given us twice, and the daily ration was four crackers.

On entering the Stockade Prison at Camp Sumter, we found it crowded with 28,000 of our fellow-soldiers. By crowded, I mean that it was difficult to move in any direction without jostling, and being jostled. This prison is an open space, sloping on both sides, originally seventeen acres, now twenty-five, in the shape of a parallelogram, without trees or shelter of any kind. The soil is sand, over a bottom of clay. The fence is made of upright trunks of trees, about twenty feet high, near the top of which are small platforms, where the guards are stationed.

Twenty feet inside, and parallel to the fence, is a light railing, forming the dead line, beyond which the projection of a foot or finger is sure to bring the deadly bullet of the sentinel.

Through the grounds, at nearly right angles with the walls of the stockade flows a stream ankle-deep, and near the middle of the inclosure spreading out into a swamp of six acres, filled with refuse wood, stumps, and debris of the camp. Before entering the inclosure, the stream, or more properly sewer, passes through the camp of the Guards, receiving from this source and others further up, a large amount of the vilest material, even the contents of the sink. The water is of a dark color, and an ordinary glass would collect a thick sediment. This was our only drinking and cooking water. It was our custom to filter it as best we could, through our remnants of haversacks, shirts, and blouses. Wells had been dug, but the water either proved so productive of diarrhea, or so limited in quantity, that they were of no general use. The cook-house was situated on the stream, just outside the stockade, and its refuse of decaying offal was thrown into the water, a greasy coating covering much of the surface. To these was added the daily large amount of base matter from the camp itself. There was a system of policing, but the means were so limited, and so large a number of the men was rendered irresolute and depressed by imprisonment, that the work was very imperfectly done. One side of the swamp was naturally used as a sink, the men usually going out some distance into the water. Under the summer-sun, this place early became corruption too vile for description, the men breeding disgusting life, so that the surface of the water moved as with a gentle breeze.

The new-comers, on reaching this, would exclaim, "is this hell!" yet they soon would become callous, and enter unmoved the horrible rotten mass. The Rebel authorities never removed any filth. There was seldom any visitation by the officers in charge. Two surgeons were at one time sent by President Davis to inspect the camp, but a walk through a small section gave them all the information they desired, and we never saw them again.

The guard usually numbered about sixty-four, eight at each end, and twenty-four on a side. On the outside, were fortifications, on high ground overlooking and perfectly commanding us, mounting twenty-four twelve-pound Napoleon Parrotts. We were never permitted to go outside, except at times, in small squads, to gather our fire-wood. During the building of the cook-house, a few, who were carpenters, were ordered out to assist.

Our only shelter from the sun, and rain, and night-dews, was what we could make by stretching over us our coats or scraps of blankets, which a few had, but generally there was no attempt, by day or night, to protect ourselves.

The rations consisted of eight ounces of corn bread (the cob being ground with the kernel), and generally sour, two ounces of condemned pork, offensive in appearance and smell. Occasionally, about twice a week, two table-spoonfuls of rice, and, in place of the pork, the same amount (two tablespoonfuls) of molasses was given us about twice a month. This ration was brought into camp at 4, P.M., and thrown from the wagons to the ground, the men being arranged in divisions of 270, subdivided into squads of 19 and 30. It was the custom to consume the whole ration at once, rather than save any for the next day. The distribution being often unequal, some would lose the rations altogether. We were allowed no dish or cooking utensil of any kind. On opening the camp in the winter, the first 2,000 prisoners were allowed skillets, one to fifty men; but these were soon taken away. In the best of my knowledge, information, and belief, our ration was, in quality, a starving one—it being either too foul to be touched, or too raw to be digested.

The cook-house went into operation about May 10, prior to which we cooked our own rations. It did not prove at all adequate to the work (30,000 is a large town); so that a large proportion were still obliged to prepare their own food. In addition to the utter inability of many to do this, through debility and sickness, we never had a supply of wood. I have often seen men, with a little bag of meal in hand, gathered from several rations, starving to death for want of wood; and, in desperation, would mix the raw material with water and try to eat it.

The clothing of the men was miserable in the extreme. Very few had shoes of any kind; not 2,000 had coats and pants, and those were the late-comers. More than one-half were indecently exposed, and many were naked.

The usual punishment was, to place the men in the stocks outside, near the Captain's quarters. If a man was missing at roll-call, the squad of ninety to which he belonged was deprived of ration. The "dead-line" bullet, already referred to, spared no offender. One poor fellow, just from Sherman's Army—his name was Roberts—was trying to wash his face near the dead-line railing, when he slipped on the clayey bottom, and fell, with his head just outside the fatal border. We shouted to him, but it was too late. "Another guard would have a furlough," the men said. It was a common belief among our men, arising from statements made by the guard, that General Winder issued an order that any one of the guard who should shoot a Yankee outside of the "dead-line" should have a month's furlough, but there probably was no truth in this. About two a day were thus shot, some being cases of suicide, brought on by mental depression or physical misery, the poor fellows throwing themselves or madly rushing outside the "line".

The mental condition of a large portion of the men was melancholy, beginning in despondency and sending to a kind of stolid and idiotic indifference. Many spent much time in arousing and encouraging their fellows, but hundreds were lying about motionless or stalking vacantly to and fro, quite beyond any help which could be given them within their prison walls. These cases were frequent among those who had been imprisoned but a short time. There were those who were captured at the first Bull Run, July 1861, and had known Belle Isle from the first, yet had preserved their physical and mental health to a wonderful degree. Many were wise and resolute enough to keep themselves occupied—some cutting bone and wood ornaments, making their knives out of iron hoops—others in manufacturing ink out of the rust from those same hoops, and with rude pens sketching or imitating bank notes.

As far as we saw General Winder and Captain [Henry] Wirz, the former was kind and considerate in his manner, the latter harsh, though not without kindly feeling.

It is a melancholy and mortifying fact, that some of our trials come from our own men. At Belle Isle and Andersonville there was among us a gang of desperate men, ready to prey on their fellows. Not only thefts and robberies, but even murders were committed. Affairs became so serious at Camp Sumter, that an appeal was made to General Winder, who authorized an arrest and trial by a criminal court. Eighty-six were arrested, and six were hung, besides others who were severely punished. These proceedings effected a marked change for the better.

Some few weeks before being released, I was ordered to act as a clerk in the hospital. This consists simply of a few scattered trees and fly-tents, and is in charge of Dr. [Joseph] White, an excellent and considerate man, with very limited means, but doing all in his power for his patients. He has twenty-five assistants, besides those detailed to examine for admittance to the hospital. These examinations were made in a small stockade attached to the main one, to the inside door of which the sick came or were brought by their comrades, the number to be removed being limited.

Lately, in consideration of the rapidly-increasing sickness, it was extended to 150 daily. That this was too small an allowance is shown by the fact that the dead within our stockade were from thirty to forty a day. I have seen 150 bodies waiting passage to the "dead-house", to be buried with those who died in hospital. The average of deaths through the earlier months was thirty a day; at the time I left the average was over 130, and one day the record showed 146.

The proportion of deaths from starvation, not including those consequent on the diseases originating in the character and limited quantity of food, such as diarrhea, dysentery, and scurvy, I cannot state, but to the best of my knowledge, information, and belief, there were scores every month. We could at any time point out many for whom such a fate was inevitable, as they lay or feebly walked, mere skeletons. For example, in some cases the inner edges of the two bones of the arm, between the elbow and wrist, with the intermediate blood vessels, were plainly visible when held toward the light. The ration in quantity was, perhaps, barely sufficient to sustain life, and the cases of starvation were generally those whose stomachs could not retain what had become entirely indigestible.

For a man to find on waking that his comrade by his side was dead, was an occurrence too common to be noted. I have seen death in almost all the forms of the hospital and battle-field, but the daily scenes in Camp Sumter exceeded in the extremity of misery all my previous experience.

The work of burial is performed by our own men, under guard and orders, twenty-five bodies being placed in a single pit, without headboards, and the sad duty performed with indecent haste. Sometimes our men were rewarded for this work with a few sticks of fire-wood, and I have known them to quarrel over a dead body for the job.

Dr. White is able to give the patients a diet but little better than the prison-ration—a little flour porridge, arrow-root, whiskey and wild or hog tomatoes; in the way of medicine, I saw nothing but camphor, whiskey, and a decoction of some kind of bark—white oak, I think. He often expressed his regret that he had not more medicines. The limitation of military orders under which the surgeon in charge was placed is shown by the following occurrence: a supposed private, wounded in the thigh, was under treatment in the hospital, when it was discovered that he was a Major of a colored regiment. The Assistant-surgeon, under whose immediate charge he was, proceeded at once not only to remove him, but to kick him out; and he was returned to the stockade to shift for himself as well as he could. Dr. White could not or did not attempt to restore him.

After entering on my duties at the hospital, I was occasionally favored with double-rations and some wild tomatoes. A few of our men succeeded, in spite of the closest examination of our clothes in secreting some greenbacks, and, with these, were able to buy useful articles at exorbitant prices. A tea-cup of flour at $1; eggs, $3 to $6 a dozen; salt $4 a pound; molasses, $30 a gallon; nigger beans (a small, inferior article, diet of the slaves and pigs, but highly relished by us) fifty cents a pint. These figures, multiplied by ten, will give very nearly the prices in Confederate currency. Though the country abounded in pine and oak, sticks were sold to us at various prices, according to size.

Our men, especially the mechanics, were tempted with the offer of liberty and large wages to take the oath of allegiance to the Confederacy, but it was very rare that their patriotism, even, under such a fiery trial, ever gave way. I carry this message from one of my companions to his mother: "My treatment here is killing me, mother; but I die cheerfully for my country."

Some attempts were made to escape, but wholly in vain, for if the prison-walls and guards were passed, and the protecting woods reached, the blood-hounds were sure to find us out.

Tunneling was once attempted on a large scale; but, on the afternoon proceeding the night fixed on for our escape, an officer rode in and announced to us that the plot was discovered, and, from our huge pen, we could see, on the hill above us, the regiments just arriving to strengthen the guard. We had been betrayed. It was our belief that spies were kept in the camp, which could very easily be done.

The number in camp when I left was nearly 36,000 on August 16.

PRESCOTT TRACY, Eighty-second N.Y. Vols.

City and County of New York, as: H. G. Higginson and S. Noirot, being duly sworn, say: That the above statement of Prescott Tracy, their fellow-prisoner, agrees with their own knowledge and experiences.

H. C. HIGGINSON, Co. K, Nineteenth Illinois Vols.

SYLVESTER NOIROT, Co. B, Fifth New Jersey Vols.

Prescott Tracy, age 30, was six feet tall with blue eyes and brown hair. He enlisted in Company G, 82nd New York Infantry on Jan. 22, 1862; two months later he was promoted to first sergeant. On Oct. 20, 1862, Tracy was reported sick at Bolivar, Va. On Oct. 30, he deserted and was later reduced in ranks. Tracy was arrested in New York City and eventually returned to his regiment. On June 22, 1864 near Petersburg, Va., Tracy was captured and sent to Andersonville. Of the three exchanged prisoners, his stay was the shortest. No further information on Tracy is available.

Henry C. Higginson, age 21, enlisted on June 17, 1861 in Company H, 19th Illinois Infantry was captured in the battle of Chickamauga, Ga., on Sept. 20, 1863. No further information on Higginson is available.

Sylvester Noirot, age 31, enlisted on Aug. 11, 1861 in Co. B, 5th New Jersey Infantry; he listed his occupation as a printer. Noirot was captured at Mine Run, Va., on Dec. 1, 1863 and sent to Andersonville on Feb. 6, 1864. He died on March 21, 1905.

September 25, 1864
SIXTY-FIFTH REGIMENT, N.Y.S.V.V.
BERRYVILLE, VA., Sept. 20.

Since I last wrote, no material change either in position or duties has taken place. We still occupy the same camp, and are busily engaged in drilling and preparing ourselves for the coming campaign. When we shall move is not known, but it is believed that we will not remain much longer inactive. The Rebels are in our immediate front, and if they don't "hike out", we will not have to go very far before we meet them. Our pay-rolls have been made out, and sent to Washington, and it is hoped that our kind Uncle will send on the greenbacks, as speedily as possible, for as winter is fast approaching, we shall need his bounties to provide for our families. Yesterday, we had a grand review and inspection by Brigadier-General Emory Upton, the whole brigade paraded, and the display was elegant; the soldierly-bearing, good marching, and fine appearance of the chasseurs elicited universal praise. That article of humanity formerly known as contrabands, but latterly styled, by good authority, American citizens of African descent, are beginning to make their appearance. One curious-looking darkey came in our lines a few days ago, and on his arrival at our camp, he was met by a delegation of the Tycoons, who proceeded to invest Sambo with the rights of citizenship, by writing on his back, viz,

"Pass this disenthralled African to the realms of Benjamin F. [Butler]."

Whether he reached that place or not, I am unable to say; for these last few days—strange to say—we have heard nothing from the ubiquitous Mosby; he has kept himself very quiet, and we infer from his quietude, that he is watching for nappers. Our neighbors on our left (the Nineteenth Corps) have been frequently disturbed of late, by having their pickets attacked during the night. Small parties of the enemy advance during the night to annoy them; and while picket-firing is unpleasant at all times, it is doubly so at night, for it deprives the main body of necessary sleep. The weather, for the past few days, has been very fine, and still continues so. The previous heavy rains had nearly inundated us; and when Old Sol appeared, it was a great relief. How the soldiers will vote, seems to be an anxious inquiry. In my next I hope to give you the result of a vote that is to be taken in the regiment, although I feel certain in saying, before hand, that the supporters of Little Mac are largely in the majority. The health of the regiment continues good, and there is nothing that adds so much to their happiness as the arrival of the mails, and the SUNDAY MERCURY.

ANOTHER SUNDAY MERCURY CORRESPONDENT KILLED—Our readers will miss in future, and some will regret with us the loss of our special correspondent, A. K., and A. F. K., whose acceptable communications were always marked by choiceness of matter as well as ease and aptness of style.

The writer, Albert Finbar Kennelly, was killed on the 1st instant, in leading on his Company A, Seventeenth Regiment, N.Y.V., of which he was Orderly-Sergeant; he was before the line, and next to Colonel Grower, when both were shot down in the assault on Atlanta.

His friends, and they were many, will deplore the loss of one so loving, so gifted, and so young. He was but twenty-one years of age.

October 2, 1864
SEVENTY-THIRD REGIMENT, N.Y.V. (SECOND FIRE ZOUAVES)
NEAR PETERSBURG, VA., Sept. 26.

As you are the friend and defender of the soldier, and take delight in heralding their fame to the many readers of your most invaluable paper, I take great pleasure in informing you of the present state of affairs in our regiment, the Second Fire Zouaves, which, of late, amid the daily occurring military items and the silence of its former correspondent, has well-nigh become forgotten. There being a great many of the "fire-laddies" yet left in the regiment who have been on the Virginia war-path for over three years, and who have so splendidly run the "gauntlet" of all the lead and iron that the enemy have so unmercifully and indiscriminately "have" at them during that period, I deem it a favor on my part to acquaint their numerous friends who are running the "machines" at home, that they are as yet all right side up with ears, most of them being unbulleted, unbayoneted, and unsubdued, not withstanding the fiery ordeal through which they have already been launched. This is saying much, at the expense of a handful of men; but is nevertheless so, and they are sensibly proud of it.

The regiment is at present snugly ensconced in one of the largest and most formidable earthworks, in the shape of a fort, on the front of the Union lines. Getting thus relieved from the arduous duties consequent upon being in line behind breastworks, the "Zous," have all come to the conclusion that garrison-duty, so much heretofore lorded over by the Regulars, is not to be laughed at after all—as the daily routine of "biz" all comes so handy, easy, light, and all that sort of thing. In fact, they are doing the soldier up in magnificent style here, under the cover of irresistible bombproofs, big guns, and high ramparts, and the idea is prevalent among them that they will be let remain here. They are now shaping things to order for a regular siege, should one ever occur; and it will remain to be seen whether we can hold a fort as well as we have heretofore held rifle-pits and breastworks.

The fort is in close proximity to the Rebel works. It is just one mile and a half from the doomed "Cockade City", which looms up plainly to our sight, and not over three hundred yards from the front line of the Rebel works. Directly opposite us is the celebrated work of the enemy, known as "Fort Hell" and which contains the famous and chivalrous Washington Artillery—the pride of all their great guns. Frowning upon one another at so close a range, of course the two forts belch forth some awful thunder at times. This is generally called an artillery duel—but duel or no duel, the Yanks generally content themselves with the second retirement, amid cheers and flying colors. Of late, this has been the custom at every going down of the sun, but during the last day or two the Johnnys have kept themselves "silently mum."

Picket-duty has been and continues very severe in our immediate front, since the day that a portion of Hancock's forces so gallantly surprised and gobbled up the Rebel picket-line. They will not forgive the Yanks for perpetrating this little piece of barbarous conduct. So they keep up a ramping and incessant fire upon our pickets. But did they know the extent of their damages they would save their powder and lead for a better purpose. They will need it all by and by. Although our boys are pinned in their little rifle-pits, for the whole term of their twenty-four hours, they generally all come back none the worse off, having invariably a good budget to relate about the Rebs as seen through a shower of bullets.

Political and Presidential talk is in full rage among the "Zoos" just now. They know that the affair is already financed down to two powerful opponents, and that matters are already shaped for the fray, so they begin to give their ideas more publicity in regard to the election and merits of the candidates, viz: Little Mac and Lincoln. The regiment goes in for Democracy and Mac, as the following canvassed figures will plainly show, they having been carefully and fairly gotten this afternoon:—McClellan 120; Lincoln, 11. To-night, the dull monotony heretofore existing along the lines for some time has been broken. Loud cheers rend the air both from the picket-line and breastworks. Official rumor has it that [Philip H.] Sheridan completely whipped General Early in the Shenandoah Valley. This is what we have been expecting for the last week or more. I think Early has gathered his last crops. If Lee's granaries are again empty he must get them replenished from other quarters. It is our greatest hope that Sheridan has become the master of the situation in that important region.

Rumor is very fertile at present. Another important item is afloat that General Lee has just found out that his position around Petersburg and Richmond has become untenable by the loss of the Weldon Railroad, and Grant's threatening attitude toward the Danville road. Hence, he is believed to be removing all his siege-guns and trains to Danville, where he is forming a new base and shoveling up mother earth with a vengeance. This may be the truth or mere rumor; but, mark my words, the Confederacy is up to some trick, which may prove to be a giant Rebel skedaddle or an impetuous onslaught on some point of our lines. General Grant is eagerly watching his wily opponent, and is minutely posed in regard to his every move. When the storm comes it will come unexpected. It will be met gallantly and stubbornly at every point, so the sooner it comes the better for us and the country.

More anon,   SHELLPROOF.

FORTY-EIGHTH REGIMENT, N.Y.V.
NEAR PETERSBURG, VA., Sept. 27.

The men whose time expired, and who were not foolish enough to re-enlist, went home from here on the 17th ult., over one month after their time had expired. It is a shame for our Government to act in this way. There were men killed in our regiment after time had expired, but, by an edict of the War Department, they were forced to go into battle after having faithfully served their three years. This kind of work does not give those who are going home any inclination to again serve an Administration which has once deceived them. It would have been much better for the Administration to have sent these men home when their time had expired, and two-thirds of them would have re-enlisted, and also helped to support the Administration. Now it is different. Not one of them will vote for Lincoln and his shoddy-contractors who surround him.

There is another thing I wish to speak about—viz., our pay. It is now seven months since we were paid. Our dear ones at home are suffering for the necessaries of life, while those who are in power do not heed or trouble themselves. Why are we not paid? It is a burning shame, that those who are in the field exposing their lives for their country should thus be made to suffer. It makes a man unfit for military duty; it gives him no desire to battle and fight with the same vigor he would, if he knew his wife and children, or aged mother, were not actually suffering for the bare necessities of life; money that he has risked his life for, and braved all the hardships incidental to a soldier's life, is withheld from him. Go among the men of this Army, and you will constantly hear them talking about these things, and wishing that Lincoln was out and Little Mac was in. If the soldiers' vote will put him in the White House, he will get it; and we all hope that he will look to the interest of those who are braving their lives in defence of the Union. Deserters are constantly coming in, in squads of from five to twenty per day, and they all seem very glad to arrive within our lines. They are more closely watched than formerly. No enlisted man is allowed to go on vidette. Their officers do this duty, and any one who is seen by them trying to cross over, is shot down; but still, with all their watchfulness, they still come in. When an army comes down to such straits, it is time for them to quit and close up books.

Everything is quiet here. Picket-firing and occasional artillery-duels take place without any material damage to us. We very often converse with the Rebels. One of our boys asked a Johnny, "What Weldon

Railroad stock was worth?" And the answer was, "You go to the devil." Tonight, they asked our men what fresh beef was worth per pound (alluding to the recent capture of our cattle). Day by day is passed away in this style; but we are in hopes that Grant will lead us not only into Petersburg but Richmond, for winter-quarters.   LEO.

THIRD REGIMENT, N.Y.V.
PETERSBURG, VA., Sept. 27.

I was surprised to learn, through your correspondent "Leo", of the Forty-eighth N.Y.V., that another Rebel fort was undermined. I having as many opportunities as most men in our corps to get the latest news, I would have known it had anything of the kind been going on in our front. I think "Leo" must be quizzing the Rebs, knowing that your paper circulates very freely among our "wayward brethren" on the other side, they being very anxious to trade off their trashy sheets for the SUNDAY MERCURY. If "Leo" is in earnest let him take a second look, and he will find it to be a counter-mine.

The fever and ague is very prevalent here. Most of the regiments have a number of cases. Ours is an exception, the men being very healthy. Notwithstanding the good health, we are compelled by a general order to have our whisky dosed with quinine, which causes some very wry faces. Every morning at four o'clock the Commissary-Sergeant with his two pails and ladle, makes his appearance in the trenches. Then a cry is raised, "Fall in for your quinine!"

This morning, while receiving our medicine, the big mortar Dictator gave the signal for a salute, and all the artillery along the line opened right, left, and centre, raining shot and shell thick and fast on the devoted heads of the Johnnys. What told we have yet to learn, but suppose it to be another victory of Sheridan's.

The men of this command feel restless after hearing the news of so many brilliant victories, while they are compelled to remain inactive; but I suppose our presence here is of as much importance as more active duty.

Every day, large numbers of recruits arrive for every organization in the Army except the ancient Third. Deserters are coming in all the time; they say more would come, were it not for the extra vigilance of their officers. Every thirty men on outpost-duty have three officers to keep them from deserting. We have lately had a valuable acquisition in the shape of a loyal sutler, who issues red, white, and blue checks, and a sermon in favor of Father Abraham. The first is very acceptable, but the latter is labor lost; for a stranger visiting the Army would suppose the soldiers know of but one candidate, and that one is the hero of Antietam, Geo. B. McClellan.

We are anxiously waiting our share of the last loan. If there are any of Uncle Sam's agents sporting around All. Cenery's; we hope you will send them down here with the greenbacks, for we have not seen one in six months. The sight of the paymaster, I think, would cure many who complain of being moon-blind.
                                                                                    HOOLIHAN.

SEVENTY-SEVENTH REGIMENT, N.G.S.N.Y.
ELMIRA, N.Y., Sept. 26.

As many of the readers of the SUNDAY MERCURY are somewhat interested in the Seventy-seventh, I will endeavor to let them know a little of their whereabouts and doings. We arrived in Elmira on the 3rd day of August, and "put up" at Barracks No. 1, where we spent two days and nights, after which we were transferred to Camp Chemung, Barracks No. 3, where we have been doing duty ever since, guarding the "Rebs" whom the fortune of war has thrown into our hands. There are more than two thousand "graybacks" at this post, and a very hard-looking crowd they are; judging from their physique, they would be a great acquisition to the Rebel ranks just about this time. However, unless Father Abraham desires they should be exchanged, there is not much probability of their being in Dixie until "this cruel war is over".

New York city is well represented here, and Brooklyn comes in for a fair share also. Our regiment was mustered into the United States service for one hundred days from the 2nd day of August, the date of our leaving New York city. Battalion and company drills are the order of the day, and of course a dress-parade every evening. The guard-duty is very severe, about one-third of the whole effective strength of the regiment being on duty at one time in various places. Captain [William] McNally and a detachment of men left here about one week ago, in charge of a large number of substitutes, recruits, bounty-jumpers, etc., for the army of General Grant; they have not yet returned.

                    More anon from   MAC.

<u>October 9, 1864</u>
SIXTY-FIFTH N.Y.S.V.V.
NEAR HARRISONBURG, VA., Oct. 1.

My last letter was written early on the morning of the 19th, and I then better know what was to happen the same day. Shortly after the mail had left camp, the order came to strike tents and pack up, and in a few moments we fell in line, and moved off. We had anticipated a forward move, from the fact of General Grant having been on a visit to Gen. Sheridan's headquarters; so it did not take us by surprise. When we arrived at Opequan Creek we found our cavalry heavily engaged with the enemy. After crossing the stream, the Nineteenth Corps moved to the right, while our corps, the Sixth, moved to the left. Lines of battle were immediately formed, and at about 11, A.M., the whole line moved forward. The Rebels were posted in woods and undergrowth, and as we came near enough they gave us some terrible volleys. But the impetuosity of our gallant boys could not be restrained; and, with cheers rending the air, they rushed on the enemy with the bayonet, and drove them like sheep from their cover. The Rebels, flanked and routed, fell back in disordered flight to their fortifications outside of Winchester. The enthusiasm of our men at this signal triumph is beyond description, but the advantage had cost us dearly, for our division lost its lion-hearted leader, General D. A. Russell, who fell early in the action, while gallantly leading his Red Cross Division to victory. On the death of General Russell, our Brigade-Commander, Brigadier-General Upton, assumed command of the division, but he was also wounded, while bearing forward the standard of the One Hundred and Twenty-first New York, in the final charge. You have long before this had an account of the battle, so I will confine myself to the part taken by the Chasseurs in the battles of Winchester and Fisher's Hill. When General Upton assumed command of the division, Colonel [Joseph E.] Hamblin took charge of the brigade, while the command of the regiment devolved on Captain [Henry C.] Fisk. I shall not make any attempt to flatter, but I believe I speak truthfully, when I say that the Sixty-fifth behaved with their usual gallantry and won additional laurels to those already gained. Our officers were conspicuous for their bravery, Colonel Hamblin was always where the bullets flew the thickest, and had his horse shot from under him, still he continued undaunted to cheer his men on, himself setting the noble example. Lieutenants [Michael] Devine and [John] Wilber were always in front of the line, encouraging the boys by their bravery and example. One instance among the many acts of individual bravery, I will mention: Private Richard Bennett, of Company H, observed a party of Rebels between the lines, who were evidently trying to reach their own lines; and as he thought they would be better off as prisoners, he rushed out amid a galling fire from the Rebel main line, and brought in the whole party—one captain and eight privates—as prisoners of war. The daring act was loudly applauded by the entire regiment. Many other feats of like daring were done, but they would occupy too much space to enumerate. When night closed upon of the evening of the 19th, it found the Rebel Army routed and defeated, and Winchester in our possession. We rested for the night, and on the morning of the 20th we started in pursuit. The road from Winchester to Middletown and Strausburg was strewn with broken muskets, burnt wagons, etc., showing that their retreat was hasty and disorderly. We arrived in front of the new Rebel position at Fisher's Hill the same evening, and in the morning the lines were advanced, batteries planted, and reconnoissances made. At 2, P.M., the signal for attack was made, and again our boys, with that good old Union cheer, rushed on the Johnnies. The Rebels held a very strong position on the ridge of a steep hill, and our boys had to use their hands and feet to get up the hill, while the Rebels were giving our boys a murderous fire of grape and musketry. But the indomitable will of men who were determined to do or die could not be checked, and the earthworks of the enemy were gallantly carried. We took a great number of prisoners and ten pieces of artillery. The Rebels flew panic-stricken, and left us masters of the field. We pursued them all night, and halted at Woodstock for breakfast. We marched all that day, while our cavalry, who were in the advance, were rapping the retreating Johnnies, constantly bringing in prisoners, who reported that Early's Army was demoralized. We are now resting here awaiting supplies. When they arrive we will probably push on to Lynchburg. Where the enemy is at present it is hard to say, as Early has been forced to divide his army to save it from capture or annihilation. Heavy firing in the direction of Port Republic implies that our cavalry has met with a snag. Wherever the chasseurs go, your readers shall be duly informed by
                                                                                FRANCONI.

FIFTH REGIMENT, N.Y. HEAVY ARTILLERY
October 3.

Last week, forty men from each of the four companies of our battalions were detailed to escort stragglers, bounty-jumpers, convalescents, and recruits, to the front. They left with four days' rations, and got back on Sunday night [Oct. 2]. Returning, they had fifteen pieces of artillery in charge, and about five hundred wagons loaded with wounded soldiers, captured arms, etc. During the march, a band of guerillas made their appearance; but the road being all the way of ample width, and in excellent condition, the teams were doubled up, and the enemy were kept at bay. They marched a distance of sixty or seventy miles, and came into camp quite weary and footsore.

The Baltimore & Ohio Railroad and Chesapeake & Ohio Canal are now in full operation, and the supply of coal by these routes will soon be abundant. It is sincerely hoped that the poor of the land as well as the thieves and suckers who have absorbed so many millions of the people's substance, will be able to survive the inclemency of the ensuing winter-season. The beneficial influence and effect of General McClellan's nomination are already beginning to be observed. The grim war-god, Mars, with his accustomed plumes of temporary might and grandeur, is at last becoming sick and tired of himself, as everybody else of him; and while with one hand he grasps the sword of strife, he is ready with the other to extend the olive-branch of peace. The fierce national struggle, now in the fourth year of its existence, is apparently drawing to a close; prices are rapidly declining to a proper standard of valuation; visions of prosperity and happiness loom brightly in the future, and every tree, stone, and running brook seems to smile with joyous consciousness of approaching good. In the event of his (McClellan's) elevation to the Chief-Magistracy, a new epoch and a new era will be established, and harmony, Union, and peace will take the place of fraternal discord, estrangement, and strife. God speed the right, and "may the best man win!"

DIOGENES, JR.

SEVENTY-SEVENTH REGIMENT, N.G.N.Y.S.

CAMP SPICER, ELMIRA, N.Y., Oct. 3.

Since my last letter, nothing of unusual interest has occurred in this region. Colonel Thomas Lynch of our regiment, is now in command of the brigade guarding prisoners of war. The regiment, together with several batteries of artillery, are encamped around Camp Chemung where the "Johnnys", to the number of more than ten thousand, are domiciled. They are all very hard-looking citizens, and if not properly "cared for" by Uncle Sam's representatives, would prove very ugly customers. Under present circumstances they keep very shady, and have very little to say. If our poor fellows who to-day are imprisoned in the rebellious States were only cared for half as well, there would be many thousands living who to-night "sleep the sleep that knows no waking" in inhospitable graves.

Great numbers of recruits are sent away from this place every few days for the front, and the cry is still they come. Political discussions are becoming more frequent as the eventful day approaches, and McClellan stock is at a very high premium in this locality. Many of the men in this regiment, and in fact many of the men in every regiment at this post served under "little Mac" in many a hard-fought field, and when the time comes they will show they have not forgot their old commander; it is said that several of the regiments here will vote for the McClellan ticket "en masse".

Our time will expire on the 16th day of November, about which time this neighborhood will have no charms for   MAC.

October 16, 1864

HOW THE SOLDIERS AND SAILORS ARE TO BE PREVENTED FROM VOTING.

PEEKSKILL, N.Y., October 13.

The following is a copy of a letter received by Isaac Valentine, of this village, from one of the crew of the U.S. steamer Young Rover, dated October 6, 1864, at Hampton Roads, containing something vital to our interests as Democrats:

"I write you these few lines to inform you that I am well. I have been in the Navy now two months and like it very well; at all events a great deal better than soldiering. I am in a first-rate ship now. I do not mean that the ship is first-rate, but that we have first-rate times on board of her. The Paymaster of this ship received the other day a lot of blank votes for the men to fill up and sign, and send it home and vote it; but he being a Lincoln-man would not give them to any man who wanted to vote for McClellan, so I could not get one. And as I do not care about losing my vote, you will do me a favor by getting one of those blank votes and fill it up and send it down for me to sign, and I will then send it up to you to vote it for me."

FIFTY-FIRST REGIMENT, N.Y.V.

NEAR POPLAR GROVE CHURCH, VA., Oct. 9.

The real object of to-day (Sunday) is the more impressive from the stillness which pervades the vicinity. As far as the ear can hear, not a sound can be heard to mar the pleasure indulged in on the Sabbath day. Few bands are out, if any at all, as a cold wind is blowing from the northeast, which makes our overcoats of much use.

Very little is said about the coming election—the boys seem satisfied, so they bother their heads but little about it; still, when called upon to cast their votes, they will not shirk. One thing of which I am certain, that the officers do and will not trouble themselves about influencing the men when they are to cast their votes, and I am sure that every man thinks his opinion the correct one. So away with such notions.

                                                                                    SUCCOTASH.

October 23, 1864
SIXTY-FIFTH REGIMENT, N.Y.V.V.
NEAR MIDDLETOWN, VA., Oct. 18.

After two weeks of incessant marches and countermarches, up the valley, and then down again, we have come to a halt, and are at present enjoying a much-needed rest on the north bank of Cedar Creek. In the early part of last week we were ordered from Strasburg to Front Royal, and we had scarce time, on halting, to prepare our meals, when the order came to fall in for picket, which we did, and at the end of our three days' tour, when we anticipated relief and rest, the bugles of the different head-quarters sounded the unwelcome pack-up call. The order to march was our relief, and rumors as to our destination were as numerous as they always are when soldiers are on the march, destination unknown; but not a few whispered Petersburg, and the most reliable opinion was that we were going there; heavy firing in the direction of Strasburg, soon after we left Front Royal, seemed to imply that the Rebels were already commencing to take advantage of the absence of the Sixth Corps. When we arrived at a point within three miles of Snicker's Gap, a courier rode by us in breathless haste on his way to the head of the column, and in a few moments the bugler from Corps Headquarters, sounded the halt, and in a few moments the column was faced about, and marched into camp for the night, the order for Petersburg was countermanded. At four A.M., the next morning, we again fell in and took up our line of march for our present encampment. Our campaign up the Valley, in point of complete throws into the shade anything that has been done by any previous commander or army in this Department. General Sheridan is a man who evidently don't do things by halves, as Jubal Early no doubt thinks after the lesson Phil taught him at Winchester, and Fisher's Hill. The Rebel Government, dissatisfied with Early, have relieved him from command, and placed in his stead an infinitely inferior officer, Longstreet, who was whipped by Peck, at Suffolk, and snubbed by Burnside at Knoxville. What hope has he to judge from his career, to cope with a General like Sheridan?

The general health of the regiment continues very good. The most welcome of all visitors, the Paymaster, visited us a few days ago, and paid us two months' pay. Lieutenant-Colonel T. H. Higginbotham, having recovered from his wounds as well as from the effects of a long imprisonment in the Confederacy, has returned to us, and he is now in command of the regiment; his return is hailed with gratification by the boys, to whom he has endeared himself by his urbanity and soldierly qualities. The cause of McClellan is everyday receiving new supports here; and could the exile of New Jersey but be with us for an evening around the camp-fire, he would feel that the followers whom he led at Fair Oaks, Malvern, and Antietam, are still with him, and will stand by him to the last, for they have not forgot his sentiment, "Stand by me and I'll stand by you; no more retreats, no more defeats." The weather in this region of the country is beginning to grow cold and shelter-tents are getting uncomfortable. The quartermaster has been busy in issuing clothing, and when Jack Frost comes we shall be tolerably well prepared for him. The SUNDAY MERCURY comes regular, as usual, and is perused with the greatest interest. More anon.

                                                                                    FRANCONI.

TWENTY-FIFTH NEW YORK CAVALRY
PLEASANT VALLEY, MD., October 17.

The last letter I wrote to you, I dated on the banks of the Shenandoah, not knowing the name of the spot, but have since learned that it was Conrad's Ferry, or Ford, or Store, being marked on different maps by all three names.

About midnight of the 4th instant, we received orders to leave that place, and to do it as quietly and quickly as possible, as there was a brigade of Rebel infantry and a regiment of cavalry within three miles of us, while there was no Union troops nearer than Cross Keys, about ten miles distant. The fact, however, was not sufficient to cause Lieutenant-Colonel [Aaron] Seeley to hurry off the regiment in unseemly haste, and he made up his mind that if the Johnnys did come there in the morning they would find nothing left that could be of any service to them. He burned a large mill which had been used by the Rebels for the manufacture of cloth, and the looms of which contained quite a quantity of unfinished webs. He also destroyed a bridge across the millstream, which is unfordable, and which would retard considerably the progress of any army advancing from the direction of Swift Run Gap.

We reached the Cross Keys, where the balance of the brigade were encamped, by daylight, on the 5th, and about noon we commenced the retrograde march, General Sheridan having come to the conclusion to follow the enemy no further, as he was then well over the Blue Ridge, and it was not advisable for our Army to move any further from such an exposed base of supplies as Harper's Ferry or Martinsburg; the roads between these points and our position being infested by strong and active parties of guerillas, and the danger also existing of a force being sent up from Richmond toward Manassas or Thoroughfare Gap, which would throw them directly in our rear, and perhaps bring our glorious campaign to a disastrous end.

On the 7th inst., the hazardous and disagreeable duty of laying waste the country on the left of the line of march was assigned to the Twenty-fifth, and we destroyed an immense number of barns and storehouses; but, perhaps, the most important work done during the day was the destruction of a gun stock-factory, on which we accidentally stumbled, in which were about two thousand gunstocks already finished, and an immense quantity of lumber. The machinery was all new, and in excellent order, and its destruction occupied considerable time; but Colonel Seeley made clean work of it ere we renewed our march. The point of rendezvous was Edinburgh; and, when we arrived there we found the division in line of battle, and some skirmishing had been going on previous to our arrival, the enemy having mistaken our movement for a retreat, and plucked up heart to follow us. We drove him back, however, and encamped for the night. Next morning, we renewed our march, and, on reaching Woodstock, one of the strongest secession holes in Virginia, our brigade being the rearguard, we found a fierce conflagration raging, which, fanned by a strong wind, threatened the whole destruction of the town. The fire had caught from some of the burning barns. Colonel [James H.] Kidd, on whom devolved the command of the first brigade after the removal of General [George A.] Custer, to take charge of the Third Division, immediately halted the brigade, and ordered back the Seventh Michigan to stop the progress of the flames. This work occupied some hours, and by this time the advance-guard of the Rebels had come up, and actually fired on the men who had been working to save the town. This was not to be endured, so the rest of the brigade was brought up and pitched in, but the main body of the Rebels, under General [Thomas L.] Rosser, having by this time come up, we were overmatched, and had to fall back to where the rest of the division was halted. The skirmishing had lasted all day; so we camped for the night, expecting a big set-to in the morning.

Long before daylight the bugles blew, and we were in readiness to meet the expected attack; but the Rebels, elated by their partial success on the previous day, were too dilatory to suit General Torbert, and we accordingly went out to look for them. We soon found him posted in a strong position, with two six-gun batteries, pouring shell into our advancing columns; but we marched steadily on, our regiment being deployed as skirmishers on the extreme right of the First Division, and connecting with the left of General Custer's division (the Third). They were soon hotly engaged, but our advance was not for a moment checked, and we sent their skirmish-line skedaddling on the gallop. A charge now made by our portion of the line gave us possession of five pieces of artillery and about three hundred prisoners, and this was the signal for a general stampede of the Rebels. Such a run as they made of it has never been witnessed, and far outdoes the first Bull Run stampede. They put, helter-skelter, every man for himself; their boasted General Rosser, proving himself the fleetest. They left the balance of their artillery in our hands, their entire wagon-train, and a large number of prisoners. We pursued them fifteen miles, and then leisurely returned to our old camping-ground of the morning, both horses and men being thoroughly played out. The conduct of the Twenty-fifth on this day elicited the warmest praise from General Custer, who said that our charge of the morning, when we broke the enemy's line, "had never been surpassed". The men, encouraged by the brilliant example of Lieutenant-Colonel Seeley, and the other officers, fought with a courage and valor which could not be excelled, and, as a natural consequence, we suffered severely. Company I, a new company, which only joined the regiment the night before, suffered considerably. Toward the close of the action, Lieutenant-Colonel Seeley was wounded in the foot, and the command consequently devolved on Major [Charles] Seymour.

On the 11th we marched through Strasburg, past the formidable Rebel works at Fisher's Hill, and encamped near Cedar Creek. Next day there was an inspection of horses. So many of our men being dismounted entirely, and quite a number of the horses which were still in the regiment being used up, General [Wesley] Merritt thought it most advisable to dismount the balance of the regiment, and send it all here to be remounted. We were accordingly furnished with condemned horses, and, in company with about two hundred men from the other regiments of the division, were sent hither. I hardly think that our regiment will go out again this winter, as horses are scarce, the fighting-season nearly over, at least in the Valley; and so I think we shall remain here and drill until spring.

During our march here we saw several bands of guerrillas prowling along the road; but, owing to the quality of our horse-flesh, were unable to turn aside to pursue them.

B. O. B.

SIXTEENTH ARTILLERY, N.Y.V.

BEFORE RICHMOND, VA., Oct. 8.

As I stated in my last, Colonel J. J. Morrison sent all detached men to their companies at the front, and you might expect some stirring news—I can gratify you. We arrived in time to join the boys in the forward march to Richmond; and although the rain was pouring in torrents, we stepped merrily, for the indications were, that we were going right through, and we thought we would quarter as victors in any building we might select in the Rebel Capital. But we found that the Rebs had a serious objection to our entry, excepting we confined ourselves to the hospitalities of Miss Libby. However, we can claim, with justice, the honor of forming in line of battle closer to Richmond than any other regiment in the Union service has done since the war began. We could see the spires of the churches, hear the clanging of the alarm-bell, the shrill whistle of the locomotive, the yell of the Johnnys, and even the encouraging shouts of the women to their Rebel friends. But, it was decidedly a warm place, and the batteries shelled us beautifully; being in a ravine they did little harm, but getting an enfilading fire upon us, we were glad to beat a retreat. We could do them no damage from our position, and if we had went up that hill, very few indeed would have come back, as we had too few troops in our rear to support us, or protect us from a flank movement. From some prisoners we learned that we were distant from Richmond just one mile and a half. We were marched back five miles, and pitched our tents in the woods without any intrenchments.

The enemy appeared in strong force on Friday, Oct. 7, endeavoring to turn our right flank. [Gen. August V.] Kautz's cavalry being first attacked, broke and ran in the most disgraceful confusion, and the scene that ensued beggars description. Horses, riderless, came dashing through the camps, destroying everything in their way; men, hatless, coatless, and shoeless, hurriedly sought the rear; pieces of artillery lay scattered over the fields; and the largest part of the army seemed panic-stricken. Officers were endeavoring, with threats and blows, to rally the men, and finally succeeded in forming a line of battle with the First Division of the Tenth Army Corps. The Second Brigade, called *par excellence* the fighting brigade, stood comparatively calm, awaiting the exultant Johnnys, who, after cautiously surveying the line, chose our regiment's position as the most salient point to attack, hoping we would give way, when the day would be their own, and our army forced back over the James, or be annihilated. But they were mistaken. Our men never fired a gun till they approached within fifteen yards, when a Rebel captain, planting his colors in the ground, shouted, "Now, you d—d Yankees, there is our flag; we will fight for it." These were his last words on this earth; a ball entering his eye sent him to settle accounts with his Maker. The blaze from the musketry was terrific. Not a man flinched. Major Frederick W. Prince coolly cheered his men; and, without his order, no wounded man was borne to the rear. When one dropped, another immediately stepped into his place, and, after three-quarters of an hour of as fierce fighting as old veterans declared they ever witnessed, the Johnnys were glad to retire. The men were anxious to charge after the flag; but it was not permitted, as it was presumed the Rebs would not have displayed so much bravado if they were not well supported by artillery. Being in close line, individual bravery had no opportunity of exhibiting itself; but the conduct of Capts. [Isaac] Green, [Orrin] Beach, and [Morris] Sheppard, and Lieuts. [Sylvester] Cook, [Frederick] Lawrence, [James] Smart, [Russell] Hall, and [Albert] Foster deserves praise. Majors [Frederick W.] Prince and [Charles] Pearce acquitted themselves very creditably, and the boys of the Sixteenth have shown themselves worthy of the good opinion always entertained of them by their Colonel, J. J. Morrison, and are entitled to his gratitude. General [Alfred H.] Terry complimented the regiment twice during the day. I give you a list of the casualties to relieve the minds of the dear ones at home, as a cankering doubt is the severest pain.

JACKSON.

HAREWOOD HOSPITAL

WASHINGTON, D.C., Oct. 18.

About one mile from this hospital stands the Old Soldiers' Home. Immediately in the rear of the Home a flagstaff marks the spot which a grateful nation has dedicated to the repose of its heroic dead. The site, which comprises about seven acres, was selected for its present uses at the outbreak of the Rebellion, and through the interments made therein were properly systematized.

The Cemetery is inclosed by a handsomely-painted and substantial wooden fence, the high square-capped post being set about six feet apart; it is embowered on three sides by rather heavily-timbered lands, the fourth side facing the road. The visitor as he alights is confronted by a neat lodge dressed in sober gray, with light Gothic trimmings. The interior of the lodge charms the person of thoughtful mind. By a large bay-window stands a pyramid of plants and flowers, whose odors fill the room. The furniture is good and of chaste design; not a picture is seen against the walls, but in lieu thereof are brackets, and in some of these little birds from their wiry homes send forth their pleasant songs; while on others are seen pretty bouquets gathered from the handsomely-laid out and well-trimmed flower-garden that surrounds the lodge. Inside the gate of the main entrance is placed a large signboard containing rules to be observed by the visitors to the Cemetery, and as he reads and recognizes the spirit of care, affection, and reverence which dictated such rules, he unconsciously doffs his hat, and feels as though he stood on holy ground. The land is slightly undulating, and has been so thoroughly drained that there is not a moist spot throughout the whole place. The walks, which run at right angles with each other, are graded with an arched elevation, and have well-laid gutters on either side. At five different points are erected arches of trellised work, under which the tired visitors rest themselves, and around which the choicest kinds of grapevines cling, and wild-flowers love to climb.

Each grave is well sodded, and has a neatly-painted white head-board, with black figures denoting the name of the deceased, his rank and company, the regiment to which he belonged, and the date of his death. As the soldier is the subject of a strict discipline in life, so here it is appropriately observed after death in his burial. Some of the "missing", the "absent without leave", and probably the "deserted", commingle with those whose identity is established beyond a doubt. All lie in "open order", and severally await the sound of the great reveille which none who hear will dare to disobey. Here, too, is the unity of the States reaffirmed; for not only are the loyal States represented, but the poor, misguided Rebels, the victims of others' wickedness and their own blindness, having paid the debt their own folly had incurred, rest from their sorrows. Here the monotonous beauty of the scene is somewhat broken by the cedars interspersed not too thickly among the graves, and the marble pyramids and headstones which occasionally are seen, and which tell you of a comrade's tribute or a friend's affection. Many persons having soldier-friends buried in the Cemetery have visited the place for the purpose of removing their remains, but when they saw the tender care bestowed by the Government toward the dust of its defenders, they wisely concluded it was better not to disturb them, and have returned to their homes with contented thankfulness in their hearts.

To the traitor against our Government, to the disloyal in practice, and to the weak of faith in Christian and human progress, I would suggest a visit to this burial-place. It may quiet the traitor, rebuke the disloyal, and strengthen the faint-hearted; while to the loyal and confident a visit will prove a lasting memorial of beauty and joy.

GUARDIAN.

October 30, 1864
SIXTEENTH N.Y. HEAVY ARTILLERY
NEAR RICHMOND, VA., Oct. 16.

On the 12th, we received our usual marching orders, for tramping appears to be the order of the day, and although we enlisted for heavy artillery, the heaviest infantry-duty appears to be imposed upon us. However, we understand our Colonel, J. J. Morrison, is making an effort to have us returned to garrison-duty, and we will be duly grateful if his efforts are successful. We started out and marched a few miles in a semi-circle, for the purpose, I presume, of making a reconnoisance but in reality, it only served to display our forces to the enemy. We succeeded in getting soaking wet, as a heavy rain fell, and, coming back to our little shelter-tents, lay down on the ground with wet clothes, and the wind blowing completely through us, with the prospect of being aroused any minute of the night to start out on another tramp. This did not appear till 4 o'clock, A.M., the 13th; and as it was questionable whether we should march forward or retreat to the South side of the James—we made preparations to take our little traps with us in the latter alternative. The command being light marching order, our trouble was useless, and we sallied out over the same ground we had traversed the night before, and met the Rebs in a new line of intrenchments thrown up on the very ground occupied by Kautz's cavalry before their shameful rout. Being incomplete, they afforded little protection to the Confederates, and they soon took the back track, but merely to assume a better position. The musketry was very severe, all the regiments in our brigade are armed but ourselves with the Spencer repeating-rifle, a most efficient weapon and splendid for skirmishing. The fighting was kept up nearly all day; three charges were made upon the enemy's works, but I am sorry to say we were repulsed. The American citizens of African descent have to bear the brunt of these assaults now—how the philanthropists can justify themselves I cannot understand. They wish to relieve them from what they call the horrors of slavery, the horror of which I cannot see, and precipitate them into the horrors of war without giving them equivalent political privileges. I should not wish to fight for a country where I was denied the right of suffrage, and I do not think it fair that the blacks should do all the work. I am here for the restoration of my Government to what it was—I want my children to enjoy the same laws and same system I enjoyed and none other, and am just as willing to carry my musket against those who insidiously attack it by proclamations and suspensions of the safeguard of human liberty, the Habeas Corpus, as those who have outraged the flag and committed the crime and folly of secession in the South. The lack of fairness which characterizes the proceedings of the military authorities in regard to the soldiers' votes, is going to deprive Little Mac of many votes from his adherents. A Democratic paper or document is an unseen thing at the front, but Republican placards are plentiful—the

Sanitary Commission deal out note-paper and Republican lies in an undue proportion of the latter. The SUNDAY MERCURY is scarcely comeatable, and the World is positively prohibited.

Americans, what farce is this you are allowing yourselves to gaze at? Is Abraham Lincoln emperor, or are you slaves? Do we want merely the name without the reality of Liberty? Shame on you to submit to it! Awake, and by the potential voice of the ballot, which you should see for yourselves to be potential, oust those who are ruining the country with their absurd notions of negro equality, and their selfish ends of filling their own pockets with the trash called greenbacks worth forty-four cents on the dollar. I understand that at Williamsburg, which erstwhile I affected, some of the best citizens are ordered from their homes, because, forsooth, they would not perjure themselves by swearing to protect and support Abe's Emancipation Proclamation. I say, if they communicate with the enemy, hang them; that is the punishment of a spy, but when men have never taken up arms against our Government, are driven from their homes for not subscribing to an oath I would not take, I blush to say I am an American.

                                                                            JACKSON.

November 6, 1864
SIXTY-FIRST REGIMENT, N.Y.V.V.
CAMP BEFORE PETERSBURG, VA., Oct. 30.

Since writing my last, picket firing has raged without cessation, until the 28th inst., when it ceased somewhat, and, at the present time, but few shots are interchanged between the pickets. By means of this cruel and barbarous practice, William Peck, of Company H, was shot through the breast and instantly killed, on Thursday morning last. On Monday, the 24th inst., this regiment received orders to go on picket, which duty we are still performing. It has not been a very pleasant duty to perform, owing to the wet weather we have had lately. Friday morning opened clear and pleasant, with a strong wind from the westward, which has been the means of drying up this detestable "sacred soil" mud which we have had to wade through. The prospect for fine weather is very encouraging at present, and none will enjoy it more than the soger-boys. We have been expecting lively times around here, but as yet, nothing of importance has occurred to mar the quietness pervading our lines.

About 2, A.M., on the morning of the 26th, the Second Division of the Second Army Corps received orders to take up the line of march for the Southside Railroad. The division met the Johnnys about 7½, charged and drove in their picket-line. Shortly after, the Rebs rallied and turned our flank, and retook possession of their line; the Division still kept advancing toward the railroad. At 11, A.M., our troops charged upon the Rebel line near the edge of Stoney Creek, about one mile from the railroad. We succeeded in taking their line. At 12, M., the artillery on both sides opened; the firing was continuous until 3, P.M., when the Rebs were discovered coming up in our rear, over the same ground which we had advanced upon. The Eighth N.Y. Heavy Artillery turned face about, and poured volley after volley into the Rebel ranks, which was the means of holding them at bay, while the division held its ground. The Rebs then massed and charged upon the battery, and succeeded in capturing four pieces. We then charged and retook the battery, along with two of the Rebel cannon. These two pieces we spiked, dismounted, and threw into a pond near by. Night now coming on, fighting ceased, and at 10, P.M., we took up the line of march for Petersburg. Not much was gained on either side as far as ground was concerned. We tore up about one mile of the railroad, and captured about 1,200 prisoners. The Rebel loss must have been heavy, as our artillery kept up a raking fire into their ranks. Our loss, in killed, wounded and missing, will not, I think, amount to over three hundred, if it does that.

At 10, P.M., on the night of the 27th, a detachment of one hundred men from our picket-line made a charge upon and captured a Rebel fortification on the line of their breastworks. At 12, P.M., same night, the Rebels rallied, and retook the fort, but not without an obstinate resistance on our part. Before we left we spiked their guns; we also captured some eighteen prisoners, among them four officers. Our loss will not amount to more than thirty.

This is Sunday morning, and as I now write, I can hear the church bells ringing in Petersburg, and thoughts of home and loved ones come through my mind.

                                                                            S. G. C.

Private Samuel G. Collins, age 24, enlisted in Co. D, 61st New York Infantry on September 1, 1864. He listed his pre-war occupation as a "Gauger." He served until the end of the war as "Adjutant's clerk." Collins died on August 31, 1881 after being run over by a train near Philadelphia.

FIFTH NEW YORK CAVALRY

CAMP NEAR STRASBURG, VA., Oct. 31.

I suppose you have heard ere this of another brilliant victory over Early, on the 19th ult., and ended in one of the most complete routs that ever befell the Rebel army.

On the morning of the 19th, just before the dawn of day, we were aroused from our slumber by a volley or two of musketry, accompanied by the most dismal howling on the part of the Rebs that ever emanated from the throats of men, resembling more the howlings of beasts than that of human beings. We were on our feet in a twinkling, and ten minutes after we were in our saddles, and formed a line of battle. Our infantry had formed a line on our left, and had hardly time to do so when the Rebel line was seen advancing in the double-quick, pouring volley after volley into our ranks, with deadly effect. As our line was but partially formed, the Rebs, pressing their advantages, broke it when it wavered and staggered like a drunken man, and fell back individually. The whole cavalry force was transferred into a line immediately in front of our infantry and for a time checked the Rebel mass. Several pieces of artillery were abandoned and had fallen into the hands of the enemy, which were immediately turned upon us. This was before 10 o'clock in the morning, and when the Army was commanded by General Wright, of the Sixth Corps. On, on, came the Rebel lines, their battle-colors flaunting gayly in the breeze, while their fifty or sixty cannon belched forth shot and shell with such precision and accurate range, that it told fearfully on the devoted little band of cavalry that were straining every nerve to check the heavy columns of the enemy. Our infantry had fallen back some three miles at this time. Gradually, the cavalry was being pressed back, and nothing but an inglorious retreat, or perhaps rout, began to find its way into the heads of many; and I actually wished in my heart for some unseen circumstance to arise and change the fortunes of the day. General Custer, our Commander, for once wore a downcast and melancholy look, as he ran his eyes upon the advancing foe. But hark! what means that cheer and yell in our rear? Again the cheering is heard, and "three cheers and a tiger" reverberates for miles through the Valley of the Shenandoah. We turn our heads, and a cloud of dust is seen arising from the pike, and a single horseman, wrapped in a cloak, his coal-black steed foaming and perspiring to that extent that plainly told the speed he was put to for many a mile over the turnpike. All eyes are directed toward the stranger, and "Sheridan!" was heard emanating from thousands of throats. "Three times three" now rang along the whole line, and the greatest enthusiasm pervaded the whole Army. But, what means the sudden quietude now apparently pervading the Rebel line? It halts, and, as the smoke from its cannons vanishes into the air, looks on quietly for some time, as if anticipating some sudden reaction on the part of our boys, and calmly awaited the onslaught shortly to be made by them. Our cavalry is now swung across on the right flank, and the ball opens anew. "Forward, men! and drive them!" shouted Sheridan to the whole line; and, with a cheer that struck terror to the hearts of the Johnnys, the whole line advanced on the double-quick, driving the now panic-stricken Rebs before them like chaff before the wind. The Rebs were actually dumbfounded by this sudden change of tactics on the part of our boys, whom they were driving but an hour ago, and, as they thought, victory already perching on their banners. They, in turn, were unable to stand the shock of our now enthusiastic advancing line; and, after incessant volleys of musketry on our part, of one or two hours duration, they began to stagger; and Sheridan, perceiving his advantage, hurled his whole corps of cavalry on the now thunderstruck Rebs, who broke and fled in the wildest confusion imaginable, and ended in one of the most complete routs that ever befell an Army. Pell-mell, helter-skelter, over ditches, cornfields, fences, stone walls, up and down ravines, and in every hole and nook where hardly a dog could conceal itself, fled the panic-stricken Rebs, and dead and wounded found on the field afterward, fully testified to the important part of the cavalry played in the rout. Our regiment had the advance on the charge, the Fifth Vermont behind us, the Second and Third Brigade following. Over fifty pieces of artillery fell into our hands, some thousands of prisoners, a wagon-train of some miles in length, besides mules, caisson, etc., and thousands of small-arms. Sergeant [David S.] Schofield, of the Fifth, captured the battle-colors of [Gen. J. B.] Kershaw's Division, of Longstreet's Corps, which were torn in shreds. Corporal [John] Welch, of the Fifth, recaptured the battle-colors of the Fifteenth New Jersey, infantry, which they had lost in the morning. General Sheridan has given them both thirty-five days' furlough. Yesterday, General Merritt, commanding the First Division of the Cavalry Corps, and General Custer, commanding the Third Division, had a dispute about the trophies captured, Merritt claiming one-half the artillery; but General Sheridan soon settled the point by awarding all the honor to Custer, he having captured over forty of the pieces, twenty-two of which were awarded to the Fifth New York and nineteen to the First Vermont.

Yesterday, we were highly complimented by both Sheridan and Custer, and the following receipt, signed by both Sheridan and Custer, was handed to Major [Abram H.] Krom, and by him read to the regiment:

22 guns, 2 battle-flags, 15 caissons, 1 battery-wagon, 17 army-wagons, 6 ambulances, 83 sets of artillery-harness, 75 sets of wagon-harness, 102 horses, 57 mules, and over two hundred prisoners, being the trophies of the Fifth New York Cavalry.

Had we but one or two more hours of daylight I dare say the whole Rebel Army would have either all been captured or annihilated. However, you may rest assured that it will be months before the remnant of Early's ragamuffins is got together; and, after this their third rout, will be more apt to shun their wily antagonist Sheridan, the hero of the Shenandoah Valley and the terror of the Rebs. Among the most conspicuous generals who led the charge, none shone more resplendent than he of the golden locks, Custer, the dashing cavalry-leader. May he live long to wear the laurels he has so honestly won, and which can never be erased from the memories of those who served under him, and watched with feelings of admiration his glorious and successful career as a cavalry-leader.

T. McG.

SIXTY-FIFTH NEW YORK VOLUNTEERS
MIDDLETOWN, VA., Oct. 28.

Our regiment, in the late battle, sustained a loss of eleven killed, seventy-one wounded, and one missing. The Chasseurs, as usual, officers and men, did their entire duty. Our tried leader, Col. Hamblin, led the brigade gallantly, and I regret to state that he was severely wounded. Captain [Henry C.] Fisk, Lieutenant [John J.] Wilber, and Adjutant [Charles H.] Woodman were, as usual, self-possessed, brave, and cool; the latter had his horse shot from under him. The boys never felt better for fighting, and the Empire City may well feel a just pride in her gallant Chasseurs. We are now in our old camps that we occupied previous to the battle, and doing the same old duties. Many were the acts of bravery performed, and were all done so well, it is hard to make distinctions; but I will mention a few instances of gallantry, in justice to the heroes who performed them, after carrying the rifle-pits near Cedar Creek. Sergeant Gill, Company C, of Brooklyn, rushed out amidst a party of Rebels and ordered them to surrender or be shot. They concluded that discretion was the better part of valor, and accordingly gave themselves up—one lieutenant and four privates. The Sergeant retains the Rebel officer's sword as a trophy. Archie Birdsall, of Company G, a mere youth, also captured a number of fleeing Rebels, and succeeded in taking a Major and eight privates prisoners. Many other feats of similar daring were done, but they would occupy too much space to enumerate.

The Fifteenth New Jersey Regiment, in a hand-to-hand fight with the Rebels early in the day, lost their colors, but the color-bearer only gave up the flag when his head was severed from his body by a sabre-cut. The colors were afterward recaptured by the Fifth N.Y. Cavalry, and returned to the gallant Jerseymen. In speaking of colors, I am reminded of the fact that we have had no colors since the three-years' men went home. We have heard that the Common Council made an appropriation some time ago for the purpose of supplying the city-regiments with flags, and we hope that the Committee on National Affairs of that illustrious body will supply this want of the Sixty-fifth New York as soon as they can find it convenient to do so. The cavalry of this department have earned fame and reputation they may well feel proud of, and they could not well be other than successful when led by such gallant spirits as Torbert, Custer, and Merritt. The fruits of the victory just gained the country owes to them. Our captures are immense, and are set down as follows:

Forty-one pieces of artillery, ten thousand prisoners, one hundred wagons, besides munitions of war, camp-equipage, etc. This is by far the most glorious victory yet achieved in this valley, and it was only gained by dint of hard fighting, energy, and wisdom, backed by the bold spirits and willing hearts.

Among the captured is the Rebel General [John] McCausland—the latter individual is noted for his barbarity and inhumanity in burning the town of Chambersburg, in his raid across the Potomac. The ballots have arrived to the regiment, and affidavits are being made busily. We gained a glorious victory on the 19th of October.

We trust our friends and countrymen will work as zealously for the Union on election-day in voting and laboring for General George B. McClellan. More anon.

FRANCONI.

NINETIETH REGIMENT, N.Y.V.V.
IN THE FIELD, NEAR MIDDLETOWN, VA., Oct. 31.

We have gained another great victory over the Rebels, and General Sheridan is now master of the Shenandoah Valley. About 5 o'clock, on the morning of the 19th instant, we were suddenly surprised to hear heavy firing on our left flank. We formed line of battle, and then found out that the Eighth Corps had been surprised in their breastworks, and had been driven out of them. We were then ordered forward at a double-quick, but before we could form line again, the enemy charged upon us, and after firing about four or five volleys we were ordered to fall back. We fell back slowly about three miles, the Rebels following us up closely, until about 2, P.M., when we formed line and drove the Rebels back, the cavalry following them to Fisher's Hill. General Sheridan has got the full confidence of all his men, and when he came down the line the air rang with cheers. He was as good to us as twenty thousand re-enforcements; a new spirit entered us, and we were determined to drive the Rebels back, or die in the attempt. It was fun for us to see the Rebs run; for when they once started, they did not stop until they got to Fisher's Hill. They stayed there until 12 o'clock that night, and then left; and we do not know where their next stopping-place will be, but expect it will be at Staunton. This regiment lost eighty-five in killed, wounded, and missing. Lieut.-Col. M. Shaurman had command of part of the picket-line. He was knocked off his horse by a solid shot, but it did not hurt him much. It went across his breast, tearing the front off his coat, and just grazed the skin. He is expected up here to-day to assume command of the regiment again. Major J. C. Smart, who was in command of the regiment was killed. He just gave us an order to fall back, when he was shot dead. His body has been sent home. When we found his body in the evening, it was stripped. All he had on was his undershirt. I have talked with some Rebel prisoners since the fight, and they tell me that General Early reviewed them the day before the fight, and told them that he was going to make another attempt to take the Valley, and that if he failed, he should leave the Valley altogether. I suppose that he has left before this.

The Rebels captured about twenty-five pieces of artillery from us in the morning, but we took them all back, and about thirty more for interest. We are now lying in our old camp quietly. As it is getting very cold, I must now close; but if Early makes another attempt to occupy the Valley, you shall hear of it.

EXCELSIOR.

November 13, 1864

A WORD OF ADVICE TO MR. LINCOLN—Now that the election is over, it is the duty of every good citizen to submit to the decision of the people; and there is not the slightest doubt that all are willing to do so. This is the time for Old Abe to make for himself a place in the hearts of his countrymen that shall be second only to that occupied by Washington. Peace! is the nation's prayer. If Mr. Lincoln will bring about peace and re-union on the basis of gradual emancipation—say in thirty years or fifty years at the outside—we can promise to him the enduring gratitude of a suffering nation. Not only do we offer to him all the influence of the SUNDAY MERCURY in strengthening his attempts to bring about reunion and peace on some such basis we have recommended, but we tender as well the unanimous support of the people of this great city and of this great State. More than this—we guarantee to support him with all our zeal, and that the country will do likewise, if he desires to seek for a new lease of power at the expiration of his present term of office. Only give the nation peace, Mr. Lincoln, and the nation will keep you in the Presidential chair, if you so desire, to the end of your natural life.

NORTHERN PRISONS FOR REBELS

At Elmira, New York, there is a large and well-constructed place of confinement for Rebel prisoners, which contains about ten thousand men. The management of the prison is of a character that reflects the highest credit upon Northern humanity. So far from any measures of retaliation being adopted, for the sufferings which our men are obliged to endure at Belle Isle, Andersonville, and other places, every arrangement for the comfort and health of the captives, possible under the circumstances, is devised and applied. It is proper that the public at home, and especially foreign exponents of opinion, should be informed of the difference between the lenient kindness with which Rebel captives at the North are treated, and the brutality, the oppression, and deprivations which are the lot of Northern soldiers unfortunate enough to experience the miseries inflicted by the chivalry of the South on those who fall within their power by the fortunes of war.

The place of confinement at Elmira is an inclosure of several acres, surrounded by a simple board-fence some twelve feet in height, guards being stationed on platforms at the top of the fence every twenty or thirty feet. The business of guarding the prisoners, however, is rather a sinecure. The officers on duty state that the captives evince no disposition to escape. They have no desire to return to the felicities of Southern soldiers. Undoubtedly, should single individuals attempt to burrow under the fence, or should a large number make a rush against it, their chances for escape would be very good; but apparently the captives would not leave if the fence and guards were entirely removed. The plot constituting the prison is finely situated on an excellent piece of ground about a mile from Elmira, and though entirely inclosed, as stated, the prisoners are not deprived of a view of external nature; for on one side rise pine-clad hills, up into the air, visible from all parts of the prison. The prisoners are all provided with bunks in the same kind of rough barracks as used for sheltering our own men at the various places of rendezvous, before going into the field. A very large building is appropriated to the culinary department, and is fitted up like the kitchen of a great hotel, and with about a dozen ranges, containing boilers, etc., and there is also a large oven, where sufficient bread, from good flour, is baked daily. The cooks and bakers are, of course, prisoners. Clothing is furnished to the prisoners by Government when their own becomes too much worn to be serviceable. The whole appearance of the camp is very neat, working-parties from among the prisoners being constantly employed in policing the grounds. The daily ration is as follows: Pork or bacon, 19 ounces in lieu of fresh beef; or fresh beef, 14 ounces; flour or soft bread, 16 ounces; or hard bread, 14 ounces; or corn-meal, 16 ounces. To the 100 rations: Beans or peas, 12½ pounds; or rice or hominy, 8 pounds; soap, 4 pounds; vinegar, 3 quarts; salt, 3¼ pounds; potatoes, 15 pounds. Sugar, coffee, and tea are issued to the sick and wounded on the recommendation of the surgeon, at the rate of 12 pounds of sugar, 5 of coffee, or 7 of green, 1 pound of tea to every 100 rations every other day. To working-parties of the prisoners nearly the same ration is given in all reports as to our soldiers in the field. Notwithstanding the rations for the prisoners is somewhat less than that issued to our own soldiers—and very appropriately so, since they do no hard work—yet, in reality, they get the benefit of the entire ration. For the difference between the prison-ration and that of the United States soldier is credited on the books of the commissary to the prison, and expended for the benefit of the prisoners in such ways as the commanding officer may direct. This fund, it will be seen, grows rapidly to a large sum. These arrangements apply not only to the prison at Elmira but to all others. The Elmira prison is for private soldiers; and if they live so comfortably, it can be imagined that the officers on Johnson's Island and at other places, who have money of their own for the purchase of little luxuries, must pass their time as agreeably as the conditions of prison-existence will permit. How utterly false, therefore, are the statements made from time to time by Jeff. Davis to the world, that Southern prisoners are badly treated!

Enough has been published, founded on the statements of returned prisoners, to exhibit the state of matters in Southern prisons; but lest these reports should be considered exaggerated, we refer to a very readable book by Colonel [Frederick] Cavada, giving an account of his life in the Libby Prison. This place, it will be recollected, is used for confining officers only, and, consequently, the brutalities experienced by private soldiers at their particular prisons are not here practiced. But notice the petty annoyances, the absence of provisions for cleanliness and comfort, the pillaging of boxes sent from the North, the heartless insults of the guards, which are detailed by the writer of this book. How does the management of a Southern prison contrast with that of a Northern? In the one, the unhappy inmates are treated as brutes; in the other, as men.

The particular distinguished characteristic between Northern and Southern feeling, manifested not only in prison-arrangements, but in every other manner, is the presence in the hearts of the Southerners of an intense animosity, while in those of Northerners there is an entire absence of all bitterness, all desire to insult and oppress. The Northerner feels kindly toward his erring Southern brother, and after the battle is done all desire to do him injury vanishes. But hatred of the Yankees continues, on the part of the Southerners, unappeasable under all circumstances. To this distinguishing characteristic of the chivalry are to be ascribed the petty oppressions and cowardly brutalities exhibited toward our prisoners. Northern officers, in charge of prisoners, who should attempt to imitate the Richmond examples, would be scorned as unfit to associate with gentlemen.

SIXTY-FIRST REGIMENT, N.Y.V.V.

CAMP IN THE FIELD, VA., Nov. 5.

I should have headed this dispatch "Camp in the Woods", as we are at present encamped in the midst of a Virginia forest, the tall pine-trees surrounding us on all sides, but the former appellation, sounding more appropriate in these war-times, I will let it remain so. We left our former position in front of Petersburg, on Monday evening, Oct. 31, at 7:30, P.M., and took up the line of march South. We reached our present position at 1:30, A.M., Tuesday morning. All hands were pretty well tired out, and were glad to obtain some rest. The morning was raw and chilly, but notwithstanding that all hands lay down to rest, and at 9, A.M. we were commenced at once to clear ground and pitch tents. Company-streets were laid out, and all hands went to work trying to make themselves as comfortable as possible. Wednesday morning opened with rain, which continued all day, and was the means of rendering the situation of some of the men anything but desirable. As it was, they all managed to get through with it, and on Friday morning Old Sol came out in all his brightness, and tended toward putting a more cheerful aspect upon our situation.

A great many are of opinion that we will winter here. If we do, we will have plenty of firewood, but water is scarce. Time will tell what we will do. I am entirely ignorant in regard to army-movements this week; shut up as we are at present, details of news are hard to get.

I mentioned in my last about Colonel [K. O.] Broady awaiting a higher commission. I was at fault there, and I am sorry to say has left us for good, having been mustered out of the service. We were in hopes that Col. Broady would remain with us, and we were much disappointed when we learned differently. If the old "Vets" keep on, we will have but a few left after a while, their term of service expiring almost every week. But one "vet" remains in Company E, and that one is its present commander, Second-Lieutenant James H. Grady. On Friday, our Division (the First and Second Army Corps) was reviewed by Brigadier-General [Nelson A.] Miles. The Division turned out with pretty full ranks, and presented a good appearance. This (Saturday) morning, we were again reviewed, but this time by our favorite General (Hancock), who, previous to his departure for Washington, wished to see, once more, the men who have followed him through many a hard-fought battle. The Division was brought up in line, and as the General passed by, hat in hand, we gave him three rousing cheers. We are all sorry to lose him. Hancock's fighting Second Army Corps have gained for themselves a name to be envied by many. We wish the General success wherever he goes. To his successor, whoever he may be, we wish the same.

It seems quiet here to what it was in front of Petersburg. No pickets or shells to "pepper" us; but we can hear firing once in a while in the distance. Only one casualty this week, and that accidental. Maurice Piereault, Company G, who was seriously injured by a tree falling upon him. He was conveyed to the hospital.

By the time this reaches you, election will be over, and in a few days thereafter we will know the result. We will look anxiously for the SUNDAY MERCURY, which, we are sure, will give us a full and complete return. Hoping that the result will be such as to gladden the hearts of our soldiers, but still remembering the old American motto, "May the best man win!" I subscribe myself, yours, etc.,

S. G. C.

ALBEMARLE SOUND BLOCKADING SQUADRON.
October 30.

The little steamer, size of a frigate's launch in charge of Lieutenant Cushman [William B. Cushing], U.S. Navy, accomplished one of the most daring and brilliant deeds ever known of since this useless war. The party were eleven in all—Paymaster [Francis Swan] of the Otsego (who wanted to distinguish himself, but showed himself a coward when the drama was performed), Master's Mate of the Shamrock, Ned Houghton, Wm. Smith, and Bernard Harley, all of the Chicopee, an Ensign, and others.

The tiny steamer got under way at 12, M., going up the Roanoke River; they passed the battery on Fisher's Hill without discovery; passed the old Southfield without being discovered by the sentinel stationed thereon, who was taken prisoner, besides three others.

Everything went on smoothly, and agreeable to their satisfaction. When in sight of the ram (the night being very dark and favorable—they were within six yards of the ram before knowing it), when the boat was hailed. "Who comes there?" No answer. "Who comes there?" comes the second time. Lieutenant Cushing answered, "You'll d—d soon find out." During this minute, they moved nearer the ram, when some one shouted, "What do you want?" It just struck six bells, or 3 o'clock in the morning. Ned Houghton says, "That's the last six bells you'll ever strike." Bang goes a gun from the ram. Bang goes another from the little steamer, who carried a twenty-pound howitzer. The same instant the torpedo gives its report, and up goes the ram! The little steamer, being so near, got upset by the whirl of the waves, so that each one had to make the best of it and save himself. There were life-preservers on board, but during the excitement no one thought of them.

Our hero No. 2, Ned Houghton, while sitting on a log near the place of action, busy pulling off his coat and throwing off his arms, to lighten himself, as he had half a mile to swim, had his arm just touched by a rifle-shot, and picked a spent one off his knee, after which he made his way across the river, where he promenaded through the woods and swamps for nearly forty-eight hours without a particle of food. Lieut. Cushing returned on Friday night.

The gunboat-fight came off yesterday, but very little of it. The fleet did not move on Friday last, not knowing positively that the ram was blown up. At 11, A.M., the fleet got under way, the Valley City ahead, next the Commodore Hull, next the flagship, then the Chicopee, and so on the other vessels.

We came in sight of the battery at 12. The Valley City passed the obstructions in the river and the battery without firing a shot, to which one of the Rebel rams responded. The Shamrock then opened her battery, advancing all the while until the obstructions were noticed, which are impassable by a double-ender. I presume that the obstructions (all Schooners) were sunk during Friday. There were about twenty shots fired in all; the whole lasted about an hour.

The Chicopee is the only one damaged. She got a shot through the port-paddle. The Valley City returned last night, bringing with her Ned Houghton. He was picked up by her while swimming. One of the party got drowned. What became of the rest is unknown at present.

The Rebels removed everything to Halifax on Friday, having expected the Yankee fleet.

ALBEMARLE.

November 20, 1864
ONE HUNDRED AND THIRTY-SECOND REGIMENT N.Y. VOLS.
BACHELOR'S CREEK, N.C. November 15.

We are at present comfortably situated in our winter quarters.

We have received a few recruits lately; they are enlisted for one year, and have plenty of greenbacks.

An "intelligent contraband" and lady came into camp this morning, having run away from their master. It seems that the lady's clothes were somewhat torn in coming through the "Pacassin" and her "lord" had to give her a pair of his "unmentionables", so she made her appearance in camp in a costume half woman and the other half man, the "breeches" fitting her skin-tight, revealing enough of her charms to shock our modesty; but she seemed undismayed at her novel situation. The boys enjoyed a hearty laugh over it. They have arrived in all sorts of "togs", but this beat all yet.

We see or hear very little of Johnnys around here. Gens. Grant and Sheridan so effectually engaging their attention, that they can't find time to bother us; but we are ready for them when they come.

The reign of Yellow Jack is over in Newbern—Gen. Jack Frost completely routing him. It is estimated that 2,200 citizens, soldiers, etc., have died of the fever. The health of our regiment is "right pert", to use a phrase much used by the citizens in this neighborhood, to denote "right well". The boys are becoming very proficient in the language of the Southern chivalry; our friends in New York would hardly understand us.

All we want is for the Paymaster to "hurry up the cakes", and we would be all O. K. Our sutler seems to be waiting for him also, as he keeps very little to supply our wants; but as soon as we have money he will have a large stock to take it away from us. As we have no chance to spend the money any other place. It would be very beneficial to the regiment if the Council of Administration would give him an overhauling, as his prices are rather steep. Butter ninety cents per pound, and other things in like proportion, can't be afforded by the "poor soldier".

JUNIOR.

November 27, 1864
SIXTY-FIRST REGIMENT, N.Y.V.V.
CAMP IN THE FIELD, VA., Nov. 18.

We have been expecting marching orders every hour, almost. They have at last arrived, and we break camp to-morrow morning; but our destination at present is unknown.

The weather has been so changeable of late that our condition has not been very comfortable, and the uncertainty of movement has deterred us somewhat from making ourselves comfortable. We hope that we may be able to render our next camping-ground more pleasant, wherever it may be.

On Sunday, the 13th, we received our long looked for camp-orders. They were immediately issued to the men, who soon assumed a more cheerful appearance, both in spirits and looks, and we all thanked Uncle Sam for sending them to us before King Frost makes his appearance in earnest.

On Monday, the 14th, we were inspected by Brigade-Inspector Captain Oldershaw, and I but reiterate his own words, when I say that our regiment made the best appearance of any in the brigade. I do not wish to disparage the other regiments, in the brigade, who, no doubt, are deserving of praise as well as we; yet, at the same time, when we have a compliment paid us we claim the privilege of using it. The men did, indeed, look well, clean, well equipped, and with their new uniform presented a fine appearance. Our time is pretty well taken up with drilling, and every afternoon a brigade-drill, when we go out on company-drill. We are in plain sight of the "Johnnys", who at once commence to shell us; we hunt up our bombproofs, and by that time our batteries have opened, and we then leave them to fight it out. Picket-firing still continues in order, especially at night, when firing is pretty brisk. This afternoon, while Company I were out on drill, a bullet came from the Rebel picket-line, and went through four of their tents, and at last brought up in a crutch of a tent—lucky escape for some of the I boys. All conceivable means are adopted by us to pass away the time; when not otherwise engaged, "we go in" and have a "sham" fight, and such charging you never seen; and then again we "play" ball with the numerous ten and twelve-pounders laying around our camp. George Chandler, of Company B, while busily employed in removing a cap from a shell, was wounded in the left leg by the bursting of the shell. I hope it will prove a warning to others not to fool with those dangerous "insects". His wound is not considered bad. He escaped luckily as it was. If I were to enumerate the many narrow escapes which come under my observation, I could easily fill a volume of such. I will but enumerate one this time. Lieutenant [Hugh] Montgomery, of Company F, had his leg grazed by a ball from the picket while standing in one of the company-streets. All the damage he sustained can be easily remedied by the tailor. Yesterday morning (the 17th) a detachment of 125 men from our regiment, in charge of Captain J. D. Cook, of Co. A, and in heavy marching order, started off for Division Headquarters. They returned to camp on the evening of the same day, having been busy performing fatigue-duty on our left.

On Monday morning last, the SUNDAY MERCURY came as usual. If it did not, we would miss it very much, and the news soon spread throughout the camp that Lincoln had been re-elected.

Some of our officers are returning from Furlough; among them, Lieut. [Clarence Y.] Beecher. All hands were glad to see him, and hope that he will now remain with us.

Several promotions are under way. As soon as they are made known, I will apprise you of the same. And in the meantime, I am yours, etc.,			S. G. C.

December 4, 1864
SECOND FIRE ZOUAVES
FORT SEDGWICK, NEAR PETERSBURG, VA., Nov. 27.

The regiment is still garrisoning the large and important work known as Fort Sedgwick among military critics; but among us soldiers, it goes, far and near, by the euphonious title of Fort Hell—a name which it justly merits, as it is the hottest, and, all the same time, the most dangerous position on the whole of this extensive line. To give you a correct idea as to how we live, or exist here, I will give you a small sketch of affairs, holds good for the whole twenty-four hours; and if you will not pronounce it a terror to the Fire Zouaves, then there is no terror whatever in the Rebel minies and mortars. In fact, we are subject to almost every missile thrown Unionward by the excited graybacks. Old Fort Hell seems to be the target for all the soldiers of Jeff that lie around Petersburg; and the way in which they crack loose on us sometimes is a sin. We are not, yet fixed up like being in no state to stand a regular siege—we having but precious few bomb-proofs—the majority of the men being in nothing but their shelter-tents. This makes things appear very critical, especially when the Johnnys open upon us. Then a comical scamp presents itself. Such a plunging of Fire Zouaves for bomb-proofs, traverses, and breastworks that takes place, is truly comical and dangerous, at the same time, as it is. It forcibly reminds us of a diminutive Bull Run. Then again, we are not to blame for it, as every shot, or shell, or mortar, that is hurled at the Johnnys within our hearing we must suffer the anxiety for it, for then they revenge themselves upon poor Fort Hell, and at our devoted salvos are pitched all the furies of countless forts; in the shape of seething and fiery mortars. But I am happy to say that they seldom do any serious injury in our midst. At this portion of the line the enemy still show a pretty solid front; but, as a natural thing, the cold weather keeps them considerably bomb-proofed. They do not seem to stand the cold half as well as our men. This is owing, no doubt, to our superior style of clothing and food. They already huddle themselves up in their blankets and squat around their fires as though, they were on icebergs. To us this is nothing but good wholesome weather. The only thing that comes hard on the boys now is the enormous amount of picket and fatigue duty that we have to perform daily. We soon hope to have present affairs altered, which done, we will be a happy-band of cadets in Fort Hell—hot as it is.

The New York troops enjoyed their Thanksgiving dinner hugely. The material, which they hastily packed into our stomachs, far surpassed their most sanguine ideas of the feast. In fact, the good people of the North, who so graciously remembered the soldiers, and got the affair up for them, have an abundance of thanks. Our bill of fare, in particular, ran thus: Roast turkey, do, chicken, pound cake, ginger do., jellies, apples, pies, onions, potatoes, etc. Considering the magnitude of the undertaking, and the difficulties surrounding it, it could not have been gotten up better. Our only regret is, that our days of thanksgiving are not so numerous as our battles.

Colonel M. W. Burns is still in command of the regiment. He is a trim and efficient soldier, as well as the soul of the regiment. No man has ever got better fighting or better conduct out of a lot of men than has Mickey Burns out of the Fire Zouaves. What is left of us all stick to him like a plaster. Our gay and undaunted Adjutant, Geo. B. Daris, is also present, performing his intricate routine of business with a precision that not only reflects credit upon himself, but also upon the organization to which he belongs. By the way, to condense the whole thing into a nutshell, George is what us lads call a whole-souled and extremely clever fellow, and just the man that a soldier would care to meet with, either in the walks of regimental camp life or on a fatiguing march; for as sure as night succeeds day, so sure is he of having the friendly smile extended.

As usual, the pickets still continue their dead-aim style of warfare, causing no small amount of wounds and loss of life on either side. But soon the Frost King will cause them to handle their cold iron less. At present everything appears to be in the usual state, and there are no signs of a move on either side. But there is no telling how soon one will spring up.

SNAKE.

December 11, 1864
SIXTY-FIRST REGIMENT, N.Y.V.V.
December 4.

"Well, we're off again", was the word, as at 11, P.M., on the evening of the 28th, we received orders to "pack up". The boys were loath to leave their quarters, some having erected for themselves very comfortable log huts, and supplied themselves with every thing requisite for passing the winter. As it was, every thing was soon packed up, and at 2, A.M., on the morning of the 29th, we started "for the left". After marching until sunrise, we halted, and rested until about 8, A.M., when we were off again. At 12, M., same day, we reached our destination, which proved to be the position formerly occupied by the Ninth Corps, and who, thanks to them, left us very comfortable log huts. Tired as we were, we set to work at once to rig ourselves; and such running and looking for boxes, boards, and the like, would make a civilian laugh.

We had hardly thrown ourselves down to rest before we were called upon to go on picket. Our rations were out, and had been for two days, and we were in hopes that rations would be dealt out before we started; but we were doomed to disappointment. The detail was called out, tired and hungry as they were, and in a short time reached the picket-line, under charge of Lieutenant Beecher.

During the night, I am sorry to say it, twenty of our men went over to the enemy; and yet I, with others, are glad to get rid of them. These same twenty men never enlisted for this regiment, but by some hocus pocus arrangement, were sent to us a few months ago as substitutes. They were continually growling and grumbling at their fate, but what must be their feelings now? I'll wager my head that they wish themselves back again. We as a veteran regiment, feel this deeply; yet, at the same time, we are not ashamed to own it, neither are we afraid of losing our "Old Vets".

On picket, can see the Johnnys plainly, and, in fact, can do so from our present camp. Near us is a "white house", and, a few days ago, we saw a man and little girl walking around it, followed by a dog. It was the first "home-like" scene we have seen for a long time, and put us all to thinking of our white homes in the North. On Thursday evening, Colonel [George W.] Scott called us out in line, and then informed us of Sherman's great victory, which has, ere this, thrilled the country. We received the news as "Vets" should, with three rousing cheers for Sherman, and three more for his men. Everything here is, at the present writing, as quiet as mice. Now and then a deserter from the enemy comes in our picket-line, and tells the same woeful tale of suffering in the South. If we winter here, we shall make ourselves as comfortable as possible, and to pass the time, we have erected a bowling alley, in the shape of two upright posts, a crossbar, ten wooden pins, a cord about twenty feet in length, with a cannon-ball attached to one end, and with which we knock the pins down as fast as they can be set up. Great fun for us "sogers".

More anon,   S. G. C.

December 18, 1864

SIXTY-FIRST REGIMENT, N.Y.V.V.

NEAR SOUTHERN RAILROAD, VA., Dec. 13.

At the date of my last dispatch, we were in hopes that the position we then occupied would be retained by us, for winter-quarters, but such was not to be the case, for at least the time being. Rumors of movements on hand were rife throughout the camp for several days, and at last culminated in a movement toward the Vaughn Road, by our brigade. We broke camp at an early hour on Friday morning, the 9th instant, and leading the brigade, proceeded toward the left. The morning was bitter cold, and it was with reluctance that we turned out; but bound not to be behind, we fell into line, and in a short time we were off. We halted about 10 A.M., same morning; line of battle was formed (we on the right), and shortly afterward, brisk firing was heard in our immediate front, caused by our cavalry engaging the enemy. We then received orders to march forward on the double-quick, and, after proceeding about half a mile, came to a stream, which proved to be Hatch's [Hatcher's] Run; it was strewn with fallen trees, which made it almost impossible to pass. The Rebels occupied the opposite bank, and we, with the Second N.Y. Artillery, were ordered to charge upon them. We made an effort to do so, but found the water too deep to admit of fording, being in some places of such a depth as to completely submerge our men. Major [George] Hogg, commanding the Second N.Y. Artillery, swam across on horseback; with three others (one of which was Lieutenant George St. Joice, of Company D, Sixty-first Regiment) holding on to the tail of the Major's horse, they were the first to land on the opposite bank, and shortly after they were joined by some cavalry; we, in the meantime, had proceeded a short distance down the stream, when we came to a pontoon-bridge. Crossing it, we (with the One Hundred and Fortieth Pennsylvania, Second New York Artillery, and several companies of cavalry) charged upon the Rebels, and succeeded in driving them from their earthworks. Our cavalry pursued them several miles, and then returned. Our loss in killed, wounded, and missing was about forty, among which were two of the Second New York Artillery, who were drowned while attempting to cross the stream above referred to. Our regiment then received orders to form a picket-line, which was soon done, and we then held the front, right, and left of the road. At 5, P.M., it commenced to snow, accompanied with rain and a cold chilling wind from the northward. Our position being on elevated ground, and exposed to the full force of the elements, we were soon in a pleasant situation—our clothes wet with rain, which froze as fast as it fell; and it took considerable blowing to keep our fire burning. Toward evening, it ceased raining, and the programme changed. At 8, P.M., a heavy hailstorm set in, which continued all night and until 6, A.M., of the following morning (the 10th). Altogether it was a very disagreeable night. Several of our veterans declared they had passed through colder ones, but none more uncomfortable. At daylight Saturday morning, the aspect of the surrounding country was decidedly winterish; but toward noon (the wind having moderated) the snow and ice began to melt, and a general thaw all round was the result. While the ground was thawing under our feet, we were busy thawing out our bodies and clothes by the aid of large fires.

At 1½, P.M., a lady, accompanied by her two little sons, applied to Lieutenant [Thomas] Miller (then in charge of our left line) for a pass into our lines, stating that she had resided in the South for eleven years, and was tired of living in Rebeldom. She was sent under guard to head-quarters.

At 2, P.M., the Johnnys were heard giving vent to their unearthly yells in our front. We were up in arms at once, and were prepared to meet them. Our cavalry then advanced, and sharp skirmish ensued between them. Companies C and D, of our regiment, under charge of Lieutenants [William] Malcom and Beecher, then advanced to aid the cavalry, and succeeded in keeping the Rebs at bay for a time. The infantry were then ordered to fall back to their breastworks, and to keep possession of them at all hazards, as far as possible. Our regiment was drawn up in line of battle behind some works, and for a short time firing ceased. Suddenly the enemy were discovered on our flanks, and we were then ordered to fall back, which we did, in good order, with the brigade drawn up in line in a cornfield to their rear. Our regiment lost seventeen men and captured some thirty prisoners. What the loss of the brigade was I am unable to state.

No further prospect of an engagement appearing, we took up the line of march for our old camp, arriving there at 8, P.M., Saturday evening, and right glad were we glad to be back in our quarters once more.

The weather is still unpleasant, and appearances indicate another storm.

S. G. C.

December 25, 1864
FIFTY-SIXTH REGIMENT, N.Y.V.V.
MORRIS ISLAND, S.C., Dec. 14.

To-night, the report comes to us, through Rebel sources, that the great city of Savannah has fallen into the hands of our gallant Sherman.

Before proceeding further, perhaps it would be well for me to say that the regiment, with the exception of about two hundred men, have gone off on an expedition into the interior of the State. They left here on the 26th of November, and proceeded up the Broad River, and made a landing at Boyd's Point, and were engaged in the battle of Honey Hill, on November 30, in which we lost a number of men.

Since then they have been in two more battles, and the total loss is about one hundred. Our regiment behaved splendidly, as it always does, when in front of the enemy.

They are still there, and what they are now doing I know not, as I have not heard from them for the past week. The men who are left here are only those who are unable to endure the march and fatigue of such an occasion.

There has been no firing from our batteries for the past week, owing to the flag-of-truce fleet, for the purpose of receiving our prisoners from the hands of the enemy lying in the harbor. To-day, they were receiving them all the afternoon, and I am sorry to say, over forty of them have died since they were exchanged. Such a ragged, filthy set of men I never saw as they were when they came on board our ship. They were washed, and supplied with new clothing, and now look respectable. While I write, the mournful tones of the muffled drums greet my ear as the cortege pass my tent. Forty-five of our brave officers are to be consigned to the tomb through the neglect of men who claim to carry on a Christian war. Their prisoners whom we returned to them were sound, and able to go into the ranks immediately, while every one whom they return to us is subject for the hospital.

But I must attend to the funeral and will leave you, and if anything occurs you will again hear from,

PET.

SIXTY-FIRST REGIMENT, N.Y.V.V.
NEAR SOUTHSIDE RAILROAD, VA., Dec. 18

For a wonder, we have remained in our present quarters one long week, and have not been disturbed, by orders to "pack up", etc. We have all been glad to remain quiet for a while; for we have, indeed, roved considerably since the beginning of the present campaign.

I have no important news to communicate to your readers this week, everything in our neighborhood being very quiet. We are performing the usual duties peculiar to camp-life, such as picket-duty, and fatigue. Our regiment performs the picket-duty, as formerly, so, you see, the Brigadier-General commanding has not lost confidence in us, as many supposed, owing to a few desertions from our ranks.

A painful example was set to all deserters from our lines on Friday of last week. Some time ago, a number of men belonging to regiments in our division deserted over to the enemy. They were in hopes that (taking advantage of the Rebel President's proclamation) they would be sent to their homes; but found themselves mistaken. They were sent to Kentucky, and at that place were captured by Union soldiers, and sent on to City Point in irons. On trial, they were found to be deserters, and were sentenced to be hanged. The sentence was carried into effect as above stated, on Friday. The whole division turned out, and all witnessed the execution. Orders were read to the troops, warning them to beware of a similar fate.

Yesterday, our monthly inspection took place, and we again received the praise of the Brigade-Inspector (Captain Boyd), who, by the way, is an excellent officer, and well liked by all in the brigade.

We are now daily expecting re-enforcements to our regiment, by a late consolidation which has been effected. The Fifty-seventh Regiment, N. Y. V., is now part and parcel of the Sixty-first Regiment, N. Y. V.; and, from the former good reputation which the Fifty-seventh enjoyed, we are led to believe that the consolidation will be for our benefit in every way.

This morning Colonel Scott read to us a dispatch from General [George] Thomas, Commanding Army of the Cumberland, stating that he had whipped the enemy at all points. Altogether, it was cheering news, and we hope that he may continue to be successful.

We have had some very cold weather here during the week; and this morning it commenced to rain, and, at the present writing, still continues.

S. G. C.

Chapter V

<u>1865</u>

by

William B. Styple

"The war-worn veteran," wrote a correspondent to the *Sunday Mercury*, "who for four years has stood the brunt of a soldier's hardship, sees at last the Rebellion tottering to its downfall. His heart yearns to his loved ones, and with undisguised joy and delight he looks forward to a speedy reunion."

By early 1865, the prospects of victory and peace were never better for the Federal Army. Whether through peace negotiations or military action, triumph for the Union seemed a certainty, and at long last the struggle was coming to an end. With Sherman in the Carolinas, Grant at Petersburg, Sheridan in the Valley, and Thomas in Tennessee, the *Sunday Mercury* correspondents were all convinced that final victory was only a campaign away, but few realized it would be over by the ides of April. An optimistic Federal wrote from the trenches of Petersburg: "There is one thing which must impress the civilians who visit this Army, and that is the cheerfulness and buoyancy of feeling everywhere prevailing."

Over in the opposite trench, there was no "cheerfulness and buoyancy" in the Army of Northern Virginia. The noose was tightening, and to everyone (with the possible exception of Jefferson Davis) the collapse of the Confederacy seemed a certainty. Lee's starving army, once vaunted and feared, was now rapidly disintegrating. The *Sunday Mercury* correspondents repeatedly tell of scores of Confederate deserters coming into Federal lines each day and night, draining the Army of Northern Virginia of its manpower. In a desperate measure to fill their depleted ranks, the Confederate Congress approved a plan to enlist slaves as soldiers, but this futile idea did not amount to anything.

Hope of a negotiated peace between the two nations was another non-reality for Jefferson Davis. On February 3, representatives of the Confederacy, including Vice President Alexander Stephens, met with President Lincoln and Secretary Seward to make overtures of peace, but the firm stance of the Lincoln Administration in not recognizing the existence of the Confederate Nation doomed the negotiations. The peace bubble had burst and one disappointed correspondent commented: "the boys have made up their minds that what they desire can only be had through the instrumentality of the bullet and bayonet."

After the surrender of Lee on April 9, any celebratory feelings of triumph felt by the soldier correspondents were soon tempered by the assassination of President Lincoln on April 14. "All the joy we felt," wrote a correspondent, "was suddenly changed into mourning." Like most newspapers in the North, the editors of the *Sunday Mercury* had been highly critical of the Lincoln Administration, especially after disastrous defeats on the battlefield, and one can only wonder how much regret the editors felt for their old salvoes against the martyred Lincoln.

With the war over, things military no longer held much appeal for the correspondents of the *Sunday Mercury*; all thoughts turned to going home. One frustrated veteran complained: "We shall be glad when we are able to throw the yoke of military rule off and return to civil life, we have had four years of it; we have been fighting for freedom and independence, and now we have gained the victory we want our freedom."

Freedom, but little else, arrived for the slave with the passage of the Thirteenth Amendment. The climate for the freemen was nearly as hostile in the victorious North as it was in the defeated South.

For the surrendered enemy, there seemed to be more pity. One correspondent wrote of the defeated rebels: "What of them? Without clothes for their backs, and perhaps their homes in ashes, what have they to look forward to? We must forgive and forget past injuries; and turn to with willing hands, and help to rebuild the broken-down parts of the land."

This feeling of brotherly goodwill among countrymen was demonstrated as the terms of surrender were being negotiated at Appomattox. Lee mentioned that his troopers and artillerists owned their own mounts and asked if these men might be permitted to turn their war-horses into plow-horses. Grant agreed. "This will have the best possible effect upon the men," said Lee, and "will do much toward conciliating our people." The bloodshed and destruction was over; the time for planting and growth had begun.

The occupation of soldier-journalist was gone. While awaiting discharge, a veteran *Sunday Mercury* correspondent visited the war-torn grounds surrounding Arlington, the former home of Robert E. Lee, now a cemetery for thousands of Union soldiers. As the soldier looked out over the fields he saw the numerous earthen fortifications being dismantled and leveled to the ground with the valuable soil being made ready for planting by the farmer. The poignant words of the veteran soldier heralded a new era of healing:

"Cornfields are blooming, and their green plumes tossed by the wind, seems to echo the divine sentiment, 'Peace on earth and good will toward men'."

With the passage of time, most of the wounds caused by this bitter conflict have healed, though some scars still remain. In the interim, the authentic voices of the Civil War have all departed; fortunately, we have their correspondence, and if we are to learn from history, we must listen to their words.

William B. Styple
Kearny, New Jersey

January 8, 1865

"Knapsack-Drill."

A soldier's life is hard enough.
He takes the smooth part with the rough.
'Tis nothing strange, but a bitter pill;
For he is oft put through the knapsack-drill.

If by chance we should go to town,
To see the sights and Mrs. Brown;
With "lager" there our canteen fill,
We are certain of a knapsack-drill.

Our dress-parades, should we not go,
But in our tents lie snug and low,
With colic-pains and other ills,
We are certain of that knapsack-drill.

The officers, so nice and prime,
Whene'er they chose can have a time;
Their goblets to the brim can fill,
And never fear that knapsack-drill.

Our service-time will soon be up,
And if we live the gun we'll drop;
Of pleasure then we'll take our fill,
Without fear of "knapsack-drill".

> LEO, Forty-eighth Regiment N.Y.V.
> PETERSBURG, VA., 1864.

HAREWOOD HOSPTIAL

WASHINGTON, D.C., Jan. 3.

The year of 1864 has closed with great victories, and the military situations never looked better than what it does now. The indications most certainly are, that the Rebellion is in a dying state. The deathlike chills have already seized it, and a few more heavy and vigorous blows will knock the breath of life out of it. Sherman's triumphal march through Georgia has put good courage into the Army, and to the whole North. Gen. Grant is still holding Lee in a vice-like grasp.

"New-Year's comes but once a year." What heart does not dilate with mingled pleasure and regret at the recollection of the scenes of hospital-life? While at home, we could enjoy many a happy New-Year's evening spent in the society of those whom we have left behind us, and who are dearest to us upon the earth, where happiness was reflected upon every face. The wounded soldier spends his holiday in games in the hospital; and the young and tender female sitting by his bedside in sweet retreating modesty, or blushing and smiling in all the charms of innocence and budding beauty, all remind us of our pleasant homes. The Harewood Zouaves were to have a grand dinner on New-Year's day; the day has come and gone, and the great feast went with it. The bill of fare at this large hotel was, for breakfast, mush and molasses (about half done), a cup of coffee, and a down East cut of bread; dinner, one piece of beef, one cup of soup (very hard to tell what it was made of), two small potatoes, and bread; supper, one cup of oyster-soup, with no oysters to be found (and about half done), and a slice of bread, free of charge to all sick and wounded soldiers of the Harewood Brigade. I could not say what they had for Christmas, because I was not here; but at Augur Hospital everything was carried on in good shape. There is a great difference in the hospitals out here. We are all getting fat and ready for duty, and to be sent to the front. Some are going to the front every day, and there are many sent back again, on account of running wounds. There was a large train of ambulances filled with wounded arrived at this hospital last week, not from the front, but from Camp Distribution, where they were sent to join their regiments for duty. They are examined at the above camp before returning to duty; if not fit for duty, they are sent back again to the same hospital where they came from, with a little note to the chief-surgeon in charge of that hospital, warning him to be a little more attentive to his duty. They have in this hospital a temperance society, numbering about one hundred and fifty members, who are mostly all cripples. They all bear an honorable scar of the Rebellion.

                                                                                GUARDIAN.

FIFTH REGIMENT (DURYEE'S), N.Y.V.V.

CAMP NEAR WARREN STATION, VA., Jan. 2.

Ever since our raid on the Weldon Railroad, we have been busily engaged in constructing winter-quarters (the second one this season), and we trust we may be allowed to enjoy the comforts of these for awhile; for that eagerness for active movements on our part, so persistently heralded by newspaper-correspondents, does not exist at this time.

Yesterday, we had the first snow of the season in this vicinity, and this morning the ground is slightly covered. There is considerable tribulation among the shoulder-straps of the Fifth Corps, owing to an order recently promulgated by General Warren, making commissary whisky non-accessible to officers, except on application to and approval of medical directors. In consequence, temperance among that fraternity is, to a certain extent, imperative; though some have found a new base, by establishing communication with friends in other corps, whose commanders have not been so unkind as ours. Various reasons are hinted at as to the cause of the order; but I am not one of those who are so uncharitable as to think that General Warren anticipated to much of a jubilee during the holidays, and therefore cut off the supplies, not withstanding "commissary" is a peculiar weakness with that class of individuals, our own regiment always excepted (?). Many of the boys are enjoying a Happy New-Year, in the receipt of boxes from home, filled with delicacies and mementos for the absent ones. An occasional package of "cordial", so original and invention as to escape the rigid scrutiny of the Provost-Marshal, anon finds its way to the owner, when the ostensible bitter or catsup is pledged in unpretending tin goblets, to the permanence of the Union. Long live the Yankees! We have rather a dull picket-line at present, being somewhat removed from our main line, with no enemy in our front that we can discover, so no interchanges occur. An occasional scouting party venture out, but I surmise they go more for their own interest than the good of the Union. At least, I hear of no good results attained. Trusting that another New Year may dawn on a restored and peaceful Union. I am yours, truly,

                                                                                SEYLUS

January 15, 1865

CITY POINT CORRESPONDENCE

CITY POINT, VA., January 9, 1865.

An elegant flag, purchased by the employees of the Government bakery at this place, was raised last week. The flag is twenty-four feet long by sixteen feet wide; the staff is painted white, and consists of two spars—the main and the topmast—which are eighty-five feet in height. Across the tree or top is the inscription in large characters: "One Union, one and inseparable", together with the date, "January 1, 1865". As soon as the flag was run up to the masthead, three hearty cheers were given with a will by all present; and thus one more bright starry emblem of our nation's pride and boast was given to the breeze, adorns City Point, and bids defiance to traitors. The cost of the flag was $100.

A large barracks is in course of erection at City Point, for the reception of soldiers passing to and fro; such a building has long been needed here, owing to the great number of troops continually arriving. A portion of the Second and Fifth Corps shipped from Bermuda Hundred and City Point, last week, in transports. Their destination is of course a secret. There has been much irregularity in the arrival of the mails from the North during the past three weeks, owing, doubtless, to the quantity of ice in the Potomac River. One can hardly realize the disappointment occasioned by a delay in the mails and Northern papers. Little firing has been heard here since the commencement of the holidays; whether it is that the enemy are keeping these days as formerly, or whether they are but preparing for another effort to pierce our lines, it is hard for us to surmise.

From a Southern refugee, named Joseph Griffin, who ran the blockade of Rebel pickets around Richmond on Saturday night last, we learn, that he with six other men, residents of that vicinity, after several repeated attempts succeeded in getting safely through. He states that, the greatest gloom pervades the community since the capture of Savannah, and that the general opinion in Richmond is that but one more great effort is likely to be made, and that if unsuccessful in that they must then accept the only alternative of submission to the General Government. Troops from the South are daily pouring in and taking position around Richmond and toward Petersburg. He says it is thought Gen. Lee will speedily make an attack in front of Petersburg, where doubtless the great fight will come off. He says they look for much assistance from the seven gunboats which they have on the James. The secession leaders look entirely to Lee for aid now, and have lost all confidence in Jeff Davis, blaming him for the "disasters" of the past year, and his interference with the plans of Gen. Lee. Provisions are not so scarce, but prices are enormous. Flour brought last week, $750 per barrel, and coffee $35 per pound; other eatables in proportion. Greenbacks are worth $35 and $40 on the dollar; one gold dollar is worth $75 Confederate money. The authorities at Richmond have recently opened a souphouse, where large numbers are daily fed on fresh beef and corn bread. Much suffering exists among poor families; neither women nor children will be allowed through the lines. Yet there are several persons who make a business of piloting refugees through. For this service they readily receive $1,000 "Confed". The Government has been sending off the machinery of their works in Richmond to Salisbury, N. C., for some days past; this is a fact of much significance, from which we can draw our own inference.

A. O. P.

SIXTEENTH N.Y. HEAVY ARTILLERY
WILLIAMSBURG, January 8.

The lines of communication between Grant's Army and Washington by telegraph, passing for some miles through the enemy's country, the Confederate authorities detail operators with instruments to tap the wires, so as to gain valuable information, and Colonel J. J. Morrison, commanding at Williamsburg, Va., has as much as he can do with his small force to preserve the line unbroken. By unceasing vigilance, however, he gets track of them, and of late, one operator was caught with his arms, horse, and instruments. Last night, hearing that another one had been detailed to fill the captured one's place, Lieutenant [Law] Washburn, Co. I, Sixteenth N.Y. Artillery, was ordered with twelve men to find him; the inhabitants getting sight of our men, gave the operator timely notice, but hardly a moment too soon, for when the Lieutenant found his blanket, it was still warm, and his instrument, a very fine one, of English manufacture, with some fine English wire, all of which ran the blockade. The woods being thickly covered with underbrush, afford an impervious shelter to the Rebel scouts. Lieutenant Washburn and his men lay in the woods all night, keeping a bright look-out, but failed to see any enemy. In a house he searched, were found some of these infernal explosive bullets which are deadly poison, and a disgrace for civilization. From the appearance of smoke above the trees shortly after leaving the Lieutenant says he wouldn't be surprised if that house took fire.

Colonel Morrison, commanding on the Peninsula, has made his name a terror to the evil-doers on the outside, he will not allow his men to be murdered in cold blood without vengeance upon their heads; he has now over fifteen of these bushwackers, who are confined at Fortress Monroe awaiting their trial.

The town of Williamsburg, once noted for its high society, pure morality and unbending respectability, is, under the base influence of our soldiers, rapidly degenerating. A horrible scene took place the other night. A young woman who was a refugee from Hampton, was married for three years or the war to a member of the First New York Mounted Rifles. Being ordered to the front, he, of course, left her behind. In course of time, the natural result was produced; but her sisters, who were very anxious for admiration, and continually had their house full of officers and men, murdered the infant a short time after its birth. The body of the child was placed in an outhouse, formerly used as negro-quarters, and the house set on fire. The danger to the surrounding houses was great, but the presence of an old fire-laddie, Lem. Van B., of the 28 Hose, who seemed in his element, confined the fire to the one building. He was only assisted by the provost-guard, he being their Sergeant (a higher position awaits his acceptance). The babe's body was discovered, the legs charred off, and the whole family have been sent to Norfolk for trial.

JACKSON.

January 22, 1865
SIXTY-FIFTH REGIMENT, N.Y.V.V.
BEFORE PETERSBURG, VA., Jan.16.

Yesterday, our regiment was inspected by Brigadier-General [Ranald S.] McKenzie; the neat, clean, and tasteful appearance of the men elicited the highest praise from that strict and stern soldier. Our camp and quarters were also minutely inspected by Major-General Fran. Wheaton, who complimented the captain commanding the regiment for the cleanliness everywhere exhibited in his command. It is needless to say that we feel highly flattered at these encomiums, coming as they do from distinguished officers, who, by their brilliant services in the cause of the Union, have made their names household words in the loyal North. The Sixty-fifth Regiment may well be pardoned if they thus openly give vent to their delight for nearly four years have elapsed since they parted down your great roadway, on their way to the seat of war. On every battle-field fought by the Potomac Army there lies their dead, while a goodly portion sacrificed their lives to the Shenandoah Valley. It is useless for me to extol them. Our record speaks for itself in plainer words than mine. No less than three generals have sprung from our regiment, two of whom are now rendering the country the most valuable service.

The Rebels are very quiet. They have kept their guns mysteriously silent for these last few days. Whenever they open their artillery-fire they generally receive a fair exchange of the same, as they send from

Fort Hill and other works of ours directly in front of Petersburg. The Cockade City—if the reports of deserters are to be relied on—has sustained great damage from our fire. They say there is not a house but what has been pierced by our shot and shell. Those of its inhabitants who still remain in the doomed city live in underground cellars, and their condition is said to be very miserable. All who come in our lines agree in the conviction that the Rebellion is a failure.

The only exciting duty at present is picket. A few nights ago, the Rebs, to the number of thirty, made a raid on the Second Division picket-line, for the purpose of stealing overcoats and blankets. But it happened, unfortunately for the Rebels, that our boys had anticipated the intentions of the seedy Secesh, and had brought but few of those articles with them. On reaching our line, the first sally was, "Give us your coats and blankets". But the answer they received was more significant than elegant. After gobbling the haversacks with contents, which was hard-tack, they returned to their own lines. Their speed doing so was made speedier by a volley of musketry. Two or three wounded Rebels fell into the hands of our men. Should they try this game over again they may not get off so easily.

The health of the boys continues very good. All letters or papers for the regiment should be directed via Washington, D.C.

FRANCONI.

TWELFTH REGIMENT U.S. INFANTRY

ELMIRA, N.Y., Jan. 17.

Having a leisure-hour to myself, I thought it best to devote it to jotting down the doings of the Twelfth New York Infantry for the year 1864.

Up to April 30, 1864, nothing of importance transpired to the regiment from the 1st of January in that time, being engaged guarding the railroad, near Nokesville, Va. On the 30th of April, the regiment commenced their march, crossing the Rappahannock on the 1st of May, and encamped near Brandy Station, Va.; on the 3rd, moved to Culpepper Court House, crossing the Rapidan on the 4th; on the 5th, first met and engaged the enemy at the old battle-ground of the Wilderness, the fight lasting until the night of 7th; on the 8th, the regiment moved to Laurel Hill, and became engaged with the enemy on the morning of the 10th; on the night of the 10th, we threw up intrenchments, remaining in them suffering from a galling and heavy artillery-fire of the enemy; on the 12th, we again became engaged with the enemy; on the 13th, we marched to Spottsylvania Court House, threw up earthworks under a terrific fire from the enemy, remaining there until the 20th. On the 21st, advanced toward Hanover, crossed the Tar River on the 22nd. On the 23rd, crossed the North Anna, and repulsed the enemy handsomely, who attacked in force. This little affair is one that the boys look upon with pride; they not only carried by assault formidable works thrown up by the enemy, but drove thrice their own number out of them, capturing also quite a batch of prisoners. On the 25th, advanced two miles, the 26th and 27th were occupied in marching toward the Pamunky; on the 28th, crossed the Pamunky, the 29th and 30th were passed in skirmishing with the enemy; on the 31st were relieved as skirmishers and advanced in line of battle one mile; on the 2nd fell back half a mile and threw up earthworks, where we remained until the 5th when we moved to Coal Harbor, holding our position until the 11th of the month; the readers of your valuable paper will remember the desperate sorties that were made by both sides, the horrible slaughter, the great loss each met during these memorable never-to-be-forgotten five days; on the 12th commenced our march toward the Chickahominy, which historic river we crossed on the 13th, at Long Bridge; on the 14th, moved toward the James River, crossing on the 16th and marched towards Petersburg, Virginia, arriving in front of the enemy's works, on the 17th or the 18th, assaulted or carried the first line of works of the enemy, after which we commenced throwing up earthworks, after which we succeeded in finishing—not withstanding our loss was great from the fire of the sharp-shooters and the enemy's batteries; the regiment remained the same in their works until the 30th of July, when they moved one-half mile along the Norfolk & Petersburg Railroad as a reserve.

You will remember that was the day that the famed mine exploded under one of the enemy's forts, resulting so disastrously to our arms; from that time until August 18th, we lay under a sharp and continuous fire from the enemy's batteries. On the morning of the 18th, we commenced our march for the Weldon Railroad, striking the road at the Six Mile House, Virginia. Our regiment was the first that reached the road, being on the right of the brigade of Regulars and New York Volunteers. We were immediately thrown out as skirmishers driving the enemy to the "White" or Davis House. At about five in the evening, the enemy advanced in force, but were kept at bay; the whole of the night, the men worked like beavers throwing up breastworks. On the 19th, the enemy assaulted with a fierceness and desperation the whole of our line, finding a weak spot on our right held by a skirmish-line only of the Third Division of our corps; they succeeded in breaking through gaining a temporary advantage, and flanking completely the whole of our division. It is on great occasions like these, brave men are produced, and true heroism shows itself. Our color-bearer was wounded, our men entirely surrounded, our colors gone. Lieutenant August Thiemann, seeing our battle-worn flag, which we had carried, though tattered and torn, with honor through the campaign, in the hands of the enemy, struck down with his sword the Rebel who had it, and bore it off in triumph, amidst the shouts and cheers of the men. That little episode gave new life to many a heart, who, emulating the gallant deed of the lieutenant, succeeded in cutting their way through. Lieutenant Thiemann was immediately placed on the staff of the brigadier-general, and has been breveted Major by his grateful country—a promotion well-earned, and properly bestowed. The Major has just reached this place, having just left the field, preferring the active life of a soldier to that of the garrison. On the 21st, the enemy made another effort to repossess themselves on the Weldon Railroad, but got driven back in confusion, leaving all their dead, some eight hundred prisoners, seven battle-flags, and a few pieces of artillery, in our hands. The enemy made no further attempt to regain what they knew was irretrievably lost, so we remained in our position until Sept. 30, nothing occurring in the meantime, except the usual picket-firing. On the 30th, moved two miles to the left, and participated in the battle of Peeble's Farm, near Poplar Grove Church. On the 28th October, was again on the move, taking part in the engagement on the Vaughan Plank Road. On the 2nd of November, 1864, the regiment was relieved for the present from duties in the field, scarcely a vestige of its original elements remaining. On the night of the 7th, we reached Elmira, N. Y., and have since been engaged guarding the Rebel prisoners stationed at this post, the men doing guard-duty every other day. In my next, I shall give you a sketch of the military position here, the Rebel barracks, etc., but en passant, will remark that the prisoners have warm and comfortable quarters, and are seemingly well fed and clothed. The sleighing here is excellent.

Truly, yours,   SOLITUDE.

SECOND N.Y. HEAVY ARTILLERY
CAMP NEAR PETERSBURG, Jan. 13.

The anxiety mentioned on the part of the gallant Second, to behold once more that periodical distributor in greenbacks, the Paymaster, increases daily. It is now upward of four months since we had the pleasure of seeing that official; and, should he honor us with a visit, I doubt not he will meet with a reception worthy the Second New York, and of the occasion. I can imagine nothing better calculated to absorb greenbacks and fractional currency than the sutler's exorbitant prices. We would willingly acquiesce to a fair certain percentage, but to demand thrice the market value of an article is not according to "Gunther". Furthermore, the man who would unhesitatingly practice such extortion toward a soldier in the field, can have but little patriotism in his organization.

Desertions from the enemy appear to be on the increase, at least on our section of the line. On an average we bring in, say fifteen a night. The Johnnys approach our lines generally on the run, their coat tails occupying a horizontal position, and making, on the whole very credible time. Decidedly the coolest thing of the season transpired yesterday morning. Toward daylight, a tall, raw-boned Johnny was seen to emerge abruptly from the edge of the wood, directly in front of a vidette pit. He was smoking a pipe with the greatest sang froid imaginable; and, on being observed by the vidette, the following colloquy took place:

Vidette.—"Halt!"
Johnny.—"I say, Yank, have you got an axe?"
Vidette.—(somewhat surprised),--"An axe?"
Johnny.—"Yes; I've been detailed to cut wood for the Yanks, and I've got no axe!"
Vidette.—"Are you armed?"
Johnny.—"Not by a d—d sight!"
Vidette.—"Advance; we will try to accommodate you."

Johnny did advance and was handed over to the corporal of the post; after which he was transferred to headquarters. A broad grin meanwhile holding possession of his countenance.

MERCUTIO.

FIFTH REGIMENT (DURYEE'S) N.Y.V.V.
NEAR THE WELDON RAILROAD, VA., Jan. 16.

Just now, the Army is apparently in the best of spirits. The papers, teeming with the news of victory and prospects of peace, have served to stimulate these feelings. Along with this also comes the welcome intelligence that City Point is full of Paymasters en route for the front, with plethoric valises, suggestive of greenbacks. Furloughs too, are expected to be soon granted, by general order, and everything tends to stamp Uncle Sam a "right power", and his generals nearly all trumps.

Our hearts are large in charity, and every man in the Army of the Potomac is ready, willing, and anxious to grasp in fellowship the hand of a repentant brother in Rebeldom. May they be as ready to meet us, is our earnest hope.

The Sixth Corps occupy the line of works held by us (the Fifth Corps) before the Weldon Railroad raid, but it seems to meet with more annoyances than the Fifth did. The pickets have been driven in on several occasions, called by the boys "haversack raids", and the Johnnys succeed in getting up a pretty large scare, a goodly number of blankets, a few prisoners, and a successful retreat, all within an hour. There is no corps in the Army between which more sociability and good feeling exists on the part of the enemy than the old Fifth. Picket firing, when not actually engaged in a campaign, is rarely practiced. This induces no lack of vigilance, however, for whenever an advance has been made on our lines, we have never been surprised.

For the past thirteen days a half-ration of whisky has been daily issued to our brigade. The ground on which we are encamped is very swampy, and sickness is quite prevalent. Fears are entertained that we may be visited by the small pox, and every precaution is taken to guard against it. A neighboring regiment, the Two Hundred and Tenth Pennsylvania is losing men daily, but it is not known among us that small pox is the cause. It is a new regiment, and the men not being acclimated I presume to be the principle cause of so much sickness among them.

Trusting that the shadow of coming events may soon assume tangibility, and that our next furlough may be a permanent one before the winter closes, I am yours,

STYLUS.

January 29, 1865
UNITED STATES FRIGATE MALVERN
OFF FORT FISHER, Jan. 20.

On the morning of January 12, 1865, after getting the fleet underway—including the New Ironside, Monadnock, Mahopac, Saugus, and Canonicus—the Admiral [D. D. Porter] started with his flag-ship the Malvern, and in a short time overhauled the fleet outside the bar, and took the lead, heading S.S.W. The transports, with the troops under command of Major-General Terry, in his splendid flag-ship, the General McClellan, comprised some ten thousand troops and about seventy-five iron-clads, frigates, and gunboats. We had fine weather all the way down, and the fleet maneuvering and signalizing was a splendid sight, indeed, to gaze upon. After a sail of nine hours, we came in sight of the coast, and off in the distance we could observe Fort Fisher and the mound looming through the haze. The fleet came to anchor about twelve miles off shore for the night. In the morning, we signalized the fleet to get underway, and stand in shore. At 7½ o'clock on the morning of January 13, the United States Frigate Brooklyn opened the ball by shelling the woods. The mound returned the fire, but the shot fell a long way short. During this time the New Ironsides and double-turret Monadnock, were advancing steadily up toward Fort Fisher. At 12, M., the iron-clads opened on the Fort, the frigates also getting into action. The bombardment that was poured into Fort Fisher was terrific indeed—the Fort not replying very briskly. In the meantime, our troops were being landed under cover of the fire of our gunboats, about three miles up the beach, the firing was so rapid, that if there had been any Rebs in the woods they stayed there, as they did not show themselves outside Fort Fisher.

After the troops were landed, took possession of Half moon battery (the Rebs having skeddadled), throughout skirmished and pickets and at nightfall the fleet hauled out of range, with the exception of the ironside's and monitors, who kept up a fire on the fort at intervals, all night, the beach being illuminated with the campfires of the soldiers. In the morning, the frigates and gunboats all stood in again and opened their ponderous batteries on the doomed fort, which was kept up without intermission during the whole day. The bombardment on Fort Fisher, was equally grand, and it seemed impossible for any fort to hold out against it. I may remark here that the mound only fired a few shots during the first days' fight, and since then has not fired until the night of the 15th. On Sunday the 15th, the fire was kept up with more vigor than any other of the preceding days. In the afternoon, at 3:10, signalized to the fleet to cease firing, and at 3:15, the signal to charge on the fort was given by blowing a long whistle, when the sailors and soldiers made the attack, the sailors taking the sea-face of the fort, drawing the attention of the Rebs at this point, while the troops charged and poured in through the sally-port of the fort, where a dreadful hand-to-hand encounter took place between the opposed and the opposers. Every inch of ground was dearly bought, and the excitement was intense on board the ships, among the men who remained to man the guns; but at last, at 10:50, P.M., on Sunday-night, January 15, 1865, Major-General Terry signalized from the parapet of Fort Fisher to Admiral Porter, that the fort was ours, also capturing 2,500 prisoners, an immense quantity of ammunition and commissary-stores, and over one hundred guns, besides small arms in any quantity. Among the prisoners are General [W. H. C.] Whiting and Colonel [William] Lamb. There was a grand illumination through the fleet, rockets bursting, bells ringing, whistles screeching, burning cotton-lights, and portfires, cheering, and everything that would tend to show our joy in this, the greatest victory of the War. The Stars and Stripes now float over the ramparts of Fort Fisher, the Rebel stronghold.

I regret to record the death of Lieuts. B. H. Porter and S. W. Preston, of this ship, while gallantly leading the blue-jackets belonging to the Malvern, in the charge on the fort, they being in the advance. Capt. [K.R.] Breese came out safe. We also lost one of our crew, Chas. Love, a messenger-boy.

On the morning of the 16th, an explosion took place in one of the magazines in the fort, killing a large number of our soldiers, mostly of the One Hundred and Sixty-ninth N.Y.V. It is hard, after the struggle they passed through to obtain possession of the Fort. The sailors and soldiers did nobly.

To-day, some of our double-enders are in the river grappling for torpedoes in the channel; got up thirteen to-day.

The Stars and Stripes will soon be floating over the city of Wilmington. The officers of this ship have been getting up a splendid leather medal for presentation to General Butler for his distinguished services, performed while here on Christmas, when he expressed it as his candid opinion that Fort Fisher was impregnable, and could not be taken by assault.

Three cheers Admiral D. D. Porter and Major-General Terry the two heroes of Fort Fisher, and the officers and gallant sailors and soldiers of the army and navy. How are you, Jeff Davis and blockade-runners?

Yours truly,   BLUE JACKET.

SIXTY-FIFTH REGIMENT, N.Y.V.V.

BEFORE PETERSBURG, VA., Jan. 24.

Nothing has occurred since my last letter to disturb the almost universal quiet which pervades along the entire line from right to left, save that desultory picket-firing which is practiced momentarily in front of the Ninth Corps. Still the quietness that I have spoken of does not at all embody the active duties of the camp. From the time that reveille awakes us from our slumbers until we are admonished by tattoo to retire, there is a general hubbub for fatigue parties and details for various purposes. Still, the boys do not grumble, but render a cheerful obedience to every command, conscious of the fact that faultfinding and growling only have effect of making their labor the harder and more difficult to perform. Besides grumbling availeth naught.

We have been furnished with a new style of belt-equipments; there is as much harness about it as would suffice to rig out an army mule. The cartridge-box by this modern invention is worn on the breast, instead of on the hip, and is held in its position by two straps which run over the shoulder, on these straps are hooks to which the knapsack is fastened and held. The whole arrangement is cumbersome and unhandy; for when the occasion comes to take off knapsacks in a hurry, knives will be used more freely then fingers; in short, the mule-rig, as the boys classically style it, is a humbug. And if the prayers and blessings that daily offered up in behalf of the inventor [William D. Mann] avail, I fear that the individual in question will come to an unhappy end; for he will either shuffle off this mortal coil in double-lasting or else die with leather on the brain.

The boys are jubilant over the great victory at Fort Fisher, and we all now cherish fondly the hope that the war will be brought to a speedy close. Poor Benjamin F., his name is now but a joke on every soldiers' lips. Alas, what changes there are in life. Butler, the brilliant, who knew not mercy to others, must feel the want of it for himself now. Chickens generally come home to roost.

The several headquarters—regimental, brigade, and division—present an appearance of neatness and comfort that would surprise any civilian who might see the wondrous ingenuity displayed in all the arrangements—gravel-walks, inclosed by rows of cedars tastefully arranged, while the huts though not in the style of gothic structures, are still paragons of taste and neatness; the whole present an aspect so pleasing that it is a smooth feature in the roughness of war.

Numbers of deserters come in every night, and their story is the old familiar one—nothing to eat, nothing to wear; and certainly their appearance supports the latter assertion. Their tales of suffering in Dixie have been told so often, that to repeat them would only sound like a thrice-told tale on a sick man's ear. One of these dissatisfied Rebels came in last evening, and reported that some ten miles of the Danville Railroad had been washed away by the recent heavy rains. If this proves true, Bob Lee's Army will suffer some days for hard-tack and bacon.

A number of new faces, with commissions in their pockets, have arrived, and signified their readiness to be mustered in. With one exception, these aspirants for military fame are all strangers to the regiment, and their coming here to fill existing vacancies is a positive injustice to the capable and deserving non-commissioned officers of the regiment. No doubt these gentlemen are fully capable and deserving; but still that does not alter the fact that sergeants who have carried their chevrons proudly should have the precedence in promotions to the line. The Sixty-fifth has therefore been able to make its own officers, and undoubtedly they can do so in the future.

Brigadier-General McKenzie has gone North, on leave of absence. During his absence, Lieutenant-Colonel [Henry C.] Fisk will command the brigade. Colonel Fisk returned but a few days ago, having been on a brief visit to his home, looking very well. The Colonel is a man of fine qualities, and is very popular with the men.

Being a soldier who has fought his way from the ranks up to his present position, he is familiar with the wants of the men; and though exercising a rigid discipline, he is ever ready to listen to the supposed grievances, and the redress them if real.

Among the benefits, that we are now enjoying, not the least is the company-mess—it saves the men the trouble of cooking their own food, and materially enhances the comfort, if it can be called so, of camp-life.

The health of the boys continues good, and all are cheerful and high-spirited. And I must truly say, that in our estimation, after the bibles comes the SUNDAY MERCURY.

Hoping my next will contain something more of interest, I remain, patriotically yours,

FRANCONI.

February 5, 1865
SIXTY-FIFTH REGIMENT, N.Y.S.V.V.
BEFORE PETERSBURG, VA., Jan. 30.

We are still here; and if there was previously a possibility of a move, it has been rendered improbable by the recent heavy rains, which deluged the roads and made them impassible. It has now cleared off, however, and a frost has set in which threatens to make terra firma anything but sound footing.

The bad weather is a blessing in one sense, for it has the effect of waking up our deluded foes to a realization of their hard situation; and whenever rain or cold sets in, it generally causes a stampede of the indifferent Rebels to our lines. They have to run the gauntlet of fire from their own men, but this does not deter them in the least; for those who fire and those who desert, understand each other very well. Either the bullet goes too high or too low, to do any damage. Your correspondent observed a party of Rebels, yesterday, who had just come into our line; they consisted of a Major and ten privates; they were on their way to Army Headquarters. Their costume was anything but respectable; and if it is Rebel fashion to have their linen and cotton sticking out in a suspicious part of their pantaloons, I hope, for decency's sake, that Confederate tailors will abandon it.

A pleasing feature has been introduced in the duties of camp, namely, a brigade guard-mounting. The ceremony takes place daily in front of our regimental parade-ground. The affair is conducted under the auspices of the Assistant-Adjutant General of the brigade. And if it took place in Union square, instead of before Petersburg, there no doubt would be a great many spectators.

A continuous heavy artillery-fire was heard a few nights ago on our right. Reports were numerous as to its cause. Some few admirers of Bombastes Furioso B. [Benjamin F. Butler] asserted that our gunboats had succeeded in passing through the famous canal, and were engaged in bombarding Fort Darling, but it afterward turned out that three of the enemy's rams had come down for the purpose of destroying the shipping at City Point. They evidently thought that our iron-clads had all been sent down to assist Porter; but they found their mistake, for there were several cheese-boxes on hand, which furnished the Rebel rammers with a liberal luncheon, gratis; and Johnny Ram had to give out. The natives who reside in the rear of our lines are rapidly becoming Yankeeized, both in manners and taste. They know to some extent the power of the Rebellion, while daily they see the power of the Union. They are sensible people, and honestly admit that Jeff ain't got a ghost of a chance to win the desperate game that he is playing, and they have shaped their course accordingly to save their property and stick up for the old flag. I may say here that numbers of the fair Virginia lasses have entered into the bonds of matrimonial union with some of our gallant Union savers, thus practically putting into execution their theory.

Numbers of our boys who were wounded in the Valley in Sheridan's campaigns are returning. Among the late arrivals of this class are Lieutenants [John T.] Douglas and [Patrick] Hopkins, who were both severely wounded in the battle of Cedar Creek.

There is one thing which must impress itself deeply on the minds of the civilians who happens to visit this Army, and that is the cheerfulness and buoyancy of feeling everywhere prevailing. The reason for this is found in the late brilliant victories and the prospect of a speedy peace. The war-worn veterans, who for four years has stood the brunt of a soldier's hardship, sees at last the Rebellion tottering to its downfall, and that success complete and final is about to gild the banner he has toiled and suffered for. His heart yearns to his loved ones, and with undisguised joy and delight he looks forward to a speedy reunion.

The health of the regiment continues good, and those few that are ill receive the greatest attention from the experienced surgeon whose duty it is to attend to bodily ailments.

To-morrow we are to have an inspection, and as your correspondent is ambitious to win that furlough promised to the tidy, I must therefore commence those cleaning innovations, and close this letter by remaining,   Furloughly yours,   FRANCONI.

FIRST LINCOLN CAVALRY.

CAMP AVERILL, VA., Jan. 26.

We are busy as troopers can be—nothing but picket and fatigue duty all the time. Last week, Brigadier-General [George H.] Chapman assumed command of this division, and immediately made a personal inspection of every regiment in his command. It was quite unexpected to us poor dragoons, for we never heard a word about it till the distinguished gentleman opened our tent-door and walked in. The visit was so unexpected that we did not recognize him till we saw the little star on his cap. However, he found everything to his satisfaction in the "Old First", as we are ready at all times and all places to receive friend or foe.

At present, we are not troubled much by the chivalry; but Mosby's gang will not leave off their old work. Last week, one of this division was killed by those infernal villains. Three men went out a short distance from the picket-post, to a house close by, to get some milk. While in the house, a squad of guerrillas pounded upon them killing one, wounded the second, while the third escaped. Colonel [Alonzo] Adams' brother was in a house not far from where the affair took place; and the folks, mistaking him for the Colonel, were very much alarmed for his safety. But "old boy Ben" was not to be captured. Last night was very severe on picket. It rained nearly all night long; and we had no shelter save our ponchoes. As we were dozing by the fire, we were startled by hearing the sharp report of the carbine at the middle post. We were in the saddle in a second, expecting to see Messrs. Johnnys upon us. When we reached the vidette, he said two men were approaching him, and would not stop when challenged. I guess it was all imagination, as he was a young boy, and a recruit. But I was sure we would be attacked, as some bushwhackers were hovering around all night.

Our old friend, the MERCURY, is received regularly by hundreds in camp, and is read by hundreds more. It is very interesting to sit in our little shanty, and peruse the different military correspondence from all parts of the country, in your valuable paper. "Lights-out" have been blown, therefore I will bid you good-night. Yours as ever,

ENLISTED MAN.

FIFTY-FIRST REGIMENT, N.Y.V.V.

BEFORE PETERSBURG, VA., Jan. 28.

'Tis said, "a calm precedes a storm." I trust the remark holds good, succeeding a storm; for I think that we will need a little calm after the storm that is prevailing at the present time. Mud is not exactly up to our knees, but in spots its overhead. For the last three days it has been drip, drip, drip—raining three days outside and six within; as a matter of course, we do not always expect to be satisfied. It is talked, that the corps [Ninth] is shortly to be relieved and put in a spot where the troops can go through a course of drilling. The men seem all satisfied with their present position, and say that they might as well remain here, partially sheltered, as to move and have no shelter of any consequence for the remainder of this winter. Moving camp, at present, is not one of the most agreeable features of our calling.

All the members of the regiment are anxiously awaiting to be drawn out of the brigade and put in a brigade commanded by Brevet-Brigadier General [G. H.] McKibbon. The General commanding our brigade is liked well enough, but the officers composing his staff are very unpopular; and, as a matter of course, our regiment is snubbed in every possible manner by the aforesaid parties. The Brigade-Inspector has forwarded such a report as never before appeared, anything but complimentary to the regiment, both officers and men. The Assistant Adjutant-General of the brigade, who is only acting in the capacity, does not allow papers to be forwarded through his office, without being returned two or three times, on some paltry pretext; and it is thought by members of the regiment who are concerned, that it is done to cause delay and confusion; perhaps, their career will have an end.

I judge from the noise that something must be doing up in (late) Butler's Department—firing of heavy guns occurs about once every two minutes.

The pickets are quite sociable, scarcely exchanging a shot. No artillery firing has occurred of late, worthy of note.

The boys are thankful to hear of the fall of Fort Fisher. It was rumored here, a few days ago, that General Burnside was to take command of the Army of the James. It seems to have been all a rumor.

A letter was received, a few days ago, from one of our officers, who writes from Danville, Va., which says that all of our officers who were captured on the 30th of September, 1864, were confined there; and from his writing, I am led to think that they are in a destitute condition, hard bread and pork being in demand. Their friends and relatives might lend a helping hand. The enlisted men were last heard from at Salisbury, N. C.

SUCCOTASH.

February 12, 1865
TWENTY-FIFTH N.Y. CAVALRY
CAMP RUSSELL, VA.,

I have to fall back on the old stereotyped line "all quiet in the Valley of the Shenandoah."

We had a grand review of the Cavalry Corps on the 1st inst., and about fourteen thousand cavalrymen responded to the order. We were reviewed by General Sheridan who rode that black horse of his, now famous in song. To see the two, you could hardly tell which to admire most, the horse or the rider; but you could not separate them, each is "but part of one stupendous whole". The fable of the old Centaurs seems to be realized in the two. To separate them would almost be a sin. It was amusing to see the officers of his escort to keep up with him; spurs and reins were used, and the poor horses snorted and panted at a rate that spoke well for the revocation of General [Montgomery C.] Meigs' order that no more horses should be purchased. As he galloped down the line, he was received with the blare of trumpets, arms presented, and banners drooping—banners that never had dipped in the field when the Rebel rag was visible—but down they went when our all-conquering "Phil" was passing.

There were quite a number of Northern ladies witnessing the review, which was held on the old battle-ground of the 18th of September. Perhaps you may suppose that I am rash in saying they were Northern ladies, but we knew they were, from the fact that not one of them had a pipe in her mouth! However, all the Southern ladies don't smoke pipes; the more exquisite ones, who consider pipe-smoking vulgar, tone the thing down and only chew snuff!

Lieutenant-Colonel Seeley commanded the First Brigade, and, as might be expected, "did take the thing up to the handle", to use the classic Bowery phrase.

The Ordinance Department is busy refitting the Army here, and we are in daily expectations of orders to move to—somewhere. Infantry are piling into the Valley by shovelfulls, and the only sure thing is that something is up. What is it. Time will tell.

A word to the ladies now. Ladies, at our grand review the other day, we could not use the standard of our regiment, as the storms of shot and shell to which it has been exposed has torn it into ribbons. The few shreds of it that are left we will send home to take their place among the relics which stand amongst the archives of New York, as witnesses of the daring deeds of her gallant sons. When can you send us a new one?

Your most obedient,   B. O. B.

FOURTEENTH REGIMENT, N.Y. HEAVY ARTILLERY
NEAR PETERSBURG, VA., Feb. 7.

We are under marching orders, with four days' rations. There is considerable speculation as to where we are going. Some think we are off to Washington, while others suppose we are bound on an expedition to the Southside Railroad. I think that the latter are right.

I wish to inform your many readers of the treatment this regiment has received. It was raised, by fraud and false representations, as heavy artillery, but has been serving as infantry in the front since April last, while other regiments of heavy artillery are doing garrison-duty. We think it would be no more than right for us to have a turn at it. On New Year's eve, while a number of our officers were imbibing quite freely, Captain [Homer] Foote remarked that he was accused of being a coward. To test his courage and bravery, he requested the Major to give him permission to go out and capture the enemy's abatis and bring them in for firewood; but the Major, doubting his veracity, did not consent.

The pickets have been in the habit of trading pork, hard-tack and coffee for tobacco, but last night they were taken aback slightly. A sergeant and two men of the Fifty-ninth Massachusetts, were out trading, when they were surrounded and captured by the Southern Confederacy. They are now reported as deserters to the enemy. That will put an end to trafficing on the picket-line.

We have just received orders to move out and leave our bombproofs in possession of the rats, which are very annoying, because they steal our hard tack by the dozen, and play tag on the bed at nights, regardless of the occupants.

The Fifth and part of the Sixth Corps are already on the move, and we expect to follow immediately.

HEAVY DOG.

SIXTY-FIFTH REGIMENT, N.Y.V.V.
BEFORE PETERSBURG, VA., Feb. 6

The quietness that has so long reigned supreme has at length been broken by marching-orders. We have been ordered to hold ourselves in readiness to move at a moment's notice. The necessary supplies have been issued, together with the usual amount of leaden pills, and we are all prepared to march forth when the order is given for us to do so. Various speculations are indulged in as to where we are going. Some think that our corps will go on the north side of the James to assist the Army there in a direct move on Richmond, while others opine that we are to charge the Rebel fortifications in our front and capture Petersburg by assault. This is generally discredited and the only report that finds any credence is, that we are going to the left to tap Bob Lee's communications. Marching-orders have not surprised any of the boys, for the unusually numerous inspections had created in our minds the suspicion that something was going to turn up, and that very shortly.

Last night, there was a continuos roar of artillery-firing on the right. The flash of our own and the enemy's cannon was plainly visible from our camp, and when the shells passed through the air they left a streak of fire in their wake which made the heavens look sublime and beautiful. The cause of the firing was said to be, that the Rebels were endeavoring to build a breastwork directly in front of one of our forts, when our artillery opened on them, and to which the enemy responded.

Picket-firing has not been so frequent or fierce of late. When the Rebel Peace Commissioners arrived in front of the Ninth Corps, that practice ceased, and when they passed through from their own to our lines, the pickets of both armies left their pits, and, standing on the embankment, they gave vent to their feelings in loud and prolonged cheers for peace. [Alexander H.] Stephens, [Robert M. T.] Hunter, and [John A.] Campbell will not easily forget the acclamations that rent the air for the dove of which they were the supposed ambassadors.

Brigadier General Joseph R. Hamblin, our former Colonel, returned here a few days ago from New York, and has been assigned to command the Third Brigade, First Division, Sixth Corps. The General is one of the most popular officers in the Army, and his career, since he entered the service, is ample proof of his gallantry and ability as a soldier. General Hamblin, at the outbreak of the present war, came out as Adjutant of the Fifth Duryee Zouaves, and left that regiment to become Major of the Sixty-fifth. By the promotions of Colonels John Cochrane and Alexander Shaler to be Brigadier-Generals, General Hamblin was made Colonel, and served in that capacity until the battle of Cedar Creek, where he was severely wounded in leading the Second Brigade, which he then commanded. His wounds caused his absence from the field, but his return now is hailed with delight. He has brought with him what he so justly deserves, the Brigadier's star, and may he ever flourish is the earnest wish of every man in the Sixty-fifth Regiment.

The weather at present is very cold, and the roads have been frozen to such an extent as to render them favorable for locomotion by troops or teams.

In my last letter, I alluded to the good feeling prevailing between the natives of the sacred soil living in the vicinity and our soldiers. Since then, an instance has occurred in the shape of a bona fide wedding between one of Uncle Sam's nephews and a fair daughter of Virginia. Your correspondent was accidentally in the neighborhood of the place where the ceremony was to occur, and recognized in the bridegroom an old friend, who invited me to be present. An army-chaplain did the business in style, and soon Miss was Mrs. Your correspondent was introduced to a fair one by the happy Benedict, with sundry hints to follow the illustrious example thus set forth. But realizing that I enjoyed a previous engagement, I concluded not to enter into any engagements of the kind, and therefore declined his mediating proposals.

The regiment has been on the qui vive for the paymaster; but that gentleman has not, as yet, appeared. I agree with some of your correspondents, who think the negligence of the Government in not paying the troops a positive injustice to the gallant defenders of our country, who more or less have families depending on them for support; and it is to be hoped that our kind uncle, for these reasons, will send on the greenbacks, and that promptly.

The regiment is enjoying fine health, which in a measure is due to the excellent sanitary rules enforced by the commanding officer of the regiment.

The MERCURY comes regularly as expected, and is read and re-read by the boys.

Should your correspondent not prove a bullet-stopper de facto in the coming operations, the part the Sixty-fifth plays will be fully depicted by yours hopefully,

FRANCONI.

FIFTY-SIXTH REGIMENT, N.Y.V.
COOSAWHATCHIE STATION, S.C., ON CHARLESTON & SAVANNAH RAILROAD
Feb. 4.

Since I last wrote you, we have been moving around considerably. On the 15th, we received orders very early in the morning to proceed to the railroad in light marching order. We were soon on the way, and after a short march we arrived there, and found, to our regret, that the enemy had left the night before, and thus spoiled our chances for a fight. After resting an hour or two, we received orders to tear up the railroad track and cut the telegraph wires. We worked till 3 P.M., when orders came for us to move down the road to the fort at the station. Here we found the telegraph-office and the ruins of the depot, inclosed by a large fort which had been built nearly for two years. We pitched our tents and rested for the night. The next day, we worked on the railroad, and tore up the track for many miles. The next day, we sent out a party of two hundred men into the country for the purpose of foraging. They returned about 4 P.M., and every man had a pair of turkeys or chickens hanging to his musket. They also captured some horses and wagons, some beef-cattle, and hogs; had burned several plantation-houses, and carried off everything that was needed by our troops. The next day, went with a party to Gillisonville under command of the Colonel [Charles H. Van Wyck], and captured some more horses and cattle. Visited the courthouse and jail and many other public buildings, including the post-office, which we broke open and captured a mailbag with its contents, and Rebel papers of Jan. 12.

Every day has been spent in foraging, and the men are living on poultry and fresh beef, and enjoy themselves finely. There are no people left here but the poor whites, and the aged and infirm slaves. They are nearly starved to death, and are a poor miserable set of beings. They hail the Yankees with joy, and we give protection to all. All the wealthy have moved up into the interior of the State, and left their homes in charge of the old slaves. The contrabands are flocking inside our lines with their families and are all sent to the rear.

The Adjutant was out with a party of men one day, and brought in a quantity of tobacco, which came very handy, as we were all out, having no money for eleven months. They also brought in a horse and buggy, some chickens, crockery, and many other things which were needed by us. I chanced to be one of the party, and captured six fine fowls and a small hog. As the Commissary had cut down our rations, I found they did not come amiss. Since then, a small party went to Grahamsville and burned the town. The same day Gillisonville, with all the houses, was burned, and everything laid waste. [Gen. Joseph] Wheeler, with his Rebel cavalry, is about sixty miles from here, but does not seem inclined to molest us. How long we will remain here I know not, but I think not many days will elapse before we are again on the move. The weather is cold and disagreeable, but we have very comfortable quarters, and are prepared for cold weather.

PO'KEEPSIE.

February 19, 1865
SIXTY-FIRST REGIMENT, N.Y.V.V.
IN THE FIELD, VA., Feb. 13.

In the field, sure enough. In my last I mentioned the likelihood of our being "near" somewhere else; and, true enough, we are nearer the "left" than formerly. At reveille, on the morning of the 9th, we were somewhat surprised on hearing the order issued to tear down our huts, and pile the wood in the rear. With heavy hearts, we went to work, and, in a short time, our camp, which lately presented such a fine appearance, was one vast heap of logs, bricks, etc. At 9, A.M., same morning, we fell into line, and casting a lingering look upon our now desolate camp, took up the march for, some said Wilmington, others declared we were going to garrison forts in the neighborhood of Washington, while others, more knowing than the rest, said we were going to re-enforce—somebody. None of the above conjectures were right, and all soon discovered the truth of the old saw: "Nothing known, nothing lost". At last we came to a halt, arms were stacked, and all hands set to work clearing a space wide enough for three Broadways.

In this work we were not alone, the whole brigade participating. Dusk now approaching, work was suspended, and the query now was, "Where are you going to sleep?" Tents of all descriptions and sizes were soon pitched; some contained one inmate, while others, boasting of larger dimensions, contained from three to five boarders. The larger the number the better for all, for reasons well understood by those who have slept alone. In this condition have we remained until the present time; our duty being now fatigue, varied with picket. The weather has been very cold and also windy; tent after tent has been blown down, and the "fires" scattered in every direction.

I desire, at the present time, to render my thanks to "MERCUTIO" for that "song", and wishing for "Valentines", I am, etc.,

S. G. C.

FIFTY-SIXTH REGIMENT, N.Y.V.V.
COOSAWHATCHIE BATTERY, S.C., Feb. 9.

Nothing of very great importance has transpired although all the rest of the troops have moved to Pocotaligo, which is about eight miles distant. Our Colonel is now commanding the First Brigade, Coast Division, with his headquarters near Pocotaligo. Our boys are enjoying themselves finely by foraging on the country for all they require in the shape of poultry and furniture. To give you an idea of the extent of our foraging, I will relate one day's work: The Major, Quartermaster, and Adjutant started out one morning with only two mounted orderlies, and brought in with them at night three wagon loads of poultry, pork, beef, and furniture. They went to the plantation of Mr. Overstreet, a notorious Rebel, who was supplied with all the comfortables of life, and found there two men and about a dozen women, who were dressed in homespun cloth, and were pictures of poverty. They stripped him of all he had, consisting of four horses, two mules, three wagons and harness, and about one hundred fowls. The Adjutant captured a handsome pony only four years old, and a splendid saddle-horse. The people did not deny that they were Rebels, and there cry was: "Take everything, but leave me my horse." But the Adjutant could not see it in that light, and the pony was brought along.

Sherman's Army have all passed by, and are on their way through South Carolina. Where they will turn up no one knows; but we will hear good accounts of him ere long. The name of Sherman is a terror to the Rebels in this vicinity. The weather for many days has been warm and pleasant, but to-day a cold, drizzling rain set in, and it is very disagreeable. Where our next movement is to be, and when, time only can tell.

Our mails are very irregular, and it is only seldom our favorite SUNDAY MERCURY strays into camp. As always as our mail is distributed many are the inquiries to know who has received a SUNDAY MERCURY. The regiment is now under the command of Major Eliphas Smith, who is a valuable officer, and deserves great credit for the manner in which he governs his command. On all occasions, under the fire of the enemy, he has shown unflinching bravery and coolness. Our regiment is blessed with valuable field-officers, and a loss of any of them would be regretted by us all. Every one is now wondering what we are to do next, but no one seems to know.

SUFFICIENT.

SIXTY-FIFTH REGIMENT, N.Y.V.V.

BEFORE PETERSBURG, VA., Feb. 13

We are again back in our old camp, after going through some trying scenes of battle and bivouac. We started from our present encampment a week ago last night [Feb. 5], and took up the line of march for the left of the Army. After marching all night, we halted at a place some three miles to the left, and in front of the Second Corps. Here we lay until the afternoon of the day following, when we moved out to support the Fifth Corps, who were in advance on the Boynton Road. We had not proceeded upward of a mile before we could plainly hear the rattling of musketry in front, which indicated that Warren's men had met with an obstacle in their way to the Southside Railroad. The First Division of the Sixth Corps, after resting a few moments, were ordered to relieve Warren, and in a moment, we were on the double quick up to the front. Arriving on the battle-field, our division formed, and was proceeding to relieve [Gen. Samuel W.] Crawford's Division, of the Fifth Corps, who had been engaged all day, and whose ammunition was exhausted. We filed into the woods, and commenced doing the relieving, when the Fifth Corps commenced to retreat. This surprised us, and in a few moments the retreat turned into a disastrous flight. All was confusion for some time; but by the exertions of many gallant spirits the troops were rallied, and in a few moments the whole line again moved forward and recovered the entire ground that had been lost. Our regiment, as usual, took an active part, and was very fortunate, losing but few men. Our brigade (the Second) was justly complimented for the gallantry and steeliness they displayed, and the credit thus bestowed is but the mood of praise they should justly have, for it was evident that, but for their coolness and bravery, the evil caused by the panic might have terminated in a serious disaster. Some time ago, one of your Fifth Corps correspondents alluded to the overcoat raids on our picket-line. He did so in a jocose manner. I trust this time he will admit that the joke is on his side.

This late move has gained for us a position from which raids can be made on the Southside Railroad, and it is believed that the Rebel Chief will in future find that "a hard road to travel". It is a victory which the boys duly appreciated and are jubilant over. We are now engaged in erecting an earthwork to be known as Fort Fisher. When finished it will be a very formidable fortification. It is calculated to mount twenty guns; and should the Rebels take it into their heads to test its metal, they will receive a sweetening that they will long remember.

The peace-bubble has exploded, and there is a feeling of keen disappointment that the conference terminated so unfavorably. The soldiers hoped that peace would be had on the basis of the Union, but it seems as if the Rebels cannot agree to those terms; therefore, the boys have made up their minds that what they so heartily desire can only be had through the instrumentality of the bullet and the bayonet; and, confident of victory, we yet hope before spring comes, another party will visit the authorities, who will be more reasonable in their views and who will readily accept the terms they now reject.

The Rebel soldiers, despite the assertions of the Rebel press, were in favor of peace on our terms, and their disappointment was bitter indeed. Your correspondent has conversed with prisoners and deserters, and they represent the feeling in Lee's Army to be for peace on any terms.

During our raid on the left, the weather was very disagreeable, and the boys suffered greatly from exposure to the wind, rain, and sleet; still there are but few of the boys sick, and doctor's call is but feebly responded to.

Our mails do not come as regularly as usual, and the reason of its delay is greatly inquired for, but no satisfactory answer is given; but we hope that whatever may be the cause of the delay, that it will be remedied. There is a rumor afloat that the Paymasters are down to City Point, and that they will shortly be up to pay the troops. So mote it be. The MERCURY is around as usual, and is eagerly sought after. The boys hope soon to be loose, financially; so they will be able to peddle. Joining in their wishes, I am, yours loosely,

FRANCONI.

ONE HUNDRED AND THIRTY-NINTH REGIMENT, N.Y.V.

NEAR FORT BURNHAM, VA., Feb. 10.

My object in writing this article is not for the purpose of slandering our officers, or to insult them, as they often do us (especially when on inspection), but whoever of them may chance to wear the shoe, let it fit him well. It is rather to give our friends at home, and the public in general, some idea how we soldiers are treated by our officers. After undergoing all the privations and hardships, impossible for my pen to describe, during the unparalleled campaigns of last spring, summer, and fall, in reference to getting furloughs this winter, and the way we are swindled out of at least half the rations allowed us by the Government, we can well stand all the insults from our officers (considering that shoulder-straps do not care much now a days who wears them), but we cannot sustain life long on half-rations.

Who is to blame for us getting only half-rations, we do not pretend to say, but it strikes us very forcibly that it is somebody about the size of our Brigadier and Regimental Quartermaster. They have not made a pile of greenbacks large enough to suit their taste yet; therefore we cannot expect full rations until their pockets are filled. Our regiment has been in the service two years and five months, and but few of its members have ever received a furlough. We have inspections twice a week. Each company-commander selects from his company the neatest soldier, and sends him to Regimental Headquarters. There they are inspected again by our Major. The best one is sent to Brigade Headquarters, where they are inspected for the third time, by Colonel [Edgar] Cullen. Being an officer of the regular service, he is far more particular in inspecting the boys than our volunteer army officers are; not only inspects knapsacks, arms, and equipments, but also the person, looks down your neck to see if it is clean, turns up the wristbands of your shirt, looks into your ears, pulls off your shoes and stockings to see if your feet are clean; after this, the best one in six—there being six regiments in the brigade—is sent to Division Headquarters, to be inspected for the fourth time. If you are lucky enough to be the cleanest soldier of three, you are promised a furlough. So you see our chance to win a furlough is small. I must now close, for the drum will soon beat for battalion-drill. We are on picket-guard, drill, and fatigue all the time, consequently we have but little time for writing when at the front.

HERO.

SECOND NEW YORK FIRE ZOUAVES

CAMP YELLOW HOUSE, February 14.

As my old friend "Snake", your regular correspondent, has evacuated our camp, for the purpose of recruiting his health for a short period in the big city of Gotham, I take the liberty of transmitting a few lines to you, for the purpose of informing our numerous friends of our present situation.

We are occupants of the same quarters as when you last heard from us. We expect to remain here but a short time. There has been too protracted a season of fine weather for the invincible Grant to let us longer remain inactive, and besides, the troops are in splendid spirits. The cheering along the line, from the extreme right to left, nightly, is sufficient to convince the listener of the above fact. It is so every night. We are so used to hearing of victories, that we will have our cheer out. How must our bitter enemy take it? His repeated question on the picket-line is, "What are you cheering for, to-night gents?" and the repeated answer is: "Another of your secesh forts taken." No wonder, then, that they are inspired with a deadly fear of the coming avalanche that is soon to hurl them into eternity.

They tell our boys on the picket-line that they expect to evacuate Richmond, and the greater portion of them wish for peace, though they say they don't like the idea of giving in to the North. The fact being that they are so totally ashamed of themselves as to prefer awaiting the result of the coming campaign. Yet you ask them what particular benefit they expect to obtain at the termination of the coming campaign; then they drop their chins and change the subject completely, carefully avoiding any allusion to the subject again whatever. These conversations transpire daily on picket, though strict orders are given to the contrary—forbidding any communication whatever between the pickets.

Col. Burns has gone to New York on leave of absence, and it is rumored here that he has succeeded in making arrangements with Governor [Reuben E.] Fenton for five companies of recruits for our regiment, which will be very acceptable here just now, as we will have ample time to break them in for the coming campaign. If our little band of vets are compelled to pass through such another campaign as the last one was alone, we will be exterminated, without being able to show any beneficial results from our victorious arms, as we now muster the strength of but one company. While I am writing this letter, there are active preparations on foot. The Army, it seems, is entirely in motion, while here the Second and Fifth Corps are warmly engaged with the enemy; and within the past few hours many a brave soldier has been made to bite the dust.

We are in the vicinity of Hatcher's Run, having driven the enemy a distance of ten miles; and now the Fifth Corps is in position on the other side of the creek. The Third Brigade of our (Third) Division, better known as the "Jersey Brigade", fought more desperate than ever I saw troops fight before. They were charged three times in succession by the Rebels; but there was no give way by the "Jerseys". With compressed lips, determined looks, and a convulsive grasp of their death-dealing rifle, on which the glistening bayonets were fixed, all giving the appearance of a fixed determination to do or die, they would calmly await the impetuous foe (who compelled by their officers to still advance, regardless of the fearful death that surely awaited them), when, with a yell that would seem to startle the dead from their resting place, they madly rush on their furious enemy, and make such terrible havoc in their ranks as to cause their hasty retreat, leaving their killed, wounded, and prisoners in our hands. Proudly, indeed, may Jersey speak of her noble sons in this glorious contest for the Union. Where was the little band of Fire Zouaves all this time? The question will naturally arise, as it is a well-known fact that there is very little going on they do not participate in. I will tell you. We are calmly awaiting the result of the contest. We are massed in rear of the front-line, under fire, and kept here for the purpose of re-enforcing any part of the line that may be driven back, or, in other words, as the forlorn hope. The suspense attending this important duty cannot be described; in fact, I firmly believe there is not one of our party who would not prefer to storm any part of the enemy's works than perform the present task assigned to us. We all patiently await the result of the affair, and hope when it is concluded that there is another nail put in the coffin of the Southern Confederacy (as the Irishman says). Our loss so far has been pretty large, yet it cannot be compared to that of the enemy's. We have also taken a number of prisoners. Doubtless by the time this reaches you, you will have a full and more authentic account than I can give you; I can vouch only for proceedings in our immediate vicinity. Our Colonel (Burns) has just arrived, amid the many warm congratulations of all that know him; and, as I mentioned above, he has succeeded in obtaining permission to fill the regiment.

SHELLPROOF.

February 26, 1865
ONE HUNDRED AND SEVENTY-SIXTH REGIMENT, N.Y.V.
SAVANNAH, GA., Feb. 17.

The weather seems to continue about the same as at last writing. At night it is a great deal colder than usual, but we soon forget that after we are once under our blankets. Every Sabbath the streets are thronged with "bright eyes", and they are now getting so used to the blue-jackets that a smile is generally the passing salutation, which, of course, keeps the streets crowded with the latter.

The bands of the Second Division, Nineteenth Army Corps, gave a grand promenade concert the other day, and kept up their "wind" from 4 to 6, P.M., making the multitude joyous with their notes. Everybody could be seen with their "gals" and ladies, from the drummer boys up to major-general walking to and fro, enjoying the afternoon and its scenes. Many things were there that would make the sourest of men laugh. Along the walk could be seen a small man, about six feet three inches, walking along with a huge piece of gingerbread in his hand, seemingly unconscious of what was going on. Close behind can be seen something glittering, but when it approaches near enough to be distinct, a man can be seen with an army-corps badge about four inches square. Whether it is tin or silver remains to be explained. A crowd could be observed drawing one side. The first impression is that it is a fight, but when you get to the great attraction it is to found that it is two ladies of color, dancing to the time of the music, taking no regard of the crowd gathered by their fandangos, showing that the music was spreading its effects. Rustlings of silks and ribbons could be heard, and as one would pass one of the "Southern belles" too close, he would be apt to have his eyes put out by one of the ribbons attached to those fair creatures.

Heavy fatigue-parties are being detailed daily from our regiment to throw up breastworks; but it seems as if they were busy on a fort—which is going to be built—and part of it is to take up part of a cemetery which lies about one mile and a half from the city. To build the fort, of course the graves have to be covered or removed, and the news of that reaching the city sent hundreds out to the place to remove their friends and relations. Being an eye-witness to the scene of resurrection, I can relate some scenes that might interest you. I came to a grave where two stout men were busy digging, and there was an old woman leaning over the grave weeping. They soon came to the object desired, which proved to be the husband of the lady present. He had been dead eleven years, and, of course, nothing but bones remained. As soon as the lady saw the skull of her deceased husband, she begged hard to let her have it, about in this way: "Give me the skull! O! give me the skull. For God's sake, do! do!" but the request was not granted. Soldiers and citizens were busy digging up the dead; but still the people could not get our men spades enough to accommodate all. They all "wish the Yanks to the devil"; but I guess the day will come yet when they will "bless the Yanks".

                    Yours truly,   ORFX.

SIXTY-FIRST REGIMENT, N.Y.V.V.

IN THE FIELD, VIRGINIA, Feb. 21.

The formally oft-repeated "all quiet on the Potomac", is emphatically true at the present time. No rumbling of cannon or whistling of bullets is now heard. The pickets of both Armies show themselves with perfect impunity, not dreading a "beadline", as was formerly the custom, when a head appeared above the breastworks. Whether the cold weather of late has rendered the handling of rifles and cartridges unpleasant or whether the animosity formerly existing between the pickets has given place to better feelings, is a problem yet to be solved.

We have again resumed our usual occupation, viz.: picket and fatigue. Of both, fatigue is decidedly the hardest task. The line we now occupy being new, a vast amount clearing etc., remains to be done. Orders were received a few days ago, for the troops of this brigade to proceed at once toward erecting comfortable quarters. "Where's our wood coming from?" Was a question but few could answer. Our anxiety on that subject was soon relieved, however, as teams were furnished and details of men, with axes, were sent out into the woods to procure the necessary article, and once more we are at work erecting our quarters. The work, however, proceeds slowly, for the reason that we are reluctant to build quarters for a short time, our former experience having demonstrated the fact that our locations are of but short duration.

Never have I seen such avidity to purchase Northern papers, as was manifested during the past week, owing to the interest felt by all regarding the late peace movement, and Sherman's movements as he progresses through the Carolinas. Some of us entertain the opinion that ere long, Sherman and his once lost, but soon found Army, will form a connecting link with the noble army of the Potomac. If so, good-bye Rebellion, and all us sogers decidedly say "amen." On the evening of the 16th inst., we were astonished by being visited by a thunder-storm, accompanied by vivid flashes of lightning—something new for this latitude at this time of the year. The morning of the 17th was decidedly wet, damp and dismal—nevertheless, we had to don our best, for it was our monthly inspection day. Brigade-Inspector was as particular as usual, but for some reason the time consumed inspecting was far less than usual. Toward evening, Grandfather Boreas thinking, doubtless, that it was his turn to blow, did indeed blow with a vengeance, and continued the performance all night. The morning of the 18th was pleasant, and we all thought that daylight appeared very suddenly. Yesterday (Sunday) was pleasant, more like spring than mid-winter. Our usual Sabbath routine was gone through with, but no service as this regiment is minus a Chaplain. With a request for Uncle Sam to forward the Paymaster without delay,

                    I am his most obedient,   S. G. C.

March 5, 1865
SIXTY-FIFTH REGIMENT, N.Y.S.V.V.

BEFORE PETERSBURG, VA., Feb. 27

We have been kept in a state of feverish excitement for the past week, by rumors and reports that the Rebels were evacuating our front. Up to this time, they have not left their stronghold; but it is the general impression that Bob Lee will have to "hike" out, and that very soon. We have lately been kept quite busy; for duties have been imposed upon us like falling rain, and thick and fast. Picket-drills, parades, fatigue, besides the ordinary camp-duties, which, in any event, have to be performed, have left the boys very little time for themselves. We are not even sure of night being a season for repose; for the powers that be have had us up several nights, to stand in line at the breastworks to watch for the advance of some imaginary Rebel line-of-battle. But, amidst these inconveniences, there is heard no word of murmur. Some days ago, we were reviewed by a foreign officer. His name I did not learn exactly; but it sounded very much like "Gen. Bic-mi-nose-off" or "Kick-up-enuff". Which of the two is his appellation, I cannot say; but certain it is that we stood in line long enough waiting for his arrival. He was attended with a brilliant staff, and simply rode along the line, the ceremony of marching in review being dispensed with. He seemed well-pleased with the appearance of the troops, and the camps—not that he could find any praise for the camp-ground (for it is knee-deep with mud), but for the regularity and neatness of the huts.

Yesterday we were to have a general inspection by the Brigadier-General [Ranald Mackenzie] commanding the Brigade, and the regiment marched out on the parade-ground for that purpose, but it was postponed by the order of the General until some finer day. In a camp like ours, where the least drop of rain causes a rise in mud, it is impossible for the men to keep in as trim as they otherwise could do, and for an officer to reflect in harsh terms on the appearance of men under such circumstances is as unjust as it is unwarrantable.

The late brilliant success of Sherman and [John M.] Schofield has truly set the boys on fire with enthusiasm; we see in the fall of Charleston, the shattered fragments of the Keystone of Rebellion; the arch is broken, and another blow will send the shaky structure tumbling to ruins; the insult to law and order given by South Carolina is at last wiped out, and the nest of treason sees again the flag they affected to despise floating over them in all its glory. Every enemy of this wicked and unjustifiable Rebellion will thank God fervently that the old flag waves again over Sumter; every additional victory gives the soldier more hope, more heart, and we see in these great triumphs the beginning of a speedy end to war and its calamities.

Every day and night brings its quota of deserters from Dixie Land. A few evenings ago, while our regiment was out on picket, no less than thirty deserters, belonging to one regiment, the Eighteenth North Carolina, came in and gave themselves up. Their journey from the Rebel to our lines was not very agreeable, as their former friends fired a volley of musketry at them as a parting salute. One of the deserters, an orderly-sergeant, informed us that his regiment existed only in name, that the majority of the men had already deserted, and that there was none left but the color-guard, and that we might expect them over as soon as they got an opportunity. This regiment was raised in the vicinity of Wilmington; and as they had good reason to believe that that place would soon be ours, they made up their minds to get home, and the surest way of doing this was to desert, and they did so. They assert that as soon as Sherman gains possession of the State, so soon will North Carolina troops refuse to lend further aid to the rebellion.

The Paymasters are here, engaged in paying the troops four months' pay. The Sixty-Fivers look for a visit from him in a few days. The health of the boys is comparatively good, and they are cheerful in spirits. The MERCURY comes regularly, and is always sought after. In my next, I hope to give you a list of our officers, field, staff and line. Until then I am your friend, as you are the people's advocate and the soldiers' friend.

Truthfully,   FRANCONIA.

FIFTY-FIRST REGIMENT, N.Y.V.V.

BEFORE PETERSBURG, VA., Feb. 24.

Shotted guns were fired this 4, P.M., as a salute in honor of the capture of Wilmington, N.C. This news, with the confirmation of the fall of Charleston, has placed the boys in the best of spirits. During the firing of the salute, the men were out on the top of their bombproofs witnessing the effect of the shell and shot as they would burst or strike over in the works of the Johnnys. Deserters from the enemy state that the rank and file of their Army are becoming quite dissatisfied, and that a large body of North Carolinians had, a few days ago, made a bolt for home. Cavalry tried to stop them, but the latter soon dispersed. They stated that the reason of the North Carolinians making tracks was that they had waited for something to be made out of the peace-negotiations; but, as it has proved a failure, they were about tired of the struggle; and that they would either go over to the "Billies" (new name for Yanks) or go home; so they chose the greater of the two evils.

There is a rumor that the Commissaries of Subsistence will be furnished tobacco to be issued to the men— as it is done in the Navy. I hope it will amount to more than rumor. I can see no reason for it not being done. Another nuisance has been dispensed with of late. Embalmers who would charge prices varying from $40 to $60. I understand that the bodies of deceased soldiers are embalmed before burial, by the Government—so that friends of the deceased can have the body conveyed North. This is not, however, the case, where the party died of contagious disease.

Miniature mortars, made from Rebel bullets, picked up on the picket line, are all the rage. Quite a number of the little jokers have been carried home by men receiving furloughs.

SUCCOTASH.

SECOND NEW YORK HEAVY ARTILLERY

CAMP NEAR HATCHER'S RUN, Feb. 27.

The confusion attendant upon camp-moving has, to a great extent, subsided. We are ensconced comfortably (all things considered) within the twelve-by-eight of our mud-plastered shanties. Yet the axe is still plied with unabated vigor, clearing the ground of stumps that have held "old possession", and removing thereby obstacles the most serious to tender feet during nocturnal peregrination.

On the whole, our recent move has been advantageous, inasmuch as our camp is pleasantly situated, being built upon a gradual slope, commanding an extensive view of the surrounding country. We have also an abundance of wood, having driven the "Johnnys" back three-quarters of a mile, and take possession of the gigantic pines.

In consequence of some mysterious movements of the enemy in our immediate front, one-tenth of our regiment were last night stationed at the breastworks in addition to the usual picket-force. Thus we were prepared to repel any attack that might be made upon our line by the deluded followers of Jeff. The night, however, passed off quietly, and with the exception of a slight shower we met with nothing calculated to disturb our equanimity.

A death has just occurred in the regiment, under circumstances highly censurable. A young man of Company A, long respected and beloved by his comrades in arms, being taken suddenly ill, sought one Assistant Surgeon, in order to be excused from duty; his serious illness, although apparent to the most casual observer, could not, it seems, be discerned by this acute disciple of Esculapius. Being returned to duty, he stood for a few moments at a tent-fire—suddenly fell, and in five minutes expired! The Assistant Surgeon, meanwhile, reached the spot, where he doubtless saw the practical result of his inexperience painfully illustrated. Cannot medical men of known ability and experience be sent to the field? Or shall young men, fresh from college, be permitted to finish their education at the expense of our lives and limbs?

The news of the surrender of Branchville and the evacuation of Charleston, was received with thundering cheers, and a tiger, the echoes of which penetrated the lines of Rebeldom. Sherman is a brick, which, being launched at the head of the Confederacy, certainly strikes terror into its most prominent bumps! His name is but another word for victory! Rebellion flies at his approach; and the rotten institution, as he stalks majestic through it, grows "small by degrees and beautifully less".

The other night, as one of our videttes was walking his beat, ruminating perhaps on the past, thinking of home and its old associations, his reverie was suddenly broken by a mysterious sound, or rather combination of sounds, that emanated from a knot of pines directly before him. Straining his auricular organs to ascertain, if possible, its cause, what was his surprise on seeing a dog extricate himself from the underbrush and suddenly confront him. His dogship, on taking a view of the premises, and being evidently well satisfied with the appearance of the vidette-pit, headed directly for the picket-line, and while in the act of taking further observations, was taken captive. On being brought to the picket-fire, he was found to be a thorough bloodhound, and, judging from his aristocratic bearing, he was certainly no cur of low degree. He had, however, a criminal aspect, maintaining a dogged silence as he stood before us, fastened to a stake (the tape of a canteen being used in lieu of hemp). The speculations concerning him were various. "He is a spy," said one. "Perhaps a bearer of dispatches," suggested another. "A member of the Peace Commission," said a third. Leaving the question undecided, I would simply say that the distinguished canine shall for the present receive our protection; and should he, by court martial, be found deserving of the stocks, our quiet neighbors of the Sixty-first will doubtless see the penalty inflicted, as a set of these reformers have recently been erected for their special benefit.

Deducting a natural inference from the above circumstance, it appears evident that the sagacious quadruped actuated by principles of genuine instinct, deserted the doomed Confederacy, for the same reason that rats are said to abandon a sinking vessel.

Yours, dogmat cally,   MERCUTIO.

March 12, 1865
FIFTH REGIMENT RHODE ISLAND HEAVY ARTILLERY
NEWBERN, N.C., March 3.

The unusual quietness of this department has been disturbed somewhat of late by rumors that active operations were soon to be commenced. The arrival of several regiments here has partially substantiated these reports. Time will doubtless develop some important movements in this vicinity.

The health and discipline of this regiment still continues to be good. A few recruits have lately been added to our numbers. But there is still room for more of the same sort. They are mostly one-year's men. Privates [John] Conley and [Edward] McQuade, belonging to Co. A., have recently escaped from Rebeldom, and joined the regiment. The former was regularly exchanged among a lot of other prisoners, and the latter exchanged himself by his own devices from the Confederate to the Federal lines while the Rebels were removing their prisoners during the march of Sherman through Georgia. They report that twenty-eight of their comrades had died while in prison at Andersonville. Co. A was "gobbled" by the Rebels last May, while stationed at a small place called Croatan, a few miles from Newbern. The whole number of men, including the captain and chaplain of the regiment, then with the company, was, I believe, about forty. It is safe to assert that not ten men of these forty will ever again return to the regiment. The majority of them now lie mouldering beneath the soil of Georgia. Is this not overwhelming evidence of the fearful mortality of our unfortunate soldiers now languishing in Southern prisons? I would give some further details as reported by these two soldiers, but I know your space will not allow it.

Captain [George W.] Graham and Horne, who train in the cavalry, made a successful raid last week to Greenville, distance some forty-odd miles, and captured twenty-seven Rebels, including a lieutenant, all belonging to a Georgia cavalry-regiment. The feat was accomplished without losing a man of the blue-blouse order. Captain Graham was formerly, I understand, a member of the Third New York Cavalry, which body of "hoss" was, and still is, a terror to the Rebels. He now leads a company of loyal North Carolinians.

It is said that the Captain was once one of the "Fire-laddies" of your city. Horne, a few months ago, deserted his love, the Confederacy, joined the Federals, and now travels with Graham.

H. P. R. R.

FORTY-SIXTH REGIMENT, N.Y.V.V.
FRONT OF PETERSBURG, March 6.

Along the banks of the silent Appomattox our regiment still continues the watchful picket. Drenched with rain and wallowing in the mud, the front lines are, betimes, no very pleasant or desirable position, yet our boys keep up their spirits in the hope of better days fast approaching. The detachment of our regiment garrisoning Fort Mansfield, also picket its waterfront, and often, in the darkest hours of night, can trace on the smooth surface of the water the outlines of an approaching boat, generally laden with a mixed cargo of white and black refugees from Dixie; our picket-fires on the beach being the beacon of their hopes. Deserters from the enemy's ranks also increase nightly, and cold as the weather is, many venture to swim the dividing stream; many are successful, whilst others are doomed to perish in the attempt. Any assistance which our men can possibly render in such cases is always promptly given, even at the risk of their own lives. A few nights since, when one of the Forty-fifth Georgia attempted to cross, but, failing, was obliged to partially return, his appeals for assistance were so truly pitiful and constant that your humble correspondent, who happened to be on picket, determined, if possible, to save his life. So jumping into an old scow-boat that lay convenient, and, with the generous assistance of Corporal Charles Ferror of Company G, we managed, by aid of a shovel used as an oar, to reach the shivering object of our search, standing up to his middle in the water on the opposite swamp. He was a fine clever young fellow, although a very poor swimmer. He says he would never be taken alive. Should he have had to try again, he would even prefer drowning to being returned to the ranks of a tyrannical Confederacy.

The paymaster is hourly expected with four months' pay; the sutlers are laying in a new stock and employing every help necessary to relieve the poor soldier from the care and burden of all superfluous greenbacks. The doctor's list will no doubt be considerably increased; for but a short time, however, as such diseases generally disappear with the currency. We begin to feel considerable improvement in the weather, much to the joy of the picket, since wood is getting to be scarce and as eagerly sought after as whisky; however, so far, this regiment has been more fortunate than many others as regards to firewood. Everything is quiet in this direction at present, and the boys have time to read their favorite SUNDAY MERCURY, and learn of the Union successes of the invincible Sherman, whose victories are saluted by the three-times-three true hearty cheers of a loyal and majestic Army, who only wait with impatience for the season to arrive, when they can vie with his veterans in dealing the death-blow to the bogus Confederacy at the capital of treason, and scatter forever to the distant corners of the globe the guilty and audacious outlaws who dared to raise a voice or hand against the honored flag of freedom and constitutional liberty.

F. K.

ONE HUNDRED AND THIRTY-THIRD REGIMENT, N.Y.V.
WINCHESTER, VA., March 5.

Our Colonel has left us again on a leave of absence, so he will be in New York in time to see the uprising of the people. Look out for stirring news from Sherman, not in South Carolina, but before Richmond. God grant him, nothing but success! You may look for glorious news from the Valley soon. General Sheridan has taken fifteen thousand cavalry on a raid for parts unknown among the ranks; but the supposition is, he will strike the Lynchburg Railroad, and cut off all communications leading to Richmond; they took ten days' rations with them. I understand he intends to form a junction with some other general who is on his way in that direction. Rebels, your doom is coming; Richmond, as your capital, is flanked.

There are orders in camp not yet been read off, to hold ourselves in readiness for an active campaign. I understand the Rebels have shown themselves not a great way from here, and so it is necessary for us to be in readiness to move. The Army of the Valley have been so successful the past year; they don't want to meet with any reverses now. We are looking daily for stirring news from Phil. and hope fervently it will be all glorious for our arms. All these victories are encouraging to us, and act beneficially for a speedy termination of this unholy Rebellion. By the appearance of General Grant's Army, he is about to make a forward movement, which will tell heavily upon the enemy. General Grant's position before Petersburg and Richmond, and the Rebels also, are probably impregnable.

I would mention a complaint, made by those who have the facts, as to how respectably-dressed ladies have been repeatedly insulted in the Twentieth Ward Relief-Station for soldiers wives. A lady who may be well dressed is questioned by the clerks as to "How do you get along without your husband?" and so on, in a very insulting manner. Means should be taken to discharge these clerks and put new ones in their places. The city-authorities should attend to it for decency's sake.

HUNCHBACK.

March 19, 1865
TWENTY-FIFTH N.Y. CAVALRY
WINCHESTER, VA., March 13.

At 4 A.M., on the 27th of February, the bugles through the corps rang out with the reveille, quickly followed by "the general" and "boots and saddles". Many a heavy sigh was heaved, as we tore down, one by one, the many little contrivances for comfort which had been put-up, in hopes of a prolonged stay. But soldiers—more especially cavalry-men—are birds of passage, and "have no abiding city here".

We were soon in the saddle and on the march, led by Sheridan himself. Our route lay by what is called the Valley Road—that is, the macadamized pike, which runs, unbroken, from Harper's Ferry to Staunton. It is an excellent road, and the horses pranced and curvetted along in high mettle, their long rest and good feeding having got them in excellent condition. We had been supplied with three days' rations and forage, and anticipated from this that our trip would not be a very long one. Many jokes were made by the men as they passed through the village, such as inquiring from the sour-looking villagers whether they had any letters for Lynchburg, Richmond, etc.; all of which were taken in exceedingly ill part, and many prophesies uttered (no doubt accompanied by a mental prayer) that we would come back quicker than we were going.

The only incident worthy of note on our first day's march was the finding of a dead Rebel scout lying by the roadside. He, in company with seven others, had been surprised by a party of our scouts; his comrades surrendered, but he refused to do so, and was accordingly shot. A sufficient explanation of his contumacy was found in the revelation made afterward by his comrades, that he was a deserter from our Army. We marched on and passed through to Woodstock, and encamped about three miles on the other side of W. Our boys were just getting their horses picketed and their fires lighted, when an order came for the regiment to go on picket. Lieutenant-Colonel Seeley, never dallies with an order—promptness and dispatch are his great characteristics; and the men were in the saddle and ready to proceed ere the staff officer who was to point out the line was ready to accompany us.

At daylight on the morning of the 28th we were drawn in. During the night and toward morning we had been occasionally annoyed by squads of Rebels feeling our lines, but they were driven off by the pickets. All being ready for the march, orders were read prohibiting foraging, and also announcing the unwelcome news that we must spin out our three days' rations, so as to make them hold out eight days. This was indeed, unpleasant tidings, but we could only "grin and bear it". The bugles sounded the "forward" and we were again on the march. Before we reached Edinburgh, the Rebels began to appear in large numbers on our right flank, and our regiment was halted at the bridge to protect the crossing of the train. This having been accomplished, we were trotting forward to retake our position in the line of march, when we heard some shots in front, and Colonel Seeley dashed forward with the regiment at the gallop, and arrived on the spot in time to save some of the wagons which were about being stampeded by the Rebels, the guards having been overpowered. We captured a couple of gray-coated gentry, and sent the balance of them flying into the woods as if the devil was after them. This was a good lesson to the wagon-drivers as they managed after this to keep the train together, and not have it scattered and strung out, as it had been. Shortly after this, firing was again heard in our front, which proceeded from a brisk skirmish which our advance was having with the Rebels. The latter, of whom there were about twelve hundred, were routed, leaving their dead and wounded on the field, and twenty-three prisoners in our hands. We had eight men wounded in this affair; but none of them dangerously.

We pushed on and through Mount Jackson, where there is a fine Rebel military hospital, and halted on the banks of the Shenandoah, while a pontoon was being laid. Gen. Custer, with his usual impetuosity, chafed under the delay thus imposed on our march, while the insulters of the flag he loves were in front, and undertook to swim the river, as the retreating Rebels had done. The latter could easily do it, as they have no load whatever on their saddles, because they can get their food for themselves and their horses wherever they go, while we have to carry all these with us. General Custer led the way, and arrived on the other side safely; but in the attempt to follow him, three men and nine horses were drowned, and the project was accordingly abandoned. The bridge being declared finished, we all crossed in safety, and proceeded on through New Market, and encamped for the night within four miles of Harrisonburg.

Next morning, the 1st instant, we were on the move at the earliest appearance of daylight, and passing through Harrisonburg pushed on toward Mount Crawford, driving the Rebels before us all the way. At the latter place we had quite a lively skirmish, as the enemy attempted to burn the bridge, and the burning party were protected by a strong force behind breastworks on the other side of the river. The destruction of the bridge would have been a serious impediment to us, as it would have necessitated the laying of a pontoon under fire from the enemy, who, protected·by his works, might have rendered the construction of the pontoon impossible; and the river was so swollen that to attempt the swimming of the turbulent stream, would have been sheer madness; and even if that could be accomplished, we would then have been compelled to destroy our artillery and train. But a sabre charge drove off the burning party, and, while some of our men went to work to extinguish the flames, another party stormed the heights and breastworks, and sent the Johnnys to the right-about. In this affair we captured fourteen prisoners, while our loss was only three wounded. We pressed on through Burk's Mills to Mount Sidney, close on the heels of the flying Rebels, and were catching up to them so quickly that, at the latter place, they abandoned their train, in which was the private wagon of General Rosser containing all his clothing, papers, etc. We reached Kline's Mills about 3 o'clock P.M., and (the order prohibiting foraging having been rescinded) after a bully supper of Rebel mutton and poultry, were about composing ourselves for a good night's rest, when "Boots and Saddles" rang out. Oh, what tall swearing. The very air turned blue. But, growl as we might, the decree had gone forth, and we had to do the same as the decree and go forth also. Our brigade was the only one that moved, and we started in the direction of Rockfish Gap, making, en route, a movement around the left flank of Rosser's camp. We captured his pickets easily, having obtained his countersign, and gained his rear without any obstruction. We now supposed that we were about to make a dash into his camp, but soon discovered that our mission was the destruction of a railroad-bridge. The bridge was an extensive trestlework, and we soon had it in flames. The light from it was the first indication which Rosser had of a force being in his rear, and he quickly got up and made tracks, carefully avoiding the vicinity of the railroad, as he supposed that, to penetrate to such a point, we must have had a much larger force than we really had. For this caution we were much obliged to him; because, if he had come that way, we should have been gobbled to a certainty. Our regiment was instructed that, if challenged by any party as to who we were, we were to answer, "the Eighth Georgia." I should have mentioned that, to reach this point, we had to pass through the City of Staunton, the main depot of supply of Early's Army. Our mission having been accomplished, we returned to Staunton, which place we reached at daylight, and there met the balance of the Army, which was moving forward—Custer's Division, the Third taking the advance. Here we halted for breakfast, and to feed the horses, which were thoroughly played-out. Foraging commenced on a large scale, and flour, bacon, hams, and tobacco were unceremoniously appropriated in immense quantities. A few of us had breakfast in the town, and we actually sat on chairs, ate from plates set on a table, on which a snowy cloth was spread, used knives and forks, and poured our coffee into saucers without the slightest accident happening, or the faintest symptom of cramp being felt by one of the party!

About noon, March 2, we started after the Army, which had taken the Waynesboro' road—that is, the people of the neighborhood call it a road, but I would most respectfully suggest that they change the name to mud-canal. The horses sank to the knees in it, and the only sound audible above the curses showered on the maker of it, was the constant pluff, pluff, as the horses pulled their legs out of the mud. One of our boys very sensibly suggested that the gunboats ought to be sent on this expedition, as it was certainly no place for a land-force to operate.

While we, the rear-guard, were plowing through this slough of despond, we heard the great guns thundering in our front, and knew that Custer, with his usual luck, had "struck ile"; but anxious as we were to have a hand in the game, fortune was against us, and "the battle was over, the victory won" before we reached Fisherville. Here we learned the extent of the work which had been done, and the fruits of the victory were 87 officers, 1,165 enlisted men, and thirteen flags, eight pieces of artillery, one hundred wagons, and the possession of Rockfish Gap. Later in the day, our advance captured a train of cars, just from Richmond, on which were six pieces of artillery—on one of which some Confederate wag had put a label addressed, "General Sheridan, care of General Early, Winchester, Va., via Staunton." You may perhaps fancy that this address was a thing of the imagination, but I assure you it was an actual fact, and was on the gun when the battery was captured. We encamped at Fisherville, and all night the rain poured on us in torrents, putting out our fires, and, as we had no tents, you can picture to yourself what a forlorn-looking lot of beings we were when the welcome notes of the reveille gave the sun permission to rise. Had our patriotism not been true blue, that drenching would certainly have washed it out. But all bands went briskly to work preparing for a resumption of the march; and as our brigade was to take the advance, visions of hot pursuit of flying Rebels made us work with an ardor that drove away all thoughts of our soaking garments. Our regiment was already in the saddle, when an order came to Colonel Seeley that we were to constitute a portion of the guard, who were to conduct the captures of yesterday to the rear. The day was spent in victualing ourselves and prisoners for the backward march; and next morning, we started in company with the Fourth, Fifth, and Twenty-second New York, First Rhode Island, and the dismounted men of the whole corps, for Winchester. When we reached Staunton, Colonel Seeley received information of a large quantity of Rebel stores being secreted in the Insane Asylum; these he immediately seized, and amongst them were a large number of shoes, which he distributed to the most needful in the command. There were also about five hundred splendid hams, which were soon adorning the saddle-bows of our gallant troopers. Quartermaster [Isaac V.] Truss, accompanied by Captain [Stephen W.] Wheeler, having gone some distance from the command to search for forage for the horses, were captured by a portion of Rosser's command. We now learned that Rosser had come back with his force to endeavor to rescue the prisoners from us, and great watchfulness on our part had therefore to be observed. We encamped that night about five miles from Mount Sidney; and Captain James Smith, with two squadrons of our regiment, started ahead to hold the bridge at that point. The undertaking was an exceedingly critical one with such a small force, but it was successfully accomplished; and next morning (March 6) we all crossed the bridge safely. Constant skirmishing with the enemy was going on, on both flanks and rear, but he was invariably driven off. This state of matters continued until the next day, when we reached the Shenandoah, and found the enemy in possession of the fords, and the river in a very swollen condition. Here we expected to have met a force from General Hancock, with pontoons, but the scouts who started from General Sheridan with the order to General Hancock, had all been captured and shot. We passed rather an anxious night, as our position was really a critical one. We were encamped on a narrow peninsula, with a formidable force in our rear, an almost impassable river on three sides of us, with all its fords guarded by intrenched riflemen. About an hour before daylight next morning (the 7th) the Rebels made a desperate assault on our camp, with the hope of taking us by surprise and stampeding the prisoners, but we were too wide awake for them. The Twenty-fifth were in line and ready in one minute from the first alarm being given by our pickets. The pickets were driven in and the Rebs came along, yelling like demons, thinking they had everything their own way; but as soon as they came within good range of our line a withering volley emptied many a saddle, and sent them skedaddling to the rear as fast as their horses could carry them. We killed eleven of them, and took nine prisoners. One of them penetrated in the outer edge of the chain of guards which encircled the prisoners, and shouted, "Break and run, boys!" But he was unceremoniously told by some of the prisoners to go to hell, and one of our guard acted on the hint and shot him dead. Had there been any inclination on the part of the prisoners to escape, many of them could have done so; but the majority of them—indeed, all with whom I conversed—expressed satisfaction at having been captured. Their only regret, and it was unanimous, was that we did not get General Early. No wonder the men would not fight under a leader whom they hate with such a bitter hatred. One of them, a captain, speaking to me of the battle of Winchester, mentioned that the division to which he belonged was the one which repulsed the cavalry charge at Brucetown. I told him that our regiment was in that charge. "Ah," said he, "we could fight then; Jubal Early, G—d d—n him, hadn't spoiled us yet, and made us the milksops we are now." They all spoke highly of John C. Breckenridge, who was their former division commander; as also of Gen. [John] Gordon, who had been removed, they affirmed, by the machinations of Early, as his talents showed the imbecility of the latter in too strong a light. Poor Early! he's down now; and every one wants to have a kick at him.

Shortly after daybreak on the morning of the 8th inst., there being no sign of the expected re-enforcements from General Hancock, and every minute's delay making our position more precarious, as it was enabling the enemy to concentrate his forces, it was determined to force the passage of the ford. The river had fallen considerably during the night, and the water was now about waist-deep, although the current was very strong. In accordance with this determination, the Twenty-second New York and First Rhode Island charged across the river, stormed the enemy's breastworks, and sent him howling in the direction of Mount Jackson. The whole of the prisoners and dismounted men were then got across, the weak and sickly being ferried over behind mounted men. Captain [James] Waters and Adjutant [Robert M.]Cumming distinguished themselves by their great exertions on this occasion. The whole crossing was under the immediate supervision of Lieutenant-Colonel Seeley. All had been got over, except the rearguard—the Fifth New York—when Rosser made a charge on the latter, expecting to overwhelm them by his vastly superior numbers; but Major [Theodore] Boice, commanding the Fifth, by an instantaneous change of front and countercharge, cut Rosser's force completely in two, and whipped them in the handsomest style, killing about twenty and capturing about thirty. General Rosser, in this fight, rode the horse which Captain Wheeler was using when captured. Lieutenant-Colonel Seeley, seeing the precarious position in which the Fifth were placed, drew the Twenty-fifth up in line on the bluff on the north bank of the river, to cover the crossing of the former regiment, but in the unexpected daring and brilliant move of Major Boice, and its admirable execution, rendered our firing one shot unnecessary. We marched that day and night until we reached Cedar Creek, which stream we forded about 2 A.M., of the 9th instant, and lay down for the balance of the night in one of the old camps of the Eighth Corps.

At 7 o'clock we were again on the move, and when near Newton were surprised by a sudden order to form line of battle. It proved to be a false alarm, occasioned by a scouting-party of our own men from Winchester, unaware of our approach, firing into our advance guard. The mistake was found out luckily before any blood was shed. We reached Winchester about 1 o'clock that day, and having handed over our prisoners, were conducted to a camping-ground where there was not wood enough to make a tooth-pick, and no water nearer than a mile and a half. We remained in the Sahara until next day, when, thanks to the untiring efforts of

Lieutenant-Colonel Seeley, we were moved to our present spot, about a mile from the town, where we had an abundance of splendid water and no limit to our supply of wood. We will remain here until our dismounted men are remounted, and then we will go—where?

No sign of the Paymaster yet, although Uncle Sam now owes us nearly nine months' pay.

B. O. B.

FORTY-SEVENTH REGIMENT, N.Y.S.V.

NEAR WILMINGTON, N.C., March 12, 1865.

For many months past, no—one apparently has been sufficiently afflicted with the cacoethes scribondi to attempt sending any account of the movements of this old regiment for insertion in the columns of the SUNDAY MERCURY. This was to be regretted for several reasons; for not only are the public interested in reading news from the regiments, but those having friends or relatives in the Army, all anxiously look in the MERCURY for a letter from the particular organization in which they may be serving. I propose, therefore, with your permission, to break the epistolary silence which has so long hung over the gallant Forty-seventh, and put in at least "an appearance".

I shall not attempt any account of the share which the regiment took in the capture of Fort Fisher, in the flanking of Fort Anderson, or the operations more immediately in front of Wilmington. I shall only say that in all these movements the Forty-seventh sustained its ancient reputation, and is now, along with the rest of the Second Division, enjoying repose after the fatigues and dangers of the past two months. How long our spell of inactivity may last, depends, in all probability, upon the direction of General Sherman's movements.

You will have heard of the large number of released Union prisoners which the Rebels have sent into our lines here, since the capture of Wilmington. The hospitals and buildings improvised as such in the city are crowded with these men, many of whom are in a sad plight from the effects of famine and disease. They say that those unfit for the march were sent on to Richmond. It is hard to imagine how much more unfit for marching any men could be than the hundreds of gaunt, hollow-cheeked, and wasted figures which were lately sent into our lines. Walking skeletons these men are, but wonderfully high-spirited, and burning to avenge the cruelties practiced upon them in Southern prisons. Among those mentioned for brutal treatment, I heard the name of Captain Henry Wirtz, keeper of the prison at Sumter, Ga. This Wirtz is the identical Dutchman who had charge of the Richmond prisoners in 1861-2. I well remember, as will many others, his ill-omened visage, and his oft-repeated threat, uttered, revolver in hand, to blow us "to hell mit gunpowder!"

So far as our experience has gone, the people here are disposed to return to the old flag. Previous to our advent, many Union-men were compelled to live in the swamps, to avoid [Robert F.] Hoke's brutal cavalry, whose principal business is said to have been to plunder indiscriminately. "When we saw the Stars and Stripes in the city," said one man to me, "you should have heard the cheer which rose up from the swamp."

VIDETTE.

SIXTY-FIFTH REGIMENT, N.Y.S.V.V.

BEFORE PETERSBURG, VA., March 12.

The heavy rain which nearly inundated our camps, and made them in such a horrid condition, has at last abated; and to-day, for the first time in a week, has old Sol shone down upon us in all his glory, and there is now a prospect of fine weather, for some days at least.

Picket-skirmishing, which has been for some time not practiced, was resumed yesterday by the pickets of the enemy in front of the Second Division of our corps. The firing from morning, until 12, A.M., was very brisk, reminding us of past, as well as those to come, of future scrimmages. After the hour named, the firing died away to an occasional shot.

Fort Fisher, of which I have frequently spoken, has at last, attained completion; the last few shovels of dirt were thrown yesterday, and to-day the huge earthwork stands forth in bold relief, bristling with defiance. The erection of this fort has been a work of great labor; details from every regiment in the corps have been to work upon it, from the time it was commenced until completed, and without exaggeration, I may truthfully say that the Sixty-fifth have contributed their entire part in its ditch-digging and clay-piling.

Camp-duties have been less severe, in consequence of the rain, and we have been allowed to stay in quarters lately for a moment, without being called upon to perform some nonsensical business; this has been a great relief to the boys, who before had scarce spare time to perform their tonsorial operations.

The Paymaster (may his shadow never grow less!), has been to see us, and while here distributed four months' pay to the regiment; the result of his visit is, that the boys are loose, financially. Bourbon, rye, and Commissary receive a fair premium, and, of course, many are spiritually elevated. It is curious and novel to see the different modes enterprising individuals have invented to supply the soldiers with articles that are contraband.

Warren Station, on Grant's Railroad, presented quite a business-like appearance. Long rows of tents and huts first meet your gaze, wherein sutlers have everything to dispose of, from a pin-cushion to a diamond-ring. A hotel also here flourishes, where veterans are served, a la Delmonico. There is also here a Daguerrean gallery, which is constantly crowded from morning until night, by Uncle Sam's nephews, who want their images taken to send to their girls. Of course these pictures would not compare with Brady's style, but still they are fair enough bearing in mind the difficulties under which the artist labors. Your correspondent had his profile incased the other day, and on returning to camp I showed it to a friend, asking him at the same time if he knew who it was. After examining it very closely, he answered, by saying that it looked very much like Mr. Clarke, the comedian, in the character of Toodles. From the above you can, perhaps, imagine how correct are army-photographs.

On Wednesday-evening next, the Tycoons are to give their final performance this winter, should war drag its slow-length along for another season of winter-quarters. We hope that war's devastation will fall but slightly on them, for their music has served to cheer many a sad hour, and has dispelled that monotony which is so oppressive to the soldier.

FRANCONI.

March 26, 1865
ONE HUNDRED AND TWENTIETH REGIMENT, N.Y.V.
CAMP NEAR HATCHER'S RUN, VA, March 20.

We are now having fine weather for this time of the year, and the boys are enjoying themselves by playing ball, or lying upon the ground to feel the warm rays of the sun, and to gaze upon the enemy that are only a little way apart. Both parties are very friendly. A great many deserters come into our lines from the enemy, bringing with them all of their equipments, and they receive pay for them. They have a great many rumors on the other side of the Run (Hatcher's). One tall big strapping Virginian came into our lines with some news, saying that Lee intends to drive us into the James River, and to strike a panic in our army. They have marching orders, but he don't know where they are to move, whether to go forward, or to take the home-stretch toward Richmond. We have rumors ourselves. Some say that we are to join Sherman's gallant band, others that we are to join Hancock in the valley. That is the Second Corps. I think that we are needed where we are at the present time.

Last Saturday, to our surprise, our division was called out to witness the execution of a deserter. John Smith Company H, of a New Jersey regiment. It seems that he deserted some time ago, and went over to the enemy, expecting to be sent home through some blockade-runner. He did not play his game right.

The boys of this regiment have furlough on the brain. The most soldierly-appearing enlisted man out of the whole brigade receives a furlough for twenty-five days. I see the One Hundred and Twentieth took the shine this time. Sergeant Sidney Carrington, formerly of the old Seventy-first, was the best-looking and the best-drilled soldier, and he has proved himself a hero on many a field. James Cronin leaves for home to-day. His term of service has expired, and he has been wounded several times, and we all hope he may enjoy his future life as well as he did in this Rebellion. This regiment, as far as I can see for the short time that I have been with it (I have just returned from the hospital), is A No. 1 in drill, and in everything done up to the mark. It is composed of good stuff, the vets from the old Seventy-first and Seventy-second New York Volunteers, of the old Iron Excelsior Brigade, who have stood the brunt of many a hard-fought battle, are now consolidated with this regiment. The rest of the old Excelsiors are scattered throughout the division; but we have a rumor flying around in this regiment that the Seventy-third N.Y.V. are coming into our brigade again. I hope it is so, because we would like to see our zou-zou fire-boys once more in our brigade. If the weather continues on so pleasant, I think you will hear of something big. The Rebs seem to be happy this morning, their bands are playing and they themselves are cheering. The cars are running to and fro. Something is up; perhaps some great victory or a grand colored jubilee looking out for some house to let on the 1st of May.

GUARDIAN.

April 2, 1865
SIXTY-FIRST REGIMENT, N.Y.V.V.
IN THE FIELD, VA., March 28.

At the date of my last dispatch I little thought that our near vicinity would be the scene of a sanguinary and bloody battle; but such is the fact. During the week we were prepared to move at a moment's notice, when suddenly on Saturday-morning we were ordered out on the color line, and in rear of the breastworks, stacked arms, and remained there about half an hour. At 7½, A.M., a detachment of two hundred men under charge of Lieutenants [Thomas] Miller, [Thomas N.] Sares, and [William V.] Hudson, proceeded to the picket-line to open the ball. Great anxiety was manifested by all, to see what success they would meet on arriving at the line. Skirmishers were thrown out, and shortly after our boys reached the Rebel line drove out their pickets and captured twenty-five prisoners—among the number one Rebel Lieutenant who surrendered his sword to Lieutenant Miller, saying at the time, "You have fairly won it." We then made another charge upon the Rebels, and drove them pell-mell into their main works. The ball was now fairly opened and the whole brigade, under command of Colonel Seeley were soon engaged. Charge after charge was made upon the Rebs, and we rapidly gained ground. About noon, the Second Brigade of our division hotly engaged the enemy on our left, and from that time until dark, one continuous roar of musketry deafened the ears of all, especially from half-past 4 to half-past 6, P.M. During that time our division being all engaged, and charging upon the Rebs, succeeded in obtaining ground advantageous for the posting of artillery, which was accordingly done. In a short time the Rebs were treated to a tremendous cross-fire from our batteries, which poured volley after volley into [their] ranks.

Dusk coming on, fighting ceased; and throughout the night it was comparatively quiet, except a few shots, now and then, from the pickets. At half-past 12, P.M., midnight, our regiment returned to its old position, and there remains, up to the present writing. All our officers and men are worthy of praise for the gallantry and courage displayed. Many criticisms were placed upon our conduct, and all of a very flattering nature.

Among the officers who distinguished themselves in particular it would be a difficult matter to state, as all did well and nobly. Major [George W.] Schaffer commanded the regiment after 11, A.M., and by his coolness and bravery commended himself to all. This regiment's loss is as follows: 4 killed, 27 wounded, and 16 missing.

With tired limbs, we sought repose, sleeping on our arms, not knowing the moment we may be called upon, and the same uncertainty exists.

S. G. C.

SECOND REGIMENT, N.Y. FIRE ZOUAVES

NEAR HATCHER'S RUN, VA., March 28.

When I wrote last, we were in the midst of a busy preparation, and every patriot seemed bent upon having his weapon in good order for the coming fray. The idea was prevalent that there was soon to be a movement somewhere, but in what direction we were to go, or at what point the blow was to be struck, was a mystery to all; since then the above movement, or one equivalent thereto, has been accomplished and that it has culminated in a signal and complete victory to our arms—that is, as complete as the nature of the engagement would admit. The enemy precipitated the attack upon us and took the cloak of a "sable midnight" to hide his real designs, and make it a most fitting opportunity to pierce our line. This was done on the front of the Ninth Corps, and, for the time being, they were very successful in the dangerous undertaking, as our picket-line was surprised and captured before the true nature of the onslaught was divined. Before their impetuosity could be stayed, they were in possession of our formidable line of breastworks, which border for a considerable distance both on the right and left of the famous stronghold of Yankee creation known as Fort Hell. There was a very weak line of our troops at the front on this unexpected attack; they being mostly in quarters back around the railroad at the time, hence the success of the enemy. Otherwise they could not have crossed the neutral ground with impunity. Some of them, elated with their short-lived victory, penetrated as far back as the railroad, but it is doubtful whether the same ever got back to their lines again; for when General [John G.] Parke made his formidable and magnificent advance upon them, he swept the Rebel columns before him in terrible disorder, recapturing his former line of works gallantly, and with but very small loss. In conversing with those who witnessed the affair on this point of the line, I have been informed that the enemy were mowed down fearfully in their retrograde flight by our well-directed musketry, and grape and canister from double-shotted artillery. Between two or three thousand prisoners were cut off from their retreat toward Petersburg. The cannonading was so loud and incessant that long before daylight the whole Army was in line. How the enemy withstood the crash of artillery that went howling after them over the picket-line, I am unable to say.

When the news of General Parke's success reached the Second Corps, which lies several miles to the left of the Ninth, General Humphreys soon put his veterans in motion. After filling the breastworks, and ascertaining that nothing serious hovered around our front, long continuous lines of troops, by regiments and brigades, were seen wending their way out to the woods, on the other side of which was the position of the enemy. This looked like work, and all hands anticipated a red-hot day of it, and I believe they were not much disappointed in their anticipations; for, before night set in, the Second Corps was in defiant possession of no less than three lines of Rebel rifle-pits, and so completely invested in their front line of works that they took discretion as the better part of valor, and remained behind them. They did not like the idea, it seems, of rushing in their usual style upon the goodly number of bayonets that were "pointed to the height of the eye" for their reception in the deep woods fronting them. Luckily for the enemy that they did not come out, for

General Humphreys would have been under the painful necessity of dealing them a few blows as hard as what Parke administered to them on the right of us.

Now for the Second Fire Zouaves. I suppose you are anxious to know on what part of this vast line they were assigned. I will tell you, and I will also inform you how the little band of spoiled patriots behaved themselves on this occasion. Gen. de Trobriand, always having a sharp lookout for the success of his brigade, deemed it expedient to throw out a skirmish-line, upon the merits of which he could rely. He was not long in riveting his eye upon the right regiments. We were not in the breastworks at the time—there not being room sufficient left for us on account of our numbers, I suppose—we only having about one hundred and ten men; so we were trotted out on the skirmish line. The Twentieth Indiana had the good luck to be our right bower. Marching out over our picket-line, we formed in the woods, about two hundred yards from the front pits of the Graybacks. Capt. James McKenna was in command of the regiment, and was subject to the orders of Col. [Albert S.] Andrews, of the Twentieth Indiana. Being now put in trim for the emergency, it soon became apparent that a charge was on the "wing", and before we had barely sufficient time to consider over the affair, the peremptory command came, and away we went double-quick through the dense woods. We soon came to another barrier in the shape of a swamp, deep and putrid through which we wended our way as best we could, with the Rebel skirmishers pegging away at us like good fellows. But no such thing as flinching was there in the two little regiments that went dashing through the mud and water of the swamp. They got through finally in pretty good style and, hastily reforming under the cover of the knoll, in the immediate front of which were the Rebel pits, occupied by a strong and determined lot of Rebels. In a few moments we were again prepared, and the ringing reports of our rifles soon told the enemy that they broke helter-skelter for their next line. Immediately occupying their front-lines which were very strong ones, we soon again pinned them. Here the Fire Zouaves rallied and they determined to make a dash at them in their other pits. They did so, and succeeded to a miracle, capturing more Rebels than what their own regiment numbered.

The result of this magnificent little charge was as follows: one hundred and twenty-seven prisoners of war, three of whom were commissioned officers, with all their guns and accoutrements; but, on account of the terrific shelling that the enemy now began to harass us with, some sixty stand of arms were demolished in the second captured line, as they could not be taken to the rear. This was done thoroughly under the command of Capt. John Noonan, a better soldier than whom did not stand upon the field that day. No body of men could have done the same more bravely and completely than did the old Seventy-third, and with so slight a loss as we sustained. Both officers and men vied with each other in acts of heroism and gallantry, and were I inclined to do them all the justice that they merit, my foolscap would not hold out. But, suffice it to say that we held the pits until late at night, when we were relieved. The enemy made four attempts to recapture them, but ignobly failed each time.

We are again in our old camp, but how long we will be permitted to stay is unknown. Things look very warlike just now, and we may be on the move again before night.

SNAKE.

SIXTY-FIFTH REGIMENT, N.Y.V.V.

BEFORE PETERSBURG, VA., March 26.

Here we are still, and in spite of all rumors and reports, it is very likely that we will not move for some weeks yet, unless we are forced to do so by some move of the enemy. The principal feature of the past week was a review of our (the First) division, by Major-General Meade and staff. The day was very warm for his season, and a great many of the men were overpowered by the heat of the sun; but the display was elegant. Every regiment looked and marched well. As the Sixty-fifth dipped their colors and marched by, the Commanding-General was heard to ask a distinguished officer near him, "What regiment is that?" On being told, he added the compliment, "They march very well." Among the prominent men who with General Meade witnessed the review, was Admiral [Hiram] Paulding of the Navy. He seemed well pleased with the display.

I feel gratified in stating that Brigadier-General Hamblin has assumed command of this brigade. The General is very popular with the boys, who repose the greatest confidence in his military abilities.

The most pleasing feature that has taken place with us for a long period, occurred a few evenings ago, in the shape of a camp-banquet, given by the Tycoon Socialist, in honor of the late brilliant victories achieved by our comrades in arms. The club, numbering thirty members, had met some evenings previous, and had appointed the necessary committees for the procurement of the materials to furnish a fitting repast. By the kindness of influential individuals, everything was obtained that was possible, and on the evening of the 21st inst. the Tycoons gathered around the festive board to eat, drink, and be merry through a legitimate channel, enough of the good commissary, which had been got to enliven their spirits, and toasts were drank, and songs sung, and speeches made. Every one appeared merry, and, for the time, the stern duties and realities of war were forgotten. After the solids had been removed, the Tycoons indulged in their favorite propensity—music. Mr. Nat Yessel, formerly of the London concert-halls, favored the company with an operatic travestie on "Macbeth" and "Robinson Crusoe", which called forth great applause. The others also did well their different parts; but time and space will not permit me to mention them. Messrs. Thirion, Dingee, McDermott, Laydon, Thompson, and Millington were particularly successful in their efforts to please. In speaking of the latter gentleman, I am reminded of a painful accident that occurred to him before the party broke up. The author of "Lannigan's ball" speaks of Timothy Dougherty sticking his right foot through Miss Flannigan's hoops; but as there was no crinoline present, Mr. Millington was not so fortunate, for instead he stuck his left foot into a camp-kettle full of boiling hot tea, the effect of which can be better imagined than described.

The news of the fall of Goldsboro' has reached here, and causes great rejoicing, and the boys anticipate that the next fall in the market of Jeff will be the surrender of Lee to U. S. Grant. The Rebel Chief must see the utter folly of attempting to hold out much longer against the vastly superior forces opposed to him, and the scion of Light-horse Harry will find it worse than useless to attempt to elude the combinations that are rapidly enveloping him and his uncouth followers. May Heaven speed the cause of justice and right, so that before long our glorious flag will float in triumph from the tempestuous Atlantic to the golden shores of the Pacific, and from the St. Lawrence to the Gulf of Mexico. When this happy epoch has arrived, and the war-worn soldier is permitted to return to those he loves, he can point with pride to the glories achieved by the national arms, and can truly say, that he was instrumental in part in securing the desired blessing.

FRANCONI.

EIGHTH N.Y. HEAVY ARTILLERY
HATCHER'S RUN, VA., March 26.

Yesterday morning, we were awakened by the booming of artillery on our right, and much reflection was adduced in consequence, but within a few minutes everything was ordered to be packed and ready to move at any moment. We could then judge what was transpiring. We were sanguine that the long anticipated movement of the Army was at hand. The boys prepared themselves for a general campaign, and as we marched off, bade farewell to our winter-houses with sighing hearts and fond recollections of bygone moments of pleasure and comfort found in our little cottages. Being so very near the Rebel lines, there was not much time for consideration before skirmishing was actively going on, which lasted until late in the afternoon, when the fighting assumed a fierce and sanguinary form. Simultaneously, we received the report of the morning's fight on our right: "That the Rebels had captured Fort Stedman and guns."

Recollections imperishable, as memory of those days of 1864, when we used to beat time with our craniums around her walls, to music written in English arsenals and played by Rebel sharpshooters, are yet as the morning-air. But that flag, ever too sacred to yield to the power of rebellious fiends, soon waved over Stedman again, and Wright's boys gave three victorious cheers in the presence of thousands of Jeff's subjects then, "as harmless as sunbeams", begging for bread.

Foiled again, the Rebels thought to wreak vengeance by dashing for our left, but here again "horida-bells" sent terror to Bob Lee, and destruction to his soldiers, for night closed the fighting, leaving Lee and his mob most cleverly whipped; while Grant and his Army were filling their ears with enthusiastic shouts of victory and success. The battle being fought and won, we returned to camp this morning, and are now resting in quietness.

A private of Co. I, of our regiment met a strange fate, a few days since. While in the act of filling his canteen from a barrel half-filled with water, he was seized with a fit and fell headforemost in the water. When discovered, he was perfectly dead. His name was Abbott, and lived in West Thirtieth street, New York.

Yours, SAM.

April 9, 1865
FORTY-SIXTH REGIMENT, N.Y.V.V.
FRONT OF PETERSBURG, VA., April 2.

The right wing of this regiment, which has for some time past been doing picket-duty along the river-bank, has been removed a short distance to the works opposite the city; while that portion of the regiment assigned to garrison Fort Mansfield still continue that duty; so the entire regiment is now situated in and around two adjacent forts—Mansfield and McGilvray. Although the position is an exposed one, the boys seem to relish the risk and excitement attending artillery-duels, which frequently occur here.

On Saturday-morning, the 25th ult., they had an extra opportunity of testing their nerves beneath the concentrated fire of the Rebel batteries, which seem to hold eternal spite against Fort McGilvray. Good reason have they to hate and dread her, especially since their late attempt to capture and hold our forts met with such prompt and terrible punishment from the Ninth Corps. While the infantry of this regiment stood firm to their works, in readiness to receive the enemy on their bayonets, the excellent artillery-pieces, under command of the brave and skillful Major Romer, actually tore the ranks of the assailants into fragments with his constant and terrible shower of grape. During the engagement, however, the gallant Romer got hurt; nevertheless, his guns were not allowed to cool on that account, since Captain Victor Traxmarer, of this regiment, being in the fort at the time, immediately volunteered his services to work the guns; and well did he prove his skill, courage, and claim, as a first-class artillerist. In fact, all our officers and men in the fort determined that the Forty-sixth should not be captured alive; and although the enemy's shells burst in every direction over and around us, we fortunately had but few casualties; so, after the entire assaulting column had been either captured, slaughtered, or otherwise totally annihilated, the work of attending to the dead and wounded commenced on both sides. When this necessary and humane duty was performed, and the flag of truce again withdrawn, both sides returned to their respective defences, our brave men cheerfully congratulating each other upon the result; while the sullen, gloomy looks of the defeated graybacks told plainly the hopelessness of their cause.

The weather, for the last two weeks or so, has been all that could be expected, and already the long-threatened but sure, steady moves of the indomitable Grant begin to spoil the plans and lessen the boundaries of Davis, Lee & Co., who, ere long, as their space grows smaller and smaller, will be obliged to tread on each others' corns for standing-room. Then look out for a rough and tumble free fight among the chivalry, while U. S. G. moves steadily on to bag his game, and hands them over to the judgement and sentence of a just and powerful people, who will never tolerate the laws and Union framed by their fathers to be broken by a few knavish and political adventurers.

FRANK.

CITY POINT CORRESPONDENCE

CITY POINT, VA., April 5.

The past week has been one of intense excitement, doubtless throughout the whole country—as it has been one pregnant with the most vital and important movements in the annals of the history of the greatest rebellion of modern times. And right gloriously too have the great and strategic combinations and calculations of Lieutenant-General Grant, aided and assisted by a most brilliant staff of generals, such as Sheridan, Sherman and Meade, culminated. Our Army entered Petersburg and Richmond on Monday at daybreak. The enemy is now fast retreating by the Danville Railroad, toward Lynchburg, Va., with Sheridan and our gallant Army, flushed with continued victory and success, fast in pursuit. The battles of Saturday and Sunday were desperate in the extreme. Never was greater valor and sacrifice required of the Army in their repeated and terrific assaults; and never was it more freely made by our men—who feel that Rebellion is on its last tottering legs—though vainly making a bold front, for a time, whenever assaulted in their strongholds, from which they have at last been driven. Our captures of the enemy amount to upward of twelve thousand men, most of which have arrived at City Point and immediately shipped on transports, which are here in great numbers—and all required. Admiral Porter has some thousands of his blue-jackets on shore for guard-duty, etc., which relieves soldiers for the field who, would otherwise be required in considerable force to guard prisoners and public property at City Point and to and from the front. One train last night brought down two thousand three hundred "Johnnies", of every size, color, and condition. Some fat, some lean (the lean being in the majority); some were dirty—few were clean; nearly all needed clothing. They all agreed that "you'ns" got the best of "we'ns" in yesterday's battling. This dialect is peculiar to the Johnnies, when referring to the Yankees. In conversation with our men, they say "you'ns", and of themselves "we'ns." Several colored soldiers were among the Rebel prisoners brought here yesterday. The trains have been busy day and night in taking down prisoners, wounded, captured artillery, caissons, ammunition and small-arms in great numbers. Our losses so far have been heavy, the hospitals here are pretty well filled, though the wounded are sent off daily in hospital-transports to Washington, etc.; during their stay at the Point, they have every attention, from both the surgeons and the Christian and Sanitary Commissions, the amount of good work performed by the agents of the former Commission is almost incalculable. Their nurses never tire in tendering to wounded the delicacies with which they are provided for the soldier. Of the Sanitary Commission it would appear as much cannot be said, notwithstanding, their supplies are less limited. Still both are invaluable to our hospitals in cause of humanity—and are a great blessing at the present time of need. Several hundred citizen employees, of both the Commissions of Subsistence and Quartermaster's Departments tendered their services through the heads of their several Departments, to the Military Authorities at City Point, for the purpose of guarding public property or prisoners here, should they be needed. This patriotic tender was duly appreciated, but they have not yet been called upon. Send forward re-enforcements from the North now—let not an hour be lost; hurry up the drafted men; don't wait to send "subs", come on, all ye loyal men, come ye peace-makers, irrespective of party or faction, all who prefer peace to war join now in the last hours of Rebellion, and aid in arresting the last armed foe to the Union, to peace and harmony—the combined army of Lee and Johnston. Now that Petersburg and Richmond are conquered and has fallen and that Grant is fast gaining on the track of Lee, with his gallant Army, send forward "new" men, men of whom there are thousands who are capable, yet never have borne arms since the war began; send such men forward now, even in this the "eleventh hour", and let them have it to say in the coming years of peace and prosperity, that they served their country, if only for a few weeks, in garrisoning the strongholds and portions which the more loyal citizens of the Republic have fought and suffered for years to gain.

The weather here is beautiful, mild, and spring-like. The roads are in excellent condition for marching. More stirring news and lengthy details will have reached your readers—long ere this arrives, so that further comment is unnecessary from your correspondent.

A. O. P.

FORTY-SEVENTH REGIMENT, N.Y.S.V.

FAYSON'S STATION, April 3.

The division broke camp near Wilmington on the 15th, and crossing northeast Cape Fear River the next day, marched on toward Goldsboro, to co-operate with the movements of Sherman and Schofield. We moved rapidly, and although we had to encounter swamps, and wade waist-deep through creeks, made as much as twenty and twenty-two miles a day. The country through which we passed is for the most part uninteresting, being low and swampy, thinly populated, and the buildings generally in a dilapidated condition. On reaching Kanawaville, however, a change for the better is observable, and residences of a highly superior description are not uncommon. On the 19th we heard the sound of Sherman's cannon, and on the 20th we could easily distinguish the rattle of musketry. On the evening of the last-mentioned day we passed a vacated camp which had evidently been occupied by a portion of our forces, and on the morning of the 21st we had formed a junction with Sherman's Army at Cox's Bridge on the Neuse River, about eight miles from Goldsboro. The fight, which commenced on the 19th, was still going on, but the defeated enemy retreated in the night.

We remained at Cox's Bridge until yesterday morning, when we were ordered to this point, situated twenty-two miles from Goldsboro, and about sixty-two from Wilmington. On the afternoon of the 24th, the pickets of the colored division, attached to Terry's command, had a brisk encounter with the enemy's cavalry, on the north side of the Neuse River, resulting in the Rebels being driven back with loss.

You will, I presume, have received General Sherman's congratulatory order to the troops on the success of the campaign. The reading of the order to each camp was followed by great cheering.

We all looked forward with great interest to our meeting with the great Army which has victoriously swept over three States; nor was the interest abated one whit on witnessing its appearance. A corps of infantry came by, preserving little or no order of march. One-half of a regiment would be mounted, and the other half on foot. Their dress was of every conceivable variety, and, like their manners, free and easy. One would ride by, sitting on a side-saddle, and behind him would come a carriage and pair, the occupants being two high privates, fully accoutered, but wearing stove pipe hats and smoking cigars. High-bred and well-conditioned horses, broken-down jades, mules, donkeys, and oxen, harnessed in every kind of style, and driven according to the caprice of the possessor, moved along in mass.

In the rear of the column came all manner of vehicles, laden with pigs, sheep, goats, forage, and negro women and children. The spectacle was strange, picturesque, and brimful of the comic element. There was nothing strictly "military" about it, but these men had, just a little while previous, been engaged in deadly conflict, where they had displayed the highest qualities of the soldier.

Sherman's men are all enthusiastic over "old Bill", as they familiarly call him. He is done with raiding now, they say, and will open a "campaign".

"Do you want to know old Bill when you see him?" said one, "I'll tell you. He wears an old coat, blue pants, and Kossuth hat; rides a mule, and holds in his mouth the stump of a cigar which he has carried with him all the way from Atlanta."

The men tell many amusing stories of the General. A rich farmer complained of being plundered. "There they are now," said he to Sherman, "in my smokehouse, taking everything they can lay their hands on."

"I would advise you," was Sherman's rejoinder, "to pitch in with the rest; you have quite as good a right as they have!"

Situated as we are I can send you no news. We are suffering from a temporary scarcity of supplies, but this will, no doubt, be speedily remedied, and the railroad will soon be in running order.

It is rumored that General Sheridan is expected here from the Shenandoah valley, with his entire mounted force.

VIDETTE.

SEVENTEENTH REGIMENT, N.Y.V.V.

GOLDSBORO, N.C., March 31.

Being at leisure in camp for the first time since we left Savannah (20th January) I will devote a few hours of my rest, principally to the relatives and those interested in the welfare of this veteran regiment.

Leaving Savannah in haste, we were anxious to know our destination. We were aware of some great campaign being in progress, but where to, no one knew. The first place of any note was Sister's Ferry, about forty miles from Savannah, the boat ran up and down Savannah River, holding communication with the city. We encamped here about five days, but were constantly employed in building roads through the swamps of South Carolina. When we refitted for the expedition, and the roads clear, the news spread over camp that we were to raid the heart of South Carolina, toward Branchville. By doing this, we compelled the enemy to evacuate Charleston. Our movements were not known, nor were they fully developed until the 16th of February, being then about to strike a blow against Columbia, the capital of South Carolina, previously making a feint for Augusta, Ga., the Rebels concentrated their main force there, only to be the victims of Sherman's strategy. Our forces entered Columbia without much opposition.

Gen. [William J.] Hardee, it was rumored, had his command there, numbering 10,000, but that force being insignificant, they evacuated six hours previous to our taking possession, bringing with him light ordnance and supplies. We followed closely in pursuit of the retreating enemy, capturing a great many wagons heavily laden with supplies. Kilpatrick assisted us in troubling the enemy's rear, cutting off and capturing troops and supplies.

Our Army marched on several different roads, scouring the country as they went.

On the 11th of March, after some lively skirmishes, we entered Fayetteville, a river town of much note; here we were delayed sufficient time to have a rest of ten hours, whilst the pontooneers were busily engaged in laying pontoons across Cape Fear River (the bridge being burnt by the retreating army). About sunset, the pontoon-bridge was laid, and crossed by the First Brigade, Second Division, Fourteenth Army Corps. Crossing in such haste was not expected by the enemy, for we came across the enemy's pickets about three miles from the bridge. Re-enforcements were continually increasing the force ahead of us, so that they became very stubborn and tried to check our advance; although the roads were in a miserable condition (through rain), we moved ahead with but slight trouble from the enemy.

On the 16th of March, close to Smith's Ferry [Averasborough, N.C.], the enemy made a determined stand, being strongly fortified. The First Division, Twentieth Army Corps, was first to engage. They tried to drive them, but to no purpose. The Second and Third Brigades of the Fourteenth Army Corps came to their assistance. The Rebs then began to waver and fall back. At this moment, the First Brigade, Second Division, Fourteenth Army Corps, were relieved from wagons and sent to the front; on the road were dreadful scenes of dead and wounded, making prospects rather gloomy. Our brigade was brought quickly into line, and the order "Commence firing!" was given. Volley after volley was sent and returned, with a strong inclination to do mischief. The line was as follows: Fourteenth Michigan Volunteers on the right, Seventeenth New York Veteran Volunteers in the centre, Sixteenth Illinois Volunteers on the left, the Tenth Michigan Volunteers and Sixteenth Illinois being in the rear for support. The firing was so heavy from the enemy's centre that the Seventeenth New York Volunteers were ordered to lie down under such shelter as nature afforded. There it was that our Lieutenant-Colonel, James Lake, was wounded, while paying attention to our safety, forgetting his own. Everywhere, up to the time of his wound, he was engaged in encouraging his command to keep cool, and before he left the field he saw that the men had good shelter, such as it was.

On hearing that Captain [William G.] Barnett (Company I), was killed, there was a look of melancholy sadness spread over the features of most every man in the regiment. He was beloved by his company and respected by those who knew him. He was a gentleman of high standing in society, and a soldier of refined qualities in the field. He formerly belonged to the Hawkins' Zouaves.

Toward evening of the 16th it grew chilly, and rained heavily; we abandoned our line, leaving only a skirmishing party under command of Captain [James B.] Horner (Company H). The Rebs evacuated next morning at 3 o'clock. At daylight we followed them up, and overtook them about twenty-six miles of Goldsboro. Two days was sufficient to concentrate our force.

On the morning of the 19th, we engaged the enemy and drove them six or seven miles through swamp and morass. They gained an elevated position for their artillery. Here they had strong works, which caused us to build works also. The First Brigade, or "Fighting Brigade" was again wagon-guard, but was soon relieved and sent to the front. About 600 yards from the enemy we threw up a strong line of works; we had them almost completed when an attack was made along the entire line by the enemy. They broke parts of the line held by the First Division of the Twentieth and First Division, Fourteenth Army Corps, which completely cut off and surrounded the Second Division, Fourteenth Army Corps. The First Brigade, accustomed to danger, thought slightly of the imminent peril which surrounded them; for no sooner had the enemy occupied our own works in our rear, than we about-faced and fought them from theirs. Whilst we were firing they hoisted a white flag and the order was given to cease firing. Captain [William H.] Dunphy, of the Tenth Michigan, with a squad of men approached to hold conversation. They asked them to surrender—that they would parole them on the spot. Captain Dunphy replied that he would fight them, but never surrender. At this utterance of the bold soldier the Rebs opened fire upon them before they had time to let us know the result. But their treachery was dearly paid. The Tenth and Seventeenth opened a most galling cross-fire, which caused them to waver. We then charged their works, capturing two stand of colors with 650 prisoners. Their loss exceeds 3,000 killed, wounded, and missing. Our loss is about 150. The prisoners state that Joe Johnston had parts of four corps engaged. Our whole force composed of three divisions. About 7 o'clock the firing gradually ceased, and at 8 o'clock we made fires and cooked whatever we had to eat; that wasn't much.

Great credit is attached to Captain Horner of Co. H (formerly of Hawkins' Zouaves), for the discipline and soldierly behavior of those belonging to the Seventeenth N.Y.V.V., for he it was that kept showing a good example, and encouraging the men to keep cool. Captain [Alexander S.] Marshall being in command of the regiment was busily employed seeking for staff-officers for the purpose of receiving orders; not finding anyone, he concluded to hold council with Captains Horner and [William E.] Fisher, Co. D. As an organization nothing can excel the Seventeenth; but they stand greatly in need of line-officers. Leaving New York, our aggregate was 660; now it is 285, having but 6 line-officers present for duty. Up to the present date no regiment can show a clearer or more honorable record than the Seventeenth since we joined the Western Army. Let the scholar take the map and follow it up from place to place we have been to; it puzzles as well as surprises the soldier in enumerating the thousands of miles we have marched. The raids and forced marches through Mississippi, Tennessee, Alabama, Georgia, North and South Carolina, that the Seventeenth has borne an active and prominent part in, will surprise the historian when he relates the trials of fatigue, fasting, wading through creeks and rivers, sometimes with no clothing nor shoes, but always with courage, patriotism, and good-will. Well may Sherman be proud of this gallant Army—an Army that is proud of him.

Yours, truly,   OLD ROCK.

April 16, 1865

DEATH OF PRESIDENT ABRAHAM LINCOLN.
THE FEELING IN THE CITY

The people of the City of New York were shocked yesterday morning by the announcement of the assassination of President Abraham Lincoln and his Secretary of State, Wm. H. Seward, accompanied as it was by the news of the death of the former and believed fatal wounding of the other. Coming at any time when the great public heart was still bounding with joy because of the prospect of a speedy and honorable relief from the sufferings and anxieties consequent upon four years of cruel war, the people were stricken with horror. The first impulse was to utter imprecations upon the head of the vanquished South, as the author of the fearful crime; then, as the thought arose that the course of the President, since the surrender of General Lee, has been indicative of an intention to adopt such measures as were deemed best calculated to soften the asperities between the North and the South, and secure reconstruction, there was a feeling that the pistol and the knife might have been directed by the hand of an unsatiated Northern fanaticism. These feelings, however, soon gave way to an assurance that the deed had been done by a madman; and then that the profoundest sorrow took and held the place of that which, early in the day, gave alarming promise of frenzied indignation. It was not until the morning had passed, that the suspicion as to who had committed the crime became generally known, but even when all that had been received in that relation had been perused, the last convulsion, and the feeling resulting from it, were, if at all changed, only strengthened and confirmed. Of all that a great city said and did on the occurrence of a great calamity, we give the following reports:

PEOPLE'S THEORIES ABOUT THE MURDER.

The speculations among the people about this awful crime are as latitudinous as are the theories and the motives that led to its commission. Perhaps the fact that all of these opinions were based partly upon imperfect information, and more of them on the merest surmise, will account for their wild and improbable character. Yet, such as they are, we note them as impressions among the populace.

Said a well-known loyal business-man, on Wall street, to an acquaintance, "I believe that Jeff. Davis sent these scoundrels from Richmond to do it." The other responded, "I can't think so. Jeff. Davis and his crew are too smart for that. They knew the kind impulses of the President, and his conservative views. Besides, the fact that Andy Johnson would be his successor would have deterred them from it. They know he is extreme, and hates the South. I think it is some fanatic or madman." Another said, "It's all nonsense about Wilkes Booth being the assassin. He wouldn't harm a chicken. I have known him since he was a child." A gentleman said, in reply, "That may be true, Booth is subject to eccentricities, if not freaks of madness, but he may have been crazed by drink."

"There is no evidence whatever," said the first speaker, "that it is Booth, if Laura Keene did think so; women are especially liable to mistakes in such a furore and frenzy of excitement; and, anyhow, if Wilkes did it, he was crazy."

"This may be true; but if there was an accomplice there was too much method in the madness. A madman don't consult a brother madman when he contemplates murder."

A person at the St. Nicholas Hotel, who has been in the Army, and who detests Butler and the Radical party, said flatly that he would sooner believe that the deed was consummated by some fanatic of that class, than anybody else, because they hated the conservatism of Mr. Lincoln. Another person, a foreigner, who looks at this from a European standpoint, contended that it was a plot of Southern men who are driven to desperation and madness by their ruin and the desolation of their country; and that other assassinations of public men would follow. That picked men had banded themselves together to seek revenge, since all was lost. Another pointed out the singularity of his death on this day, the anniversary of the day, four years ago, when Mr. Lincoln issued his proclamation calling for 75,000 men to defend the capital. And still another reminded a friend that an ex-Governor of this State predicted last Fall that the "next President would die by an assassin's hand". Yet men of all classes and of all shades of political opinions concurred in denouncing the atrocious crime, not only as to the manner of "his taking off", but as a great national calamity, for reasons painfully obvious to the whole country.

April 23, 1865
TWENTY-FIFTH N.Y. CAVALRY
Camp Seeley, Berlin, Md., April 18.

It would be in vain for me to attempt to depict the horror and indignation which was aroused in this camp when the news of the murder of President Lincoln was received here. At first no one would believe it, considering it one of the canards which are constantly flying around this, as around all camps; and it was universally stamped as emanating from the same source which the penniless beggar, Beau Brummel, said had originated, the report of his death, "mere stockjobbing". In the present case, doubtless, the wish was father to the thought. It was too gigantic a horror for the mind to entertain. But when full confirmation was received—when an official dispatch to Colonel Seeley placed beyond dispute that which we had looked upon as a lie, when told by the passengers on the train, that first brought the news—profound sorrow became universal. The meridian of joy, in which all had been basking, at the glorious events which had crowned the nation's brow with such thick woven wreaths, was at once overcast by the darkest thunder-cloud which ever arose in the horizon of the Republic. The wail of lament was but the echo of that which has rent the nation's heart. If J. Wilkes Booth—who has apparently been recognized as the murderer—receive but a little of the execrations and anathemas which were poured out upon him, hell would be a paradise for him. Amongst the punishments suggested for him, were crucifixion, impalement, and roasting before a slow fire; while another said, that he should be chopped up and distributed, no person to receive more than a quarter ounce of him; the recipient of each piece to be a sworn avenger of his victim.

Scouting-parties into Loudoun County continue to be the order of the day, and Colonel Seeley is determined that, as he is able, that beautiful valley shall become too hot for the guerillas who have made it their head-quarters. The fruit of his efforts is shown in the fact that Mosby has sent in an offer of surrender of himself and his whole command provided they receive the same terms as were accorded to the Army of Northern Virginia, of which he claims to be a component part.

We are anxiously awaiting to hear of the surrender of Joe Johnston, which will be about the final act of the suppression of the rebellion; as "old Billy"—as General Sherman is called by his "boys"—has doubtless ere this "moved on his works". As soon as a general becomes popular with his men, he is invariably dubbed with a nickname. Thus we have "Little Phil" for Sheridan, "Old Grizzly" and "Pop" for Thomas, "Old Billy" for Sherman, "Curly Cus" for Custer, and so on. It is the highest compliment a soldier can pay to his commander. Napoleon felt prouder of the nickname of "Little Corporal" than any of the titles which he subsequently bore.

B. O. B.

OUR CITY POINT CORRESPONDENT
City Point, Va., April 17.

We learn that the Chief-Magistrate of our nation, Abraham Lincoln, has fallen by the hand of the assassin. That he whose name has been a household-word throughout the nation for the past five years; that he, whom all, irrespective of party and creed, have learned to love and respect, for his devotion and honesty to that Government which he had twice sworn to support against all enemies; and that he who has so faithfully kept that oath, and now just witnessing the good fruits of those untiring years of labor, should meet with so untimely and sorrowful an end. We mourn his loss. All honest men, North and South, East and West, will recognize in the death of Abraham Lincoln, at this particular crisis of national affairs, a vacancy in the Executive-Chair which cannot be replaced by any member of the Cabinet. Though it was known in high official circles as early as Saturday morning, it was kept a profound secret throughout the Army until yesterday morning, when it was first made known. At City Point, the public buildings, including the "Chief Depot-Commissary", "Chief Quartermaster", "Ordinance", "Harbormasters", Office, etc., were hung with crape. While the shipping lowered its flags to half-mast, and gunboats fired blank charges every ten minutes in honor of the distinguished dead. To-day again the minute guns are reverberating through the solemn stillness of the bright spring-day, and we have no hesitation in saying there are few discharges which find not an echo in the hearts of all within earshot. It is but two short weeks ago since your correspondent saw the President at City Point, in the centre of a large circle of men, who even crowded around Mr. Lincoln during his stay at this place, while Grant was taking Petersburg and Richmond. Then he looked certainly care-worn, delicate, and anxious, as indeed he must have been during so critical a period in the life of the nation. He stood calmly there, towering far above every one else in the crowd, making, occasional remarks to Admiral Porter, who was beside him, while rapid salvos of artillery in the direction of Petersburg told him how pregnant with importance were the passing moments. We little dreamed then that in a few short days his career of usefulness would be ended by the hand of the assassin.

A daring and damnable attempt was made to blow up the ordinance-stores and wharf here last Friday-night, by some of our paroled prisoners; but our guard being too early for the villains, the diabolical act was frustrated, and the culprits being seized—four in number—suffer the penalty of death; to-day, the Provost-Marshal will cause them to be hung by the neck until they are dead. This short, sharp, and decisive act of justice may prove as a good warning to other would-be Southern heroes, as few men approve of the heapen cravat arrangement. Had those villains been successful the other night, millions of dollars' worth of property and hundreds of lives would, doubtless, have been forfeited. But little mercy must be looked for by all such "Rebel Vandals", when caught by the Government forces. Our Army is greatly incensed against the South since the receipt of the sad news of yesterday. Indeed, had Booth 10,000 lives, so bitter is the existing and freely-expressed detestation of the act perpetrated by him, each one would be taken in explanation of his crime. We just learn of another attempt having been made by a "Cornfed" to burn the Commissary buildings on the wharf last night, but it was detected in time, and the incendiary shot by the officer of the guard. Guerrillas thicken in the country on the south of our lines, and nightly visit houses in the vicinity of the railroads. A scouting force of Union soldiers yesterday came upon and captured some twenty-seven guerillas, near Charles City Court House, which are now in safe keeping, and will be dealt with in a most "becoming manner." All of the above little incidents indicate the vindictive feeling still existing amongst many of the Southern renegades throughout Virginia, and show the necessity for the continued presence for months to come of a large force upon Southern soil—until at least all the public highwaymen and outlaws are brought to justice.

We learn that a public meeting is called by the citizens of Petersburg to-day, in order to express in a becoming manner the union of sympathy on behalf of the people of that city with the nation in the death of President Lincoln.

Au revoir,   A. O. P.

FIFTY-FIRST REGIMENT, N.Y.V.V.

NEAR FARMVILLE, VA., April 13.

On the night of the 31st of March, brisk firing commenced on that portion of the line where the Johnnies displayed one of their retrograde movements, a short time ago, in Fort Stedman. Fort Morton replied with mortar and rifle-shells; the scene witnessed from our camp put one in mind of the demonstrations on 4th of July, only not quite so harmless; at about one o'clock the firing died away. On the night of the 1st of April, the same occurred—the pickets also keeping up a continual fire—rumors were current that the Johnnys intended an attack, as a matter of course we were on the qui vive. Our regiment took up their position in the works, the Fifty-eighth Massachusetts and Thirty-ninth [New Jersey] were moved to the rear of Fort Hell (Sedgwick); at about four o'clock the charge was made upon the works of the Rebs, directly on front of Fort Hell. The distance at this point, between the two lines, was very small. The Johnnys were completely taken by surprise, not having an opportunity to reply with their guns, the latter being immediately turned upon the other Johnny forts near at hand. The position was held till the morning of 3rd, although several desperate charges were made by the evening to recapture their works. Shortly after day-light on the 3rd, it was reported that the enemy had evacuated Petersburg; soon the bells of the city rang out the joy of the Yankee possessors. The cheering could be heard for miles. Orders were received to move forward. Did so, halting about one mile from Petersburg; ate dinner, and had the pleasure of seeing the "Father of his Country", President

Abraham Lincoln. His appearance in so short a time after the evacuation of Petersburg, had a marked effect upon the troops, who cheered him on his approach, and while passing them.

On our passage through Petersburg, but few whites were to be seen. The number of negroes was large. "They were so glad to see the Yanks," "Bress de Lord!" The First Division, Ninth Corps was left here, the rest of the corps going on. Our brigade was detailed to guard a portion of the baggage-trains of the Army, and have got it this far. The railroad was left in good condition; the first destruction by the enemy was at this place—burning of a bridge. The rest of the Army is some distance off; we cannot tell how far, or what is going on. From seven thousand to eight thousand prisoners started yesterday for Petersburg. The men are rather footsore, not having marched to any amount since June last. If we stop for a day or so on the road, we generally get orders to move on about 12, M.; start at 1, and in many, if not all instances, march till 10 and 11, even 12 o'clock at night.

Lee has surrendered.

The country is being foraged for miles around. Some of the men act more like highway-robbers, taking food from a house where there is no one but women and children, leaving the latter to starve.

I neglected to state that Brevet Major-General Robt. B. Potter, commanding Second Division, Ninth Corps, was seriously wounded in the charge of the 2nd inst. Also Brevet Major P. E. Peckham, A.A.A. General, staff of General [John I.] Curtin, commanding First Brigade, Second Division, Ninth Corps.

One more promotion among the veterans—Sergeant Chauncey W. Waldron to Second-Lieutenant.

                                                                SUCCOTASH.

April 30, 1865
SECOND OHIO CAVALRY
PETERSBURG, April 25.

On the 6th of the present month, our regiment, in conjunction with the Third New Jersey, was ordered to charge the wagon-train of the Rebels, at a point near Jetersville Station, on the R. & D. RR. In front, and in full view of us, the enemy had thrown out a strong skirmish-line of infantry, supported, as we supposed, by a heavier line in the woods to their rear. We moved steadily on in column until within a few hundred yards of the foe, then rapidly deploying into line, charged as only Custer's men can. Our determined onset caused the Rebel Infantry to break and fly in all directions for the shelter of the woods; but few of them ever reached their protective shadow, the major part being either cut down in their flight, or captured and hurried to the rear; the few who made good their escape owed their safety more to an early start than anything else. Much to our surprise we found that nothing now remained between us and their train, of which fact we took advantage by charging pell-mell among the wagons. The negro drivers, Rebel dead-beats, sick and wounded men presented quite a ludicrous appearance as they scampered off assisted in their flight by the musical hum of Spencer's patent metal pills. Among the captured wagons were those belonging to General Lee's Headquarters; these contained the most miscellaneous assortment of articles that ever were dignified by the name of baggage, for instance, a medicine chest, formerly owned by Uncle Sam, but then used as a trunk by Lee's A.A.A.G., was, upon examination, found to contain besides a faded suit of Rebel Uniform: One horn comb, a bootjack, age unknown, though to judge from appearance I should say was a family relic; two pair leather stocks (U. S. model); a large bottle, sometimes called a tickler, the smell of which at once betokened its owner's fondness for "red-eye"; one pack of playing-cards very well thumbed, and which, no doubt, if able to speak, could tell of almost fabulous sums of Confederate money (?) risked upon the turning of one of their number; lastly, though not the least interesting of its contents were a package of love-letters, neatly tied with a leather shoe-string, and carefully wrapped in a dirty towel; these interesting epistles breathed nothing but fire and brimstone toward the Yanks. I must say that while I honor the young ladies for their devotion to their country (or lovers) that I am very sorry that there are no public schools established in the "Sunny South", for the benefit of rich and poor children. Enough of that for the present.

We had succeeded in partially destroying two hundred wagons. Six men of my own regiment, myself included, came unexpectedly upon a brigade of Rebel infantry drawn up in line-of-battle across the road. Without stopping to consult we broke for the brush on either side of the road, four of us taking to the right and remaining two to the left. Each party, if I mistake not, were induced to lie as flat on the horses as possible, while the Johnnys were endeavoring to have us take, whether or not, pills of a nature much easier to take than digest. We had scarce gotten out of reach of their kind attentions before we ascertained that we were cut off from all support. After scouting about for nearly an hour, during which time we were twice fired on, we were forced to surrender to [William] Mahone's Division, of Hill's Corps, by whom, to their credit is it said, we were kindly treated, nothing but Government property being taken from us. After three days of hard marching, we reached Appomattox Court House, the scene of Lee's surrender. Here we were formed in four lines, running parallel to each other, and told we were to remain for some time. We could hear the rattle of musketry in front, mingling with the roar of artillery in the rear and left flank. By this we knew, long before the guards intimated as much, that Lee was hopelessly cut off. Our spirits rose with the roar of battle, and many offers were made to the guards to learn the true state of affairs. About noon on the 9th, Generals Lee, Mahone, Heth, Fields, Longstreet, and Gordon passed us at a very short distance, giving us a fine chance for observation. Lee appeared the plainest among them, but there was an air of quite solemn dignity about him that to every observant mind at once stamped him the man he was. About 4, P.M., we first heard the news, or rather report of Bobby's surrender. Although only a report to us, it was confirmed by the actions of the Rebels themselves. Officers and men commenced to plunder the wagons, discarding their old clothing and donning new attire. At this time, the feeling among them seemed to be one of disquiet more than despair; some even went so far as to say they were glad of it. While talking with one of the guards, I heard several quick reports, and looking round, saw a man, clad in the habiliments of a Rebel colonel, in the set of breaking the revolver he had just discharged over the tire of a wagon-wheel. This accomplished, he drew his sword, and, after glaring at it for a moment, broke it over his knee, throwing the pieces into the stream near by. His belt and scabbard, after being cut, he consigned to a similar fate. This man, I afterward learned, was a Colonel Clark of Mississippi. At 5, P.M., we were ordered to fall in to march to our lines. When this became known, the joy of the prisoners, some eighteen hundred in number, knew no bounds. A march of two miles brought us to General Grant's headquarters. Here we were counted, and, without delay, informed of the whereabouts of our commands, and ordered to report to them without delay. More anon.

VERACITY.

SIXTY-FIRST REGIMENT, N.Y.V.V.

NEAR BURKESVILLE, VA., April 24.

Since my last we have shifted position, being now located on the brow of a hill, overlooking the camps of the entire Division. Our regiment is posted on the extreme right of our brigade. "Next door" to us is situated Brigade Headquarters, around which juvenile members of both masculine and feminine gender are continually running, hooting and crying at us Union men. The eldest of the juveniles visit us daily, dispensing pie-tarts to the hungry ones. Said tarts rapidly diminish, being of a size equal to a dollar bill. The brigade-sutler has arrived and pitched his tent, and his stock of eatables are also rapidly disappearing. The men, after their arduous march, appear extremely voracious, and the lucky possessor of greenbacks soon finds his pile grow small and beautifully less.

We are enjoying comparative quiet. No duty exacted except the usual camp and picket—the latter for the purpose of arresting all stragglers who may wish to enter our lines. These stragglers when arrested, are sent to head-quarters, and there disposed of.

The news of the assassination of President Lincoln was announced to the troops by a special order from General Meade, and has caused great excitement among all. If the assassin was to appear here, the mercy shown him would border somewhat on the piratical. It is curious to overhear the discussions among the men in regard to the Rebellion, some declaring the war over, and expecting to be discharged instanter. We all hope that the war is over, and that we may all be permitted to return to our homes before the lapse of many months. We are now anxiously awaiting news from Sherman, which news we are led to believe will be of a gratifying nature. Our supplies of clothing are daily expected, many of us being ragged and shoeless; our clothes in many instances exposing rather more of Nature than modesty demands. Rumors of our leaving camp are already in circulation, but I cannot trace it to any reliable informant. Major-General [Nelson A.] Miles rode through our camp to-day, looking as well as usual. The men all turned out to have a look at him. During the recent engagements, General Miles bore a conspicuous part, and in General Humphreys' "thanks to the Second Corps", Major-General Miles' name was particularly mentioned. By the way, a brief resume of our operations during the early part of the campaign, with incidents, etc., may not prove uninteresting to your readers. The country through which we passed bore but few traces of cultivation. The houses were few and far apart, and bore in general a dilapidated appearance. But, few male inhabitants were seen, and those were either young boys or gray-haired men. The women presented an appearance anything but fashionable, being clad in the coarsest of garments, and oracularly testified to the misery they had been subjected to.

The hasty retreat of General Lee was plainly discernable on all sides. Ammunition wagons were passed on the road, destroyed and some on fire, which, communicating with the powder, caused an explosion like unto an earthquake. Other wagons were passed which had been abandoned, their contents scattered in all directions—said contents consisting of almost every conceivable article, from writing-paper to horse-shoes, and railroad-spikes. The rapidity with which papers were overhauled, to find some valuable document, or the signature of some distinguished Rebel officer, was astonishing; for the time being, many a one made a Barnum of himself, endeavoring to procure some lasting relic of Lee's once grand Rebel Army, and many a one was successful. On the day we captured the wagon-train the trophies were alarming in number—some had flags, others articles of clothing and equipments. The wagons of themselves being curiosities indeed, bearing a strong resemblance to the Confederacy, "rotten and worthless". The country traversed was of every description, good, bad, and indifferent; hills, valleys, marshes, woods, sand, mud, and water. In many places the woods were on fire and covered many acres, having caught by the picket-fires of the enemy. At the commencement of an engagement a hospital would be established a short distance in the rear for the purposes of attending temporarily to the wants of the wounded; some of the wounded bore the amputation of a limb without giving escape to a groan. One brave fellow belonging to the One Hundred and Seventy-eighth Pennsylvania Volunteers, while having his leg amputated, sang the song "Rally Round the Flag Boys". The Surgeons were prompt and attentive, and did all in their power for the wounded. After the surrender, great anxiety was manifested to visit the scene of the same, and those who visited it procured several mementos of the place in the shape of stones, barks, and limbs of trees, etc. Our march from the scene of the surrender to the present place, was exceedingly disagreeable—it raining heavily most of the time—traveling through mud knee-deep and wading through water waist-deep; glad were we when orders were given to halt and rest. During the march we were frequently out of rations, and the begging of hard bread, etc., from one another was the order for a while. The officers themselves were "minus" rations also, and suffered as much as the men.

S. G. C.

ONE HUNDRED AND THIRTY-THIRD REGIMENT N.Y.V.
NEAR SUMMIT'S POINT, VA., April 24.

The glorious victories that have come to our greeting by our armies, has now turned to a melancholy feeling in the death of Mr. Lincoln. The news spread through the ranks like an electric shock, to think that the champion of liberty, and the great and noble man, and the leader of the States, has departed this life by a traitor in heart, by a miscreant in principle.

The day before we left our camping-ground near Winchester, we had a brigade-review by Gen. [James D.] Fessenden, commanding the Third Brigade. Gen. [William] Dwight and staff were there to look at it, and not satisfied in looking at a brigade review, but must order a division review at 3 o'clock in the afternoon, in heavy—even tents were included. Before the tents were struck it commenced to rain. What could we do under the circumstances to lessen the weight—we the Third Brigade had to carry it for three miles. Such are the orders we have to obey under such a General.

On the 20th, the First Division received orders, about 12 o'clock in the night, to embark on the cars for Washington. The orders were not given out to the different companies, but the drums were a sufficient evidence that something was up. We got our coffee, struck tents, and received two days' rations of pork and crackers, and left for the cars at the Point, and found the same-awaiting us. About 11 o'clock, we left for Washington, hoping never to see the Shenandoah Valley again. On the way, Co. A, One Hundred and Thirty-third Regiment, was shocked by a collision between a freight-train, which came near doing more damage than it did. The cars, thank God, were the only things injured. The men jumped out, and landed safely on the ground. Still there were more breakdowns. There was a car, the wheels came from under it, and there was a delay of about two hours; finally a company of soldiers upset the car over the embankment, and set fire to it, and on we went then and arrived in Washington about 10 o'clock, the next morning, traveling almost one hundred miles in twenty-three hours—very slow traveling. In fact, it is the worst route there is; nothing but continually turning curve. After we arrived in Washington, the boys summoned to get off the cars and fall in. The Third Brigade marched to what is known as Camp Stoneman, just outside the capital. We are in camp inside of a race course. The First Veteran Corps, or better known as Hancock's Vets, are organizing here. It is a question of thought what we are here for, but conjecture is now out of the question.

HUNCHBACK.

SIXTEENTH N. Y. HEAVY ARTILLERY
CITY POINT, VA., April 26.

This battery of the Sixteenth New York Volunteer Artillery is now, per order, located at City Point, where, after a squatting down among a multitude of blackened stumps, and an ocean of water, four inches deep in our tents, we are pleasantly situated in the old camp of the Twentieth New York, in respectable quarters, though not at all equal to those we built at Fort Magruder. Our duty is not exceedingly heavy, but the boys become scattered as the duty varies. We have camp-guard, picktet-guard, headquarters-guard, provost-guard, guard on railroad-trains, safeguards, and guard prisoners-of-war to various prisons. I was one of the latter, on a week's excursion to Washington, which city we found presenting a mournful and sad picture of the grief that has overcome the nation on the death of the good and humane President. We were favored with a contemplation of his rigid figure, deposited in the coffin, and, as we gazed, we thought how much the nation lost, and, particularly, the misled people who have been in armed rebellion. The great magnanimity of his heart had opened the door of reconciliation and repentance, and the sons of our erring sisters would have been welcomed back as erring brothers, the fatted calf been killed, and all made merry, if they had shown the disposition of the Prodigal Son. Although evidence of sorrow met us at every step, every house, even to the poorest, bring draped with the sombre black; all places of public amusement closed, and the street-conversation almost entirely bearing in the awful and detestable crime perpetrated, and the great virtues of the deceased; yet I could not help noticing the hollowness within. Washington is a mass of corruption; business was carried on briskly, although sub rosa; and though theatres and concert-halls shut their doors, houses of ill-repute and gambling-halls were crowded to excess; and it was disgusting to hear the sounds of music and laughter preceeding from houses decorated with the outward insignia of sadness. But a truce to this; it becomes the chaplain, not me to moralize.

FRANK.

May 7, 1865
CITY POINT CORRESPONDENCE
CITY POINT, VA., May 2.

Nothing can equal the joy and pleasure which glistens from the eye of every soldier in the Army since the receipt of the late order of the Adjutant-General, commanding an immediate reduction of the Army, etc. the surrender of Johnston has been for some time back a foregone conclusion with the boys; from which they argued that their services would be no longer required; and thus joyfully have they anticipated the order which has now been promulgated, promising to them a speedy return to their homes, family, and occupation. So that neither the surrender of the last of the Rebel forces nor the order for their discharge, have been unlooked for; nevertheless, they are none the less cheering and gratifying to the soldier. Few but he who has suffered and endured all the trials incidental to the past terrible struggle for the maintenance of the Government during four long bloody years, can realize the happiness which they now experience, after having "fought the good fight", and triumphed therein, are permitted to return home to the walks of civil life once more, there again to don the garb of the citizen in exchange for the "blue", which has shown for so long a time through the smoke and flame of battle beneath our "starry banner", from whose firmament not a single bright star has been plucked by the traitors, who, after so desperate and fruitless a struggle, are now compelled to rush beneath its folds for protection, seeking forgiveness, in tears, for the misery and disgrace they have brought upon themselves and their posterity.

The Commissary and Quartermasters' Department pursuant to "orders", are closing up business at this place, as rapidly as possible; vessels with supplies for the various departments which have arrived within the past few days, are returning with their freight unloaded. Many citizen-employees of the Government will thus find their occupation gone; as one conductor on the railroad remarked jokingly to another, in our hearing, "You will have to go back to your old job again ere long, old fellow." "What is that?" was the response. "Why hire out to some old farmer, as you did before Uncle Sam started military railwork!" There may, perchance, be more truth than poetry in many such witticisms, which are so often expressed around Government-works. There is no doubt many will be out of employment who have heretofore held fat Government-jobs, with good pay and little to do.

A sad affair occurred here yesterday morning, resulting in the death of a soldier of the Twenty-first Massachusetts Volunteers. It appears that the guard of the Eighth Heavy Artillery (colored troops) are in the habit of going down to the bank on the railroad, each morning as soon as relieved, to discharge their muskets. On the opposite bank of the road a detachment of the Twenty-first Massachusetts Volunteers are encamped. Yesterday the darkeys poured their volley into the soldier's camp opposite, mortally wounding one (who is since dead) and slightly wounding another, while their tents bore evidence of the fact that many had narrow escapes, being pierced with bullet-holes. The poor fellow who lost his life by the carelessness of those who have not sufficient judgement to handle a musket, had served four years, was ever considered a brave soldier, and now in anticipation of home, with the knowledge that he has aided in bringing about a happy and glorious peace to his country, is shot down by a lot of "good for nothing" worthless niggers, who laugh in their sleeve at any mischief done to a white man. Indeed, in return they find but little sympathy from the soldier. It is but a couple of weeks since they shot a soldier on the Point. The question now naturally arises "What is the hungry nigger going to do?" and echo answers, "What?" No one whom we have asked can furnish us with any plausible idea as to how they are to be disposed of. The war being over, the many thousands employed by Government in the various departments—at $25 per month with rations and quarters—will be thrown out upon the world and their own "dark" resources. We don't want, and won't have them North; all agree on this point. Their services are no longer required by their "old massa" at the South, who won't have their former slaves around them, when they can no longer call them their property. We are in favor of sending them all off to Liberia, on the west coast of Africa, there to assist in the cultivation of the land, in raising sugar, rice, tobacco, and even cotton, to which the soil is said to be well adapted. A wag recently suggested that it would be well to start an "ink factory" with them. Seriously, it would have a most unwholesome effect to allow the emancipated negroes of the South to go North, there to settle down, filling positions in various walks of life, to the exclusion of the whites, as eventually, to a great extent, they would do. But the coming session of Congress will remedy this evil, doubtless.

We are enjoying most beautiful weather out here, the days being, for this advanced season, mild and cool. The citizens of the North are availing themselves of the recent order permitting them to visit City Point, Richmond and Petersburg, and great numbers of sight-seers arrive daily on the mail-boat. We understand it to be the intention to start a new line of steamers for the accommodation of travelers.

A. O. P.

FORTY-SEVENTH REGIMENT, N.Y.V.

NEAR RALEIGH, N.C., April 29.

We suffer once more from the "regular routine" of camp-duty—I say "suffer"; for after all the excitement of marching, maneuvering, and living at large, although one may sigh for rest, he certainly disliked the restraints of camp-life. Who, after roaming through wood and over meadow, with a change of scene and incident each succeeding day, would desire being confined to two acres of ground day after day and week after week? A soldier's life, under such circumstances, is monotony itself; and although one may get used to it, I question very much whether anybody can ever get to really like it.

We are stationed in the suburbs of Raleigh—a pretty little city with beautiful surroundings. The contrast between the topography of this district and that to the south and east of Goldsboro' is striking and agreeable. Instead of one vast flat stretch of pine-barren swamp, black ground and black water, here we have actual hills and valleys, green fields, clear running brooks. The camps are arranged with a view to the promotion of cleanliness and health, and these ends are enforced by frequent and rigid inspections. The weather is cool and bracing; and everything, like the prospect of peace, looks bright.

All the joy we felt, however, at the approach of peace was suddenly changed into mourning on the receipt of the intelligence of the death of President Lincoln. When the news was first announced, few professed to believe it; yet the grave and anxious looks of all told what they feared, and when their fears were confirmed the deepest regret was expressed. No occurrence could have caused more bitterness of feeling in the Army. Strong guards were at once posted to keep the men in their camps, and undoubtedly the precautions taken against riot, and perhaps worse, were wise.

You will observe that the *Standard* and *Progress* newspapers of Raleigh have come out true Union advocates since the advent of the Federal troop. These papers indeed, have never indorsed the Rebel cause, and I have often marveled why Jeff. Davis should have permitted their outspoken censures upon him and his government. The true secret of their immunity from seizure and confiscation no doubt lay in the fact, that an uncomfortably large number if the inhabitants of North Carolina who believed in their doctrines were considered safer in being permitted a little freedom of speech than they otherwise would have been.

Although everybody in the Army believed that the war would be virtually ended this campaign, still few, if any, regarded the end as being so near. One's debatable friend for once can't turn round and boldly say "I told you it would be so!" for he also is compelled to express his astonishment at the almost miraculous chapter of events, so rapidly recited, which has amazed the whole world, and confounded the most astute and the wisest of our enemies. Without feeling any glorification over events which should cause in the minds of all a feeling of deepest reverence and thankfulness to Providence, still we might ask what will the London *Times*, and its host of echoes, say to this rude upsetting of all their pet theories, so plausibly uttered and heroically stood by? In a moral point of view, the consequences will be more terrible than a commercial crash; and the paying down in the present of so much sterling truth as will balance the terribly bad logic and worse assertions of the past, can have but the effect of utterly ruining the name of the Thunderer and its satellites for trustworthiness. "Facts are chiel's that winna ding!"

All the talk is now of getting home, and your "sub" of two weeks standing is the most anxious to know when that time will come. Home! The majority of those in the Army can look forward with feelings of pleasure to the time when he may once more see home and friends. But the poor fellows on the other side, Jeff Davis's dupes, what of them? Without one cent of pay, without clothes for their backs, and perhaps their homes in ashes, what have they to look forward to? The world is all before them, and they have to begin again under circumstances of great difficulty the struggle for existence. I observe that Gen. Sherman has resolved to distribute all his spare horses among the farmers of North Carolina, and I have no doubt that Southern Aid Societies will in time be formed at the North. The terrible ordeal through which the country has passed has just one region rich and prosperous, the other utterly ruined and half depopulated. We must forgive and forget past injuries; and, in view of the common calamity, turn to with willing hands, and help to rebuild the broken-down parts of the land.

VIDETTE.

THIRTEENTH N. Y. CAVALRY
CAMP RELIEF, WASHINGTON, D. C., May 1.

Last week, the Sixteenth New York Cavalry broke camp at Vienna, and are now camped with us. The Sixth [West] Virginia Cavalry, who have been with Sheridan in the Valley, arrived here about the same time. Where the destinations of the two regiments are to be, I know not. Mosby's men have been coming in at Camp Lowell very fast and giving themselves up, as they know full well that the guerilla warfare will no longer be allowed, since the surrender of Lee, as they would be hunted down like dogs. Mosby offered to surrender on the same terms as General Lee, but Grant will not receive him, he having been declared an outlaw; there has been a reward of $2,000 offered to any of his men who will take him and bring him in. His men are now scouting through Virginia after him.

Lieutenant [Edward] Doherty, of the Sixteenth New York Cavalry, with twenty men, has at last succeeded in ridding the country of the assassin of our beloved President; Sergeant [Boston] Corbett, of the Sixteenth, having fired the shot which took the life of one of the worst criminals on record. This death was almost too easy for one who has caused the greatest sorrow through the country. A squad of twenty men, belonging to Co. M, returned to camp last week, having been looking after the assassin, Booth, in Maryland; and having got track of him, they followed him up to the swamps in St. Mary's County, Maryland. Here Booth and [David] Herald found a temporary refuge until they found means to cross the Potomac. The swamp is four or five miles from the Potomac. The swamp is about twenty miles long, and in some places almost impenetrable.

Yours,   EUPHCANISTIFICAN.

May 14, 1865
SIXTY-FIFTH REGIMENT, N.Y.V.V.
NOTTOWAY COURT HOUSE, VA., May 9.

At last, after a weary pilgrimage through the Old Dominion, from Burkesville to Danville, and then to this place, we have come to a halt, and the regiment is now enjoying a much-needed rest.

Our duties are comparatively light in comparison to the wearisome trials and privations of an active campaign. The headquarters of the brigade have been established at the Junction, which place, heretofore insignificant, has suddenly become quite important.

Contrabands have and are flocking there in great numbers in search of life (hard tack), liberty, and pursuit of happiness. I understand from one of the assistants in the Commissary Department there, that employment had been furnished to a great many, but that the constant arrival of fresh darkeys rendered it necessary for them to send the freed people further on toward Richmond.

The white population—or, as we have sometimes styled them, the chivalric natives—bear their fortunes with remarkable fortitude, and express themselves contented with the turn of affairs have taken. They confess that since the battle of Gettysburg they have had no hopes of ever gaining their desired ends, and that they looked upon the further resistance of the South as hopeless and as a useless effusion of blood. They think that the Government will not trouble them or their property when they signify their readiness to take the oath of allegiance to the Government. Their condemnation of Jeff Davis, [Judah] Benjamin, Breckenridge, and other leading Rebels are loud and sincere; and they hope that in the event of their being captured that Andy Johnson will hang them, while, on the other hand, they profess the deepest respect for General Lee, whom they love for his sincerity and frankness. These people will not believe that Lee, as the chieftain of armed rebellion, is in a manner more responsible for the woe and desolation of our country North and South than any other traitor, and they cling to him now in his downfall with an admiration worthy at least of a nobler motive.

The boys at present are continually discussing the all-absorbing topic: When are we going home? Rumor, based on hearsay, officially reports that we are going to start for Washington on Monday next (to-morrow), to participate in the grand review that is to be held there of the Army of the Potomac. The same questionable authority there goes on to show that after this auspicious event we will be immediately mustered out of the service and sent to our homes. I hope in this case that the individual from whom this information is obtained will prove a prophet, and that we will realize the fond hopes that he has raised among us.

The battle-scarred braves of the Sixty-fifth are already building castles in the air that may, however, descend, and stand erect in reality on terra firma. That portion of the boys who have wives to welcome them anticipate with joy the meeting, while those who are not blessed in that manner look with delight to their meeting with their Marys, Hatties, Susans, and Josephines.

Should it prove so that we are to return to our homes you will be duly advised of the fact, by

Yours, Manhattanly,   FRANCONI.

CITY POINT CORRESPONDENCE

CITY POINT, VA., May 9.

The new line of steamers commenced their trips on Wednesday last, between Baltimore and Richmond, the "George Anna", which stopped here on her way to Richmond, for the first time, was crowded with passengers, civilians of both sex. Many of the passengers get off at City Point, and go by rail to Richmond, passing through Petersburg, and thus have a better opportunity of seeing the late seat of the war, than by continuing up the river.

Large quantities of railroad iron has been recently unloaded here, is to be used in the repairs of the various roads connecting with Richmond, Petersburg, Danville, and Washington City. Most of the roads are badly in need of repair, and nothing will go so far to encourage our "erring brethren" of the South, in the knowledge that they have been waging war against the best, most forgiving and generous government in the world, whose desire it is now to open to them again the roads to happiness and peace, as well as to commerce and trade, with loyal states, from which they have been so long and willfully estranged. Already the planters in this vicinity are leveling earthworks, clearing brush and undergrowth, and preparing their land for crops; in this work, the want of proper farming-implements is greatly felt, as is also the want of horses; but this latter necessity is fast being remedied, viz: the sale of horses, wagons, etc. condemned by the Quartermaster, takes place to-day simultaneously at Richmond, Petersburg, and City Point, and if we can judge from the great numbers of Southern farmers assembled at the sale here to-day, they will have an abundance of "horse flesh" to answer their immediate requirements in the tillage of the land this spring and summer. As for laborers, the provost-marshals have ordered many of the negroes, wandering around looking for Government work, of which there is none for them, as many of those already employed will, like Othello, soon find their "occupation gone"—to go to work for the farmers, and accept such wages as they can give, whether it be one dollar a day or twenty-five dollars per day. In this many farmers hereabouts find much encouragement in their exertions to get their crops in the ground; and already do they begin to draw bright pictures of prosperity and plenty against the dark landscape of want, misery, and starvation, presented to them by their late leaders, in a hopeless procrastination of the Rebellion. Yes, it is a freely acknowledged fact among the people of the South to-day, that they have been made the dupes of Jeff. Davis and clique, and it is to him they owe losses of life, property, all.

Au revoir,   A. O. P.

RETURN OF THE SOLDIERS TO THEIR HOMES.

The war being over, the soldiers who have survived the perils of the battle-field are on their way to their homes. For years they have borne the shock of war, and the dangers of the conflicts, the tedious monotony of camp-life, the toils and privations of long marches, and all the discomforts incident to a soldier's life. Through all these years of trial, through every vicissitude of fortune, they never quailed before the enemy, and never doubted for a moment their ability to accomplish the objects for which they took the field. Their deeds are now historic, and never in the annals of warfare has it fallen in the lot of the historian to record the incidents of a struggle more fierce and terrific, or marked by greater intrepidity, or a higher degree of the qualities which exalt the soldier into a hero. Our enemies abroad, who began by a sneer at our inexperience, have been forced to accord to us the character established by the bravery of our troops, and acknowledge us the greatest military power of ancient or modern times.

The returning soldiers, crippled and debilitated as many of them are, have the satisfaction arising from the reflection that their conduct exhorted the admiration of the world; and that they not merely reaped the laurels due to such bravery, but that they accomplished the object for which they forsook their peaceful avocations, and preserved intact the unity and integrity of the Republic. If we permit our liberties to be trampled upon by political usurpers, it is no fault of theirs; for they periled their lives not more to prevent the disintegration of the nation than to preserve inviolate its liberties, and the laws by which those liberties are secured. They will not fail to maintain at the ballot-box the principles in whose behalf they faced death and danger without the shrinking of a nerve.

During the balance of his life the returned soldier will be the favorite of his neighborhood. Not only will the patriotism which led him to the front endear him to those who reap the benefit of his services in having a united country to inhabit and afford them protection, and laws to secure their rights, and who share in the glory and fame of his achievements, but his participation on the battles whose particulars have been devoured by all classes with an eager and unsatiable avidity, will render him a living history and chronicle of the war, around whom old and young will cluster to hear from his own lips accounts of the "moving accidents by flood and field" which befell himself and his comrades, and the hair-breath escapes of some from the missles of death which strewed others at his feet. He will be welcomed by all with a warmth surpassing the ties of kindred, and reap in his own approval and in the gratitude of his fellow-citizens the reward due to patriotism and bravery.

May 21, 1865
ONE HUNDRED AND FIFTY-EIGHTH REGIMENT, N.Y.V.
RICHMOND, VA., May 14.

Knowing you to be a lover of truth and justice, I hope you will pardon me if I occupy a space in your valuable journal, there being no one who has chronicled the operations of this command. I deem it my duty, if not too late, to inform your millions of readers of our late operations. On the 27th of March, 1865, we left camp at Deep Bottom, Va., and marched to Hatcher's Run, where we (the Fourth Brigade, First Division, Twenty-fourth Army Corps) relieved a division of the Second Corps. On the 30th, the enemy attempted to carry our works, but was repulsed with slaughter. On the morning of April 1, our brigade attacked and carried the strong picket-line of the enemy; but reenforcements not coming up, we were compelled to fall back. On Sunday, April 2, one-half of each regiment in our brigade being on the picket-line, the balance were under arms from 3, A.M., and at the breastworks, awaiting orders. At 7:30, A.M., an order came that General [Thomas M.] Harris had broken through the enemy's line, and we would come up and assist. Never was the order, "forward, march", obeyed with such alacrity as on that morning. We marched along the works until arriving at Humphrey's Station, when we marched to the front and through the numberless lines of abatis of the enemy, until arriving inside their inner line of works, when we were immediately put in line of battle by brigade, and marched from one point to another, our brigade being designated to support the Third Brigade of the Independent Division; until, at last, arriving within one thousand yards of that Rebel stronghold, we halted to await orders. In the meantime, the Third Brigade of our division received orders to charge Fort Gregg. With an enthusiastic cheer they charged, and arrived near enough to plant their standard on the ramparts; but there being a determined set of men in the fort, kept them at bay. There lay nothing but four feet of earth between our boys and the enemy. At length General [Robert] Foster, our division commander, gave orders to Colonel [Harrison S.] Fairchild, without hesitation, said, "I will, General," and immediately gave orders for the Eighty-ninth N.Y.V., 87 officers and men, and One Hundred and Fifty-eighth N.Y.V., 176 officers and men, to forward and take that fort (Gregg). The order was cheerfully obeyed. We marched in line of battle, at quick time, until arriving within about two hundred yards of the fort, when, with a cheer, we charged up to the ramparts of the fort. All the time we were shouting to the Third Brigade to make room for us to go right in the fort; but, they, I suppose, not understanding us, remained still, thereby preventing us from going into the fort. Matters began to look rather serious. After a few moments rest, we made one grand rally, and were the first in the Rebel stronghold. When arriving in the fort, the scene there beggars all description. The enemy refused to surrender, appearing to prefer that which they received most bountifully, the bayonet.

I regret to say we lost our beloved comrade, First-Lieutenant Edward Rielly; also Major F. W. Tremain of the Eighty-ninth N.Y.V., and Color-Sergeant Jas. Howard.

From the time of leaving Deep Bottom, the 27th of March, until the 27th of April, we marched 327 miles, and had the pleasure of fasting four days, our rations having been given to the Rebel Army.

BREVET.

FROM A WASHINGTON CORRESPONDENT
WASHINGTON, D.C., May 19, 1865

Business at present in and about Washington is pretty good, caused by the great accumulation of troops about here. Yesterday I took the Alexandria boat Keyport, fare five cents from Washington. Walked out four miles and a half to the camp of the Fifth Regiment New York Veteran Volunteers. Boys were much pleased to see me again, and I accordingly whiled away a few hours very pleasantly. Many anxious inquiries were made about going home. They are not all pleased at the idea of being retained a day longer than necessary, for the anticipated review or anything else. They think that they have been reviewed enough, and having fought the fight through are now anxious to go back to their homes, and quit soldiering. The accounts of the late battles the soldiers delight in giving, but when speaking of their sufferings since the taking of Richmond and surrender of Lee, a great deal of suffering seemed unnecessary, and wrongly inflicted. In eight days the Fifth Corps marched two hundred and fifty miles, and were deprived of food for four days. They tell me that the time they made was so fast that the trains were unable to keep up with the troops. The roads were in a very bad condition part of the time, and during the rainstorms several of the soldiers were struck by lightning and killed, many died from exhaustion along the march, and now a great many are very sick from the irregular diet they have been subjected to. When Lee surrendered his army our supplies were given to the Rebels, while our men were actually famishing. Somebody must be to blame, for if any body are to starve, the Union soldiers, I think, should be counted exempt. They have suffered all the necessary hardships and privations without a murmur, but they know that the fault rests upon subordinates under our Government—not on the Government. The terrible marchings—worse they say than most of the forced marches—there certainly must be some fault in some of the leading commanders, for it cannot seem possible that it was so highly necessary with propriety. Many of the re-enlisted veterans—who sprung to arms at the first call of their country, and at the time their country was in its greatest peril, offered themselves a further sacrifice to freedom, think they are not being justly treated by being retained, now that the war is over. They appeal to the better sense of justice of that civilized Government which they have defended so nobly, and ask only their right—to be discharged the service, and allowed to return to their fond families and friends, where they may attend to pursuits of a more congenial nature, now that their services as warriors are no longer necessary. Many ideas may be set forth why our Government should not discharge veterans, but it would seem that some consistency should be used. The veterans and reliable regiments have always been used for the hardest, and sacrificing, while shirks of the Army, who could not be depended upon, are sent to the rear. The soldier has suffered all this complimentary bosh, fought the fight through, and now it would seem that, because of his devotion and bravery, he is to be punished, instead of, in justice, being allowed to be the first to enjoy the comforts of home and the blessings of civil life.

I will close now by saying that the Fifth New York have just received a set of splendid new colors, viz.: a State flag and guidons, of beautiful silk; also, a very handsome regimental flag. They are presented by the city of New York, and the regiment is very proud of them. The old colors are so battle scarred, that of the regimental colors there is not enough left to unfurl. Shot, shell, and bullets have passed through it. Good-by for the present. Yours,

J. J.
Formerly of the Brooklyn Fourteenth, New York.

ARMY CORRESPONDENCE

To Our Army Correspondents—As the time is approaching when our different war correspondents in the field will be mustered out and retire to civil life, we would suggest to them the idea of still keeping up communication with us, and giving from time to time incidents and scenes of their war life that have not as yet been made public. It is well known that several of the dailies maintained corps-correspondents who wrote frequently and at considerable length, giving accounts of what the generals did, and how this or that corps d'armee moved up to support another, or was held in reserve, etc. This was all very well in its way; but we want to go a little further, and find out what the men—the privates, we mean—composing our victorious armies did. We want to give to the world, in sketch form, the thrilling scenes of actual warfare realized during the late Rebellion, depicting its deeds of daring, its changing camp-scenes, its marches, its hours of trial and triumph. Many a wonderful story of life is treasured up in the minds and hearts of our war-correspondents, which to the hurry of departure from place to place, or the violent contention of battle, was then temporarily forgotten. Now, they can sit down quietly at home, and give us these descriptive papers, which will one day be interesting to refer to.

June 18, 1865
SIXTH REGIMENT, U.S.V.V.

With your kind consent, I will try to give you a faithful view of the movements of the First Army Corps, or better known as Hancock's Vets, composed of private soldiers who have seen service, and officers who have, with very few exceptions, seen none, except in provost-marshals' offices and barrooms. Their former occupation is gone, and no more trust in the latter. They, as a last resort, fell back on this new corps, bringing with them a lot of new-fangled notions but no military tactics. God only knows what would have become of those tinsled gents, were it not for Major-General Hancock. You must be aware that the men composing this gallant corps are men who have seen service in all its branches, during the Rebellion, and have been under some officers who have had some queer (if not strict) ideas of military discipline, and when they joined this corps, expecting to be under the very best of officers. Judge of their disappointment, when they arrived at this rendezvous, to find themselves officered by men who are incapable of drilling a battalion. As singular as this may appear, 'tis nevertheless true. The whole movements in a drill comprised the following: Head of column to the right or left, and a walk around. But if they are deficient in drill, they make it up in other ways. The Lord knows there is no end of reviews, inspections, and roll-calls. Of the latter, the first-sergeants have enough. They have to count-noses no less than seven times per day. One cannot go to the cook-tent to get his pint of bean-water, unless his name is first called by the Orderly, so as to see if he is the genuine John Smith or Bill Brown, as the case may be.

As regards arms, we were told we were to have the best arms that could be produced. Some of the regiments have what is called the Joslyn rifles, a sort of a double-back-action concern, warranted to kill the man who fires it; more have the Sharpe rifle. One regiment has the Jacobs rifle, sixteen-shooter; while we, not wishing to be like the others, are to have the mountain-howitzers. Of what calibre it has not yet been decided.

Very many of the boys are now visiting Washington for the purposing of seeing their friends; and the weather being so warm, they extend their trip to the watering-places, North; only until the cool weather comes, you know, then they will come back—in a horn.

Discussions are the order of the day. The Western-men claim the honor of subduing the Rebellion, and consider the Army of the Potomac as mere lookers-on. This raises the dander of the boys who have followed Little Mac, Burnside, Hooker, Meade, and last, though not least, Lieut.-General Grant—men who held Lee in their tight grasp while the Western troops marched through Dixie with nobody home. Both deserve equal praise, I think.

We are enjoying fine weather at present, but it is very warm; still we are on elevated ground, and the little breeze that blows we have our share of. There are rumors of a move, but when or where I know not, still I hope it will be soon.

Yours, very respectfully,   LYNX.

June 25, 1865

ONE HUNDRED AND NINETY-SECOND REGIMENT, N.Y.V.

CAMP AXTELL, SUMMIT POINT, VA., June 18.

Since my last, we have had lively times here. Struck tents several times to move, but have not got off yet. The men are going fast; the regiment is about gone up. We left Albany in March with over nine hundred men, and have not now over four hundred; expect by the Fourth of July that the regiment will not number one hundred men. Both officers and men are becoming demoralized. The men have a great "stall" for getting away. When a party of them make up their minds to go, they go. One of the party goes on picket; after taps, another of the party blows up a canteen of powder, which makes a report equal to a twenty-pounder, the officers all run to find the guilty parties, and while they are looking for them, they (the men), accompanied by the one on picket, are gone. The General orders the regiment turned out, rolls called, and ammunition inspected, and while his aids are inspecting ammunition, another canteen goes off; all run to find the one who set it off, but he is off also. This kind of work goes on nearly every night. Very few of the men that desert are caught, although over eight hundred men have left the Valley inside of two months. The One Hundred and Ninety-second and One Hundred and Ninety-third Regiments have lost heavy. Captain R. W. Cross, while making his rounds as division officers of the day, caught two of the One Hundred and Ninety-third trying to get through a swamp. He brought them back to headquarters, and had them put in the pen for safekeeping. When arrested and asked where they were going, they replied that they were demoralized and going home.

Two very interesting subjects were brought to our notice, while on parade the other evening, in the shape of two deserters. They were marched through the camp with placards on their backs, and escorted by a very heavy guard, while the band played the "Rogue's March". They belonged to the One Hundred and Ninety-third. They deserted, and succeeded in getting to Baltimore, where they were arrested. They represented themselves as belonging to [Harry] Gilmore's (Rebel) Cavalry. They wore the Rebel uniform when arrested, but it was no go. They were brought back under heavy guard, and paraded through all of the camps in this division. One of them seemed to look at it in a Philadelphia point of view. "What can't be cured, must be endured." On Monday-morning, the 12th instant, a man might be seen sauntering across the parade-ground with a gun on his shoulder. A close observer might easily have seen that he was laboring under a temporary aberration of the mind at the time, for he would occasionally look around to see if any one was watching his movements. He crossed the parade-ground and entered a shrubery, situated about 150 yards from camp; he halted, and, placing the guard of his gun on a small limb of a tree, he cocked his piece, and placing the muzzle of the gun to his breast he pulled it; the cap snapped, but the piece did not go off. He went to a sentry at a spring close by and procured a cap; he then returned, placed the cap on the gun, and placed the muzzle to his breast; a report followed, a heavy crash, and the man was dead. On examining the body, it was found to be Private John McCann, of Company B, One Hundred and Ninety-second New York Volunteers, alias Clarence Hoy, of Albany.

I am unable to learn the cause of this rash act, but it appears that he was defrauded out of his bounty, which worked upon his mind; and that morning, not being well, and being ordered on picket, the Surgeon would not excuse him. He resorted to the means of getting rid of the picket by getting rid of his life. He was a man who gained the good-will of the officers of his regiment, and was beloved by the members of his company. He was buried, but without the honors due to a soldier, by order of the Colonel.

The daughter of the regiment has gone; the line-officers are not sorry, but the field mourn her loss. The Colonel did not like to let her go, and placed a guard on her tent to prevent her from leaving camp; but she became so insubordinate and unmanageable he let her go.

VOLUNTEER.

NINETIETH BATTALION N.Y.V.V.

NEAR WASHINGTON, D.C., June 22.

The Ninetieth is still in existence, notwithstanding reports to the contrary, which have found their way to the City of New York, through discharged men. Yes, the Ninetieth is still in, the field, and from all I can learn, we shall stay here for some time yet.

We are now laying in camp about four miles east of the Capitol, and near Fort Lincoln; but we are under marching orders and liable to move at a moment's notice. Nearly all our (Dwight's) Division has gone South. Since our arrival at this place we have been re-enforced by about 150 men belonging to the following regiments: One Hundred and Fourteenth, One Hundred and Sixteenth, and One Hundred and Thirty-third N.Y.V.V., which have been mustered out, under late orders; most of the men thus transferred are veterans, having been on the war-path since 1861. We have now on the ground about two-hundred men for duty, and about two-thirds of them are Vets.

The boys do not like the idea of going down South again, some of them gone to New York to visit their friends and bid them good-bye before they go, but most of them have forgotten to come back again.

We shall all be glad when we are able to throw the yoke of military rule off and return to civil life; for it is not very pleasant to be kept in a small camp of about six acres, and fed on pork, coffee, and hardtack, and all the duty we have to do is to guard each other, and see that no man leaves the allotted space unless provided with the proper pass.

We have had four years of it; and now the War is over, we do not want to learn any more of military discipline, for we do not intend to make it our trade; we have been fighting for freedom and independence, and now we have gained the victory we want our freedom. Give us our discharge, and we will be independent enough.

The weather is very warm and sultry here at present, although for the past four or five days we have had a good deal of rain, which made it very unpleasant for us in our shelter-tents, besides, we are swarmed out with flies, which will give us no rest. We have company-drills every morning, and inspections every evening.

We would like it very much if that lazy paymaster would wake up and pay us a visit, for we have now about six months' pay due, and all of us are very short of cash.

Yours truly,   EXCELSIOR.

FORTIETH REGIMENT. N.Y.V.V.

NEAR BAILEY'S CROSS ROADS, VA., June 23.

Our camp was exceedingly lively this morning at receiving the welcome intelligence from Headquarters that the Seventy-third, Eighty-sixth, Ninety-third, and Fortieth N.Y.V.V. were to at once be mustered out of the service. At the call some few minutes later for the men to fall-in for a growl, only one was found who dared give vent to his feelings in that peculiar manner, and his dissatisfaction was to be ascribed more to bilious temperament than to any just cause.

We hope to get to New York to spend the Fourth with you, and I doubt not that the citizens thereof will gladly welcome the return of our regiment, which has done good and efficient service, as its oftentimes depleted ranks testify, in battling for the right.

We shall not forget that we, as well as every regiment in the service, are under many obligations to your valuable journal for not only furnishing us the latest intelligence, but in carefully guarding the soldiers' interests while we have been performing our duty at the front. We shall call en masse to electrify you with three hearty cheers and a tiger, such as has often woke up the perceptive qualities of the Johnnys. The Fortieth and Seventy-third Regiments have not forgotten the soldier's champion and friend—the SUNDAY MERCURY.

MOZART.

July 2, 1865

A REBEL PRISONER'S EXPERIENCE OF NORTHERN TREATMENT.

EASTERN HOTEL, NEW YORK CITY, June 27.

Will you please give my note a space in the columns of your paper, as I desire to inform the inquiring people of your city how a Rebel released prisoner has been treated in their midst, and since my capture, etc.? I was captured on Hatcher's Run, on the right of Petersburg, Va., March 25, 1865, by the Fifth Corps, with a large number of officers and men. We were sent direct to corps-headquarters, thence to City Point, and on Sunday-morning, the 26th, we were taken on board a steamer for Washington City, and arrived on the 7th, at 8 o'clock, and were placed in the Old Capitol Prison. The prison was under the superintendence of Mr. [William] Wood, who treated all very kindly. Remaining there a few days, we were then sent to Fort Delaware, Arrived at the said place April 1, and remained there until June 19, when we took the oath of allegiance to support a great and good government; but allow me to inform you what I think of Fort Delaware and the treatment we received there. Brigadier-General [Albin F.] Schoepf was commanding, who is highly respected by every man of good sense who came under his jurisdiction, for he certainly gave us every privilege that he was allowed—and sometimes, I thought, he went beyond the length of his cable-toe. Rations were thought to be small by a great many, but I learned from the Federal soldiers that we drew the same that they did. Our rations consisted of half a dozen crackers, one-third of a pound of pork or beef, and soup, for dinner, which I ate, being hearty; and I think, could you see me, you would think I had not suffered much. Rascality was practiced at Fort Delaware, but it was by the cooks and Rebel officers, who had plenty of money, which they obtained from their friends. The Rebel officers would purchase extra meals from the dining-room, for which they paid two dollars per week, getting about two pounds of meat and one of bread, and all of the beans and rice that should have been in our soup; therefore, you see that all men are not called Yankees that practice rascality to their comrades. The soldiers received a great deal of clothing and money from their friends, and I did not see one man in prison that suffered more than I did, and I knew I was not injured, you perceive, by my visit to Fort Delaware. On the 19th instant, 500 officers were placed on board a steamer for Philadelphia; arrived by 11 A.M., and there, some went North, some South, and they were sent in different directions; but I had a pleasant time in Philadelphia. I was invited to dine with a friend, which you know was accepted, and, after eating and smoking for the Union, we bade each other adieu. I left for this city at 5, P.M., and arrived on the 20th at 8, A.M., without one cent in my purse, and I had no friends as I thought; but, alas! not so. 'Twas here and since I came here that I have found the teaching of the political demagogues South to be false. They preached that we had no friends North, only a few, and they worked only for interest. But through life my motto has been to believe what political demagogues say, for I look on them as being murderers and robbers. As I before said, I came here without one cent and poorly clad, but not long did I remain in that condition. I have received many donations from friends and brothers—from those whom I have been fighting. Have I suffered? No; I have lived well, and good tidings will I carry to my country when I return; and always shall I recollect the people who have shown so much hospitality toward me, and not only me, but the wants of every needy man has been supplied.

I sail, this day at half-past 3, P.M., from Pier 46, on board the Mississippi for New Orleans, La., thence to Mobile, then to Demopolis, Ala., and I return South fully convinced that this war was a cruel and an unjust one, and ever shall I support the Union which I have never fought against with my own free will and accord; and I now believe that the South was not duly and truly prepared, and I did never think that England and France would vouch for. Therefore, I could never hope of any success, notwithstanding I fought on many a bloody field, and received two wounds. But many a Southern man had to enter service against his will and good judgement. Then, his honor being at stake, before disgracing himself he would die. I shall never forget my friend, J. B. Greene, an officer in the Federal Army; for, after fighting each other for three years, we met as strangers, and never did I enjoy myself more with a friend and a brother. I hope soon to sail; and when I step aboard the steamer, and cast a look at the city, my prayers will be for the Union and the people of New York city, hoping to return home, and be an instrument in the hands of our God of doing much good. Forgive me for so trespassing, and believe me a friend to all honest and good people.

AN ALABAMA SOLDIER.

FORTIETH REGIMENT, N.Y.V.V.

June 28.

In your last copy of the SUNDAY MERCURY, I took particular notice of your special notice to correspondents and I certainly think that your desires are based on good grounds, as after the disbandment of the volunteers now in the field, you will certainly find (as I am afraid the small private diaries of some of your humble ignorant privates will reveal great military secrets hitherto unknown to a rapacious public for intelligence, which, perhaps, it would not suit Army Headquarter correspondents to reveal; the history of this war is yet to be written) that some of your old correspondents will not desert the columns which have so nobly and fearlessly advocated the soldiers' rights and claims, and particularly so for the valuable information and amusement which you have afforded us in our self-proscription from the pale of civilized society.

We have at last attained almost the acme of our desires. Impatiently and anxiously have we been viewing the departure of our brave comrades-in-arms, thinking of course, that Government was overlooking us; at the same time, Rumor exciting us to the highest pitch of disappointment. But at last all doubts are banished and fears allayed, for the order for our muster-out has at last arrived, along with our veteran comrades, the Seventy-third, and in a few days we expect to be en route for the far-famed city of Gotham. We fully expect to participate in your Fourth of July parade.

If we must judge from our present feelings, we should certainly acknowledge that we are amply repaid for the services rendered our suffering country in her trying hour of need; and now that our perilous career is ended, we retire as peaceful citizens, hoping that, with the Divine assistance, our statesmanship shall be brought out in such unanimity and perfection as to insure peace for all succeeding generations. Not wishing to descend into the theological, I am, as ever,   WATERFORD.

July 16, 1865
SIXTY-FIFTH REGIMENT, N.Y.S.V.V.
HALL'S HILL, VA., July 11.

At last, that long-expected, much-desired, and truly-welcome order has been issued for our muster out from Uncle Sam's employ. The muster-out rolls are being rapidly completed, and I have every reason to believe that before Tuesday, next we shall be on our way homeward bound. The news that we were to be immediately mustered out reached camp a few nights ago, and our gentlemanly Adjutant, Charles A. Baker, eager to impart the joyful news to the men of the regiment, went to each company and read the order; the result of which was, that the boys made the welkin ring with cheers for home. The veterans who have suffered and toiled for the honor of their country through four long years of war, now see with undisguised delight the certainty of ere long meeting with those from whom they have so long been separated.

Camp-life at present is almost unendurable. The excitement which formerly gave spirit to the profession of arms is dead, there is nothing doing to make it agreeable. Even the Tycoon Socialists, who, in times past, were festive fellows, can afford none of the enjoyments which made them so popular in the brigade. The only talk is home. Even the late excursions in Washington attracted no attention.

The vicinity of Arlington Heights and the surrounding country, is beginning to look like its former self (before the war). The rude car of war's devastation has been withdrawn, and in its place the plow and plowshare now reign supreme. Many of the forts have been dismantled and leveled to the ground, in order to give the farmer the benefit of the valuable soil they occupied. Cornfields are blooming, and their green plumes tossed by the wind, seems to echo the divine sentiment, "Peace on earth and good will toward men."

Arlington, the former residence of Robert E. Lee, is one of the most beautiful places that I have encountered while in Virginia. The house and surroundings exemplify the taste and culture of Virginians. The greater part of the domain is devoted to a cemetery for the burial of soldiers.

The men are in excellent spirits and health, and will wait patiently for the word go. In behalf of the regiment, allow me, Mr. MERCURY, to offer you our sincere thanks for the generous manner in which you have advocated the rights of the soldier. Wishing the MERCURY what it so deserves, every success, I am yours for home,   F. G. T.

Chapter VI

2000

by

Robert Lee Hodge

Seventeenth Regiment
New York Veteran Volunteers
Before Atlanta, Georgia
August 19, 1864.

We are now, as you have perceived by the heading of this letter, in front of Atlanta. We left Decatur on the 5th inst., and arrived here on the 7th. The trip was a very interesting one, as there are many beautiful landscapes along the bank of the Tennessee River, which cannot be surpassed even in classic Italy. Chattanooga, Lookout Mountain, and the numerous fortifications around were, of course, objects of great interest; and from thence to Dalton, and on to Marietta, along the railroad, were the numerous and powerful lines of earthworks thrown up by both armies in their different positions. That spades were trumps, we had here ample testimony, especially so when they are played on the Union side. If those works could be preserved by law, for the benefit of our curious posterity, they would last for many generations. Each battle-field would thus have its own monuments to celebrate the events that transpired there; each rifle-pit and battery speaking more to the heart of the spectator than would whole volumes of history.

Thus wrote Orderly Sergeant Albert Finbar Kennelly, of the 17th New York Veteran Volunteers to the New York *Sunday Mercury* in 1864. Distinct in their dark blue Hawkins' Zouave pattern uniforms, they had recently been reorganized and transferred to William Tecumseh Sherman's western Federal Army. What is amazing and refreshing, yet odd, to hear from Kennelly's voice during these desperate moments in America's annals is his desire to protect the trenches of the battlefields while he is still fighting in them. In the engagements before Atlanta he knew the importance of not only the events transpiring around him, but additionally that the physical remains of the engagements had validity and meaning as a historic shrines. That the earthworks were relevant to the understanding of the conflict, not purely in a literal sense, but in a spiritual sense also, provides a wealth of information for historians and preservationists alike to reflect upon. Then they must use that type of information as an instrument to seize their, and our, modern sense of duty…protecting our physical history.

For the student of the subject—academic or not—and more importantly the interested layman—to be able to make a connection with Sergeant Kennelly's concerns for the preservation of the battlefields is a reinforcement to the spiritual virtue of defending our cultural roots. We owe that to him. For he, like hundreds of thousands of other men, who not only died, but suffered, to achieve victory in what they believed to be right and true to the Constitution is a plaudit to the human soul.

Perhaps Kennelly was articulating on something more profound than he himself even realized. It almost seems as if through his concern for the battlefields that he could foretell their future.

- *The National Park Service owns just 3% of our major Civil War battlefields.*
- *Every ten minutes 1 acre of a Civil War battlefield is bulldozed for "development."*
- *In the next five to ten years most of these historic lands will be gone.*

If you are not shocked by those statistics, then I am shocked at you.

I would be embarrassed to show Albert Kennelly how Atlanta, or just about any other battlefield from the struggle of the 1860's has been, or not been, preserved. How would he feel looking at these sites today? The words dismayed, shocked, horrified come to mind when I dwell on the ever encroaching sprawl. Those negative terms loom in my thoughts when I think about how American society regards our history. Kennelly was saying from the "front," almost 140 years ago, what I have been pondering for a decade. How peculiar to find an ally from that long ago war...or maybe it isn't so strange.

I remember in the evenings, growing up as a child in northeastern Ohio, when my mother would tuck me in under the covers to say our prayers. Then she would treat me to the nightly quota of Civil War readings from the books I had scooped-up on my latest raid on our local library.

While she was reading from these treasured pages of history, I would close my eyes and imagine myself in many distant places, in another century. At times I would be with Henry Heth's southern butternut division, marching down the Chambersburg Pike at dawn, July 1, 1863; during other readings I would move with John Sedgwick's Federal units through the pastures at Salem Church, or on occasion advance with Braxton Bragg's rebel army into Kentucky in the late summer of '62.

I had felt the roots of American History through those Civil War books. My mother's readings probably did more to create my 1860's addiction than anything else. Those stories had instilled in my mind a certain type of adoration for those men and battlefields.

I would take these coveted books to school and have them stealthily splayed out under my desk during the often uneventful instruction of math and science. Even though these courses had no appeal to me, I was fine—leaning over my desk, eyes looking attentively and gleefully at the sketches, photos, and maps of Rebs and Yanks.

However, those were books—two-dimensional surfaces that had their limitations in representing the real world and events. In my daydreaming and drooling over the armies of Blue and Gray I could not stop thinking of getting to the battlefields someday to see where the major defining moments of America were forged. It was the next logical step to go to the land and make a literal *and* spiritual connection with the past. I remember specifically dreaming of walking the same ground as the Army of Tennessee had in their swan song advance at Franklin. The books, and then more-so the battlefields, had become an odd type of Pavlov dog experiment. Obviously I had "the Bug."

Lincoln said at Gettysburg that the world could never forget what the soldiers did on those fields, and that they had not died in vain. I grew up feeling that kind of resonating reverence for the soldiers and the land they fought on; hearing and reading of areas inside those hallowed grounds named for intense action that have become part of the American vernacular like: The Peach Orchard, Snodgrass Hill, The Bloody Angle, Devil's Den, The Cotton Gin, and The Orange Turnpike. Those names were, and are, sacred to me, and will be throughout my life.

Starting in the mid 1970's, my folks began taking me to the battlefields; my first was Fort Donelson, then Gettysburg, Chickamauga, Shiloh, and Antietam. These parks looked fine in my mind's eye as a child, and I assumed that many of the other battlefields in this country were maintained in some similar fashion.

However, my naiveté would be shattered in 1991, when as a young adult, I visited for the first time the battlefields of Chancellorsville, The Wilderness, and Spotsylvania. At Chancellorsville in May 1863, one would have had to duck minié balls zipping over your head. Today, next to the battlefield we have a resort where you have to occasionally "take cover" from slicing salvos of golf balls zipping through the trees from the nearby driving range.

The forested area around the Old Plank Road at Chancellorsville—where Lee and Jackson last saw each other, and where the Rebel brigades of Kershaw, Posey, and Mahone assaulted the Federals of Slocum's command—has recently been bulldozed for a housing development named the *Estates of Lee-Jackson*!

On my 1991 visit I could not imagine what was going on in the heads of the original combatants that struggled in the burning woods of The Wilderness because of the drowning sounds of circular saws and hammers, throwing up the latest identikit homes for the nouveau riche on streets named *Musket Ridge Lane*, *Grant Court*, and *Lee-Jackson Circle*. Maybe this is our modern way of commemorating our historic richness?

The rural character of this historic property was becoming suburban, and I was standing as a witness to a cultural crime called by some "growth." I realized right away what this all meant: That the National Park Service was again helpless as the county board of supervisors rezoned the area from rural to higher density residential. This was another instance where one feels so helpless against what is called "progress." Whether it is between the Union and Confederate at Chancellorsville, or in suburban Atlanta, there are blossoming subdivisions that appear to be springing-up overnight. I sometimes scratch my head in puzzled amazement at the rapidity of the sprawl, wondering if it is possible that the building was done by metaphysics. I have facetiously thought that when everyone is asleep the "developer fairy" comes to a battlefield and plants little red and green Monopoly size homes with a sprinkling of Miracle Grow!

The very serious crisis and theme of battlefield preservation is a sensible constant in this growing chaos of overpopulation. Preserving battlefields may be seen as one possible direction towards focusing on the bigger picture of how we are going to plan our communities and attempt to build a better society for future generations.

Oddly enough the uncomfortable contemporary issues of race, immigration, religion, population control, land rights, capital punishment, and other issues involving planning and growth, tie our interest in history and battlefield preservation. Understandably it is hard, very hard, for many people and politicians to talk about these issues. The population density combined with poor planning is crowding out a quality of living where historic land can play a vital role in current society. Even if we cannot turn someone onto history, and the significance of historic land, we should be able to get folks thinking about saving these sites to be maintained as open green-space—which would benefit all people, not just history enthusiasts.

Many parts of Georgia, Virginia, and Tennessee are no longer threatened with being overrun by hundreds of thousands of Federal troops with cannon. But those areas are being blitzkrieged by thousands of developers with thousands of bulldozers, building hundreds of thousands of press-board and hot glue gun McMansions for millions of people trying to escape from the criminal, or ignorantly planned, suburbia of metropolitan Atlanta, Northern Virginia, and now central Tennessee. The mass exodus created by the bourgeoisie escapees, is turning the surrounding historic countryside into the very thing they are running from…sprawl! What we run from we are bringing with us. Automobiles and jammed highways are nothing more than great instruments to run from work to home…and our inner city problems. Politicians at the local, state, and federal level think that the answers are simple, and talk of relieving traffic pressures and solving commuting dilemmas, by building more roads.

Most road designs are nothing more than weak, short-term copying mechanisms…not solutions. Building a road is like putting a band aid on a mortal wound—it doesn't heal the scar, it perpetuates the problem. The wound festers and it spreads like cancer, and no real solution is explored because of the sensitivity of the issues that revolve around fixing the problems.

This type of trend in thinking *and* actions will continue—there is no reason why it wouldn't, and it will not be isolated to the areas I just mentioned. Why would it be? The destruction of the many battlefields around these metropolitan areas is a sentinel for what is coming to the rest of America; it is just a matter of time.

We may not be able to change all the massive forces in motion, but we can at least *do* what we *can do* to help save historic land from the rapid and thoughtless growth while there is still time left—and this action must take place *now*.

There has been no strategy in place to combat the lightning-fast growth of suburbia *and* the destruction of the many unprotected historic sites. And that major "growth" created by a few folks fueled by greed, negatively impacts millions of Americans for decades—if not centuries.

Throughout my travels over the battlefields I have felt too numb, and too sad to be upset at what I have thought to be a great betrayal by past and present governments and generations. Somebody, at sometime, had somehow violated something I have held so close to my heart.

At Salem Church, Virginia dense haphazard growth, that has sprung up practically overnight, surrounds the bullet marked church and covers the battlefield. The historic countryside that was there has been bulldozed for a growing culture that worships the automobile-driven world of instant gratification and obscene, intoxicating wealth.

It is not just development that is a problem here; but more importantly the *type* of growth around it— McDonalds, Burger King, Exxon, Pizza Hut, Blockbuster, Taco Bell, and many other corporate chains, are creating a homogenizing, numbing oneness—going against celebrating diversity. The main reason the corporate chains are there is because the county board of supervisors, or the city council, did not care enough to protect their—and our—historic resources.

These battlefields, where the corporate chains lurk, were paid for years ago…consecrated in American military blood. Do the gross planning mistakes of the recent past have to continue? No. Does historic green-space always have to lose to concrete? No. Does every tree have to be cut down for another Wal-Mart? No. Do we continue to let our city councils and county boards ruin our historic landscapes? No.

Let me reiterate that in the next ten years there will be no more battlefield land left in question as to its future preservation—because it will vanish under cement…or it will be saved.

We need to learn to be stewards *forever* of historic property—protecting it, so that future generations have the opportunity to see these sites and get in touch with our cultural roots. We need to educate the masses, especially the children, that these places are relevant. Without a constituency for the few parks that already exist they will perish. Most battlefield parks are woefully incomplete, and they need to at least grow with the populous. Places like Salem Church, Virginia, Franklin, Tennessee, and Atlanta, Georgia will never be able to grow, unless it is through reclamation.

However, despite the hurdles that damage preservation efforts, victories can happen: A major Formula-1 racetrack was thwarted at Brandy Station, Virginia—the site of the largest cavalry battle in the western hemisphere, and the Army of the Potomac's massive encampment in the winter of 1863-1864. Disney was chased back to Florida when it threatened to build a "historic theme park" near Manassas. Thousands of acres have been bought by various preservation groups around the country. So David can conquer Goliath, but the victories take work with sacrifice. These efforts must take place immediately. We cannot afford to put the responsibility off for the next generation because the advancing sprawl is too expedient to think otherwise.

It is hard, very hard, to figure out how solutions to our historic green-space problems are to be resolved—if they are to be resolved. But while we should be *thinking* about how to protect remnants of our physical history we must take *action*. Let the words of Albert Kennelly help spur you to take that action and save what we can save right now. Tomorrow is too late....I guarantee it.

Sergeant Albert Finbar Kennelly was killed alongside Colonel William Grower, leading Company A, of the 17th New York Veteran Volunteers at Jonesboro, Georgia on September 1, 1864. The Federal victory that day, just outside of Atlanta, did more to solidify Abraham Lincoln's presidential reelection that following November than any other action during the War Between the States. The Jonesboro battlefield is now under concrete.

Did Albert Kennelly die in vain?

What will our legacy be?

"Never doubt that a small group of thoughtful, committed citizens can change the world. Indeed, it is the only thing that ever has."—Margaret Mead.

Robert Lee Hodge
Alexandria, Va.

Research guide to the Civil War letters in the New York Sunday Mercury.

Libraries with New York Sunday Mercury holdings: New-York Historical Society—1862, 1863; New York Public Library—1861, 1862, 1863, 1865; Center for Research Libraries, Chicago, Il., —1863, 1864, 1865 (incomplete); Library of Congress—1862, 1863, 1865.

List of letters appearing in each issue of the New York Sunday Mercury during the Civil War.

1861

May 5
13th Regt. of Brooklyn
(2 letters)

May 12
Fire Zouaves
(3 letters)
8th NYSM
(2 letters)
13th NYSM
12th NYSM
71st NYSM
(3 letters)

May 19
Fire Zouaves (2 letters)
13th NYSM
6th NYSM
8th NYSM (2 letters)

June 2
Fire Zouaves
71st NYSM
69th NYSM
13th NYSM
8th NYSM

June 9
8th NYSM (2 letters)
71st NYSM (2 letters)

June 16
Fire Zouaves (2 letters)
8th NYSM (2 letters)
13th NYSM (2 letters)

June 23
71st NYSM
Fire Zouaves
79th Regt. NYSM
69th Regt. NYSM
5th Regt. NYSV
Hawkins' Zouaves
13th NYSM

June 30
13th NYSM

(2 letters)
8th NYSM
(4 letters)
71st NYSM
79th NYSM

July 7
10th NYSV
8th NYSM
(3 letters)
69th NYSM
6th Regt. NYSM
13th Regt. NYSM
79th NYSM

July 14
Ninth Regt.
8th NYSM (4 letters)
79th NYSM

July 21
10th NYSV
1st Wisconsin Regt.
71st Regt. NYSM

July 28
Fire Zouaves
2nd Regt. NYSM
Mozart Regt. (40th NYSV)
9th NYSV
71st NYSM

August 4
79th NYSV

August 11
9th NYSM
79th Regt. NYSM
10th Regt. NYSV
Russian Vols.
Hawkins' Zouaves

August 18
Russian Vols.
9th NYSV
Mozart Regt.

August 25
1st Cav. NYSM

14th Regt. NYSM
Mozart Regt.
10th NYSV

September 1
Russian Volunteers
2nd Regt. NYSM
1st NYSV
9th NYSM

September 8
Russian Volunteers
Second Fire Zouaves
Mozart Regt. (40th NYSV)
4th NY Art.
USS Niagara

September 15
Russian Vols
Second Fire Zouaves
14th Regt. NYSM
US Chasseurs

September 22
Russian Vols.
40th NYSV
First US Chasseurs
9th Regt. NYSV
9th Regt. NYSM
Second Fire Zouaves
USS Savannah

September 29
Russian Vols.
14th Regt. NYSM
Second Fire Zouaves
8th Regt. NYSM

October 6
47th NYSV
14th Regt. NYSM

October 13
9th NYSM (3 letters)
55th NYSM
Continental Guard
Anderson Zouaves

October 20

79th NYSM
Second Fire Zouaves
14th Regt. NYSM
48th Regt. NYSV

October 27
55th NYSM
10th NYSV
3rd NYSV
US Niagara

November 3
Hawkins Zouaves
US Chasseurs
79th NYSM
Anderson Zouaves
Continental Guard

November 10
9th NYSM
First Chasseurs
Second Fire Zouaves
Continental Guard

November 17
55th Regt. NYSM
79th Regt. NYSV
First Chasseurs
Hawkins' Zouaves
USS Frigate Niagara

November 24
Hawkins Zouaves
48th NYSV
12th NYSM

December 15
Hawkins' Zouaves
48th NYSV

December 22
Second Fire Zouaves
First Fire Zouaves

December 29
Hawkins' Zouaves
USS Niagara

1862

January 5
79th NYSV
9th NYSM
47th NYSV
10th NYSV
25th NYSV
2nd NYSM
48th NYSV

January 12
25th NYSV
9th NYSM
Mozart Regt.
69th Regt. NYV
10th NYSV
Second Fire Zouaves
4th NYSV

January 19
25th NYSV
Mozart Regt.
First Long Island
5th Regt. NYV
9th NYSM

January 26
Mozart Regt.
40th NYSV
10th NYSV
2nd Regt. NYSM
4th NYSV
55th Regt. NYSM
First Chasseurs
3 Month Western Vol.
2nd Del. Inf.
8th NJVI
79th NYSV
A Private
3rd Regt. Excelsior

February 2
First Michigan Infantry
9th Regt. NYSM
87th NYSV
9th NYSV
Mozart Regt.
1st USSS
Second Fire Zouaves
55th NYSV
62nd NYSV

February 9
2nd Regt. NYSM
 (4 letters)
25th Regt. NYSV
40th Regt. NYV
First Chasseurs
5th New Hampshire Inf.
61st NYSV
9th Regt. NYSM
 (3 letters)
69th Regt. NYSV
4th NYSV
38th NYSV
36th NYSV
First Michigan Inf.

February 16

Mozart Regt.
9th Regt. NYSM
87th Regt. NYSV
2nd NYSV
48th NYSV
66th NYSV
36th NYSV
62nd NYSV
Trip to Mt. Vernon
79th NYSV
D'Espineuil Zouaves
USS Niagara

February 23
40th Regt. NYV
First Michigan Inf.
9th Regt. NYSM
First Chasseurs
55th Regt. NYSM
57th NYSV
4th NYSV
36th NYSV
62nd NYSV
72nd Pa. Inf.
96th NYSV
48th NYSV
Second Fire Zouaves
25th NYSV
5th NYSV
1st USSS
38th NYSV

March 2
69th Regt. NYSV
1st Regt. Excelsior
Brigade
32nd NYSV
10th NYSV
2nd NYSM
36th NYSV
Second Fire Zouaves
1st USSS
47th NYSV
38th NYSV
45th NYSV
61st NYSV
25th NYSV
Naval Corresp.

March 9
A Gunboat Volunteer
48th NYSV
From a Scout
36th NYSV
38th NYSV
9th Regt. NYSM
Berdan's Sharpshooters
10th NYSV
25th NYSV
9th Regt. NYSM
Second Fire Zouaves
2nd Regt. NYSM
55th NYSV
62nd NYSV

March 16
5th Regt. NYV
First Fire Zouaves
Mozart Regt.

15th Regt. NYV
1st Regt. Excelsior Brig.
10th NYSV
9th NYSM
48th NYSV
32nd NYSV
From Our Scout
62nd NYSV

March 23
From Our Scout
95th NYSV
62nd NYV
Second Fire Zouaves
1st USSS
79th Regt. NYV
55th NYSM
9th NYSM
Transport Service
69th NYSV

March 30
95th Regt. NYSV
First Chasseurs
51st Regt. NYV
61st NYV
First Regt. NYV
25th Regt. NYV
62nd NYSV
2nd NYSM
Second Fire Zouaves
9th NYSM

April 6
48th NYSV
32nd Regt. NYSV
9th Regt. NYSV
Mott's Battery
10th Regt. NYV
4th NYSV
Second Fire Zouaves
5th NYSV
Station Service
9th NYSM

April 13
9th Regt. NYSV
40th (Mozart) Regt.
1st Regt. NYSV
9th Regt. NYSM

April 20
On the Battlefield
Pittsburg Landing
From Our Scout
95th Regt. NYV
Mozart Regt.
79th Regt. NYV
Second Iowa Infantry

April 27
57th NYSV
9th NYSM
First Fire Zouaves
Second Fire Zouaves
First Regt. Excelsior
Brig.
25th NYSV
9th NYSV

95th NYSV
2nd NYSM

May 4
79th NYSV
99th Regt. NYSM
Berdan's Sharpshooters
66th NYSV
From Our Scout
First Long Island

May 11
9th NYSV
Letter from Col. Ferrero
First Fire Zouaves
95th NYSV
Old Guard

May 18
55th NYSV
40th (Mozart) Regt.
38th NYSV
69th Regt. NYV
Second Fire Zouaves
9th NYSM
First Fire Zouaves
18th Mo. Inf.
First Long Island

May 25
95th NYSV
9th Regt. NYSM
4th NYSV
6th NYSV
70th Regt. NYSV
First Long Island
87th Regt. NYSV
25th NYSV

June 1
38th NYSV
5th Regt. NYSV
66th NYSV
31st NYSV
Second Fire Zouaves
First Long Island
9th NYSV
62nd NYSV
Wilson's Zouaves
US Gunboat Galena

June 8
7th Regt. NYSM
9th Regt. NYSM
First Long Island
13th Regt. NYSM
From a Staff Officer
6th NYSV
90th NYSV
71st Regt. NYSM
13th Regt. NYSM

June 15
25th Regt. NYSV
7th Regt. NYSM
66th Regt. NYSV
9th Regt. NYSM
37th Regt. NYSNG
71st Regt. NYSV

69th Regt. NYSV
31st Regt. NYSV
First Long Island
48th Regt. NYSV
8th Regt. NYSNG
13th Regt. NYSM
14th Regt. NYSM

June 22
71st Pa. Inf.
40th NYSV
First Chasseurs
25th NYSV
71st NYSM
37th NYSM
57th NYSV
8th NYSM
9th NYSM
2nd NYSM

June 29
Second Fire Zouaves
47th Regt. NYSV
4th Regt. NYSV
Our Own Special
Correspondent
9th Regt. NYSV
8th Regt. NYSM
71st NYSM
79th NYSV
4th NY Art.
22nd NYSM
From a Dragoon

July 6
12th NYSM
4th NYSV
14th NYSM
71st Regt. NYSM
22nd NYSM
37th NYSM
95th NYSV
8th NYSM

July 13
8th NYSM
9th NYSM
12th NYSM
Artillery Camp
4th NYSV
65th NYSV
Howland the Scout

July 20
Our Own Special
Correspondent
US Dragoon
8th Regt. NYSM
4th NYSV
62nd NYSV
90th NYSV
79th NSYV
9th Regt. NYSM
51st NYSV
71st Regt. NYSM
USS Sabine
USS Wabash

July 27

12th NYSM
Second Fire Zouves
22nd NYSM
95th NYSV
102nd NYSV
9th NYSM
57th NYSV
36th NYSV
71st NYSM
4th NYSV
7th Regt. NYSM

August 3
8th Regt. NYSM
2nd NYSM
95th NYSV
90th NYSV
57th NYSV
9th Regt. NYSM
87th NYSV
71st Regt. NYSM

August 10
38th NYSV
12th Regt. NYSM
71st Regt. NYSM
9th NYSV
13th Regt. NYSM
90th NYSV
Second Fire Zouaves
31st NYSV

August 17
1st Excelsior Brigade
57th NYSV
90th NYSV
71st NYSM
12th NYSV
37th NYSM
40th NYSV
65th NYSV

August 24
12th Regt. NYSM
71st Regt. NYSM
8th NYSM
37th NYSM
90th NYSV
95th NYSV
4th NYSV
USS Fernandina

August 31
12th NYSV
36th NYSV
31st NYSV
A Paroled Prisoner
4th Regt. NYSV
12th Regt. NYSM

September 7
Howland the Scout
4th NYSV
12th NYSM
4th NYSV
6th NYSV
55th NYSM

September 14
90th NYSV

Second Fire Zouves
48th NYSV
41st NYSV
9th NYSM
65th NYSV
Paroled Prisoners
US Hospital Newark

September 21
125th NYSV
14th Regt. NYSM
US Hospital Newark
1500 Paroled Prisoners
6th NYSV
Second Fire Zouaves

September 28
Ebenezer Hospital
US Hospital
47th Regt. NYSV

October 5
2nd Regt. NYSM
90th NYSV
4th NYSV
36th NYSV
Ebenezer Hospital
51st NYSV
51st NYSV
47th NYSV
4th NY Cav.

October 12
4th Regt. NYSV
Mozart Regt.
From Our Western
Troops (Iowa)
48th Regt. NYSV
Mounted Rifles
99th NYSV
47th NYSV

October 19
9th Regt. NYSM
Howland the Scout
13th NYSV
4th NYSV
38th NYSV
36th NYSV

October 26
12th NYSV
57th NYSV
40th NYSV
36th NYSV
Sketch of Bushwackers
31st NYSV
Mounted Rifles
Second Fire Zouaves
5th Rhode Island V.
99th NYSV
55th NYSM

November 2
Mounted Rifles
62nd NYSV
14th NYSM
57th NYSV
Second Fire Zouaves
2nd NYSM

38th NYSV
USS Fernandina

November 9
12th Regt. NYSV
99th NYSV
48th NYSV
9th NYSM
40th NYSV
36th NYSV
Second Fire Zouaves
6th NYSV

November 16
145th NYSV
6th NY Art.
36th NYSV
133rd NYSV
132nd NYSV

November 23
First Mounted Rifles
5th NY Art.
Second Fire Zouaves
36th NYSV
19th NYSNG
99th NYSV
Paroled Prisoners
90th NYSNG

November 30
Second Fire Zouaves
55th NYSV
12th NYSV
9th NYSM
162nd NYSV
4th NY Cav.
132nd NYSV
5th RIV
1st NY Art.

December 7
132nd NYSV
57th NYSV
21st NJVI
62nd NYSV
4th NYSV
Thrilling Incident of the
War
56th NYSV
5th NY Art.
36th NYSV
90th NYSV
51st NYSV
32nd NYSV
170th NYSV

December 14
5th NY Art.
51st NYSV
36th NYSV
19th NYSNG
12th NYSV
132nd NYSV
95th NYSV
5th RISV

December 21
Mounted Rifles
12th NYSV

99th NYSV
139th NYSV
36th NYSV
10th NYSV
5th NY Art.
79th NYSV

December 28
79th NYSV
25th NYSV
12th NYSV
25th NYSM
9th NYSM
Mounted Rifles
55th NYSM
5th NY Art.
31st NYSV
56th NYSV

1863
January 4
36th Regt. NYSV
NY Mounted Rifles
14th Regt. NYSM
47th NYSV
51st NYSV
99th NYSV
62nd NYSV
15th NY Eng.
170th NYSV
1st Excelsior
Second Fire Zouaves
5th Regt. NYSV Art.
Mounted Rifles

January 11
170th Regt. Irish Legion
127th NYSV
51st NYSV
47th NYSV
99th NYSV
48th NYSV
5th Art. NYSV
USS Lockwood

January 18
12th Regt. NYSV
170th Regt. Irish Legion
40th NYSV
99th NYSV
42nd NYSV
90th NYSV
9th NYSM
USS Fernandina

January 25
49th NYSV
36th NYSV
99th NYSV
5th NYSV Art.
4th NY Cav.
12th NYSV
170th Regt. Irish Legion
Second Fire Zouaves
New Camp
Convalescents

February 1

5th Regt. Heavy Art.
9th Regt. NYSM
10th Regt. NYSV
6th Regt. Heavy Art.
62nd NYSV
56th NYSV
90th NYSV

February 8
Corcoran's Legion
79th Regt. NYSV
On the Blackwater
5th RI Vols.
12th NYSV
4th NY Cav.
US Cuyler
5th Heavy Art.
6th NY Heavy Art.
6th NYSV

February 15
Mounted Rifles
57th NYSV
9th Regt. NYSM
5th RI Vols
90th NYSV
99th NYSV
10th NYSV
Howland the Scout
USS Fernandina
118th Ill. Vol.

February 22
12th NYSV
38th Regt. NYSV
NY Mounted Rifles
10th NYSV
51st NYSV
90th NGNYS
62nd NYSV
102nd NYSV
105th NYSV

March 1
48th NYSV
1st Cav. NYSV
99th NYSV
NY Mounted Rifles
132nd NYSV
168th NYSV
15th NY Engineers
9th NYSM
170th NYSV

March 8
90th NYSV
12th NYSV
127th NYSV
176th NYSV
10th NYSV
5th NY Heavy Art.
79th NYSV
147th PA. Vol.
31st NYSV
Mounted Rifles

March 15
Mounted Rifles
12th NYSV
63rd NYSV

170th Irish Legion
168th NYSV
47th NYSV

March 22
NY Mounted Rifles
5th NYSV
14th NYSM
12th NYSV
Fire Laddies
USS Fernandina
6th Regt. NY Art.
10th NYSV
38th NYSV
From Meagher's Brig.
79th NYSV
48th NYSV
132nd NYSV
51st NYSV

March 29
10th NYSV
82nd NYSV
40th NYSV
165th NYSV
9th NYSV
56th NYSV
48th NYSV
99th NYSV
132nd NYSV
127th NYSV
79th NYSV

April 5
162nd NYSV
6th NY Heavy Art.
67th NYSV
9th NJ Vol.
5th NYSV
5th RI Vol.
139th NYSV
48th NYSV
9th Regt. NYSM
79th NYSV
USS Fernandina

April 12
162nd NYSV
12th NYSV
14th NYSM
48th NYSV
90th NYSV
38th NYSV
158th NYSV
9th Regt. NYSM
USS Stars and Stripes

April 19
12th NYV
51st NYSV
31st NYSV
10th NYSV
Second Fire Zouaves
132nd NYSV

April 26
170th NY Irish Legion
NY Mounted Rifles
Brook's Division
9th Regt. NYSM

158th NYSV
14th NYSM
12th NYSV
51st NYSV
139th NYSV
Charleston Expedition

May 3
Shaler's Brigade
Second Fire Zouaves
175th NYSV
12th NYSV
170th NYSV
176th NYSV
99th NYSV
79th NYSV
158th NYSV
132nd NYSV
48th NYSV

May 10
Letter from Ned
Buntline
Marriage in Camp
176th NYSV
51st NYSV
99th NYSV

May 17
Mounted Rifles
Hospital Dept.
36th NYSV
79th NYSV
127th NYSV
USS Fernandina

May 24
5th RI Regt.
Third Div. 6th Corps
162nd NYSV
51st NYSV
NY Mounted Rifles
10th NYSV
165th NYSV

May 31
5th RI Regt.
Mounted Rifles
15th Regt. Engineers
56th NYSV
132nd NYSV
Third Div., Second
Corps

June 7
79th NYSV
165th NYSV
36th NYSV
132nd NYSV
90th NYSV
51st NYSV
88th PA. Inf.
USS Tahoma

June 14
1st Brigade, 2nd Div. 6th
Corps.
139th NYSV
4th NY Battery
175th NYSV

June 21
48th NYSV
99th NYSV
USS Kanawha

June 28
A Military Sketch
14th Regt. NYSM
132nd NYV
From Bank's Army
36th NYSV
176th NYSV
23rd NYSNG
8th Regt. NGSNY

July 5
8th Regt. NGSNY
NY Regiments at Port
Hudson
51st NYSV
90th NYSV
23rd Nat. Guard
71st NYSNG
139th NYSV
48th NYSV
USS Tahoma

July 12
8th Regt. NYSNG
6th Regt. NYSNG
Army of the Peninsula
47th Regt. NYSNG
79th NYSV
4th Regt. NYSNG
133rd NYSV
90th NYSV

July 19
8th Regt, NYSNG
14th Regt. NYSNG
47th Regt. NYSNG
18th Regt. NYSNG
158th NYSV

July 26
176th NYSV
Howland the Scout

August 2
133rd NYSV
48th NYSV
84th Regt. NYSNG
59th NYSV
99th NYSV

August 9
Second Fire Zouaves
14th Regt. NYSM
5th RI Heavy Art.
118th Ill. Regt.
47th Regt. NYSNG
90th NYSV
5th NY Art.

August 16
5th RI Heavy Art.
Invalid Corps
Corcoran's Irish Legion

August 23
139th Regt. NYV
Army of the Potomac
99th NYSV
48th NYSV
176th NYV

August 30
178th NYSV
170th NYSV

September 6
40th NYSV
5th RI Art.
170th NYSV

September 13
9th Regt. NYSM
170th NYSV
176th NYSV
Corcoran's Irish Legion

September 20
170th NYSV
132nd NYSV

September 27
Irish Legion
From a Paroled Prisoner
4th NY Heavy Art.
159th NYV

October 4
56th NYSV
48th NYSV
Second Fire Zouaves
Irish Legion

October 11
40th Regt. NYV
38th Regt. NYV

October 18
99th NYSV
170th NYSV
3rd NYSV
48th NYSV
Independent Battalion
Western War News
2nd Regt. Corps
D'Afrique
Letter From Knoxville

October 25
40th Regt. NYV

November 1
Independent Battalion
132nd NYSV
145th NYSV
170th NYSV
175th NYSV

November 8
14th Regt. NYSNG
Howland the Scout
159th NYSV
170th NYSV
First Chasseurs
57th NYSV

November 15
158th NYSV

November 22
40th NYSV
3rd NYSV
17th NYV
5th RI Heavy Art.
47th NYSV
51st NYSV

November 29
Mounted Rifles
Independent Battalion
1st NY Cav.
117th NYSV
5th RI Heavy Art.

December 6
Independent Battalion
170th NYSV
145th NYSV
48th NYSV

December 13
5th RI Heavy Art.
14th Regt. NYSNG
158th NYSV
99th NYSV

December 20
7th Regt. Corps
D'Afrique
71st NYSV
17th NYSV
132nd NYSV

December 27
Independent Battalion
1st Mounted Rifles
Second Fire Zouaves
39th NYSV
117th NYSV
158th NYSV

1864
January 3
139th NYSV
71st NYSV
158th NYSV
146th NYSV
170th NYSV

January 10
17th Regt. NYVV
170th NYSV
51st NYSV
15th NY Cav.
US Wanderer

January 17
170th NYSV
51st NYSV
17th NYSV

January 24
170th NYSV

5th Art. NYV
146th NYSV

January 31
17th NYVV
51st NYVV
132nd NYV
2nd Regt. NYSM
Excelsior Brigade
3rd Regt. NYV

February 14
19th Regt. NYV
17th NYVV
14th NYSNG
178th NYV

February 21
47th Regt. NYV
2nd NJ Cav.
132nd NYSV
133rd Regt. NYV
71st NYV
170th NYV
2nd Regt. Fire Zouaves
168th NYSV

February 28
12th Regt. US Inf.
5th NY Cav.
5th RI Heavy Art.
US Bark Fernandina

March 6
47th NYSV
16th Regt. NYV Art.
120th NYSV

March 13
71st NYV
2nd Fire Zouaves
2nd NY Art.
51st Regt. NYV
146th Regt. NYV
16th Regt. NYV Art.
US Steamer Comm.
Barney

March 20
132nd Regt. NYVI
17th Regt. NYVV
40th NYSV
162nd NYSV
170th NYSV
90th NYVV
2nd NY Art.
US Steamer Comm.
Barney

March 27
47th NYSV
178th NYSV
3rd Regt. NYV
158th NYSV
46th NYSV
17th NYVV
9th Regt. NYSM

April 3
17th Regt. NYVV

79th Regt. NYV
1st US Chasseurs
90th Regt. NYVV
40th Regt. NYV

April 10
132nd Regt. NYI
120th NYV
14th Regt. NYSM
5th Regt. NYVV
Matters and Things at
the West
US Bark Fernandina

April 17
40th Regt. NYV
170th Regt. NYV
1st US Chasseurs
90th Regt. NYVV
16th NYH Art.
170th Regt. NYV
146th Regt. NYV

April 24
4th Regt. Excelsior Brig.
90th Regt. NYV
4th NYH Art.
3rd Regt. NYV
79th Regt. NYV
5th Regt. NYVV
16th NYH Art.

May 1
16th NYH Art.
14th Regt. NYSM
40th Regt. NYV

May 8
5th NY Art.
5th Regt. NYVV
1st US Chasseurs
162nd Regt. NYV
90th NYV
132nd Regt. NYV
13th NYH Art.
South-Atlantic Squad.

May 15
162nd NYV
170th NYV
25th NY Cav.
US Steamer Grand Gulf

May 22
5th NY Art.
13th Regt. NY Art.
12th US Inf.
13th NY Cav.
37th Regt. NGSNY
17th Regt. NYVV

May 29
37th Regt. NGSNY
25th NY Cav.
81st Regt. NYV
56th Regt. NYVV
5th RI Art.

June 5
158th Regt. NYVV

16th H Art. NYV

June 12
5th NY H Art.
90th NYVV
162nd Regt. NYV

June 19
162nd Regt. NYV
165th Regt. NYV
56th NYVV
68th NYVV

June 26
No issue available

July 3
No issue available

July 10
12th US Inf.
25th NY Cav.
178th NYV
12th NYSV
48th Regt. NYV
13th NY Cav.
5th NYH Art.
US Hydrangea

July 17
95th Regt. NYV
84th Regt. NGSNY
146th Regt. NYV

July 24
17th NYV Art.
170th Regt. NYV
25th NY Cav.
162nd Regt. NYV
5th Regt. NYVV
90th Regt. NYVV
1st NY Mounted Rifles

July 31
56th Regt. NYVV
90th Regt. NYVV
13th NY Cav.
68th Regt. NYV
57th Regt. NYV
84th Regt. NGSNY
69th Regt. NGSNY
6th NY Cav.
5th NY Art.

August 7
From an Old Soldier
69th Regt. NGSNY
5th NY Art.
25th NY Cav.
146th Regt. NYV
Army of Tennessee
178th Regt. NYV
90th Regt. NYVV
84th Regt. NGSNY
3rd Regt. NYV

August 14
65th Regt. NYSV
84th Regt. NGSNY
170th Regt. NYV

13th NY Cav.
48th Regt. NYV
69th Regt. NYSNG
16th Regt. Wisconsin VV

August 21
68th Regt. NYSVV
13th NY Cav.
95th Regt. NYV
5th RI H Art.
84th Regt. NGSNY
69th Regt. NYSNG
US Malvern
US Ironclad Roanoke

August 28
69th Regt. NGSNY
6th NY Cav.
178th Regt. NYV
48th Regt. NYV
5th RI H Art.
93rd Regt. NGSNY
45th Regt. NYV
56th Regt. NYV
13th NY Cav.
Harewood Hospital

September 4
13th NY Cav.
17th Regt. NYVV
132nd Regt. NYV
69th Regt. NYSNG
47th Regt. NYV
3rd Regt. NYV
48th Regt. NYV
133rd Regt. NYV
65th Regt. NYV

September 11
69th Regt. NYSNG
45th NYVV
3rd Regt. NYV
5th NY Cav.
16th NY Cav.
99th Regt. NGSNY
65th NYSV
93rd Regt. NYSNG
40th NYVV

September 18
No issue available

September 25
95th NYSV
65th NYSVV
132nd NYV
40th NYVV
69th Regt. NYSNG
56th NYVV
84th Regt. NGSNY
13th NY Cav.
51st Regt. NYV
NC Blockade Squad.

October 2
68th Regt. NYVV
16th NYH Art.
93rd Regt. NGSNY
Second Fire Zouaves
13th NY Cav.

84th Regt. NGSNY
77th Regt. NGSNY
16th NY Cav.
48th NY Regt. NYV
71st Regt. NYV
3rd Regt. NYV

October 9
77th Regt. NGNYS
65th Regt. NYSVV
51st Regt. NYV
(Remnant)
84th Regt. NGSNY
5th Regt. NY H Art.
178th NYV
93rd Regt. NGNYS
16th NYH Art.
13th NY Cav.
56th Regt. NYVV

October 16
93rd Regt. NGNYS
16th NYH Art.
25th NY Cav.
13th Regt. NY Cav.
51st Regt. NYV
95th Regt. NYV
84th Regt. NGSNY
USS Malvern

October 23
51st Regt. NYV
65th Regt. NYVV
25th NY Cav.
84th Regt. NGNYS
13th NY Cav.
61st Regt. NYVV
A Voice from the Sailors
Harewood Hospital
16th NYH Art.
5th NYH Art.
93rd NGNYS
77th NGNYS

October 30
99th Regt. NGNYS
16th NYH Art.
170th Regt. NYV
102nd Regt. NGNYS
61st Regt. NYVV
132nd Regt. NYVV
A Voice from Kansas
13th Regt. NYV

November 6
61st Regt. NYVV
77th Regt. NGNYS
65th Regt. NYV
2nd NJ Cav.
13th NY Cav.
90th Regt. NYVV
5th NY Cav.
Army of the Border

November 13
Lookout Mountain
2nd NJ Cav.
61st Regt. NYVV
Albermarle Squad.
170th Regt. NYV

November 20
132nd Regt. NYV
Albemarle Squad.
5th NYH Art.
61st Regt. NYVV
25th NY Cav.
51st Regt. NYVV

November 27
65th Regt. NYVV
1st Brig. Cav. Div.
13th NY Cav.
2nd Fire Zouaves
61st Regt. NYVV
25th NY Cav.
162nd Regt. NYV

December 4
City Point
5th RI Art.
48th Regt. NYV
51st NYVV
61st NYVV
From Grant's Army
65th Regt. NYVV
25th Regt. NY Cav.
Second Fire Zouaves
95th Regt. NYV

December 11
61st Regt. NYVV
164th Regt. NYV
13th NY Cav.
178th Regt. NYV
16th NYH Art.
Harper's Ferry
5th NYH Art.

December 18
71st Regt. NYV
25th NY Cav.
133rd Regt. NYSV
5th RIH Art.
51st Regt. NYVV
2nd NJ Cav.
16th NYH Art.
61st Regt. NYVV

December 25
132nd Regt. NYV
61st Regt. NYVV
56th Regt. NYVV
Hatcher's Run
57th Regt. NYV

1865
January 1
16th NYH Art.
61st Regt. NYVV
90th NYVV
3rd Regt. NYV
133rd Regt. NYV
176th Regt. NYV

January 8
25th NY Cav.
Harewood Hospital
132nd Regt. NYV
5th Regt. NYVV

61st Regt. NYVV

January 15
2nd NJ Cav.
City Point
176th NYV
162nd NYV
65th NYSVV
46th NYV
16th NYH Art.
61st NYVV
2nd NYH Art.
57th Regt. NYV

January 22
33rd USCT
2nd NYH Art.
65th Regt. NYSVV
61st Regt. NYVV
12th US Inf.
133rd Regt. NYV
Second Fire Zouaves
51st Regt. NYVV
56th Regt. NYVV

January 29
46th Regt. NYV
133rd Regt. NYV
65th Regt. NYVV
25th NY Cav.
2nd NJ Cav.
61st Regt. NYVV
Army of Tennessee
139th Regt. NYV
USS Malvern
13th NY Cav.

February 5.
25th NY Cav.
61st Regt. NYV
65th Regt. NYSVV
Second Fire Zouaves
Nineteenth Army Corps
5th NYH Art.
First Lincoln Cav.
51st Regt. NYVV
Harewood Hospital
3rd Regt. NYVV

February 12
From Hilton Head
25th NY Cav.
13th NY Cav.
Second Ohio Cav.
56th Regt. NYV
65th Regt. NYVV
139th Regt. NYV

February 19
61st Regt. NYVV
Dept. HQ
65th Regt. NYSVV
25th NY Cav.
139th Regt. NYV
46th Regt. NYVV
5th NY Art.
133rd Regt. NYV
Stationary Guard
178th Regt. NYV
51st Regt. NYVV

February 26
25th NY Cav.
68th Regt. NYV
City Point
2nd NJ Cav.
61st Regt. NYVV
133rd Regt. NYV
179th Regt. NYV
51st Regt. NYVV
8th NYH Art.
132nd Regt. NYV
2nd NYH Art.
Harris Light Cav.

March 5
Dept. HQ
61st NYVV
51st NYVV
133rd NYV
65th NYSVV
2nd NJ Cav.
2nd NYH Art.

March 12
8th NYH Art.
5th RIH Art.
46th NYVV
68th NYVV
61st NYVV
133rd NYV
51st NYVV
66th NYV
65th NYSVV
176th NYV
90th NYV

March 19
25th NY Cav.
47th NYSV
73rd NYVV
65th NYSVV
133rd NYSV

March 26
5th NY Cav.
First Cav. Div.
61st NYVV
120th NYV
13th NY Cav.
133rd NYV
65th NYVV
51st NYVV
165th NYV

April 2
61st NYVV
90th NYVV
51st NYVV
Second Fire Zouaves
8th NYH Art.
16th NYH Art.
25th NY Cav.

April 9
City Point
17th Regt. NYVV
47th Regt. NYSV
46th Regt. NYVV
90th Batt. NYVV

13th NYH Art.

April 16
25th NY Cav
192nd NYSV
56th NYSV

April 23
25th NY Cav.
City Point
176th Regt. NYV
51st Regt. NYVV
68th Regt. NYVV
13th NY Cav.

April 30
61st NYVV
46th NYV
8th NYH Art.
133rd NYV
Second Ohio Cav.
16th NYH Art.
73rd NYV

May 7
47th Regt. NYV
City Point
90th Batt. NYVV
13th NY Cav.

May 14
City Point
25th NY cav.
17th Regt. NYVV
13th NY Cav.
176th Regt. NYV
65th Regt. NYVV
Second Corps Hosp.

May 21
158th Regt. NYV
Washington Corresp.

May 28
46th NYVV
39th NYVV
2nd NYHA
192nd NYV
51st NYVV
120th NYV
47th NYVV
City Point
139th PA. Inf.

June 4
176th NYV
8th NYHA
192nd NYV
40th NYVV

June 11
65th NYVV
16th NYHA
13th NY Cav.
2nd NJ Cav.

June 18
City Point
73rd Regt. NYVV
2nd NYH Art.

6th Regt. USVV
Second Ohio Cav.

June 25
12th Regt. USRI
90th Batt. NYVV
192nd Regt. NYV
40th Regt. NYVV
73rd Regt. NYVV

July 2
40th Regt. NYVV
First NJ Cav.
A Rebel Prisoner
6th Regt. USVV
16th NYH Art.

July 9
4th NYH Art.
73rd Regt. NYVV
61st Regt. NYVV
First NJ Cav.

July 16
47th Regt. NYV
65th Regt. NYSVV

July 23
165th Regt. NYV
13th NY Cav.

July 30
165th NYV
3rd Prov. Cav.
90th NYVV

Index

The Contributors

Brian C. Pohanka served as a senior researcher, writer and consultant for Time Life Books, and is a frequent speaker to Civil War Round Tables. He has authored numerous articles and several books, and was Series Consultant for the television documentary *Civil War Journal*. He is active in battlefield preservation and serves as Captain of the 5th New York Zouaves living history organization.

Edwin C. Bearss was born in Billings, Montana and served in the U. S. Marine Corps during World War II. Mr. Bearss studied at Georgetown University and received a B. S. degree in Foreign Service. His career with the National Park Service began in 1955 at Vicksburg, Mississippi, where he was Park Historian. Currently, Mr. Bearss is Historian Emeritus for the National Park Service and is considered the dean of all Civil War guides.

James M. McPherson is George Henry Davis Professor of American History at Princeton University. He is the author of several books on the Civil War. His book *Battle Cry of Freedom: The Civil War Era*, won the Pulitzer Prize in 1989.

Richard J. Sommers was born in Indiana and raised in Illinois. He received his bachelor's degree from Carleton College and his doctorate from Rice University. Since 1970, he has lived and worked in Carlisle, Pennsylvania. His numerous publications on the Civil War include *Richmond Redeemed: The Siege at Petersburg*, which earned the Bell I. Wiley Prize as the best Civil War book published in 1980 and 1981.

William B. Styple is a graduate of Catawba College, and operates a business in his native Kearny, New Jersey, where he is also Town Historian. He has edited, co-authored, and authored several works on the Civil War. His book *The Little Bugler* won the Young Readers' Award from the Civil War Round Table of New York. He is currently writing the biography of General Philip Kearny.

Robert Lee Hodge is a life-long student of the Civil War and has committed himself to battlefield preservation. His life and adventures have been documented in the award-winning best seller *Confederates in the Attic* by Tony Horwitz. Rob has been involved in numerous Civil War films and television programs, and has recently formed his own production company dedicated to the preservation and interpretation of Civil War sites.